THE COMPLETE BOOK OF YOUTH MINISTRY

THE COMPLETE BOOK OF YOUTH MINISTRY

EDITED BY
WARREN S. BENSON
MARK H. SENTER III

MOODY PRESS
CHICAGO

An excellent resource tool for workers in almost any area of youth ministry is the 32-volume *Ideas* series (Ideas Library), edited by Wayne Rice and published by Zondervan in Grand Rapids and Youth Specialities in El Cajon, California.

All Scripture, except where otherwise noted, is taken from the *Holy Bible: New International Version*. Copyright © 1973, 1978, 1984 by the International Bible Society. Used by permission of Zondervan Bible Publishers.

Chapter 28, "Youth and the Sunday School," is © 1985 by Emory Gadd.

Library of Congress Cataloging in Publication Data

The Complete book of youth ministry / edited by Warren S. Benson and
    Mark H. Senter III.
        p.   cm.
    Bibliography: p.
    Includes indexes.
    ISBN 0-8024-9849-3
    1. Church work with youth.   2. Church work with young adults.
I. Benson, Warren S.   II. Senter, Mark.
BV4447.C57   1987   87-18441
259'.2—dc19

4 5 6 Printing/AF/Year 93 92 91 90

Printed in the United States of America

Contents

Part 3: Principles of Church Youth Ministry

Part 4: Strategies for Church Youth Ministry

Introduction

Ira Levin's book *The Stepford Wives* was the basis of a television movie entitled "The Stepford Children." The film depicts a small town in an idyllic setting where not only the wives, but also the teenage children, behave in a manner that is too perfect to be real. The "Men's Association" controls the town and its people by science fiction techniques that "change" the attitudes and behavior of any who deviate from the prescribed patterns. In the process people are reduced to automatons. That is one way to address behavioral problems, but it is simply fiction.

The analysis of the nature of man by Søren Kierkegaard and M. Scott Peck takes another tack. Though one might expect them to rail against humankind's sinfulness (they readily acknowledge it), their complaint is that people are passionless and apathetic. Philosopher Kierkegaard claims that people will die, not from sin, but from a lack of passion. Psychotherapist Peck in *The Road Less Traveled* argues "that we are all basically lazy and too lethargic to execute the changes in life which will give us healthy dispositions and personal joy." Tony Campolo agress with Kierkegaard and Peck that a passion for life is ultimately a gift of God's grace (Eph. 2:4-9). Campolo further suggests that youth "have experienced too much too often too young." Media have jaded youth with artificially induced excitement. Sex has been emasculated of its mystery and beauty because of overstimulation and lack of moral absolutes in our culture. Many, if not most, youth have lost their eagerness and vigor for vocations that contribute to the enhancement of society. A shallow "me-ism" has gained front and center stage.

The editors and authors of *The Complete Book of Youth Ministry* are committed to the concept that although some students may be apathetic and shot through with an overdose of narcissism, the gospel of Jesus Christ enables students to be more selfless while gaining a slice of God's viewpoint of themselves and others.

The presence of the Holy Spirit illuminates one's picture of concerns and vocation. But the gospel is no magic potion. Working with junior high (middle school) and senior high school students in churches is tough. In fact, it may be more difficult than ministering to them in a parachurch setting.

The Complete Book of Youth Ministry specializes in working with youth within the context of the local church. It is directed to both youth pastors and volunteer staff people. Church youth ministry is dissimilar and unique from that of parachurch organizations. Paul Borthwick suggests that "it differs from the idealistic models often presented in manuals and seminars. The contrast between actual youth work and many leaders' expectations frequently leads to frustration, discouragement, and 'early retirement.'" (*Youthworker,* Spring 1984, p. 74).

In what ways does church youth ministry differ? In the church, youth workers often have responsibilities to perform other than those specifically related to students. Parachurch staff people are accountable to one boss; in the church, one often is accountable to many. In the church more youth are at different levels of spiritual formation, and some attend meetings against their will. If you attempt to minister to nonchurched youth, some of the church parents may complain. Further, many church kids know the Scriptures intellectually but fail to personalize their faith. Competent strategies are needed.

We believe in church youth ministry. The editors have spent more than thirty years total in that field. Each contributor is first and foremost a practitioner. In our choices of writers we have boycotted the arm-chair theoretician. If we are to present to you experience-honed solutions, we must draw on the practitioners.

The following statements are intended to give the book a common perspective of ministry:

1. Youth ministry begins when adults find a comfortable method of entering a student's world.
2. Youth ministry happens as long as adults are able to use their contacts with students to draw them into a maturing relationship with God through Jesus Christ.
3. Youth ministry ceases to happen when either the adult-student relationship is broken or the outcome of that relationship ceases to move the student toward spiritual maturity.

An exposition of these three principles will be found in chapter 1, "A Theology of Youth Ministry." The rest of the volume provides further elaboration of them.

The editors want to express particular appreciation for the fine contribution of Lenore Benson in assisting us throughout the editorial process. Her precision and high standards in word usage and grammatical form have enriched and enhanced the volume.

Part 1

Background to Church Youth Ministry

Warren S. Benson

1

A Theology of Youth Ministry

Jack has become a theological zombie because of a penchant for methodology. He has been a youth pastor for eight years. Since seminary his reading schedule has constantly deteriorated. In fact, he has not read a book of intellectual substance in three years. His idea of exercising his theological muscles is to read an issue of *Christianity Today* or *Youthworker.* Jack lives from one Youth Specialties conference to another but finds that those experiences provide only a temporary fix.[1]

Nearing a state of collapse because of his frenetic pace, Jack goes on vacation. With time to read, he develops even greater guilt when Richard Foster's *Celebration of Discipline* and Gordon MacDonald's *Ordering Your Private World* devastate him.

Although this entire volume may provide some much-needed direction and focus for Jack, the present chapter will supply only a partial solution.

1. This is not necessarily the fault of Youth Specialities or any other conference approach. Youth workers often fail to reflect on and summarize how their ministry philosophically and experientially should respond to new data or reinforced concepts. Possibly, more events such as those that Youth Specialities so ably provides should conclude with an hour of private reflection and/or small groups in which a person is given the opportunity to articulate the difference the conference has made in his or her own thinking about ministry.

WARREN S. BENSON, Th.M., Ph.D., is vice president of academic administration and professor of Christian education, Trinity Evangelical Divinity School, Deerfield, Illinois.

Still, it is eminently worthwhile to think through *why* we do what we do. Peter Drucker contends that what we do is our value system. Actually, a common thread found in the Foster and MacDonald books is that we are to rethink and reshape our priorities in light of biblical principles. That is the reason for the inclusion of a chapter on the theology of youth ministry: not just getting back to basics but reconstructing, if need be, our philosophy and praxis.[2]

A Rationale for Youth Ministry

My coeditor, Mark Senter, has formulated some experiential touchstones for conceiving and initiating a ministry with youth. These help evaluate whether or not we are beginning to reach into young people's lives. According to Senter,

1. Youth ministry begins when adults find a comfortable method of entering a student's world.
2. Youth ministry happens as long as adults are able to use their contacts with students to draw them into a maturing relationship with God through Jesus Christ.
3. Youth ministry ceases when either the adult-student relationship is broken or the outcome of that relationship ceases to move the student toward spiritual maturity.

Those principles form the basis of our direct encounter with youth. Yet there are a number of theological and philosophical premises that give emergence to them. Most important, they rest on a framework that finds its basis in Scripture, which is viewed as authoritative by all the writers of this volume. Because a high view of Scripture is germane to the various thrusts of the book, we will begin our discussion at that point. The principles themselves will be examined from a theological perspective later in the chapter.

Scripture: An Authoritative Base

Donald Bloesch, in a critique of churches and theological seminaries, comments that if seminaries are to "resist the lure of the technological society" they will be forced "to stress the rediscovery of the historical roots of the faith

2. I am using the term *praxis* in the sense of practice or methodology, not as those who employ the term as the liberation theologians do in which praxis is equated with theology. Gustavo Gutierrez in his *A Theology of Liberation* (New York: Orbis, 1973) states that truth is constituted at the level of personal engagement through concrete acts of charity and compassion because, as he maintains, God does not communicate "truths" from some heavenly, suprahistorical realm. Therefore, there are no such things as preexistent eternal propositions that wait to be discovered. Liberation theology per se will be discussed later in the chapter.

over communication skills and church growth strategies."[3] Bloesch contends that content rather than methodology is to be the centerpiece in our paradigm of ministry. He is fearful that a "generation of technocrats with all the spiritual warmth and fervor of a computer" will be unleashed on the church.[4] Unquestionably, the Word of God and praxis must be kept in balance.

Educationists, not only secular but also some Christian, have been captivated by the potential of sociology and educational psychology to solve our problems. Reinhold Niebuhr critiqued this inclination insightfully when he said:

> The most persistent error of modern educators and moralists is the assumption that our social difficulties are due to the failure of the social scientists to keep pace with the physical sciences which have created our technological civilization. The invariable implication of this assumption is that, with a little more time, a little more adequate moral and social pedagogy and a generally higher development of human intelligence, our social problems will approach solution.[5]

Although secular education continues to be a valuable resource, it should be remembered that it is often in flux, on the move, changing.[6] At times it follows trends that are short-lived. A biblically informed philosophy of education will endure and remain stable in a sea of societal change. Scripturally generated principles for youth ministry should be given primacy because they are always relevant. The Bible provides an unchanging yet dynamic base. Scripture retains its contemporaneity and transcultural character; it does not place us in a methodological restraint.

It should be noted that evangelicals do not denigrate the insights and wisdom of sociology and educational psychology, or any other of the social sciences. Our enthusiasm for the concept that all truth is God's truth militates against a provincialism that implies that the Bible has all the answers. What the evangelical unabashedly calls for is the concept that Scripture stands in judgment. It is Scripture that evaluates other disciplines and provides a framework for content.

THEOLOGY OR PHILOSOPHY?

Theology denotes a system of beliefs about God, human nature, the world, the church, and other related topics formulated to enable Christians to

---

3. Donald G. Bloesch, *Crumbling Foundations* (Grand Rapids: Zondervan, 1984), p. 111. This should not be construed as diminishing the cruciality of communication skills and church growth strategies. Rather it is to establish a proper hierarchy in building a philosophy of ministry.
4. Ibid.
5. Reinhold Niebuhr, *Moral Man and Immoral Society* (New York: Scribner's, 1932), p. xiii.
6. This is true whether one follows secular or religious educationists whose theological moorings are insecure or questionable.

comprehend and make sense of their faith. Classically, philosophy was and is engaged in the development of systems for interpreting reality. Lately, thanks to the thrusts of analytic philosophy, it is seen more often as a source for clarifying meanings and relationships. Charles Gresham states: "Philosophy as a METHOD is concerned with careful thought. It is an attempt to see things as a whole and to interpret the data presented by all aspects of reality. As CONTENT, philosophy attempts to set forth a comprehensive answer to the ultimate questions."[7]

Theology answers such questions as: What is the nature of humankind? What is our purpose in living? Though the Scriptures throw profound light and speak on the following questions, it is philosophy that interacts directly with: What is the nature of reality (metaphysics)? What is the origin of the universe and man? What is the nature of knowledge, and how does one come to know (epistemology)? What is the ultimate destiny of man and the world?[8]

Theology and philosophy are not only tangential; their interrelationship is abundantly obvious. But as Colin Brown indicates, the "relationship between philosophy and the Christian faith" could not be described as an "ideal marriage."[9] The church Fathers Justin Martyr, Origen, and Clement of Alexandria were certain that many pagans had been brought to Christianity through philosophy and "that philosophy was to the ancient Greeks what the Old Testament was to the Jews."[10] Tertullian, among others, rejected that premise, advocating, instead, that "philosophy was often the root of heresy and that worldly wisdom without faith could never bring men to a knowledge of Christ."[11]

The apostle Paul seems to be on Tertullian's side of the discussion, but that conclusion rests on a faulty interpretation of Colossians 2:8, "See to it that no one takes you captive through hollow and deceptive philosophy, which depends on human tradition and the basic principles of this world rather than on Christ." Paul was speaking about the danger of being spoiled by a false philosophy, that is, by any branch of learning that removes Christ from the center of one's life. Christ is the Lord. No knowledge, no matter how seemingly brilliant, is to be compared with Christ. Anyone who loves any wisdom that draws him away from Christ is loving an empty idol. Christ is to be the Lord of our minds.

Ultimately then, theology is to be the determining discipline in construct-

7. Eleanor Daniel, John W. Wade, and Charles Gresham, *Introduction to Christian Education* (Cincinnati: Standard, 1980), p. 51.
8. Ibid.
9. Colin Brown, *Philosophy and the Christian Faith* (Downers Grove, Ill.: InterVarsity, 1966), p. 7.
10. Ibid.
11. Ibid.

ing a philosophy of youth ministry.[12] It furnishes direction regarding our view of authority, God, the world, and how we are to work with non-Christians as well as Christians. One's view of theology, then, is eminently crucial to a youth ministry. For example, if one's theology does not include bringing people into a right relationship with God and with each other, it is not biblical theology (Deut. 6:5; Matt. 22:37-38; 28:16-20). A biblical theology vibrates with reality; namely, the reality of Christ's life that impacts the character and concerns of people, which, in turn, creates a desire to become mission-oriented. That brings us to the person whose life we as leaders are to emulate: Jesus Christ.

THE INCARNATION: MODEL FOR MINISTRY WITH YOUTH

World War II brought many radical changes to North America. The area of youth work was one of them. Both the church and the parachurch youth movements were at the forefront of those changes. In the main, the parachurch organizations set the pace for the churches.

In the late 1930s Jim Rayburn, a seminary student, was serving part-time in a Presbyterian church. Desiring to reach nonchurch high school students, he became frustrated with the stereotypical methods and materials then being used. Fortunately the pastor with whom he worked encouraged him with the statement "Don't monkey around with the people who come to the church. I'll take care of them. You go down to that high school."[13] He instructed Rayburn to go to them rather than hoping that high school students would come to the church building. This may have initiated a new pattern and strategy of youth ministry.

Subsequently, Rayburn founded Young Life. He and his associates were creative pioneers in the philosophy and methodology of youth work.[14] (See chapter 4 for a more complete historical panorama.) They emphasized the

---

12. The term *philosophy* is used in its nontechnical sense here, and often so within this chapter. I will use the term to denote the body of principles that undergird a work with adolescents, as in a philosophy of ministry.
13. Jim Rayburn III, *Dance, Children, Dance* (Wheaton, Ill.: Tyndale, 1984), p. 46.
14. In my judgment it was the creative genius of Walden Howard and Jim Rayburn that spawned many of the fresh concepts that made the Young Life movement so distinctive in its approach. Without question, the visionary and chief spokesman of the movement was Jim Rayburn. The methodological principles practiced by Young Life are: (1) go where kids congregate, (2) accept them as they are, (3) learn how to walk in wisdom to those outside the faith, (4) see the dignity of each unique person, (5) find a neutral setting for the club meetings, (6) create a climate that is informal, (7) speak naturally in terms familiar to he vocabulary of the kids, (8) communicate your certainties rather than flaunt your doubts, (9) consider it a sin to bore kids, especially with the gospel, (10) build on their instinct for adventure, and (11) capitalize on the elements of good fun and music to establish an openness to the gospel. Char Meredith's *It's a Sin to Bore a Kid: The Story of Young Life* (Waco, Tex.: Word, 1978), p. 53. It is interesting to note the number of these principles that have been utilized by the renewal movement within centrist evangelicalism.

incarnational ministry of Jesus Christ as the correct model and motif for touching the lives of youth, particularly the nonchurched. Wise youth workers go where high school people are, as Jesus did.

The incarnational nomenclature projects an analogy of what God accomplished in the person of His Son. In Jesus, God came down to us, became one of us, and identified with us, even though we were separated from Him because of the impasse of our sin. Christ's substitutionary atonement made it possible for us to be reconciled with the Father and have the impasse removed. Through faith in Jesus Christ we can come into a right relationship with God the Father (2 Cor. 5:10-15).

At this point the analogy breaks down. We as sinful but redeemed people go to alienated youth, identify with them by getting to know them and, in a sense, by becoming one of them. In the absence of Christ's physical presence, people working with youth (or any age group) become His representatives. When Christians speak in His name and evidence love and concern, youth see Christ living in those representatives. And we, like Christ, are encouraged to go to the nonchurched as well as to minister to Christians (Acts 20:24). Lawrence Richards and Gib Martin comment:

> To incarnate Jesus in this world, the Christian must experience an inner transformation in which he not only behaves as Jesus behaved, but also shares His love, His valuing of persons, His compassion, and His zeal for justice and righteousness. This character, stamped indelibly on his heart and mind, will be read by all men (2 Cor. 3:2). The incarnation of Jesus in the LAOS of God is to be an incarnation of God's love in personal relationships.[15]

Some of the implications for youth ministry from the above are obvious. Several extrapolations, however, should not be missed. For example, Jesus renounced His rights and became one of us. He took a deep personal interest in people's lives. Doug Stevens adds some insightful perspectives on Christ's ministry patterns:

> He was close to people, empathizing with their hurts and joys and aspirations, and He never adopted the typical style of the guru, aloof and distant. . . . He actively and naturally participated in the culture of His day. . . . Jesus demonstrated authentic love for people (John 11:5, 33-36) and appreciated their true value. He was relentlessly and unhesitatingly committed to people, always viewing relationships as gifts from His Father (John 17:6). . . . He kept an astonishingly low profile. . . . He used no razzle-dazzle. He refused to overwhelm others with exhibitions of His extraordinary power (Mark 8:11-12). Jesus [took] time to devel-

15. Lawrence O. Richards and Gib Martin, *A Theology of Personal Ministry* (Grand Rapids: Zondervan, 1981), p. 101.

op credibility so that people might respond to Him with the right motivation. (John 6:22-59)[16]

To reiterate a principle with which the chapter began, Jesus moved into people's worlds with a comfortable style of ministry. "As we draw close to teenagers (without closing in on or cornering them) and extend our friendship, our adulthood is not compromised. Only mature adults are secure enough to relate to young people this way."[17]

Christ never forgot why He had come, as He gently and lovingly brought people into a redemptive relationship with Himself and His Father. With those who remained with Him, He generated maturing commitment through a discipling relationship. The enabling relationships Christ established were broken only when His followers turned away from Him. He never turned His back on them. Jesus' style of ministry was so remarkable and, indeed, so contemporary that it behooves us to study the gospels on a continuing basis.[18]

THE CONSTRUCTS OF EDUCATIONAL PHILOSOPHY

Jay Kesler has suggested that one's theology is ultimately more important than strategy or methodology. It is not that theology will replace the study of methods, but that methods must flow out of a sound theology.

> Your personal theology will have an effect on everything you do in youth work. It will influence the type of message you bring, the response you expect, the progress of the youth among whom you minister, your method of counseling, your attitude toward others, and how you measure results. In short, all we do relates to what we actually believe.[19]

In essence, one's theology determines his educational philosophy, which in turn undergirds his practice. If an educator believes there is no theology and that all processes are natural, education (youth ministry) will be naturalistic. If one subscribes to supernaturalism and existential theology, education (youth ministry) will be existential and experience-centered at the possible expense of surrendering objectivity and factuality. If, however, our theology is rooted in

16. Doug Stevens, *Called to Care: Youth Ministry and the Church* (Grand Rapids: Zondervan, 1985), pp. 19-37.
17. Ibid., p. 30.
18. See my discussion of Jesus' ministry priorities in "Discipling Youth," in Roy B. Zuck and Warren S. Benson, eds., *Youth Education and the Church* (Chicago: Moody, 1978), pp. 210-11. The following are also suggestive of other materials that are available on Jesus' principles of ministry: Robert E. Coleman, *The Master Plan of Evangelism* (Old Tappan, N.J.: Revell, 1973); A. B. Bruce, *The Training of the Twelve* (Grand Rapids: Kregel, 1971); Carl W. Wilson, *With Christ in the School of Disciple Building* (Grand Rapids: Zondervan, 1976).
19. Jay Kesler, "Determining Your Theology of Youth Ministry," in Gary Dausey, ed., *The Youth Leader's Source Book* (Grand Rapids: Zondervan, 1983), p. 23.

supernaturalism, its task demands the supernatural. If it deals with objective truth, then there is content to be communicated. If this truth is dynamic, then our educational and youth ministry should be dynamic in experience.

THEOLOGICAL PERSPECTIVES EMANATING FROM THE LADDER OF EDUCATIONAL PHILOSOPHY

The authority in which we place our confidence is exceedingly determinative in building a philosophy of youth work. That becomes apparent when we see the philosophic ladder we all use, whether or not we possess sophisticated expertise as educationists. It is not only ironic but tragic when people who hold to a high view of Scripture fail to think through their ministry theologically and philosophically.

Evaluation
Implementation
Structural Organization
Goals/Objectives
Nature of Man
Basis or Authority

Merely a high view of Scripture is not enough. The Word of God gives authoritative directives, principles, and patterns for our philosophy of youth ministry, both in terms of process and content.

FIRST RUNG

We have observed the cruciality of the basis or authority that forms a strong first rung of the philosophic ladder, the trustworthiness and authority of the Bible.

SECOND RUNG

The second rung directs our attention to the human dilemma, the sinfulness of people. John Locke's view regarding persons' having a mind that is a tabula rasa (which extrapolates to sinlessness) is categorically denied. Locke, acclaimed by many as one of the intellectual giants of the eighteenth century—and, indeed, he was—argues that reason rather than revelation should form the basis of education. In wrestling with the relationship between Christian revelation and natural religion, he ultimately "came down on the side of the autonomy of the human knower"[20] and, in his own words, concluded that "reason must be our last judge and guide in everything."[21]

From a biblical perspective, we are created in the image and likeness of God (Gen. 1:26-27). That image is seen in humankind's personality and capacity to know and obey God. Because of the Fall, man stands condemned by the knowledge he has. The result is not the demolition but the distortion of God's image. God created man "a little lower than the heavenly beings" (Ps. 8:5) and "wonderfully made" (Ps. 139:14). The New Testament also speaks of the divine image in unredeemed persons (1 Cor. 11:7; James 3:9). Man is magnificent, yet fallen.

Through Adam all of us received a sinful nature (Rom. 5:12), are spiritually dead (Eph. 2:1), are in rebellion against God (Rom. 2), and, therefore, are unable to receive salvation apart from God's atoning grace in the death of His Son (Eph. 2:8-9). Through faith in Christ as Savior and Lord one is given new life by a sovereign act of the Holy Spirit (Titus 3:5). In youth ministry, then, there should be a recognition of our depravity, human inability, and God's sovereign grace (Eph. 2:4-5).

It is at these first two rungs that evangelicals have a major disagreement with those to the left of us on the theological continuum. The authority of Scripture (2 Tim. 3:16-17; 2 Pet. 1:21) and the depravity of humankind (Rom. 3:23; 5:12)—first and always theological matters—are of great consequence in building a theology or philosophy of education and youth ministry. Although we evangelicals desire to be contemporary, we must not give ground on either of these issues.

THIRD RUNG

The third rung of the philosophic ladder answers the questions: What are the spiritual results we want to see in the lives of our teenagers? What are the goals, purposes, and objectives that we desire for these students? The process of education is related to the nature of our priorities. The Christian should derive his value system from that which is eternal rather than from that which is transitory. A growing and progressive relationship with Jesus Christ is to be valued above all else (Phil. 3:7-10). Some of the ultimate objectives in a youth ministry are to lead them into

1. A consciousness of God as the supreme reality in human experience, to a personal relationship with Him through Christ, to a sense of moral re-

20. Bruce A. Demarest, *General Revelation: Historical Views and Contemporary Issues* (Grand Rapids: Zondervan, 1982), p. 81.
21. John Locke, *An Essay Concerning Human Understanding*, ed. A. D. Woozley (New York: New American Library, 1974), p. 423, cited in Demarest. Paul Henry indicates that American evangelicals have unconsciously incorporated Locke's self-centered individualism into their version of the American dream, Paul Henry, *Politics for Evangelicals* (Philadelphia: Judson, 1974), pp. 29-48.

sponsibility to Him, which shall bring glory to God;

2. An understanding and appreciation of the personality, life, and teachings of Jesus Christ; to an experience of Him as Savior from sin, friend, companion, and Lord; and to obedience and faithfulness to Him, in all of life;
3. A knowledge and experience of the Person and work of the Holy Spirit as comforter, teacher, guide, and source of power;
4. A knowledge, love, and effective use of the Bible as the Word of God and the final authority in faith and conduct;
5. An appreciation of the nature and ministry of the church and to vital participation in its life and work;
6. An appreciation of the meaning and importance of the Christian home and the desire and ability to participate constructively in its life and responsibility;
7. A progressive and continual development of Christlike character;
8. An enthusiastic and skillful involvement in propagating the gospel to the whole world and particularly to others in their own schools;
9. An intelligent and scriptural participation as a Christian citizen who cares for people as Jesus did—for the poor, the neglected, and the forgotten;
10. A Christian interpretation of life and the universe, and to a philosophy of life built on that understanding.[22]

Underlying much of the foregoing is the issue of moral behavior. Although that is the major thrust of chapters two and three, it bears mention in this context. Two of the most helpful books written on youth ministry come from the research skills and perceptions of Merton P. Strommen and his associates.[23] In *Five Cries of Parents* Strommen and his wife, A. Irene Strommen, cite moral behavior as the fifth cry of the parents of fifth through ninth grades. The Strommens follow the line of reasoning advanced by C. S. Lewis in his *The Abolition of Man.*[24]

Lewis suggested that it is possible to identify one judgment of values among the civilizations of the world. The writings of all time imply that the following constitute the moral judgments of all societies:

22. These have been constructed over a period of time by Howard G. Hendricks, Charles M. Sell, and Warren S. Benson in introductory classes in Christian education and adapted to ministry with youth.
23. Merton P. Strommen, *The Five Cries of Youth* (New York: Harper & Row, 1974); Merton P. Strommen, Milo L. Brekke, et. al., *A Study of Generations* (Minneapolis: Augsburg, 1972); Merton P. Strommen and A. Irene Strommen, *The Five Cries of Parents* (San Francisco: Harper & Row, 1985).
24. C. S. Lewis, *The Abolition of Man* (New York: Macmillan, 1946), pp. 95-121, cited in *The Five Cries of Parents,* pp. 105-10.

The "law" of mercy
The "law" of magnanimity:
    Generosity in forgiving
    Willingness to die for another
The "law" of doing good
The "law" of caring for one's family:
    Duties to parents and others
    Duties to children
The "law" of justice:
    Sexual justice
    Honesty
    Justice in court
The "law" of good faith

C. S. Lewis's views express quite correctly that there is a moral structure to the universe built into the very fabric of life. Indeed, there are intrinsic and inherent values. This observation in no way negates the formerly stated theological construct that people are separated from God as the result of sin. Rather, it substantiates that people know right from wrong by virtue of their God-given conscience. That is clearly taught in Romans 1-2.

When youth come to faith, the Holy Spirit assists them to spiritual maturity. That includes the further development of the moral structure God has placed in every human being. And when a person becomes more Christlike, he brings glory to God (Rom. 8:29).

FOURTH AND FIFTH RUNGS

The fourth rung of the educational philosophic ladder identifies the kind of organizational structure or setting where the aforementioned goals and objectives may be achieved in a most natural and effective manner.

The fifth rung forces us to determine what methods and materials to use in bringing about the desired changes. Methods and techniques inevitably focus on the kinds of experiences to which we want students to be exposed. Therefore, the organizational implications of rung four and the experiential and methodological ramifications of the fifth rung will be discussed together, because they cannot logically be divided or developed separately.

How, then, may changes be effected and by what agent? It is the Holy Spirit who convicts the non-Christians of their sin, their mistaken understanding of righteousness, and their own inaccurate perception of judgment (John 16:8-11).[25] It is the Holy Spirit who also brings about growth in the sanctifica-

25. D. A. Carson, *The Farewell Discourse and Final Prayer of Jesus* (Grand Rapids: Baker, 1980), pp. 38-48.

tion of the Christian (1 Cor. 2:9–3:4; Rom. 8:5-17). Our task is to be Spirit-filled (Eph. 5:18), and thus available agents to the work of the Spirit in the lives of students.

The kinds of interaction utilized with adolescents reflect the purpose of the fourth and fifth rungs. The introduction to this chapter, and what this entire book is all about, relates to the three statements of the volume's "Rationale for Youth Ministry."

THEOLOGICAL REFLECTIONS ON THE "RATIONALE FOR YOUTH MINISTRY"

1. Youth ministry begins when adults find a comfortable method of entering a student's world.

Adults are to be relaxed and natural in working with adolescents. Though easily stated, it is difficult for some of us to accomplish this directive. However, the more comfortable we are in the presence of youths without feeling that we have to become one of them, the greater flow we will have into their world and lives.

Societally, children and youth are being narcotized by sensual and violent electronic media. Videos, films, television, and records can be provocative and potentially dangerous. In spite of public and parental pressure, the entertainment industry, based on its interpretation of the Bill of Right's guarantee of free expression,[26] will fight any attempt at regulation.

The point has been made that we are to move into the adolescent's world. A Christian philosophy of ministry should reflect the relentless drive of the triune God for a relationship with people. It is God who desires that closeness, and our interaction with students may be instrumental in bringing it about.

George W. Peters, in discussing the history of God's redemptive plan, indicates that in the Old Testament the Father's concern for the nations was facilitated through Israel, His chosen people. The mission of Israel was centripetal, and in God's hands the nation became a kind of "sacred magnet." As Israel lived in the presence of God she drew the attention of other nations toward Jehovah.[27]

In the New Testament, God's mission becomes centrifugal. The philosophy of ministry in the Old Testament was a "come" philosophy, whereas the New Testament calls for a "go" methodology. Christ sends us as His disciples into the environment of adolescents. Kent R. Hunter notes that this was not a change in ministry, but a change of method.[28]

26. "What Entertainers Are Doing to Your Kids," *U.S. News and World Report,* 28 October 1985, pp. 46-49.
27. George W. Peters, *A Biblical Theology of Missions* (Chicago: Moody, 1972), pp. 22-31.
28. Kent R. Hunter, *Your Church Has Personality* (Nashville: Abingdon, 1985), p. 58.

2. Youth ministry happens as long as adults are able to use their student contacts to draw students into a maturing relationship with God through Jesus Christ.

As we become students' friends, we will gain their trust. As we gain their trust, we shift to a new level in the relationship that facilitates dialogue and authentic response to the lordship of Christ. Ephesians 4:13 identifies our ministry goals as seeking to reach "unity in the faith and in the knowledge of the Son of God and become mature, attaining to the whole measure of the fullness of Christ." Colossians 1:28 encourages us to "proclaim Him, admonishing and teaching everyone with all wisdom, so that we may present everyone perfect in Christ."

That brings us back to the previously discussed concept of incarnating the message, which includes the process of modeling. This may take the form of being at a pizza parlor, a Bible study, going shopping together, a mission trip, having youths in your home, or fifty other informal as well as formal interactions and contexts. Camps and retreats fit in here (see chaps. 22 and 23), and so do small group Bible studies (see chap. 29).

Yet the more profound question concerns the kind of models we are. The more authentic we are as godly persons, the greater the likeness of Christ youths will see. So the quality of our lives is a critical factor in the equation. This fosters a further question: Who will serve as a model or spiritual mentor for us? Eugene H. Peterson suggests that each Christian who desires to be used in ministry should find a "spiritual director,"[29] one who can shepherd him or her in faith development. Without a mentor, the Christianity we are passing on may be effete and nonproductive.

> Spiritual direction takes place when two people agree to give their full attention to what God is doing in one (or both) of their lives and seek to respond in faith. More often than not, these convergent and devout attentions are brief and unplanned; at other times they are planned and structured conversations. Whether planned or unplanned, three convictions underpin these meetings.[30]

One, God is always doing something: an active grace is shaping this life into a mature salvation.

Two, responding to God is not sheer guesswork: the Christian community through the centuries has acquired wisdom that provides guidance.

Three, every person is unique: no wisdom can simply be applied without

29. Eugene H. Peterson, "On Finding a Spiritual Director," *Leadership*, vol. 4, no. 2 (Spring 1983): 38-42; "The Inglorious Work of Spiritual Direction," *Leadership*, vol. 7, no. 1 (Winter 1986): 50-54.
30. Ibid., p. 50.

discerning the particulars of each life, each situation. "Most spiritual direction takes place spontaneously and informally in unplanned but 'just right' moments. . . . The 'unimportant' parts of ministry might be the most important."[31] The Holy Spirit is inventive.

3. Youth ministry ceases when either the adult-student relationship is broken or the outcome of that relationship ceases to move the student toward spiritual maturity.

This principle of our rationale for ministry places the emphasis again on our ability to build relationships with individual persons. Often workers with youth spend too much time planning meetings and too little time building bridges. Without question, Bible studies and other meeting contexts provide consequential growth experiences. However, relationships should take precedence over meetings. Do the adults pray together, strategize, and establish priorities regarding who has best entry into a given student's life? Recruitment of an adequate number of adults and training in relational skills are primary concerns.

Why do adult-student relationships break down or cease to motivate youth toward spiritual maturity? No patent solution can or should be offered. It is easy to assign blame or dismiss it on the basis of parental inadequacies, the erratic behavior patterns of the adolescent, the failure of the church to provide finances or a suitable meeting place. Paul, Silas, and Timothy modeled the shape of significant ministry to students and adults. Their work with the Thessalonians was characterized by spiritual power, pure motives, and godly concern (1 Thess. 2:1-6). Furthermore, they were winsome and wise, tender and caring as they unselfishly gave themselves to others (1 Thess. 2:7-8). They saw the people as individuals rather than as a crowd. Ministry was tailored to personal needs. The phrase "we dealt with each one of you" (v. 11) denotes individualized instruction. It brings the aspects of preaching (the larger context of ministry) together with the particularized aspects of discipling.

The call to each youth worker is to determine, in light of his spiritual gifts, abilities, and talents, how he may contribute to the group's spiritual development. Both the paternal and maternal characteristics of leaders should be utilized in actualization of the three propositional statements in our rationale for ministry.

THE BALANCE OF THEOLOGICAL CONTENT AND PRAXIS

In our discussion of a theology of youth ministry we must not omit a crucial development in the broader field of theology. Liberation theology is

31. Ibid., pp. 53-54.

shouting loudly for a primary position on the agenda of the church. It deals profoundly with the concept of praxis previously mentioned. Bear in mind, however, that when evangelicals employ the term *praxis*, it is generally in light of a dictionary definition, such as practice as distinguished from theory, which is application or use, as of knowledge or skills. Some background may be helpful to set the stage for an understanding of liberation theology's distinctive use of that term.

THE RISE OF NEO-ORTHODOXY

By the 1930s new theological winds were blowing. Evangelicals (fundamentalists to some) had sustained a considerable loss of prestige through the fundamentalist-modernist controversy. On the other hand, Karl Barth, Reinhold Niebuhr, and the neo-orthodoxy they espoused seriously challenged the liberalism of that day, not only in seminar classrooms but also in the ministry of the local church. Kendig Brubaker Cully identifies this significant movement that touched religious education dynamically in his *The Search for a Christian Education—Since 1940.*[32]

In 1940 Harrison Elliott, a colleague of Niebuhr at Union Theological Seminary in New York, wrote *Can Religious Education Be Christian?*[33] Elliott championed liberalism and was critical of neo-orthodoxy. In fact, there were a number of celebrated debates between Elliott and Niebuhr on the Union Seminary campus.

In 1941 H. Shelton Smith, a religious education professor at Duke Divinity School, penned a stinging attack of Elliott's position and advocated a neo-orthodox approach to theology.[34] Norma Thompson, in commenting on Elliott's position, noted that "by 1944 the controversy had assumed sufficient magnitude to become of pressing concern to the leaders of the International Council of Religious Education,"[35] to which only a few mainline denominational evangelicals belonged.

EVANGELICALISM

In 1946 Frank E. Gaebelein led the Commission on Educational Institutions of the National Association of Evangelicals to study the philosophy and practice of Christian education. The results were presented in *Christian Education in a Democracy.*[36]

Gaebelein subsequently developed a series of lectures on the integration

32. Kendig Brubaker Cully, *The Search for a Christian Education—Since 1940* (Philadelphia: Westminster, 1955), p. 17.
33. Harrison S. Elliott, *Can Religious Education Be Christian?* (New York: Macmillan, 1940).
34. H. Shelton Smith, *Faith and Nurture* (New York: Scribner's, 1941).
35. Norma H. Thompson, ed., *Religious Education and Theology* (Birmingham: Religious Education Press, 1982), p. 6.
36. Frank E. Gaebelein, *Christian Education in a Democracy* (New York: Oxford, 1951).

of evangelical theology with Christian education that were given at three seminaries. These were published under the title *The Pattern of God's Truth.*[37] Gaebelein saw Scripture as the base for the integration of faith and learning. The centrality of the Bible furnishes the core and unity of learning around which educational settings, whether formal, nonformal, or informal, may be built. Recently, Bruce Lockerbie, long-time colleague of Gaebelein's at the Stony Brook School, Long Island, New York, brought together some of the best of Gaebelein's material on integration in *The Christian, the Arts, and Truth.*[38]

Reformed philosopher Gordon H. Clark published *A Christian Philosophy of Education*[39] in 1946 and Lois E. LeBar wrote *Education That Is Christian*[40] in 1958, but it was Gaebelein who brought evangelical Christian education into perspective through the paradigms and constructs of theology. Though none of those thinkers interacted authentically with the neo-orthodox and liberal religious educators—they were more concerned with establishing a systematic evangelical philosophy of education—they did provide a much-needed structure for evangelical Christian education.

More recently, among evangelical writers, only Lawrence O. Richards has written extensively on youth work and educational philosophy. (I am not aware of any neo-orthodox, liberal, process theology, or liberationist theologian who has written extensively in both of these areas.) Richards develops a socialization model that opts for nonformal and informal learning. He makes a strong case for a youth ministry that will not allow students merely to assent to the truth of Scripture. Too often our Bible studies with youth are information centered and weak in life response. But according to Richards, sharing feelings, attitudes, and even beliefs is not sufficient. Scripture is God's revelation of reality. It demands decision and commitment that culminates in action, both attitudinal and behavioral change.

Furthermore, Richards avers that both Old and New Testaments (Deut. 6:4-9; 31:12-13; Prov. 1:2-5; Matt. 28:19-20; 1 Thess. 2:7-12; 2 Tim. 2:2; 3:10-11) establish that the truth of God comes "from outside the realm of human experience." It focuses "on a personal relationship with God" and the way in which "that relationship is expressed in a godly lifestyle. . . . Effective teaching demands participation in a community in which that Word is put into practice."[41] Therefore, intimate, ongoing relationships with good models—those who demonstrate the truths they articulate—are mandatory.

37. Frank E. Gaebelein, *The Pattern of God's Truth* (Chicago: Moody, 1968). It was originally published by Oxford University Press in 1953.
38. Frank E. Gaebelein with D. Bruce Lockerbie, ed., *The Christian, the Arts, and Truth* (Portland: Multnomah, 1985).
39. Gordon H. Clark, *A Christian Philosophy of Education* (Grand Rapids: Eerdmans, 1954).
40. Lois E. LeBar, *Education That Is Christian* (Old Tappan, N.J.: Revell, 1958; rev. 1981).
41. Lawrence O. Richards, *Expository Dictionary of Bible Words* (Grand Rapids: Zondervan, 1985), p. 592.

Richards's thinking about youth ministry has gained wide acceptance among evangelicals. As indicated above, he has moved from a formal, cognitive position regarding the teaching-learning process. His 1985 revision of *Youth Ministry: Its Renewal in the Church* indicates a continuing shift toward the socialization model and its emphasis on nonformal and informal learning.[42]

LIBERATION THEOLOGY

Without question, liberation theology poses a challenge to all theologies, including evangelical theology. To be accurate, we should use the plural. Theologies of liberation find contemporary expression among blacks, feminists, Asians, Hispanic Americans, and native Americans (that is true for Canada as well). The most significant and articulate expression has taken place in Latin America through the teaching and writings of theologians such as Gustavo Gutierrez and Juan Luis Segundo and educationists such as Paulo Freire and Ivan Illich.

The development of liberation theology in Latin America should be seen as an endeavor to unite theology, sociology, and political concerns. Philosophically and sociologically its major input came from Immanuel Kant, George F. Hegel, and Karl Marx. Evangelical theologian Bruce A. Demarest has described the evolution of Gutierrez's seminal thinking in particular.

Gutierrez argues that the church historically has seriously misunderstood the nature of the theological enterprise. During the early centuries of its life, the church concentrated on the spiritual function of the discipline—defining theology as "wisdom." From this perspective, the theological task focused on withdrawal from worldly concerns, meditation on the Bible, and the mystical quest for perfection. However, from the eleventh or twelfth century on, theology increasingly came to be viewed as a body of formal knowledge. Here emphasis was placed on the rationality of Christian faith, the systemization of faith into a body of truths, and the defense of a doctrinal position. The high-water mark of this latter approach to theology was achieved during the time of Thomas Aquinas, who firmly established theology as a rational science. Gutierrez adamantly insists that these two traditional models—theology as wisdom and theology as science—must give way to the 20th century vision of theology as praxis. In a world whose horizons are dominated by masses of poor, oppressed, and despoiled people, a radically new way of doing theology is mandated.

Gutierrez thus envisions theology not as pietistic spirituality, nor as reflection on doctrine, but as ACT, or practical INVOLVEMENT in the plight of the poor and the powerless of the world.[43]

42. Lawrence O. Richards, *Youth Ministry: Its Renewal in the Church*, rev. ed. (Grand Rapids: Zondervan, 1985), pp. 168-69.
43. Demarest, *General Revelation*, p. 210.

Certainly any Christian should attempt to contribute to the elimination of injustices and halt the exploitation of those in bondage. But to Gutierrez, that may necessitate revolutionary involvement that would mirror the dictates of Marxist socioeconomic analysis. Furthermore, to the liberationists, praxis means far more than the application of theological truth to a life situation. Gutierrez defines theology as "critical reflection on historical praxis."[44] That is, doing theology calls for the discovery and formation of theological truth that emerges out of a given historical context in the class struggle for a new socialist society.

David D. Webster declares that "liberation theology rightly exposes the fact of oppression in society," but its weakness and error "stems from the application of misleading hermeneutical principles and a departure from historic Christian faith."[45] For liberationists, praxis has in effect become their theology.

Evangelicals need not appropriate the Marxist scheme to legitimize the use of a praxis as doing. Rather, theology and praxis, separate activities engaged in together, can be thoroughly biblical, Pauline, and evangelical. In other words, it is truth that should set the agenda and provide the motivation for praxis, that is, ministry with all people.

Liberationists reverse the biblical order by upholding the priority of doing over knowing, or praxis (their use of the term) over revealed truth. "Gutierrez and other liberationists often do little more than hang biblical window dressing on the framework of a sociological theory."[46]

Praxis, in effect, has become their hermeneutic and their theology. Scripture is forced to accommodate itself to culture and meet the standards of society rather than society meeting the standards of Scripture. Also, liberation theology often presents salvation and participation in the kingdom of God as the inalienable birthright of humankind. Thus, a universalist strain tends to pervade its literature. Gutierrez insists that "all men are in Christ efficaciously called to communion with God." That is, "the salvification of God underlies all human existence."[47] Liberation theology has distanced itself from the ortho-

---

44. Cited in Douglas D. Webster, "Liberation Theology," in Walter A. Elwell, ed., *Evangelical Dictionary of Theology* (Grand Rapids: Baker, 1985), p. 635.
45. Ibid., p. 637.
46. Demarest, *General Revelation*, p. 215.
47. Gustavo Gutierrez, *A Theology of Liberation* (Maryknoll, N.Y.: Orbis, 1973), pp. 71, 153. I am aware that Gutierrez attempts to distinguish three components of salvation in this book: "political liberation, the liberation of man throughout history, liberation from sin." Gutierrez does affirm that sin is the root problem and that ultimately liberation from sin is a gift of God through Christ. Nevertheless, he asserts that progress on the other components of liberation do in fact cooperate with and promote liberation from sin. In other words, human reconciliation was not equated with reconciliation to God, but *was* intrinsically related to it. To Gutierrez, you cannot have complete liberation from sin in Christ without being involved in the liberation of others politically. The liberationists' criticism of evangelicals' tendency for theology becoming an end in itself is at times justifiable. Good works are mandatory, but they are not the equivalent of salvation. Gutierrez remains Pelagian in his view of salvation.

dox manner of thinking about the central doctrines of salvation. As the foregoing has clearly implied, theology and praxis are inextricably bound together. The deeper question is, Which judges which?

An inevitable problem that liberationists have addressed concerns the frightening social and political conditions found on all continents, particularly Latin America and Africa. The call to minister to the whole person is right, proper, and biblical. The liberationists have ministered to the poor, but evangelicals have, too, although often inadequately. The gospel must penetrate the individual; then its implications for the social order are legitimate. However, Demarest is correct in contending that this fails to legitimize the "assertion that man comes to know God savingly by identification with the poor and oppressed." Rather, as he points out, "God is redemptively known not in the neighbor but through the divine Savior" and that "participation in the plight of the poor and oppressed represents the *fruit* rather than the root of one's knowledge of God."[48]

Educators Ivan Illich and Paulo Freire have become heroes to some North American religious educators because of their substantial efforts in assisting Latinos and others to learn to read and develop economic skills. But they, like Gutierrez and so many other liberationists, have a defective theology that holds that man is inherently good. They reject the biblical assertion that sin originates in the human heart (Mark 7:20-23) and that all of mankind stands condemned because of original sin (Rom. 3:9-18).

David Webster concludes his discussion of liberation theology as follows:

> Liberation theology stirs Christians to take seriously the social and political impact of Jesus' life and death but fails to ground Jesus' uniqueness in the reality of his deity. It claims He is different from us by degree, not by kind, and that his cross is the climax of his vicarious identification with suffering mankind rather than a substitutionary death offered on our behalf to turn away the wrath of God and triumph over sin, death, and the devil. A theology of the cross which isolates Jesus' death from its particular place in God's design and shuns the disclosure of its revealed meaning is powerless to bring us to God, hence assuring the perpetuity of our theological abandonment.[49]

As evangelicals we must hear the cries of the poor and the oppressed. We are challenged by Scripture to respond to cries for social justice. William H. Taylor boldly states:

> Escapism [is] a denial of the balance between Bread and breads. It is nonbiblical, unrealistic, and a negation of responsibility beyond physical comfort.

48. Ibid., p. 215. For background on the differences of pure theory and praxis-oriented theory see Nicholas Wolterstorff, "Theory and Praxis," *Christian Scholar's Review,* vol. 9, no. 4 (1980): 317-36.
49. Webster, *Evangelical Dictionary,* p. 637.

What we need are more Evangelicals who are at the same time biblically literate and compassionate, and who with the highest view of the Scriptures will contextualize their theology in the lives of precious humans. Believers and nonbelievers live in the bitter reality of historical oppression and poverty, injustice and violence. They need and deserve a biblical evangelism which does justice and preaches grace.[50]

How much will liberation theology impact the youth ministry of your church? Directly, not very much. But idealistic youth will respond positively to the cries of those in need. Workers with youth should lead the way as they struggle with the clear call of Scripture to become involved and not turn their backs.

In many geographical contexts the needs of urban North America are multifaceted. A vital component of service should be direct participation in activities such as food and clothing distribution and remedial educational centers, as well as backyard Bible clubs and Bible studies. Any ministry that will be appropriate for junior high or senior high students should be considered.

It becomes apparent that liberation theology's focus on good works has minimized the biblical message of repentance and salvation. This flawed theory/practice renders it a form of religious humanism that is more sociological and political than theological.

CONCLUSION

In discussing evangelical ministries to youth, Canadian researcher Donald Posterski forces us to go back to the basic questions regarding the theology of the church (and therefore of youth ministry) when he asks:

Is the church a place where we call people to come and live their Christian life out within the confines of the institution, or does the church exist to equip people to go into the world and be the church? If our mentality is that we do ministry when we gather people inside the church, we're not going to be effective. Does the institution exist to serve, or to be served? Until we get that straight, until the energies of the church and the resources of youth workers are poured into people, we will have a shallow understanding of what it is to be a follower of Jesus Christ, and thus a shallow, ineffective ministry to our culture.[51]

50. William H. Taylor, in Robert E. Coleman, ed., *Evangelism on the Cutting Edge* (Old Tappan, N.J.: Revell, 1986), pp. 66, 69. See Emilio Antonio Núñez, *Liberation Theology* (Chicago: Moody, 1985); John Perkins, *A Quiet Revolution: The Christian Response to Human Need . . . A Strategy for Today* (Waco, Tex.: Word, 1976); Miriam Adeney, *God's Foreign Policy: Practical Ways to Help the World's Poor* (Grand Rapids: Eerdmans, 1984); Richard Cizik, ed., *The High Cost of Indifference: Can Christians Afford Not to Act?* (Ventura, Calif.: Regal, 1984); Vinay Samuel and Chris Sugden, eds., *Evangelism and the Poor: A Third World Study Guide* (Oxford: Oxford Centre for Mission Studies, 1982).
51. Donald Posterski, in *Youthworker,* vol. 3, no. 4 (Winter 1986), p. 62.

Repeatedly in this chapter we have attempted to answer these and other crucial theological queries that drive us back to Scripture. Initially, we established that Scripture is authoritative and capable of providing a base on which a theology of youth ministry may be constructed. Second, we answered the question of theology or philosophy by asserting that though theology is our authoritative foundation, we must also think philosophically as we build our ministries. Third, we discussed the incarnational model of ministry that Christ embodied and that we would do well to follow. Fourth, we looked at theology and ministry in light of the constructs of educational philosophy. And fifth, we discussed the balance between theological content and practice, or praxis, that gives intentionality to our ministry with students.

Our thesis has been that theology is not incidental to building a philosophy of ministry with students. A working knowledge of theology is a most important consideration. Kurt Lewin's suggestion that there is nothing more practical than a good theory is indeed correct. And good theology has much more going for it than good theory. According to the evangelical, we can embrace Scripture and the theology it teaches with certitude. C. Ellis Nelson's statement that "the limitation that is most distressing in our day is the inability of theology to establish a common authority for faith," though essentially accurate, is patently unacceptable to the evangelical.[52]

Though our methodology remains sensitive to changes in society, we move forward with confidence and humility to construct a theology that is based on a wholly dependable Word from God. Certain understandings of Scripture and theology will change, but that trustworthy record is impregnable.

For Further Reading

Bloesch, Donald G. *Crumbling Foundations.* Grand Rapids: Zondervan, 1984.

Dausey, Gary, ed. *The Youth Leader's Source Book.* Grand Rapids: Zondervan, 1983.

Demarest, Bruce A. *General Revelation: Historical Views and Contemporary Issues.* Grand Rapids: Zondervan, 1982.

Erickson, Millard J. *Christian Theology.* Grand Rapids: Baker, 1983.

Peterson, Michael L. *Philosophy of Education.* Downers Grove, Ill.: InterVarsity, 1986.

Richards, Lawrence O. *Youth Ministry—Its Renewal in the Church.* Rev. ed. Grand Rapids: Zondervan, 1985.

Stevens, Doug. *Called to Care.* Grand Rapids: Zondervan, 1985.

Zuck, Roy B., and Warren S. Benson. *Youth Education in the Church.* Chicago: Moody, 1978.

---

52. Ellis C. Nelson, "Theological Foundations for Religious Nurture," in Marvin J. Taylor, ed., *Changing Patterns of Religious Education* (Nashville: Abingdon, 1984), p. 13.

2

Anthony Campolo

The Youth Culture in Sociological Perspective

There is no single youth culture in the technological, urban, industrialized societies of the Western world. Instead, there are a variety of subcultures existing side by side, each with its own language, value system, and worldview. A survey of a typical American high school will give ample evidence, even to the casual observer, of a kaleidoscope of subcultures. There are *the preppies, the burn outs, the punkers, the jocks,* and *the God squad,* among others. Each of these groups has unique characteristics, and the members of each group recognize themselves as distinct and "superior" to those who belong to other groups. Ridiculing members of other subcultural groups within the given high school social system is a favorite pastime of youth.

There is a great temptation to treat young people as though they belonged to a single cultural system. It is easier to design programs and curriculum for ministry if we yield to that temptation. Sweeping generalizations about young people's needs, psychology, and beliefs provide us with an imagined cultural mind-set for which we can develop "relevant" ministries. Youth work for the church is by no means that effortless. Instead, we should be prepared to relate to a variety of subcultural types as we endeavor to communicate the gospel. Teenagers of one subcultural group will require a linguistic approach, a program style, and a psychological understanding that will be different and distinct from that required to reach another subcultural group.

ANTHONY CAMPOLO, Ph.D., is professor of sociology, Eastern College, St. David's, Pennsylvania.

However, in spite of their varied and distinguishing traits and characteristics, there are some commonalities to the young people who make up the teenage cohort. There are social forces that have influenced all youth, and it is possible to analyze these forces and their social-psychological consequences on character formation. Such an analysis can prove useful in our endeavors to understand the special people those in youth ministry have been called to serve.

INDUSTRIAL REVOLUTION AND THE ROLE OF TEENAGERS

Among the many forces at work molding the general consciousness of youth, the most important are those derived from consequences of the Industrial Revolution. The urban life-style created by industrialization has forced a redefinition of the societal role of young people, and with that redefinition has come a stress and strain that we are still trying to alleviate.

First of all, we must face the fact that children were necessary when we lived in a basically agrarian society, but are unnecessary in the urban industrial system. On the farm there was always important work for children to do. There were cows to be milked, fields to be plowed, and barns to be painted. Children and teenagers knew they were needed. Young people were major contributors to the economic well-being of their families, and they were well aware of their value. In fulfilling their role expectations, they were required to do exhausting work, but it was that work that established their significance and identity. Their economic role in the preindustrial world was a source of healthy pride. Then came the steam engine; which, in turn, gave birth to the factory system; which, in turn, gave birth to the urban-industrial society. In its earliest stages the emerging industrial economy still provided important work for young people. The wages of factory workers were so despicably low that the survival of many families was dependent on every member being gainfully employed. Unfortunately, the work available to youth was often inhumane and psychologically destructive. The history of the industrialization of the Western world is marked by too many chapters outlining the exploitation of children and teenagers in such places as the coal mines of Pennsylvania, the textile factories of New England, and the sweat shops of New York City. Children were brutalized by a socio-economic system that, at the turn of the century, was undeterred by government regulations and unchallenged by unions. Yet, even in those bitter days, the children of factory workers and miners knew they were *needed.*

In the years following World War II, the youth of America gradually made an unhappy discovery about themselves that had never been true of young people in any other generation in human history. Those human by-products of an advanced industrial society gradually came to realize that they were superfluous. The wages of factory workers and office clerks had risen to a level high enough to enable them to support their families without the earnings of their children. Children no longer were expected to serve the economic needs of their families but instead came to view themselves as persons to be served by their families. In the new social order, people might desire children to meet their emotional needs and to become the objects of gratifying love, but one thing was certain: they were no longer economic necessities. In the brave new world of postwar affluent America, married couples were not likely to view children as economic assets. Instead, they tried to figure out if they could afford to have children, who in many ways had become economic liabilities.

Parents in an urban industrial society may *want* children, and they may *love* them when they are born. But children are no longer economically necessary. The consequences of this new state of affairs are threatening. Young people *know* they are unneeded, and it is a short step from *being* unneeded to *feeling* unwanted. Stripped of the necessity of laboring for the well-being of their families, life in many ways has become easier for contemporary youth (as their parents often remind them). But on the other hand, young people do not always find it easy to cope with the truth that they are, in economic perspective, useless liabilities.

Existing solely for the emotional gratification of parents is by no means desirable for most teenagers. They often resent the burden of being responsible for the happiness of their parents. They labor with the awareness that their successes and failures are of undue concern to their parents. Getting good grades, being popular, dating often, and making varsity teams are more than individualistic accomplishments for teenagers, because they know the happiness of their parents is tied up with such achievements. The burden of being responsible for the emotional fulfillment of parents is often too heavy for teenagers, and in many cases they simply give up trying.

In our new urban industrial society, all most parents ask of their children is that they be happy. However, achieving happiness is no easy task and is seldom attained by seeking after it. Rather, it is a by-product of giving and serving. Though this is a truth that modern psychologists like Erich Fromm[1] and M. Scott Peck[2] have promoted over the past few decades, the New Testament has presented the same message for nineteen hundred years. As society has denied young people the opportunity of doing meaningful work and contributing to the well-being of their families, it has simultaneously denied them an important way to achieve the happiness that accompanies self-giving. It is more blessed to give than to receive, and most of today's young people are being denied the possibility of being blessed.

1. Erich Fromm, *The Art of Loving* (New York: Harper & Row, 1956).
2. M. Scott Peck, *The Road Less Traveled* (New York: Simon and Schuster, 1978).

THE DECLINE OF PARENTAL AUTHORITY

It is well known that the authority of parents has declined over the past two generations, but sometimes we fail to associate this decline with the consequences of an emerging urban industrial society. In the agrarian society of yesteryear children were obedient to their parents. Fathers ruled the homes, and their word was law to all who lived under their roofs. When America lived on farms, fathers could exercise patriarchal control of their families because they were always at home. Because they resided and labored at the same locale, they could make decisions, establish rules, and mete out punishments. However, the urban industrial life-style changed all of that by establishing a work schedule that has removed fathers from their households.

In recent years we have debated the consequences that working mothers have on the character formation of children. But we have given little attention to the significant effects of the removal of fathers from the home in our urban industrial world. The typical American father leaves for work at seven in the morning and does not return until six in the evening. For the better part of the day fathers are not available. Preachers may eloquently declare that fathers should be the heads of their families, but it is impossible for them to be rulers and disciplinarians if they are absent from their homes most of the time.

Mothers would seem to be the likely successors to power in the absence of fathers, but unfortunately they have not, for the most part, moved into the leadership gap. In America we have been victimized by what I call the cult of momism. Both the psychology of Freud and the principles of behaviorism have led mothers to believe that their primary task is to be "love machines." They think that the psychological well-being of their children is dependent on the children seeing mother as always lovable. Mothers are warned that all sorts of neurotic behavior will evidence itself in their children unless the children can constantly view them with love. Mothers who are preoccupied with being sure that their children love them at all times are not able to exercise decisive leadership. Good leadership in the home requires discipline and the making of unpopular rulings. If mothers are afraid of having their children dislike them even temporarily, they cannot provide the controlling authority that children need in their everyday lives. There is role conflict between being a strong leader and being well liked. Unfortunately, American mothers have chosen to be well liked.

If the fathers cannot rule because they are absent most of the time, and the mothers are afraid to rule because they dread incurring their children's resentment, we are inclined to ask, "Who rules teenagers?" But we know the answer to that. The teenagers themselves have taken the reins of control, and ours is quickly becoming a society dominated by teenagers. The problems associated with this set of circumstances have been explored brilliantly by Erik

H. Erikson, the famous Harvard psychologist.[3] Erikson contends that, in the maturation process, the child goes through distinct stages of development. With each of those stages there are privileges and responsibilities. He argues that if children are forced to accept the privileges and responsibilities that belong to a stage of development into which they have not yet moved, they will become disoriented, confused, and neurotic. Looking at contemporary young people, Erikson concludes that the demise of parental leadership in American families has left teenagers with the burden of making decisions they are ill-equipped to make. The authority vacuum in American family life has forced young people to accept privileges and responsibilities they cannot handle. In short, the inability of families to cope with changes brought on by the urban industrial revolution has placed teenagers in a burdensome position. They are being forced into a state of freedom that their immaturity has not equipped them to handle. The depressions and despondencies so typical of contemporary teenagers are, in part, related to this. The rising rate of teenage suicide is also a likely concomitant. Moreover, drug use and alcoholism among teenagers probably are related to the lack of regulations in the teenage world, a situation sociologists call anomie.

Young people need structure to their lives if they are to survive psychologically, and they seem incapable of creating that structure for themselves. To meet this need, the church should take action. It would be useful if the church would sponsor parenting workshops so that parents can get together in Christian community and collectively decide the guidelines for their children's behavior. Proper and fair norms for dating, times to get home at night, responsibility for family chores, and allowances can be established at these parental get-togethers. Biblical requisites for sexual behavior can be ascertained and established. Parents can gain the confidence they need in order to stand up to their children's demands for leniency.

Once the norms and regulations are defined in the context of Christian community, parents should discuss with their own children what the fair punishment should be for violation of the rules. If punishments are established *prior* to violations, with teenagers agreeing to the punishments' fairness, there will be minimal pressure on parents as they carry out their responsibility for establishing authority over their children. For instance, my son had agreed with my wife and me that if he received another traffic ticket for speeding, he would lose his driving privileges for six months. When subsequently he did receive a citation for breaking the speed limit, he meekly surrendered his car keys. Because the punishment already had been established with his consent, he did not argue with us or express any hostility.

3. Erik H. Erikson, *Identity, Youth and Crisis* (New York: Norton, 1968).

FAMILY SIZE AND TEENAGE CHARACTER

Because children are economic liabilities in an urban industrial society, families are smaller than in previous generations. In contemporary America we tend to have two children families, whereas a century ago families of five or six children were common. The differences between children who are raised in small families and children who are raised in large families is rather obvious to any who take the time to observe them. Primarily, children raised in small families are conditioned to having their families adapt to their needs and expectations, whereas children raised in large families are prepared to adapt to the needs and expectations of their families. For instance, if there is one child in a household, that child might be asked at what time he or she would like dinner served. But if there are eleven children in a family, the hour for dinner is set, and the individual child is told to be there at that time.

TELEVISION AND THE YOUTH CULTURE

Marshall McLuhan, more than any other modern-day scholar, has sensitized us to the influences that the various modes of communication have in the forming of our personalities. He makes clear that the character of teenagers has been dramatically shaped by television.[4] The sheer amount of time teenagers spend watching television gives us ample warning that it is a powerful force in their development. Consider that the typical teenager in America watches television five hours a day but converses with his or her father only seven minutes. In light of that, it is easy to ascertain which is likely to have the greater influence when it comes to the communicating of values. Many teenagers would be affected more by the loss of TV from their lives than they would be by the loss of their fathers.

Most of us are aware that the violence and sexual material on television have bombarded the consciousness of youth to the point where they seem indifferent and jaded when it comes to the violence and sexual deviance in everyday life. We all have questioned the content of television programming. However, McLuhan leads us to explore the more subtle influences of television on youth, influences that go far beyond the analysis of programming.

Perhaps most important is the discovery that television has brought an end to any concept of childhood. Sociologists have come to recognize that for childhood to exist as a stage in personal development there must be secrecy. Some information must be withheld because it is considered offensive or obscene to the sensitivities of the young. Sexual knowledge and the realities about the violence and corruption of human nature are purposely concealed

4. Marshall McLuhan, *Understanding Media: The Extension of Man* (New York: McGraw-Hill, 1964).

from children so they can grow up in a world surrounded by people whom they believe to be basically good and pure.

McLuhan and his successors (e.g., Neil Postman) contend that childhood existed when reading was the primary mode of communicating information. As children learned to read, there was progressive development, not only of their skills, but also of the content of reading materials. "Adult knowledge" was kept out of children's books, and therefore they had very limited access to the secrets of adulthood. For a child growing up forty years ago, pornography consisted of viewing the native women in *The National Geographic,* and the concealed world of adult sexuality could be glimpsed only by peeking into medical books in the public library. Children were protected from the harsh realities of life. And from the Renaissance until the introduction of electronic communications (radio and television), it was possible to maintain this protection.

Childhood came to an abrupt end with the advent of electronic communications, particularly television. Now, youngsters of nine and ten years of age are aware that rapes and violence exist in their own neighborhoods. The evening news, television talk shows, and special reports on television have them well versed on such subjects as abortion, homosexuality, and incest. By the time they reach the age of twelve, modern young people have an understanding of life that is already cynical and far beyond what we generally assume is appropriate for those at such a "tender" age. In reality, the media makes them adults in awareness, if not emotionally, well before they reach the teenage years. Anyone who has ever tried to explain the facts of life to a high school youth group is aware that childhood has been abolished by the media. Often those involved in religious education deny this reality and try to introduce young people to aspects of life about which teenagers already know much and about which they already have fixed opinions and judgments.

Another way in which television conditions youth is by making the events in their everyday lives seem boring by comparison. Television holds attention through the use of what Jerry Mander calls technical changes.[5] Mander, the author of a recent book on the effects of television, explains that television presents pictures of a subject from different angles and in rapid succession. With zoom lenses, viewers are first moved in close to a character or scene, then transported to distant perspectives. Images can be rapidly changed, superimposed on other images, or distorted for desired effects. In the average television show, viewers are exposed to upwards of fifteen technical changes per minute. In an effort to hold the viewers' attention, the producers of television commercials increase the number of technical changes. In an expensive Pepsi or Coke ad, the number of technical changes can run as high as a

5. Jerry Mander, *Four Arguments for the Elimination of Television* (New York: Morrow, 1978).

hundred per minute. Interest is maintained by throwing multiple images on the screen in rapid succession so that the viewer is mesmerized by the presentation.

A generation of young people reared on television has been conditioned to view reality as dull. After all, reality does not offer rapid image changes. Today's typical teenagers are not impressed as they stand at the edge of the Grand Canyon. They have already seen the beer ad on TV in which the canyon is shown from twenty different angles in a period of thirty seconds. The real Grand Canyon just sits there doing nothing. When teenagers go to school, they find teachers boring by comparison to "Sesame Street," in which the letters of the alphabet dance and sing their way through a multiplicity of technical changes. Certainly church seems dull and boring to the youth of our day. They are used to having their attention held by rapid changes in image and sound.

Still another way in which television has conditioned the consciousness of modern youth is through the creation of celebrities. Celebrities have taken the places of heroes as persons to be emulated by youth. Celebrities, whose talents have made them temporary luminaries, dazzle the imaginations of young people, whereas heroes, who distinguish themselves through the risking of their own well-being for the sake of humanity, have faded as role models. There is no question that young people are more prone to imitate Michael Jackson than Mother Teresa, and Paul McCartney rather than Martin Luther King. The death of John Lennon gave evidence of the ability of the media to create bigger-than-life personages that elicit worship from the teenage populace. These media celebrities seldom portray a life-style or suggest a value system that is acceptable for Christians.

I used to host a television interview show on one of the Philadelphia stations. One day I invited one of the most prominent rock disc jockeys in the city as a guest. I had thought that I would create a heated dialogue by starting off the show with a statement that judged contemporary rock stars to be, for the most part, a morally twisted, sexually obscene group of self-centered egotists who were major contributors to the emerging American drug culture. Much to my surprise the disc jockey agreed with me wholeheartedly. He went on to say that in his business he was required to get to know rock stars personally, and he had not met one that he would allow into his home as a guest. He explained that the rock stars were destroyed by the very media that had given them fame.

Television is able to rocket a twenty-year-old performer into international stardom and make that performer into the idol of tens of millions of people overnight. No ordinary person can escape the perversion that usually follows such awesome glory and adulation, my guest explained. He believed that most rock stars become self-indulgent, rebellious against the norms that restrain ordinary folk, and end up immersed in a life-style wherein their every wish or whim, be it sexual or material, is immediately gratified. The teenagers of our society not only listen to the music of the stars they meet via television videos but also study the details of the personal lives of those performers via a host of publications aimed at the youth market. Rock stars set a style that is admired and imitated by youth more than most of us want to admit. No honest secular sociologist would deny that television has created by means of its rock stars a life-style that glorifies the defiance of societal norms and the acceptability of drug use, and one that engenders permissiveness in sexual matters.

There was a time when those who work with young people urged youth not to adopt the values and life-style prescribed by their peers. Although peer groups still play a significant role in conditioning the behavior of young people, peer groups are no longer primary value creators. The media create the values for contemporary youth. It is from television that they learn dress styles, language, sexual norms, and purposes for living. The peer group only serves to reinforce those values. It is the peer group that ridicules the young person who does not conform to the life-style and value system that has been defined by television sit-coms, dramas, soap operas, and videos. The peer group is an enforcer, not the creator of behavioral norms. The youth of our age, with all of their varied subcultural manifestations, are media productions.

Limitations on time and space prevent a complete survey of the sociological factors influencing young people, but even a limited survey must give some attention to the impact of the dating system. Youth seem to be preoccupied with dating, and teenagers tend to see themselves as failures or successes in terms of how well they do at the dating game. In his book *Coming of Age in America,* American anthropologist Edgar A. Friedenberg gives ample evidence that the status of young people within the high school social structure is almost completely determined by how well they come across to members of the opposite sex. Boys evaluate other boys and girls evaluate other girls in terms of their popularity as dates.[6] Willard Waller, one of the founders of American sociology, wrote a brilliant essay entitled "Dating and Rating" in which he outlined how young people are constantly evaluating themselves and others in terms of how they do in the dating game.[7] It is no exaggeration to suggest that most young people are grading each other on a numerical scale of one to ten.

The dating system is an American invention and has evidenced itself as a mating pattern since the end of World War I. Prior to that, mates were selected by means of courting. In courting, as opposed to dating, young men were expected to gain permission from the parents of prospective partners before there could be the kind of social interaction that might lead to marriage. The breakdown of the small rural community brought an end to the age of courting. In today's world young people get to know each other in settings that may

6. Edgar A. Friedenberg, *Coming of Age in America* (New York: Vintage, 1963).
7. Willard Waller, "The Rating and Dating Complex," *American Sociological Review* (1937): 731.

be completely alienated from those with which their parents are familiar. Young people meet in huge consolidated schools that are a far cry from the one-room schoolhouses that marked rural America. The automobile makes it possible for them to escape parental supervision when socializing, and movie theaters, rock concerts, and sporting events give them new places to go on dates.

In the dating system young people must engineer their own dates, plan their own entertainment, and arrange their own transportation. Attracting dates puts a great emphasis on physical appearance. William Kephart, one of the leading researchers on dating, refers to our present age as the era of good looks. He points out that those who lack attractive faces and proper builds will find themselves excluded from the dating game.[8]

The emotional agony of young people who "lose" in the dating game is greater than can be imagined. Senior proms are the ultimate symbol of the dating game, and they have become synonymous with pain for the two-thirds of high school seniors who do not attend them. Those without dates for the senior prom are usually viewed as social rejects, not only by their peers and themselves, but also by their parents. Females who lack the personality or pretty face to get dates quickly learn that boys will be interested in them if they deliver various sexual favors. Consequently, there is significant moral compromise on the part of many young people who are desperate to be included in the dating life of the high school world.

Churches tend to aggravate the horrors of the dating game. Often they plan social activities (such as a banquet on the night of the senior prom) that also require a partner of the opposite sex for participation and thus perpetuate the same value system that dominates the secular society. If churches are to communicate Christian values, they should never sponsor social activities that require dates. Dating tends to diminish the feelings of worth of those who already feel degraded and usually further enhances the self-concepts of those who already think too highly of themselves.

Many church youth groups have fostered group dating as an alternative to the normative dating patterns of our culture. Groups of young people go out together rather than as separate pairs, and young people can get to know each other and establish relationships without the sexually charged conditions generated by the American dating system.

Today's style of dating is largely responsible for the increasing sexual permissiveness of our society. According to one of the most reliable estimates, 49 percent of males and 42 percent of females engage in coital activity prior to high school graduation. These figures do not include that behavioral phenomenon that Alfred Kinsey, the foremost researcher of American sexual behavior, referred to as technical virgins. Kinsey applied this term to young people, most

8. William M. Kephart, *The Family, Society, and the Individual,* 5th ed. (New York: Houghton Mifflin, 1981).

of whom would fall into the category of "intensely religious," who do not engage in sexual intercourse, but who nevertheless "pet" to orgasm.[9]

M. Scott Peck, the psychotherapist from Harvard University, states that it is easy to explain psychologically how social conditions make young people emotionally sick. What he finds difficult to explain is why so many of them turn out to be fairly well-adjusted persons. From Peck's perspective, the sociological forces being exercised on young people should make them all psychologically ill. It is his conclusion that the only reason that so many are relatively healthy is through the grace of God.

FOR FURTHER READING

Bibby, Reginald W., and Donald C. Posterski. *The Emerging Generation: An Inside Look at Canada's Teenagers.* Toronto: Irwin, 1985.

Coles, Robert, and Geoffrey Stokes. *Sex and the American Teenager.* New York: Harper & Row, 1985.

Elkind, David. *All Grown Up and No Place to Go: Teenagers in Crisis.* Reading Mass.: Addison-Wesley, 1984.

———. *The Hurried Child: Growing Up Too Fast, Too Soon.* Reading, Mass.: Addison-Wesley, 1981.

Erikson, Erik H. *Identity, Youth and Crisis.* New York: W. W. Norton, 1968.

Stott, John R. W. *Christian Counter-Culture.* Downers Grove, Ill.: InterVarsity, 1978.

Strommen, Merton P. *Five Cries of Youth.* New York: Harper & Row, 1974.

———, and A. Irene Strommen. *Five Cries of Parents.* San Francisco: Harper & Row, 1985.

Yankelovich, Daniel. *New Rules: Searching for Fulfillment in a World Turned Upside Down.* New York: Random House, 1981.

9. Alfred Kinsey et al., *Sexual Behavior in the Human Female* (Philadelphia: W. S. Saunders, 1953), chap. 7.

Perry G. Downs

3

Faith Shaping: Bringing Youth to Spiritual Maturity

Tom was every youth leader's dream. A national honor society scholar and quarterback of the high school football team, Tom was a natural choice for president of the youth group. His peers elected him enthusiastically.

Tom was quiet about his faith but not to the point of silence. Although a bit reticent about speaking up in front of groups, he gave a clear witness of his faith in Christ when encouraged. It was with a great deal of confidence that I saw Tom off to college that fall.

When he returned home for Christmas it was evident that Tom was questioning Christianity. There was a hint of arrogance as he raised some rather cynical questions in the college age Sunday school class. When I talked with him privately he was more like his old self. But it was clear that he was going through some struggles regarding the truth of the Christian faith.

When Tom came back for spring break he openly announced that he was no longer a Christian. He believed that there were purely natural explanations for spiritual phenomena and that the Scriptures could be explained in terms of sociological principles. As I listened to Tom, I wondered how my star leader

PERRY G. DOWNS, Ph.D., is associate professor of Christian education, Trinity Evangelical Divinity School, Deerfield, Illinois.

could have come to this point. What happened to that faith that seemed so evident in high school? Could it be that he was never a true believer or that he had lost his salvation? My theological framework could not allow for the latter option, and I doubted the possibility of the former. Had I understood something of the theories of faith development, I might have had some better understanding of what had happened to Tom.

SPIRITUAL MATURITY: THE ULTIMATE OUTCOME

The goal of youth ministry in the church is outreach and nurture. Discipleship includes both. Effective youth ministry will always have an evangelistic passion, but it must also focus on building up teens in their faith. The outcome for which we strive is the spiritual maturity of the teen.

The literature of faith development offers a variety of definitions of faith. In that most theorists are concerned with process rather than content, their definitions tend to be more psychologically oriented than theological. That tendency can cause confusion as we try to integrate these theories into a distinctly evangelical context.

It is best to define faith, and the subsequent growth toward maturity, from a theological perspective. It is critical to youth ministry (and indeed to all Christian ministry) that a clear understanding of faith be determined. That will serve to direct the activities of youth ministry, for the ends dictate the means.

From a theological perspective, faith may be defined as "a certain conviction, wrought in the heart by the Holy Spirit, as to the truth of the gospel, and a hearty reliance (trust) on the promises of God in Christ."[1]

Faith is an activity of the person in response to the work of the Holy Spirit in his heart. It is a complex activity that is made up of three elements.

The *intellectual element* is concerned with the knowledge of faith. Christianity is a propositional religion with truth to be known. When a person comes to Christ it must be with some foundational knowledge about the object of his faith.

The *emotional element* of faith accepts this knowledge as important. There is a deep conviction about the validity of the knowledge with an active embracing of it.

The *volitional element* of faith is the crowning aspect. This is the choice of the will to respond and act on that which is believed. The importance of obedience is stressed so that the person is changed by his faith. These three elements together constitute the full biblical concept of faith.

The critical concern for youth ministry is, How much should we expect from our teenagers? Any faith that is authentic must have these elements within it. But how much knowledge, conviction, and obedience should we

1. Louis Berkhof, *Systematic Theology* (Grand Rapids: Eerdmans, 1941), p. 503.

expect from our teens? It is at this point that the theories of faith development become helpful.

THEORIES OF FAITH DEVELOPMENT

Three major theories of faith development are currently in the literature. These have been developed by James Fowler, John Westerhoff, and Bruce Powers. In addition, Ben Marshall has suggested an interesting addition to Fowler's work.

Fowler has suggested six stages through which common human faith may progress.[2] It is important to note that he is interested in faith as a normal human experience and not as particular Christian activity. His definition of faith is both existential (experience oriented) and relativistic (not rooted in the absolutes of Scripture).

Fowler's formal definition of faith is formidable. According to Fowler, faith is:

> people's evolved and evolving ways of experiencing self, others and world (as they construct them) as related to and affected by the ultimate conditions of existence (as they construct them) and of shaping their lives' purposes and meanings, trust and loyalties, in light of the character of being, value and power determining the ultimate conditions of existence (as grasped in their operative images—conscious and unconscious—of them).[3]

This dynamic triad of self, others, and shared centers of value and power makes faith something that is evolving, existential, and relative. It has to do with how we see ourselves, others, and the ultimate values that are held in common.

Fowler contends that there are predictable stages of structure, or shape, to one's personal faith. As in all stage theories, Fowler's stages are understood as invarient and sequential. All people's faith will emerge through the same stages in the same order. The content of the faith will differ and change, but the structure will always be according to the same six stages. What varies is the extent to which one's faith will develop. Some people may reach only stage three, whereas a few may develop all the way to stage six. But the route to the higher stages will be the same for all people.

Fowler describes the six stages of faith in chapter length treatment. For the sake of brevity, only a simplified description is offered here.

Stage one, *Intuitive-Projective Faith* (early childhood), is a fantasy-filled, imitative phase in which the child can be powerfully and permanently influenced by examples, moods, actions, and stories of the visible faith of primarily

2. James Fowler, *Stages of Faith* (New York: Harper & Row, 1982).
3. Ibid., pp. 92-93.

related adults. A dominant aspect of this mode of faith is thinking in terms of magical explanations of events.

Stage two, *Mythical-Literal Faith* (ages 6-12), occurs when the developing ability of logical thinking helps the person sort out reality from make-believe. This stage is characterized by literalness in understanding. The narratives of the faith communities are added so that stories become increasingly important.

Stage three, *Synthetic / Conventional Faith* (ages 12 and beyond), is also tied to cognitive development. With the ability for abstract thinking comes the need to integrate faith into a systematic whole. Developing self-identity causes one to identify with others in a unity of belief, with God being perceived as an extension of interpersonal relationships and as a close personal friend.

In stage four, *Individuative-Reflective Faith* (early adulthood and beyond), self is separated from the group, and beliefs are critically reflected on by the individual. A demythologizing of religious rituals occurs as the person seeks meaning in religious practices and assumes greater personal responsibility for his faith.

Stage five, *Conjunctive Faith* (mid-life and beyond), occurs as deeper self-awareness develops. One becomes alive to paradox and open to other religions and people. It becomes axiomatic that truth is multidimensional, and one seeks significant encounters with others.

Stage six, *Universalizing Faith* (mid-life and beyond), is reached only when issues of love and justice become all important as one is grounded in oneness with the power of being. As people are drawn to this stage by God, they learn to *live* radically the kingdom of God as a means of overcoming division, oppression, and brutality.

Fowler's third stage, "synthetic/conventional," is the stage that characterizes most adolescents. This stage typically begins about age twelve or thirteen, when a person is able to reflect on his or her own thinking. It is called synthetic in that the person is concerned with pulling together values and self-image. It is conventional in the sense that it is concerned with the expectations and judgments of significant others. It is a clear attempt to make order out of one's life and to conform to a respected group. God is perceived to be one's best friend and an extension of one's personal relationships.[4]

Some adolescents may still be in stage two, "mythic/literal faith." This stage is characterized by a more magical orientation and an extreme literal understanding. This teen needs to move to a more mature faith that utilizes his full cognitive capabilities.[5]

When ready, usually in later adolescence, the teen may move to "individuative/projective faith." This stage is characterized by drawing away from

4. Ibid., pp. 151-73
5. Ibid., pp. 135-50.

the group and emphasizing one's own understandings of the issues of faith. In this process of personalizing faith, one usually needs to draw some distinctives from the group. To the person observing the process, this may be perceived as rebellion. However, in reality it may actually be an important part of the process of faith development.

Fowler is primarily a theologian, and as such he does very little in helping us to understand how we can help someone grow in faith. He has tried to describe the shape of faith as it develops, but he does not speak to the subsequent issues of ministry.

Working off the base of Fowler's stage three, R. Ben Marshall has suggested sub-stages of faith characteristic of seventh to twelfth graders.[6] He has focused on a structural perspective by attempting to locate and describe the characteristics of faith during the period from seventh to twelfth grades.

Position One teens (seventh–ninth grades) are still concrete in their conceptions and egocentric in their relationships. God is perceived as an old man with white hair who is distant and not directly involved with their affairs. Their primary concern is for acceptance by the group. They can state their own beliefs but are not sure what others may believe.[7]

Position Two teens (ninth–eleventh grades) develop a deep concern for others' viewpoints. Truth becomes what is right for the individual, and relationships with peers become increasingly important. A new sense of self-confidence emerges that influences their relationship with God; God is now seen as a cooperating friend.[8]

Position Three teens (eleventh–twelfth grades) relate to God as a source of value and principle. An increased concern for others develops, along with an interest in fulfilling life potential. Characterized by a greater realism, these youth have a more responsive love for God than those in the earlier positions.[9]

Marshall admits that his research is only tentative. However, it is a good indication of how people view faith development in adolescents. It also provides some helpful models for considering how teens exercise faith.

John Westerhoff III uses the analogy of the rings in a tree to describe faith development. Each ring remains, even as another ring develops around it. He defines faith as "an action which includes thinking, feeling, and willing. It is sustained, transmitted and expanded through our interaction with faithing selves in a community of faith."[10]

Westerhoff suggests four stages of faith. These stages emerge one from the other so that a clear developmental process is evident. *Experienced Faith*

6. R. Ben Marshall, "Faith Inquiry: An Exploration of the Nature and Nurture of Adolescent Faith," *Perkins Journal* (Fall 1979): 33:36-50.
7. Ibid., pp. 38-39.
8. Ibid., p. 39.
9. Ibid., p. 40.
10. John H. Westerhoff, *Will Our Children Have Faith?* (New York: Seabury, 1976), pp. 89-91.

(preschool and childhood) is foundational to faith. The child experiences, explores, tests, and reacts to faith. He copies the faith of others, and by observation and interaction begins to develop a faith of his own.[11]

Affiliative Faith (adolescence) is characterized by a strong sense of belonging to a group. There is a strong affective aspect to this faith that is influenced by music, drama, and even dance. Moreover, there is a sense of authority that the community's way of understanding faith will influence values and actions.[12]

Searching Faith (late adolescence) is characterized by doubting and questioning. There may be some experimentation with other religions or ways of expressing faith, and there is a growing need to commit oneself to one or several causes.[13]

Owned Faith (adults) is when the person comes to peace with his faith and wants to be characterized by it. This person will strive to witness for his faith, and Westerhoff suggests that this is God's will for all people.[14]

Westerhoff contends that the adolescent must question and even doubt his faith if he is to own it. The context in which this should take place is the community of faith (e.g., the church). He argues that enculturation (nonformal relational experiences) rather than instruction (formal teaching settings) is the best means of nurturing faith. In addition, he advocates helping adolescents question their faith as a means of helping it to grow.

Under the influence of both Fowler and Westerhoff, Bruce Powers has suggested another means of understanding the process of faith development.[15] His five stages are the result of both integrating Fowler and Westerhoff and an intense reflection on his own faith pilgrimage. Rather than describing stages per se, Powers describes five phases of faith development.

The first phase, *Nurture,* is the first exposure to the meaning of life. This usually occurs from birth to age six. For Powers, the most influential people in this phase of his development were his parents and Sunday school teachers. The issue was not so much what they said; rather, it was that they loved him.

The second phase of *Indoctrination* takes place in the ages of seven through eighteen. During this phase, the primary agenda becomes the acquisition and mastery of the content of the faith. This is more than the memorization of data, but is also influenced by the beliefs of peers. Together the teens decide what they will believe.

Ages nineteen to twenty-seven are characterized by *Reality Testing.* During this phase, the individual tries out his faith in the arena of life to see if it

11. Ibid., pp. 91-93.
12. Ibid., pp. 94-96.
13. Ibid., pp. 96-97.
14. Ibid., pp. 98-99.
15. Bruce P. Powers, *Growing Faith* (Nashville: Broadman, 1982).

will stand up. Also during this phase, some of the idealism of youth is tempered and changed by the realities of life.

Making Choices is the work of faith development during ages twenty-eight to thirty-five. In this phase the person truly owns his faith, and his life is now to some degree shaped by what he believes. This process culminates in the phase of *Active Devotion,* which is accomplished after the age of thirty-six.

Powers's second stage, Indoctrination, involves working to master the content of one's faith. This content is gained not only by learning the Bible stories and the content of the sermons but also from interaction with other adolescents. Those in this stage need to share with their peers as they strive to understand their faith tradition.

Significant to Powers's perspective is the idea that adolescents cannot yet truly own their faith. It is not yet incorporated into them because they have not had sufficient experience to test what they believe. By means of responding to life issues in the ways their faith suggests, youth will have the ability to begin to incorporate their faith into their own personalities. Unlike Fowler, Powers offers practical suggestions for helping people grow in their faith.

Perhaps the strongest of Powers's contributions is his description of the underlying progression in faith development as a cyclical learning process that continually helps a person adjust to life needs. This cyclical process involves awareness of a growth need, recall of Christian teaching, understanding possibilities for response, conviction of certain action, and application of one's knowledge and talents in Christian service. The process of learning the content of Christian faith and reflecting on life needs in relation to that information makes teaching adolescents a critical means of enhancing their faith development. Therefore, Powers stresses that the role of parents and youth leaders as teachers is critical to helping teens grow in faith.

The common thread that runs through each of these theories of faith development is that adolescence is a time when faith will probably be questioned. It is not axiomatic that all adolescents will go through periods of question and doubt, but it is likely that they will. Their new found cognitive abilities (what Piaget calls formal operations) and their need to establish independence from their parents may result in some form of questioning Christianity. This is not a spiritual problem, but, rather, a normal developmental phenomenon.

When Tom went off to college he was armed with some information regarding the validity of Christianity. But his high-school-level answers could not stand up to his college-level questioning. Moreover, his need to establish some independence from the group was expressed by his attacks on the faith. In reality it was a rather immature response from a college freshman, but it was understandable.

What is to be our response when teens question Christianity? If the theories of faith development tell us anything, it is that the process of questioning and doubting is quite natural. It actually may be an indication that Christian growing is occurring.

We need to be sure that we are at peace with the validity of Christianity. If we as leaders communicate anxiety about the questions teens raise, we may indicate to them that we are not confident that our beliefs can stand up under close scrutiny. But if we respond with openness, not condemning their questions, we help them discover that doubt is a normal part of growing as believers.

RESPONDING TO DOUBT

If it is true that questions and doubt may be a normal aspect of faith development for the adolescent, it is incumbent on the youth leader to have an adequate theological perspective on doubt. In addition, those who work with youth must also know how to help people with their doubt.

From a biblical perspective, doubt is not a sin. Both Testaments provide examples of believers who doubted. Jeremiah 20 provides a striking example of the prophet's struggle with doubt. When he despaired over God's dealing with him (vv. 7-8, 14-18), he was expressing doubt. In the same manner, when John the Baptist questioned if Jesus was the Christ (Matt. 11:1-6), he was expressing his doubt.

Doubt is not the same as unbelief. Os Guiness states:

> Doubt is not the opposite of faith, nor is it the same as unbelief. Doubt is a state of mind in suspension *between* faith and unbelief so that it is neither of them wholly and it is each only partly. This distinction is absolutely vital because it uncovers and deals with the first major misconception of doubt—the idea that in doubting a believer is betraying faith and surrendering to unbelief. No misunderstanding causes more anxiety and brings such bondage to sensitive people in doubt.[16]

Because doubt is a natural part of adolescent faith development and is not the same as unbelief, we are free to allow the adolescent to question his faith. Biblically, doubt is not antithetical to faith, but almost a necessary corollary to it. That is, by means of the process of doubt one's faith can actually be strengthened.

If we are to help teenagers with their doubt, there are three things we must do for them. The first is to provide a context where doubts can be expressed. If the message is given that no good Christian ever doubts or that we are uncomfortable with their questions, they may feel the need to go elsewhere. But by accepting their questions, and even at times encouraging

16. Os Guiness, *In Two Minds* (Downers Grove: InterVarsity, 1976), p. 27.

them, we can provide a safe context in which questions can be raised.

The provision of this context is not as much a matter of program as it is one of attitude. Those who work with teens must feel comfortable with their Christianity and with the hard questions that teens are likely to raise. Being an open and accepting person who can identify with these questions ("Yes, I was bothered by that issue for some time myself") is essential to providing an environment where teens can grow in their faith.

Second, we can provide some answers for their questions. This does not mean that when a teen questions we must quickly provide the answer so that their doubts may be resolved. But it does mean that those who work with youth should be familiar with the basic issues of apologetics (the rational defense of Christianity).

When teens question the authority of Scripture or the existence of God, it is because these are real questions to them. If the leaders are not able to provide adequate answers, logic will force them to conclude that there are no answers. But these sorts of questions have been raised down through the ages, and there is a rich heritage of literature that deals with these issues. An effective youth leader should have a foundational grasp of this material so that he or she can help the adolescent deal with his questions in an intellectually responsible way.

The answers we offer must be in keeping with the level of the student's development. The first questions of the junior high student will be handled by relatively simple answers. But the more difficult questions of the college age students will require more thoughtful responses. But in either case, the adolescent needs the security of knowing that others have raised these questions and that satisfactory answers are available.

Third, we must provide for the adolescent a true Christian *experience*. Though doubt is an intellectual issue, teenagers are also very experience oriented. Philosophically they are existentialists, that is, oriented to believe their experience. If they can *feel* the truth of Christianity in their family, church, and youth group, they will have a basis that transcends their intellectual questions. The fact that Tom continued to come to church while he was doubting was an indication that he still felt some reality even though he doubted.

If youth group is a place where the teen is accepted and supported, if it is a place where the presence of God is felt, the teenager has a basis beyond the intellectual to believe. This would not be very helpful to the doubting adult, but it is quite powerful for the adolescent. They are both relativistic and existential in their orientation to life; experience plays a critical role in their faith.

Each of the major theorists who deal with the ministry questions that are related to faith development support these strategies. The emphasis will vary, but these essentials remain. Critical to helping youth through doubt is a context of acceptance, answers to their questions, and experiences with true Christianity.

ADOLESCENT FAITH DEVELOPMENT

The question remains, What is spiritual maturity for teenagers? What can we realistically expect from them in terms of their development as Christians? Obviously it would be wrong to attempt to develop a list of criteria by which we could measure spiritual maturity. (The Pharisees attempted this strategy and found it to be lacking.) Rather, what we can do is develop some guidelines that incorporate both the theological and developmental concerns mentioned in the preceding sections. It is then the task of the youth worker to apply or modify these guidelines to fit his or her own local and theological situation.

The first guideline is to desire and expect some change in the teenager as an outcome of spiritual development. As a person grows, change is inevitable. The reason many people fail to grow is that they are not willing to change. Of course, the kind of change we expect in our teens should be according to Scripture. We are not after conformity as an end in itself, but we should seek to see observable results from the process of nurture in the lives of our teenagers.

The second guideline is closely related to the first. The kind of change we want to see in our teens should be related to the teachings of Scripture. But it also should be related to the unique life of each individual teenager. In other words, we should not expect the same kind of change in each person, because each teenager is an individual, and in a different place in the process of transition we call adolescence. For one teenager we might expect to see growth in the capacity to participate in the worship of God, and for another we would desire that he might reduce his need for drugs. Both of these involve a change in the person, but the kind of change desired is different for each individual.

For some teenagers the period of adolescence is quite easy, and for them · our expectations for spiritual growth will be quite high. But for others, adolescence is an extremely difficult period, and most of their energy is given to surviving the period. For those teens, our expectations for spiritual maturity will be much less, but still it is proper to desire and expect growth from them. For those persons, expecting some kind of change in them can be a means of encouragement and a way of showing them that you believe in them. To have no expectations for them will only serve to show that you really have no hope for that person's growth. Therefore, we should expect change in all of our teens, but the kind of change we expect should be related to where that person is in his own life experience.

The third guideline is that we should seek growth in the areas of knowledge, values, and behavior, because those are the foundational aspects of faith. Again, the nature and level of the change should be in keeping with the level and ability of the individual; but for all teenagers spiritual growth includes a growing knowledge of the content of the Christian faith, a deepening adoption of the values of the kingdom of God, and a life-style characterized by a more radical obedience to the teachings of Scripture.

The specifics of what these changes will be like for any given teenager will be dependent on the background experience of the individual. If, for example, a teenager comes from a home where Christian instruction was a normal activity, his growth will be much more advanced than the teenager whose background is apart from the church. But in either case, growth in the areas discussed above should be desired.

The next guideline grows out of the data on adolescent development and states that we should desire to help teenagers go through the process of development in ways that are in keeping with the Christian faith. We should accept that God has so designated human beings that there is a period of transition from childhood to adulthood called adolescence, and that in this period there are going to be some difficult issues to be resolved. But we should also accept that if a teenager considers himself to be a Christian, then God does have standards for him that are to be followed. For example, an important part of adolescent development is sexual maturation. As a result, teenagers tend to be very sexually oriented. This is not sin; it is merely adolescent. But we should expect and help teenagers to handle their increased sexuality within the boundaries established in the Scripture. It is normal and right for people of the opposite sex to be attracted to and stimulated by one another, but it is not right for them to have sexual relations outside of the commitments of marriage. Also, it is quite normal to expect teenagers to want to break away from their parents in some form, so as to establish their own identity. But while they are in this process, they must still be expected to honor their mother and father, as this is a biblical absolute that is non-negotiable.

The point is that we must not deny the normal issues of adolescent development, but that it is appropriate for us to expect teenagers to go through these transitions in a way that does not violate the teachings of Scripture. Helping teens to talk about the struggles of adolescence, and then helping them to integrate their Christianity into these struggles in positive ways, can be an effective means of nurturing them in the faith.

The final guideline is for the youth worker rather than the teenager. This guideline is that we must always seek to encourage rather than to discourage the teenager. Adolescence can be a rather negative and cynical period in a person's life. If we enter into it with criticism and scorn for the teenager, we will only serve to confirm in their own minds that they cannot live up to the standards of the Christian faith. Especially if our expectations are too high, we will have a tendency to be critical and abusive in our relationships with them.

That will only serve to hinder the process of growth.

Perhaps the best antidote is to remember our own adolescence, with all of its difficulties (real and imagined) as well as its successes. By attempting to remain sensitive to this period in our own lives we can protect those teens we work with from the burden of unrealistic youth worker expectations. But, by maintaining a clear theological perspective on the issues of faith development, and being sensitive to the issues of adolescent development, we will be more capable of establishing realistic goals for the spiritual growth of our teenagers.

FOR FURTHER READING

Dykstra, Craig, and Sharon Parks. *Faith Development and Fowler.* Birmingham: Religious Education Press, 1986.

Fowler, James W. *Stages of Faith.* San Francisco: Harper & Row, 1981.

Joy, Donald M. *Bonding: Relationships in the Image of God.* Waco, Tex.: Word, 1985.

Kesler, Jay, with Ronald Beers. *Parents and Teenagers.* Wheaton, Ill.: Victor, 1984.

Posterski, Donald C. *Friendship: A Window on Ministry to Youth.* Scarborough, Ont.: Project Teen Canada, 1985.

Powers, Bruce P. *Growing Faith.* Nashville: Broadman, 1982.

Sparkman, G. Temp, ed. *Knowing and Helping Youth.* Nashville: Broadman, 1977.

Westerhoff, John H. *Will Our Children Have Faith?* New York: Seabury, 1976.

Dean Borgman

4

A History of American Youth Ministry

History should never be a mere chronicle of events or of the development of structures. History, especially a history of youth ministry, should describe the spirit of the times and its cultures, and it should depict visions and trends. From history we need inspiration, a few lessons, and encouragement.

The early 1980s produced five books in three short years from significant social critics on a single subject: we developed childhood and adolescence for our young, and then we stole it from them. The critics' conclusions are strikingly similar and present a common challenge to youth ministry. Those will be considered at the close of this chapter.[1]

Age has always been a factor in history. The critics mentioned may overstate the "invention" and "disappearance" of childhood and adolescence. Certainly much more was made of childhood and adolescence during the nineteenth and twentieth centuries. And recent factors rush the young through

---

1. David Elkind, *The Hurried Child: Growing Up Too Fast* (Reading, Mass.: Addison-Wesley, 1981); *All Grown Up and No Place to Go: Teenagers in Crisis* (Reading, Mass.: Addison-Wesley, 1984); Vance Packard, *Our Endangered Children* (Boston: Little, Brown & Co., 1983); Neil Postman, *The Disappearance of Childhood* (New York: Dell, 1982); Marie Winn, *Children Without Childhood* (New York: Pantheon, 1983).

DEAN BORGMAN, M.A., is associate professor of youth ministries, Gordon-Conwell Theological Seminary, South Hamilton, Massachusetts.

childhood to adulthood. But children have always had to become adult through a transition that included training and rites of passage. Aristotle noted a generation gap in ancient Greece, and several biblical characters were very aware of "being a mere child," or still being adolescent, as we would put it. Medieval scholars knew that town and gown riots and the Children's Crusade were youthful phenomena of their times.

Childhood, adolescence, and generation gaps have always been present to one degree or another, but the nineteenth and twentieth centuries have produced a youth culture new to history. Though young people have become tremendously important as social and political factors, notice of their importance by serious scholars has come only slowly. It is just recently that random notice and novels about generational differences have grown into serious study. The past fifty years have produced systematic studies. These show that from the revolutions of 1848 through the rise of German and Italian national socialism and Russian communism, to the Iranian revolution, to guerilla and regular army forces of Africa and Latin America, we are talking about adult-led youth movements as a major force in modern history.[2]

This new importance of youth can be traced to the Industrial Revolution in a general way. During that period it was recognized that children and youth are something more than creatures waiting to be adults. They were beginning to be seen as people with new significance, freedom, resources, and needs. Such a perspective represents the beginning of modern youth ministry.

Ministry, from our Lord Jesus Christ on, is a response to needs met in terms of one's calling. Youth ministry follows the changing needs of what has, in the past century, become an exciting youth culture. Modern youth ministry begins with the social evolution of modern adolescence and the view of that development taken by church and society. Dynamic changes in the youth subculture have affected the growth of youth ministry.

In the 1840s Bennet Tyler wrote a book analyzing twenty-four revivals during the period from 1797 to 1814. In his opinion fifteen of those started among youth. In fact, many criticized revivals in those days for being principally among youth.[3] At the turn of the twentieth century, American psychologist Edwin Starbuck concluded, "This much we can say with certainty, that spontaneous awakenings are distinctly adolescent phenomena."[4] That observation would apply to both the Great Awakening in the mid-eighteenth century and the Second Great Awakening from about 1790 to 1840. The Second Awakening spilled across the Atlantic from John Wesley, William Wilberforce, and the Clapham Sect.

2. Anthony Esler, ed., *The Youth Revolution* (Lexington, Mass.: Heath, 1974).
3. Joseph Kett, *Rites of Passage: Adolescence in America 1790 to the Present* (New York: Harper & Row, 1977), p. 64.
4. Edwin D. Starbuck, *The Psychology of Religion: An Empirical Study of the Growth of Religious Consciousness,* quoted in ibid., p. 62.

In an important chapter from his history of adolescence in America, Joseph Kett traces the religious youth movement of the nineteenth century from the Second Awakening, through the collegiate Christian societies, to the missionary movement climaxing at the turn of the century.

The immediate progenitor of missionary enthusiasm in colleges and seminaries was the Second Awakening. . . . The writings of British evangelicals were factors in stimulating some of the original interest in the home missions in America.

New England towns had long contained moral and religious societies composed of earnest young men between 15 and 25, but such voluntary associations reached their apex of influence in colleges between 1790 and 1850 (Harvard's Adelphoi Theologica, Yale's Moral Society, and various Philadelphia societies). . . . Viewed in retrospect, the most influential was the Society of Brethren, formed in 1808 at Williams "to affect in the persons of its members a mission . . . to the heathen."[5]

The 1880s and 1890s were exciting times. England was an industrial giant with great colonial pride. In America, the Civil War had accelerated the progress of the Industrial Revolution. Rail travel across the continent was becoming commonplace, and by 1898 half the world's railroad mileage was in the United States. The last frontier in the Middle West was closing. Thomas Edison and others were perfecting the telegraph and telephone and developing uses for electricity. The phonograph, kinetoscope, and stereopticon were providing entertainment and spreading popular culture. Cities were growing, and they were filled with young people. Those developments prepared the climate for a new era of Christian youth movements.

EARLY YOUTH MOVEMENTS

Sunday school, the Young Men's and Women's Christian Associations, and faith missionary societies were all significant movements of the nineteenth century. Originating in England, they quickly spread across the Atlantic. The idea of Sunday school is attributed to Robert Raikes in Gloucester, England (1780). George Williams helped a dozen young men found the YMCA in London in the middle of the 1840s. By the end of the 1850s it had spread to New York. Another decade saw the beginning of the YWCA in Boston.

The YMCA and YWCA became inextricably connected with another great youth movement of the nineteenth century. In 1806 a freshman at Williams College in Massachusetts challenged his prayer group about foreign missions one afternoon. They had been caught in a thunderstorm and took shelter under a haystack. That famous Haystack Prayer Meeting led to the Society of the Brethren at Williams College and nearby Andover Theological Seminary.

5. Kett, *Rites of Passage*, pp. 70-71.

Further impetus for foreign missions arose from the Inter-Collegiate YMCA Movement (IYMCAM) and the Inter-Seminary Missionary Alliance.

Two hundred fifty-one students from eighty-six colleges gathered at the Mount Hermon Conference in Massachusetts in July 1886. It was a relaxed and open format. But out of the concern of a few students, a powerful challenge for world evangelization grew until, on the last night, the Mount Hermon One Hundred pledged themselves as volunteers. Students like Robert Wilder (of Union) and Robert Speer (of Princeton) toured the country enlisting additional recruits and organizing campus groups into what was to become the Student Volunteer Movement for Foreign Missions. John R. Mott of the YMCA and Nettie Dunn of the YWCA were other significant leaders of the movement.

In the climate of the Progressive Era, Christian college students rallied to a most difficult and sacrificial challenge: The Evangelization of the World in This Generation. The Student Volunteer Movement grew steadily from 1891 to 1910. In the following decade its conventions drew some five thousand students as five hundred new missionaries were sent out each year. Church historian Kenneth Scott Latourette credits those students with recruiting "a large proportion of the outstanding leaders in the world-wide spread of Protestant Christianity in the twentieth century." Back in 1887, President James McCosh of Princeton College asked, "Has any such offering of living young men and women been presented in our age, in our country, in any age or in any country since the days of Pentecost?" After 1920 that movement faced gradual decline.[6]

THE CHRISTIAN ENDEAVOR MOVEMENT

During those same last decades of the nineteenth century, one of the greatest youth movements of all times also had its beginnings. One cold February evening in Portland, Maine, the pastor of the Williston Congregational Church called his young people to the parsonage for cocoa and cookies. Francis Edward Clark always admitted that he built on a growing religious interest among New England churches and young people in 1880-81. "The Society, let it ever be remembered, was born in revival."[7]

Francis Clark sensed the growing lack of spiritual vitality in Sunday schools and YMCAs. Yet he felt the earlier eighteenth century societies had come to young people with a "rugged theology that had more often conceived of God as a King and Judge than as a loving Father." Clark objected to the old tendency to expect conversions to be only of the Pauline rather than the

---

6. Two fine books on the Student Volunteer Movement are Timothy C. Wallstrom, *The Creation of a Student Movement to Evangelize the World* (Pasadena, Calif.: William Carey, 1980) and David Howard, *Student Power in World Missions* (Downers Grove, Ill.: InterVarsity, 1970).
7. Francis E. Clark, *Christian Endeavor in All Lands* (Philadelphia: n. p., 1906), p. 33.

Timothy model. And he did not want to come at young people with a "tithing-man's stick, with which to rap naughty boys over the head," but rather with a "shepherd's crook wherewith to guide them into the green pastures of loving service."[8]

Those words of Clark do not indicate a softness on his part; he knew that young people would truly respond only to a hard challenge. The failure of contemporary youth movements and local groups of the late nineteenth century was due to their expecting too little from the young. "Most of these mistakes lay along the line of doing too much for the young people rather than allowing them to do what they could for themselves."[9]

Anticipating a twentieth century youth leader to be noted later in this chapter, Clark believed that "the life of Christ and His teachings appeal especially to the young: how natural, almost inevitable, it is for a young person to be drawn to Christ and to accept Him as Pattern and Guide when He is winsomely presented."[10]

Clark was familiar with Cotton Mather's early eighteenth-century principles for organizing religious societies. And in an ill-spelled document by the young people of Brockton, Massachusetts (1741), he found the basic principles of the prayer meeting, experience meeting, the pledge, and active membership. So he had been thinking how he might start something new and different "from the old type of young people's meetings that made so manifest a failure."

The principles he laid out to his group that crisp February evening were not immediately seized on. In fact, Clark had to twist the arm of one he recognized as a leader before the others would follow. But there was little modification in what was presented that day to what was to become the Six Essential Characteristics of the International Christian Endeavor Society.

All members must strictly commit themselves to:
1. The Pledge—an active commitment to the service of Jesus Christ as Lord and to actively participate in the Society's prayer meetings
2. The monthly experience or consecration meeting
3. Systematic, definite and regular committee work—training by doing
4. Private devotion; daily prayer and Bible reading
5. Denominational loyalty including attendance at midweek prayer and Sunday evening services
6. Interdenominational fellowship—an early Protestant and evangelical ecumenism described as "a very complete and beautiful system of unions"

For Francis Clark and his wife, Harriet, who led the girls of the Mizpah Circle, the essence of the Endeavor was that it was thoroughly Christian,

8. Ibid., p. 23.
9. Ibid., p. 26.
10. Francis E. Clark, *Christ and the Young People* (New York: Revell, 1916), p. 14.

strictly disciplined, and dedicated to service.

The creation of that first society in 1881 so revitalized youth life in Williston Church that other churches requested to be brought in on the idea. Within sixteen months a convention was held for six thriving societies. In a remarkably short time conventions were attracting thousands. Imagine some fifty thousand persons at one of the great conventions in Boston in 1895. That same year, Christian Endeavor became international with Francis Clark as its first president (to be followed by Daniel A. Poling, 1927-62).

Thousands of members jammed trains all across the country and headed for a convention in San Francisco in the early 1930s. But Christian Endeavor would begin to experience a decline in general vitality in the 1930s, and the consolidation of denominational fellowship groups in the 1940s brought further loss to the Society.

During the first two decades of this century, Christian Endeavor was one of the strongest and largest youth movements of modern times. Denominational fellowships of the mid-twentieth century were descendants of the movement, and no history of American revivals and missionary movements would be complete without a study of this world endeavor. Although most outside observers would see a decline in the vitality of the Christian Endeavor movement during the 1930s and 1940s, it presently claims 5 million members of all ages from eighty-three different denominations in seventy-six countries.[11]

Many would argue that several factors brought a decline of spiritual dynamism in youth ministry during the middle of this century. Those factors are identified as enlightenment philosophy, scientism, theological liberalism, and a sophisticated materialism. Certainly, tremendous changes were coming to the youth culture in the 1930s and 1940s. It took an economic depression to fulfill the liberal dream of "universal" high school education. The Great Depression and universal high school appear to have been prime factors in the creation of modern youth culture.

Put most American teenagers in high school and you have football, cheerleaders, and the Saturday night dance. And that was happening just as the big dance bands were coming into vogue, along with radio, phonographs, soda fountains, juke boxes, and available cars. Suddenly there was a youth culture as never before. Compared to basketball games, school dances, and movie dates, youth group seemed pretty dull. Singing the old gospel hymns did not quite match Kate Smith's "When the Moon Comes over the Mountain" or, later, "Mr. Saturday Dance." Fundamentalism meanwhile was trying to separate its youths from much of pop culture and theological liberalism.

11. David G. Jackson, General Secretary of the International Society of Christian Endeavor and the World's Christian Union 14 August, 1965. See also *The Christian Endeavor Story* (Columbus, Ohio: World Christian Endeavor Union, n.d.).

PERCY CRAWFORD

Turned off by the strict rules of a Bible conference and a "bawling out" he received for skipping a meeting to be with a pretty girl, and yet filled with passion to reach young hearts for Christ, a Philadelphia seminary student was trying all available ways to attract young hearers. His vision and drive have been written about, his style of sincere and compelling preaching noted, but it was his use of current, popular music that especially affected youth evangelization in this era. Long before Larry Norman penned the words, Percy Crawford did not want the devil to have all the good music.

Percy was born in a log cabin in Minnedosa, Manitoba, Canada, on October 20, 1902. He had two older brothers, Earl and Alfonse. Margaret Crawford wanted something more for her three boys than the small village of nine hundred could offer, so she convinced her husband, Thomas, to move to Vancouver on the West Coast. Thomas was a blacksmith, a quiet man until his temper erupted. He was hard and authoritarian. From his father Percy received rawhide whippings for missing church or other misdemeanors. And it was his father who made him quit school. Finally, Margaret could no longer endure her husband's coldness and the cruelty to the boys. Father was asked to leave home, and he did, for good.

The hatred Percy felt toward his father may also have caused his rebellion against church and his doubts about God. A new freedom was found drinking, in pool halls, at dances, and in the arcades. He left home for bigger cities, made money, and was unexpectedly converted. With his new life came a passion for evangelism and a desire for further education, Bible school, college, and seminary. He chose Westminster Seminary partly because it was located in a large city, and Philadelphia was to be his base from then on.

Ruth Duvall, at fifteen, was already beautiful, as well as a talented pianist and vocalist. The arranged date with a student sounded exciting until she learned he was twenty-nine. Still, the date came off, and when Percy heard her sing and play, he immediately recruited her for his evangelistic team. Romance and marriage followed.

Percy finally graduated from Westminster in 1931. Always the driving individualist, his zeal for preaching the gospel was unmistakable. His preaching was lively, simple, and clear. His own difficult childhood and adolescence gave him a special heart for teenagers, and he understood all about rebellion.

Ruth and Percy knew young people must be attracted through music, and they were in tune with the musical culture of their day. Sounds like that of Fred Waring and the big bands impressed them. The Crawfords brought swing into Christian music, especially in the new gospel choruses that came out regularly in *Pinebrook Praises*. Pinebrook was their camp in East Stroudsburg, Pennsylvania. To it came musicians and songwriters, including Norman

Clayton, Wendell Loveless, and John Peterson, with Peter Slack and Ruth at the organ and piano respectively. It was a new sound with an exciting spirit and beat. Crowds of young people sang and listened in Pinebrook's great old wooden tabernacle. Songwriters from around the country and even Great Britain sent their scores to Ruth Crawford. Look through songbooks for youth used by Young Life, Youth For Christ, and other organizations in the 1940s and 1950s, and you will see the names of musicians who gathered around Percy and Ruth.

Crawford developed the Saturday night rally, new-style Bible conference, and camps and bookstores. He was on radio, and when radio time became too expensive, he bought his own FM station. In the 1950s he was one of the first youth leaders on television with a musical program of the finest quality. Many youth organizations rose from his inspiration and help: Youth For Christ, Word of Life, Singspiration, Song Time, High School Born-Againers, and New Life Boys' Ranch.[12]

The evolution of a new kind of youth culture in the 1930s continued dynamically in the 1940s. What the Depression had begun, World War II accelerated. With young adults off to war, teenagers were "the biggest men in town." And they had money in a new booming economy. With this new label of *teenager* and money to spend, they quickly caught the merchants' eyes, and teen magazines, music, and clothes were soon on the market. A Purdue University survey in the 1940s revealed that of teenagers questioned, 33 percent felt they could do nothing to prevent wars, 50 percent of all girls considered their figures to be their major concern, 37 percent of all boys were primarily interested in having a "good build," and 33 percent of two thousand questioned believed the most pressing teenage problem in America to be acne.

A reader of *Seventeen* magazine wrote: "I think you should have more articles on dates and shyness and put in some more about movie stars. Stories like those on atomic energy are very boring." About this generation, social scientist Murray G. Ross said, "Few young people share deeply in the life of a group dedicated, and actively devoted, to the highest goals of mankind."[13] It was an age of high group-conformity, fads, bobby socks, Friday night slumber parties, pop songs, dancing, and high school sports. It was fun and very much alive. They were moving away from adults and adult institutions.

JIM RAYBURN

One adult encountered and anticipated this culture more vibrantly than most. He was a young engineering student sensing a call to Presbyterian ministry with an emphasis on youth. An assignment by that denomination to

---

12. Bob Bahr, *Man with a Vision: The Story of Percy Crawford* (Privately published and out of print). Material obtained through the courtesy of Calvin Waldron, Ossining, N.Y.
13. *1940-1950*. This Fabulous Century. 8 vols. (New York: Time-Life Books, 1969), 5:28.

young Mexican-Americans and the advice of a Dallas pastor challenged him to a revolutionary kind of ministry. That challenge involved a moratorium on developing youth programs and on inviting teenagers to church or youth group. It demanded that one go from the church to where youths were. There one was to meet and listen and laugh and learn. Out of relationships formed, a whole new kind of program might emerge.

Jim Rayburn is well known for believing "it's a sin to bore a kid." As much as any, he wanted young hearts to hear the gospel, but more than most, he was willing to go to any extreme in order that the opportune time and situation might be provided. He wanted each young person in America to be relaxed and happy enough to enjoy a special meeting with Jesus of Nazareth. He shuddered to think of the conditions under which most teenagers hear of Jesus and with what they associate Him. He demanded that each youth evangelist earn the right to be heard by a ministry of presence. Rayburn and those around him developed singing, humor, and telling the gospel in stories to a fine art.[14]

Under such leadership, Young Life was born (officially in 1942). It has pioneered in relational recruitment work, camping at teenage resorts, Christian wilderness camping, international, indigenous, and urban youth work, as well as graduate-level, professional training. Its influence on contemporary youth ministry is broad and unmistakable.

Youth For Christ Movement

Facing the challenge of the 1940s and responding with stirring Saturday-night rallies was Youth For Christ. There was an exciting background in the 1930s for those rallies. Lloyd Bryant had begun to attract religiously unaffiliated youth through a youth broadcast and with rallies at Manhattan's Christian and Missionary Alliance Tabernacle in New York City in 1929. In the middle 1930s he toured the country with his film *Youth Marches On* and stirred interest in city-wide youth rallies. Frederick Wood of English Young Life Campaign (founded 1911) spoke at some of Bryant's rallies and brought Bryant's name to Jim Rayburn's attention. The name *Youth For Christ* was first used by an Australian, Paul Guiness, who attracted crowds to a Brantford, Ontario, theater in the 1930s, and whose idea and name spread to other Canadian cities. At about the same time in southern California, Oscar Gillian was organizing interdenominational rallies run by gospel teams. So it was on the foundation laid by those men, Percy Crawford, and Jack Wyrtzen that Youth For Christ emerged.

Torrey Johnson, Bob Cook, and six other men may be considered the founders of Youth For Christ (YFC), which was born out of a prayerful

14. Emile Calliet, *Young Life* (New York: Harper & Row, 1963); Char Meridith, *It's a Sin to Bore a Kid* (Waco, Tex.: Word, 1978); Bill Milliken, *Tough Love* (Old Tappan, N.J.: Revell, 1968); Jim Rayburn, *Dance, Children, Dance* (Wheaton, Ill.: Tyndale, 1984).

conference at Winona Lake, Indiana in 1944. Billy Graham was YFC's first full-time staff person as traveling evangelist. Skeptics labeled it a passing fad, and critics found its excesses and mistakes, but Youth For Christ became and continues to be a mighty force for youth evangelism around the world. Its leadership has spawned many other vital ministries, such as World Vision and Youth Specialities.

Increasingly, Youth For Christ followed a parallel course to Young Life with the development of home clubs called Campus Life. Its ideas of mixers and discussions on current issues are invaluable and have spread in many directions. Youth Guidance (of YFC) has done admirable work among troubled youth and is highly respected by many municipal experts.[15]

Other evangelical, paraparochial (or parachurch) leaders have accomplished what both Young Life and Youth For Christ could not do alone. Organizations such as Youth Specialities and Group Magazine have developed the creative ideas of those organizations in a sophisticated way and passed them on to church groups around the country. Their various publications and workshops not only support but add to the professionalism of youth ministry today.

Meanwhile, what was happening in the churches? Of church youth fellowships Oliver deWolf Cummings wrote:

> Before the development of the Youth Fellowship, a state of affairs existed in the churches which was quite chaotic. Several organizations competed for the loyalty of youth with overlapping functions, gaps unprovided for, and with limited coordination . . . Sunday School, Sunday evening youth societies, missionary organizations, Boy and Girl Scouts, Camp Fire Girls, Hi-Y, athletic clubs, and many others.

> Gradually, a simpler and more effective approach of the church to its youth work was discovered. In one denomination after another, steps were taken to establish an improved organizational pattern. . . . In these developments, young people themselves, lay leaders of youth, ministers, and national officials have had a part. Now, a new force, the Youth Fellowship movement, is abroad in America, and the end is not yet.[16]

MAINLINE DENOMINATIONAL YOUTH MINISTRY

The denominations had profited from the momentum of Christian Endeavor, adjusted to the changing culture of youth, and sought to organize past ideas that had fallen into disarray. The youth movements and societies of the nineteenth and early twentieth century gave way to the youth fellowship idea

---

15. James C. Hefley, *God Goes to High School* (Waco, Tex.: Word, 1970).
16. Oliver deWolf Cummings, *The Youth Fellowship* (Valley Forge, Pa.: Judson, 1956), pp. 16-17, quoted in David Evans, *Shaping the Church's Ministry with Youth* (Valley Forge, Pa.: Judson, 1965).

of the 1930s–1950s. But the end of that era was closer than Cummings imagined when he wrote in 1956, "The end is not yet."

By 1960 several things were becoming clear to church leaders. Young people had either been misjudged, misguided, or were emerging from their apparent social and political lethargy. They were looking for something more than fellowship groups. It also became evident that over-organization and competition needed to be reduced within youth ministries. Denominational leaders were questioning the segregation of youth from the overall life of the church.

So among most of the Protestant mainline denominations there was a dramatic dismantling of youth bureaus and services in the early 1960s. The aim was to integrate young people into the mainstream life of the church. Soon, however, dramatic issues were arising: civil rights, minority and third world needs, the Vietnam War and draft counseling, drugs, and the sexual revolution. Ministering to such demanding issues moved churches toward a concept and into an era of youth ministry almost without design.

In the 1970s the mainline denominations began to direct more of their attention to a wholistic curriculum for youth. Joint Education Development (JED) brought some thirteen denominations together, in some ways replacing the old ICRE (International Council of Religious Education). Their work contained covenant community, prophetic, and servant themes often missing in the evangelical paraparochial organizations and conservative denominations. By the late 1970s some of the major denominations were experimenting with national youth events. Producing those events, which have been attended by thousands, regained networks within denominations that had earlier been dismantled.

Church youth ministry has been very successful in the Southern Baptist Convention. With too little contact with, and often respect from, other churches, Southern Baptists are nevertheless proud of their ministry to youth. A thousand ministers of youth with about fifty different job titles join eight thousand more in youth-related positions in eleven thousand churches. While other denominations slashed national youth ministry staffs, Southern Baptist agencies and institutions called on fifty professional consultants and specialists.[17]

SOUTHERN BAPTIST YOUTH MINISTRY

Southern Baptist youth work has followed the general currents of other churches for more than 140 years. During the era of the Christian Endeavor and other societies, the Baptist Young People's Union (BYPU) developed from the 1890s. Slogans, theme songs, and cheers with meetings at area, state, and

---

17. Bob R. Taylor, *The Work of the Minister of Youth* (Nashville: Convention, n.d.), p. 5.

national levels attracted college-age youth. Soon senior and junior high schoolers were included.

As BYPU's success inspired Sunday evening programs in local churches, the fellowship era began. A full-time youth director appointed in 1937 at the Third Baptist Church, St. Louis, Missouri, is considered among the first of that profession. Such adult directors and youth programs with events and projects were characteristic of the youth fellowship era of the 1930s–1950s.

Helen May, Betty Jo Lacy, Roxie Jacobs, Philip Harris, and other Southern Baptist leaders questioned the recreational tendencies of that era's fellowship groups. They sought a stronger educational base that would be more closely integrated to families and the rest of the church. So, in line with other denominations, the era of youth ministry came in the late 1950s or early 1960s.

The distinct emphases of youth ministry are described by Bob R. Taylor as:

1. A youth minister working with a team of church leaders
2. Youth ministry growing out of needs of youth
3. Youth ministry developing out of the involvement of shared leadership—youth and adults[18]

CURRENT STATUS OF YOUTH MINISTRY

The renaissance of Roman Catholic youth work, after the decline in some areas of CYO and CCD, has also produced interesting results, sometimes emerging out of charismatic and evangelical renewal. Catholic professionals were forced to give the grass roots people the evangelistic and discipling skills for which they asked. They sometimes benefited from the more prophetic emphasis of their Protestant counterparts. Evangelicals, though retaining their evangelistic roots, have been challenged to a more prophetic and service orientation by World Vision, by Billy Graham's growing social concern, by contact with Third World evangelicals, by the Lausanne Covenant, and other factors. Thousands of youth are streaming around our world reaching people with the good news of Jesus Christ and caring for the hungry and the poor.

There are certain nagging problems in youth ministry in the 1980s. In a survey of seminaries by Youth Leadership of Minneapolis, 95 percent of respondents saw youth ministry as one of the critical needs of the church, and yet only 5 percent said they intended to do anything about it.[19] The church continues to see youth work as a stepping-stone to a "real" ministry. Requests for youth leaders pile up, but what churches are usually looking for is a single,

18. Ibid., pp. 9-19.
19. Gary Downing, Lilly-funded survey by Youth Leadership, Inc., Minneapolis.

dynamic person—usually male—who will serve at a low salary for a few years before moving on.

Tensions exist between suburban and urban ministries; there is a great lack of understanding and appreciation for international forms of ministry. Within our ministries we have not learned to appreciate other theological emphasis or philosophies and styles that differ from our own.

A higher professional sense and a unity in the Spirit under the lordship of Christ is needed. We must grow in appreciation of all that the gospel proclaims and in understanding of the full counsel of Scripture. Conferences by Group, Youth Specialities, and Son Life are attempts toward this end. Each national organization has something valuable for us all; we must continue to learn from one another. Much could be gained if denominational and paraparochial leaders could exchange expertise with evangelical ministries and, on occasion, from those on the theological left: compromise, no; exchange of strategies, yes.

Knowledge about adolescence and changes in the youth culture are proliferating at a stupendous rate. Valuable information gathered by Search Institute and Gallup polls should be supplemented with the growing knowledge gained by market analysts specializing in youth. Information must be made available easily to leaders through a simple, dynamic, and interactive network. Training for youth ministry at the graduate level must be given greater attention.

Elkind, Postman, and Packard, referred to earlier, emphasize the impact of the electronic revolution. Youths are being bonded to television right after mother, often before and more effectively than they are bonded to father. We continue to see figures as to how much time youths spend watching television and how many murders and adulteries they see before high school graduation. The 1980s are the age of MTV (music videos), VCRs, rented videos, and cable TV. These need to be monitored and used effectively by youth leaders. Experts plead for concerned adults to supplement parents in wholistic relationships with adolescents.

Youth Ministry in the late 1980s also needs to take note of the resurgence of the Peace Corps and other service organizations. The strongest youth groups are those including a strong program for serving. Work-study-celebration programs bond a group in vital community so longed for and needed by adolescents. They allow young people to participate in the commands of the gospel and to discuss and integrate its truth. Denominational helps for such a program and Tony Campolo's *Ideas for Social Action* (Youth Specialities) are necessary and exciting handbooks for these ventures. Organizations like Quest can help us in our enabling of youth for service, as the Navigators, Serendipity House, and organizations mentioned above offer aid in discipling.

This history of youth ministry, among many other things, suggests that the vision and special expertise of paraparochial movements are continually absorbed into church programs. Many astute leaders believe that youth leaders in the local church will be learning from this history and developing the most exciting and wholistic ministries of the late 1980s and early 1990s.

FOR FURTHER READING

Caillet, Emile. *Young Life.* New York: Harper & Row, 1956.

Christian Endeavor Essentials. Columbus, Ohio: International Society of Christian Endeavor, 1956.

Eavey, C. B. *History of Christian Education.* Chicago: Moody, 1964.

Esler, Anthony, ed. *The Youth Revolution: The Conflict of Generations in Modern History.* Lexington, Mass.: D. C. Heath, 1974.

Hefley, James C. *God Goes to High School.* Waco, Tex.: Word, 1970.

Meredith, Char. *It's a Sin to Bore a Kid: The Story of Young Life.* Waco, Tex.: Word, 1978.

Pugh, Donald E., and Milford S. Sholund. "A Historical Survey of Youth Word." In *Youth Education in the Church,* edited by Roy B. Zuck and Warren S. Benson. Chicago: Moody, 1978.

Rayburn, Jim, III. *Dance Children, Dance.* Wheaton, Ill.: Tyndale House, 1984.

Byron D. Klaus

5

Societal Patterns That Contribute to Adolescent Problems

The first cup of coffee in the church office had not even been drunk when the phone rang and Jesse, a "problem kid," shared his desperate story.

"Dad went crazy again last night. I don't know how long I can put up with him going crazy when he drinks."

You encourage him, tell him you are pulling for him, and then you set up an after school meeting that day. As you hang up the phone, your mind goes back to another difficult situation from yesterday: a single mother who cannot handle her sixteen-year-old daughter any longer. These kinds of "normal" happenings face all youth workers; they are part of the terrain. Searching for the answers to the problems faced by teenagers seems to be like shooting at a moving target.

Youth ministers must acknowledge that their attitude toward such problems has much to do with their willingness to face the factors surrounding the problems. In our attempts to find some kind of meaningful solution, we should realize that the observable problem is usually only the tip of the iceberg. Below the surface lurks the ever-changing agenda of a developing adolescent. Home,

BYRON D. KLAUS, D.Min. is chair, department of church ministries, Southern California College, Costa Mesa, California.

school, and society-at-large are all presenting their evaluations, approvals, and condemnations of certain behaviors and activities. The emerging identity issue superimposes itself on all aspects of adolescent life. That makes the "problems" we wish to solve with mere cause-effect logic very difficult to evaluate, let alone minister to.[1] The youth worker must deal not only with the observable nature of adolescent problems but also with the foundational issues of development and culture that so deeply impact the form those problems take.

Before we attempt to consider the observable "problems" of youth, it is worthwhile to examine the context in which they occur. The uprootedness of contemporary society tends to intensify adolescent problems, which presents us with the distinct possibility that unsuccessful movement through adolescence is becoming more the norm than the exception.

David Elkind says that even our relatively new understanding of adolescence has had its demarcations obliterated. In his book entitled *All Grown Up and No Place to Go,* he observes that today's teenagers are being denied the time to develop identity. Compounding that, the significant adults in their lives are not secure in their values either.

Thus the process of constructing an identity is negatively affected by the teenager's being unplaced in society. The pluralism of our society presents numerous options and choices to the teenager who increasingly self-destructs because of the lack of capability to take hold of life.[2] Erik Erikson describes this contemporary phenomenon using an analogy from Arthur Miller's *Death of a Salesman:* "I just can't take hold Mom, I just can't take hold of some kind of life."[3]

Growth through adolescence is increasingly by substitution: the construction of self is composed of the summation of feelings, thoughts, and beliefs copied from others. Elkind describes the teenager who opts for that kind of growth as developing a *patchwork self.* Such a person is easily swayed by others because he does not have a clear definition of his own self. There is no inner core of consistency and stability in the patchwork self, which renders the young person vulnerable to stress from peers and society.[4]

An awareness of the culture through which a teenager is negotiating life is certainly not what solves the problems he may have. However, the youth worker should acknowledge that teenagers are growing up in a world unlike that of any previous generation. The youth minister's own experience as a young person can no longer stand as the sole standard for present youth to follow. Today, the youth reply to their leaders (including youth workers), "You have never been young in my world."[5]

1. Dave McCasland, *The Culture Trap* (Wheaton, Ill.: Victor, 1982), p. 8.
2. David Elkind, *All Grown Up and No Place to Go* (Reading, Mass., Addison-Wesley, 1984), pp. 5-9.
3. Erik Erikson, *Identity, Youth and Crisis* (New York: Norton, 1968), p. 9.
4. Elkind, *All Grown Up,* p. 17.
5. Margaret Mead, *Culture and Commitment* (Garden City, N.Y.: Doubleday, 1970), introduction.

The task before the contemporary youth worker is certainly not a hopeless one, but it necessitates the highest level of commitment. Youth workers must truly understand their constituency and the context in which their ministry efforts take place. They also must trust the one true minister, Jesus Christ, whose power to transcend the complexities of culture and human development is the very foundation on which life change occurs.

DEFINING THE PROBLEMS

SUBSTANCE ABUSE

The term *substance* is usually used to include both alcohol and drugs, legal and illegal, as well as anything (such as glue) that might be used in an excessive way to produce physical and emotional effect. Attitudes toward substances, whether legal or illegal, are developed partly by social and cultural factors. Substances that are acceptable in one culture may be rejected in another. In the United States, using a small amount of marijuana is illegal, but drinking excessive amounts of alcohol is not. Whether a society considers substances legal or illegal, however, the fact remains that both alcohol and drugs are potentially addictive.

Our world has undergone significant changes in its perception of drugs. We have moved from viewing drugs as a cure for the body, through a period where drugs were used to cure the mind, to the expectation that drugs should alter the body for convenience and pleasure. We are fast entering Aldous Huxley's *Brave New World*.[6] As the adolescent's milieu becomes increasingly ill-defined, there is a natural correlation to the increasing problem of substance abuse among teenagers. The Norman-Harris report documented that

- 1 out of 4 high schoolers drink more than once a week
- 40% of teenagers smoke marijuana regularly
- 7 out of 10 high schoolers have tried marijuana
- The majority of teens feel their parents know they drink, but only 29% say their parents know they smoke marijuana
- 50% of teens will lie to parents about pot use
- 55% say that their parents have never discussed drugs
- 62% of teens believe drinking is bad for their health but continue to drink[7]

Commonly abused drugs include *sedatives*, which help induce sleep and relieve pain (opium, morphine, heroin, phenobarbital, Seconal, alcohol); *stimulants*, which provide tremendous stimulation of the central nervous system, euphoria, and create elevation in mood (cocaine, Benzedrine, Dexedrine; i.e.,

6. Oakley Ray, *Drugs, Society and Human Behavior*, 3d ed. (St. Louis: Mosby, 1983), pp. 4-5.
7. Jane Norman and Myron Harris, *The Private Life of the American Teenager* (New York: Rawson, Wade, 1981), p. 87.

bennies, pep or diet pills, or uppers); *hallucinogens,* which create vivid distortions in the senses (LSD, mescaline, and sometimes marijuana, with an increasing variety of synthetic "designer drugs"); *tranquilizers,* which relieve tension (Valium, Equanil, Xanax, Librium); *antidepressants,* which impact the hormone levels in the brain causing the individual to feel alert and energetic (Nardil, belladonna); and *antihistamines and volatile liquids,* which produce drowsiness and sleepiness (glue sniffing and excessive use of nasal sprays).[8]

As teenagers interact with the intensity of their own development and the pressures of society, they react in three main ways that deeply influence substance abuse. *Conformity* is one response. A culture that desires euphoria and media campaigns that paint alcohol consumption as "normal" all intensify the call to conform. Beginning to drink or to experiment with drugs is almost always a social experience. Substance abuse results most frequently from peer pressure.

Rebellion may be another reaction to the pressures of moving through adolescence. Outrage against restrictions at home or at school may bring on such a response. Substance abuse may be an act of defiance.

For more and more teenagers, substance abuse is a way of *retreat.* The world is increasingly perceived as hopeless and the value of involvement or contribution in society as worthless. Thus, retreat to a state of altered consciousness is becoming increasingly an option for teenagers.[9]

The youth worker must realize (and help parents realize) that homes and circumstances do not force teenagers to abuse alcohol or drugs. No matter what problems exist in the family, the teen who decides to try a substance does so of his own free will. It is a behavior, and as such is continued on the basis of enhancement of pleasure or reduction of discomfort. A teenager chooses to involve himself knowing that it violates certain values. The fear of being caught and knowing the difference between right and wrong impact that choice. But the teenager himself makes the choice; that must be acknowledged.[10]

The youth worker should be aware of the several stages that occur in all substance abuse. Most youths will encounter availability of alcohol or drugs before they actually use them. In stage one a substance is taken only when it is convenient. It is hard to spot drug use during this period because the teen looks and acts normal. In stage two consumption increases from occasional to every weekend and many weeknights. In stage three the user loses control. Activities are not finished, and attention span decreases. There are abrupt mood changes, and the teen spends a lot of time alone. Stage four users can no longer distinguish between normal or high. The teenager will look "wasted" all

8. Gary Collins, *Fractured Personalities* (Carol Stream, Ill.: Creation House, 1972), pp. 172-73.
9. Billie Davis, *Teaching to Meet Crisis Need* (Springfield, Mo.: Gospel Publishing, 1984), pp. 108-9.
10. Ray, *Drugs, Society and Human Behavior,* p. 10.

the time. The eyes will be glazed, and there is loss of weight. Relationships are out of the question.

PREMARITAL SEX

The last twenty years have brought about massive reevaluation in our societal expectations of sexual conduct. The so-called sexual revolution is a fact of life to teenagers. Open nudity and "sexual awakening" are all glorified in movies geared to the teenage audience. Legalized abortions, birth control pills, and the lowering of the age of first sexual experience cloud the horizon. Teens see their divorced parents bring home lovers, and the "blended family" is the context in which nearly half of all teenagers will live their teen years.

Contemporary scholars decry the loss of innocence among the adolescents of our society, and yet sex is constantly being examined clinically on radio, television, and in magazines. The advertising industry creates erotic ads and sells sexuality as part of the total dress package. Statistically,

- Nearly 6 out of 10 sixteen to eighteen-year-olds have had sex.
- Nearly 1 out of 3 thirteen to fifteen-year-olds have have had sex.
- The average age of first sexual experience is fifteen to seventeen.
- Nearly 6 out of 10 sexually active teens do not use contraceptives.
- Nearly 75% of today's teens have never discussed birth control with their parents.[11]

The pressure to conform is no less for the Christian teenager. "Everybody's doing it" is a very difficult pressure to withstand. In the teenager's world, decisions are made based on what is "in" as opposed to eternal truth. In some high schools more teens are nonvirgins than virgins. The girl is pressured into having sex to prove that she is a woman. Even more pressure is put on the young man to prove his sexual prowess.[12]

Sex is really a mystery to the growing teenager. The mystery and wonder of sexuality helps keep sex on their minds out of simple curiosity. Youths want information and answers and yet receive mixed responses from society.[13] "Don't do it!" may be the message the teenager receives from parent and church, but "how to do it" is the teaching many teens receive in public school sex education programs. That is compounded by the message teenagers receive from peers: "We do it all the time!"

The youth worker's response to this confusing situation must be both sensitive and decisive. The problem will not go away, and yet it is a volatile topic in many church settings. To act may bring controversy, but not to act

11. Norman and Harris, *Private Life*, pp. 42-43.
12. Barry Wood, *Questions Teenagers Ask on Dating and Sex* (Old Tappan, N.J.: Revell, 1981), chaps. 18-21.
13. James Dobson, *Preparing for Adolescence* (Santa Ana, Calif.: Vision House, 1978), pp. 80-81.

may bring unnecessary trauma to teenagers and their families. Christian sex education should seek to affirm God's design (i.e., sexual relations within marriage). The youth worker must also seek to discover the church's readiness for such a program and his own skills and qualifications for carrying out such a task.[14]

Though the primary emphasis is to prevent the misuse of sex, the youth worker will encounter teens who have felt the guilt and damage that engaging in premarital sex can bring. In this situation it is important to stress that repentance still brings God's forgiveness (1 John 1:8-9). The scars of sexual irresponsibility may remain, but God does not intend guilt to be one of those scars.*

ABORTION

In January of 1973 the United States Supreme Court granted women the right to abortion on demand during the first six months of pregnancy. Also, during the final trimester of pregnancy, an unqualified right to abortion for "health reasons" was given. Abortion, heretofore a crime, now became a right. Since then, legal abortions have increased drastically. Over a million teenagers become pregnant every year, thirty thousand of them under the age of fourteen. Annually, 400,000 girls will have an abortion.[15]

Woven into an already sex-laden society is Donald Joy's observation that the sexual identity question is central to an adolescent's life. The teenager has been given confirmation that the sexual gift "works," i.e., the menstrual cycle or ejaculation. The increasingly early sexual activity of teenagers is met with a high resistance to the use of contraceptives. Not only is this true because of the lack of information, but because teens sense they possess wonderful powers in their fertility. Readily available abortion tends to trivialize the mystery and power of sexuality and particularly the moral agenda surrounding teenage sexuality.[16]

The convenient option of abortion carries with it a set of rather traumatic consequences. Abortion centers provide a clinical and emotionally sterile procedure that allows a teenage girl to go through the abortion with very little psychological involvement. Her child *and* her sense of responsibility are both aborted. That is testified to by the fact that fifty percent of teenage mothers

---

*The problem of Acquired Immune Deficiency Syndrome (AIDS) is a major factor influencing teenage sexual activity. It is entirely possible that teenage sexual activity may change dramatically because of the fear of the disease or at least the stigma associated with it.

14. See Shirley Palmer in "How to Teach Sexuality Without Getting Fired," in *Youthworker Journal* (Winter 1985).
15. Jay Kesler, ed., *Parents and Teenagers* (Wheaton, Ill.: Victor, 1984), pp. 505-7.
16. Donald Joy, *Bonding: Relationships in the Image of God* (Waco, Tex.: Word, 1985), pp. 159-60.

have a second pregnancy within thirty-six months. Sixty percent of teenage mothers have a second pregnancy before age nineteen.[17] On the other hand, adults who encourage a girl to get an abortion may be leading the girl to think they have no respect for her as a woman. Feelings of being a murderer or remembering the date of the abortion with guilt and grieving are quite common.[18]

Much of the debate on abortion centers on the question of when human life begins. This discussion must look to Scripture as the final source of authority. Whereas Scripture does not explicitly prohibit or permit abortion, it is very clear about the sanctity of human life.

1. Life begins in the womb (not at birth)
   a. John the Baptist leaped in Elizabeth's womb (Luke 1:41)
   b. David claimed God was his God from his mother's womb (Psalm 22:9-10)
2. God is actively involved before birth
   a. We are formed from the womb (Isaiah 44:2)
   b. The unborn child is protected and has his/her future ordained by God. (Exodus 21:22-25 and Psalm 139:13-16)[19]

Support systems for the pregnant teenage girl are very few within the church. If we are going to preach against the evil of abortion, we must work to supply the services necessary for girls facing unwanted pregnancy. The lack of such support in the name of Christ many times gives the illusion that abortion is the only way to avoid traumatic circumstances.

Jim Oraker offers some solid advice on counseling the pregnant teen.

1. *Establish a relationship of trust.* The situation surrounding the pregnancy is always hard to unravel. You do not have to establish guilt; that most likely is already present.
2. *Clarify your own convictions.* You must clarify your own convictions about abortion. Oraker suggests two that he holds. One, God's intent is to sustain the life of the unborn child to the highest degree. The "quality of life for the mother" argument is contradictory when we consider that it involves terminating the life of another. Two, each individual facing unwanted pregnancy must be treated with love and compassion.
3. *Explore a girl's approach to decision-making under pressure.* Previously learned decision-making patterns will influence her present decisions.
4. *Provide accurate information.* The girl needs to know the physical and emotional consequences of abortion.

17. Lawrence Simkin, "Consequences of Teen-age Pregnancy and Motherhood," *Adolescence* (Spring 1984).
18. Keith Olson, *Counseling Teenagers* (Loveland, Colo.: Group Books, 1984), p. 411.
19. Kesler, *Parents and Teenagers*, p. 509.

5. *Making the best decision.* Though the final decision rests with the girl, the best decisions are made by involving others affected by this traumatic event, i.e., parents, the father of the child, and friends. These people sometimes are abusive and judgmental. The youth worker must hold together those whose pain can drive them apart. Pregnancy and child-rearing are serious consequences for moral irresponsibility, but abortion simply cannot be condoned. However, if the girl decides on abortion, she should not be abandoned. She must continue to receive God's love in action, as well as the truth of Scripture.[20]

CRIME

Urbanization and the changing configuration of the family have had a significant influence on juvenile and adolescent crime. The number of delinquent teenagers appearing before juvenile courts has increased significantly. David Elkind reports that every month high schools experience 2.4 million thefts, almost 300,000 assaults, and more than 100,000 robberies. Adolescent males between seventeen and twenty are arrested for virtually every class of crime (including homicide) with greater frequency than any other age group. An even more sobering statistic is the record number of children under ten years of age (55,000 arrests in 1980) who are involved in crime. This grows seven times worse by age fourteen. A traumatic appendage to these statistics is the more than one million young people who run away from home every year. Prostitution and pornography thrive on vulnerable young runaways, causing untold grief and a shameful situation for many urban areas.[21]

Over two-thirds of those polled by a CBS News/*New York Times* survey suggested that social conditions such as poverty and leniency of the law were major contributors to juvenile delinquency. Other factors cited as contributors were the justice system and the breakdown of religion and morality in the family. Major differences regarding the causes of delinquency can be seen by the variations in the perceptions of people based on occupation, age, education, political party, and region.[22]

One could search in vain for *the* reason for the sudden surge in juvenile delinquency, but, as we noted, the teenager is negotiating life in an era unlike any in history. Teenagers are confronted with the implications of growing up much sooner than in previous generations, attempting to meet the challenges of life without the societal moorings of previous generations. The results are seen in activities that reflect both self-destructive hopelessness and peer-group affinity.

Terms that a youth worker should be aware of as he ministers with the adolescent delinquent include:

20. James Oraker, "How to Counsel in a Pregnancy Crisis," *Youthworker Journal* (Winter 1985).
21. Elkind, *All Grown Up*, p. 8.
22. Gary Jenson, ed., *Sociology of Delinquency* (Beverly Hills, Calif.: Sage, 1981), p. 8.

1. *Arrest.* An investigation by a police officer because of a law violation or a reported law violation. The juvenile is taken into custody, usually to a juvenile court intake officer.
2. *Intake.* The process of determining whether or not the case should move ahead for court processing. The intake officer may release the child to the parent or guardian with a reprimand. Or the case may move ahead for prosecution, at which time the juvenile may be detained in a juvenile detention center or released to his parent or guardian pending a hearing.
3. *Petition.* A formal document that initiates the court process, if the prosecutor upholds the recommendation of the intake officer.
4. *Adjudication.* The process by which a juvenile court judge reviews all the evidence presented at a hearing and determines to sustain or reject the allegations made on the petition.
5. *Disposition.* The review of the recommendations of all concerned parties as to what should happen to the young person.
6. *Aftercare.* The carrying out of the disposition. This may be probation, counseling, enrollment in a community program, and the like.

Juvenile courts deal with matters pertaining to parents and their children. Parents are legally responsible for the reasonable care and supervision of the children. Courts do try to help rather than punish parents of willfully unruly children so the family unit can remain intact.[23]

CHILD ABUSE

Adolescent abuse makes up nearly fifty percent of the caseloads of the nation's child protective agencies. It has been reported that more than seventy-five percent of all adolescent runaways experienced abuse in their homes. In a study abstracted by Lynn and Voigt, the following statistics were noted. Eighty-eight percent of teens were abused by at least one birth parent, and, contrary to some studies, step-parents represented a minority of the cases. Fifty-seven percent of abuse was carried out by the birth mother, whereas thirty-one percent was the work of a birth father. The remainder of the abuse was carried out by siblings, grandparents, step-parents and mothers' boyfriends. Sixty-eight percent of those abusing teens were abused themselves as children. Most abuse that occurred during adolescence had been over a protracted period of time, worsening from childhood to adolescence. Interestingly enough, adolescents who ran away from abusing home situations were labeled as problem adolescents. Those teens who sought help in a hospital or protective services agency were more often labeled abused adolescents and were extended considerable help.[24]

23. "Facts About Youth and Delinquency," U.S. Department of Justice, in Kesler, *Parents and Teenagers*, pp. 533-34.
24. David Lynn and Jay Voight, eds., "Research Briefs," in *Youthworker Journal* (Fall 1985).

The incidence of severe physical abuse and neglect is increasing annually. Expert researchers show a clear relationship between child abuse and adolescent criminal activity. Abusing and neglecting parents have many of the same kinds of characteristics. These include low self-esteem and an inordinate need for love and response that they desire the children to provide them. Abusive families are from a variety of socioeconomic backgrounds.

Abuse occurs most frequently in broken or disintegrating homes. Many times a potentially abusive parent is attracted to a mate with similar tendencies or to a person who is so passive as not to hinder the abusing parent from his destructive activity. The circumstances that usually produce abusive episodes include attempts at discipline, hopelessness, and medical and social stress. Sexual abuse and incest usually includes both parents. When not the actual abusers themselves, they often contribute to the act through apathy, neglect, or even cooperation with the parent who is abusing the adolescent.[25]

Several states have begun to require doctors, social workers, school teachers, and in some cases ministers to report suspected instances of child abuse. Such legislation has been developed because of the growing awareness of physical and sexual abuse among young people. Those new laws are paving the way for impingement on "clergy-penitent privilege" that heretofore has been respected by the state. The privilege has provided that clergy cannot be compelled to testify in a court of law regarding information shared by a "penitent." However, given the precedent that may be developing in pending decisions, the youth minister should be advised to exercise greater care in how he or she is dealing with troubled youth.[26]

SUICIDE

Newspaper headlines and television documentaries are reporting one of the greatest tragedies of our time: the epidemic of teenage suicide. Nationally, teen suicides have tripled during the past two decades. There are about five thousand reported suicides among teenagers every year, with fifty to one hundred unsuccessful attempts for every person who dies. Teenage suicide is 33 percent higher than the rates for the overall population and is the third leading cause of teenage death, behind homicide and accidents.[27]

The reasons teenagers take their own lives lie in developmental assets and liabilities formed from earliest childhood. The nature of society, the family one lives in, and how the teen learns to handle the stressful conflicts and traumas

25. Robert C. Trojanowicz, *Juvenile Delinquency, Concepts and Controls,* 2d ed. (Englewood Cliffs, N.J.: Prentice-Hall, 1978), pp. 207-8.
26. John Eidsmoe, *The Christian Legal Advisor* (Milford, Mich.: Mott Media, 1984), pp. 513-22.
27. Peter Giovacchini, *The Urge to Die, Why Young People Commit Suicide* (New York: Macmillan, 1981), p. 5.

of growing up all weave together an understanding of this tragedy. Some of the motivations for teenagers to commit suicide include:

1. *Escape from an intolerable situation.* Intolerable conditions may just be in the perception of the teenager, but most suicidal people want to escape a difficult situation.
2. *To punish the survivors.* Suicide is certainly a hostile act in most cases. The anger of the suicidal person is many times directed toward the survivors. Getting even in this vicious way is many times the goal.
3. *To gain attention.* To attempt suicide grabs attention like few other activities. The people close to the attempt are startled, guilty, concerned, and respond with much attention to the suicide attemptee. Regardless of how troublesome it may be, the person who seems only to be trying to gain attention by suicide attempt should be taken seriously.
4. *To manipulate others.* To manipulate through a suicide attempt is to gain more than attention. It usually means the person is seeking a specific action or result.[28]

Clues that suicide may be contemplated by a teenager would include:

1. *A history of problems.* Suicide is a process and hardly ever an impulsive act. A good clue to possible problems is a history of problems.
2. *A recent traumatic event.* Remember, the term *traumatic* is defined differently by teenagers. It may be some significant event like an accident or divorce of parents, but it may also be something like a failing grade on a test, romantic breakup, or just a parental denial of a request.
3. *Communication problem.* Sometimes in a last-ditch effort to communicate, suicide is attempted. This ultimate cry for help is an avenue that many teenagers use.
4. *Withdrawal.* Withdrawal from family life that borders on isolation can be very dangerous. When the teenager ventures away from home and never really "rejoins" the family, a warning sign is present.

Rich Van Pelt offers the following suggestions for the youth worker dealing with a suicidal crisis:

1. Do not panic. Someone needs to be in charge.
2. Believe that you can help. The relationship you have with the teenager provides the basis for that.
3. Do not call a teenager's bluff. You can push people over the edge.

28. Bill Blackburn, *What You Should Know About Suicide* (Waco, Tex.: Word, 1982), pp. 20-22.

4. Do not leave the person alone.
5. Alert parents or guardians.
6. Share the responsibility. Find the available resources in your community *now* so you will be prepared for a difficult situation.
7. Prayer must be a foundation to helping the young person in crisis.[29]

The teenager who survives a suicide attempt needs the special care of a youth worker. The guilt and the feeling of being labeled will definitely be obstacles to emotional recovery and healing. The youth worker should rely on a keen belief in the power of the Holy Spirit to bring restoration to the young person. Regular Bible study and memorization are keys to transforming the destructive "self-talk" of the teenager who has attempted suicide.

EATING DISORDERS

Anorexia nervosa and bulimia are emerging as problems unique to Western culture. Anorexia is self-imposed starvation. Anorexics restrict their intake of food, and the result is the slow deterioration of the body. Death usually occurs from heart failure. The mystery of why this problem has become so rampant is a difficult matter to unravel. Third-world cultures know nothing of the disorders we are experiencing. As with the other adolescent problems already discussed, we must employ the idea of the seen and unseen dangers of the iceberg. The real problem begins with a culture that tells us that thin is beautiful and that physical perfection is to be highly prized. Young women seem to be the most susceptible to this societal priority, as 95 percent of anorexics are female. The victims are usually from middle- or upper-class white families. These women are usually intelligent and well-mannered and are perceived by those around them as having a bright future. Part of the mystery of anorexia is that though these young girls seemingly have ideal family settings, they somehow are struggling to gain their own personal identity. The mastery of food control becomes the domain in which a sense of power and control establishes a feeling of autonomy and self-esteem.

The identity struggle shows itself in distortion of body image. Anorexics perceive themselves as fine and healthy when they actually may need hospitalization. An interweaving of individual, family, and cultural factors predispose the person to become anorexic. A significant stress or event usually precipitates both the onset of the disorder and the circumstances that sustain it.[30]

Bulimia is an eating disorder that is characterized by episodic binge eating and subsequent elimination of the food through induced vomiting called "purging." Binges are the rapid consumption of high calorie foods that can be

29. Rich Van Pelt, "The Suicidal Adolescent," *Youthworker Journal* (Spring 1984).
30. David Benner, ed., *Baker Encyclopedia of Psychology* (Grand Rapids: Baker, 1985), p. 61.

swallowed easily (i.e., ice cream, doughnuts, breads). Three thousand to five thousand calories are consumed in an episode. Forty to 65 percent of bulimics admit to at least one episode per week, with 15 to 35 percent being involved in daily binges. A very depressive mood usually sets in after an episode. This contributes to bulimics being highly secretive and thus hard to detect. Even when diagnosed, they tend to underestimate the severity of the problem. Wrestlers and gymnasts, whose activities are so connected to weight standards, are particularly susceptible to developing bulimic tendencies.[31]

Youth workers should be aware of the following signals that might alert them to the existence of an eating disorder:

1. *Continual dieting.* If you see dieting that goes beyond 25 percent of normal body weight, beware. Is a person who is already thin, trying to get thinner and thinner?
2. *Unusual interest in food without an interest in eating.*
3. *Consumption of great quantities of diet sodas or laxatives.*
4. *Excessive rigidity in an exercise schedule.*
5. *Cessation of menstruation.*
6. *Impulsive behavior, major social changes, or isolation from friends.*
7. *Unusual weight consciousness and self-deprecating speech* concerning one's own appearance when compared to the current standards of physical perfection.[32]

HELPING PARENTS UNDERSTAND THEIR TEENAGERS' PROBLEMS

The youth worker should realize the uniqueness of the relationships necessary with parents of adolescents. Youth workers are co-workers with the home; they should not replace parental responsibility but should support it. Two biblical principles guide the youth worker in understanding his or her relationship with parents. Deuteronomy 6:4-9 makes quite clear parental responsibility for the nurturing of faith in children. Ephesians 4:11-16 discusses pastoral leadership's function of equipping for service. These two biblical principles come into focus in the role of youth workers and parents. The equipping function of the youth worker includes *both* parent(s) and teenager.

The recent work of Merton and Irene Strommen has documented the desire of parents to receive information and help from outside sources to aid them in their relationships with teenagers. The Strommens' research shows that church-related personnel are the first choice of parents turning to someone for help during a personal crisis. Along with the high priority that ministers be those who can help people in times of stress, the research showed that

31. Ibid., pp. 144-45.
32. Kesler, *Parents and Teenagers,* pp. 514-15.

people desired that the congregation be equipped to serve as a caring community and a friendship/support system.

The following are the percentages of the 10,457 parents who declared their interest in outside help in specific areas:

70% How to help a child develop healthy concepts of right and wrong
68% How to help a child grow in religious faith
66% More information on substances
62% How to communicate better with one's children
47% Effective discipline
44% More about sex education
42% How to participate in a parent support group[33]

A YOUTH WORKER'S STRATEGY FOR DEALING WITH ADOLESCENT PROBLEMS

We do not lack methods and procedures to do the tasks of youth ministry. What we do need are youth workers with the will and desire to ask the tough, reflective questions that make methods of youth ministry truly effective and relevant for a particular situation. In creating a plan or strategy for dealing with adolescent problems, youth workers should be able to discover the limits of their own gifts and skills. They also should be able to develop awareness of the resources available to help in times of real crises.

A YOUTH WORKER'S PERSONAL AWARENESS OF ADOLESCENT PROBLEMS

Much of one's strategy for dealing with teen problems will be tempered by an honest evaluation of oneself as a youth worker. Ask the following set of questions as part of a personal evaluation process:

1. What level of training have I received for the problems I am being asked to deal with?
2. How much experience do I have in dealing with the particular problem?
3. Do I understand adolescents developmentally?
4. Am I capable of "feeling" with *both* teenager and parent in a crisis situation?

If an honest appraisal of the level of training or experience in a particular area shows a lack, see it as a motivation to action. Lack of experience in one area does not mean personal immaturity.

In evaluating adolescent problems as they relate to parents and family, ask the following questions:

33. Merton and A. Irene Strommen, *Five Cries of Parents* (San Francisco: Harper & Row, 1985), pp. 189-91.

1. How do I work with parents who are not Christian, but whose teenagers are?
2. What are the limits to a single parent's influence on his or her teenager?
3. Do I understand the dynamics of "blended families"?
4. About what kinds of issues do I consult with parents?
5. What "rights to privacy" do teenagers have in my counseling with them?
6. Do I understand the unique passages that teenager and parent (most likely middle adult) are going through that might give me a key to why they behave the way they do?
7. Are the "problems" simply expressions of normative family interaction?

REFERRAL STRATEGY SKILLS

Part of the youth worker's response to adolescent problems is to be a resource person. Not only does one need to be aware of personal resources and skills but those that are available through referral. Three basic rules of thumb to consider when deciding if you need outside resources for help include:

1. *Time.* Youth workers face a constant juggling of activities, personal preparation, and administration. Ask yourself whether or not you can be effective if you take on the problem by yourself. Can you still continue to handle your other responsibilities?
2. *Skill or experience.* Be honest about your capability to help in a particular situation. Do not bluff yourself or other persons.
3. *Emotional security.* Are you facing problems you have never personally resolved in your own life? As you are helping teenagers resolve problem relationships with family members, can you say you have done the same with your own family? Considerable stress and strain in your own life can come from overwork, lack of sleep, and strained personal and church relationships. Be aware of putting relationships with significant persons at stake while attempting to help in problem and crisis situations.

Part of your strategy should start with appropriate disclosure to those you work with on how you will hope to react in certain crisis situations. Examples of some principles you would want to make clear might include (examples are not meant to be normative): (1) I consult with family on substance abuse issues; (2) Problems in boy-girl relationships are kept confidential except in the case of pregnancy and resulting necessary choices; (3) I am here to help both parent and teen; and (4) I do not see myself as the only resource for the handling of teen problem situations.

RESOURCE NETWORKING

Your first line of help should be other *church staff personnel and mature lay persons*. Build solid relationships with fellow staff and laity in the church, and see them as a rich source of help for crisis situations.

Much of the process of dealing with problem situations has to do with work that is done previous to the actual problem's occurring. This should necessitate developing a file of brochures, contacts, and easy-reference phone numbers or addresses that can be obtained quickly when the problem occurs. Potential sources should include:

1. *Professional therapists.* Child psychoanalysts and psychiatrists, clinical psychologists, family therapists, and clinical social workers may all be persons whose help may be needed in a crisis. Always try to be aware of the resources you are using. The recommendation of friends or peers is good; however, do your best to use professionals whom you have checked for competency.
2. *Parachurch agencies,* including Campus Life, Youth Guidance, Young Life, Salvation Army, YMCA, YWCA, and rescue missions. The specialists or the facilities of such parachurch agencies may be a tremendous help in crisis-problem situations.
3. *Substance abuse counseling,* such as Teen Challenge, Al-Anon (for family members of alcoholics), or local self-help groups. These can serve as both informational and therapeutic resources.
4. *Pregnancy counseling:* homes for unwed mothers, denominational sources, foster care situations. When asked what the alternative to abortion is, make sure you can give an answer.
5. *Crisis hotlines.* Awareness of this kind of information can help immediate crisis situations. Awareness of hotlines for suicide, substance abuse, and venereal disease are important.
6. *Foster homes.* Physical abuse and the necessity of temporary housing as a result of family separation should motivate the youth worker to be aware of these resources. They might even exist within your own church membership.
7. *Social services.* Be aware of city, county, and state services and agencies that might provide someone the temporary help they need. Get to know the social worker in your area, particularly the juvenile justice system case workers.
8. *School counselors.* Build solid relationships with local school counselors, not only for vocational counseling help, but for insight and help with the teenagers you work with.

The Body of Christ possesses an amazing potential for meeting the multifaceted needs of adolescents. The church may play an enabling role in helping students and their families as they face the problems endemic to adolescence. Together with the community agencies available, Christians may form muchneeded networks to demonstrate compassion and concern that reflects the ministry of Jesus.

FOR FURTHER READING

Barnes, Frace M. *Alcohol and Youth: A Comprehensive Bibliography.* Westport, Colo.: Greenwood, 1982.

Baucom, John. *Fatal Choice: The Teenage Suicide Crisis.* Chicago: Moody, 1986.

Collins, Gary R. *Christian Counseling: A Comprehensive Guide.* Waco, Tex.: Word, 1980.

Cretcher, Dorothy. *Steering Clear: Helping Your Child Through the High Risk Drug Years.* Minneapolis: Winston, 1982.

Furstenburg, Frank, ed. *Teenage Sexuality, Pregnancy, and Childbearing.* Philadelphia: U. of Pennsylvania, 1980.

Perkins, William Mack, and Nancy McMurtrie-Perkins. *Raising Drug-Free Kids.* New York: Harper & Row, 1986.

Powell, John S. J. *Abortion, the Silent Holocaust.* Allen, Tex.: Argus Communications, 1981.

Spotts, Dwight, and David Veerman. *Reaching Out to Troubled Youth.* Wheaton, Ill.: Victor, 1987.

Part 2

Personnel of Church Youth Ministry

6

Paul Borthwick

The Person of the Youth Minister

Consider three different youth workers. John works in an urban setting. He spends days with students, counseling some to stay in high school, helping others as their parole officer. He has few youth programs, although his house is a beehive of activity almost every day. He loves the young people of his neighborhood, and he works to help his neighbors to do the same.

Loretta works part-time at her church. Her youth group averages about twenty, and she has recruited a team of others to join her in the ministry. Her church leaders are not too supportive, but for fear of the church's teenagers they let her continue her ministry.

Bill is a full-time youth worker. He has a situation that John and Loretta would consider heavenly: a big budget, lots of support, many helpers. But Bill still does not look at these things as the measure of his ministry. He looks for students that have come through the youth group and have continued following Jesus. He evaluates success in the same way that John and Loretta would—changed lives that have been served, helped, built, and loved.

The contexts of these three ministries are very different, but their work does have one common denominator: it requires them to give extensively from their own personal lives. As they work, they find out quickly that their views of themselves and their ministries affect everything they do.

PAUL BORTHWICK, M. Div., was formerly minister to students at Grace Chapel, Lexington, Massachusetts.

The Socratic advice to know thyself is one of the great challenges of youth ministry. Who am I? Where do I fit into God's plan? Why am I doing youth work in the first place? Those and other questions loom large in the mind of any person who has given serious thought to youth ministry and to his or her respective call.

Self-concept is a sensitive issue for the Christian. Some go to one extreme by ignoring the questions about self-discovery and self-actualization. Such thinking is, in their minds, an expression of a secularized way of being selfish and self-centered, qualities contrary to Christian faith.

Others, however, pursue self-discovery with zeal. Psychology, studies on the question of "my spiritual gifts," and repeated soul-searching are all part of an apparent obsession to find oneself. Knowing who I am and what makes me tick becomes the life goal.

The problem with either extreme is the lack of balance. The former extreme ignores the benefits of self-understanding as a part of personal growth before God. The latter extreme focuses too much on the self; in the words of Robertson McQuilken, president of Columbia Bible College, South Carolina, they fail "to ask the question, 'What am I going to do with myself once I find me?' "[1]

MASKS WORN IN YOUTH MINISTRY

Working with teenagers puts us into a world where self-discovery and self-knowlege are hard to come by. In the book *Is There Life After High School?* Ralph Keyes points out that the high school environment is a very competitive arena where false standards of success are formed that continue to influence us throughout adulthood. Because of that, Keyes suggests that much of our adult self-image is based on either a reaction to the lack of popularity we experienced in high school or an effort to reconstruct the acclaim we had as popular high schoolers.[2]

Thus, many will reenter the teen world through youth ministry with insecure self-images (based on comparison to their high school experiences) and will manifest their insecurity through wearing various masks with the youth.

Some fall prey to the stereotypical youth minister image. Rather than thinking about who they are and how God wants to use them in a unique way, they try to become what they perceive a youth minister must be. The athletic, musical, popular, joke-telling, do-everything-well youth minister usually exists only in fables. Most youth ministers are strong in some areas but weak in others, yet those weaknesses are never dealt with as long as the Mr. Everything youth worker image hangs over them.

1. From the Grace Chapel (Lexington, Massachusetts) International Missions Conference, April 21, 1985.
2. Ralph Keyes, *Is There Life After High School?* (New York: Warner, 1977), pp. 24, 39.

Others desire acceptance so badly from their youth that they fit right into the teen culture. That is especially true of the youth worker who subconsciously is hoping that the youth ministry will provide him or her the popularity that was never achieved in high school.[3] At age twenty or twenty-one, that may not be so bad, I suppose, but at age thirty a man or woman should not be identical with a teenager when it comes to levels of maturity. The danger of perpetuating our adolescence by working with youth is a temptation that we all face, and we can conquer it only through a strong sense of who we are before God.

"Being 'real' in the youth culture," writes Pat Hurley, "does not mean trying to be a 'kid'. You are an adult who relates to the youth mindset. Being a free person, a person they can trust, will provide an environment of spontaneity and flexibility wherever you go."[4]

A third problem related to self-esteem and self-image for the youth worker manifests itself through an authoritarian, gestapo style of leadership. Tony Campolo speaks to this problem:

> Other youth workers may have a psychological need to exercise authoritarian domination over others. They thrive on having young people depend on them for answers to their everyday problems and questions. They gain delusions of grandeur as they see themselves as the primary shapers of the lives of their youth group members.[5]

Aberrant behavior with our youth groups, whether it be trying to be someone that we are not, or being everybody's buddy, or being the boss, ultimately comes back to the question, What do I think about myself?

> Having a poor self-image is a problem we all face at one time or another in our ministry with youth. How do we feel secure enough to be ourselves with our youth? How do we build the confidence needed to be stable in our self-images?[6]

SELF-CONFIDENT

It could be argued that insecurity and unstable self-concepts will be with us all our lives, but youth ministry holds some inbred tension areas that tend to exacerbate the problems.

First, there is the matter of our own age. If we are young, we are still feeling our way around in adult life. We are indeed unsure of who we are, and the youth ministry becomes the testing ground. We identify closely with the

3. Ibid., pp. 75, 89.
4. Pat Hurley, *The Penetrators* (Wheaton, Ill.: Son Power, 1980), p. 27.
5. Tony Campolo, "Hidden Reasons Behind the Revolving Door Syndrome," *Youthworker* (Summer 1984), p.24.
6. Paul Borthwick, "Do You Know the Real You?", *Group* (June-August, 1984), p.11.

teenagers, but then, about age twenty-five, we become acutely aware that we are no longer teens. Our worlds are different, and we start facing tough choices. Do I stay in youth ministry at the risk of feeling that I am curtailing my adult maturation? Do I resign in an effort to start a pilgrimage into adulthood, or can I cultivate adult maturity while continuing to work with students?

A second tension is the matter of our performance. Do I know how to accept myself well enough so that I can feel comfortable when I discover that I am not popular with my youth group? Can I tolerate the feelings of personal failure that sometimes occur after one of my key students abandons the faith? How will I respond when my performance is lauded by church leaders but the accompanying salary for youth work seems to say, "Your job is not really too important"?[7]

A third tension is the youth program itself and the accompanying expectations that others have of the leader. The youth minister is quick to learn the proverb "You cannot please all of the people all of the time." When students are happy, the parents might be furious. If the youth minister identifies with the parents, the students may feel that he has abandoned them.[8] And on top of all that, if there is no growth in the youth group, the church leaders begin to wonder if he should be the youth leader in the first place.

When those tensions are added to our personal questions about God's will for our own lives and His plans for us, we can come out as very confused men and women. Where do my dreams fit into all this? Is failure a sign that God is not with me in youth ministry? How do I measure myself?

I KNOW—I AM THERE

I write not as a psychologist who is evaluating the personality types of those who choose youth ministry, but as a youth minister who has been working with youth for more than ten years. I have stayed with youth ministry for all kinds of reasons. There have been times when I have wondered if the motivation is to perpetuate my own adolescence or to be the authority over others who are younger than me. At other times I have wondered if I am not in youth ministry to try to give teenagers experiences I wished I could have had in my own teen years.

Although there is always room for personal growth with respect to developing an adequate self-image and getting God's honest yet loving view of

7. Perhaps nothing is more of a tension or frustration to youth workers than the negative message that the church subconsciously sends by underpaying youth leaders or by failing to support the youth ministry financially. This financial pressure can drive people out of youth ministry.

8. For a good discussion of this tension, see Darrel Pearson, "Whose Side Do You Take?" in *Parents as Partners in Youth Ministry* (Wheaton, Ill.: Victor, 1985).

ourselves, teenagers need leaders who are at peace with the person God has made them. To put it another way, teenagers, who are themselves wondering who they are, what they are worth, and where they fit in, must have leaders who are models of appropriate self-images. The youth leader need not be perfect, but he or she should have a good sense of "who I am" as well as "who I am not." The self-image and self-concept of the youth worker is critically important in setting the pace of growth for the teenagers in the group.[9]

As leaders of moldable teenagers, before God we must pursue security in the knowledge of ourselves and be at peace with that. We must learn to accept the changes, the weaknesses and failures, and the short-comings and successes in order to lead our young people in the manner Paul the apostle described in Romans 12:3: "For by the grace given me I say to every one of you: Do not think of yourself more highly than you ought, but rather think of yourself with sober judgment, in accordance with the measure of faith God has given you." Paul himself exemplified this pattern in 1 Corinthians 15:10, where he writes, "But by the grace of God I am what I am, and His grace to me was not without effect. No, I worked harder than all of them—yet not I, but the grace of God that was in me."

TOWARD GREATER GROWTH

The key word in developing as people with solid self-images is growth. We may all fall prey to the weaknesses and insecurities of leadership, but as we grow in understanding ourselves, we can be more like Christ. The next paragraphs describe the youth minister's building project. It's an ongoing project that will not be completed quickly.

QUALITIES AND COMMITMENTS

As followers of Jesus Christ, one of the most important gifts we can give to others is the gift of ourselves. Paul wrote to the Thessalonians that his ministry was to share not only the gospel of God "but our lives as well, because you had become so dear to us" (1 Thess. 2:8). Our lives as leaders, examples, models, and advocates are among the most significant aspects of youth leadership. With that in mind, the question arises, What kind of people do we want to be? Effective youth ministry requires the development of several key qualities and commitments.

Self-acceptance. As stated earlier, teenagers need leaders who are confi-

---

9. David Elkind (*All Grown Up and No Place To Go* [Reading, Mass.: Addison-Wesley, 1983]) states that the teen years are crucial in the development of "a sense of self, a sense of personal identity" (p. 15), but he worries that adults are not providing "a clearly defined value system against which to test other values and discover their own" (p. 9). The result? "The process of constructing an identity is adversely affected because neither the proper time nor the proper ingredients are available" (p. 9).

dent in God and secure about who God has made them. When I was first invited to lead the high school ministry at Grace Chapel, Lexington, Massachusetts, I turned it down. The former leader was dynamic, a good singer, an excellent speaker, and somewhat charismatic in his ability to lead. I perceived none of those qualities in myself, and I knew that I would be crushed under the comparison.

A year later, however, I accepted the job. In the time that intervened I became convinced that God wanted to use my skills and abilities at Grace Chapel. I learned that I could accept myself before God, that it was wrong to compare myself to someone else.

Leroy Eims's book *Be the Leader You Were Meant to Be* was instructive at this point. When God called Moses to be Israel's deliverer, He said in effect (Ex. 3 and 4):

> Moses, it really doesn't matter who you are — whether you feel qualified or unqualified, whether you feel up to the task or not. The point is that *I* am going to be there. . . . I am going to deliver them, and I am going to give you the privilege of beingein it with me.[10]

In the midst of my own inadequacy, I could accept myself because God had called me. He required my availability to Him rather than dynamic personal abilities.

The ability to accept myself as God has made me has been exceptionally liberating. I am free to recruit others who have strengths where I am weak, and I am free to say to parents and youth what our youth group does and does not offer.

Self-acceptance has also enabled me to define my target of youth ministry. Rather than feeling constantly guilty about the millions of teenage runaways and thousands of distraught young people contemplating suicide. I am able to say, "This is where God has called me; how can I serve, care for, and build the teenagers *here*."

The starting point of my coming to peace with who I am in God's sight was intertwined with the reading of Paul Tournier's book *The Strong and the Weak*. The following quotation helped me to accept myself as the weak person that I am:

> All men, in fact, are weak. All are weak because all are afraid. They are afraid of being trampled underfoot. They are all afraid of their inner weakness being discovered. They all have secret faults; they all have a bad conscience on account of certain acts which they would like to keep covered up. They are all afraid of other men and of God, of themselves, of life and of death.[11]

10. Leroy Eims, *Be the Leader You Were Meant to Be* (Wheaton, Ill.: Victor, 1975), pp. 10-11.
11. Paul Tournier, *The Strong and the Weak* (Philadelphia: Westminster, 1964), p. 21.

My fears and insecurities, I found, need to be brought before God. I needed to acknowledge my own weakness so that God could use me as I was.

In the process of growth toward greater self-acceptance, I have been able to be an example to our young people. For instance, as I learned to accept that I was going bald, I relearned God's love, regardless of my appearance. As I shared this with our students, they, in turn, were helped through their traumas of acne and the disproportionate growth of their bodies.

Flexibility. Growth implies change, but the older we get the less we desire change. We like to have things stay the same, and we prefer to think about "the good old days" more and more. Teenagers, however, are in a world of growth and change. Their classes, their bodies, their career aspirations, and even their family make-up (due to death, divorce, and remarriage) are in a perpetual state of change.[12]

Although teenagers need the stability of those who are committed to youth ministry for the long-haul (see chap. 18), they also need people who are open to change, new ideas, and transitions. Youth leaders must be people who cultivate the ability to *laugh* (especially at themselves) so that teenagers see them as models of flexibility.

One of the greatest qualities of Jesus was His ability to change the *status quo.* He surprised people with His answers, and when some desired very rigid standards on issues that He knew were peripheral to the kingdom of God, He knew how to get them to consider bigger issues. He was a model of the "new wine" (Luke 5:37-38), and He gave us an example to follow.

For the youth leader, being flexible does not mean being contrary to church systems or rebellious against the *status quo.* It means being willing to ask, "Why are we doing this?" and, "How could we do it better?" It means openness to growth and a willingness to address the truth of the gospel to the contemporary world of the teenager.

In practical terms, "new wine" flexibility for our group has meant that we have had to avoid rigidity with respect to issues like rock music. With the same spirit of flexibility, we have cancelled programs that had outlived their effectiveness, opened our doors to students who did not look like the teenagers in our group, and pursued discussions with those of theologically different views so that our students could see that not everyone who calls himself a Christian speaks in the same jargon.

Personal growth. I have often told my youth team that a healthy staff begets a healthy youth group. When the leaders are growing, the youth find it easier to follow suit. The principle is basically that of being a *model.* "The inner life of the leader will either make him or break him. If he neglects the cultivation of purity, humility, and faith, he is in for big trouble."[13]

12. Elkind (*All Grown Up,* p. 33) cites the rapid transformation of adolescence as the cause of the teen formation of the "imaginary audience," the feeling that everyone else is as concerned about the teen's changes as the teen himself.
13. Eims, *Be the Leader,* p. 39.

Paul taught Timothy that he needed to be an example to the believers "in speech, in love, in faith, and in purity" (1 Tim. 4:12). He also commanded that bishops and deacons be the husbands of one wife and men who managed their own households well (1 Tim. 3:2,4,12). The basic idea was that they needed to have their own lives in a growing, orderly mode *before* they could lead others.

We too must think in those terms. Growing in our own walks with God, building our marriage and family relationships, and being responsible adults must be a part of the life foundation on which we develop our ministry to youth. "We stay fresh in the ministry when we are growing as a person and a pastor. 'Growing' is a present progressive verb that means the process continues every day."[14]

Perhaps the greatest challenge in terms of personal growth boils down to how we use our time. Am I reading books beyond those directly related to youth work? Is my youth group schedule so full that I have no time to take my wife on a date? Are there people that I need to be pursuing who will help me to grow? If I subtract every aspect of my life that is directly linked to my youth ministry, is there anything left?

I once mentioned to our senior pastor, Gordon MacDonald, my acquired conviction that I would rather burn out than rust out. He responded, "Neither seems too desirable to me. I'd rather last." If we are going to last in youth ministry, we must commit ourselves to growth so that over the long haul we continue to have something to offer to the youth we serve.[15]

Thoughtfulness. One of the problems of youth ministry is that many of us enter it without much advance planning. Like the mountain climber, we accept youth leadership because it's there, yet we really do not know what we will do with it when we get it.[16]

Effective youth ministry and an effective youth minister require a commitment to thoughtfulness, carefully mulling over what we are doing and why. Rather than just following the lead of others and implementing other people's programs and strategies in our youth ministries, we must be people who grow with respect to what God wants to do in *our* ministry.

John Musselman, minister of youth at Coral Ridge Presbyterian Church in Fort Lauderdale, Florida, at one time was having 300 or more students at

14. Earl Palmer, "Strategy for Sanity," *Youthworker* (Summer 1984), p. 5.
15. One principle has helped me be more balanced in my growth: rather than trying to do everything in the first two years of youth ministry, I preferred to take more of a plodding style. I told church leaders, "We all face a choice: I can either work ninety hours a week for the youth ministry for eighteen to twenty-four months (before I burn out), or I can work fifty to sixty hours per week for a long time. I prefer the latter option." Fortunately for me, they did too.
16. This is not only my personal story (I started in youth group leadership at age nineteen, one year out of high school), but it is also substantiated by interviews with fellow youth leaders. The *Youthworker* survey (Fall 1984, pp. 78-79) showed that the average youth leader was twenty-seven, with four and one-half years of youth ministry leadership, which implies that most had entered youth ministry leadership right after college or Bible school.

his youth programs. But when he evaluated the situation, he realized that he did not know where those students were in relationship to Jesus Christ. He made bold decisions that reduced his numbers and changed the program, but it was the thoughtful change needed for long-term effectiveness.[17]

Jay Kesler, former president of Youth For Christ (and now president of Taylor University), addressed this issue under the category of personal theology:

> Your personal theology will have an effect on everything you do in youth work. It will affect the type of message you bring, the response you expect, the progress of the youth among whom you minister, your method of counseling, your attitude towards others, and how you measure results. In short, all we do relates to what we actually believe.[18]

What do we believe? And why are we doing what we are doing? What impact are we trying to have in the lives of students? The answers to these and a variety of other self-searching and ministry-evaluating questions are necessary if we are to be at peace with ourselves and our ministries.

Perhaps thoughtfulness about ourselves and our ministries will help us to gain credibility as professionals; perhaps it will challenge us to incorporate work with parents into our ministries. But whatever else thoughtful examination of ourselves and our ministries may achieve, it will give us a greater sense of direction and purpose. "The most productive thing a leader can do is to train himself to think ahead. A leader has been described as a person who sees more than others see, who sees further than others see, and who sees before others do."[19]

In 1978, I set out to do some thinking about our youth ministry. I evaluated myself, the caliber of the students in our church youth group and in our community, and the tone of the church. At that point, I decided before God that developing leaders would be one of the primary goals of our group. Now, when the questions arise as to why we do not have more fun and games, I have an answer. On the other hand, when parents are challenged by the growth they see in their own teenagers, I am encouraged to know that the young people are affecting their homes for Christ. In short, we thought about where we wanted to go, and we are getting there.

Integrity. One of the themes of Paul's teaching to Timothy and Titus

---

17. From an interview with John Musselman in April 1981, as well as personal contact again in November 1985. Coral Ridge's youth group has never again achieved such high numbers, but it now has more than a hundred students in intense discipleship groups, scores in its Youth Evangelism Explosion program, and dozens that have gone out on short-term mission teams.
18. Jay Kesler, "Determining Your Theology of Youth Ministry," in Gary Dausey's *The Youth Leader's Sourcebook* (Grand Rapids: Zondervan, 1983), p.23.
19. Eims, *Be the Leader*, p. 55.

regarding church leadership was blamelessness.[20] In an age of fluctuating morals and debatable ethical practices, it is necessary that the youth leader be a person of integrity, that he or she be above reproach.

Such integrity manifests itself in a variety of ways in the youth ministry. It includes our relationship with parents and church leaders. It means that we strive not to become defensive when attacked or blamed. It means telling the truth about problem teenagers and resisting the temptation to exaggerate the successes of the youth ministry.

Integrity must also be evident in our relationship with young people. We must seek to be men or women of our word, not people who make promises that go unfulfilled. It means that we seek to help students confront their problems head-on rather than side-stepping the issues with evangelical clichés like "God will work it all out."

Finally, integrity should be reflected in our personal morality. By resisting the temptation to pilfer from the discretionary cash fund or by acknowledging that our desire to give a hug of affirmation to a teenage girl may be more sexual than sincere, we engage in the personal struggle to maintain uprightness before the Lord and the people we serve.

Priorities. David Bryant states that many of us are "spiritually and psychologically fatigued. Ruth Graham calls the modern evangelical 'packed man'. We have so many options that we are paralyzed with over choice and fatigued by trying to carry out too much, too soon, too fast, too often."[21]

In light of the excessive demands for our time and energies, we must grow both in our ability to make good decisions regarding our commitments and in our ability to carry out those commitments in a disciplined way.

The most basic priorities and commitments—to God, our families, and our ministries—cannot be established and carried out through a onetime decision. We must discipline ourselves to meet with God, pray, and immerse ourselves in the Word of God regularly. We must evaluate and revise our schedules so that our spouses and families are getting more than lip-service love.[22] We must prayerfully balance our perspectives on our ministries so that we see that God is the one in charge.

Endurance. Robert Service wrote a poem entitled "The Men That Don't Fit In." I loved the title, so I went looking through the local library until I found it. Rather than telling me what I had expected—that it was the "men that don't fit in" that changed the world—he stated quite the opposite. The "men that don't fit in" wander the world aimlessly, restlessly trying to sink

---

20. See 1 Tim. 3:2; Titus 1:7.
21. David Bryant, *Concerts of Prayer* (Ventura, Calif.: Regal, 1984), p. 117.
22. In this respect, I am convinced that one of the greatest needs of today's teenager is to see positive, godly marriages and families. The irony is, however, that we, by our compulsive drives to be good youth workers, often exemplify just the opposite of what we want the students to see.

their roots, but it is the *"steady, quiet plodding ones* who win the lifelong race."[23]

To be a steady, quiet, plodding one sounds neither romantic nor adventuresome, but those are the characteristics that make for effective ministry to youth. To endure through the ingratitude, tensions, and insecurities related to youth ministry is hard work, but it is worth it.

Endurance might seem fruitless at first, but over the long-term it yields priceless results. By endurance, I have seen rebels converted and apathetic teenagers motivated. By endurance, I have been privileged to lead students to Christ, disciple them, see them through college and off to seminary or the mission field, marry some, and even bury others.

But remember, such war stories have not come quickly. I estimate that I have about ten favorites since becoming involved in my present ministry in 1973. That works out to less than one war story per year. The rest is endurance.

SKILLS AND TRAINING

Developing the person that God has made us includes more than personal commitments to growth and being an example. It goes beyond our desire to be thoughtful or flexible people. By the very nature of leadership, it must extend to the ways that we lead. Our skills and abilities, as well as our training and education, must work cooperatively to help us be effective leaders of youth.

Some people are very gifted; others feel dull and unskilled. For each leader, however, the point again is growth. Realizing weaknesses and strengths, we must be committed to developing the skills that we do have and getting help in the areas where we fall short. There are at least four areas in which we all need to grow with respect to the youth ministry. Some skills can be developed through practice in ministry. Others may require attendance at youth seminars or continuing education courses. All are necessary.

Communication. I have two friends in youth ministry who are extremely different as communicators. One has a terrible stutter and takes a long time to work his way through a sentence when he speaks. The other is a masterful, polished speaker. Both are effective communicators, however, because they talk in terms the students understand, and they make the Scriptures relevant to daily living. They know how to answer their students' questions from a Christian perspective, and their teenagers listen.

Communication in youth work does not always demand exceptional oratorical ability or the ability to preach. Effective communication usually requires knowledge of the audience, a commitment to be relevant, a willingness to

23. Robert Service, "The Men That Don't Fit In," from *The Collected Poems of Robert Service* (New York: Dodd, Mead, 1907), p. 42.

address the hard issues of daily living with honesty and compassion, and an ability to express Christian truth in an understandable way.

The person who wrote, "I'd rather *see* a sermon than hear one any day," would have done well in youth work, because our primary method of communication is by example. As Paul wrote to the Corinthians, "Follow my example, as I follow the example of Christ" (1 Cor. 11:1), so we must state to our youth, "If you want to know how to follow Christ, watch me."

The first responsibility of a youth worker as a communicator, therefore, is to build on his or her own personal example, to show teenagers how to live.

> One basic result of the role-model relationship is that it shows the teenager that the Christian life has practical, daily implications. . . . A teenager who watches a respected person can be reassured that the Christian life can be lived.[24]

The second responsibility *does* require good oral and written communication. (Incidentally, one way my stuttering friend makes up for his impediment is by his excellent skills in writing for his students and their parents.) There must be an awareness of the teenager's world combined with a knowledge of the Scriptures. Our goal as leaders must be to enable our young people to interpret and respond to their culture and society with biblical values and attitudes. They need to be trained to distinguish good from evil (Hebrews 5:14), and we must be the pacesetters through our talks, newsletters, and Bible studies with them.

A third responsibility is to communicate with those outside the youth group: parents, church leaders, and other interested adults. Too often, youth leaders are either afraid of parents and adult leaders, or they assume that they are not interested in the youth group. As a result, communication breaks down, parents feel ignored or untrusted by the youth leader, and the youth leader feels that the youth group is operating on an isolated island in the sea of church life.[25]

Communication by example requires personal growth. Communication with teenagers requires study of the world of adolescents as well as intimate knowledge of the Bible. Communicating with parents and other adults requires the dissemination of information as well as the willingness to explain and answer questions. Effective oral and written communication, as a skill, may mean that we take active steps to improve—a speaking or writing course, a personal coach to help us grow, or some extra reading—so that we can do our best to communicate to these people who are looking to us for answers.

Administration. Youth programs are not an end in themselves; they are

24. Bill Muir, "The Youth Leaders As Model," in Dausey, *Youth Leader's Sourcebook*, p. 55.,
25. Parents' meetings, newsletters, or even a Parents' Council are all avenues of communication that often serve to restore good communication between parents and youth leaders.

merely a means to do outreach, build relationships, and train students. But youth programs do not just happen. There is a lot of work and coordination required, from making the deposit to secure the hayride to providing for the refreshments after the Bible study.

Few people enter youth work with an understanding of the administrative work load that is often required.

> The complexity of relationships and the anxiety of multiple responsibilities are in direct conflict to much that is taught or written about in youth ministry. Many of the youth ministry ideals that are upheld assume forty or more hours per week dedicated to youth. This is seldom the case in church ministry.[26]

Because of administrative details related to the youth group (newsletters, phone calls, money management, study time) and administrative matters unrelated to the youth group (like writing letters to financial supporters or sharing in the worship services at church), every youth worker feels at one time or another that the red tape is overwhelming. "I was spending more time *with kids* when I was a volunteer!"[27]

Managing our work is a skill that can be developed. It starts by organizing our time and getting a clear understanding of what is realistically accomplished in a block of time. It also means using the skills of others (see the section on teamwork, below) and delegating responsibilities. It involves conditioning our self-expectations with the realistic demands of our jobs. In 1984 a survey of youth leaders revealed that 92 percent had jobs with multiple responsibilities (youth and music, youth and education, etc.).[28] Realizing that we have only twenty hours to spend on youth group matters helps us to modify our goals and aspirations, and it helps us accept that we simply cannot accomplish as much as someone who is truly a full-time youth worker.

Counseling. If counseling is defined as coming alongside others to help them, then youth ministry is indeed a counseling–oriented ministry. We counsel teenagers, parents, and others who are concerned about youth. We are, as youth ministers, those who have been called alongside to help.

Good counseling with youth and parents requires certain skills that must be developed and acquired. We must be able and willing to listen. That is especially the case with the troubled teenager and parents. What is *really* happening? Can we hear the pains that are unstated? Do we listen compassionately rather than defensively? Good counseling requires that we follow James's

---

26. Paul Borthwick, "Church Youth MInistry: A Breed Apart," *Youthworker* (Spring 1984), p. 77.
27. Walter Henrichsen *(Disciples Are Made, Not Born* [Wheaton, Ill.: Victor, 1974], p. 93) states: "In the final analysis, the trainer can only contribute to a person's development in two areas: (1) the giving of time and (2) the opportunity to learn." One of the frustrations many encounter with administrative work is that it takes away from the first basic contribution, the giving of time.
28. *Youthworker* (Fall 1984), pp. 78-79.

instructions to be "quick to listen, slow to speak, and slow to become angry" (James 1:19).

Good counseling also requires that we be strong at outreach. "A true ministry to teenagers," conclude Gallup and Poling, "will *never* wait for them to appear at the church door; rather it will reach out to that age group wherever they are to be found."[29] Only the very good parents and teenagers (those who want advice on how to get even better) or the very needy parents and teenagers (those who turn to me as a last resort) pursue me. The rest I must pursue. Such initiative means making myself available to students by seeing them on campus. It means opening myself up to parents by holding meetings where they can ask questions. Outreach makes it possible to reach the vast majority of adults and teenagers who are average, with average problems, and average needs.

Teamwork. Jethro counsels Moses in Exodus 18:18, "You cannot handle it alone." That is sound advice for the youth worker. The days of the one-man-show style of youth ministry are over (perhaps they never existed). Teenagers are diverse, in need of models, and desirous of one-on-one attention. We cannot lead a youth ministry alone. We must learn that early and develop our skills as team leaders.

I was fortunate in the earliest days of my own ministry to realize that I was not multi-talented. I needed all kinds of help—from people who were better at reaching the fringe students, from musical people, athletic people, and those who could identify with the students who had never really strayed from Christ. I needed a team, and I needed to be secure enough in my own self-image to let others share the leadership with me.

Working with a team takes time and requires a concerted effort by the leader. It is never easy to delegate responsibility to someone who might do it differently than you would. Working with a team means that some responsibilities will be mismanaged, some will fail, and others will be negative examples to the youth.

But the team approach to youth ministry is the only way to survive. The diversity of students in grades seven through twelve requires a diversity of leaders. The greatest leadership skill that the youth leader needs is the ability to draw the best out of each member of the team: managing the team so that both team members and youths grow.[30]

Teamwork takes a variety of shapes and sizes. In some situations volunteers handle the entire program and report to an associate minister. In other circumstances volunteers are involved only as chaperones on retreats and activities. The optimum situation seems to be a blend of both professional and

29. George Gallup, Jr., and David Poling, *The Search for America's Faith* (Nashville: Abingdon, 1980), p. 33.

30. Some good resources regarding volunteers include Mark Senter's *Art of Recruiting Volunteers* (Wheaton, Ill.: Victor, 1983) as well as the issues of *Leadership* (Summer 1982) and *Youthworker* (Winter 1986) that are dedicated to the subject.

volunteer leaders, using the skills, resources, and commitments of each to build the youth group. Discipleship, teaching, outreach, and activities can all be shared in the youth ministry where the team works together in leadership.

Education. One of the skills required for ministry with youth is that of being a resource person, but that does not come without effort. Formal and informal education is demanded if we are to be effective youth leaders, teachers, speakers, and Bible study leaders. Adolescent psychology offers insights integral to our work, and a thorough understanding of Scripture provides the theological foundations for all that we do.

Youth ministry is now taught as a formal discipline at several Christian colleges and seminaries. Such training can provide essential theological, psychological, and practical foundations. For some, formal education may mean a temporary withdrawal from youth ministry, but this will be well worth it in the long term.

Informal education is also available, in the form of seminars, newsletters, and journals,[31] but the youth worker must be cautious to study foundational issues (like theology and psychology) as well as the practical ideas or contemporary trends that tend to dominate newsletters and youth-related publications.

ROLES WE FULFILL

When we think about the youth worker as a person, something must be said about the roles we are expected to fill, not just by the church or parachurch organizations but also by ourselves. Commitments, qualities, skills, and training all include aspects of that expectation. But to gain a solid understanding of who we are to be as youth leaders, we have to set some specific goals and expectations for ourselves.

Those that I have listed have been learned from others, or they have emerged as recurrent needs in youth ministry. Some youth leaders will not have to fulfill all of these roles; they will delegate some of them to others. Others will modify them in light of their own ministries. In general, however, the youth worker who pursues effectiveness as a leader will need to consider at least nine roles.

Youth expert. Dean Borgman, associate professor at Gordon-Conwell Theological Seminary and long-time veteran of Young Life, has expressed a concern "that the church see youth work as a professional, ordainable ministry rather than just a steppingstone to the pastorate."[32] If that is ever to be the case, however, youth workers must become youth experts, knowledgeable

31. Some of the best periodicals for youth workers are *Youthletter*, published monthly by Evangelical Ministries, 1716 Spruce Street, Philadelphia, and *Youthworker* (quarterly) and *Sources and Resources* (monthly), both published by Youth Specialities, 1224 Greenfield Drive, El Cajon, CA 92021.
32. Dean Borgman, interviewed in *Youthletter* (June 1981), p. 45.

about adolescent trends, psychological development, and effective measures for helping teenagers grow up. We face a great challenge, being asked to address the gospel to the world of the teenager. To do that successfully, we must become skilled in understanding and discerning what motivates teenagers, and we must respond accordingly.

Friend. Teenagers need faithful, adult friends who will hear them and love them. That is our job. We are not merely analysts (as experts) nor tyrants (as disciplinarians; see below). We are often the key figures in their lives, exemplifying unconditional love and faithfulness. Teenagers need youth leaders who will say by words and actions, "I love you; I believe in you; I am here to help you."

In this capacity of friend, we build our most rewarding discipling relationships. In so doing, we follow the example of Jesus.

> The time which Jesus investedvin these few disciples was so much more by comparison to that given to others that it can only be regarded as a deliberate strategy. He actually spent more time with His disciples than with everybody else in the world put together. He ate with them, slept with them, and talked with them for the most part of His entire active ministry. They walked together along the lonely roads; they visited together in the crowded cities; they sailed and fished together in the Sea of Galilee; they prayed together in the deserts and in the mountains; and they worshipped together in the Synagogues and in the Temple.[33]

Disciplinarian. Becoming the friend of a teenager, however, does not mean that we lose our posture as leaders. Teenagers need to be led as well as loved, and that means we must be willing to discipline and correct them. "Wounds from a friend can be trusted" (Prov. 27:6), and we must be willing to "wound" teenagers through disciplining them for their good.[34]

Of any of the expectations of ourselves, this may be the hardest because it puts our reputation and our popularity with students on the line. Until we are faced with the decision to discipline, we may not realize just how important it is to us to have the youth group like us (if we love our students, we will desire their love in response). Yet leadership means making the courageous decision to do what is right, even if it is unpopular. In the long run, it yields fruit (Heb. 12:11).

Team leader. We cannot lead our ministries without others' help, but we cannot expect others to join alongside us in youth leadership without effort on our part. The youth leader must be the team leader who recruits others, trains them in adolescent work and encourages them in their ministry. In the role of team leader, the youth worker fulfills the pastor-teacher function of Ephesians

33. Robert Coleman, *The Master Plan of Evangelism* (Old Tappan, N.J.: Revell, 1963), p. 43.
34. With reference to this, see the article by Gordon MacDonald, "The Difference Between Discipline and Punishment," in Jay Kesler, ed., *Parents and Teenagers* (Wheaton, Ill.: Victor, 1984).

4:11-12. The youth team leader equips the saints (the team in this case) to do the work of the ministry so that the Body of Christ (including the youth) may be built up. As team leaders, we find ourselves in the role of discipler for our youth team as well as for our young people.

Father figure. When thinking of being a father figure to young people, most of us shy away, feeling that the responsibilities and the expectations are too great. Nevertheless, whether we like it or not, many of our youth will look to us as "parents." We must respond with a desire to give good advice, faithful love, and a consistent example.

Bill Stewart, a long-term advocate of this fathering kind of youth ministry, states it this way: "We have a lot of motivators and teachers, but we have few who care for others with the love and strength of a father. Young people in our society need dads. As Paul was to the Corinthians (1 Corinthians 4:14-16), so we must be to our youth."[35]

Programmer. "Around here, we care about people not programs." That is an easy statement to make, but it reflects a very simplistic and somewhat exclusive (as if it were one or the other) view of ministry. People indeed must be our target, but programs can be the arrows that help us hit that target.

As a result, the effective youth worker must always be on the lookout for useful and well-thought-out program ideas. Relying on the old bag of tricks is not wise. Research must be done to design programs that meet needs, stimulate relationships, and promote a deeper understanding of what it means to be a Christian.[36]

Advocate: teens to parents. Sometimes teenagers are victimized by the bad press they get. "Because 64 percent of kids at some high school in another state said that they tried drugs," complains a teenager, "my mother now suspects that I am a junkie."[37]

As youth leaders, we need to see ourselves as advocates of teenagers to their parents. We should devote ourselves to using whatever resources we have to help parents discern what is normal for a teenager versus what is aberrant. We serve as advocates, working to help parents see the positive strides that their teenagers are making or are capable of making.

Advocates: Parents to teens. Although many teenagers will complain, "My parents do not treat me fairly," they are often guilty of doing the same. They generalize, criticize, and hurt their parents.

The youth leader must stand up for the parents at times. Teenagers must be reminded that their relationship with their parents is a two-way street for

35. Bill Stewart, interviewed in *Youthletter* (August 1981), p. 63.
36. *Youthworker* and *Group* offer some of the best program suggestions in this respect. Also, the *Any Old Time* books (Wheaton, Ill.: Son Power) may be helpful.
37. We have found this response from parents after they read newspaper articles that contain alarming statistics or after they examine books like *The Private Life of the American Teenager* (New York: Rawson & Wade, 1981) and *Teenagers Themselves* (New York: Adama, 1984).

which they carry responsibility, too. We need to teach young people to encourage, appreciate, and respect their parents so that parents can enjoy the years with their teenagers.

Servant. "A disciple is not his own," writes Elisabeth Elliot, "left to seek self-actualization, which is a new word for selfishness."

A disciple is one who seeks to do a "great work for God. "What constitutes a 'great work for God'? Where does it begin? Always in humility. Not in being served, but in serving. Not in self-actualization, but in self-surrender."[38]

Jesus washed His disciples' feet and, in so doing, gave us an example to follow (John 13:3-11). We must accept our roles as servants. We are to fulfill our roles and goals and tasks because we are serving our Master and the people to whom He has called us.

A sophomore in our ministry was talking with two youth leaders from other churches. They asked him, "Do you realize that your youth leader is a national leader in youth mnistry?" He was very shocked. "Paul Borthwick? He's just the bald guy who runs the youth group."

If I am to fulfill my role as a servant of our students, being "just the bald guy who runs the youth group" is enough.

The youth worker's self-expectations will not be fulfilled overnight. Nor will every role be performed satisfactorily. But outlining goals provides a target that will help us be balanced leaders in our ministry to others.

The common thread in the ministries of hundreds of other youth workers that I have met is a love for teenagers, a sense of call from God, and enough confidence to give themselves away in service to youth. As persons, they are all very different, but as youth leaders, their commitment to serve is the same.

FOR FURTHER READING

Blanchard, Kenneth, Patricia Zigarmi, and Drea Zigarmi. *Leadership and the One Minute Manager.* New York: William Morrow, 1985.

Engstrom, Ted W., and David J. Juroe. *The Work Trap.* Old Tappan, N.J.: Revell, 1979.

Hershey, Paul. *The Situational Leader.* Escondido, Calif.: Center for Leadership Studies, 1984.

MacDonald, Gordon. *Ordering Your Private World.* Nashville: Oliver Nelson, 1985.

Powell, John. *Unconditional Love.* Niles, Ill.: Argus, 1978.

Taylor, Bob R. *The Work of the Youth Minister.* Nashville: Convention Press, 1978.

Willey, Ray, ed. *Working with Youth: A Handbook for the Eighties.* Wheaton, Ill.: Victor, 1982.

38. Elisabeth Elliot, *Discipline — The Glad Surrender* (Old Tappan, N.J.: Revell, 1982), pp. 25, 127.

7
William H. Stewart and William E. Yaeger

The Youth Minister
and the Senior Pastor

Recently, a senior pastor called and expressed frustration regarding his youth pastor. In the course of the conversation several concerns were noted. First, the youth pastor was "too much of a kid." Second, he was not communicating with the rest of the staff. Third, parents were indicating a loss of confidence in his ministry. Fourth, sometimes youth-related events seemed poorly administered. Finally, at times the youth pastor appeared to be "in another world."

The pastor sent him to stay with us for three days. The youth pastor lived with one of our full-time youth ministry couples and attended many of the activities. At the conclusion of his stay the concerns expressed by his pastor were reviewed with him. The youth minister seemed totally devastated. He thought his pastor had sent him to spend time with us as a refresher or vacation from his ministry. None of the concerns mentioned had ever been communicated to him.

Perhaps the single greatest problem facing men and women in the youth ministry today is the inability to communicate or develop a good relationship with his or her senior pastor. After years of academic and practical training in the ministry, we have found that most misunderstandings, the greatest disillu-

WILLIAM H. STEWART, M. Div., is associate minister, youth ministries, First Baptist Church, Modesto, California.
WILLIAM E. YAEGER, D.D., is senior minister, First Baptist Church, Modesto, California.

sionments, and a major cause for job abandonment stem from the lack of healthy relationships between youth ministers and senior pastors. Dealing with problems involving drugs, rock music, sexual immorality, and family conflicts are not the real cause of youth minister drop-outs. On the contrary, the lack of cooperation and support among members of church staffs is what sends many youth ministers packing.

The youth minister is involved in three critical relationships that must be maintained at all costs. The first is that of the man or woman with Jesus Christ Himself. That relationship must be kept ever new, ever fresh, ever vital through the devotional study of God's Word and the filling of the Holy Spirit. The youth minister must believe and be committed to the Word of God. There is no other source for all that we are and teach.

The second relationship is that of the youth minister with his spouse and family. When that is not nurtured and cultivated, the youth minister will find himself outside looking in on his or her home and missing the blessing of God.

Third, the youth minister must carefully plan and develop the relationship with the senior pastor. That will require a clear understanding of his own role and responsibilities and how these interconnect with those of the senior pastor in the context of the local church.

THE YOUTH MINISTER

A SENSE OF GOD'S CALL

The average stay of a youth minister is brief. For the youth growing up in our churches, that reinforces family instability in our society, as well as the insecurity of many relationships with adults. In an earlier day a young person attending a one-room school would often establish a strong relationship with the teacher, who had responsibility for all classes and grades, frequently for a period of years. Today, many of our students see several teachers in a day, and then, after a few months, they have a whole new set of teachers. The sense of family, the sense of security, and the sense of adult models is greatly diminished.

If youth ministry is to provide the strength and stability needed, we must be serious about the place of God's call. Some time ago one of us spoke with a man who had served his church as youth pastor for nearly twenty years. In his judgment a youth minister should feel called to that responsibility. We agree. A youth minister must believe not only that God calls people to such a ministry but also that he or she has received God's call.

To many people, youth ministry is considered a stepping stone to the "real" ministry. Perhaps as a result, the call of God to youth ministry has not been properly taught. We need to be reminded that God places men and women in strategic supportive roles. In the Old Testament, Joseph and Daniel are examples. Neither of those men ever became the ruler of a kingdom, but there is no doubt of their importance or contribution. A "second level" role is not necessarily of less significance in God's eyes.

In the New Testament, Jesus called the Twelve to be with Him. Some served in secondary capacities. Just so, the Lord calls men and women today to be with Him, some as senior pastors and others in serving youth. Either way, in order to minister effectively, there needs to be a sense of God's call.

The call to youth ministry is primarily a call to be a spiritual parent to students. Paul provided a model in 1 Corinthians 4:14-17. In that passage he stressed the importance of the parental relationship in ministry.

> I am not writing this to shame you, but to warn you, as my dear children. Even though you have ten thousand guardians in Christ, you do not have many fathers, for in Christ Jesus I became your father through the gospel. Therefore I urge you to imitate me. For this reason I am sending to you Timothy, my son whom I love, who is faithful in the Lord. He will remind you of my way of life in Christ Jesus, which agrees with what I teach everywhere in every church.

TWO IMPORTANT CHARACTERISTICS

What do churches and senior pastors look for in a youth minister? Two characteristics are particularly important. First, the youth pastor must be content where he is. In Philippians 4:10-19, the apostle Paul discusses the importance of being content whatever the circumstances. Too often the person involved in youth ministry allows his head to be turned by the prospect of greener pastures or a better salary elsewhere, especially when the going gets tough.

Second, the youth minister must be a finisher, one who takes care of details. There are few things as frustrating as having a whole list of unfinished tasks hanging over one's head. The unfinished in one's life affects his or her self-worth. Set a goal never to have to be asked twice to do a thing. Even when the task has little to do with youth, it is important to complete it or to report on its status.

Luke reminds us that if a man is faithful in little things, he will be faithful in much. If he is unfaithful in little things, he will be unfaithful in the things that pertain to the kingdom of God (Luke 16:10-12). Many youth ministers have jeopardized their ministries through unreturned phone calls, unanswered mail, and broken promises. Whether the task or event is large or small, it is important to pay close attention to details.

RELATING TO THE SENIOR PASTOR

How may a youth minister develop a relationship of excellence with the senior pastor? He should *pursue the pastor for time.* A youth minister may have to do all kinds of creative things, including studying carefully his pastor's routine and program. He may have to learn to play golf or how to participate in some other activity in which he does not normally take part. If his pastor runs, he may have to find out when and where and run with him occasionally.

Often, the walk the pastor takes from the church to his vehicle on Sunday morning or Sunday night after preaching is a long one. Take that walk with him and encourage him. The best way to learn how your pastor ticks is by spending time with him, informally as well as formally. Do not use these opportunities to manipulate him or to promote your concerns. Be authentic. Be available to him for listening or exhortation.

In addition to spending time with him, the youth minister must *encourage the pastor.* Build him up. When he does well, let him know. Never forget that your pastor is human and, like us all, he needs kind and positive words. When your pastor preaches well, let him know. When the message has a special impact on your life, let him know. When the Holy Spirit touches your life through your pastor's spoken word or personal ministry, thank him. Remember, in a ministry that reflects the work of the Holy Spirit, edification through encouragement is critical.

Make your pastor your project. His weaknesses, his concerns, his family, and especially his children need your attention. Look for ways to help him, love him, and support him. Many youth workers are highly motivated, quick to seize the opportunity in promoting their own interests. Humanly, they may be self-centered and focused only on those things for which they feel responsible. They need to broaden their horizons, lift their eyes, expand their ministry, and include the senior pastor in the circle of their concern.

Pray for your pastor regularly. Is he on your prayer list and part of your prayer life?

Learn to *love your pastor.* The ministry is much like a marriage. A youth minister accepts a call to a church because he likes and desires to work with the pastor. At some point after he arrives, he begins to discern the pastor's humanness and weaknesses. At that juncture, a critical decision is made: will I love the man or will I begin to look elsewhere? At times, after a call is accepted to a church, answers to questions asked earlier are changed. That is not to say people would mislead you because they want a youth director, but occasionally misunderstandings *do* occur. It is during those times you have to decide, "Am I here for 'better or for worse'?"

Earn your pastor's trust. Faithfulness and continued support will produce the desired effect.

Do not allow others to divide you. Nearly eighteen years ago, when Pastor Stewart came to his present pastorate, a family invited him to Sunday dinner. At the table the man of the house said, "Pastor Yaeger says thus and so about situation number one." A little further on in the conversation, another issue was brought up. Finally, toward the end of the meal, a third issue was raised and then Pastor Stewart was asked, "What do you say?" He replied, "I say what Yaeger says. Please pass the potatoes." Later, he filled Pastor Yaeger in on the situation. The effort clearly was intended to divide us.

Efforts to create division are common. What do children do when one parent says no? They often go to the other parent. In the same way, adults and young people dissatisfied with one counselor's advice often look for a second opinion. More destructive are those who seek to divide friends in order to protect themselves. Satan began his effort at creating division in the Garden of Eden. He has continued ever since, and he works hard at sowing dissension in the church (see 1 Corinthians 1-3).

A friend described a situation in which he was invited to supper with a family. During the meal a bitterness was expressed toward the senior pastor of the church. The issue was pressed and my friend got up from the table, went over to the phone, and called the senior pastor. He said, "Pastor, some questions have been raised here this evening. I would like you to come over and help me answer them." The pastor came immediately, and together they sat down with the family and dealt with the bitterness. Things were taken care of honorably, and the family was restored to fellowship with the Lord and the church. Although the youth minister took a few minutes of heat while awaiting the arrival of the pastor, that discomfort was well worth the reconciliation that resulted.

Along the same line, *do not betray confidences.* If the pastor asks you to keep a confidence about a matter, do what he requests. Talking about a situation when there should be silence, that is, the silence of love and confidence, is undermining. A pastor had confided in his fellow workers regarding a major plan for the future of the ministry. Before he had worked out the details of the plan and developed a strategy, leaders in the church were made aware and responded negatively. The pastor became discouraged and accepted a call elsewhere. The staff was left with the negative membership.

Do not blame the pastor for decisions. If a decision has to be made regarding the use of a facility, music, or something else, the worst thing the youth minister can do with the young people is to say, "The pastor said we have to do it this way." Years ago in another ministry one of us let go some sponsors who were active in the high school program. They were told, "The pastor and I discussed this and we agreed together. We feel . . ." The pastor did agree with the decision and the subject had been discussed, but it would have been better to have said, "I feel before God that this is the better thing to do." It is too easy to shift the responsibility for difficult decisions onto the pastor.

Finally, *adjust to your pastor.* You will find that he has priorities in his approach to the ministry. These may or may not have been discussed prior to your coming. You may have asked the right questions and discovered your pastor's real priorities. You may have asked the right questions and not found them. The point is, adjust to your pastor's desires and priorities with an honorable, godly spirit.

OTHER CRITICAL CONCERNS

When you discuss priorities, be sure to discover what is most important in youth ministry for the church. Is it most important for you to be working with the high school area and concentrating there, or should you be working more directly with the junior high school students? The senior pastor should not set all of these priorities. Together the two of you should come to an agreement of focus and emphasis. That gives you good protection when a parent complains that you are neglecting some area of ministry. The pastor can provide a more supportive response to that parent if you have discussed priorities with him.

The second area of adjustment has to do with standards. Agree on standards, whether they have to do with hair, music, dress, or whatever. We know of a church with standards very different from those of many other churches, including our own, that is reaching hundreds of young people. Although it is often criticized because of its extremely conservative code of conduct, that church is successful in its ministry. The leaders have agreed on their approach, and they work together. Young people are very flexible. Sometimes the problem is not with the standards we set but with the individual and the way in which the standards are presented.

Finally, we come to the cardinal sin of impatience. Many involved in youth ministry do not like to wait. They become impatient when facilities, budget, or personnel are not available. A key word of advice is, no surprises.

Years ago a youth minister spent hundreds of dollars redecorating the area his young people used on Sunday mornings. He had communicated well with the pastor and the administrator of the church. However, the president of the women's support group had not been informed. The youth area was painted again.

Surprises may also come in the form of angry parents. You should inform your pastor of any potentially volatile situations. That alerts him to the problem and allows him time to formulate an appropriate response if necessary. He also may be able to provide helpful support and advice.

Another area where surprises are unwanted is in personnel. Before approaching people to work in the youth ministry, be sure your pastor is in agreement. He may know something about the situation that is really important to you. If you are working in a large church, it will also be important for you to discuss names of people with senior staff members before you invite them to be involved.

The Senior Pastor

Many young men, and some not so young, go into youth ministry without having evaluated the men with whom they will work. That is unfortunate. The senior pastor sets the tone, either enhancing or limiting the total ministry. One should look for several qualities in the senior pastor. These may be categorized into three areas: what he must believe, what he must be, and what he must do.

WHAT YOUR PASTOR SHOULD BELIEVE

In the area of belief the pastor must be firmly committed to Christ and His Word. That would seem to be obvious, but some pastors are committed to other concerns: retirement, business and sales, or some interest other than fulfilling the Great Commission. A pastor who is committed to Christ and His Word will not be easily distracted or manipulated. When a pastor gets involved in making extra money and doing things other than the ministry, it always takes the edge off his effectiveness. Paul told Timothy very clearly, "Don't get involved in civilian pursuits" (2 Tim. 2:4).

It is important, of course, for a minister to have a hobby or interest other than the ministry. In the long run that will bring greater creativity to his life and work. However, anything that unduly usurps his time or energy is a hindrance to the ministry.

A second area of belief concerns how the pastor views youth ministry. Does he recognize it as a profession? Some churches are finally coming to see that a ministry with youth may well be a life career. A pastor who believes and expects that all men in the ministry will sooner or later be senior pastors will tend to have that in mind when hiring youth workers. Do not expect a person to remain long in youth ministry if he plans to go on into another field, such as the senior pastorate. One's agenda will inevitably surface.

Dan Veerman wrote an article in *Moody Monthly* entitled "Too Old for Youth Work." He commented, "Let's rethink our ideas of the typical youth worker and start recruiting mature Sunday school teachers, youth group sponsors, and youth ministers. Let's begin to consider youth work as a possible lifetime career and not a brief stop along the way."[1]

Recently, Phillip Briggs of Southwestern Baptist Theological Seminary in Fort Worth, Texas, indicated that for many years he had been asking a series of questions of those individuals he thought had made a great contribution to the work of Christ. One key question was, Who had the greatest influence on you during your younger years? A second question was, How old was that influential person? He was surprised to discover that the great majority of those who had influenced these Christian leaders most as young people were adults in their forties and fifties.

During the 1960s and 1970s it was believed by many that you cannot trust anyone over thirty. To the contrary, often those who make the greatest impact reflect a more mature perspective. Unfortunately, most people involved in youth ministry are looking for another field by the time they are thirty. If the senior pastor reflects this, it may well be a self-fulfilling prophecy. The pastor must believe it is possible that people will want to give their lives to youth ministry in the church.

---

1. Dave Veerman, "Too Old for Youth Work," *Moody Monthly* (May 1983), pp. 63-65.

WHAT YOUR PASTOR SHOULD BE

First, the pastor must be a person of vision. Does he have a vision for the community? Is he genuinely concerned for a ministry that is going to reach and touch the entire area, or is he somewhat satisfied with what the church has accomplished? Periodically we will meet or see a pastor who has been in a church five, ten, or twenty years, and complacency has set in. He has said in effect, "We have enough members." In today's world you must be growing just to maintain stability. Therefore, be sure the pastor with whom you work has a vision with which you are comfortable.

Second, the pastor should be a father figure. In some churches the loss of a pastor can be a very traumatic event to some of the young people, almost akin to losing a parent. They may have lost parents already through death or divorce. Some may have gone through several divorces in their families. The pastor (or youth pastor) may be seen as the one who loves them, the one through whom God speaks to them. He may be the one who led them to Christ. The sense of loss and feeling of aloneness experienced by people in the church, especially young people, may be devastating. If your pastor is a short termer, his plan is always to go to the larger ministry. He will be with you only until his great opportunity comes; he will move along sooner or later. Meanwhile, he will never give 100 percent of his commitment where he is. The person who plans to move is already looking toward the future. Ask yourself, Is this man going to stay here, or is he likely to move?

Third, a pastor must be a shepherd. The apostle Peter referred to himself as an undershepherd. A shepherd is not just one of the flock. He must be the leader. Some men would prefer to flow with the momentum of the church. That is not the role of the shepherd. As the shepherd, he must be one who fears God and leads his people.

Fourth, a pastor also must be a leader. Anything short of that brings frustration to the staff working under him. Leadership in a pastorate is expressed both publicly and privately. Public leadership is most frequently seen in excellence in the pulpit. When the pastor keeps the preaching ministry strong, the church as a whole will sense direction and the youth ministry will experience a greater freedom to fail, which is, of course, the freedom to succeed.

Private leadership is expressed in many styles, but the end product is that everyone on the church staff, as well as the elected leaders of the church, understands the mission of the church and is working with the pastor to accomplish that mission. He has earned the right to be followed.

Fifth, a pastor must be a lover. We have been motivated afresh by a recent remark that a man can put up with a lot if he knows he is loved. Love is the first fruit of the Spirit. Too often it is the last response of those working in the ministry.

Sixth, the pastor must be a team worker. He must understand how to work together with a group of individuals. A team worker is concerned about each person in the group. He wants everyone to receive proper recognition for his or her contribution. A pastor must have a godly concern for others.

Seventh, the pastor must be a listener who carefully weighs concerns expressed by his fellow workers. Jerry W. Brown points out that listening is a learned skill. "Effective listening is not passive but requires concentration, self-discipline and genuine concern for the other person. It often provides a thera-peutic release for the speaker . . . the listening encounter usually results in establishing an atmosphere of trust and rapport."[2]

The listening pastor will allow the Holy Spirit to open his own understanding as a result of his contact with other men and women of God.

Finally, the pastor must be a self-disciplined man. Pastors and youth workers deserve the same respect shown to other professionals. However, if one's office, personal life, or family do not demonstrate discipline, respect may be slow in coming. More important, the godly disciplines of life are required if a man wishes to serve Christ well.

WHAT YOUR PASTOR SHOULD DO

First, the pastor must be willing to stand up for members of the staff when necessary. That establishes an atmosphere of confidence, commitment, and support. It also increases mutual loyalty and respect.

Second, the pastor must insist on staff meetings. Furthermore, he must set a regular time and place for them. If a group of people is to become a creative team under the direction of the Holy Spirit, it is essential that time be set aside for productive thinking to come to fruition. The youth minister should be eager for such meetings, and he should communicate that eagerness to the pastor. On occasion he may even have to take the initiative.

For some, a staff meeting means business only. Do not be caught in that trap. Our staff spends four days together three times a year in prayer, planning, trouble shooting, and recreation. When the recreation time is limited, creativity in ministry programming and ministry between staff members is impaired. The joy of working together has come with the inclusion of all the above.

Third, the pastor must encourage "a wholesome, friendly, spiritual environment for the church where believers can worship and feed and go out again into the world to be salt and light."[3] The pastor must not allow jealousy to interrupt his ministry of love with the staff.

Finally, the pastor must never publicly criticize the staff. That can destroy the ministry of Jesus Christ in a church. Criticism before the deacons or con-

2. Jerry W. Brown, *Church Staff Teams That Win* (Nashville: Convention, 1979), pp. 88-89.
3. William E. Yaeger, *Who's Holding the Umbrella?* (New York: Nelson, 1984), p. 25.

gregation casts a shadow over the one rendering the critique as well as the one who is being evaluated.

How much more a public or private expression of appreciation will gain. A senior pastor needs to recognize and acknowledge the ministry of the people with whom he works. In his book *Church Staff Teams That Win,* Jerry Brown examines the three levels on which pastoral appreciation can be shown: personally, publicly, and financially.[4]

THE CHURCH

We have discussed the responsibility of the youth minister and the senior pastor in a team relationship. What may we expect from the church?

First, a job description should be expected by the youth minister. A good job description will not only clearly outline the youth minister's tasks and responsibilities, it will also indicate to whom he reports. In some churches the youth minister reports to everybody. We believe the youth minister should have only one boss. A sample job description for a youth pastor is attached.[5]

Fig. 7.1 BASIC RESPONSIBILITIES FOR DIRECTOR OF YOUTH MINISTRIES

POSITION: **Director of Youth Ministries**
REPORTS TO: **Pastor of Christian Education**

The purpose of the position of Director of Youth Ministries is to provide overall direction to the development of the high school and junior high school students of the church for the purpose of introducing them to a relationship with Jesus Christ and assisting them in maturing in their understanding of how this will impact on their future. It is the function of the Director of Youth Ministries to assist the students in understanding the role that the church plays as explained in the Statement of Purposes found in our constitution. The ultimate goal is the preparation of lives for future service to Christ.

Responsibility	*Activities*
Pastoral ministry to young people	1. Study and minister God's Word effectively and faithfully to the youth of the church.
	2. Understand the needs of young people and be a facilitator in meeting these needs.
	3. Be available for ministry in time of crisis in the lives of young people and their families.

4. Brown, *Church Staff,* p. 85.
5. Courtesy Mark Senter III. Also see Leonard B. Wedel, "Exhibits and Sample Job Descriptions," in *Church Staff Administration* (Nashville: Broadman, 1978).

Responsibility	*Activities*
Recruitment and development of volunteer staff	1. Recruit people gifted in ministry to young people. 2. Train and coach staff members in their capacity to minister to young people. 3. Provide at least annual evaluations for each staff member. 4. Meet with staff members individually and as a group on a regular basis. 5. Aid staff members in establishing and attaining personal ministry goals.
Shepherd volunteer staff and students	1. Hold staff members accountable to develop their own capacities to minister. 2. Establish personal relationships with each staff member. 3. Insure continued spiritual growth on the part of each staff member. 4. Model youth ministry through shepherding a small group of students. 5. Insure that each student in the program is being ministered to by a staff member.
Curriculum development	1. Record the educational and spiritual development needs for each age level. 2. Recommend appropriate curricular materials and developmental goals to the Christian Education Department for approval. 3. Evaluate the effectiveness of curricular materials on an annual basis.
Program development	1. On the basis of approved curriculum concepts, implement a program that accomplishes the goals. 2. Evaluate the effectiveness of the implementation process on an annual basis.
Planning	1. Establish quarterly and long-range ministry goals. 2. Prepare annual budgets and program budgets for youth activities. 3. Project needs for space.

Responsibility	Activities
Department relationships	1. Attend and participate in Christian Education Department meetings. 2. Submit monthly reports to Pastor of Christian Education. 3. Temporary task force assignments.

Second, a youth worker should expect adequate remuneration from the church. The Word of God is eminently clear on this issue. The man who would serve Christ must be paid well enough to rear his family and honor Christ with his resources. One of the major reasons people leave youth ministry is poor salary and benefits. As a rule of thumb, we encourage churches to consider public school teachers' salaries as a base. Then add somewhere between thirty and forty percent, for the youth minister works more months and often many more hours weekly than his counterpart in public education. Also, a youth minister carries heavy administrative responsibilities.

When children come into a youth minister's home, it helps for him to own both. He should not have to pay for his child on credit. Also, his family will need a home that can provide safety and security. He will be away from his family evenings during the week, not to mention long stretches of time for camps, trips, and other activities. One church offered a $25,000 interest free loan to its youth minister as a down payment on his first home. He agreed to repay the money when he sold that home, which motivated him to stay. This represents a wise investment on the part of the church.

Finally, the church should be expected to provide a professional atmosphere of respect for the youth minister.

CONCLUSION

Like a fine-tuned mechanism, a senior pastor, the youth minister, and the church can work closely together to produce a holy and effective work to the glory of God. Such coordination can and does happen, but not without effort. We all remain human. It takes prayer, work, and the power of the Holy Spirit to bring unity, "firm in one spirit, contending as one man for the faith of the gospel" (Phil. 1:27).

Not long ago a youth worker from the Midwest was in California for a conference. Realizing that he would be close to the new church of his former pastor, he made an appointment to see him, and the two sat down to share their lives with each other. Forgotten were the sophomoric mistakes made by the youth worker. Forgotten were the management blunders made by the pastor, who was never trained to handle a multiple staff. Instead, the two men reflected on the grace of God in allowing them to minister together and to help each other during the five years they were a team. Theirs was and is a bond forged in the context of ministry by the formative hand of their heavenly Father.

FOR FURTHER READING

Borthwick, Paul. "How to Keep a Youth Minister." *Leadership* (Winter 1983): 75-81

Brown, Jerry W. *Church Staff Teams That Win.* Nashville: Convention Press, 1979.

Campolo, Anthony, Jr., *The Power Delusion.* Wheaton, Ill.: Victor, 1983.

Christie, Les. *Servant Leaders in the Making.* Wheaton, Ill., Victor, 1984.

Donnelly, Dody. *Team: Theory and Practice of Team Ministry.* Ramsey, N.J.: Paulist, 1977.

Schaller, Lyle E. *The Multiple Staff and the Larger Church.* Nashville: Abingdon, 1980.

Westing, Harold J. *Multiple Church Staff Handbook.* Grand Rapids: Kregel, 1983.

Wiebe, Ronald W., and Bruce A. Robinson. *Let's Talk About Staff Relationships.* Alhambra, Calif.: Green Leaf Press, 1983.

Christie Stonecipher Cistola

8

Women in Youth Ministry

Sharon is a forty-one-year-old black woman working in an independent Baptist church located in an economically depressed neighborhood of Detroit. Sharon was reared in that low income, often violent, neighborhood. After graduating from high school, Sharon attended a small junior college where she completed her associate degree and subsequently found employment. During that time, she developed a desire and interest to work with troubled youth.

Sharon began teaching Sunday school in her former church. That position later evolved into a full-time salaried position as youth minister. Sharon was the first woman to be employed on the ministerial staff of her church. Her role was initially viewed by many of the congregation as a mother-figure to the youth. She would spend her time talking with the youth and finding activities to keep them off the street. When Sharon assumed other roles, such as directing a church-wide volunteer ministry of adults to be big brothers and big sisters to troubled youth, she received criticism from those members who had tightly defined her role. Sharon was described as too aggressive and goal-oriented, and she was rebuked for desiring to expand her ministry by recruiting, training, and supervising adults to work with youth. That criticism caused her to experience self-doubt.

Eventually, she withdrew from leadership roles and halted the new programs that were being developed. As Sharon withdrew, she witnessed the death

CHRISTIE STONECIPHER CISTOLA, M. Div., formerly Campus Life staff member and ministry associate, Park Street Church, Boston, Massachusetts.

of the ministry she had been building. When she saw the consequences of the criticism on her ministry and on her own self-esteem, Sharon realized that what was being said about her was untrue and unwarranted. She decided to dialogue with and appropriately confront the individuals who had criticized her so heavily. By reeducating members of her congregation concerning the special needs of the youth in the church and in the neighborhood, Sharon was able to enlist the support of many of the people who had criticized her work. Because she did not bury her abilities and gifts, but exercised them wisely, Sharon was able to walk through that difficult phase in her ministry.

Carol, a thirty-year-old woman living in an upper-middle-class suburb of Boston, teaches journalism and English in a public high school. Prior to teaching school, she served for five years in a parachurch organization that focused on youth evangelism and discipleship. While Carol served on the ministry staff, she was known to her co-workers as one of the "guys." Carol had learned that if she expressed her ideas, feelings, and ministry style in the same manner as the men on her staff team, she would be accepted. If she deviated from the unspoken ground rules for participation, she was either ostracized or told she was acting like a "girl."

After five years of ministry, Carol began to experience both a restlessness and loneliness in working with youth on a daily basis. She also realized that she was not really one of the guys and that in denying her often unique insights or manner of approach, she was in actuality denying a part of her sexuality.[1] On reflection, Carol realized that being the only woman on an all-male staff was not healthy for her at that season of her life, that is, not until she was better able to express herself without compromising something of her own sense of personhood.

Eventually Carol left full-time ministry with youth and accepted a teaching position in the public school system. In time Carol developed a support-study group with other women like herself who wanted to explore and better understand the male-female issue. To satisfy her desire to remain in some capacity of ministry, Carol also assumed a position as adviser to the Christian education board and youth ministry staff of her church.

Nancy recently graduated from a Christian college. As a Christian education major, she had prepared for a full-time professional career in youth ministry. Nancy is an outstanding administrator and program developer. Her ultimate goal is to receive a Ph.D. in Christian education and to serve as a seminary professor in order to train future students for youth ministry.

1. When I speak of sexuality, I am not referring to the mechanism of sexual reproduction or to sexual behavior, but rather to one's core gender (the sense, I am female, I am male) and gender role behavior. See Ethel Spector Person, "Sexuality as the Mainstay of Identity: Psychoanalytic Perspectives," in Catherine Stimpson and Ethel S. Person, eds.,"*Women, Sex and Sexuality,* (Chicago: U. of Chicago, 1980).

In the church where Nancy was reared, her family had both male and female teachers. It was not until Nancy entered a Christian college that she learned about the wide spectrum of beliefs on women's roles in ministry. After her college graduation, Nancy accepted an associate youth minister position where her major responsibility was leading youth Bible studies; thus the issue of Nancy's exercising authority and teaching men was not an immediate problem.

However, as Nancy considers graduate studies and a faculty position, her role as a woman in the church is becoming much more of an issue. Even though Nancy is comfortable in her present job, she realizes that she will need to continue working out her own understanding of Scripture in order to pursue her long-term goal.

These situations illustrate several issues that face women in youth ministry in the church. How women deal with those issues can drastically affect their effectiveness and desire to continue in youth ministry. The purpose of this chapter is to present some of the most common issues that only women face in youth ministry and to suggest skills that may help them work through those issues. In addition, the chapter provides perspectives and information that will enable women contemplating a career in youth ministry to make a well-informed choice.

VALUE OF WOMEN IN YOUTH MINISTRY

It is important for women to serve in ministerial capacities within the evangelical church. Women entering youth ministry should be hired and recognized as trained, professional staff. However, for perspective on their role, it is important for women to know about those who have served in the ministry before them, both to provide role models and also to help them learn from their predecessors' experiences. Ruth Tucker, in her book *From Jerusalem to Irian Jaya,* discusses why women historically have not been accepted into official ministerial roles within local churches and why they consequently sought ministries in the foreign mission fields.

> Foreign missions attracted women for a variety of reasons, but one of the most obvious was that there were few opportunities for women to be involved in a full-time ministry in the homeland. Christian service was considered a male profession. Some nineteenth-century women, such as Catherine Booth, broke into this male-dominated realm, but not without opposition. Wrote Catherine, herself a Bible scholar, "Oh, that the ministers of religion would search the original records of God's Word in order to discover whether . . . God really intended woman to bury her gifts and talents, as she now does, with reference to the interests of His church." Other women simply entered secular work. Florence Nightingale above all else wanted to serve God in Christian ministry, but there were no opportunities.

"I would have given her (the church) my head, my hand, my heart. She would not have them." So the mission field, far away from the inner sanctums of the church hierarchy, became an outlet for women who sought to serve God.[2]

Today, women who serve as youth ministers or as part of the ministerial team in the youth program (rather than serving on the foreign mission field or in a parachurch organization) are blazing new trails of their own. Those trails are ones that lead to having women on youth ministerial staffs in positions of recognized authority and responsibility. Women are not serving behind the scenes and out of sight, nor are they serving in a volunteer capacity. Women in youth ministry are beginning to be recognized as a vital cog in the formalized authority structure of the church. Because they are not going solely to foreign mission fields or parachurch organizations, they will affect church attitudes, decisions, and programs. The more women serve on youth ministry staffs, the more they can have influence and a voice in the local church. Tucker further comments:

> Women excelled in almost every aspect of missionary work, but the fields of medicine, education and translation work were particularly affected by their exper-tise. Hospitals and medical schools were among their achievements, including one of the best mission-run medical schools in the world, located in Vellore, India. Schools were established by them all over the world, including an eight-thousand-student university in Seoul, Korea. And Scripture was made available for the first time to hundreds of different language groups as a result of their persistence.

> Another unique feature of women in missions relates not so much to their particu-lar ministry as to their appraisal of that ministry. Women, by and large, found it easier to admit their weaknesses and vulnerabilities and to present a truer picture of living the life of a "super-saint" missionary. Their honest soul-searching and admission of faults and failures has shed light on a profession that has often been clouded in myth.[3]

As Tucker has noted, women bring a balanced perspective to the ministry. In his book *The Five Cries of Parents,* Merton Strommen says that by the year 2000 the typical family will be a step-family.[4] If that prediction comes true, it will have enormous impact on youth ministry. The problems that youth experi-ence will be increasingly more complex and demanding. It will be crucial then (as it is now) that *both* men and women be hired as youth staff, thereby providing necessary and positive role models along with bringing a balance in teaching and counsel. History has shown that women have demonstrated a

2. Ruth A. Tucker, *From Jerusalem to Irian Jaya* (Grand Rapids: Zondervan, 1983), pp. 232-33.
3. Ibid., pp. 233-34.
4. As quoted in *Youthworker,* "The Five Cries of Parents, A Conversation with Dr. Merton Strommen" (Spring 1985). See also Merton P. Strommen and A. Irene Strommen, *Five Cries of Parents* (San Francisco: Harper & Row, 1985).

capability to serve in ministry and that their contributions have been significant.

More important, women as well as men reflect the image of God, and both were given responsibility to exercise dominion and care over creation. Youth need to see healthy working relationships between men and women and to experience an active participation under the leadership of both sexes. A woman youth minister will offer insights and understanding of God to the youth in the church that men alone cannot provide. Women serve a valuable role in youth ministry.

CHURCH VIEWS ON THE ROLE OF WOMEN IN MINISTRY

Looking at various denominations within the evangelical community, one recognizes a spectrum of opinion regarding the role and status of women. Some denominations ordain women to church office, whereas others do not allow them to function in any kind of authoritative or leadership role over men. Christian education directors can be either male or female in some churches, but in practice most hire only men.

Numerous churches and denominations have an established positional statement; others are reexamining this issue and trying to formulate their own biblical understanding. Women entering youth ministry need to recognize that ambiguity, sometimes rigidity, and certainly change is occurring regarding their role and status.

As a woman considers her options in youth ministry, her decision-making process and vocational goals will be affected by the particular positional statement, or the lack of one, in her local church and denomination. How? First, the policy position affects her entry level and potential for advancement. For example, can she be only a ministerial staff person serving in an associate role, or can she be the youth minister? If she desires to leave youth ministry and move into working with adults, will that be possible? Could she eventually teach at a Bible college or seminary if she has met the necessary academic qualifications?

Second, church and denominational positional statements affect her job description. Can she interact with adult volunteers and parents in a position of authority? When Sharon first began her ministry, everyone was pleased to have a person to help with the youth, but expectations of Sharon's role were never discussed by the congregation and the church officers. As Sharon exercised leadership skills such as program development, upfront teaching, and community networking, some individuals and groups within her church expressed their displeasure.

Fortunately, Sharon and the church officers were able to resolve the oversight of an unclear job description by clarifying her role in written form. The formulation of a clear job description embodying the church's new positional statement concerning her ministerial role enabled Sharon to have something concrete to discuss with the individuals and groups that were critical of her. In addition, it was written in such a way as to encourage the use of her leadership abilities and so as not to violate the church's view regarding the role of women in ministry. If that had not been true, Sharon would have needed to relocate to a church where she was free to minister according to her understanding of God's Word.

CAREER OPPORTUNITIES FOR WOMEN IN MINISTRY

The career options for women today are far more broad and less gender-defined than they were a generation ago. They also bring opportunities for economic advancement and financial independence that previously have not been available to women. Today, for example, fewer women need fathers and husbands to pay the bills and maintain the roof over their heads.

A women entering (or continuing) youth ministry will interact with women (and men) who have made a variety of career and marital decisions, including those who marry right after college and those who never marry, those who become mothers and pursue a career at the same time, those who have to work simply to pay the bills and feed their children, and finally those who have chosen to pursue a fast-paced and financially rewarding career while remaining single and childless. All of that will create personal and professional challenges to the woman in youth ministry. For example, the position a woman in youth ministry assumes may pay a salary of $14,000 a year with a ceiling of $20,000. Her friend who entered business after college may have a starting salary of $30,000. Even her male counterpart in youth ministry earns significantly more. *Youthworker* recently reported that the median income of youth workers they surveyed is $21,000, and 88 percent of those responding were male.[5] How will salary level affect one's sense of self-worth and economic security?

Or, what about the woman who has chosen to postpone marriage, pursue a career in youth ministry, and then finds herself single, not too secure financially, and restless in her career choice at the age of thirty-three? When Carol entered youth ministry, she recognized her desire to be married one day, but at a later stage in her life. While on the parachurch staff, Carol attended twenty weddings of colleagues and friends. But she had developed few male relationships outside of the staff. Consequently, Carol found herself with few male friends that she could possibly date. Her world of support and social interactions had become one primarily of couples; it once had been primarily singles. For the first time, Carol became acquainted with feelings of loneliness and restlessness. She did not plan to become bored in her career choice, nor did she

---

5. "Here's How Much You Make," *Youthworker,* Fall 1984, p. 79.

intend to feel sad that she was not dating. It just happened. During that period of change and heightened anxiety, Carol became envious of her female friends whose lives seemed more exciting and relevant.

Regardless of how motivated and purposeful a woman feels as she enters or remains in youth ministry, occasions will arise that force her to face and interact with "the other woman," whose life she will desire and at times fantasize about. That is when the call of God and vocational goals are reexamined with greater seriousness.

In the process of writing this chapter, I surveyed a significant number of evangelical pastors regarding their hiring practices. One comment surfaced numerous times. When money was a major consideration in hiring ministerial staff, it was not uncommon for pastors to choose male applicants over females. Why? First, the possibility of relocating because of a spouse's job change is less likely if the staff person is male. Second, the problem of maternity leave and benefits does not exist if the staff person is male.[6] Third, there is less tension regarding supervising and teaching adults if the youth minister is male. As the pastors admitted, discrimination in hiring is a reality, and it can affect a woman's opportunity for placement. It is one thing to acknowledge a call to youth ministry; it is another to possess grace and security when situations such as salary differences arise, when one's financial needs change, or when one is unable to find placement in the position she desires.

WOMEN IN YOUTH MINISTRY FACE A DOUBLE TENSION

Women entering youth ministry face two obstacles simultaneously. The first problem concerns the ministry itself. Youth ministry is just now finding its own credibility and recognition within the church. That new recognition is evidenced by more reasonable salaries and the hiring of trained professional staff rather than looking for volunteers from the congregation to direct the youth program. (For further discussion of this issue see "A History of American Youth Ministry," chap. 4.)

The second obstacle a woman faces is that she is entering a professional arena that historically has been male. Simply because of her gender, she will cause rigid stereotypes and hidden expectations to surface. When Nancy began her first job, she was expected to do all of her own typing (as her female predecessor had done), though her male peers on the ministerial staff utilized secretarial services. Sometimes Nancy was even asked to help the men with their paperwork. In 1983, when Carol was serving in full-time youth ministry, some women made less money than men for the same job. The reason given was that men were the main supporters of the homes, whereas women were working only for extra income or until they were married. (I also can remember

6. See the February 1984 issue of *Working Woman,* "Company Maternity Leave Policies."

being told that when I first began ministry.) Both Carol and Nancy had experienced inequality on their jobs because of sexual stereotyping, even though both women's job responsibilities were equivalent to those of the men with whom they served.

The women's liberation movement has raised the issue of gender stereotyping, career opportunities, career advancement, and salary equity for women and minorities to the forefront of our society. R. C. Sproul has made a keen observation regarding the feminist cry. Sproul says, "Behind almost any militant protest movement there is always some element of authentic complaint to be found . . . behind the anger somewhere there is pain . . . the action may not be legitimate (appropriate) but the pain is real and has its roots in something legitimate."[7] Both women and men in our society have experienced the pain of sexual stereotyping and rigid gender definitions. Jean Baker Miller comments in *Toward a New Psychology of Women* that such stereotyping is both harmful and limiting. "In Western society men are encouraged to dread, abhor, or deny feeling weak or helpless, whereas women are encouraged to cultivate this state of being."[8] Sharon had been told by certain members in her congregation that she was too aggressive and that women are not to be aggressive. Carol found that when one of the men with whom she had served had cried during a ministry staff meeting, the others had isolated him and warned him of being weak. Carol's male associate and Sharon both had been hurt by a mindset that said men do this and women behave like that. Although these illustrations may seem extreme and are unfair descriptions of many churches and congregations, there does exist for women the double tension of youth ministry's credibility and the entering of a male-dominated arena.

POSSESSING A HEALTHY IDENTITY AND A SENSE OF LIFE DIRECTION

A woman entering youth ministry needs to possess a healthy understanding of herself personally and as a woman. She needs to have a solid grasp of who God is and how she relates to Him, and she needs to have some sense of life direction, or purpose. In other words, she needs to know herself as a whole person in relationship to her Creator.

One step a woman takes in answering the question of identity is to understand the abilities and gifts she uniquely possesses. These should be identified and examined in light of her motivations. By doing this, a woman has something tangible by which to describe herself. Ralph Mattson's and Arthur Miller's book *Finding a Job You Can Love* can serve as a good resource for this process.

Second, in respect to possessing a healthy identity, a woman needs to

7. R. C. Sproul, "Role of Women in the Church." Cassette tape. 1984.
8. Jean Baker Miller, *Toward a New Psychology of Women* (Boston: Beacon, 1976), p. 29.

recognize and value her sexuality. The tension Carol faced as the only woman on a multiple staff team was how to be herself both as a person and as a female. If a woman allows herself to be viewed only as one of the guys, she has misunderstood and devalued her own sexuality. Those who place her in such an unnatural position are guilty of doing the same to themselves. Conversely, a similar lack of understanding also can be witnessed when a woman is accepted solely because of her sex, and her role and responsibilities are rigidly defined, as with Sharon and the critics of her ministry.

One way to gain insight into oneself is through the use of diagnostic tools such as the wholistic assessment tool designed by Rick Wellock and David White, formerly of the Ligonier Study Center. The tool was designed to assist individuals in assessing their knowledge of God, their understanding of relationships with others, their attitude concerning their own sexuality, their physical stewardship, their vocational direction, and their expression of their core aspirations or purpose in life. Neither this chapter nor book is designed to explore in depth the means by which one comes to understand his or her identity and life direction. Those are issues that need to be probed in relationships with skilled and knowledgeable individuals. However, an assessment tool may help a woman to isolate key issues she needs to explore. If she does not possess a healthy sense of identity along with a sense of life direction, she may be crippled in her effectiveness in ministry.

YOUTH MINISTRY — COMING IN OR GOING OUT

There are many reasons that a woman may choose to enter youth ministry. Regardless of how a woman describes her calling, biblically and/or personally she should be able to answer these questions:

1. How has God led you in the past?
2. How do you understand the Scriptures to be speaking to you in your choices and directions now? Are the biblical norms and principles clear or at least focused enough for you to begin?
3. What counsel have you received from your parents, elders, and peers? Are you affirmed, or do you find resistance? How would the youth you have ministered to respond to your desire?
4. Are you realistic about what lies ahead? Can you anticipate, in part, where you will be strong and where you will fail? How will you face those situations?

Do women leave youth ministry? Yes, and you too might leave. Therefore, as you contemplate entering youth ministry, be aware of what might lead you out of the field. Identified are some of the factors that might provoke you to such a decision:

1. A heart for primary or secondary youth work changes: you do not want to focus your ministry on youth any longer.

2. Economics, low salary, or lack of job possibilities: you cannot save money or stay abreast of your financial obligations.
3. Balance of life decisions: you might desire to marry and/or start a family, and you do not want to balance the relationships of a family with that of the youth in your church.
4. Lack of support or supervision from staff, parents, or youth: regardless of how motivated and effective one is, burnout creeps in when affirmation and support are missing.
5. Your skill level has peaked: you are not sharp anymore, and you are facing situations beyond your ability.
6. A change in your personal belief system: your philosophy of ministry or goals may be different from when you began.
7. You have reached a plateau personally, professionally, and spiritually. You need to move in a new direction to accommodate a new interest and growth inside you.
8. You possess unrealistic expectations of yourself: a negative attitude or continual sense of failure and inadequacy surround you.
9. You cannot balance your personal life and your ministry: you have not had a date in two years, and you want one.

Contemplating the reasons women (and men) leave youth ministry enables you to think through how these could possibly affect you and your career choices. But just as there are reasons women leave youth ministry, there are signals that will serve to confirm and validate an ongoing ministry. The signals are:

1. Listening ears: someone or some others will listen and support you.
2. Financial support: though money may be strained at times, it will be there when the needs exist.
3. Helping hands: people will be there to serve physically and spiritually.
4. Individuals will appropriately confront you in love and compassion.
5. You will know the freedom to fail.

Not every ministry situation will be perfect and encompass all five of these signs. But if all or most of these elements are missing, there needs to be a reevaluation, a touching base, and a going back to identify where the breakdown is and why.

CONCLUSION

The reward of a youth minister is to see the gospel of Jesus Christ make an impact on the lives of youth. When an individual woman recognizes God as the author and finisher of her salvation, then she becomes God's vessel in ministry. God will be God, and she will be His good and faithful servant.

The woman in youth ministry should be able to relax and know that her task is to be faithful to her call and to maintain her own sense of personal integrity. Sometimes the reward of seeing kids' lives change will be evidenced, sometimes it will not. That is why ministry with youth can be characterized by the metaphor of sowing, watering, and reaping. Some women will have a ministry like Nancy's first few months. They will begin sowing and will water what others have planted before them. Carol, on the other hand, waters and only occasionally sees the fruit reaped. Sharon has been in youth ministry for twenty years. God has blessed her faithful and constant sowing and watering. Now she is reaping by seeing large numbers of volunteers involving themselves in the lives of youth and then seeing those youth find Jesus.

Whether you are a woman entering, continuing, or contemplating leaving youth ministry, be informed of the special problems and issues facing you in this field. Following God's call into youth ministry is a high privilege and a wonderful adventure. Regardless of the metaphor used to describe your ministry, God will be faithful to you and to His Word. Allow Him to use the fullness of who you are as a person and as a woman to touch kids' lives dynamically with the saving news of Jesus Christ.

FOR FURTHER READING

Bilezikian, Gilbert. *Beyond Sex Roles.* Grand Rapids: Baker, 1985.
Briscoe, Jill. *Women in the Life of Jesus.* Wheaton, Ill.: Victor, 1986.
Evans, Mary J. *Women in the Bible.* Downers Grove, Ill.: InterVarsity, 1983.
Hurley, James B. *Man and Woman in Biblical Perspective.* Grand Rapids: Zondervan, 1981.
Mickelsen, Alvera. *Women, Authority and the Bible.* Downers Grove, Ill.: InterVarsity, 1986.
Schaller, Lyle E., ed. *Women As Pastors.* Nashville: Abingdon, 1982.
Sproul, R. C. "The Role of Women in the Church." Cassette tape. Ligonier Ministries. 598 S. North Lake Blvd., Suite 1008, Altamonte Springs, FL 32701.

Sherwood M. Strodel

9

Interns and Part-time Youth Ministers

A Protestant chaplain at a military academy, a soccer coach at a Christian university, a professor of religion at a church-related college, a pastor of a Congregational church in California, a pastor of an independent church in New Jersey, and a pastor of a Presbyterian church in New York—the above six persons have five special things in common: they all were part-time youth leaders or interns in the same church over a period of thirteen years; they all went to the same seminary; they all worked with the same minister of education; they all continued as friends; and they all purposed to follow through on their commitment to influence the world for Jesus Christ in their chosen professions. Furthermore, during the time of the researching of this chapter, a young Presbyterian minister, trained and discipled by the people mentioned above, was interviewed by the same minister of education to work with him as minister to singles.

In the past twenty-five years numerous interns and part-time youth leaders have been trained well and have served countless high school students effectively in many of our churches. Are the energies, frustrations, budgetary hassles, space problems, endless meetings, counseling burdens, and late hours involved in this training worthwhile? Observe these comments from two interns serving in similar ministries: "I wanted to write and thank you for your part

SHERWOOD M. STRODEL, M. Div., is minister of education, Highland Park Presbyterian Church, Dallas, Texas.

and support of the intern program. As time has passed, I have been able to do a bit of reflecting, and am only just now coming into a good appreciation of the internship. I can see clearly that the fifteen months I spent in Dallas have done as much to prepare me for ministry as the two years I spent in class, if not more"; "In September I will be returning to complete my M. Div. degree. To a great extent my desire to finish this degree as well as seek ordination is a result of my internship."

Similar results continue to motivate one church in Texas to budget more than $80,000 every fifteen months for the precise purpose of training a number of interns. A church in California was the recipient of a Lilly foundation grant to fund monies for twenty interns each year for three years. These and other churches have learned there can be rewards, such as a healthy camaraderie and sharing of training experiences, in having more than one intern in a church.

PURPOSE

INTERNS

An intern usually is a graduate student whose focus is supervised, practical training. Our society illustrates the value of supervised instruction in business, law, medicine, and education. Such practical training enhances the whole process of equipping a person for his profession. In a church setting the purpose of an intern program should include (1) training people who are going into ministry who have completed their undergraduate requirements; (2) having people specialize in a particular ministry yet observing other aspects of the church program; (3) having interns work in cooperation with a professional in the field of ministry, thus providing exposure to models and mentors ("heroes inspire us whereas models help us to do");[1] (4) producing quality individuals who will be better prepared to serve; (5) creating a reservoir of competent, committed resource staff who will enhance the work of our churches and denominations throughout the United States and the world; and (6) equipping people better to proclaim the good news of Jesus Christ, the work of the Holy Spirit, and the holiness of God the Father to all people, and helping interns better to live out these realities before others.

Interns may be either full- or part-time. Part-time interns work about ten to twelve hours each week. Involvement on a part-time level, especially while attending seminary or college, proves tremendously beneficial to both the organization and the intern. Though many churches view part-time youth workers as interns, in this chapter they are treated separately, recognizing, of course, that under certain situations the positions have overlapping duties.

Interns and part-time youth workers, regardless of the variation in expec-

1. Fred Smith, *You and Your Network* (Waco, Tex.: Word, 1984), p. 80.

tations and salaries, usually have three things in common: (1) a limited tenure, (2) a limited salary, and (3) a limited amount of time available each week.

An important distinction between these two ministries is that the intern places a higher priority on the learning experience, whereas the part-time youth worker centers on *doing* the work along with anticipated benefits of learning and personal growth. Clear-cut job descriptions and written philosophies can help to clarify the intentionality and design of each position.

PART-TIME YOUTH MINISTERS

Part-time youth ministers are people with a special calling to serve the cause of Jesus Christ in the church or Christian organization. These workers are of college age, in graduate work, seminary, or older. It would be interesting to find out how many men and women in Christian leadership positions today got their start and initial training as part-time youth leaders. I am sure we would be amazed at the number of them whose early part-time experience provided the training ground for their present impressive leadership.

Numerous churches have benefitted greatly by having part-time youth workers when budgetary limitations prohibited full-time professional help. Employing part-time youth workers exhibits wise use of funds and at the same time reflects a vision and concern for the youth. Part-time youth ministers can bring to the church expertise from their talents, knowledge from academic pursuits (undergraduate, graduate, and professional levels), resiliency in dealing with students, high energy capabilities and maturity commensurate with their ages, models and mentors for Christian youth, and short-term personal benefits that might help a youth leader in preventing burnout. Likewise the youth minister serving within a limited time frame can derive from the church exposure to a specialized ministry in action, contacts and references for future service, discipling by a supervisor, testing and development of his gifts in a ministry situation, a sense of fulfillment, a specific form of witness and service in the church, and financial assistance to supplement his income.

There is a mystique about working with youth that prepares men and women to deal effectively with issues we all face as adults: guilt, pride, vulnerability, honesty, forthrightness, ingenuity, perspicuity, phoniness, prioritizing, and decisiveness. Somehow, the demands to be flexible, enthusiastic, authentic, humorous, and candid enhance an individual as he seeks to cultivate leadership qualities. Many people who have worked with youth make the best pastors and leaders for Christ. For a number of men and women considering full-time youth work, this limited exposure on a part-time basis helps ascertain God's will for their lives. Conversely, someone serving in this capacity could also discover that youth work is not for him and thereby prevent a mismatch of his gifts and talents by observing early on that this is not his calling.

In many situations the learning experience is not a goal but a by-product. The energy, effort, and discipline faithfully exercised will bring to fruition a profitable learning experience in which talents in people skills, Bible teaching, communication, evangelism, pastoral care, and organization will see growth and fulfillment.

OPPORTUNITIES

Numerous kinds of internships in youth ministries are available. They include, but are not limited to, the academic school year, summer months, or year-round assignments. As an example, one church has a fifteen-month internship providing the benefits of a three-month overlap for the purpose of meeting the accelerated summer program demands and a three-month continuity of training for new interns. Another church provides a two-year internship for recent seminary graduates. Most internships are less extensive.

In youth work the intern is usually a specialist for one age-division, such as senior high or junior high. Variations on a smaller scale could include involvement with both junior-high and senior-high activities. A wider range would permit the intern to specialize in a well-defined area of ministry—a camping program, athletic coaching, puppet ministries, or administrative responsibilities—and at the same time introduce him to a broad range of ministry opportunities.

The part-time youth worker has by design less time for personal contact with the senior pastor. It is important to realize this at the outset in order to eliminate false expectations of developing a close working relationship with the senior pastor.

Regardless of the time frame, the merit of internship programs reflects the quality of the adult laypersons in the church. Because of the transient nature of interns, laypersons (e.g., volunteer sponsors, church leaders, and church families) may begin to resent the energies invested in individuals who will be lost to the church when their internships end. Resentment leads to resistance, and resistance to divisions. The church laypersons must see the internship as a means of giving rather than of receiving.

Beyond the impact of the level of maturity of the adults is the role of the senior pastor. *Any youth ministry in the local church will have merit and meaning in direct proportion to the verbal or nonverbal endorsement of the senior pastor.* This truth is fundamental to the success of the program and cannot be underscored too strongly.

ACCOUNTABILITY

"Eighty percent of success is showing up" (Woody Allen).
"But above all try something" (FDR).
"Ready. Fire. Aim" (executive at Cadbury's).[2]

2. Thomas J. Peters and Robert H. Waterman, Jr., *In Search of Excellence* (New York: Harper & Row, 1982), p. 119.

As these axioms indicate, if we are going to accomplish something we had better *be there*, we should at least *attempt* something, and we must definitely *think through* the procedure. A bias for action, one of the key principles of management underscored in the book *In Search of Excellence*, by Thomas J. Peters and Robert H. Waterman, is the goal of doing something rather than sending ideas through countless committee cycles.

Accountability begins with the interview process and the completion of an application form prepared by the church. The church will need the following information from the applicant: personal history, educational background, description of personal Christian experience, a statement of faith, work experience, ministry experience, indication of skills, vocational aspirations, availability, references—one of which must be a minister, and another an employer. Applicants should also be prepared to answer Christian growth questions, such as:

1. If the Philippian jailer asked you, "What must I do to be saved?" how would you respond?
2. Describe your relationship to Christ in the last three months.
3. Out of your Christian walk, what gifts and abilities do you feel God and others have affirmed in your life?
4. In your own understanding of ministry, what do you feel most fulfilled in doing? What brings you the most satisfaction?
5. What do you find you like or dislike doing?
6. Where do you see yourself vocationally five years from now? Ten to fifteen years from now?
7. What do you expect from an internship here?

POSITION DESCRIPTIONS

Good accountability is fostered through position descriptions that facilitate communication, evaluation, and achievement and result in wise stewardship of one's time. A well-written position description will include position title, person to whom accountable, general responsibilities, specific responsibilities, and term of service. The following position descriptions illustrate the differences between the position of a part-time youth worker and that of a full-time intern.

Part-time Youth Worker

Position title: Part-time Youth Minister.
Accountable to: Director of Christian Education.
General responsibilities: oversee the youth ministry of the senior high young people on a part-time basis (not exceeding twenty hours per week); coordinate weekday youth ministries with the Sunday school morning programs for

youth; attend church staff meeting on the first Tuesday of the month and the Christian education committee as called.

Specific responsibilities: organize at least one special retreat for spiritual purposes; visit in the homes of the youth; meet periodically with the immediate supervisor; set goals for the youth ministry; evaluate the program; teach and lead Bible studies/Sunday school classes; plan appropriate socials, outings, and outreach programs; lead a discipling program.

Term of service: (specify dates).

Remuneration and benefits: salary, auto allowance, expense account, secretarial assistance.

Full-time Youth Ministry Intern

Position title: High School Ministry Intern.

Accountable to: Youth Pastor.

General responsibilities: work with students and families; be involved with all planning, preparation, and execution of senior high meetings, programs, retreats, camps, and activities; attend all senior high activities that require employees' presence; attend monthly staff functions and weekly staff meetings; assist the minister of youth and/or pastor in a fifteen percent overlap of duties outside the general job description; support all the church-related activities.

Specific responsibilities: assist in the planning and implementation of Sunday evening programs; lead a small group and create others as approved; assist in Sunday school when needed; help in developing training sessions for Sunday school teachers and youth workers; visit the campuses of senior high schools that have their students enrolled (if the principal allows); meet with other department heads to learn more about the church activities; make personal appointments with senior high students before or after school on weekdays to keep in touch, discuss problems, and relate to as a friend; attend senior high activities where church students are involved.

Term of service: (specify dates).

Remuneration and benefits: room and board with a church family, health insurance, auto allowance, expense account, stipend.

In making final a commitment, a contract (call or covenant) is helpful. This can be as simple as the one-page memorandum suggested by Peters and Waterman.[3] Specific agreements relating to salary, book allowance, major medical insurance, moving costs, vacation time, Social Security benefits, housing and automobile allowances should be stated.

EVALUATION

Another indispensable aspect of accountability is evaluation. Lyle Schaller, in *The Multiple Staff and the Larger Church,* cites the seven Cs used in

3. Ibid., p. 150.

evaluating an existing model of staff relationships: compatibility, continuity, competence, confidence, coherence, complementarity, and the conceptualization of the role and purpose of that particular congregation.[4]

The following questions should be incorporated into an evaluation session for both the intern and the part-time youth worker. It is recommended that evaluation take place every three months:

1. Does the printed job description adequately describe your job?
2. Should your job description be changed in the light of new developments?
3. What has been added to your duties that has affected your attitude toward your work?
4. What do you find in your work or relationships that is frustrating?
5. What do you find in your work or relationships that is especially satisfying?
6. What can I do for you that would make your job easier or more satisfying?
7. What can the church do?

In his best-selling autobiography Lee Iacocca reiterates the principle of reviewing one's work when he says, "Over the years, I've regularly asked my key people—and I've had them ask *their* key people, and so on down the line—a few basic questions: 'What are your objectives for the next ninety days? What are your plans, your priorities, your hopes? And how do you intend to go about achieving them?' "[5] Iacocca goes on to say that questions like these appeared to be burdensome but resulted in employees becoming more accountable to themselves and more apt to dream of what could be accomplished.

OTHER KINDS OF ACCOUNTABILITY

In some denominations, graduate credit is offered for an intern program that is in harmony with the expectations of the seminary. Field education performance appraisal forms are required.[6] The immediate supervisor of the intern program at the church is usually required to have brief training periods with the graduate school. The end result is the kind of church internship that has both the highest spiritual and academic standards. One church assigns a family in the church to care for the intern during his training period, demonstrating a special relationship as he faces practical needs and concerns. In addition, an officer (elder or deacon) can also be assigned to this student-in-training. This broadens the opportunity for discipleship for both the officer and the intern alike.

4. Lyle E. Schaller, *The Multiple Staff and the Larger Church* (Nashville: Abingdon, 1980), p. 103.
5. Lee Iacocca, *Iacocca, An Autobiography* (New York: Bantam, 1984), p. 47.
6. Princeton Theological Seminary, *Teaching Church/Internships. Field Education Performance Appraisal* (Princeton, N.J.: Princeton Theological Seminary, 1983), p. 3.

LEARNING EXPERIENCE

Intern programs in a number of church settings are viewed as a learning experience and not as a job per se. This is critical to understanding various philosophies and implementations of certain intern concepts. A learning experience, fostered by many graduate seminaries, means the intern specializes in observing, watching, and reading in the initial stages of his experience and then progresses to a more work-centered schedule during the final six months of a fifteen-month commitment. Many supervisors wrongly look to the intern as an additional staff person, thus negating the philosophy of a learning experience. The role of the supervisor becomes critical as he meets regularly (at least one to two hours each week) with the intern to implement the objectives of the program. Some seminaries have rather formal and sophisticated requirements for the intern and supervisor if they are to gain academic credit for the experience.[7] It is important to find a senior pastor or immediate supervisor who is compatible in ministry style and philosophy. The pastor has to have the vision to train. Such training requires much additional time and effort on the part of a pastor or supervisor. A willingness to take on such an added assignment speaks well for the pastor or supervisor as he combines his efforts of shepherding people and discipling future church leaders.

The genius of an intern program depends on implementation, follow-through, and evaluation. One practical way to achieve this goal on a fifteen-month schedule is as follows. During the first three months the intern primarily watches the supervisor and the ministry. That is followed by a similar period of assisting the supervisor in the ministry. By the third three-month period the intern will be ministering while the supervisor observes his progress. Then for the final six months of the fifteen-month commitment the intern ministers on his own, without close supervision.

POTENTIAL PROBLEMS

FRUSTRATIONS

Disenchantments for both interns and part-time youth directors are inevitable when pursuing a call to such ministries. For example, limited time to do all the planning, counseling, listening, sharing, discipling, and teaching can stifle creativity. Time management courses are frequently offered to assist workers in developing good practical habits in work. An additional valuable resource is the book *Managing Our Work*, by John Alexander. Alexander talks about five major steps in planning: (1) recognizing the planning of God; (2) reaffirming our commitment; (3) formulating policies; (4) taking inventory;

7. Austin Theological Seminary, *Supervised Practice of Ministry Program*, packet for training of supervisors (Austin, Tex.: Austin Theological Seminary, 1983).

Fig. 9.1[8]

1. *First Period*—3 months (June, July, August)

   Objective: Observation of supervisor and ministry.
   "You watch me" concept.

List of specific ministries to observe as arranged by supervisor and intern	Actual ministries observed (at end of first period)
a.	a.
b.	b.
c.	c.

2. *Second Period*—3 months (September, October, November)

   Objective: Assisting supervisor.
   "You help me" concept.

List of specific ministries in which intern can help as arranged by supervisor and intern	Actual ministries in which intern helped (at end of second period)
a.	a.
b.	b.
c.	c.

3. *Third Period*—3 months (December, January, February)

   Objective: Supervision while ministering.
   "You do it while I watch you" concept.

List of specific ministries to serve under supervision as arranged by supervisor and intern	Actual ministries served under supervision (at end of third period)
a.	a.
b.	b.
c.	c.

4. *Fourth Period*—6 months (March through August)

   Objective: Ministering independently.
   "You do it alone" concept.

8. Harry Hassall, *1985-86 Intern Program Manual* (Dallas: Highland Park Presbyterian Church, 1985), p. 4a.

List of areas of service and ministry as arranged by supervisor and intern	Actual ministries served (at end of fourth period)
a.	a.
b.	b.
c.	c.

and (5) formulating objective goals and performance standards.[9] Personal improvement in this area is gained by observing people who demonstrate a balance between administration and people-centeredness. A genuine walk with Christ, like the one outlined in Richard Foster's popular book entitled *Celebration of Discipline,* only enhances one's ability to be motivated to align priorities.

Foster stresses inward disciplines of meditation, prayer, fasting, and study, along with outward and corporate disciplines.[10] Effort and availability are requirements for any meaningful follow-up ministry. Follow-up is always needed after retreats, discussions, and spiritual commitments. Personal visits, phone calls, letters, small group Bible studies, and luncheons are a few ways that demonstrate good discipleship. Resources such as tapes, books, and Christian youth magazines can assist in fostering the growth that is needed to manage this work with all its demands.

In addition to time limitations, another disappointment is in not seeing completed goals and lasting results. That makes it imperative to build a program in relationships that by the grace of God will have long-term benefits. One must combine the efforts of parents, Sunday school teachers, laypeople, interns, and youth workers to provide a setting and atmosphere that permit them to work toward goals of Christian maturity. Specific training on how to study the Bible; how to share one's faith; how to deal with peer pressure, dating issues, vocational guidance; what Christians believe; and seeking God's will are but a very few of the indispensable topics for Christian growth. It should be added that locating and training mentors for accessibility in the youth environment is another way to offset the disappointment of time limitations.

A third frustration deals with budget limitations. "Part-time staff usually get part-time money!" One must realize that restricted budgets can be frustrating, and if an intern and youth worker rely only on monetary benefits, their impact will be limited. Personal relationships are the key. Skills can be achieved without expensive buildings and equipment. One principle is vital:

9. John W. Alexander, *Managing Our Work* (Downers Grove, Ill.: InterVarsity, 1972), pp. 13-15.
10. Richard J. Foster, *Celebration of Discipline* (New York: Harper & Row, 1978).

laypersons want to know how money contributes to the Christian commitment and growth of the teenager. Also, they need personal reports of how God has changed lives and stimulated maturity.

A final discouragement concerns numerical growth. In a part-time position, a limited amount of time is available for ministry expansion. Conversely, an overconcentration on numbers could cloud one's true sense of mission. The supreme requirement God has for His leaders is to be faithful—faithful to His Word, His mission, and the needs of the youth. The quality of one's ministry is a foremost objective. Youth workers and interns have been known to start with their dynamic personalities, attract large numbers, empty their "bag of tricks," and leave shortly thereafter. Unfortunately, the group then dwindles as quickly as it skyrocketed. Part-time youth workers and interns should try to build a base of leadership that will have long-term results. That demands a ministry of discipling.

DIVIDED COMMITMENTS: BREAKDOWN OR BREAK THROUGH

Divided commitments apply especially to part-time youth workers, and yet many interns face some of the same issues. Youth ministers need to deal with the issues of divided loyalties brought about because of schooling, job, or family. With divided time commitments, a person is forced to prioritize his schedule to utilize time wisely. Key areas of ministries, such as Sunday school, retreats, youth meetings, discipleship teams, socials, outreach efforts, and evangelism, must be defined and arranged according to preference and abilities. In addition to enthusiasm and a love for youth, one must also know his limitations. Because the time frame is shorter, it is necessary to concentrate on training other adults, working closely with the youth committee, discipling key leaders, clarifying key needs and issues, writing out a philosophy appropriate to the local situation, and clearly articulating a sense of direction. Remember that the real test of any youth ministry is how it goes after the intern or youth worker leaves.

What can an intern or part-time youth minister expect to accomplish? He can make good initial contacts and establish friendships, especially if he has a charismatic personality, is upbeat and infused with enthusiasm. Awareness of time limitations should encourage him to spend his energies up front, meeting needs immediately. (Summer camp counselors, who have only one or two weeks to spend with the campers, face a similar challenge.) A student can observe spiritual commitment. Therefore, even though time is limited, good modeling also can be achieved. Good teaching is a further result. Whatever is done to communicate should be of the highest quality. One may also attain a sense of personal fulfillment; obedience to serving Christ brings the joy of a job well done. Again, the thrill of making disciples, multiplying one's ministry, and guiding young people to Christian maturity has life-long implications both for the recipient and the teacher. Finally, great fulfillment comes when a person obeys the call of Jesus Christ to share one's gifts, personally grows spiritually, and sees Christian development take place in the lives of the others.

In sum, to offset discouragement, a part-time youth leader needs to understand his sense of call, realize his limitations, creatively delegate responsibilities, work closely with people, and continually reshape his philosophy of ministry by engaging in periodic self-evaluation and being open to the critique of more experienced people.

Succession of part-time youth ministries. Because staff changes take place often—sometimes too rapidly—several cohesive factors must be kept in focus in order to avoid problems. First, a discipled and trained laity will serve efficiently. Furthermore, our ministry goal is to function as enablers and equippers (Eph. 4). Each part-time minister and intern can contribute to the success of this purpose. Second, the laity needs a well-defined sense of mission, a clear statement of purpose, and an awareness on the part of parents, staff, Sunday school teachers, and students of their commitment to excellence. Third, the governing body of the church must organize and implement guidelines. If the purpose of leadership is to bring certain objectives to fruition, good leadership is the art or science of getting the right things done through people. That will require planning. Planning, briefly defined, is spelling out goals and defining them.[11] The degree to which this is done will influence the stability of the entire ministry and reduce frustration for interns and part-time youth workers. In conclusion, whether the church be large or small, in order to provide cohesion it will need to exhibit clear communication, well-defined purpose, high expectations, accountability (position descriptions for all involved), a concern for good use of resources, the endorsement of the senior pastor, an awareness of reasonable limitations, and a vibrant and concerned optimism.

GETTING AN INTERN OR PART-TIME PROGRAM STARTED

FOR THE CHURCH

The most effective way for the church to begin an intern or part-time youth worker's ministry is to study the needs of the church, define the purpose of the ministry within that context, and prepare brief position descriptions. The church should also state clearly and realistically the expectations of both the church and the youth worker or intern, not forgetting to define financial boundaries.

That done, the church should contact other churches for illustrations of

11. Ted W. Engstrom, *The Making of a Christian Leader* (Grand Rapids: Zondervan, 1976), p. 139.

existing programs, and seminaries and colleges for pertinent information and prospective personnel. Observe what other institutions are doing, such as businesses, law firms, and medical schools. Out of all this, develop an application form and send it to prospective students and placement offices of educational institutions. Finally, set standards of evaluation and organize procedures for reviewing them periodically.

FOR THE POTENTIAL INTERN OR PART-TIME YOUTH WORKER

The potential intern or part-time youth worker should carefully follow these steps: (1) observe the philosophy of ministry as it functions in the local church; (2) seek a comfortable framework in which to work; (3) insist on clear expectations and lines of communication; (4) recommend weekly feedback opportunities with the supervisor; (5) ask for periodic evaluation sessions; (6) seek to maintain balance among the aspects of theoretical preparation, observation, and experience through participation; (7) interview other students or workers who have previously been employed by the church; (8) ask for a family sponsor; (9) be flexible as the Spirit of God directs the learning, serving, and maturing experience. The church may perceive your gifts and abilities differently than you do.

Benefits of an Internship or Part-time Program

On-the-job training for interns and part-time youth workers brings significant results that prepare men and women for meaningful ministries and helps churches meet needs that normally might not be met because of limited budgets and small church size. Both the church and the participants stand to gain immeasurably as a creative framework of experience is provided for interns and part-time youth workers. Here are some specific benefits afforded those who work out this program effectively:

1. Exposure of the participant to ministries on a practical level that will elevate the person's awareness as to the needs, opportunities, and responsibilities of ministry will permit the individual to contribute more ably and productively to the work of the church.
2. Development of a person's skills takes place in a learning/serving process that will enhance self-worth, improve the style of leadership, provide vocational guidance, and teach principles of time management.
3. Theological thought and conviction will be cultivated and broadened for personal experience in dealing with frustrations.
4. Personal limitations will be encountered.
5. Maturity will take place as both the church and the employee deal with relationships in committee meetings, staff sessions, and with parishioners.

6. Activities providing first-hand involvement in communication, caring, and administration will help prepare the workers for future ministry.
7. Professional growth can take place in an intern program that augments formal education. Too often proper practical experience is lacking in some seminaries, Christian colleges, and Bible schools. This is especially true where schools are weak in preparing professionals for Christian vocations other than the role of senior pastor.
8. Churches stand to profit greatly through the succession of talented and gifted persons.
9. The entire experience can improve each participant's likelihood of serving Jesus Christ more ably and fully in the future.

For Further Reading

Anderson, James D., and Ezra Earl Jones. *Ministry of the Laity*. San Francisco: Harper & Row, 1986.

Dayton, Edward R., and Ted W. Engstrom. *Strategy for Leadership*. Old Tappan, N.J.: Revell, 1979.

Drucker, Peter F. *The Effective Executive*. New York: Harper & Row, 1966.

Hassall, Harry. *1985-86 Intern Program Manual*. Dallas: Highland Park Presbyterian Church, 1985.

Lindgren, Alvin J., and Norman Shawchuck. *Let My People Go: Empowering for Ministry*. Nashville: Abingdon, 1980.

Rush, Myron. *Richer Relationships*. Wheaton, Ill.: Victor, 1983.

Yaconelli, Mike, and Jim Burns. *High School Ministry*. Grand Rapids: Zondervan, 1986.

10

Robert Joseph Choun, Jr.

The Church Without a Youth Minister

Can the church without a youth minister have a dynamic, exciting youth ministry? Consider a church in Grant, Oklahoma. At Grant Baptist Church, the youth ministry includes a volunteer youth director, extensive parental involvement, a closely graded Sunday school for youth, and even a Wednesday night youth prayer group. Volunteer Sandra DeFrates says, "Our youth ministry is exciting and is bringing teenagers into our church. We try to get as many parents involved as possible. Our students need models and examples of godly men and women. We will keep on with our youth ministry because it is important for our students here."

How did this happen? Did Grant Baptist Church just stumble on this success story, or was it carefully planned with specific goals in mind?

BACKGROUND OF THE SMALL CHURCH

Lyle E. Schaller, in his book *The Small Church Is Different,* says:

The small church is the normative institutional expression of the worshipping congregation among the Protestant denominations on the North American continent. One-fourth of all Protestant congregations on this continent have fewer than

ROBERT JOSEPH CHOUN, JR, D. Min., is assistant professor of Christian education, Dallas Theological Seminary, Dallas, Texas.

thirty-five people in attendance at the principal weekly worship service, and one-half average less than seventy-five.[1]

The small church is here to stay. Moreover, the small church is normative. Most small churches would be glad to have the multiple staff and attractive facilities with which larger churches can attract young people, but we should not overlook the advantages that a small church can offer.

DISTINCTIVES OF THE SMALL CHURCH YOUTH MINISTRY

There are at least a dozen distinctives of the small church youth ministry. The following items are taken from Vernon E. Olson's "Youth Work in a Small Church," a part of Denver Seminary's Continuing Education Seminar, February 1984.

Many church members' homes can be used for youth functions. People live closer to the church, and their homes are more accessible. This also provides young people with a model of a family that is Christian.

The small church is often less conscious of age differences. Usually more love and concern can be shown across age groupings. Caring can take place as people relate to other generations, as well as when junior high and high school students function in the same group.

Church leaders are usually in a better position to observe, discover, and evaluate the spiritual gifts of the people. This is the first step in placing them into ministry with youth. The same evaluation/recruitment process will apply to the way in which the young people's gifts are used within the church.

It is often easier to identify and minister to young men and women who need help. Once a problem is observed, steps are usually taken by the church family to provide assistance in a natural and informal way.

In a small church the opportunities for participation and service are often far greater than in a larger church because of fewer numbers. Youth can often be teachers and assistants in Sunday school, vacation Bible school, camps, and weekend retreats. The responsibility level is usually higher.

In a youth group of twelve or fifteen, a growth statistic of three or five is usually a major miracle. However, in a youth ministry of 100 or more, 3 or 5 percent is not earthshaking. To young people and leaders, growth in a small youth group is more evident and more exciting.

Youth in trouble or in need of counsel can often find someone ready to help instead of waiting days or even weeks for an empty slot on a counselor's calendar. That most frequently is the parent of a friend or another adult in the church with whom a warm bond has been established.

The young person in a small youth group is more likely to feel loved and

---

1. Lyle E. Shaller, *The Small Church Is Different* (Nashville: Abingdon, 1982), p. 11.

appreciated. He is not just a statistic or a number on an offering envelope. Each person is a visible part of the family.

In addition to these factors, when a young person is absent from a small youth group, he or she is more likely to be missed. Follow-up can readily take place.

In a small youth group, closer fellowship, more family warmth, and a family-like atmosphere exist. The needed support system for youth at this critical time of life happens rather naturally.

The pastor in a small church can have much closer contact with the youth in his church. The pastor might be the cook, the games coordinator, or even the camp director at a weekend retreat or campout. That first-hand experience of what the pastor is really like is refreshing. When the pastor stands in the pulpit and preaches, the youth are more apt to listen because they have seen Christianity in action in his life.

Youth and their families that come to visit can be more easily recognized. That is crucial for follow-up and assimilation into the church body, which should be the concern of both leaders and youth. As youth mature, more of this kind of contact and follow-up work can be given to them.

Of course there are problems with a small church setting, too. Finances, limited people to draw on for volunteers, lack of adequate training, and not enough youth for a complete program usually head the list. However, the advantages outweigh the disadvantages.

INGREDIENTS OF A GROWING YOUTH MINISTRY

There are two ingredients that make a growing and successful youth ministry. These are the development of a proper philosophy of ministry and the development of personnel.

In a church without an established youth program, the pastor should be the first to recognize the need for such a program and take steps to initiate it. In this situation, the pastor should take his strategy to the church board and begin the development of the philosophy and program in cooperation with church leaders and interested parents. Together they should select the adults who will work with the youth. Sadly, in many churches it is often the parents who point out the need for a youth ministry. Regardless of who initiates the plan, both pastor and volunteer workers must share in the development of the ministry. In most churches the pastor serves as a consultant and encourager only. The laypeople work directly with the students and carry the ministry.

DEVELOP A PROPER PHILOSOPHY

In assembling a proper philosophy of youth ministry there are five crucial areas that must be discussed.

Build relationships. The young people in your church learn about biblical and theological principles in the context of deep, personal relationships. The catchphrase for youth is "Show me, don't just tell me." Jesus built strong relationships with His disciples. His love in the midst of that relationship was unconditional. Ours must be the same.

Focus on the process and not just the product. What we desire for our youth, what we want them to become, is in the future. Conformity to the image of Jesus Christ is a life-long process. Consider that process. What is the ministry doing to build that image in the lives of youth? Such considerations should give guidance to the plans for the weekly meetings, monthly social events, and the totality of the program.

Model the proper attitudes and behavior. Modeling is crucial at this point in the life of young persons. What are they seeing, hearing, and being encouraged to do? Praise and encouragement go much further than correction.

Motivate youth to become involved. The youth in your church today will be tomorrow's board members and teachers. Allow them the freedom to get involved in specific activities and take on responsibilities. Give them first-hand experiences. Be prepared, however, to give them the training they need. If a young person is asked to assist in a Sunday school class, provide him with the training and support necessary to help him succeed and to show him that the work he has been given is a serious responsibility. Hold him accountable for that task with follow-up.

The small church can furnish much stimulation for the youth group by maximizing its involvement in denominational youth events. The Evangelical Free Church and Baptist General Conference are not large denominations, but they, and a host of others like them, sponsor outstanding conferences that bring identification for youth from small churches who gather with large groups of students from their own denominations.

Small evangelical churches in a given geographical area can often combine their groups to provide an adequate number of students for conducting retreats, summer camp programs, and outreach ministries. Pastors should be in the forefront of such plans so that doctrinal aspects are considered.

Create the right environment. The church must provide an opportunity for each person to grow at his own rate. Youth are no different. You will have youth who come to watch, those who come to listen, still others who come with a desire to grow. Providing opportunities for each of these is essential. You will even have a few who will come to minister to others. Give them the freedom to serve as much as they can.

DEVELOP THE PROPER PERSONNEL

The relationship of the youth workers to the pastor is crucial to the success of the program. They must be teammates in ministry. The pastor must be willing to delegate authority along with responsibility. He should encourage the volunteer workers with training, motivate them with positive direction, and improve their skills with evaluation and feedback. Once the program is in motion, volunteer workers should not be left alone to sink or swim. They must have the support of church leaders who will oversee their efforts and provide helpful direction. It is not the sole responsibility of the pastor to advise and encourage. The church leaders must share in this.

Recruiting and training volunteers in the small church has almost always been a problem. However, the excitement and the enthusiasm that the pastor and the church leadership bring to this task can show the entire church that it can be done.

How can a small church develop competent workers for a youth ministry? There are ten steps that provide the basis for successful recruiting of personnel to work with the students.

1. *Total involvement.* Everyone should be looking for qualified individuals to serve in the youth ministry. The church people should be praying for the right people to be models for youth.
2. *Publicity.* Opportunities for ministry within the youth program should be presented to the congregation on a regular basis. Through slides, bulletin boards, bulletin inserts, and by personal testimonies, people can hear and see the excitement of the church's youth ministry.
3. *List qualifications and job descriptions.* What kind of person are you looking for to work in youth ministry? List qualifications. You will want someone who is a believer, who understands today's youth, and who can aggressively meet their needs as individuals. A job description should be written. It is important to link the right person with the right ministry. What is the youth leader/sponsor to do? How much time will be required? Who is in charge?
4. *Find prospects.* Look for people who are qualified and gifted for youth ministry. Obtain a list of adult members from the pastor, the church office, or adult Sunday school classes. Go through them, keeping your list of qualifications in mind.
5. *Approve prospects.* Make sure that the people on your list are approved by the pastor and church leaders. Try not to overburden workers already involved in other ministries.
6. *Interview prospects.* Take time to set up a personal interview with each one. During the interview, give specific reasons as to why the individual has been selected. Also offer specifics about the ministry, related curriculum materials, and number of students. Allow the person to ask any questions.
7. *Observation.* Allow the potential recruit to observe the ministry in action.

If the ministry is just beginning, try a trip to another small church to observe what happens during a typical Sunday morning and midweek program. Observation provides a look not only at the program, but also at the need for additional workers.

8. *Allow time for a decision.* A week is usually enough time for a decision. Make sure that it is a spiritual decision. Volunteers are actually covenanting with the Lord for this ministry, not just the church leadership.

9. *Follow up on the prospect.* Never arm-twist. A no now may save weeks and even months of painful conflicts later. If the person responds with a yes, training should begin immediately.

10. *New staff training.* In youth ministry there should be no involvement without the proper training. This training should include: (a) age group characteristics and needs of junior and senior highers; (b) goals/objectives of our youth department/youth ministry; (c) programming and curriculum that will be used in our ministry; (d) teaching methods and materials suitable for youth; (e) evangelism and discipleship of youth; (f) working with parents—home visits and counseling; (g) organizing and scheduling youth activities and events; (h) counseling skills; (i) youth culture; and (j) adolescent problems.

Training can be provided in many different formats. It can take place during several evenings or on one or two Saturdays. Be aware of youth ministry training events that will be in your area in the upcoming months. Your local Bible college or seminary should be able to tell you about events. Investigate the many audio-visual aids that are available for training. Filmstrips, audio cassettes, and video cassettes are available at reasonable prices. These can be used for training staff in Bible study, teaching a Sunday school lesson, evangelism, discipleship, and other areas of ministry.

If it is true that youth learn biblical truth in the context of deep personal relationships, then we must strive for excellence in our recruiting strategy for youth ministry.

Programming for Youth Ministry

There are three keys to successful programming for youth ministry in the small church. Make the program comprehensive, culturally current, and committed to multiplication.

Comprehensive. The program must meet the needs of the youth. The leaders must understand the needs of junior and senior highers. The following needs are crucial factors in deciding the goals for the program:

Physical—comfort, warmth, mobility

Security—belonging to a group, abiding by a few recognized rules, being allowed to disagree, a nonthreatening atmosphere

Social—fellowship, meaningful conversation, helping each other, loving and being loved, sharing feelings, accepting others and being accepted

Self-Respect—knowing and understanding facts and concepts; giving and receiving attention, respect, courtesy, acceptance, and praise; receiving understanding

Achievement—using abilities, discovering and trying out ideas, growing as a person

Spiritual—knowing Christ as Savior, experiencing changes in the Christian life, experiencing the guidance of the Holy Spirit, becoming familiar with the Word of God, overcoming temptation, sharing what is learned, fellowship with other believers, practicing God's principles in daily living

The youth program must also focus the teaching ministry toward the broad areas of biblical truth that relate to youth ministry. These areas of emphasis are:

- God (Jer. 9:23-24; John 17:1-3)
- The Word (Ps. 119; John 15:1-17; 2 Tim. 2:14-15)
- Evangelism (Matt. 28:16-20; John 20:19-23)
- The Body of Christ (John 13:31-35; Eph. 4)
- The home (Deut. 6:4-9; Eph. 6:1-4)
- Christian maturity (Eph. 4:7-16; Phil. 3:12-16)
- Christian leadership (Eph. 4:7-16; 2 Thess. 3:7-9; 2 Tim. 2:1-13; 1 Pet. 2)

After surveying the needs of the young people in the program, a group leader would select an area of study to meet those needs. Goals for the group would be established and then a program aimed at reaching those goals. The next step would be to determine the personnel and materials best suited to the program. A schedule should be set for the recruitment and training of workers, survey of curriculum materials, publicity, and other factors in programming. An in-depth evaluation of any program should always be done, followed by a new evaluation of group needs.

Culturally current. The youth programming must be current with the times. There are several ways to become aware of what is going on in the youth culture.

1. Listen actively. Listen to what they are saying. Listen with an ear for the emotions. Listen to what needs are being expressed.
2. Spend time with them. Go where they spend their time. Where do the young go after school? Is there a "strip" or a "main drag" where teens often go on weekend nights? If the language and behavior you encounter are unacceptable to you, remember that accepting each person as a valuable individual is different from condoning unchristian words and actions. Jesus said that people who are well have no need of a physician.

3. Be a FAT person. Be Faithful, Available, and Teachable. Always be willing to learn all that you can from them.
4. Check with the police department or other agencies in the community to find out the specific problem areas that youth are facing. Be aware of some of the prevention and rehabilitation programs in your area.
5. Get into the homes of your youth. A young person is a picture window to the home. Knowing the home situation may often reveal the cause of certain behaviors. It may also alert you to the special needs of this individual young person.
6. Be willing to reach out to the youth and their friends. Remember that when youth bring their non-Christian friends to a church or home function there may be some non-Christian behavior. That is when God's unconditional love must take over.

Committed to multiplication. As stated earlier, youth leaders must move their students from an attitude of "come and listen" to "come and multiply." How is that done?

The accompanying chart that Dann Spader uses in his Sonlife Ministries Seminars has proved to be very helpful. (See Spader's discussion in chap. 14 and David Busby's in chap. 30.)

STUDENT MATURITY	YOUR PRODUCT	THE CHALLENGE
	Multiplication Level	Come and Lead Leaders
	Leadership Level	Come and Learn to Lead
	Ministry Level	Come and Minister to Others
	Growth Level	Come and Grow
	Outreach Level	Come and Listen

Fig. 10.1

As you survey your youth, you will observe that some are in each level as shown above. Perhaps most are in the outreach and growth level. About 90 percent of all youth programming is done at these two levels. Moving the ones who are growing up to the top three levels is a challenge. It can be done in the small church because of the special distinctives mentioned earlier in this chapter.

The typical youth meeting includes a time of fun, fellowship, and serious Bible study and discussion. Because it is obvious from the chart just reviewed that the young people attending such an event will bring to it different needs and expectations, activities must be planned to meet those needs and expectations. Young people who exhibit greater spiritual maturity and commitment should be provided with the individual or small group nurture that will prepare them for leadership roles. Young people less spiritually mature, who attend largely for the social aspect of the program, should be taught on the outreach or growth level. Regardless of the level of spiritual development, all young people have needs in the areas of physical, social, and emotional growth. The church's youth ministry can develop the whole person by providing a balance.

CONCLUSION

The church without a youth minister can have an impact on the young people within the community. Whether a church is large or small, the principles mentioned above still apply. However, after doing research for this chapter, I am firmly convinced that the small church can perhaps make a bigger impact on its youth than the larger church. Be committed to the Lord Jesus Christ. Strive for excellence in all that you do for your youth ministry. Above all, meet together as a group of leaders. Pray, plan, and program to glorify the Lord Jesus Christ. It is still His ministry. Cooperate with the Spirit of God as you lead His youth. The days ahead are exciting.

FOR FURTHER READING

Anderson, Ray S. *Minding God's Business.* Grand Rapids: Eerdmans, 1986.

Burns, Ridge, with Pam Campbell. *Create in Me a Youth Ministry.* Wheaton, Ill.: Victor, 1986.

Coleman, Robert E. *The Master Plan of Discipleship.* Old Tappan, N.J.: Revell, 1986.

———. *The Master Plan of Evangelism.* Old Tappan, N.J.: Revell, 1969.

Hanks, Billie, Jr., and William A. Shell. *Discipleship.* Grand Rapids: Zondervan, 1981.

Henrichsen, Walter A. *Disciples Are Made—Not Born.* Wheaton, Ill.: Victor, 1980.

Pippert, Rebecca M. *Out of the Salt Shaker.* Downers Grove, Ill.: InterVarsity, 1979.

Roadcup, David, ed. *Ministering to Youth.* Cincinnati: Standard, 1980.

Training Manual. Gordon-Conwell Theological Seminary/Young Life Youth Ministries Program, n.d.

11

Leadership Development of Lay Leaders

I approached the church parking lot excited yet apprehensive. Today was a big day, our biggest. Two hundred senior high students were converging on this lot along with some forty college, young adult, and adult age staff who were busily contributing to this year's departure.

As I walked through the diesel fumes of the six Greyhound buses, I was relieved as each little detail seemed to be under control. Dave busily loaded the PA system onto several buses. His team had finished building the system only weeks before. They masterfully jockeyed the pieces into the holds for the 1,500-mile journey from Minneapolis to Colorado.

In the church, Annie, sitting behind alphabetically labeled tables, did an orderly job of checking in people. Her staff confirmed each student's ticket and saw that everyone was assigned to a bus, cabin, and counselor.

Chuck huddled with six drivers, clarifying our food and fuel stops in Iowa, Nebraska, and Denver. The itinerary was set, and the bus captains were busily taking attendance from Annie's detailed list.

The work crew (all collegians) gave out the trip shirts. Counselors mingled with excited students and parents. The speakers for the week reviewed their notes, and the official photographer for the slide show distributed film

MARK D. WICKSTROM, M. Div., is pastor, St. Andrew's Lutheran Church, Mahtomedi, Minnesota, and formerly director, Youth Leadership, Inc., Minneapolis.

and instructions to his charges. The senior men's and women's counselors studied their schedules, and the trip doctor and his wife sealed the medical kit for the long journey west.

When the last suitcase was loaded, the last seat filled, and the last parent hugged, the last bus accelerated out of the lot. We were off on time and without a hitch. There is no greater relief for a youth minister than having a trip begin successfully. There is also great satisfaction in seeing the members of a diversely talented and well-organized staff function together.

Unfortunately, a well-organized staff does not just happen. Rather, like a garden, each person must be planted, watered, and weeded in order to produce. A good staff can be grown. It takes a lot of work, intentionality, and commitment on the part of the leaders. This chapter will address what goes into creating an interdependent leadership team.

What to Look for in Volunteers

Growing a youth ministry team can seem overwhelming, especially in the beginning of one's ministry. There are a myriad of qualities to look for in volunteers. Many look for external or physical attributes: Are the people attractive, young, robust, athletic? Other youth leaders look for internal attributes: Are the volunteers ethically moral, spiritually motivated, and intellectually competent? Still others ask only that the people be willing to show up: "I will take anyone I can get!"

PERSONALITY TYPES

I have observed three personality types that are desirable when building an effective leadership team.

The first type is the person who is good at human skills. These are outgoing, people persons, skilled conversationalists who love being with others. Geoff was the perfect human skill leader. An insurance salesman by trade, he was boisterous and adept at small talk with almost anyone. Geoff's gift of gab, his interest in sports, and his memory for trivia made him a terrific volunteer, especially with the athletic guys in our groups. Susan, on the other hand, also displayed human skills. Although somewhat quiet and unassuming, she related well to guys and girls of all kinds. She loved to talk one-on-one with kids, whether popular students or unknown wallflowers. Susan always found a way to draw each person into a conversation. Geoff and Susan represent the extremes in human skills—boisterous versus quiet, gregarious versus shy, groupie versus one-on-one. However, both were effective with teenagers. Both loved people and used their unique personalities to reach high schoolers.

A second type is adept at technical skills. These are the reliable, organizational people who love making lists and keeping track of details. Annie manifested great technical skills. She would make hundreds of phone calls to arrange special events for seniors. She single-handedly designed our retreat check-in system, which rivaled anything an airline might create. Annie was invaluable to the success of our programs. She regularly thought of thank you's, stickers, magic markers, and countless other details that needed to be considered. Ted was also a technical type. Although less prone to thorough list making, Ted always asked the technical questions. He was concerned about issues or agenda that sometimes escaped the rest of us. Ted's role also was helpful in that he always sought to hold the group accountable to the desired tasks. These two individuals demonstrate variations in technical skills, but each contributed uniquely to the effective management of our ministry.

The last type is the conceptually skilled. They are the team dreamers, visionaries, and brainstormers par excellence. I perceive myself as the conceptual type. I love looking at what is not there and finding a way to make it appear. Dave was also a conceptual type. He and I could talk for hours about schemes both large and small, and we would be energized by the exchange of ideas. Our ideas were utilized best when combined with the detail concerns of those more technically oriented and fleshed out by individuals strong in human skills.

I believe a youth ministry becomes most effective as it is able to involve people who represent each of these categories. Understandably, not every group will have these three skill groupings readily available, but they can be discovered and grown. A major task in leadership is assessing one's own avenue of strength and then recruiting volunteers from the missing categories. To do so is to begin to plan for successful team ministry.

LEADERSHIP QUALITIES

I will never forget the cartoon caricature I once saw of an effective youth worker. She had athletic gear from five different sports, a guitar, a Bible, a joke book, a counseling manual, a story book, a camping manual, a prayer book, and a radio all dangling from her body. Often youth directors have the same subtle expectations of volunteers. Do volunteers really need to be able to do everything with kids and do it well?

Absolutely not. I believe that almost anyone can work with or around kids. However, the truly effective leaders in ministry with kids will possess certain qualities.

The first quality is an authentic personal walk of faith. Adults can only lead others spiritually as far as they have gone themselves. Like guides in a boundary water wilderness area, leaders cannot knowingly lead kids into any area they have not previously explored. True, many adults can plan activities, supervise events, or chaperon happenings, but authentic spiritual change, growth, and direction require personal experience. My observation is that many church youth groups lack spirituality not because the kids are incapable or even uninterested, but because the leaders are unable to provide spiritual direction and insight from their own experience. As a result, many church youth groups are relegated to activities, events, and happenings that are compatible with the adults' experiences. Volunteer leaders need to be encouraged and enabled in their own faith walk. As their faith grows, so will their effectiveness in ministry.

A second quality worth looking for in a volunteer leader is related to the first. Not only is the person growing in faith, but he also is enlightened concerning his own abilities, talents, and gifts. In his book on spiritual gifts, C. Peter Wagner draws helpful distinctions between abilities, talents, and gifts. A youth minister in suburban Minneapolis used Wagner's book as a training tool for his staff. He said it helped his leaders see themselves more clearly and understand how they might fit on the staff more fully. Youth leaders need to be tuned in to their spiritual gifts and their personal talents. That goes a long way toward building self-understanding and confidence for effective ministry.

A third quality highly desirable in volunteer leaders is love of adolescents. Youth ministry will be most effective when leaders authentically enjoy being involved. Teens are sensitive to how their leaders view them. The Sunday school teacher who is there out of guilt, or the parent who is there under duress, or the minister who is there out of duty will pass on negative nonverbal messages. Many unsuspecting adults actually invite dysfunctional behavior through their own attitudes about being with youth. Teens need to know they are accepted and loved as people, not just tolerated as trials or endured like an illness. The prudent youth leader will look for people who really enjoy kids.

The aforementioned qualities are highly desirable, and I think they should be viewed as *essential.* They are not, however, the only qualities helpful for effective ministry with teens. Here is a brief listing of some additional attributes whose presence in people will enable them to be effective in ministry with teenagers.

Teachability. Teachability describes a leader's willingness to learn new skills, interact with new ideas, wrestle with varied perceptions about youth ministry, and even struggle with faith. Volunteers who are teachable will tend to be around, growing, and available for longer periods of service. The less teachable, the more likely people will be to leave rather than encounter new ideas or change old ways.

Adaptability. There is an almost universal need in youth work to be able to adapt to unexpected changes in people, situations, or even the best-laid plans. A few years back our annual spring ski trip left Minneapolis on time only to encounter a major winter storm in Nebraska. The highway was closed, and all six buses were forced to pull off in Grand Island. Although this prolonged stop was not in any of our plans, after a call to the state police and the local Red Cross, the next twenty-four hours were spent in the Grand Island High School gym. We ran our program, seminars, some impromptu gymnastic and volleyball tourneys, and even made headlines in the local newspaper. As the poster so aptly puts it, "When life gives you lemons, make lemonade." So, too, in youth work look for people who are willing to make the most of the situation.

Vulnerability. This quality is best observed in those who are willing to take risks with teens. They go where kids are located (at games, places of employment) and seek to live out the incarnation, God getting involved with people by becoming a person. Vulnerable adults get involved with kids on the teenage turf, and often on adolescent terms. Jim Rayburn, the founder of Young Life, referred to this as contact work, as an adult being secure enough to leave the adult world and enter the world of the adolescent. Not everyone will enter youth work ready to do that, but it can be caught, as well as taught.

Dependability. Choosing leaders you can count on is a big lesson to learn. There will be four or five people who will volunteer to "help out sometimes" for every one person who will be there no matter what. Our culture is not a supportive environment for learning to follow through on commitments. So when you find someone who is reliable and dependable, let your volunteer know you appreciate follow-through. As Mary Kay Ash (of Mary Kay Cosmetics fame) says, "Praise people to success."

Ability to model behavior. Over the years I have watched all kinds of people effectively work with teenagers: a mortgage broker in New York, a science teacher in Pennsylvania, a lawyer in Minnesota, a dairy farmer in Iowa, an unmarried ironworker in Florida. Each of these individuals represents a significant aspect of ministry to teens—modeling. Every adult becomes an adult guarantor for students. A Cornell University study discovered that parents, teachers, and adults had the greatest impact on children's long-term values even through adolescence. Peer influence is significant during the teen years, but it is often most influential on short-term values like music, language, and fashion. The long-term values about work, education, and life are influenced by adults. In choosing a staff, look for variety in ages, in life circumstances, and in situations. Each person will be a continuing reminder to teens that one can be a college student, working adult, husband, wife, or professional and still be a Christian. What a great reassurance for many teens.

This list is by no means exhaustive. Probably no volunteer you encounter will encompass all the aforementioned attributes, but an effective team will have various people each bringing his or her own unique strengths to the task. As a youth director or ministry team leader, you need to recruit volunteers who complement one another in such a way that in their cooperative and corporate ministry God is able to use them interdependently to influence the lives of teenagers effectively for the gospel's sake.

WHERE TO LOOK FOR VOLUNTEERS

As a twenty-five-year-old seminary graduate, I started my first parish youth ministry with an inherited staff of assorted veterans. As that first year unfolded, I realized how ill-equipped I was to deal with that staff. Oh, I was great with kids, but within nine months, two-thirds of my volunteers had politely said, "We need a break," or, "Maybe we're getting too old," or simply, "It's time for some new blood." At first I was devastated. What had I done to offend them? Next, I rationalized, "Who needs them anyway! We really do need some new blood." Finally, I began to understand what had happened. They were all thirty- to thirty-five-year-old couples with children. All were friends of the previous youth director (who was also thirty-five, married, with children). I was twenty-five, single, long-haired, and very different from the previous fellow. What occurred was a change of the guard, a change of the administration that was needed and healthy. I just wish someone had warned me.

That experience illustrates two helpful principles in volunteer leadership. One is that it is often helpful and healthy for a new leader to grow his or her own staff rather than expecting the old staff to change or the new leader to conform to old approaches. Second, your own situation in life will often attract the kind of staff interested in working with you. Years two and three found me working with a predominance of twenty-five to thirty-year-old single adults. In many such situations, likes do attract.

A notable church consultant once told me that on the average 20 percent of a church's membership does 80 percent of the work. My experience has found those statistics to be accurate. That presents a special challenge for youth leaders. First of all, where do you look for the volunteers to staff your program? (How to recruit that 20 percent will be discussed later in the chapter.)

Eighteen to twenty-two year olds. This group's proximity of age and interests is very attractive for working with slightly younger peers. This group also is often the most readily available. Whether persons this age are in school or working, they frequently have a high degree of free time and minimal long-term commitments. As a result, many churches rely heavily on those recently graduated from high school to provide adolescent leadership.

The cautions of using this age group are less obvious. Developmentally, persons in this age group are often dealing with similar issues as the students they seek to serve. Some studies classify eighteen to twenty-two year olds as late adolescents themselves. That does not necessarily mean it is easier for them to help solve the problems of their younger peers.

Twenty-two to twenty-six year olds. This group brings a little more life-experience to the task of resolving teenage issues. Men and women often have resolved some basic issues concerning career and/or marriage and, therefore, have some insights to offer teens.

On the negative side, if persons this age have not resolved these issues this age group comes the closest to resembling smoke. You can see them and smell them, but when you attempt to grab them, they disappear. One autumn I began with three volunteers in this age bracket, each having expressed excitement and commitment to the program. One began dating a leader from another group and within three months was gone. A second person worked faithfully for two months, then decided she wanted to live in Seattle and moved there before Christmas. The third person changed jobs three times that year and was constructively available only a few weeks per quarter. I do not want to downplay the value of this whole age-group on the basis of some unique experiences, but I do think those in early adulthood will present special challenges to any youth director.

Twenty-six to thirty year olds. One positive aspect of persons in this group is that they are often more established in a church and community. They offer teens a sense of continuity and frequently can provide long-term presence in a program.

The most common shortcoming of this group is that these persons' commitment to working with students will often be limited by personal, professional, and family demands. As a twenty-seven-year-old single person, I had time and energy to give to late nights at restaurants or almost unlimited time for personal contact. As a twenty-eight-year-old married man, my wife became a higher prority than evenings at Perkins Cake and Steak. As a thirty-four-year-old father of two, suddenly my evenings and days off were necessarily taken up by time for personal recreation, family interaction, and fulfilling my roles as husband and father. I have observed this scenario repeatedly in the lives of volunteers. An alert youth leader will be flexible in utilizing individuals who are going through personal and professional changes.

Thirty year olds and up. This is probably the most frequently overlooked age group. True, adults past thirty are often beginning the peak production years in their careers and are experiencing the greatest demands on their time. Coaching little league, serving on the PTA, or numerous church committees all clamor for these adults' time. However, why should the school, community, or local agency be the only recipients of this group's input? Some of the most mature leadership I have seen has come from adults who were challenged to share with the youth group some of their precious time and life-experience. I believe these people can be encouraged, equipped, and exhorted to do significant ministry with adolescents.

Parents. I have a bias that parents can be a wonderful resource but in almost all situations should *not* be working with groups where their teenage children are involved. I know of one mother who was a wonderful volunteer with the junior high church program until her oldest daughter reached seventh grade. Then she quit working with the early adolescents and volunteered with the high school group. When her eldest child reached sophomore age, she took a break from youth work altogether so her daughter could be in her "own" high school group and her son in the junior high group. That parent showed great sensitivity to a basic need for teens to establish independence from parents. There is no more frustrating experience than trying to separate from one's parents when your parent is leading the youth group. There are exceptions to this rule, but I believe for every parent who can effectively work with his kids in the group, there are five who cannot. Parents can be utilized very effectively with groups of all ages, but during adolescence I believe their involvement should be with groups other than their teenagers.

Peers. I cannot leave the topic of who can be a leader without encouraging youth leaders to see students themselves as effective leaders among their peers. Much of adolescence is influenced by peer networks encouraging one another in fashions, music, recreation, and life-style. I believe peer pressure can be exerted in a positive manner and that Christian values can be lifted up by seniors, juniors, or freshmen, too. These peer models can go a long way in influencing young students for the gospel's sake.

In the early 1970s two seniors from a local high school took peer ministry seriously. They began a weekly Bible study with eight friends, and within months the study grew to a weekly meeting of more than a hundred students. That Wednesday night program was conceived, planned, and run by seniors. Needless to say, it was larger and more effective than every church youth group in town. Although it is not surprising that both these young men ended up going into the ministry, the impact of their ministry with their peers has been life-changing for me.

In most of our communities employers expect teens to do an adult's share of work, coaches expect excellence, band directors demand perfection, and teachers encourage students to become all they can be. Because most adolescents live up to the expectations placed on them, the prudent youth director will be well aware of the opportunities out there for students to be enlisted, encouraged, equipped, and evaluated in leading their friends down the path of discipleship to Christ.

WHY DO VOLUNTEERS COME?

"All that glitters is not gold." That old adage is descriptive of an important element in youth ministry. Every volunteer is not necessarily the kind of person you want leading your group. Over the years I have seen people seek to get involved in youth work for unhealthy, neutral, and healthy reasons. Let me briefly describe some examples of each.

UNHEALTHY REASONS

Parateen. This person wants to work with youth as an extension of his or her own adolescence. Such persons act like kids, want acceptance at almost any cost, and can be seen living out their adolescence in an older body. Often they are looking for the strokes and affirmation they never got as teenagers.

Crusader. Crusaders often sound well intentioned. They want to make sure kids today do not make the same mistakes they made in adolescence. It is the former drug user or the former pregnant teen who returns to the group readily telling his or her story, wanting to make sure kids do not make the same choices. That sounds innocent, but it can be a subtle form of self-service.

Tonto. This volunteer is an adult looking for other adult partners, his own "Lone Ranger" to follow and fellowship with personally. This type usually creates an adult fellowship group that uses ministry to teens as an excuse for its existence. Such individuals are readily observable because they often gather together as a group and seldom interact with the teenagers they supposedly came to serve.

Empire builder. This adult often has huge insecurities or ego needs that he or she seeks to satisfy by having groups of people follow him or her. Empire builders can be very charismatic individuals, but the groups they lead tend to focus on the leader, and the group disintegrates as soon as the leader leaves.

People who get involved for unhealthy reasons can do more harm than good. One of the hardest lessons we must learn is to say no to willing people. But unhealthy reasons for getting involved will bear destructive fruit.

NEUTRAL REASONS

Melvin or Margaret Milquetoast. These people could not say no when you asked them, so even though they have little interest or ability in working with kids, they are on your team. They appear to be pluses (they were willing), but in time their inconsistency or ineffectiveness gives them away.

Mama Morganstern (named after the mother on the former TV show, "Rhoda"). This person is guilt-driven: "If no one else is going to take the group, then I guess I will." Though often concerned for kids, especially their own, their reason for getting involved is not always for the teens' best interest.

Amnesia. This volunteer shows up at your staff meeting and is not sure why he is there. Such persons may have read about the need, had a friend tell them or bring them, or even once heard they were good with kids. The "Amnesias" are there, but unsure why, and usually they are not sure how long they will be involved.

I call these neutral reasons because, depending on the person and how the leader handles him, these individuals can continue for healthy or unhealthy reasons. Each can be nurtured into healthier reasons for service, or each can be encouraged to find a more meaningful place to serve the Lord outside of youth work.

HEALTHY REASONS

Lovers. These people have a genuine love for teenagers. They often relate well to kids, and their built-in acceptance, empathy, and concern for teens is readily apparent in their behavior and demeanor.

Servant. This adult has often felt a desire to serve God, and the place he or she has chosen to serve is with youth. These individuals at times refer to wanting to pay back something to the church for all they have received.

Grateful debtor. This adult had a wonderful youth group experience and wants to give another generation of teens the same kind of experience. Such individuals are one of the most wonderful compliments to a ministry, for truly the experience of God in youth has taken hold of their whole lives. They do often have preconceived ideas as to what a youth group should be like ("we used to do"), but they represent a wonderful adult guarantee to teenagers.

Deprived provider. These leaders had either a lousy experience or no experience of God in their youth and now want to make sure kids get what they never received themselves. They do not necessarily try to control kids or groups, but, rather, seek to be what they wished they had experienced: a caring adult friend, a listener, a provider of compassion to kids.

Authentically concerned parent. This adult has a genuine love of his or her own kids and those of the neighbors. These parents want their children to be as excited about God, faith, and church as they are. They give regularly and willingly of their time and resources to ensure that God has positive healing in kids' lives.

People will arrive on your staff for these and even other reasons. And there is no denying God can use anyone to deliver the gospel to another person. As responsible youth directors, however, we would do well to create methods to filter out folks with unhealthy intentions. They need to be healed before they can effectively serve. We also should strive to encourage, honor, and train those who come with healthy intentions. They will bear much fruit in God's kingdom. We need to pray for those who arrive out of neutral intentions, for God's blessing and guidance in leading them into healthy reasons or perhaps into a ministry other than with teenagers.

LEADERSHIP TRAINING

APPROACHES

There are three commonly used models for training leaders. By far the most common is the sink or swim approach. A church I know in central Iowa once recruited a new member to become the part-time Christian education director for the church. She knew few people in the congregation and had no experience in curriculum development or evaluation. The church itself was between pastors, and she was told to build the program. Splash! She was in deep, way over her head. Although it sounds incredible, many churches perceive this as the only way to build a volunteer staff. Whoever volunteers gets the whole job, no training, no assistance, and no time. Just go and do it. Fortunately most medical doctors and dentists are not trained that way! There is value in getting people involved with ministry and real life situations, but the sink or swim approach is Darwinian in the truest sense. Only the strong volunteer will survive; the rest will often drown.

Advocates of the second style, the informational approach, are usually steeped in academia. Americans are fascinated with this method. I have observed seminars on almost everything—sex, drugs, eating disorders, time management, youth issues, real estate investment, and estate planning. It is apparently believed that the best way to prepare someone for any situation is to offer a course, a class, or a series of lectures on the subject.

The informational approach in youth ministry seeks to give volunteers cognitive information about all aspects of adolescence. That is often done through a plethora of handouts, books, and charts detailing each area of concern. Obviously there is a great deal to be gained from such courses and information. However, I have observed that an old quote is very true: "Information can breed fear; experience breeds confidence." I remember one January day spending hours with a college intern discussing the finer nuances of working with teenagers. He was interested and yet fairly aloof. We had covered every angle of contact work—the philosophy, the goals, the approaches—and he gave regular verbal and nonverbal affirmation of each thought. When I asked if he had any questions about it he said no. I replied, "Great, tomorrow you can go to school alone and tell me later how it went." His eyes enlarged, his face showed lines of tension, his voice became high-pitched, as he asked, "Alone? What will I say?" My intern had all the information, but once that information had to take flesh and bone (his), he suddenly was unsure, almost distraught. Two weeks later he was finishing his project, and after having visited the school several times alone, he was no longer fearful but confident of what he could say and do there.

Information is helpful and a continual source of personal growth, but it is rarely an adequate substitute for experience.

The work-study approach has long been used to educate teachers, doctors, and dentists. Training programs utilizing this method allow students and teachers to learn a subject and then teach a class, or an intern to study anatomy and then see patients, or a dentist to memorize the steps of a procedure and then actually clean someone's teeth. This approach has been popularized in recent years by the vocational school movement, where a student studies part of a day and then puts the lessons to work in a job situation.

The work-study approach for youth leaders' training is an excellent way to get people involved with students' lives as they continue to equip their minds and hearts with other skills: spiritual, small group, counseling. Once volunteers spend time with teens, the intent of their training becomes more clear and their questions are more personal and often more relevant. The key to using work-study effectively is the presence of a *trainer,* someone who offers advice, feedback, and reflections to the person being trained. Without supervision, the whole work-study approach becomes a glorified sink or swim approach. On the other hand, with a proper blend of "watch me; do it with me; do it alone with my observation; do it alone," our volunteer staff can quickly and confidently move into a teaching and mentoring role.

ENVIRONMENT

Growing a youth ministry staff is an intentional choice. It is important to realize that training is more than just sharing information, and it takes place over a long period of time. People must be nurtured into effective leadership. Nurture is the sharing of one's life, information, and perceptions with another. In order to train our volunteers effectively, we need to create an environment that lasts more than a couple of hours or a couple of weeks, or is limited to a few select situations. Rather, a youth director needs to create an environment that is honest, challenging, supportive, affirming, accountable, consistent, and cyclical.

Honest. "Oh, this won't take too much of your time," or, "Just come whenever you can." Those lines frequently crossed my lips as a beginning recruiter. After all, I did not want to ask too much of a volunteer. Although I often tried to soft-sell people as they came onto my staff, it was not long before I was disappointed and even angry when they took me at my word and then did not give as much time as I thought was needed. I learned the hard way. We need to be honest in our expectations of people, especially those in a volunteer position. Job descriptions, contracts, or at least minimum requirements should be clearly laid out for them from the beginning.

My minimum requirements were five hours per week (two Sunday, two Monday evening, and one in contact work), one Saturday morning per month from 10:00 A.M.-12:00 noon for leadership training, and at least two overnight retreats yearly. People sometimes could and did give more than that, but seldom less. Those guidelines were dealt with from the very beginning so that everyone knew what was expected.

Challenging. One of my pet peeves in church work is the absence of spiritual growth for volunteers. That is especially true in youth work. Leadership training should provide spiritual growth, growth in personal skills, and personal growth for volunteers. Staff times should be feeding times where the director takes responsibility for enriching his or her staff and challenging each individual to become all he or she can become as a person and as a Christian. The staff that does not get fed will soon lose strength and wither, and so will its ministry. That does not mean every staff meeting needs to be a seminary course, but it does mean that every staff time should be a time of personal study, fellowship, worship, or service for the volunteers. As staff members grow individually and in relationship with God and each other, their ministry will become more effective.

Supportive and affirming. Youth leaders are working with the church's toughest audience. Young children often come to church because their parents bring or send them. Adults will often go to church out of guilt, habit, tradition, or personal desire. However, teenagers are the most likely to be honest about church. If it does not scratch where they itch, kids often are not there. I have listened to many a distressed parent describe the anguish felt about the teenage son or daughter who thinks church is boring and will not get involved. Because leaders working with youth are dealing with such a demanding, honest, and at times fickle, group, churches need to be very supportive of the youth volunteers. Commissioning services in the fall, appreciation dinners or luncheons (at the church's expense), regular thank you notes, periodic public recognition, and the offering of encouragement and prayer are all helpful ways of showing support. The youth director must be particularly mindful of saying thanks with hugs and handshakes, smiles and words, as often as possible. To do so will help staff members feel appreciated, and it builds a growing sense of loyalty to the ministry. To fail to say thanks in a variety of ways will often serve to shorten the time a volunteer stays with the program.

Another kind of support occurs when program concerns and directions can be discussed by the staff. If a leader is having trouble with a small group or individual, or even with the staff, it can be expressed openly. I will never forget the fourth night of a senior high week at camp when at the evening counselor meeting John broke down in tears. He shared frankly the hurt he was feeling. There was a minor virus going through camp, and its symptoms of nausea and vomiting had first appeared in his cabin. He was tired of the jokes and treatment making him feel like a leper. As he spoke, the whole counseling staff was convicted. Many of us had joked about it, had kiddingly avoided him on the paths around camp, or had avoided his table in the dining hall. For John it was no joke, and as he wept, the twenty-five counselors silently moved around him and hugged him. Some cried too, but all of us experienced his hurt. A staff can and should become a trusted place to share, confront, and deal with all kinds of human emotional and spiritual needs.

Accountable. The weakest area in many youth ministries is accountability. For many youth directors, ministry is too intangible to be measured by the old business school Management by Objectives. Other youth directors tend to measure attendance, number of people saved, or other tangible items in an effort to say bigger is better, or certainly that more kids or more saved is more blessed.

I am a firm believer that youth ministries need accountability. Every group and each leader (myself included) needs to be held accountable to these two questions: Are our time and efforts accomplishing what we want them to accomplish? Are we reaching whom we want to reach? Statistics or perceptions can certainly tell any story the compiler wants to tell (the glass is half-empty or half-full). I prefer to hold myself and my staff members accountable to what

I think are significant vehicles for ministry, such as the following:

Group atmosphere. Do people feel welcome, included, important? Or do they feel excluded and uninvolved? In other words, is God's love evident in our actions?

Group content. Are people clearly hearing the gospel explained to them? Are they challenged to grow or underwhelmed with the same old stuff? In other words, is God's love being spoken?

How well am I known? Do the leaders know me? Can I talk with them and confide in them? Do they take an interest in me? Or do they know my name but nothing about who I am, where I hurt, what I need? In other words, is God's love real to each individual?

Who is being reached? What is the profile of an involved guy or girl? What kind of kids really come? Are they church members? Are they really unchurched? In other words, whom are we reaching with God's love, really?

Is our mission being fulfilled? Where are we going? If students spend three years in our program, what will they do, experience, or become that they would not if they were not involved in our program? In other words, what is it about God that we want to communicate to teens?

What needs are we meeting? What specific needs of specific kids are we trying to address? Which needs are most important to meet first? What needs can wait? In other words, how is God's love being presented?

What programs do we offer? What need(s) is each program seeking to address, relieve, and fulfill? Are all our programs aimed at the needs of teenagers or at our church's need to offer something?

Consistency. A youth staff needs to have regular elements in its training. Each volunteer needs to have individual, periodic time with the youth director throughout the year. This is most effective if done at the volunteer's place of employment, school, or home. It is a great way for the leader to get to know each individual working with him and what he or she faces daily.

As a staff, youth teams need to have fellowship time monthly, quarterly, biannually—whatever fits the group. Times of fun and laughter help build interpersonal commitments and confidence in one another, regardless of the size of the team (two or twenty). We found a monthly Saturday morning together brought opportunities for personal faith nurture. Our sessions included outside resource people, interpersonal skills workshops, and biblical studies. The content varied monthly, but it was always geared to the *needs* of the *staff*, not just my own agenda.

Consistently, a youth team needs to have retreats of its own without kids (two or three maximum). These extended times together can be a brief overnight, a full day, or even several days. It is in the shared cooking, eating, playing, studying, praying, and planning that staff intimacy is nurtured. There is no avoiding the importance of leadership teams spending time together.

When togetherness is present, interdependence is a wonderful by-product consistently harvested.

Cyclical. God has created all living things to be subject to cycles. Physically, humans need food, exercise, work, rest, and sleep in order to function properly. It is possible to go for a while without any one of those items, or to overdo others, but the body always pays a price when we do. So, too, a staff is a living organism that also requires feeding, exercise, work, and rest if it is going to function properly. We have already talked about the feeding, exercise, and work elements that a youth staff requires, but what about rest? I am convinced that the demands of effective youth work are such that no one should be expected to work at it twelve months a year. Instead, the year can be divided into separate sections, and all volunteers should be encouraged to have regular periods of rest.

I consciously recruited two different staffs. One was for the academic year (September to May); the other was for the summer (June, July, August). I discovered that when my academic year staff took the summer off, they came back more excited and refreshed. I also realized that summer was a terrific time to develop collegians or post high schoolers with leadership experience. Camps have done that for years. The church can learn from their example.

I calculate that for every three months I gave a staff person off, he or she tended to reenlist for another nine. Conversely, every person I asked to work without a break tended to drop out nine months earlier. In other words, with three months off people came back rested and ready to serve nine more months. Without a rest, I lost them the next fall. People need time away regularly.

Kids need time off too. Programs also should be cyclical with regular fellowship, study, worship, and service time, but also with regular breaks when there is no programming scheduled. Our year went from September 15 to December 20; January 3 to May 20; June 10 to August 10. Each change in program schedule enabled staff and students to have a rest. This is a refreshing cycle that a sensitive youth director should seriously consider as he programs for a year.

SEQUENCE

Carl and his wife finished their coffee and consented to be a part of my confirmation staff. I was relieved. He was an industrial arts teacher at the high school, and Sherry was a secretary. They agreed to get involved, but during the next two months my failure to have an intentional plan for their progression into the program was instrumental in their dropping out by October. I was young and inexperienced. I planted a seed but failed to nurture the soil. If a staff is to be grown, the work is not done when the seed hits the soil.

In the years following my fiasco with Carl and Sherry, I learned that a single procedure clearly outlined prevents many future frustrations. First of all, whenever possible, a volunteer needs a break-in period, usually one to three months long. Duing that time the volunteer participates in all the staff activities, but basically observes the program. Involvement is not crucial, but the person should be given a broad overview of the various parts of the ministry. This is often referred to as the Watch Me phase of youth work. The new person watches an experienced person at work.

Next comes a period of Do It with Me. When possible, the trainee takes some aspects of the group meeting. Again the trainer is clearly in charge. On a weekly or regular basis, the new staff person is given increasing doses of experience and responsibility: leading the ice breaker, teaching the lesson, designing the questions, leading prayer time, or whatever meeting elements are present. The person is given experience, as well as information.

Do It Alone with My Observation is the third phase of this ideal training sequence. The new staffer runs the meeting, and the experienced trainer merely watches and provides feedback later. As a college senior, I taught in a high school in Lancaster County, Pennsylvania. I will never forget my first experience of being in charge of the class session from beginning to end. My supervising teacher, Tom, watched, left the room, came back, and afterwards sat down and gave me feedback on the job I had done. I had watched teachers for sixteen years, but being one was really different. I longed for Tom's supportive observations and bristled at times under his watchful critique. I was learning. The feedback time was when I really grew.

The second-to-last phase of the sequence, Do It Alone, is turning the person loose to lead the group on his or her own. The staff person usually has a sense of confidence and readiness to move ahead by this time, and the ministry begins to expand.

The last phase is asking the newly trained leader to become the trainer of another volunteer. This is truly the full cycle of discipleship. There is no standardized amount of time for the sequence to take place. Rather, it should be geared to individual needs and personal capabilities.

CONTENT FOR TRAINING

What should be included in training volunteer youth leaders? There are two principles to be kept in mind. The first is that training must be geared to the volunteers' needs as much as to the leader's agenda. To borrow an old analogy, I have seen many youth leaders try to feed steak to volunteer babies who have not yet developed teeth. We should know our staff well enough to effectively design training to match their personal and corporate needs.

The second principle is that it is a sin to burn out a staff. People may tire of working with kids or need a rest from the strain, but a youth staff should never burn out. Youth volunteers always must be given the opportunity to grow personally, spiritually, and even professionally. They never should be allowed to run dry.

With these principles in mind, there are three areas that need constant attention.

Vision. The staff of every ministry needs to know where it is going, and periodically the staff needs to know if the goal, desire, and dream of its ministry are being fulfilled. A friend took the theme Make a Difference Where You Are for his suburban youth group. His staff regularly reflected on the difference they saw happening in the community, the group, individual student lives, and in their own personal lives. Whatever the goal, a youth ministry team will need regular reminders and even revisions of the direction in which the group is going.

Personal leadership skills. Several years ago at a denominational youth gathering I was appalled at the inability of the adult leaders to interact effectively with their adolescent charges. I realized anew that listening skills are essential in effective ministry with teens. Small group leadership, counseling, song leading, skit planning, program development, and effective teaching are all valuable skills for reaching teenagers with the gospel of Jesus Christ. Volunteers will need regular input, exercises, and information on how to utilize such skills with kids if a staff is going to become more effective.

Personal growth. A youth staff is more than just volunteers. It is made up of human beings with personal histories, biases, abilities, and disabilities that all play a part in their knowledge and understanding of Scripture. In each of these areas staff members need to grow in their personal lives of devotion and faith, to be what Henri Nouwen has called wounded healers.

The New Testament strongly witnesses to the importance of spiritual growth. We must work hard to provide our staff with opportunities to achieve it. Of course, we can only provide the opportunity for growth, and people may choose not to take advantage of it. Also it is important to realize that although each staff session might afford possibilities for personal and skill development, every lay leader will grow at a different pace. Each will respond differently on any given day. Our task as leaders is to be sensitive enough to the group that there can be something for everyone each time it meets. There is no excuse for not giving people the chance to become all they can be as individuals and as Christians.

Effective youth ministry teams can be grown, though there are no short cuts or easy answers. The task will always be challenging and at times difficult. Still, given the reality of God's presence in our lives, we can all work at growing healthy interdependent lay leaders.

FOR FURTHER READING

Johnson, Douglas W. *The Care and Feeding of Volunteers*. Nashville: Abingdon, 1978.

Ludwig, Glenne E. *Building an Effective Youth Ministry*. Nashville: Abingdon, 1979.

Nouwen, Henri J. M. *The Wounded Healer*. Garden City, N.Y.: Doubleday, 1972.

Stone, J. David, and Rose Mary Miller. *Volunteer Youth Workers*. Loveland, Colo.: Group Publishers, 1985.

Wagner, C. Peter. *Your Spriritual Gifts Can Help Your Church Grow.* Ventura, Calif.: Regal, 1979.

Wilson, Marlene. *The Effective Management of Volunteer Programs*. Arlington, Va.: Volunteer Management Associates, 1976.

————. *How to Mobilize Church Volunteer Programs*. Minneapolis: Augsburg, 1983.

————. *Survival Skills for Managers*. Arlington, Va.: Volunteer Management Associates, 1981.

Les Christie

12

Motivating Youth for Ministry

Mark was one of those young people who drifts through a youth group. He started attending youth activities the summer before his senior year. He was polite and friendly, but he did not fit the Southern California image. Physically, he was shaped like an ostrich. His head stuck out from his long, slender neck, and his back seemed to bend like a bow on his incredibly tall, frail frame. His voice was higher than that of most of the other boys, and he had an "absent-minded professor" stare with his head somewhere in the clouds.

Everyone liked Mark, but few took him seriously, and no one saw leadership potential in him. So when Mark announced he was going to a Christian college to become a minister, I needed cardiopulmonary resuscitation. I did not want to discourage him, so with difficulty I responded with a weak, "Great."

Mark had selected a college in another state, and when he left I thought that would be the last I would hear from him. It was not. He wrote me weekly asking several detailed questions on reaching kids in the inner city. He had started a mid-week Bible study in a large apartment complex in an extremely poor neighborhood. When I did not hear from Mark for about four months, I called to find out what had happened. He apologized for not writing and explained that his study group had grown to more than 100 and that he was

LES CHRISTIE, M.A., is minister to youth, Eastside Christian Church, Fullerton, California. A portion of this chapter was taken from the author's book *Servant-Leaders in the Making* (Wheaton, Ill.: Victor, 1983). Used with permission.

deeply involved in teaching other students how to start similar Bible studies at other apartment complexes in the same city. It was at that point in my ministry that I realized I could not always predict which kids would make a significant impact for the Lord. I understood that I needed to look at each young person as having leadership potential.

The ultimate goal of youth ministry is to bring young people to maturity in Christ, to prepare, disciple, and train them to serve God. One of the most effective methods for accomplishing that goal is to give youth real responsibility. By real responsibility I mean tasks that *stretch* them physically, socially, mentally, and most important, spiritually, so that they dream dreams and see visions of what God can do through their lives.

This concept is as old as Scripture. For example: "It is good for a man to bear the yoke while he is young" (Lam. 3:27). A yoke was normally made for two animals. Bearing the yoke expresses the idea of working alongside others who are performing similar tasks and striving for similar goals. Learning to handle burdens, tasks, and responsibilities helps prepare young people for life.

But developing leadership potential is not simply a matter of giving people jobs to do. Equally important is a principle found in a frequently quoted verse: "Train up a child in the way he should go. Even when he is old he will not depart from it" (Prov. 22:6, NASB*). Parents and youth workers have often been quick to claim this promise without heeding the command. One meaning of the phrase "train up" in Hebrew is "create a desire." The phrase was used to describe the action a Hebrew midwife would take at the birth of a child. She would rub her finger in some crushed dates, then place it on the roof of the newborn baby's mouth. That would induce the desire to suck, so the baby would begin to take nourishment. It is our job as youth workers to create a desire in young people to live for Christ and to serve Him. We can accomplish that by developing and using the gifts and abilities God has given them.

Two Ways to Motivate

One of the most frequently asked questions about developing student leadership is, How do you motivate young people to be leaders? How do you create the desire in them to be all they can be, with God working through them? To answer this question, consider two kinds of motivation, extrinsic and intrinsic.

EXTRINSIC MOTIVATION

Extrinsic motivation originates from some outside force. Something external makes the individual respond. Usually, extrinsic motivation takes the form of punishment or reward.

New American Standard Bible.

Punishment. With punishment, in order to get young people involved in training and service, we hold a shotgun to their heads. The most commonly used shotgun is *guilt.* We threaten, frighten, snarl, growl, bristle, and become just plain nasty in order to persuade kids to get involved in our programs.

Even if that kind of external pressure gets immediate results, when the pressure lets up, so does the person's response. Whether it is used to persuade a young person to become a Christian, to attend a meeting, or to accept a responsibility, punishment usually backfires. When punishment is used to generate involvement, people may get involved physically, but mentally they are miles away.

The result of motivation by punishment is illustrated by an unusual statistic I came across a few years ago regarding the amount of water used on Christian college campuses. More water is used on Sunday from 10:00 A.M. to 12:00 noon than at any other time of the week. The reason is that many college students sleep in. Then they get up, take long showers, and wash clothes instead of going to church. It seems their parents used extrinsic motivation to get them to go to church when they were younger, and now they are rebelling and doing what they want.

Reward. With this method we try to motivate young people by rewarding them. Extrinsic reward is probably the most common method used by Christian youth workers. We offer kids something to entice them, a bribe, prize, tribute, or an offer they simply cannot refuse. Howard Hendricks calls this the lollipop method of motivation. It may appear relatively harmless, but it can have negative effects.

One of the bad side effects is to produce young people who come to activities merely to be entertained. It fosters a self-centered, narcissistic attitude: What am I going to get out of this? Young people begin to think everything rotates around them, which destroys the servant concept of Christianity. Whatever you win young people with is what you win them to.

That becomes even clearer when the reward is removed. Young people stop coming because their primary motivation is the reward. They begin to look for another church that offers a more appealing enticement. The young people are not committed to the true mission of the church, but instead they are coming for the show.

The results of this lollipop method came home forcefully to me when I heard of a certain high schooler who had brought a friend to a youth group function. The program was great, packed with enjoyable activities. It was meant to attract non-Christians, and it was successful. But, as the high schooler expressed to me, her friend was disappointed that no one said anything about Jesus. Her friend was a non-Christian who fully expected to hear about Christianity at a church program and felt cheated that she did not. That visitor never came back.

Extrinsic motivation is the least effective form of motivation. The only time extrinsic motivation is legitimate is when it triggers intrinsic motivation. However, one can never be sure it will.

I became a Christian through extrinsic motivation that eventually triggered intrinsic motivation. I had attended Sunday school briefly while I was in fifth grade, but my particular class was chaotic. There was no discipline, so I did not learn much. I stopped going to Sunday school when my family moved to another city.

Later, when I was in high school, a friend invited me to his church. I made excuses not to go, until he finally mentioned that the teacher of the high school class had an airplane. My friend explained that if I came to Sunday school with him for three weeks in a row, the teacher would take both of us up in his plane. I went for the bait and was rewarded with the airplane ride. The teacher of the class then told me that if I brought a friend three times in a row, I could fly with my friend.

The class began to grow. Everyone was bringing friends. That went on for a little over a year until, suddenly, disaster struck. The man stopped teaching the high school group and took his airplane with him. We students were devastated. Our class took a nosedive in attendance. The extrinsic motivation had been removed.

But in that year's time, a few of us had caught a glimpse of Jesus. As a result, our motivation for going to Sunday school no longer depended on an airplane. We had developed an intrinsic desire to be there.

Without extrinsic motivation I might not be a Christian today. So I have a difficult time ruling it out altogether. Nevertheless, I also recognize that it is the least desirable form of motivation.

INTRINSIC MOTIVATION

Extrinsically motivated people are spiritual babies, always relying on external persuasion. But intrinsically motivated people are self-starters. They do not need the threat of punishment or the promise of reward to get them to go to meetings, read their Bibles, pray, and serve—to take responsibility in living the Christian life. Their motivation comes from within.

John was a high schooler who became intrinsically motivated. He was a leader who would follow through with tasks given to him. Furthermore, he was goal oriented in that he was firmly committed to the Lord and wanted to serve Him in some way. He would be at every meeting, listening, attentive, asking thought-provoking questions. John was interested in making films. He started a Christian film-making team and made several brief (five minutes or less) 8 mm films for our youth group. They were crudely put together, but there was a spark of creativity in each one, and John was determined to make better films. Some of these early ones were "Jonah Meets Jaws" and "The

Stink" which gives an idea of the "fine quality" of these films. They were not fantastic, but John did get the message across.

John now makes Christian films for a living. Some of his award-winning films include *Super Christian, Kevin Can Wait, The Greatest Story Never Told,* and *The Wait of the World.* This chapter is written to help you tap into that intrinsic motivation that I believe exists in every young person.

THE BASICS OF LEADERSHIP DEVELOPMENT

ALLOW FAILURE

Caution: Do not do anything for the youth in your group that they are capable of doing for themselves. Violate this principle at the risk of creating a group of spiritual babies who rely on adult leaders instead of learning to trust God.

Jesus emphasized this principle many times. When Peter asked if he could join Jesus in His walk on the water, Jesus encouraged him to jump right in (Matt. 14:29). We do not know exactly what happened next. Maybe Andrew yelled, "Watch out for the wave on the right, Pete!" But for some reason, Peter took his eyes off Jesus, got scared, and began to sink. Jesus allowed Peter to learn through failure. Through his failure, he learned to keep his eyes on the Lord.

In the parable of the prodigal son (Luke 15), the father allowed his son to fail. The father knew the boy would waste his money in riotous living, but he also knew that some things can only be learned through failure. When the son came to his senses, the father was waiting with open arms.

Becky was responsible for publicity in our youth group. We had an important activity coming up that we hoped would attract a lot of non-Christian kids. Becky completed only half of the publicity and left it unfinished with a note on my desk. She was hoping I would finish it for her.

I called her home and left a message with her mother, explaining that the publicity was Becky's responsibility and that if she did not do it, it would not get done. Becky did not complete it, and only half the number of kids we were expecting showed up.

The following Monday, Becky came into my office. I asked her what happened. She explained and said that she felt she had let down the whole group. I agreed with her and asked what she thought she should do next.

"Maybe I should just quit!" she responded.

"Quit? Quit!" I replied.

"Well, maybe I shouldn't quit," said Becky.

We talked about responsibility and commitment. Becky saw how she could change her priorities and schedule in order to get things done. We prayed together that God would use her. Becky was a dynamite publicity chairwoman from that day on. I could always count on her.

Becky is now married, and she is an active leader of a large young-married group at our church. Becky learned by being allowed to fail, dust herself off, and go at it again.

We overreact to pressure in a teen's life, especially pressure that is causing pain when we can do something to relieve it. Instead of helping them work through the pressure, we think of how we can get them out of it. Maybe instead of rescuing the perishing, we should let them learn to swim.

DEVELOP INDEPENDENT THINKING

It is alarming that students who were once involved members of high school youth groups drop out of church life at a staggering rate when they reach college years. One reason for this high dropout rate is that we treat high schoolers as if they were still in diapers. We do not challenge them to think. Instead, we encourage them to regurgitate the words we give them without thinking ideas through.

Then they hit the university campus. Some atheistic professor asks, "Who believes in the Bible?" And our little Alberta raises her hand. The prof asks, "Why?" And Alberta responds with an answer that says in effect, "Because my adult youth group leader said I should." The professor proceeds to slice little Alberta into a hundred pieces and have her for lunch. She never knows what hit her.

We need to be teaching young people that life is not a game with cheerleaders yelling, "Go, Christian, go," but rather a battlefield. Better that young people fail in the youth group and succeed in the world than vice versa.

That is not always an easy principle to practice, as I discovered when I met for a year with a group of eight high-school-age student leaders. We met every Wednesday night for forty-five minutes and spent fifty-two weeks studying the gospel of John. I would give the eight students the lesson material on Wednesday, and the following Monday night, in pairs, they would give the same material to their peers in four different homes.

On Wednesday nights, after forty-five minutes of my ramblings on the passage in John, I would ask the students if they were ready to present the lesson. They would all nod affirmatively. Then I would fire a difficult question at them about the passage. They would moan and complain, "No one will think of asking that," or, "How are we supposed to know?" or, "That's too hard." Then we would begin the process of searching for the answer in commentaries, concordances, word-study books, and Bible atlases. When the students could answer the question satisfactorily, I would ask them another. This process would go on for another forty-five minutes.

The kids would get so mad at me, I could see it in their eyes. I would tangle them up, and dangle them until they began to wonder whose side I was on. But when they left that room, they went out with eyes of steel, muttering under their breath to the world, "Ask me a question from this passage in John! Ask me anything!"

When students trained like that hit the university campus, they *look* for the atheistic profs and sit in the front row with their oversized Bibles prominently displayed. They can hardly wait for the prof to challenge their faith.

What makes the difference? Allowing young people to fail. We must allow them to fail, to fall flat on their posteriors if need be. Let them fail in the youth group so they can stand up tall in Christ when they're out in the world!

Too often we give children answers to remember rather than problems to solve. We need to teach kids to question more answers instead of answering more questions.

Parker Palmer tells of a history teacher who has learned how to open "space" in a lecture.

> At the end of this incredible lecture in a college class, the students were overwhelmed by all the knowledge he dumped on them. He said to them, "You can tear up all your notes because much of what I have said to you is untrue. Some of it was so patently false you should have been suspicious. From time to time in the coming term I will slip in more lies. It will be up to you to catch them and to challenge me if you want to get things straight. I will not accept any of my own lies as answers on exams. They are false even if I did say them. Class dismissed." Can you imagine what happened the rest of the year in that class?[1]

GIVE ENCOURAGEMENT

According to Acts 4:36, Barnabas's name means "Son of Encouragement." Young people need youth workers who will be Barnabases to them. They need someone to tell them, just as Paul told Timothy, that being young and inexperienced does not make them nobodies: "Don't let anyone look down on you because you are young, but set an example for the believers in speech, in life, in love, in faith, and in purity" (1 Tim. 4:12).

If our youth are to become God's leaders, we must become their encouragers. Our job is to build the confidence that God is working through them even when things look terrible.

Several years ago Jeff, a junior in our high school group, had difficulty with stuttering. He was also shy and tended to be an introvert. Once a month we put on a worship service at a local convalescent home. Some of our young people would lead singing, others would help bring the residents into the

1. Parker J. Palmer, *To Know As We Are Known* (New York: Harper & Row, 1983), p. 78.

recreation room, and one would preach. I was excited but a little anxious about Jeff's speaking to these people. Our adult volunteers worked with him the entire month on his sermon.

The Sunday finally came. Jeff began to speak, with very few of the residents listening to him. He was about five minutes into his brief message when suddenly one older man in a wheelchair near the back woke up and out of nowhere said loudly, "Preach it boy!" Jeff got excited. He really started to get into his sermon, and it was dynamite.

When Jeff finished the sermon all our kids gathered around him and told him what a great job he had done and how God had used him. Jeff was never the same again. He became a servant-leader in our group. Jeff is now married, and he is still active in our church. I have a cassette tape of the message he gave that Sunday. It reminds me that you can never tell what a few encouraging words will do to a young person's life.

BE POSITIVE

Youth workers try hard to maintain a positive outlook. Unfortunately, too many of us are more like the grandfather who fell asleep in his rocking chair. The grandson came in and put Limburger cheese on the grandfather's moustache. He soon awakened and said, "My, this room smells bad." He walked around the house and said, "This whole house smells bad." Then he walked outside and said, "This whole neighborhood smells bad." Of course, it was not the neighborhood, the house, or the room, it was the cheese on his own moustache that he was smelling.

Sometimes we get discouraged, ready to throw in the towel and blame the youth for our problems. It may not be the kids. We may need to examine our ministries more closely and pray that God will help us view the situation more positively.

What do you do when three kids show up for a meeting and you were expecting ten? "Three of you! No wonder our youth group is falling apart. Only three of you show up. Three of you! Can you believe this?" The three who did make an effort to attend can hardly wait to come back!

Some people see a glass half empty; they focus on the hole in the donut; they see all the empty chairs in a roomful of people. Such persons do not get very far in developing leadership potential in youth. Young people need positive youth workers.

As long as you think kids cannot, they will not. Always be looking for something positive you can point out in your youth. They never forget a good word you say about them. One of the reasons I am in youth ministry today is because, in a chaotic fifth-grade Sunday school class, a lady I barely knew mentioned that she thought I would make a good youth worker. I never forgot it.

BE ENTHUSIASTIC

Mr. B., the minister of the church I attended during high school, was a completed Jew, and I thoroughly enjoyed hearing him preach and being around him. He was about five feet five inches tall and weighed about 180 pounds, a solid ball of dynamite. He encouraged me to drop by the church office on the way home from school, and I did—often. He was a fascinating person with many wonderful stories.

I will never forget the first time I went to visit Mr. B. in his office after school. I had been going to the church only a couple of weeks, but he had encouraged me from the pulpit to start reading my Bible. I did. I had never read it before, and when I came to the Scripture about Lazarus rising from the dead, it seemed incredible to my young pagan mind. I had to show Mr. B.

Mr. B. was sitting behind his desk when I shared my "find" with him. In looking back now I am surprised he did not laugh and say, "Les, I've read that a dozen times." Instead, he jumped up from his desk, ran around it, and sat next to me. He became as excited about that passage of Scripture as I was. He said, "How about that," and he let me talk about it. It may have been old and familiar to him, but he never let on. He knew it was a fresh discovery for me. He was so enthusiastic that I could not wait to return again to share with him new insights I had gained from other sections of God's Word. Soon he was telling me about Jesus rising from the dead and what Jesus could do in my life. Mr. B.'s enthusiasm was definitely contagious, and he clearly had a positive impact on my life.

The word *enthusiasm* comes from Greek words that mean "God in us." We Christians have God living in us. How can we not be enthusiastic? The book of Acts shows how enthusiastic the early Christians were. For example: "We cannot stop telling about the wonderful things we saw Jesus do and heard Him say" (Acts 4:20, TLB*).

I hope you thank God every day that He has allowed you to be a youth worker. I know there are days when you want to give up. But remember, youth work is not a 100-yard dash, it is a 26-mile marathon. "Do you not know that in a race all the runners run, but only one gets the prize? Run in such a way as to get the prize" (1 Cor. 9:24).

SHOW UNCONDITIONAL LOVE

Perhaps the most important key to developing leadership potential in youth is to simply love them unconditionally. It is not always easy to look at every kid in your youth group as having potential, especially the kid that drives you up the wall. Do you have some you secretly pray will not show up at your next meeting? They are probably the ones that need our love the most. Love motivates and tends to bring out the best in people. Remember, if a kid is

The Living Bible.

sharp enough to get into trouble, he is probably creative enough to become someone significant.

Even though he was not a Christian, the famous Indian political leader Mahatma Gandhi used a Christian principle when he looked for the image of God in people. He often changed people by regarding them not as what they were, but as though they were what they wished to be.

I have always looked at my job as being that of an Andrew or a Barnabas. They are the ones who introduced the Peters, Pauls, and John Marks to Jesus. They were not in the limelight. They tended to blend in with the woodwork of Scripture. What a privilege to realize that I too may have a small part in God's molding of future leaders.

SELECTING AND TRAINING SERVANT-LEADERS

Be open and available to every young person God gives you to work with. That does not mean you have to give equal time and energy to each one. Just as Jesus selected twelve men—and even an inner group of three, in whom He invested most of His time and energy—select a few key students and make their development a top priority. They, in turn, will become equipped to minister to their peers. That was the idea Paul expressed to Timothy: "And the things you have heard me say in the presence of many witnesses entrust to reliable men who will also be qualified to teach others" (2 Tim. 2:2).

How do you select these student leaders? Traditionally, we have used some strange methods. Sometimes we choose a young person to be a leader because he is so hard to handle. If we put him into a leadership position, maybe he will straighten out, so the thinking goes. What does that approach say to the young person who has been part of the group for years and wants desperately to serve, but because he is quiet and well behaved, gets neglected and ignored? We are telling him that the way to be a leader is to be rowdy.

Then there is the election method, often equally unproductive. In many youth groups, election time is a time of political speeches, banners, and posters that result in jealousy, contention, confusion, and hurt feelings. For example, say we have three people running for president of the youth group. One wins, the other two are out. Or we make one of the losers the vice-president (usually not a very exciting position). Or we give them other do-nothing jobs, such as lightswitch or chalkboard monitor.

Another possible method is that of appointing students to specific leadership functions. Naturally we tend to appoint students we know best. Many times these are the outgoing extroverts. As a result, we may neglect the quieter introvert who also could be used by God. And other young people, personally less familiar to us and who might make terrific leaders, are simply skipped over. Another danger with this method is that it may cause ill feelings. All the pressure for the selection falls firmly on your shoulders. That may open you to the criticism of showing favoritism.

Scripture does not give a specific pattern for the selection of leaders. But one biblical principle is clear: *God's leaders are to be chosen primarily on the strength of their spiritual lives, not their personalities.* That does not mean God promotes mediocrity. Rather, He chooses to use and develop the abilities of those people who are living in obedience to Him, those who are willing to be used by Him.

God can use the beauty queens, the star athletes, the kids with brains or money, or the elder's kids. But they must be willing to be like clothing in His ready-to-wear department, clothes the Holy Spirit can slip into and use any time.

The method of selecting student leaders will vary from church to church according to church policy, maturity of the youth group, and the model of youth ministry employed by the church. Yet three factors are essential if the student leader is to emerge as a spiritual leader.

QUALIFICATIONS

Several weeks before youth group leaders are to be selected, ask members to pray that the right people will be chosen. On selection day, give each voter a list of your youth group members in alphabetical order. Review some of the characteristics of a man or woman of God, such as Galatians 5:22-23, Titus 1:7-9, 1 Timothy 3:8-13, 1 Corinthians 13:4-8, and 2 Peter 1:5-8. Then instruct voters to circle the names of those members they believe God wants to lead the youth group. They can circle as many or as few names as they want.

Next, with the help of other adult youth workers, tabulate the ballots. Then review the list of top vote getters with your adult co-workers. Determine if someone has been elected whom you feel should *not* be in a leadership position. If that occurs (it rarely does) then the person with the next-highest number of votes is selected. This procedure makes leadership selection a combination democracy and dictatorship.

BALANCE

In selecting young leaders, it is also important not to let one class dominate and not to rely heavily on one particular grade. Otherwise, when that class graduates you will be left with a leadership void in the group. Determine how many you will select from each grade, possibly proportionate to the size of the grade. These student leaders are selected to serve for one year. They will be allowed to serve additional terms if selected by the youth group in the future. However, we must always be on the lookout for new faces.

SUPPORT

Before announcing the results, call the parents of the newly-elected leaders. Find out if they are willing for their young people to accept the responsibilities of leadership. Parents appreciate your getting their approval and input. (In our youth group, student leaders must be able to come to most of the activities, spend as much time as needed to fulfill their leadership responsibilities, and keep a quiet-time diary.)

If the parents give approval, visit each home and go over with the parents and the youth the tasks you are asking him to do. Finally, call a leaders' meeting in which each newly elected leader is asked to describe his tasks to the rest of the group. That will help you know whether each leader understands what his job will involve.

EXPECTATIONS OF STUDENT LEADERS

SERVANT LEADERSHIP

Make clear to these newly elected leaders that they are to be servant-leaders (in our group they are responsible for cleaning up after every function). Theirs is not an elevated but a lowly position. It will cost them something—mainly time, availability, and a lot of hard work. Frank F. Warren has said, "If you wish to be a leader you will be frustrated, for few people wish to be led. If you aim to be a servant, you will never be frustrated."[2] How many people do you know who say "servant" when asked what their career ambitions are?

Whenever servants see a need, they will be the first to volunteer. They are doing this not to earn spiritual points or to be publicly recognized, but simply to serve. They are to follow the leadership style of Jesus in Luke 22:27, "I am among you as one who serves," and Matthew 23:11, "The greatest among you will be your servant."

LOYALTY

These servant-leaders are to be loyal to each other and to the adult leaders who work with them. They are to be supportive and positive about the plans made by fellow servant-leaders. They are to stand by each other and defend one another. That does not mean they cannot disagree or have their own opinions, but once a decision has been reached, they will support that decision.

I do not like voting on decisions. That tends to be divisive, when the vote turns out to be eight in favor and four against. I prefer to have our servant-leaders talk out the decision until we can come to a unanimous decision and everyone has had his say and input in molding the final decision.

If these servant-leaders are to become God's leaders they need to be willing to go for broke. They need to demand the best of themselves and be consistent and loyal to the Christian walk.

---

2. Frank F. Warren, cited in Kenneth McGuire, "Belaying: A Model For Ministry," in *Pastoral Life* (April 1982).

MINISTRY TO FELLOW STUDENTS

The main task of all servant-leaders is to care for the other kids in the youth group, including the other servant-leaders. Each servant-leader not only has certain tasks to do but also has a group of people to whom he is to minister. For example, the servant-leader in charge of socials may have six or seven other students who work with him. The servant-leader is to minister to these other young people. Paul described Timothy as a leader who had that kind of relationship with those he led: "I have no one else like him [Timothy], who takes a genuine interest in your welfare" (Phil. 2:20). Timothy genuinely cared about people. Train your servant-leaders to follow Timothy's example.

Dawson Trotman, founder of the Navigators, died in a boating accident at the age of fifty. He was in a boat when a girl fell overboard. Dawson, a good athlete, dived into the water to rescue her. He lifted the girl up safely into the boat. But then something went wrong, and he fell back into the water and died.

In reporting Dawson Trotman's death, *Life* magazine wrote, "He was always lifting others up." What a tremendous epitaph. I want my servant-leaders always to remember that *people* come first. I want them to know how the kids in their task-related group and those in the rest of the youth group are doing—spiritually, physically, emotionally, and socially. I want them to know that their main job is to "lift up" other young people.

GOAL ORIENTATION

Help each servant-leader select a group of young people to work with. Each group is responsible for a specific ministry (publicity, visitation, discipleship, missions, etc.), and the servant-leader is in charge of the group.

Try to assign one adult leader to each group as well. These adult leaders assist, but they do not run the group projects. That responsibility lies in the hands of the servant-leaders who oversee the group. The group projects become *their* successes and their failures. The adults serve merely as facilitators. For example, if one of the servant-leaders is in charge of publicity, the adult youth leader might show the student how to do the job. Once he understands how to do it, it becomes his responsibility. The process looks something like this:

I do it — they watch
I do it — they help
They do it — I help
They do it — I watch

The ultimate goal is "that we may present everyone perfect [mature, complete, whole] in Christ" (Col. 1:28) and "to prepare God's people for works of service [ministry], so that the body of Christ may be built up" (Eph. 4:12). Every activity must be considered in light of these verses.

Ask, Will this activity bring young people to maturity in Christ and prepare them for ministry? If it will not, then it should be scratched. Whatever you win youth *with* is what you win them *to*.

Clearly defined goals put handles on your dreams. I remember John F. Kennedy's pronouncement in 1961 that the United States would put a man on the moon before the sixties were over. That vision seemed unrealistic and unattainable. But goals were established, target dates were set, and the dream was kept in the forefront of people's thoughts. Then, on July 20, 1969, Neil Armstrong stepped onto the moon.

Goal-oriented people take criticism and handle rejection better than those who have no goals. It is better to have a goal and fall short of it than to fail to set a goal at all.

Setting goals is important. If your student leaders have no goals they will:

Attempt to do too much or too little
Major in the minors
Not see the significance of details
Not be related to life needs
Have few or no results

Goals are needed for efficiency. Be sure you have specific goals at committee meetings to get the task done. Goals are important so that you do not get lost from one youth meeting to the next.

Goals are motivators. They help students get going each day. Goals give their lives purpose and direction, bring the future into the present, and help them realize their dreams.

The key is to set goals and then remain open to God's guidance. After setting a goal, we must move in that direction, while continually seeking God's will and timing by praying and listening to what the Lord wants to say to us. God is faithful to guide us if we really want to do what pleases Him.

GROWTH

Too many young people in the church are constantly taking in but never giving anything out. Such a condition is not healthy. We must provide opportunities for ministry and service if we want to develop the leadership potential in young people, stretching them and encouraging them to dream dreams.

I do not want these servant-leaders to be like stagnant ponds. I want servant-leaders who are young people of commitment.

They are committed to their own personal study of God's Word. They can say with Jeremiah, "When Your words came . . . they were my joy and my heart's delight" (Jer. 15:16).

They are committed to a consistent, personal prayer life (1 Thess. 5:17).

They are committed to keeping a clear conscience (Heb. 13:18).
They are committed to their own families (Eph. 5:22-25).
They are committed to serving (Gal. 5:13).

PROBLEMS EXPERIENCED BY STUDENT-LEADERS

BURNOUT

The Bible records how Elijah suffered from burnout, even though he was obedient to the Lord and had a successful ministry. He single-handedly took on 450 prophets of Baal (1 Kings 18:17-46). Yet when Queen Jezebel said she was going to kill him, he ran 120 miles in the opposite direction (1 Kings 19:1-4).

Burnout is a depletion of emotional resources. Elijah was so exhausted, he lay under a bush and prayed to the Lord that he might die. Elijah did not want to die. If he *really* wanted to die, I know a woman 120 miles back up the road who would have been glad to accommodate him. Have you ever thanked God for unanswered prayer? I think Elijah did on that day. He simply was exhausted.

If the adult leaders know their kids, they will know how much responsibility to put on each student-leader. There is a fine line between stretching young people and burning them out. Help them each to set a pace that is best for them.

Some kids may have extra responsibilities at home or school. Some may have to help out the family financially. Be sensitive as you lead, and desire the best of these young people. I have found that the senior year is a difficult time for high schoolers. Many have to work as they get ready for college.

PRIDE

One of the greatest dangers of pride is that it implies over-confidence and, in turn, breeds a careless attitude toward spiritual realities. When a student-leader begins to place confidence in himself alone, he is on the brink of disaster. God will deal with leaders who refuse to give the glory to Him. The Bible clearly states in Proverbs 16:18, "Pride goes before destruction," and in Daniel 5:20, "But when his heart became arrogant, and hardened with pride, he was deposed from his royal throne and stripped of his glory."

Each of us has a desire for recognition, a desire to be important or influential. John calls it the pride of life. It is a desire to be noticeably superior, and it explains why student-leaders may have difficulty associating with people who do not reflect their own self-perception.

DISCOURAGEMENT

Discouragement usually comes from comparing yourself with someone else and feeling guilty because you are not doing as much. Adult leaders must also guard against comparing one leader with another. Some kids have more abilities. Some kids have twelve cylinders, some have two. It would not be fair to look at each leader from the same viewpoint.

Someone has suggested that discouragement is the devil's calling card. That "calling card" often immobilizes even the best-prepared student-leaders.

TIME MANAGEMENT

Here are some time-saving ideas for student-leaders.

1. Use a "things to do" list.
   a. Put things in groups: phone calls, errands, letter writing, homework.
   b. Do not put too many things on the list, or you will be overwhelmed and not get anything done.
   c. For self-motivation, give yourself a certain amount of time to get an item done.
   d. Tackle one thing and work on it until finished. Then mark it off with a bright red Flair pen.
2. Learn to say no. Practice saying it in front of the mirror.
3. Share the workload. Delegate by enlisting others. Some things should never be done alone: weight lifting, swimming, youth ministry.
4. Do not rely on your memory. Write things down.
5. Use your keys as a reminder. Put them on top of items you want to take with you. When it is time to go, as you grab your keys you will remember to take items under them.
6. Write thank-you notes immediately.
7. Block out time on calendar to read, relax, goof off, pray.
8. Find a secret hiding place where you can go and not be interrupted by phone calls or by people dropping by.

QUIET TIME

It is possible as a leader to get so busy that you begin to lose perspective of your ministry. The genuinely important items get placed on the back burner. We begin to run around at a frantic pace but accomplish little for the Lord or His kingdom.

Student-leaders must set aside a definite time each day to get into God's word, pray, and meditate—a time to be alone with God. Mike Yaconelli in the *Wittenberg Door* clearly states the need for quiet. He writes:

> Isn't it wonderful that, in today's technological world, most of us never have to experience actual quiet? Most of us cannot even remember those horrible days when people were forced to experience long periods of silence—when people were forced to think.

With the sudden easy accessibility of noise to the masses, with the onslaught of technological advancement, with the proliferation of TV and radio, and with the invention of the waterproof Walkman, this generation is well within reach of what generations before us have only dreamed about—The Quietless Society.

Maybe it is time for Christians to be quiet and let the still, small voice of God be heard in the silence.[3]

Encourage your young people to keep a quiet-time diary to record their thoughts from a passage of Scripture read and to record prayer requests and answers.

FOR FURTHER READING

Bridges, Jerry. *The Pursuit of Holiness*. Colorado Springs, Colo.: NavPress, 1978.

Collins, Gary R. *Give Me a Break*. Old Tappan, N.J.: Revell, 1982.

Eims, Leroy. *Be a Motivational Leader*. Wheaton, Ill.: Victor, 1981.

Getz, Gene A. *Building Up One Another*. Wheaton, Ill.: Victor, 1976.

Hyde, Douglas. *Dedication and Leadership*. Notre Dame, Ind.: U. of Notre Dame, 1966.

Kohlberg, Lawrence, *The Philosophy of Moral Development*. 2 vols. San Francisco: Harper & Row, 1981, 1985.

McAllister, Dawson. *Discussion Manual for Student Discipleship*. Englewood, Colo.: Shepherd Productions, 1975.

Moore, Waylon B. *Multiplying Disciples*. Colorado Springs, Colo.: NavPress, 1981.

3. Mike Yaconelli, "The Quietless Society," in *Wittenberg Door* (October-November 1984), p. 32.

Part 3

Principles of Church Youth Ministry

13

Mark H. Senter III

Axioms of Youth Ministry

"As excellent as last year's youth ministry was at Bloomingdale Evangelical Church, this year has been bad. Really bad," confessed Ned to the youth workers in his workshop session. "If I had done this session last year, I might have entitled it All You Ever Wanted to Know About Youth Work but Were Afraid to Ask. This year I am tempted to call it The Youth Ministry Blues, Brothers."

The development of the church's youth ministry had been like a fairy tale during Ned Burgess's first three years in Bloomingdale. Village, church, school district, and youth group all seemed to mushroom in tandem. Though a significant part of the proportion of the new students and leaders had moved to the community from the racially changing urban areas twenty miles away, Ned's greatest joy had come from the non-Christians who had been reached and were now being discipled into the church.

But that was last year.

June had seen the graduation of the key student leaders Ned and his youth sponsors had been discipling over the past three years. Now the greatest spiritual maturity and leadership potential appeared to be in the freshman class. Numbers had dropped off. Non-Christians were not being reached in any significant manner. Momentum seemed to have been lost.

MARK H. SENTER III, M.A., Ph.D. candidate, is assistant professor of Christian education at Trinity Evangelical Divinity School, Deerfield, Illinois.

Yet there was Ned, standing in front of forty-five youth workers, explaining how the ministry should be done. He had two options. Either tell the expectant audience the glory stories from the last three years or honestly confess that hard times had come to Bloomingdale's youth ministry and attempt to discern what had been beginner's luck and what had been biblically sound ministry principles.

This chapter is an effort to isolate ministry principles that apply in all of the models of youth ministry (see chap. 15, "Models of Youth Ministry"). Thus the ideas are referred to as *axioms,* or propositions regarded as self-evident truths. Though some supporting evidence will be provided for certain axioms, the various propositions are offered as insights based on the successes and failures of a generation of youth ministry practitioners.

An important distinction must be made at the outset. *Youth ministry* involves adults whose primary desire is to disciple students in their Christian faith; *youth work* is a broader term that does not necessitate Christian discipleship; whereas *youth movement* in a Christian context describes a process of discipling young people by other young people in which adults play a decidedly secondary leadership role.

Thus the Student Volunteer Movement and Student Foreign Missions Fellowship as well as many aspects of the Jesus People movement are not considered youth ministry because they were student led. Similarly, the activities of the YMCA, Boys Club of America, most aspects of Scouts, and youth athletic leagues are not youth ministry because Christian discipleship is peripheral to their primary purpose.

Axiom 1

Youth ministry begins when a Christian adult finds a comfortable method of entering a student's world.[1]

Though some adults feel comfortable spending time with adolescents, a large proportion of Christian adults would feel rather awkward attempting to build a relationship with a high school student without some kind of excuse to do so. Parents of students similarly might look with skepticism on adults who appear to be spending time with their children without apparent rationale. Consequently, the comfort zone must to some degree include student, parent, and Christian youth worker.

Entering a student's world can be described as contact work. The idea was capsulized by Young Life staff member John Mackay when he spoke of "earning the right to be heard."[2] The idea was not new, for adults had been earning

1. Ken Green, *Insights: Building a Successful Youth Ministry* (San Bernardino, Calif.: Here's Life, 1981), pp. 61-66.
2. Emile Cailliet, *Young Life* (New York: Harper & Row, 1963), p. 62.

a right to be heard by youth through organizational systems for years. Young Lifers merely applied it to a new area, that of relationships. Their contention was that the basis of evangelism and discipleship is a relationship, not a system.

Today at least four kinds of contact work can be identified. *Natural contacts* are made by people who, by virtue of their personalities and positions, attract young people to themselves. Certain schoolteachers, employers, athletes, and media people would fall into this category. Students, for one reason or another, find them fun to be around, and so the contact that can lead to discipleship has been made.

A second kind of contact is *adult-initiated contact.* This is done by people who may not be with students on a normal basis but who use a skill or interest to meet a need in the life of a student. Tutors, nonprofessional coaches, mechanics, computer specialists, musicians, and youth ministers could all use their abilities in fields of interest to young people to gain a hearing for the gospel.

Program-initiated contact is a third way for adults to gain a hearing with youth. Sunday school, youth group activities, youth choirs, camps, retreats, and clubs are activities in which adults make contact with students when the young people come to be involved with a formal organization geared to their interests or needs. Thus the program provides the comfort zone for adults, students, and parents.

A final kind of contact work is that of *parental contact.* When youth ministers were asked who had been instrumental in shaping their spiritual development, one answer was heard rather frequently: their own parents or the parent of a close friend to whom they went in time of need. Though this could be an extension of *natural contact,* it deserves special attention because so frequently parents forget that they, too, are youth ministers.[3]

IMPLICATIONS

1. The most comfortable method for an adult to earn the right to be heard by students will differ from person to person as well as from situation to situation in any one person's life. There simply is no *one* right way to enter a student's world.

2. At the same time, youth ministry will not happen unless someone has earned the right to enter the student's world. Just as redemption would not have happened if the God-man had not entered time and space to live, die, and live again, so the Christian discipleship of students will not take place without flesh and blood relationships (John 1:14).

3. Mark H. Senter III, "What Contributes to Spiritual Maturity?" *Youthworker* vol. 3, no. 1 (Spring 1986), pp. 40-44.

Axiom 2

Youth ministry happens as long as a Christian adult is able to use his or her contact with a student to draw that student into a maturing relationship with God through Jesus Christ.[4]

Maturity, like excellence, is much easier to recognize than to describe. When one focuses on an aspect of maturity as elusive to describe as spirituality, the idea of defining spiritual maturity becomes exceedingly difficult.[5] Yet, for purposes of this discussion, a definition is in order.

> Spiritual maturity for a high school student is that stage in his or her relationship to God when he or she is capable and willing to allow biblical truth to shape his or her values, decisions, and actions.

Youth ministry happens only as long as the youth minister's efforts are moving students in this direction. The progress will not be smooth, for adolescence is a period of idealism and doubt, of success and failure, of growth and relapse. There may be periods when nothing appears to be happening. Then evidences of spiritual maturity will appear. Yet all of the youth minister's activity has one objective in mind: spiritually mature students. Everything else is merely "youth work."

An important gauge of youth ministry is the question, How often and to what extent are the students with whom I am working willing to share their fears and doubts, triumphs and joys, hopes and dreams, mistakes and sins, moods and feelings with me? These are the teachable times. These are the maturing times.[6]

At least three evidences of spiritual maturity can be found in Luke's description of the church following the day of Pentecost (Acts 2:41-47). First, people were being converted, signified by their baptism (v. 41). Second, they were learning biblical truth as explained by the apostles. They evidenced its impact by participating in the church's love feast, including Communion and prayer (v. 42). Third, they were learning to love each other, accepting the implications of that love by making material sacrifices for each other (v. 44).

The various models of youth ministry provide a context in which adults can assist young people in their spiritual pilgrimages. Team competition provides an opportunity for captain to confront team members with the claims of Christ. Drama, under the wise direction of a qualified adult, becomes a vehicle

---

4. See William R. Goetz, "Adult Leaders of Youth," in *Youth Education in the Church,* ed. Roy B. Zuck and Warren S. Benson (Chicago: Moody, 1978), p. 164.
5. For a useful discussion of the subject see "Maturity—The Goal for Church Youth," in Elmer L. Towns, *Successful Biblical Youth Work* (Nashville: John T. Benson, Impact Books, 1973). pp. 155-67.
6. For further treatment of facilitating relationships, see Lawrence O. Richards, *Youth Ministry: Its Renewal in the Local Church,* rev. ed. (Grand Rapids: Zondervan, 1985), pp. 119-30.

for ministry. Core groups, when guided by a caring leader, exemplify a redemptive community. Planning teams, when coached by nurturing adults, bring about leadership skills in the next generation of church leaders.[7]

IMPLICATIONS

1. Models of youth ministry are *vehicles* for assisting the spiritual maturation process in young people, nothing more. They are neither biblical nor unbiblical, right nor wrong, appropriate nor inappropriate in and of themselves.
2. Spiritual maturation appropriate to the youth group and the individuals within the group is the ultimate standard of success for the ministry. It is also the means by which adults working with youth should measure their effectiveness.

AXIOM 3

Youth ministry ceases to happen when the adult-student relationship is broken or no longer moves the student toward spiritual maturity.

It is quite possible for a strong youth ministry, or even part of a youth ministry, to slip unwittingly from youth ministry to youth work, from assisting young people in their spiritual maturation process to providing mere activities for the same students. In fact, if youth workers are not aware of this down side of youth ministry, their efforts may become frustratingly ineffective.

The two major aspects of axiom 3 may be linked in an apparent cause and effect connection, but for purposes of this discussion they will be examined separately. The first is broken relationships. Relationships can be severed in youth ministries in three primary ways. Adults and students can physically move away from each other, and though a discipling relationship can continue, more often than not new loyalties are established.

A second and more subtle manner in which ministry relationships can be broken is through adult and student drifting apart. As a student begins to take greater responsibility for his or her own spiritual growth, he or she may find that the need the adult had previously met in his or her life is no longer an issue. Or the mutual interest that initially drew adult and student together, such as sports, drama, music, or camping, is no longer a significant part of the student's life. New interests supersede older commitments. Relationships fade.

The least obvious and most detrimental manner in which ministry relationships can be broken is through a loss of respect by one or both of the adult-student tandem. Unfulfilled expectations, perceived inconsistencies, un-

---

7. Towns, citing a study by E. Michael Rustin, points out that the "average time spent by each youth sponsor per week was highest in the most successful churches: most successful youth groups spent 11.4 [hours per week with youth sponsors]; other sponsors . . . spent 3.9 hours. Most successful churches devoted an average of .7 hours per week per youth, while the average for the others was .2" (*Successful Biblical Youth Work*, p. 197).

confessed sin, unresolved inter-personal conflict, and unkept promises undermine the authority of the adult youth worker and bring about a loss of respect, especially on the part of the young person who may not have developed skills in conflict resolution. Whereas the "drift factor" may merely be developmental, the "respect factor" has its roots in spiritual matters and therefore needs to be identified and resolved lest long-term damage results.[8]

Adult-student relationships, though not broken, may become unproductive from a spiritual standpoint and thus bring youth ministry, at least for those people, to an end. A friendship can degenerate to a "buddy-buddy" arrangement wherein the adult is more like one of the students than the loving adult role model the young person needs. That is most common when an adult youth worker has an identity problem and is gaining his or her sense of worth from the students to whom he or she is ministering.[9]

Unproductivity can result when the student outgrows the spiritual leadership that an adult has to offer, especially in later adolescence when young people are most capable of coming to grips with the social, economic, political, and moral implications of the gospel. The need at this point may be to refocus the adult's activity on young people who need what he or she has to offer.

Romantic relationship between adult and student usually brings about unproductive youth ministry. Though stories have been told of the youth minister who marries a girl who had recently been a member of his group, actual examples of that are rare. More often ministry becomes unproductive on three fronts. First, the student becomes so emotionally involved with the adult that the student loses perspective on spiritual values. Second, other members of the youth group feel ill at ease about the relationship and may withdraw trust from the two involved. Finally, parents of other students may become resistant to the youth sponsors for fear that this will happen again.

Unproductivity can also result from the adult sponsor who focuses so exclusively on the specific skills around which the ministry model is built that the goal of spiritual maturity is obscured. Athletic activities, music, and Bible quizzing can all fall into this trap. It is a matter of the good becoming the enemy of the best.

IMPLICATIONS

1. Adults must accept their adultness in order to maximize their ministry potential. Youth ministry is no place to resolve a postponed identity crisis.
2. Adults must maintain their focus on bringing students to spiritual maturity through the ministry model employed. If the model becomes an end in itself, the ministry will tend to be lost by default.

8. See David Elkind, *All Grown Up and No Place to Go* (Reading, Mass.: Addison-Wesley, 1984), pp. 109-13.
9. Goetz, "Adult Leaders," p. 170.

3. By contrast, adults must be willing to release students when spiritual independence is necessary. The youth worker's "empty nest syndrome" may be as difficult for the loving youth worker as it is for the nurturing parents. Endless accountability, however, will become counterproductive.

AXIOM 4

The influence of the student's family on his or her value system will exceed the influence of the youth worker on most occasions.

There is a tendency among youth ministers to see themselves in isolation from any other sources of influence on the young person's spiritual development. Fortunately and unfortunately that is not true. It is fortunate because a majority of youth ministers have not gained the wisdom necessary to be solely responsible for a young person's spiritual development. It is unfortunate because the spiritual convictions of many parents are discouragingly vague.

Yet research points out that for the most part the church, and more specifically the youth minister, is only a temporary, though sometimes pivotal blip on the radarscreen of a young person's life. Reginald Bibby and Donald Posterski, in their 1984 survey of Canadian youth fifteen to nineteen years of age, concluded: "Teenagers readily adopt their parents' affiliation and religious self-image, along with some basic Judaic-Christian beliefs and selected practices. However, the majority neither profess religious commitment nor want extensive involvement with 'their' religious groups."[10] Commenting on that group's view of organized religion, the same researchers observed that Canadian teenagers "exhibit 'a polite posture' towards formal religion. A two-thirds majority indicate that they have a fairly high level of confidence in church leaders, similar to the confidence they accord educational, scientific and judicial leaders."[11]

Similarly, in their study of 8,156 young adolescents and 10,467 parents, American researchers Merton and Irene Strommen suggest that adolescents

> share the personal conviction of their parents about the importance of religion. A majority of the young adolescents say it is the most important or one of the most important influences in their lives. . . . The enigma, however, is this: though religion is identified as important by both parents and adolescents, it is almost a taboo subject at home.[12]

Despite this resounding silence in their homes, the Strommens conclude that "young adolescents in this study tend to experience religion as more liberating

10. Reginald W. Bibby and Donald C. Posterski, *The Emerging Generation: An Inside Look at Canada's Teenagers* (Toronto: Irvin Publishing, 1985), p. 128.
11. Ibid., pp. 119-20.
12. Merton P. Strommen and A. Irene Strommen, *Five Cries of Parents* (San Francisco: Harper & Row, 1985), p. 133.

than restricting. In part this means that young adolescents focus more on God's love than on God as judge or rule-giver."[13] It would appear that the absence of religious instruction in the home has allowed each young person to construct a concept of God that closely resembles parental attitudes gained informally in the home.

Admittedly, neither study is looking specifically at churches that employ youth ministers, but neither did the findings indicate that a difference might be found in such populations. Young people, comments Michael Rutter, "tend both to share their parents' values on the major issues of life and also to turn to them for guidance in most major concerns."[14]

Perhaps that is why Jehovah was so explicit in explaining to the Jewish parents in Deuteronomy 6 exactly how they were to go about passing the law from generation to generation. It was not through the priests or through the synagogue (which emerged later) or even through the prophet Moses that spiritual values were to be shaped. It was the family's responsibility.

What, then, is the function of the church and, more specifically, the youth group in discipling young people today? Perhaps the best way to describe the youth group's function is as a laboratory in which to test the appropriateness of parental spiritual values in the student's life. Of course that is not the only laboratory in which young people are experimenting, but it is a very important one.

IMPLICATIONS

1. A youth worker is only fooling himself if he thinks that the few hours he spends with a young person each week can offset the many years of informal education amassed by that young person's observing mother and dad. That is not to say the Holy Spirit is bound by a family conditioning process; it is merely to suggest that the Holy Spirit does not isolate the young person to the exclusive stewardship of the youth worker.
2. By contrast, the youth worker need not feel like a baby-sitter for a previously determined spiritual being over which he has no influence. He is called of God to assist the young person in examining biblical values and making them his own.

Axiom 5

Most youth groups reach peak effectiveness when attendance reaches twenty to thirty high school students.

One of the great frustrations to a new youth minister is the manner in which youth group growth stalls once the average attendance reaches about

13. Ibid. p. 137.
14. As quoted in Richards, *Youth Ministry,* p. 27.

thirty students. The reasoning goes something like this. Because group attendance was averaging close to twenty people each week before a youth minister was employed, the average should double or triple as a result of the extra amount of time a full-time youth pastor can invest in the ministry.

But that kind of reasoning is focused on the wrong factor. Unless the youth minister is an especially charismatic person with excellent communication skills, the mere injection of additional ministry time into the youth group is not enough to overcome the social dynamics of the group.

C. Peter Wagner points out that the average person feels known and accepted by no more than thirty people. There is a natural cohesion in such groups. People know each other's names, interests, frustrations, skills, and attitudes. People sense that other people care for them, and as a result they develop a high degree of commitment to that group.[15]

Donald C. Posterski, in his book *Friendship: A Window on Ministry to Youth,* supports Wagner's idea. "Healthy young people," comments Posterski, "want to influence their environment. They are attracted to circles of relationships in which their presence matters." Based on his research among 3,600 Canadian youth, he further observes that "bigness is not necessarily better when trying to touch people who have tasted intimacy and have experienced what it is to belong. Large size alone is threatening; it can alienate the very people the organization intends to help."[16]

Adults working with such groups need to have a clear perspective on what they can and should be doing for their students. Two primary functions stand out. Adults give or assist the group in finding a sense of direction that reflects biblical priorities and insure that each student retains a feeling of belonging within a loving, caring fellowship. These can be thought of as teaching and shepherding functions.

If a youth group is to grow beyond the twenty to thirty attendance range (and in many cases that is both desirable and necessary in order to do God's work in a community), youth workers will need to insure that the students do not view one or two adults as essential to the unity chemistry of the group. Friendship clusters, as Posterski calls them, with other adults involved, will need to be established within the large group in order to provide the social security necessary to reach out to more people.

IMPLICATIONS

1. Working harder may not increase the size of a youth group beyond a certain point. The youth minister could put in eighty-hour work weeks and not be able to break through the average attendance barrier that has developed.

15. C. Peter Wagner, *Your Church Can Grow* (Glendale, Calif.: Regal, 1976), pp. 97-109.
16. Donald C. Posterski, *Friendship: A Window on Ministry to Youth* (Scarborough, Ontario: Project Teen Canada, 1985), p. 14.

Better talks, more effectively organized committee meetings, stronger links with the students' parents, and more creative activities only assist growth to a certain point. Then, in most cases, growth stops.

2. Working smarter is the key that allows growth and continuity to happen beyond that given point. Working smarter invariably focuses on multiple leadership. As Gary Downing warns, "Don't do it alone! Some things are dangerous when done alone."[17] Volunteer youth workers with significant roles in the youth ministry are essential to working smarter and thus more productively.

AXIOM 6

Long term growth of a youth ministry is directly dependent on the ability of the youth worker to release ministry responsibilities to mature and qualified lay volunteers.

Delegation has a ring of General Motors, impersonal bureaucracies, and the worst aspects of big business. The stereotype is that of dumping unwanted jobs on unwilling workers. But the image of such coercive leaders as the corporate ideal, criticized by some youth ministry writers,[18] has been replaced more recently in management literature by the concept of networking. John Naisbitt in *Megatrends* states,

> The vertical to horizontal power shift that networks bring about will be enormously liberating for individuals. Hierarchies promote moving up and getting ahead, producing stress, tension and anxiety. Networking empowers the individual, and people in networks tend to nurture one another.[19]

Robert C. Coleman, in his classic book entitled *The Master Plan of Evangelism,* suggests that one of the essential elements of the Lord's ministry was delegation.[20] The idea was not at all of purging undesirable tasks from a busy leader but of sharing crucial responsibilities with carefully selected co-workers who could work together to accomplish the goal.

Early in my ministry, Kenneth Wessner, now the chairman of the board of Servicemaster Industries, shared this idea with me: "Delegate the things you do best." When I reacted with surprise, he went on to explain that the things one does best are the easiest for him to adequately supervise because he will be able to tell at a glance if they are being done well. By contrast, tasks that a

17. Gary Downing, "The Care and Feeding of the Volunteer Youth Worker," in *Working with Youth: A Handbook for the '80s,* comp. Ray Willey (Wheaton, Ill.: Victor, 1982), p. 35.
18. L. Richards, *Youth Ministry,* p. 109.
19. John Naisbitt, *Megatrends* (New York: Warner, 1982), p. 204.
20. Robert C. Coleman, *The Master Plan of Evangelism* (Old Tappan, N.J.: Revell, 1963), pp. 82-93.

person does not do well take more time to adequately supervise because he has to figure out what should be done and evaluate how well the person is doing it.

So what does releasing ministry responsibilities mean in youth ministry? It means shifting to other people the authority to minister to young people while sharing the responsibility for the quality of that ministry with them. That definition suggests that real authority is given to volunteer workers so that they do not have to fear being second-guessed by the professional youth worker. At the same time, responsibility is shared so that both professional and volunteer youth workers have a vital interest in effective ministry to youth.

Simple enough, right? So then why is releasing ministry responsibilities so difficult? Séveral reasons come to mind.

"I want to do it" is the implied comment from some big-hearted youth workers. It is not that they distrust other youth workers or fear incompetence on their co-workers' parts. They simply enjoy the ministry so much that they never want to lose the opportunity to spend a majority of their time in face-to-face communication with students. Consequently, effective long-term growth is stymied.

"What will I do if I release my responsibilities?" questions another delegation resister. There may be a fear that the church people will mistake delegation for laziness or that volunteer workers will resent the "glory" the professional is receiving while they are doing all the work. It might simply mean that the professional youth minister does not know how to supervise once he has delegated specific aspects of the ministry to people who lack natural talents in youth ministry.

"Students will come to me anyway" is another smokescreen placed in the path of delegation. That feeling is frequently found in churches where the youth pastor is a very charismatic figure who lacks an adequate understanding of the dignity of the people of God.[21]

"I can't get qualified staff" is a fourth reason given for failing to release ministry responsibilities. Though this is a real problem in many churches, and may be the very reason a youth minister was employed in the first place, the situation must not be permitted to persist. Even if he must grow his own staff from within the youth group, qualified staff must be developed.

As a youth minister learns to delegate ministry responsibilities, he will pass through three stages. In the first stage nothing is delegated, for the youth worker is learning how the ministry should be done. Stage two is the experimentation stage in which some tasks are delegated and initial skills in supervision are learned. The final stage is the growth period when most of the primary ministry responsibilities are accomplished through nonprofessional youth workers.

21. See the discussion of the "people of God" in Lawrence O. Richards and Gib Martin, *A Theology of Personal Ministry* (Grand Rapids: Zondervan, 1981).

IMPLICATIONS

1. As a youth worker grows, the focus of his or her ministry must change from primary ministry to secondary ministry or else the effectiveness of his or her efforts will be severely limited. A resistance to change in ministry style is a vote to kill a ministry.
2. Shared leadership responsibilities coordinated by a resourceful leader is more likely to generate numerical and qualitative growth than nonshared leadership. Though one plus one may not always equal two in ministry terms, one alone will never equal two.
3. Released authority and shared responsibility in ministry is one method for inhibiting burnout. All the weight of the youth group does not rest squarely on the shoulders of only one person. This allows the youth worker to retreat from time to time in order to rebuild his ministry resources.

AXIOM 7

A high school student will not be theologically mature until he or she is sociologically comfortable.

Perhaps the most frequent critique of a high school youth group that has ceased to be a ministry to students is that many of the members are cliquish. Students from "the other high school" feel excluded by students from the school where the majority attend. Those who buy their clothes at J. C. Penney's feel rejected by the more expensive shoppers. National Honor Society members feel scorned by the athletes, and everyone looks down on the "nerds."

Though it is important to point out that small groups in which one feels loved and accepted are the building blocks of social relationships, exclusive groups (or cliques) have a highly detrimental effect on the spiritual development of youth ministry. Psalm 23 beautifully illustrates the comfort level that is important for a normal growth process. The lamb is part of a flock and finds comfort in the shepherd, the environment, and even the support system available when danger occurs.

Dennis Benson and Bill Wolfe suggest that the primary reason for the emergence of cliques in a youth group is the need for protection and security among the members, "a homemade social insurance policy."[22] In many ways this problem sounds like the in-fighting described by Paul in 1 Corinthians 3. Such strife resulted in the Corinthian believers remaining "mere infants" (v. 1).

The proponents of "mastery learning" are helpful in assisting the youth

---

22. Benjamin S. Bloom, ed., *Taxonomy of Educational Objectives: The Classification of Educational Goals; Handbook 1: Cognitive Domain* (New York: Longmans, Green, 1956); and David R. Krathwohl, Benjamin S. Bloom, and Bertran S. Masia, *Taxonomy of Educational Objectives: The Classification of Educational Goals; Handbook 2: Affective Domain* (New York: David McKay, 1964).

worker in understanding why theology and sociology are linked in youth ministry. Three domains of learning have been identified, two of which have special relevance to this discussion. The *cognitive domain* deals with knowing. The *affective domain* focuses on valuing. The two are distinct from each other.[23] Thus it is possible for a student to know a biblical principle but not to value it; or worse yet, to value abusing what is known. At best that would have to be considered theological immaturity.

A warning is in order at this point. Just because a student will not be theologically mature until he is sociologically comfortable does not mean that when he is sociologically comfortable he will become theologically mature. Unfortunately, many youth programs settle for creating social comfort zones that never lead to theological maturity. That, as distinguished earlier in the chapter, would merely be youth activity, not youth ministry.

There are several ingredients that will contribute to developing theologically mature students. The first is models of openness on the part of student and adult leaders. It is a rare freshman who will feel at ease with upperclassmen unless the older students take deliberate steps to make the newcomer feel at home. Many times it is the adult youth worker who is the key in opening the doors of friendship in the youth group by demonstrating love and concern for each youth group attender, while urging student leaders to do the same.

The second ingredient in the sociological/theological maturation process is creating structures that break across the offending social network. Sunday school classes may have to be restructured. Ministry projects may be planned and staffed with people who are not well acquainted with each other. Core groups may be created with a mix of upper and underclassmen. Teams may be organized at camp or on a retreat that include no more than two people from the same high school or other natural grouping.

The final ingredient is that of vital spiritual life within the students and leaders. One could hardly expect students who are spiritually dead to demonstrate the evidences of love described in 1 Corinthians 13. Similarly, one could not expect great theological insight from students or adults who lack theological conviction. Spiritual life breeds both loving actions and theological sophistication.

IMPLICATIONS

1. Sunday school may unteach more theology than it teaches. Students who do not feel a part of the social structure of the youth group may throw out the theological baby with the sociological bathwater. They may learn the doctrinal information and reject spiritual commitment.
2. A more subtle response that leads to the unteaching of theology is apathy.

23. *The Basic Encyclopedia for Youth Ministry* (Loveland, Colo.: Group, 1981), p. 70.

Students may learn but not value the biblical information to which they are exposed. The result is environmental Christians who have been conditioned to respond in culturally appropriate ways without allowing the Holy Spirit to grip their lives.

3. Well-developed shepherding skills, both in student and adult leaders, are as important as accurate theological convictions. The sovereign Lord, speaking through the pen of Ezekiel, gives a beautiful picture of how He would care for the flock of Israel (Ezek. 34:11-16). The product of that careful shepherding is a theological awareness as the people of Israel realize that Jehovah is their God (34:31). The skills of a shepherd produced the insights of a theologian.

4. A possibly more intriguing implication is that contemporary Christian music may become the primary source of theological perspectives for the current generation of young Christians. Unless the church provides a sociologically comfortable context in which to learn theology, young people are likely to find that context through the community atmosphere created by Christians in the performing arts. The unfortunate aspect of that is the theological inadequacy of the words sung. They may come nowhere close to the doctrinal maturity of the Sunday school materials published by the leading evangelical publishers.

AXIOM 8

The most effective youth ministries are those that rapidly move students into ministry postures.

In his book *Dedication and Leadership,* Douglas Hyde contrasts the manner in which Communists and Christians disciple new converts. The Communists, says Hyde, immediately send newly enlisted followers out to sell copies of the party's newspaper or some similar activity. The result is that the enthusiasm of the fresh party loyalty sells papers. At the same time the experience teaches the novice what he does not know about his newly embraced cause. When he returns from his assignment, he is the most willing learner in the party. He demands answers. He tests his spontaneous responses to the official party line and makes appropriate modifications in his thinking. No one has to urge him to study Communism. It rapidly becomes an obsession with him.[24]

By contrast, Hyde points out that Christians take new converts and assign them to a classroom for the first three years after their conversion under the pretense that they do not want to shove immature believers out of the nest before they are ready to provide answers to non-Christians. By that time their newly found enthusiasm has worn off, and the witnessing for which they have

24. Douglas Hyde, *Dedication and Leadership* (Notre Dame, Ind.: University of Notre Dame, 1966), pp. 21-26.

been so carefully prepared never takes place.

Glenn Heck, vice-president of National College of Education, applies this same principle in the realm of youth ministry. Heck suggests that at the very time when early adolescents begin feeling adult instincts to nurture (baby-sit, work in the church nursery, help with the little kids in vacation Bible school), traditional Christian education wisdom has insisted that those students be the receivers rather than the conveyers of nurture. So by the time they are deemed ready to serve, the lessons of nonservice have already been learned.

There are four kinds of ministry postures that are common in youth ministry today. The first is ministry within the youth group. Though most models of youth ministry make a sincere effort to reach beyond the limits of their youth groups, a majority of the youth ministry models see that as their primary ministry focus (see chap. 15, "Models of Youth Ministry"). That is especially true of the youth fellowship model, in which a majority of the activity is focused on serving the group through the presentation of Sunday evening programs by the students themselves.

The second approach involves ministry within the church but beyond the scope of the youth group. The community model, which tends to treat students as full participants in the life of the congregation, urges early and full involvement in the serving of nonpeers within the church. Teaching of Sunday school, even as early as the junior high years, service on church committees, visitation of the elderly, and participation in the worship services are advocated.

Service outside the church is a third ministry posture. The phrase most frequently heard in that regard is "reaching your campus for Jesus Christ." The competition model is as conscious of that kind of ministry as any of the models. Student leaders are constantly reminded that the only person who has free access to students on campus are those who attend, not youth pastors or Christian rock groups. No parachurch leaders or even schoolteachers and administrators have the freedom that students have to be salt and light on their campuses.

Other services outside the church could include certain kinds of musical ministries, tutoring of special-need student groups, ministries to latch-key children, and community service. Clown and puppet ministries, backyard Bible clubs for children, and other outreach activities can also fit into this category.

Ministries outside the culture would be a final kind of ministry posture. The ministry model is a primary example as it attempts to focus the entire youth ministry on "Samaria, and to the ends of the earth" (Acts 1:8). Minority groups within the country as well as specific ministry activities in other countries would be the primary concern of this ministry posture.

IMPLICATIONS

1. Perhaps the greatest hindrance to rapidly moving the young people into ministry postures is the myth of "know before do." Most of life is just the

opposite, people do in order to know. Children learn to walk by walking, they learn to talk by talking, they learn to keep their rooms neat by keeping their rooms neat (usually with strong encouragement from Mom). Patterns are formed early in life. The sooner service activities are provided, the sooner a theology of service will be integrated into a student's world view.

2. The priority of service in youth ministry may determine the curriculum or at least the curricular materials for youth ministry. Depending on the intensity and complexity of the service experience (witnessing on the street is much more intense and complex than ministry in a nursing home, though both are valid ministries), the formal educational time (Sunday school or group Bible studies) may have to be dedicated to responding to immediate student needs for answers and skills.

AXIOM 9

Student ownership of youth ministry guided by respected Christian adults is essential for the ministry to remain healthy.

Youth ministry begins when an adult earns the right to be heard by students, but it reaches its peak of effectiveness when the adult has earned the right to be silent. Students, willing and capable of providing spiritually sensitive leadership for the youth group, assume ownership. Seldom will a youth ministry reach the point where the students will have so much ownership and maturity that their adult leader will be able to remain entirely silent, but that should be the goal for at least some aspect of the ministry.

Negative ownership by students is a distinct possibility as well. The ingredient that turns student ownership sour is an absence of respect for the adult leader. The adult has attempted to impose his ideas on the students without earning the right to be heard. The result is that the adult leader cannot be heard even when he needs to be. Students are controlling the direction of the youth group, even if it means going around in ever smaller circles.

Worse than negative ownership is an absence of ownership. Some call it apathy, others refer to it as a lack of commitment, but it amounts to the same problem. The adults are the performers, whereas the students are mere spectators.[25] The weight of responsibility is placed on the adult leaders to provide constantly improving entertainment or else students do not attend youth group functions.

The best illustration of student ownership is a high school state championship team. The coach has done most of his work behind the scenes, working long hours to refine athletic skills and team coordination so that when the final buzzer sounds, all of the players, even those sitting on the bench,

25. Jim Green, "Helping Youth to Take Charge," *The Youth Worker's Personal Management Book*, ed. Lee Sparks (Loveland, Colo.: Group, 1985), pp. 67-71.

have a sense of being champions. The students have done the work. The coach has merely found a way to bring the best from each player.

Ownership is a tricky factor, and adult leaders handle it in different ways. Some will concede ownership to the students ("It is their youth group; let them do with it what they want"). Others will respond favorably to student ownership ("If that is what you really want to do, let me help you do it the best we possibly can"). A few will sell ownership to the students ("I've shared this idea with the student leaders, and they are pretty excited about it, so they've asked me to explain it to you. What if we. . ."").

Certain adults will discover mutual ownership with the students ("What do you think we could do for God's glory if we had no fear of failure?"). A relatively few have the personal charisma with students to succeed in demanding ownership by the students ("If you don't take the challenge of this ministry then God will raise up students who are willing to do His work"). Still others have the joy of seeing students adopt the ownership of an obviously successful ministry ("Welcome, freshmen, to one of the most exciting youth groups in the Midwest. I've heard many of you begging me to allow you to join earlier, but now is the time").

Styles of adult leadership will differ. Student motivation for ownership may not be the purest. But without student ownership the youth ministry of the local church will produce neither numerical nor quality results.

IMPLICATIONS

1. When students sense ownership in a youth ministry, their capacity for leadership is amazing. Their spiritual insights, creative expression, capacity for work, and willingness to persevere under adverse conditions will amaze even the most optimistic adult leaders.
2. Traditions and symbols are closely associated with student ownership. Group names, a logo, and annual activities known for reasons that the group values all contribute to the building of a greater sense of group identity. To ignore or violate such symbols or traditions without group permission will invariably bring about problems.

AXIOM 10

A youth ministry will reflect the vision of its adult leaders.

Remember, we are not talking about *youth movements*. Those reflect the vision of young people. When God sees fit to bring about a youth movement, adult leaders would be well advised to set aside their visions and assist the rising generation to do God's work in a manner that is new and at times uncomfortable to the people who have seen God work in previous years.[26]

26. For an excellent summary of youth movements read David M. Howard, *Student Power in World Evangelism* (Downers Grove, Ill.: InterVarsity, 1970).

Greg Gregoire defines *vision* as "perceiving God's desires based upon the absolutes of His Word and your circumstances. In comparison, *objectives* state those desires in measurable terms, and *programs* help you to organize activities that will fulfill those objectives."[27] Thus *vision* can be thought of as the broad strokes of the paint brush, the big picture, the dreams that others can perceive and follow.

There are two kinds of visions current in youth ministry. One is a *process vision,* which is most concerned with what will happen to the young people involved in the ministry while they are enroute to a specific objective. Success or failure of an activity is measured in terms of the extent to which the events assisted students in their spiritual maturation process.

The other is *product vision,* which is more focused on the expected outcomes of youth group activities. The reason for this greater goal orientation is that no one can measure spiritual maturation anyway, so it is a waste of time to focus on anything except the expected results.

Most visions include both process and product. That healthy blend needs to be there. The key question, however, is not, Which vision is best? Instead, it should be, Can the other adults and students catch the vision and build the ministry around it?

In order for a vision to be transferable it must be significant, attractive, and attainable. Significance has two primary foci. The first is biblical. Does the vision further the kingdom of God as revealed in Scripture? The second is cultural. Do the students of this generation view the activities implied by the vision as important? Without the former, youth ministry has degenerated to mere youth activity, and without the latter, students will tend to view the activities as petty, as Sunday school busywork.

Attractiveness has to do with the appeal that the vision has. Is the vision capable of capturing the imagination of students and adult leaders? Many activities that are theologically significant and culturally acclaimed are simply boring to youth group members.

For example, a suggestion that the youth group spend two weeks ministering in an impoverished section of an urban center would be highly significant but might not be at all attractive to suburban high school students. Does that mean this kind of vision should not be selected? Not at all. It merely suggests the vision may not be transferred into reality without a great deal of effort to make the idea attractive.

A transferable vision must be perceived by students and adult leaders as being attainable. No matter how significant and attractive a dream may be, unless the young people and their sponsors can see themselves as a part of the big picture, the leader's vision will remain just that—the *leader's* vision.

27. Greg Gregoire, "Developing a Vision for Ministry," in *Insights: Building a Successful Youth Ministry,* ed. Ken Green (San Bernardino, Calif.: Here's Life, 1981), p. 2.

Mediocrity and past failures are the primary enemies of a vision appearing to be attainable to students. If the philosophy that "it is good enough for church work" has dominated the church's approach to youth ministry, it may take a while to raise the group's sights to expect excellence. By contrast, if someone has previously raised the group's expectations and then for some reason or other failed to deliver, the resistance to trying again may be greater than if the group had not tried to live out the vision.

IMPLICATIONS

1. A youth group that is without a vision is a youth group that is doomed to perpetuate the past. It is in a rut. It tends to be governed more by sociology than by theology. The student and adult leadership tends to have a high turnover rate. Creativity is limited. The spiritual impact is minimal.
2. A leader's vision, when shared by students, is the starting point for planning. Each leadership meeting will be structured in reference to the vision. Each decision will be made with the youth group's vision in mind. Each evaluation will measure the contribution that an activity has made toward achieving the vision.

Axiom 11

In youth ministry the group performs three functions: identification, contribution, and consolation.

Scattered around my desk as I write this chapter are nearly twenty of the best-known books on youth ministry. Yet I have sought in vain to find an author who has dealt with the question, What contributions does a youth *group* make to the development of a mature Christian young person? Not the leaders of a group, not the other people in the group, but the specific dynamic that comes from the young person having associated himself or herself with a group.

Church growth literature, on the other hand, has been much more conscious of the *group factor.*[28] As adapted from the writings of Peter Wagner and Eddie Gibbs, three functions of groups might be identified. The first is that of *identification.* The youth group provides the young person with a place to belong, not in the "joining" sense but in the "place to be" sense. There is a feeling of dignity in being associated with the people who make up the group and in participating in their activities.

The second function is that of *contribution,* for it is within the youth group that a young person can first begin to discover his or her niche within

28. See Eddie Gibbs, *I Believe in Church Growth* (Grand Rapids: Eerdmans, 1981), pp. 275-312; C. Peter Wagner, *Your Church Can Grow* (Glendale, Calif: Regal, 1976), pp. 97-109.

the ecosystem of the church. "Where do I fit in?" "What do I possibly have to offer?" Those are questions felt by teenagers as they attempt to discover their personal identities by testing out different roles apart from school and home. For most, the youth group is a new beginning both socially and spiritually.

For some the niche would appear to be negative to the adult observer— clown, rebel, loudmouth, flirt, skeptic, "air-head," even "nerd." Yet the important thing is not the role but that the young person has a distinct place within the group's ecosystem.

For others the positive leadership roles are readily available. Team captain, organizer, care-giver, consistent witness, up-front communicator, spiritually sensitive person, even loyal follower are usually respected niches in the youth group. Thus the student finds a distinct place to make a contribution, hopefully of spiritual value, within a safe environment outside his or her home.

A third function of the youth group is that of *consolation*. When a student is feeling insecure, has had an argument with parents, or has broken up with the person he or she has been dating, a support system is in place. When a young person has doubts about God, moral standards, or issues of life and death, there are specific people from the group to whom that person can go. When someone misses a youth group activity or two, he or she is missed. Each of these is evidence of consolation.

In small groups these functions happen rather naturally. As a group grows, special care must be given to ensure each function, or else the group will revert to a size small enough for identification, contribution, and consolation to happen spontaneously.

Large group or small, a sense of identity generally comes from the group as a whole. Contributions, by contrast, decrease as the youth group grows in size. Once the size exceeds thirty to forty students some people are going to begin feeling as though their contribution does not count any more. From that time onward the group will need to be subdivided in order to allow every person to have a context in which to make his or her contribution. Such groups will need to be large enough for new niches to develop. Frequently that means a dozen or more members in each new subsystem.

Consolation is best provided by two to five people who genuinely care for a hurting person. In larger groups it becomes essential that a structure be established so that hurting people who do not have a high profile in the group are immediately missed or responded to as needs dictate.

IMPLICATIONS

1. The larger the group becomes the more spontaneity must be carefully planned. It is a continuing concern for adult and student leaders. A plan to provide all of these functions tends to breakdown the day after tomorrow. Therefore, they must be stressed repeatedly, monitored continually, and

repaired constantly. The purpose for all of this calculated spontaneity is the continual enfolding of all students for whom the group has a stewardship.

2. The tendency in a larger group is not to miss a person who has been away from the group activities until he or she returns. If he or she does not return for a prolonged period of time, a disengagement process begins as the absentee emotionally withdraws from the group. Should that process extend over three or more weeks without a response from a caring friend, the student may be lost to the group and possibly to the Lord.

AXIOM 12

The development of a youth ministry will not exceed the public communication skills of the primary adult leader.

Jesus Christ is a prime example of marvelous public communication skills. After all, 5,000 people do not come to listen to a person who is dull or boring. He did not do extensive expositions of Old Testament passages and show their relevance to the modern Jewish culture. He told stories (parables), used catchy phrases that were easily remembered (Beatitudes), and chose examples to which the hearer could relate (children, the weather, trees).

Let there be no mistake, our Lord's primary task, as A. B. Bruce has pointed out, was the training of the twelve,[29] but His personal communication skills provided the context in which that training would take place. The attracting of crowds in Christ's earlier ministry and the rejection by crowds because of hard sayings later in His ministry provided examples that Peter and the other apostles would follow after the Lord returned to heaven.

As a person looks at the public communication skills of the leading youth ministers of this century, four common denominators emerge. They are *story oriented*. Most are craftsmen in the art of bringing narratives to life. Many, if they wanted to go commercial, could give Garrison Keillor and Bill Cosby a run for their money. They are able to capture the seemingly insignificant details of life and weave them into a verbal picture in which each listener can place himself. Jim Rayburn, the founder of Young Life, was a master of the art. Using a conversational tone, he could spin a tale which would capture the attention of the most unsuspecting young person.

The story is not an end in itself, and yet it is. Many times the listeners will walk away without a Bible verse in mind and yet have a marvelous grasp of a theological concept due to the masterful way in which the speaker has wedded the story to the concept it illustrates.

Effective communicators to young people are *need oriented* in their presentations. They know their audience, their joys and pains, pressures and fantasies, struggles and achievements, loves and rejections. They raise ques-

29. Alexander Balmain Bruce, *The Training of the Twelve* (Edinburgh: T. & T. Clark, 1898).

tions that students are asking ("If God is love, why can't I get my locker open?") and then take them to principles of Scripture that assist them in dealing with these tensions.

For the novice communicator the tendency is to speak in abstract philosophical terms, in words borrowed from respected communicators, or in response to his own needs that are fancied to be of concern to the listener. Each approach reflects the background of the speaker rather than the struggles of the hearer. To be effective, the rookie youth speaker must move from a "Here is what I have to say" posture to a "Can I help you solve that problem?" stance.

Biblically based is a third common denominator of effective youth speakers. There is an authority to what they have to say. Though they draw from the social sciences and current events, from the arts and media, from literature and sports, from history and politics, the ultimate interpreter of human experience is the Word of God. Without that source of authority the speaker is little more than another source of entertainment, and youth ministry degenerates to youth activity.

Youth ministry communicators are *results focused*. They know which results to expect each time they speak, and they are surprised if God does not intervene in the lives of the young people being addressed. Not all appeals for response are focused on salvation, though that is appropriate some of the time. Many touch on changes in daily living that would honor the Lord of Scripture. Dedications and rededications to Christ are neither overworked nor ignored. God the Holy Spirit is assumed to be working and willing to give visible results.

IMPLICATIONS

1. Much of the identity (see axiom 11) that a youth group has will be associated with the public presentation of the primary spokesman for the group, usually a professional youth minister. Thus the youth worker would be wise to work continually on improving his public communication skills for the sake of the ministry.
2. Motivation on the part of the speaker is very important. If speaking is nothing more than an effective method for gaining the status or attention that was not afforded an individual earlier in life, the speaker has become merely a "resounding gong or a clanging cymbal." Speakers get caught in all kinds of questionable practices if their motives are not pure before God. Stories can be enhanced for dramatic effect. Emotions of immature adolescents can be manipulated in a quest for greater responses. Personal biases can be pawned off as the will of God.
3. Public speaking in behalf of God is an awesome responsibility. It must be handled wisely.

Conclusion

Webster defines *axiom* as "a maxim widely accepted on its intrinsic merit." The twelve maxims presented in this chapter have been widely accepted on their own merit. They are an indication of the manner in which youth ministry in the local church has matured in recent years.

There may be youth ministers who take issue with these axioms or who would like to offer additional axioms to further refine the ministry skills of a rising generation of youth ministers. The editors of this book welcome continuing dialogue on the subject.

For Further Reading

Boyer, Ernest L. *High School.* New York: Harper & Row, 1983.

Coleman, Lyman. *Youth Ministry Encyclopedia.* Littleton, Colo.: Serendipity House, 1984.

Green, Ken. *Insights: Building a Successful Youth Ministry.* San Bernardino, Calif.: Here's Life, 1981.

Griffin, Em. *Getting Together.* Downers Grove, Ill.: InterVarsity, 1982.

Richards, Lawrence O., and Gib Martin. *A Theology of Personal Ministry.* Grand Rapids: Zondervan, 1981.

Spader, Dann. *Sonlife Strategy of Youth Discipleship and Evangelism.* Chicago: Moody Bible Institute, 1981.

Dann Spader

14

Stages of Youth Ministry

Tom anxiously awaited graduation from seminary. He had received a call to serve as youth pastor in a small but growing suburban church. He was excited about this ideal situation.

Six months later the pastor of the church resigned. The board approached Tom and added new responsibilities such as occasional preaching, overseeing the Christian education work of the church, and additional administrative details.

After a year Tom became frustrated with the teens. They were not responding to his teaching and programming. Parents began to voice their concern, offering numerous suggestions on how to run the youth ministry. The teens clearly communicated their lack of excitement about the youth group. Tom quickly tried some new curriculum, but to no avail.

After twenty months (two months longer than the national average) Tom resigned and went to work for his dad in the carpeting business. Youth ministry obviously was not God's will for Tom. Or was it?

Gail, while going through Bible college, worked part-time as youth director in a small ministry. Having an outgoing personality, Gail easily established friendships.

After graduation, Gail took a full-time position as youth director in a large church. Her background of programming experiences and her positive outlook

DANN SPADER, D.Min., is Director, Sonlife Ministries, Chicago, Illinois.

helped Gail weather the ups and downs of the first couple of years in this new church.

The ministry grew. At the beginning of the fifth year Gail took a hard look at her calandar. She was working sixty to seventy hours per week trying to meet all the needs of this growing ministry. With twice as many students, she found herself working twice as hard and still not meeting all of the needs. She felt trapped and burned out.

Gail moved to another position in a publishing ministry. That allowed her time to slow down and get a better handle on her life. Youth ministry in a church situation was just too demanding for her. God's will was to move on. Or was it?

Don accepted a call at a young, vibrant church in a growing community. The previous youth pastor, Don's close friend, had done an excellent job of laying a foundation and equipping key students for ministry.

Don began this new ministry with excitement and intensity. He adopted a high profile program and designed small discipleship groups based on some material he had written. The programming attracted many new students, and within a couple of years the group tripled in size.

Because of the fast growth, Don was asked to conduct seminars at denominational and regional conferences. He explained his program and curriculum. Many young youth workers became excited, convinced this new program would work in their churches. Don had shown clearly why it worked in his church and how it tripled the size of his youth group. He guaranteed that if they did exactly what he had done, their ministry would grow like his. Or would it?

Tom, Gail, and Don are true case studies. They represent hundreds of youth workers across the country who become victims of a limited understanding of the processes involved in the development of a growing youth ministry.

Understanding the stages in the development of a ministry can greatly help the youth worker comprehend the dynamics of any given group. Youth workers tend to leave after either eighteen months or five years because of normal stages in the development of a youth ministry.

Knowing these stages will give us insight into the processes at work and help us adapt a strategy in accordance with those processes.

THE PRODUCT

Before we can begin to assess the stages in the development of a youth ministry, it is important that we define our desired product. The product we are seeking to develop will affect the process.

In any given community five or six different types of students can be found at various levels of commitment and personal development. The *secular* student is the student outside of the church setting who has not established a personal relationship with God through Jesus Christ. In churches, the noninterested student is all too common. He does not want to be there but is forced to come by his parents. His interests are not in spiritual matters. Often this student is the hardest to work with in a church setting. As the title implies, the *fun seeker* comes to have fun. Though not interested in spiritual matters, he does enjoy a good time and his friends in the youth group. The *curious* student is beginning to ask serious questions, perhaps because of a crisis in his life or through a friend's becoming a Christian. He is curious about God and aspects of Christianity. The *convinced* student, on the other hand, has Christ in his life and is growing in his relationship with God. Finally, the *committed* student is cause oriented. He wants more. He does not just want to be ministered to; he wants to minister to others. This student wants to share in the work of the ministry.

What then is the desired product of our ministry? Our goal should be to build a discipling ministry adapted to students at various levels of personal growth and development.

A survey of 100 churches demonstrated that 85 percent of them geared all of youth programming toward the convinced student.[1] (Bible studies, Sunday school, discipleship groups, quizzing, puppetry, and programs like these are designed for the convinced student.) Very little, if any, programming was designed specifically for the secular or the committed student. With such an approach, the secular student is seldom reached, and the committed student has to go elsewhere to continue to be challenged.

An over-emphasis of programming for the convinced student only results in stagnation, ingrown attitudes, and spiritual apathy. Thus, it is critical that the development of our ministries reflect a commitment to reach and challenge students at various levels of spiritual need.

Youth ministries should emphasize winning, building, and equipping students—winning the secular student to Christ, building the convinced student in his faith, equipping the committed student to do the work of the ministry. This is the desired product: a discipling ministry.

THE PATTERN

Howard Hendricks has asked, "How did Jesus train His men? Whenever we study the gospels, we tend to study them exclusively for content. Why don't we study them for methodology?"[2]

Christ's own ministry developed through stages. In building His ministry, Christ did not immediately begin outreaches to the masses. Neither did Christ

1. Dann Spader, "Developing for Sonlife Ministries an Advanced Training Manual Designed to Lay a Foundation for Equipping Youth Pastors in a Strategy of Developing a Discipling Youth Ministry" (D.Min. project, Trinity Evangelical Divinity School, 1984), p. 32.
2. Howard G. Hendricks, *Leadership* 1, no. 32 (Summer 1980), p. 32.

immediately choose a group of leaders and appoint them over areas of ministry.[3]

With wisdom, Christ recognized that there was a progression in the development of a solid ministry. I would like to suggest three stages in His approach.

During the first stage, Christ sought to lay a foundation for His work. From His baptism through His rejection by His hometown of Nazareth, Christ ministered in the rural areas in a relatively low profile manner. He performed only two miracles that were recorded during the first year and a half of His ministry.

In the second stage Christ began to spend more time with a small band of disciples. He challenged five disciples—James, John, Simon, Andrew, and Matthew—to follow Him in order to become fishers of men (Matt. 4:18-22; Luke 5:27-28). He intensified His ministry with a few. We immediately see Him twice in Peter's home and once in Matthew's (Matt. 8:14-17; 9:10-13; Mark 2:1-12).

Also during this stage, Christ took His small band of followers to Capernaum and began an expanded outreach to the masses through His Galilean ministry. Christ's outreach was designed not only to reach the multitudes, but also to train His ministry team.

In the third stage we find Christ appointing the twelve apostles. Because the ministry had grown, He restructured the movement to continue its multiplication, sharing the ministry with the leaders who were in training. They would carry on when He left.

From this simple development of Christ's ministry, it is obvious that there was a definite progression. Christ did not immediately appoint a group of leaders to do the ministry, nor did He immediately begin outreach to the masses. He laid a solid foundation and developed His ministry through stages.

THE PROCESS

Throughout the rest of this chapter I will suggest three stages in the development of a well-balanced discipling ministry.

STAGE ONE: LAYING A FOUNDATION

During the first stage the emphasis will be on initiating and establishing solid relationships within the youth group. Maintaining and working within the existing program structure is usually the wisest decision during this first

3. For a further development of a breakdown of Christ's ministry into stages see: A. B. Bruce, *The Training of the Twelve* (Grand Rapids: Kregel, 1978), especially chaps. 1-4.
   A. T. Robertson, *A Harmony of the Gospels* (New York: Harper & Row, 1950), especially parts VI-VIII. Observe his titles and division breakdown. Similar divisions are found in Stanley Gundry and Robert Thomas, *A Harmony of the Gospels* (Chicago: Moody, 1978).
   Carl Wilson, *With Christ in the School of Disciple-Building* (Grand Rapids: Zondervan, 1976). Though using different titles, the stages can be seen in his breakdown of Christ's ministry.

stage. The youth leader who, upon arrival, begins to change the existing program structure, may be successful. However, often he devotes his remaining time at the church overcoming tensions and disagreements that resulted from the quick changes.

Instead, during this first stage, the emphasis needs to be placed on creating the kind of environment that will be conducive to the development of disciples. There are six key areas on which the youth leader should concentrate in the first stage.

1. *Creating an atmosphere of love.* A study of the Scriptures shows the high priority God places on love. That is especially true in youth ministry. In *The Measure of a Church,* Gene Getz convincingly demonstrates that love is one of the three measuring sticks God uses to determine the health of a church.[4]

First Corinthians 13:13 tells us that our greatest priority is to be loving. Without love, our ministries will be cold and empty. 1 Peter 4:8 states that we are to "love each other deeply, because love covers over a multitude of sins." Many youth leaders burn out in youth work because they get worn out with petty little conflicts that continually arise. But if a youth worker can create a spirit of love within a group, many problems will be averted.

How do we create this loving, caring spirit within the group? We must begin with a person who genuinely loves the students and is capable of communicating God's love through his or her life. It is not enough for the youth worker to have experienced God's love, he or she must be able to express that love in such a way that students feel cared for. It has been said correctly that teens do not care how much you know until they know how much you care.

Love must be established as a major priority of the group. Study, discussion, and evaluation around the topic of love needs to be emphasized.

The approach to creating a loving, caring group should be multifaceted. Youth workers must model and clearly communicate God's love. The priority of becoming known for their love (John 13:35) ought to be a group goal. Concentrated Bible studies, along with group discussion, evaluation, and prayer, can make love become a central focus.

2. *Building relationships.* Youth ministry is relationships. Howard Hendricks has stated, "You can impress people at a distance, but you can only impact them up close. The closer the personal relationship, the greater the potential for impact."[5] Secular and Christian studies continue to demonstrate that teenagers are primarily influenced by relationships.[6]

Christ demonstrated God's love by coming into our world and initiating a

4. Gene A. Getz, *The Measure of a Church* (Ventura, Calif.: Regal, 1975), chaps. 1-5.
5. Hendricks, *Leadership,* p. 34.
6. Merton P. Strommen and A. Irene Strommen, *Five Cries of Parents* (San Francisco: Harper & Row, 1985), pp. 68-82. Merton P. Strommen, *Five Cries of Youth* (New York: Harper & Row, 1974).

relationship. Christ did not sit in the synagogue and invite people to come and see Him perform miracles. He went to the people, and He encouraged us to do the same: "Go and make disciples" (Matt. 28:19); "go . . . and preach the good news" (Mark 16:15); "I chose you . . . to go and bear fruit" (John 15:16); "as you sent me . . . I have sent them" (John 17:18). Christianity consists of going, not just asking people to come. We can expect students to come only to the degree in which we have been faithful in going. That involves entering the student's world. (See "Rationale for Ministry" in chap. 1.)

If possible, we need to get to their schools, sporting events, outside activities, home, and work. As we enter into their world, we begin to understand their real needs, become aware of their struggles and desires, and learn how to minister more effectively to them. As we enter their comfort zone, they begin to see us as genuine people in touch with reality, yet transformed by God's power.

3. *Establishing a base of prayer.* Carl Wilson states, "Prayer is one of the most important aspects of building disciples. If one is to be effective in making disciples he must pray. Indeed, if we do everything right in terms of making disciples yet fail to pray, nothing significant will happen."[7] "For our struggle is not against flesh and blood but against the rulers, against the authorities, against the powers of this dark world and against the spiritual forces of evil in the heavenly realms" (Eph. 6:12).

During stage one, youth workers cannot neglect extended times of establishing a solid foundation through prayer. Often in the business of youth ministry and the demands of a relationship style of ministry, it is easy to neglect the dimension of prayer. We need to recruit prayer warriors among the parents, the elderly, and other concerned people. The development of an established prayer base ought to be an emphasis of our time and commitment during the first stage.

As a youth pastor meets with adults and communicates the vision of the potential of the youth ministry, adults will respond, committing themselves to pray regularly for the youth. Monthly prayer letters, along with an occasional group prayer meeting, can lay a simple and yet extremely effective prayer base for the youth ministry.

4. *Emphasizing personal involvement with the Word of God.* The Bible must be central to the Christian's walk with God. A quick survey of the Scriptures emphasizes the centrality of God's Word in the growth process.

Deuteronomy 8:3: "He humbled you causing you to hunger . . . to teach you that man does not live on bread alone but on every word that comes from the mouth of the Lord."

Psalm 119:11: "I have hidden your word in my heart that I might not sin against you." (Of the 176 verses of Psalm 119, 170 refer to the centrality of God's Word.)

7. Wilson, Carl, *With Christ*, p. 223.

Psalm 119:130: "The unfolding of your words gives light."

Jeremiah 23:29: "Is not my word . . . like a hammer that breaks a rock in pieces?"

2 Timothy 3:16: "All Scripture is God-breathed and is useful for teaching, rebuking, correcting and training in righteousness, so that the man of God may be thoroughly equipped for every good work."

Hebrews 4:12: "For the word of God is living and active. Sharper than any double-edged sword."

1 Peter 2:2: "Like newborn babies, crave pure spiritual milk, so that by it you may grow up in your salvation."

Although many youth leaders emphasize the priority of God's Word, those who model the truth of Scripture are few. In today's fast-paced, quick-fix society, the Word often gets set aside for a more immediate solution.

There are two ways in which we lose the centrality of God's Word. First, frequently we talk about the Bible rather than actually study it. The teacher sees a need in the youth group, he develops a concept to teach, then goes to the Word to prooftext the concept. Scripture is not examined thoroughly and allowed to speak for itself. After a while students quit bringing their Bibles because they are used only occasionally.

Second, we allow a curriculum rather than Scripture to become the center of our study. As teachers, we find a well-packaged curriculum and then devote our study time to understanding the curriculum data and communicating it clearly. The Bible simply becomes a resource to reinforce the concepts of the curriculum. A good curriculum should get a person into the Bible more, not less. Yet that is rare in today's market.

Slowly the Bible is set aside—not totally neglected, but definitely not central to the learning process. Students graduate from high school with concepts about all the "hot" issues in youth circles, but few are adequately equipped in Bible study, and most have a surprisingly poor grasp of God's Word.

5. *Building a proper concept of grace and works.* Unfortunately, many people have a warped concept of the Christian life. Even Christian young people are often motivated to live for God out of fear of rejection and judgment. Their motivation is guilt-based, fearing God will get them if they do not do what good teens should do. They feel that through good works they become acceptable to God.

Well-meaning ministries and organizations complicate this problem by offering rewards, trophies, or special prizes for certain external actions accomplished. External motivation, though not always wrong, should not have primary emphasis over a system of developing a God-centered internal motivation and an understanding of God's grace.

How is that achieved in students' lives? During this first stage especially, our teaching and modeling need to reflect a threefold emphasis: who God is, what He has done and is still doing for us, and who we are in Christ Jesus. Our desire is to build intrinsic motivation, which comes only as we grasp a true knowledge of God and all that He has done for us.

The Bible emphasizes who God is, what He has done for us, and who we are in Christ Jesus. Our "doing" grows out of our "being." That is why, according to Richard Howard, all of Paul's writings begin with the indicative and end with the imperative mood.[8] We serve because of what He has done for us. We are what He has made us.

Only as students begin to grasp who God is, what He has done for them, and who they are in Christ will they begin to experience intrinsic motivation for their Christian living. Emphasis only on what they are to do for God quickly leads to a works motivation or legalism.

6. *Creating a healthy group image.* Every youth group has an identity. Each student has some image formed in his mind about the church youth group. Unfortunately, the image of a typical church youth group is rather negative. A secular student, when discussing the church youth group commented, "A youth group is where you go when you can't make friends. For the most part, they consist of people who can't make it in real life." That is definitely an image problem.

The way a youth group sees itself is critical for several reasons. First, it directly affects the degree to which students learn. Students who feel positive toward their group tend to be very receptive to the group's teachings and priorities. Students who have a negative image of the group tend to be defensive, even going so far as rejecting much or all that is taught in the group.

Second, the image directly affects the degree to which students feel free to bring their friends. From a Christian perspective, this is critical. Students who are positive about their group will be quicker to identify with the cause of Christ and bring their friends. Unfortunately, too many Christian students have such a poor image of their church youth groups that they will work hard to keep their friends from finding out that they attend.

The key to building a healthy biblical group image rests directly with the youth minister. He or she must be excited about the potential of the youth group. He or she must be able to see beyond the problems and focus on the potential. That involves vision, clarity of thinking, and a strong grasp of God's sovereign control in all situations. Much of communication is nonverbal. Students will reflect the enthusiasm of the leadership. We cannot avoid communicating. Over a period of time students will reflect the leader's image of the youth group.

During stage one our primary objective is to lay a solid foundation, to create the kind of environment that will be conducive to growth. We have suggested six priorities during this stage: the priority of love, a prayer base, healthy personal relationships, a positive group image, the centrality of the

8. Richard Howard, *Newness of Life* (Grand Rapids: Baker, 1975), chaps. 16-17.

Word of God, and focus on building a proper concept of God's grace. These six priorities lay a foundation for the first stage. That first stage may last from three months to three years, depending on a number of circumstances. It is a time of creating an atmosphere conducive to seeing growth take place in the ministry.

The second stage begins to build on that foundation and to tap those students who are beginning to say, "We want more."

STAGE TWO: EXPANDING ON THE FOUNDATION

As people pray, the Word enters students' lives, a positive group image surfaces, love is communicated, and relationships are established. The natural by-product will be a few students who begin to express in a variety of ways that they want more. Adults, as well, will begin volunteering to be a part of the youth ministry. They do not want merely to be taught, they want to share in the teaching. They do not want just to be ministered to, they want to share in ministry to others.

It is critical at this time that the youth worker begin to organize, mobilize, and train emerging leaders. Like Christ, the youth pastor must begin to practice "multiplication" and move toward investing his life in a few. Emphasis must be placed on building a team.

A leader's job is not to do the ministry but to "prepare God's people for works of service" (Eph. 4:12). Carl Wilson writes:

> The step of ministry training is critical to the expansion of the movement. At this point, most organizations and local churches reach their peak. If they do not train believers other than the pastor to evangelize and build disciples, their expansion stops. The maximum potential is reached without a continuing growth and broadening impact. True multiplication occurs only when disciples are trained in evangelism and disciple building. No matter how dynamic the pastor, no matter how financially stable and well organized the church, expansion will not continue if people are not trained to minister.[9]

It is at this stage that equipping can begin. Too many leaders try to enable people to do the ministry who have no desire to be equipped or who have a wrong motivation. In stage two we begin to train those workers who want more.

Several key principles will aid the process of equipping. First, selection of those for the ministry team should be based on character qualities and not arbitrary external standards. Three key qualities we should look for are faithfulness, availability, and teachability. Unfortunately, many books on discipleship emphasize arbitrary standards as criteria for selecting those to be trained. "If

9. Wilson, *With Christ*, p. 101.

you really wish to find out who wants to be discipled," they suggest, "set up meetings at 5:30 in the morning and require homework, memorizing three verses a week, and daily writing in a journal. Then you will find out who really wants more." That is not necessarily true. Some may meet all the standards, yet still not be faithful, available, and teachable. It is far more important in selecting a ministry team to look at the heart attitude and to emphasize that quality rather than external standards as priority in the selection and training process.

Second, investment of more time and energy into a few emerging leaders does not mean we love them more than the rest. Often the leader who begins to focus his efforts as I have suggested comes under the criticism of playing favorites. At this point the leader's attitude is critical. If these few *are* his favorites, then he is guilty of the charge. However, no one would argue that because Christ spent more time with the disciples He did not love the masses. On the contrary, the reason He spent time with them was because He loved the masses. Robert Coleman calls this "the genius of Christ's strategy." He invested in the few, "so that ultimately the masses could be reached."[10] Youth ministry is no different.

Third, this ministry team, which may consist of both adults and teens, begins to share the responsibility of the youth group. Teamwork is emphasized. Although the youth pastor remains as the player-coach, the team begins to share the responsibilities. All the marks of a team become visible:

- Working well together
- Having a common, clearly defined goal
- No individual glorification—instead, a team effort
- Each player has a unique role
- The team does not get down on a player if he fails
- The team is usually as strong as its weakest member
- Does not just talk about the game but plays it
- Runs planned plays
- Practice, practice, practice
- Sticks with the basics—keeps reviewing and mastering them

As this ministry team becomes operative, an evangelistic thrust is the natural by-product. A good environment has been developed; needs are being met through the ministry team, and now an increased desire to bring new friends and expand the ministry begins to surface.

As students increasingly begin to express a desire to reach out to their friends, it is essential that the leadership help them to see that become a reality. Philemon 6 states, "I pray that you may be active in sharing your faith, so that you will have a full understanding of every good thing we have in Christ." It is

10. Robert E. Coleman, *The Master Plan of Evangelism* (Old Tappan, N.J.: Revell, 1971), p. 33.

only as a person is active in sharing his faith that he can come to a full understanding of Jesus Christ. Outreach is not an option. As students begin to verbalize their faith and seek to present Christ to their peers, they will experience Christ living in and through them.

How can youth workers most effectively bring this about?

First, we should remember that our job as leaders is not to *do* evangelism as much as it is to *equip our students* to do the work of evangelism. If we can help our students reach their friends for Christ, we have greatly helped them grow in their walk with God. We must constantly ask what kind of training and programming can be used to help our young people be successful in sharing their faith.

Second, keep in mind that evangelism is a process and not an event. The Scriptures use three figures to define the evangelism process: cultivating, sowing, and reaping. Cultivating is the tilling of the soil to prepare it to receive the seed. It is the initiating of a friendship, the building of a relationship with non-Christians. Jesus was described as a friend of sinners.

Sowing is the planting of the seed in the soil. It is the injecting of God into the relationship with the non-Christian. It is the sharing of a word about what God means to me or what God is doing in my life. This is a natural process that stems from a healthy relationship between Christians and non-Christians. Done in the context of an established friendship, it diminishes tension and becomes a positive experience for both the believer and nonbeliever.

Reaping is the harvesting of the seed that has been sown and grown to maturity. It results from relating the gospel to a person who is ready to respond. Reaping is the natural by-product of the process of cultivating and sowing.

Third, an organized regular effort is needed to reach teens in today's culture. Teens are attracted to events that are well done, organized properly, and relevant to their age group. Offered regularly, evangelistic "big events" cannot only attract new students but, equally important, become effective tools in training students to reach their peers for Jesus Christ.

Specific evangelistic events can help students be successful in reaching their friends. Although some students are mature enough to reach their peers personally, the majority of teens do not possess the ego strength to witness. Unfortunately, many feel guilty; they know they should be doing evangelism but are frightened or frustrated by their awkward attempts. Well-planned events can help students overcome this awkwardness by giving them confidence and positive experiences in a nonthreatening manner.

The more the event is part of the usual program, the better tool it becomes for training. Scheduled regularly, bimonthly, monthly, or once every two months, outreach events provide a basis for training. After each event, evaluation should take place, allowing an opportunity to strengthen weak areas for the next evangelistic effort. Such a practice tends to encourage students in a life-style evangelism focus. As they develop new friends at school, they can begin to pray and work toward exposing them to other Christians through this kind of event.

Excellence and consistency must be priorities in planning these evangelistic events. The student's reputation is on the line. If two or three excellent outreaches are followed by a sloppy one, students become uncertain as to what they should expect. If they work hard to bring their friends and the event is poorly executed, we may have hindered their efforts to reach their friends.

These events are designed with the non-Christian in mind. Our goal is to bring students to Jesus Christ. To do this, we need to break down barriers the non-Christian has against Christianity. It is not a Christian social or primarily for Christians. It is an event designed specifically for the non-Christian. Three tough questions need to be asked at each outreach event. First, are non-Christians present? Second, are they exposed to Christ in a positive way? Third, is anyone likely to accept Christ or go away closer to accepting Christ?

During stage three, growth in numbers, especially non-Christians coming to Christ, should be the norm. As the ministry begins to grow and new students become involved, new problems and tensions arise. As a result, leadership cannot continue to minister as it has throughout the first two stages. Stage three thinking must now begin to dominate.

STAGE THREE: MULTIPLYING BY DIVIDING

As the ministry begins to grow, it is critical that leadership restructure the ministry to allow it to keep on multiplying. Ministries that fail to reorganize soon reach a maximum attendance point and then either level out or begin to decline. Others, aware of the increasing numbers, come to the faulty conclusion that they must work harder to meet all the needs, and eventually burn out. The issue is not to work harder but smarter, restructuring to allow multiplication to continue.

A leader is someone who has a segment of the ministry allotted to his care (1 Pet. 5:3). We often use the term *leadership* loosely, calling almost everyone a leader. But Jesus warned about that (Matt. 23:10). We need to return to a high standard of definition for a leader, always keeping in mind that with leadership comes accountability and responsibility before God.

As the ministry grows, all the ingredients that caused it to grow, such as prayer, the Word of God, enthusiasm, good relationships, investment in a few, and outreach to the masses, need to be maintained. They are what combined to produce the growth. But how can leaders continue to maintain all these things with an expanding ministry? The answer is simple. They cannot. The options before the leaders then are fourfold: work harder, stop doing some things (and usually prayer and study of the Word are the first to go), burn out, or delegate segments of the ministry to the care of other leaders. Obviously, the answer is the latter.

Under stage two, ministry training, the workers shared the ministry load as a team was developed that worked to meet the needs of the group as a whole. But now the leader must delegate segments of the group to be under the care of other leaders. Only this will ensure personalized care and attention to each member of God's family. Biblically, these leaders become "undershepherds" of segments of the ministry.

It is critical that leadership be appointed to carry these areas of the ministry. That allows the key person in leadership to back away from the burdens and concerns of the daily care of the groups (personalized attention, phone calls, counseling, rides home, etc.) and devote himself more to prayer and study of the Word. The key leader now concentrates on the other leaders.

To summarize, a diagram of the three stages in the development of a ministry would look like the following:

Stage 1: Emphasis is placed on building relationships, developing a positive group image, creating a loving, caring atmosphere, establishing a prayer base, and helping students get to know God as He really is through the Word of God.

Stage 2a: During stage two, the thrust is twofold. First, emphasis is placed on selecting and working with a few to build a team approach to meet the needs of the rest. More time is spent with the few, but all of the criteria of stage one remain. By the very nature of time limitations, the youth leader has less direct contact with students and more with the ministry team.

Stage 2b: Second, outreach becomes a priority because of the desire to reach the masses while training the ministry team. Outreach should become the norm because of the very nature and atmosphere of the group. Other students tend to be drawn to it.

Stage 3: The ministry now is broken down into four smaller segments in the large group, each with a leader who cares for the needs of his section. The youth pastor still is responsible for the entire ministry and serves as pastor-teacher, but now the daily concerns and care of the flock are primarily carried out by others.

Though the stages are not clear-cut divisions, they are nevertheless different aspects of a growing ministry. An understanding of the stages perhaps could have saved Tom (our youth pastor in the first paragraph of this chapter) from quitting after twenty months, or Gail from burning out after five years, or Don from telling beginning youth workers that his program will definitely succeed in their situation.

In stage one, laying a foundation, the emphasis was on creating an atmosphere that was conducive to students' growth. That is accomplished through a strong prayer base, healthy personal relationships, a positive group identity, an emphasis on who God is and what He has done for us, getting students into the Word of God, and building a loving, caring group. As this environment is developed, students will begin to surface who will say in various forms, "I want more."

Stage two, expanding on the foundation, is a time of pulling together both adults and students who become a team to minister to the rest of the group. This team consists of those who are teachable, available, and faithful, and are desirous of being equipped to do the work of the ministry.

An evangelistic thrust becomes a natural by-product of stages one and two. It is a time of touching others outside of the youth group and exposing them to the love of Jesus Christ. The motivation to reach out stems from a healthy growing group and the ministry of the Holy Spirit working within Christians.

Stage three, multiplying by dividing, is a way to keep the ministry healthy and growing. Leadership is shared, and segments of the responsibilities are delegated to other leaders. Multiplication becomes the key principle in this stage.

The product—a discipling ministry—has been developed and can now be maintained. Secular students are being reached, built up in their faith, and equipped to share in the ministry. The ministry's foci are winning, building, and equipping students. Regardless of one's level of personal commitment, a student can plug into this ministry because it offers a variety of categories and dimensions that are built on the concepts of development and growth.

FOR FURTHER READING

Arn, Win, and Charles Arn. *The Master's Plan for Making Disciples.* Pasadena, Calif., Church Growth Press, 1982.

Bruce, A. B. *The Training of the Twelve.* Grand Rapids: Kregel, 1978.

Dausey, Gary, ed. *The Youth Leader's Source Book.* Grand Rapids: Zondervan, 1983.

Hartman, Doug, and Doug Sutherland. *A Guidebook to Discipleship.* Irvine, Calif.: Harvest House, 1976.

Kuhne, Gary. *The Dynamics of Discipleship.* Grand Rapids: Zondervan, 1978.

Peterson, Jim. *Evangelism For Our Generation.* Colorado Springs, Colo.: NavPress, 1985.

Spader, Dann. "Developing for Sonlife Ministries an Advanced Training Manual Designed to Lay a Foundation for Equipping Youth Pastors in a Strategy of Developing a Discipling Youth Ministry." D. Min. project, Trinity Evangelical Divinity School, 1984.

Wilson, Carl. *With Christ in the School of Disciplebuilding.* Grand Rapids: Zondervan, 1976.

15

Models of Youth Ministry

The story is told of three former youth group members who met in heaven and began discussing their experiences in the different churches they had attended in life.

"Our group was so exciting," reflected one, with a trace of cheerleaderlike nostalgia. "We were constantly on the go with our teams, and the team captains were the greatest. In fact, it was Juan, our team captain, who lead me to Christ. I can remember it as clearly as yesterday. It was at the end of a Christian rock concert."

"Rock concert?" interrupted an athletic-looking companion. "Your group attended rock concerts?"

"Christian rock concerts," replied the first person, a bit unsure of the point of the question.

"Our group always stayed clear of those kinds of activities," responded the athlete. "We felt there were much better ways in which to bring people to Christ than allowing ourselves to imitate people who were living lives nearly indistinguishable from the values of the secular culture. Witnessing, for instance. Every Saturday morning our group went out witnessing. That's how I came to know the Lord."

"But what about justice?" inquired the third member of the heavenly trio. "We all know how important it is to make a personal commitment to Christ,

MARK H. SENTER III, M.A., Ph.D. candidate, is assistant professor of Christian Education, Trinity Evangelical Divinity School, Deerfield, Illinois.

but what about the role of being salt and light in the world? That's what our group did. It was never easy, but we learned to share in the sufferings of Christ before a watching world."

The conversation continued, perhaps for millennia, with each person periodically expressing surprise, disbelief, or admiration at the activities of the other youth groups. The three seemed so dissimilar, and yet there they were, in heaven, discussing their differences.

Though the preceding story is apocryphal, it points out the diversity of youth ministry at the end of the twentieth century. Had this chapter been written in the middle of the century, one or two youth ministry models probably would have been sufficient to cover the approaches found in local churches. But now, at least eight distinct models can be identified as options for those involved in ministering to students.

COMMUNITY MODEL

SCENARIO

"The best way to teach our young people how to become the church," stressed Pastor McFall, "is to allow them to be the church right now. None of this youth week stuff where we pay lip service to high school students for 168 hours and then put them back into the youth group 'cage' for the rest of the year. They have to be full participants in the life of the congregation right now."

Henry Weinberger and Walt Gibson were a bit startled by the pastor's forcefulness on the point. They had served with him on the church board for nearly three years now, and although the topic of the high school youth group had come up before, the implications of what the pastor had been saying had never been this clear.

"Then you would like to see high school students represented on the committees of the church?" Henry's statement was really a question.

"Not represented," the pastor responded. "Full members of each and every committee."

"And the church board?" probed Walt.

"Permanent elected members of the board as well," replied the clergyman. "That way the decisions of the church will belong to them. They will be participants in the community of believers."

PHILOSOPHY

Develop in students the attitudes and skills necessary to be God's presence in the world through making them a vital part of all aspects of the life of the Christian community, namely, the church.

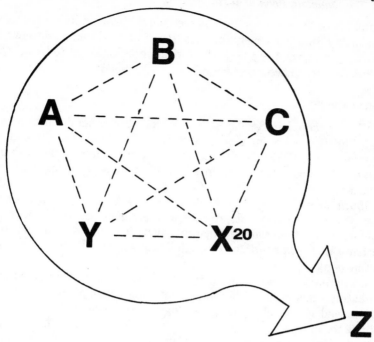

COMMUNITY MODEL
Fig. 15.1

A=Youth pastor; B=Adult sponsor; C=Parents; X=Students (super-script indicates the ideal number of students); Y=Student leaders; Z=People ministered to outside the youth group. Broken lines indicate advisory relationships.

BACKGROUND

As public education began to move away from a concept of education as the mere memorization and retention of data in classroom settings to viewing education as being an interaction among the many people and experiences in a student's life, the church began reexamining the methods by which its young people were being initiated into the Christian community. The result has been an integration of high school students into all aspects of congregational life, from teaching posts in church school to elected positions on the ruling boards of the church.

The youth group, however, has not been eliminated. It has merely been changed from an isolated function within the peer group to being "involved in the total life of the congregation" as the church grows in its consciousness of responsibility toward a society that has rejected a Christian worldview.[1] Young people are then given the power within their church context to become part of the Christian presence in the world.[2]

MAJOR ACTIVITIES

Church school, or Sunday school, is a place of either discussion of issues from a Christian perspective or ministry as high school students play significant roles in the Christian nurture of younger children. Relationships with Christian adults outside the student's immediate circle of friends and family are provided here.

Youth group meetings provide a twofold function in the community model. On the one hand, it provides a meeting place for Christian friends (sociological function), and on the other hand it provides a context in which Christian values can be forged through discussion and disagreement (stimulation function).

Corporate worship in the community model is probably more significant than in any other model. The Sunday morning worship service is viewed by students and adults alike as a meeting of the community of believers to celebrate the presence of their Lord and Savior, Jesus Christ. Thus, if a student had to choose between corporate worship and any other youth group function, at least in theory, the student would choose corporate worship as a means to express his unity with the Christian community.

Ministry activities are a logical extension of the youth ministry. Usually this will express itself in local ministry to people who are peripheral to society: minorities, the aged, widows, children, and the poor.

LEADERSHIP ROLES

Youth minister or lay sponsors, like their counterparts in the youth fellowship model (see later), serve as coaches to the students and help them by providing resource materials, ideas, and suggested direction for youth group meetings. They also take leadership in developing ministry activities.

Student leaders are the ones who lead meetings and ministry activities. Content of the meetings tends to separate the community model from the youth fellowship model.

Parents are closely identified with the youth ministry and are viewed by students and sponsors alike as a vital part of the student's community of faith.

1. Genny Ward Holderness, *Youth Ministry: the New Team Approach* (Atlanta: John Knox, 1981), p. 10.
2. See Stephen D. Jones, *Faith Shaping: Nurturing the Faith of Youth* (Valley Forge, Pa.: Judson, 1980); D. Campbell Wyckoff and Don Richter, eds., *Religious Education Ministry with Youth* (Birmingham, Ala.: Religious Education Press, 1982).

PREFERRED CONTEXT

The community model works best in churches where there is a large constituency of nonlegalistic parents who are more interested in seeing their adolescent children explore the outer reaches of their faith than in protecting them from the corrupting influences of society.

Churches employing this model tend to have smaller youth groups. Strong family ties may contribute to a lower attendance at youth group meetings, for the security at home may make the need for the security of a peer group less significant. But for these churches, low attendance tends not to be a problem, because outreach is associated with ministries to the disenfranchised of society rather than to peers that would result in numerical growth of the youth group.

Junior high youth groups may employ this model with a limited degree of success if adult leaders do not expect students to be young philosophers in order to deal with the pressing social issues of the day. Junior high students tend to be much more inclined to learn by doing than to learn by reasoning.

COMPETITION MODEL

SCENARIO

The narthex of the church is a sea of teenage faces. Dress ranges from prep to freak. Most are still hyper from the game time just completed. All are waiting for the same thing.

In a few moments the doors of the sanctuary will open and the Son City band will greet the human wave of high school students with a modified rendition of the Beach Boys' song "Be True to Your School." Only the vocalist will sing, "Be true to your *team,*" as hundreds of students pour into the sanctuary carrying banners declaring themselves to be on one of eight teams named after colors. Slides of last week's competition flash on a screen behind the band while the students stand and clap and whistle, awaiting the announcement of the scores of the just-completed competition.

But competition is not the main point of the competition model, discipleship is. Competition is merely a way to gain a hearing from secular students for the life-changing truths of the Bible. Within a half hour this same sea of vibrating teenage bodies will be prepared by music, media, and drama to listen with rapt attention as the youth minister focuses biblical truth on an area of need common to the listeners in the room.

Many will respond. Some will never return. Others will be left to reflect on the events of the evening until next week. A few will seek out team captains or the youth minister in order to commit themselves to an ongoing life of Christian discipleship.

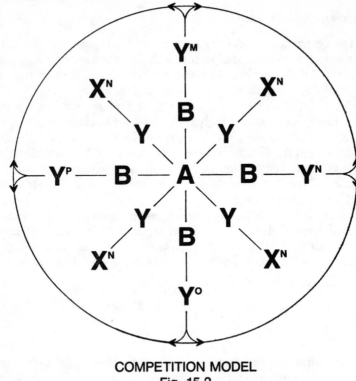

COMPETITION MODEL
Fig. 15.2

A=Youth pastor; B=Adult sponsor; C=Parents; X=Students (super-script indicates the ideal number of students); Y=Student leaders (super-script indicates the following code of talents: m=music, n=media, o=drama, p=administration). Solid lines indicate accountable relation-ships; broken lines show advisory relationships. Dotted lines suggest min-istry performed.

PHILOSOPHY

Use the natural leaders from the high school society, trained to serve as servants and motivators to their teams in the context of team competition, to attract and hold high school students for an articulate confrontation with biblical truth, both in the large group setting and in smaller discipleship groups.

BACKGROUND

In 1972 Dave Holmbo, youth music director at South Park Church in Park Ridge, Illinois, formed a musical group called The Son Company in order to reach high school students with their own kind of music. By the fall, Bill Hybels had been enlisted to develop a ministry that would utilize Holmbo's music and other ministry vehicles to evangelize high school students. Using a group of thirty high school students who were willing to discipline themselves in Bible study, prayer, and sharing the gospel, Hybels created a new mix of youth ministry ingredients that within a short time was drawing over a thousand students each week to the Son City program of the four-hundred member church.[3]

The ingredients included intense competition among teams led by student captains, music, drama and media presentations that were on a par with the best theatrical presentations of the local high schools, and articulate presentations of biblical truth as it related to specific needs of high school students. Its rapid success soon led to Son City kinds of programs springing up all over the nation, with hundreds of students making commitments to Christ each week.

MAJOR ACTIVITIES

Week night meetings are designed to gain a hearing for the gospel from the secular high school student. Using team competition, music modeled after the current popular music, dramatic vignettes related to the theme of the evening's talk, media presentations, and topical talks based on biblical truths, the student is swept along in an exciting experience that is both enjoyable and thought-provoking.

Discipleship meetings provide biblical meat for those students who want to experience further spiritual growth. These may be part of the Sunday school structure or meet on Sunday evenings, but the discipleship meetings are usually led by the youth minister. Many groups have another layer of discipleship groups as well.

Team leaders meetings are used by the youth minister to train the key student leaders and develop ministry skills in people who already have natural leadership abilities. The meetings also allow the youth minister to hold team captains accountable for their team members and their spiritual development.

Camps and retreats are relation-building times for the youth minister and his staff while the students are being guided into new levels of spiritual character development. Larger programs may run as many as eight to ten weeks of camp during the summer months.

LEADERSHIP ROLES

The *youth pastor* is a skilled communicator who has a vision for reaching the local high school population with the gospel of Jesus Christ. Most often he

3. Don Cousins, "Son City: A Youth Program That Works," in *Evangelizing Youth,* ed. Glenn C. Smith (Wheaton, Ill,: Tyndale House, 1985), p. 191.

has organizational skills that allow him to administrate a complex combination of moving parts.

Youth staff members provide technical and administrative assistance to the youth minister. They will work with talented students to provide the music, drama, media, and staging aspects of the evening's program.

Team leaders are, for the most part, high school students who organize team activities and shepherd their members. Leaders will include a captain, co-captain, and others, if needed by the team.

Parents have little contact with the youth ministry.

PREFERRED CONTEXT

The church in which the competition model is located must have a vision for reaching the current high school generation in its city or town. The pastor, as well, must provide unqualified support for the program, or else the resistance from people with special concerns will inevitably bring the ministry to an unceremonial end.

The program requires a significant financial investment. Sound systems, media equipment, athletic paraphernalia, and staff salaries are just a few of the costs the competition model will incur. It is best that these costs be paid by the church, though in some cases the youth program has been able to pay for itself through fund-raising activities.

Creative people who are committed to Jesus Christ are another aspect of the context. In most cases the competition model needs to be located near a college community in order to draw on the talent of Christian students as youth sponsors.

The competition model can be adapted to junior high students by de-emphasizing the competition aspect of the game time. Noncompetitive games that create excitement and yet do not focus on finely developed skills to the embarrassment of rapidly growing early adolescents are strongly preferred. Team captains should be taken from older age groups in order to perform the functions essential to the model.

DISCIPLESHIP MODEL

SCENARIO

"What's been happenin' this week?" asked Juan as the six sophomore guys settled into comfortable positions on the floor of his apartment. The weekly core group meeting was under way.

Juan Martinez had been involved with the church's youth ministry since he had come to know the Lord as a sophomore at Forest View High School eight years ago. For the past two years he had been responsible for building relationships with seven high school students with the purpose of helping them grow in their spiritual lives. Six of the seven were present. Tony had called earlier to let Juan know that he had been grounded by his parents and therefore would not be at the core group meeting tonight.

Juan usually began their Wednesday evening get-together with an open-ended question in order to allow his guys to tell him what had been happening in their lives. Most of the time the responses were anticipated by the young leader because he had been in contact with his charges by phone or in person earlier in the week. Yet it was important for the boys to learn to express their feelings, joys, and concerns before their peers as well.

The sharing time varied in length. Sometimes it was five minutes long. Other times it dominated the hour and a half they spent together.

Tonight it lasted about fifteen minutes before Juan focused the attention of the group on the Bible passage assigned for the evening's discussion. Part of the commitment to the group was to come prepared to share insights gained from studying the passage during the week. Though it was not always easy to guide the discussion, this evening the conversation flowed smoothly. The group members had obviously done their homework by studying the passage on their own.

The core group meeting was concluded in a prayer time. One of the key prayer requests had been mentioned by the youth pastor in Sunday school the preceding week. It involved a girl in another core group who was having tests at Mercy Hospital the following day for a suspected tumor. Other prayer requests focused on the non-Christian friends at school, problems with parents, and the upcoming high school retreat.

The clock struck 10:30 P.M. as Juan opened the refrigerator to get a cool glass of orange juice. Most of the group had left by nine o'clock, and then, as usual, the caring leader had driven Scott and Rob home. It had been a productive evening. The fellows appeared to be taking their faith much more seriously this year. Juan just hoped that the other core groups were enjoying a similar response.

PHILOSOPHY

Train students to be God's people in an ungodly world, equipped with Bible study and prayer skills developed in a caring atmosphere with a view to reproducing their Christian lives in others.

BACKGROUND

The idea of discipleship groups is nothing new. James A. Davies has pointed out that "students of church antiquity know that Baptist, Moravian Brethren, Methodists, Quakers, as well as Lutherans used petite cells for religious nurturing."[4]

4. James A. Davies, "Small Groups: Are They Really So New?" in *Christian Education Journal* 5, no. 2 (Glen Ellyn, Ill., Scripture Press Ministries, 1984), p. 43.

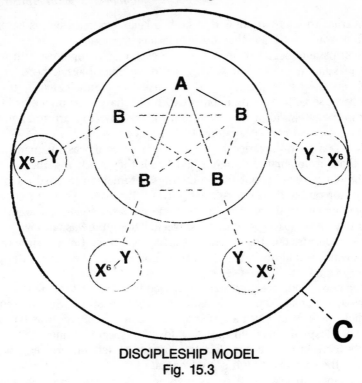

DISCIPLESHIP MODEL
Fig. 15.3

A=Youth pastor; B=Adult sponsor; C=Parents; X=Students (super-script indicates the ideal number of students); Y=Student leaders. Solid lines indicate accountable relationships; broken lines show advisory relationships.

The Wesleyan revivals were a prime example of small groups in action. Converts were placed into tightly disciplined groups, or class meetings, with ten to twelve members from the same neighborhood. The purpose of weekly gathering was to examine the needs and spiritual progress of each member of the group, thus keeping the Wesleyan movement pure. John Wesley later commented that he had found that one of these group members had "learned more from one hour's discourse [in a class meeting] than from ten years' public preaching."[5]

The Navigators, founded by Dawson Trotman, employed similar strategies during World War II in order to evangelize and disciple military men all over

5. Ibid., p. 44.

the world. With the end of the war, many of these men and women enrolled in colleges and universities where they employed the strategy to reach their campuses for Jesus Christ.[6]

It was not until the late fifties that people working with high school students began to take the strategy seriously. Perhaps the most influential location in this shift was the Wheaton (Illinois) Graduate School under the leadership of Lois and Mary LeBar. It was from this context that people like Chuck Miller and Bill Gothard emerged with a discipleship strategy for doing high school youth ministry.[7]

MAJOR ACTIVITIES

Core group meetings are the heart of the discipleship model. Usually consisting of six to eight students and an adult leader, core groups meet weekly to hold each other accountable for Bible study, prayer, and (in some cases) evangelistic efforts. Core groups sometimes have social activities and may take on short-term ministry efforts.[8]

Large group meetings provide both a sociological and theological function. Because students are divided into core groups for a midweek meeting time, it is essential that the youth group meet as a body at another time during the week for the students to feel part of the larger whole (sociological function). Usually this is during the Sunday school hour, though it may be on Sunday evening or at other times throughout the week.

During the large group meeting the youth pastor usually teaches from the Bible and relates the Scripture to the problems encountered by students in daily life (theological function). Frequently the large group meeting includes group singing, skits, media presentation, and announcements that affect the entire group.

Core group leaders' meetings are essential to keep the ministry to high school students moving in a unified direction. Held at least every other week, the meeting allows the youth pastor to provide in-service training for core group leaders, assist in dealing with problems that have arisen in individual core groups, and maintain a level of support and accountability to and from the volunteer workers in the high school ministry.

Camps, retreats, and big events are a regular part of the ministry to high

6. Vic Glovach and Milford S. Sholund, "Parachurch Youth Movements and Organizations," in *Youth Education in the Church,* ed. Roy B. Zuck and Warren S. Benson (Chicago: Moody, 1978), p. 379.
7. Lois E. LeBar, *Education That Is Christian* (Old Tappan, N.J.: Revell, 1958), pp. 161-62. See also William Gothard, "A Proposed Youth Program for Hi-Crusader Clubs" (M.A. thesis, Wheaton College, Wheaton, Ill., 1961), and Chuck Miller, "Discipling—A Holistic Ministry," in *Working with Youth: A Handbook for the 80's,* comp. Ray Willey (Wheaton, Ill.: Victor, 1982), pp. 57-59.
8. John Musselman, "Ministering Through Core Groups," in *The Youth Leader's Source Book,* ed. Gary Dausey (Grand Rapids, Mich.: Zondervan, 1983), pp. 141-51.

school students. The function of these activities is to edify the students while allowing them to have common experiences that are wholesome and entertaining. Camps, retreats, and big events play a major role in maintaining the unity of the youth group.

LEADERSHIP ROLES

The *youth pastor* has two major functions: communicator and administrator. As a communicator, he rallies the group to enjoy and respect the biblical truths that are presented in large meetings. As administrator, the youth pastor works through other people who care for students and hold them accountable for their own spiritual development.

Core group leaders are the undershepherds of the youth group. They are the flesh and blood of the whole youth ministry, for they are the people with whom students share their experiences en route to maturity. The core group leader is not primarily a communicator. His or her responsibility is to win the right to listen and then provide the structures in which students will talk about their spiritual development.

Student leaders either take on short-term tasks, such as working with the youth pastor to plan and promote a retreat, or they emerge as core group leaders for younger students.

Parents tend to provide a supportive environment for the discipleship model. Christian parents view the model as an extension of their parental function, whereas non-Christian parents tend to appreciate the care being provided for their adolescent.

PREFERRED CONTEXT

The church in which the discipleship model functions best tends to be a church where the teaching of biblical truth is highly revered. Church leaders realize that the way to produce a spiritually mature youth group is not through a constant diet of entertaining activities but through developing biblically literate volunteer leaders who are adept in passing their skills along to a generation of high school students.

The organizational arrangement of the church must permit the youth pastor to take control and, if necessary, significantly change the high school Sunday school hour rather than allow it to function in the traditional manner.

A community where college students and young working adults want to live is important (though not essential) for the discipleship model to function well. They tend to be the people with the amount of discretionary time available to perform the functions of an effective core group leader.

The model can be used with junior high students, though the intensity of accountability of students should be decreased.

FUNDAMENTALIST MODEL

SCENARIO

The youth revival drew to a close. Fifteen hundred high school students sat in silence as the organist played the third stanza of a dedication hymn. Already there were close to a hundred students standing or kneeling at the front of the church auditorium, and more were making their way forward. For them, this was an hour of spiritual decision.

The issues Tom Johnson, the youth evangelist, had focused on were not new to the students: an appreciation for the Word of God, separation from the values of the world, a willingness to live according to Christian moral standards, a commitment to winning souls for Jesus Christ, and a loyalty to their church. The key question, however, was, "What will you do with Christ?"

After a few more stanzas of the hymn, the closing session was over. Tearful farewells were said to students from the surrounding states who had come to Burnsville Baptist for the meetings. Hopefully they would see each other at next year's youth revival meetings.

The next day the students from Burnsville Baptist, most of whom were enrolled in Baptist Christian High School, were back in their normal schedules. The first real test of their newly made commitments was the following Saturday morning when the soul winners' club met.

At 9:00 o'clock sharp, Pastor Steve, the youth pastor at Burnsville Baptist Church, opened the meeting of the soul winners' club with prayer. One hundred thirteen high schoolers were present. Because there were so many first-time students present, Pastor Steve focused his talk on what the gospel is and how it should be presented.

By 10:00 all 113 students were on buses headed for neighborhoods in the city where they would go door to door presenting the gospel to people of all ages. As with hundreds of soul winners' club members of previous years, many of these high school students were so nervous that their mouths were dry. Yet, as Pastor Steve had pointed out, if Christ was willing to endure the shame of the cross for them, why should they not risk the possibility of a little embarrassment for Him?

PHILOSOPHY

Build the church of tomorrow through challenging students to lead lives separate from the values of the world and through providing opportunities to participate actively in the evangelistic responsibility of the church while enjoying the backing of the Christian school and the Christian home.

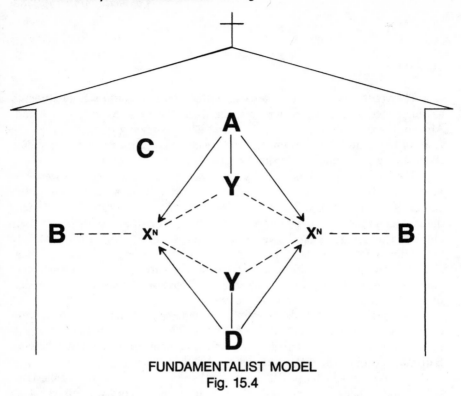

FUNDAMENTALIST MODEL
Fig. 15.4

A=Youth pastor; B=Adult sponsor; C=Parents; D=Christian school; X=Students (superscript indicates the ideal number of students); Y=Student leaders. Solid lines indicate accountable relationships; broken lines show advisory relationships.

BACKGROUND

The fundamentalist model, developed in the 1950s and 1960s, was most closely associated with the churches of the Bible Baptist Fellowship. It was characterized by a professional youth pastor who usually was a scaled-down version of the evangelistically minded senior pastor of the church—more a preacher than counselor or facilitator. The majority of youth activities featured the youth pastor preaching to large groups, yet most of the students felt as if he knew them personally and genuinely cared for them.

During the 1960s and 1970s, Bible Baptist churches mushroomed in size. Elmer Towns, Sunday school editor for *Christian Life Magazine,* publicized the movement. Their churches had some of the largest and fastest growing

Sunday schools in the nation. The youth groups were mainly an extension of the Sunday school, and many students were involved in the evangelistic efforts of the church alongside the adults.[9]

The 1970s and 1980s have seen a rising emphasis on Christian schools, and with that has come a decreased need for youth group functions in the churches that felt their impact. The more relational aspects of the church's ministry to students now takes place in the Christian high school, whereas the church has emerged as more of a training ground for Christian service. The loser is the youth who attends a public high school but attends the fundamentalist church.

MAJOR ACTIVITIES

Sunday school is biblically based and is by far the best attended youth activity in the church. Highly organized and traditionally structured, every student in the church must be accounted for each week. If absent, the student will be visited by his or her teacher or at least contacted by telephone.

The *youth group* meets on Sunday night prior to the evening service, and usually the youth pastor will preach, emphasizing an aspect of Christian character that he feels the group needs at that time. Sometimes the youth choir will practice for part of the hour in which the youth group meets. Frequently, soul winning activities are an outgrowth of the Sunday night meeting.

The *Christian high school* provides a Christian world view as well as social activities for the majority of students from Christian homes, thus decreasing the need for such youth group functions. For students who do not attend the Christian high school, Bible studies are sponsored by the youth ministry.

Camps, retreats, and revival meetings are normal parts of the youth ministry, with an emphasis on repentance from sin and commitment to Christ.

LEADERSHIP ROLES

The *youth pastor* is a skilled communicator of God's truth and leads the high school students in implementing the philosophy of the church on the high school level.

Sunday school teachers lead and shepherd classes of from eight to fifteen high school students. Part of the teacher's responsibility is to evangelize his or her students as well as to reach new youth with the gospel.

The *Christian high school* is playing an increasingly important role in the fundamentalist model of youth ministry. Seeing no reason to duplicate ener-

9. See Elmer L. Towns, *Successful Biblical Youth Work* (Nashville: Nelson, Impact Books, 1973).

gies, the youth ministry of the church has allowed the social activities of the school (formal and informal) to carry the weight of the youth group's social calendar.

Parents provide vital support for the church's approach to youth ministry, even to the extent that a growing number are paying the tuition for their adolescents to attend the church-sponsored high school.

PREFERRED CONTEXT

The fundamentalist model tends to work best in situations where there is a predominance of what S. I. Hayakawa has called bimodal thinkers in the congregation. Bimodal thinkers tend to see life in mutually exclusive categories. Things are seen as black or white, good or bad, right or wrong. In this context, authoritarian leaders who are willing and able to lead people in the "right" way are highly respected.

Similarly, the model is most likely to work in churches where success, especially numerical success, is important to the people of the congregation. Most of the efforts of the youth ministry are focused on making the church successful in evangelizing its community.

GIFT DEVELOPMENT MODEL

SCENARIO

It was 5:00 o'clock on Sunday afternoon and the youth group was meeting in the youth lounge, and in the choir room, and in the sanctuary, and in the second grade Sunday school department, and in the women's missionary society sewing room.

Several weeks before, Marty, the youth pastor, and the student leaders of the youth group had presented a plan to the high school students that would allow each one to experiment with his or her spiritual gifts and natural talents, and in the process minister to people in the community as well as the church. The plan was simple. Instead of having the whole youth group together on Sunday afternoons or evenings, students would choose a project or task force of which to be a part. They would then work with that task force until the project was completed.

Five ministries were chosen. Project Tutor was a thirteen-week effort to help Cambodian children with their English skills. Projects Myrrh and Props consisted of two complementary task forces working to produce the Christmas play entitled *And Myrrh*. One trained the actors, and the other developed costumes, props, sound, and lighting for the play.

The fourth ministry was Project Media, which was to produce biweekly slide presentations, updating the entire youth group on the progress of each task force. The last service opportunity was Project Contact. These students met briefly for prayer and then went out to contact the children who had visited the Sunday school earlier in the day.

A number of students were disappointed because they could not be in more than one project, but it was explained that there would be more opportunities for service during the winter and spring. For now, however, the project meeting times were structured to conflict so that everyone would have an equal chance to explore his or her gifts and abilities.

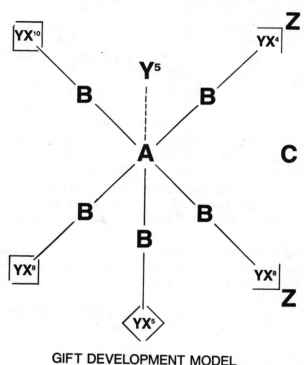

GIFT DEVELOPMENT MODEL
Fig. 15.5

A=Youth pastor; B=Adult sponsor; C=Parents; X=Students (superscript indicates the ideal number of students); Y=Student leaders; Z=People ministered to outside the youth group. Solid lines indicate accountable relationships; broken lines show advisory relationships.

PHILOSOPHY

Give students opportunities to explore their spiritual gifts and natural abilities to minister through providing short-term service opportunities, performed in small groups and coached by a spiritually qualified adult with skills in the tasks being performed.

BACKGROUND

Service projects have been a part of youth ministry for many years, but it was not until the student activist days during the Vietnam War that the gift development model emerged as a valid option for the central focus of the youth ministry in a local church. With the Jesus Movement emerging in the wake of the antiwar efforts, students at colleges and seminaries began providing short-term service opportunities for high school students, and student activism within the church rapidly became a norm.[10]

Scripture Press Publications, Success With Youth, Incorporated, and several more seminaries quickly picked up the concept and spread the idea. Though the model is not in wide usage today, the concept remains a valid option for developing Christian students in the local church.[11]

MAJOR ACTIVITIES

The *task force meeting* is the heart of the model. It is here that students explore their gifts and abilities through participation in a ministry project under the skilled and spiritually sensitive leadership of an adult sponsor.

Task force presentations are vital in maintaining student commitment. Presentations give the students goals toward which to work. Some projects, such as plays and concerts, have their presentations at the end of the effort. Others, such as media presentations and tutoring, have more frequent deadlines.

Large group Bible teaching and Sunday school provide a sense of unity to a group that may feel fragmented by the project efforts. This also provides a forum for the youth pastor to point out biblical qualifications for people in ministry.

Camp, retreats, ministry trips, and social activities also play a role in the spiritual development of the high school student.

LEADERSHIP ROLES

The *youth pastor* or *head youth sponsor* tends to be the visionary behind the model. She or he sees potential, discovers resources (both human and material), shares and even sells the vision to students and leaders, then supports and encourages the task forces to the completion of their projects.

Task force sponsors are adults with specific skills who are willing to coach a task force to the conclusion of a project and to shepherd the individual students in the task force as each explores his or her spiritual capacity to minister.

10. Mark H. Senter III, "Guiding Youth in Project Ministries," *Christian Education Monographs: Youth Workers Series* no. 6 (Glen Ellyn, Ill.: Scripture Press Ministries, 1971).
11. Mark H. Senter III, "The Project Approach to Youth Programming" in *High School Leaders' Resource Book*, vol. 2, (Wheaton, Ill.: Scripture Press, 1971) pp. 31-36.

Student leaders are vital to the success of the model. Without their commitment and enthusiasm for the various projects, the youth group will tend to fragment and become discouraged.

Parents, similarly, must understand and support the concept of project ministries. Because of the goal orientation aspect, students may have extra time demands placed on them as the project draws to a conclusion. It is then that the wholehearted support of parents is important.

PREFERRED CONTEXT

The church in which the gift development model will work best is one with a diversity of responsible adults, talented enough to coach students in accomplishing specific tasks and spiritually mature enough to shepherd the high schoolers as they discover and begin to use ministry skills.

Trust is essential for the model to function properly. Parents must trust the youth pastor. Students must trust their coach/sponsors. The church must trust its high school students, especially when the presentation of a project takes place in a public service of the church.

The number of students in the group should be large enough to allow at least three attractive and yet diverse projects to be undertaken. Seldom will one or even two projects appeal to all of the members. Consequently, students who do not become involved tend to drop out.

MINISTRY MODEL

SCENARIO

The airport terminal was jammed with little brothers, banners, cameras, and parents of all shapes and descriptions. The students who would enter the terminal through gate H5 were returning from three weeks of ministry among orphan children in Mexico. And three life-shaping weeks they had been, for many of these normal American high school students had never before ventured out of their cultural cocoon. Parents, families, and church awaited the impact of the trip.

The expectations were not the result of wishful thinking. This was the seventh summer missionary trip sponsored by the church, and each year the impact among the students seemed to be more tangible.

Last year's post-trip response was perhaps the most significant. Within days of her return from three weeks of ministry in one of the major urban centers of the nation, Dawn, a high school senior, began to ask, "What can we do here at home during the rest of the year?"

A survey of the community by Dawn, her youth pastor, and several other students revealed the presence of hundreds of "latch-key" children, preschool and grade schoolers who come home to empty apartments because their parents are working to make a subsistence living. From that survey emerged a five-afternoon-a-week ministry sponsored and led by high school students from two churches.

Demands for high school social activities decreased as the students began sponsoring parties for their latch-key children. Tithing became as natural as breathing when the students determined to raise the six hundred dollars a month required to support the latch-key ministry. Ministry had become a way of life for these high school students.

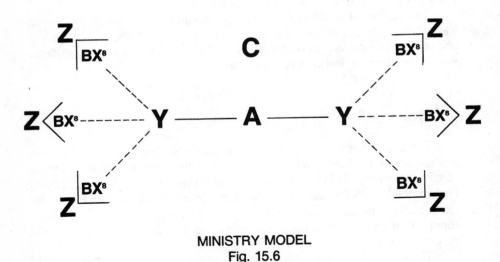

MINISTRY MODEL
Fig. 15.6

A=Youth pastor; B=Adult sponsor; C=Parents; X= Students (superscript indicates the ideal number of students); Y=Student leaders; Z=People ministered to outside the youth group. Solid lines indicate accountable relationships; broken lines show advisory relationships.

PHILOSOPHY

Develop student ministry skills and a context in which to use those skills through carefully planned exposure to human and spiritual needs outside the cultural context of the church, enhanced through meeting similar needs in the community surrounding the church and supported by accountability groups within the youth group.

BACKGROUND

The vision of students making valid though short-term contributions to the worldwide mission of the church was not new when George Verwer and students at Moody Bible Institute founded Send the Light (later called Operation Mobilization) in the late 1950s. However, the idea was never the same after Verwer began taking college students during vacation periods to distribute literature in cross-cultural situations.

Within a few years the idea of including high school students in similar efforts began to emerge in missionary-minded local churches. Initially most of those missionary trips were focused on native Americans, but quickly more ambitious trips were undertaken as high school students were sent around the world. Names like Missionary Internship, M.O.P. (Missionary Orientation Project), and Project Serve began showing up in magazine articles about the missionary involvement of students in local churches. The problem with the concept, however, was that once the trip was over, the experience of service tended to stop until the next missionary trip.[12]

Soon *Teen Mission,* with the slogan Get Dirty for God, began sponsoring missionary trips for high school students all over the world. Though their "boot camp" experience better prepared the students to serve, and though the missionary trips were more task oriented, the follow-through in the local churches during the rest of the year was still lacking.[13]

Ridge Burns and the students of the Wheaton Bible Church in suburban Chicago were among the first to turn summer missionary trips into the essential core of a church's youth ministry throughout the year. Though others had enjoyed limited success with similar ideas, Burns was able to incorporate elements of other models into the ministry model and in the mid-1980s sustain a youth ministry around the idea.[14] (See chap. 25.)

MAJOR ACTIVITIES

Student missionary trips, providing cross-cultural ministry experiences, are the activities that tend to engage the students in the model. Taken during vacation periods (usually spring or summer), the trips are designed to mix

12. Bill Bynum, "Missionary Education of Youth," in *Youth Education in the Church,* p. 330; Bette Sloat, "Operation 'MOP' " in *High School Leaders' Resource Book,* vol. 1 (Wheaton, Ill.: Scripture Press, 1969) pp. 23-28.
13. Robert M. Bland, "Involving Youth in Missions," in *Evangelizing Youth,* ed. Glenn C. Smith (Wheaton, Ill.: Tyndale House, 1985) pp. 269-75.
14. Ridge Burns, "Report from the Front Lines: New Hope for Latch-Key Kids," *Youthworker 1,* no. 2 (Summer 1984): 64-68.

manual labor with the meeting of human and spiritual needs.

Weekly community ministry is an outgrowth of the missionary trips. When functioning best, these are student led, staffed, and supported. These ministries are not an extension of the existing church program but are expressions of student visionaries.

Sunday school or a *weekly large group meeting* gives the youth group a sense of being part of a larger body of committed high school students. Bible teaching and discipleship training along with skit announcements are major features of this whole group function.

Core groups of six to eight students meet during the week to hold each other accountable for spiritual development. These are usually led by adult sponsors.

Retreats and *camp* experiences are used to build group unity, interpersonal relationships, and Christian character.

LEADERSHIP ROLES

The *youth pastor* is a skilled communicator of biblical truth, a shepherd of adult sponsors and student leaders, and a stimulator of student ministry visions.

Student leaders dream of, organize, and lead their fellow students in actual ministry efforts, including major cross-cultural trips. Though working closely with the youth pastor, the students actually are the missionary leaders.

Youth sponsors serve as coaches on cross-cultural trips and shepherds of core groups at home.

Parents are strong supporters of the concept and practice of allowing the Christian mission to be the focal point of the youth ministry. Usually this means a significant financial commitment to underwrite the expenses of the missionary efforts and may even mean being patient until their student is willing to make a commitment to the ministry concept.

PREFERRED CONTEXT

The ministry model tends to work best where the adults of the church have a strong commitment to the world mission of the church. This most frequently can be seen in a significant missionary budget in conjunction with active programs of outreach in the local community.

The model is not built overnight. In most cases the process of adapting the ministry model has taken place over a period of three or more years. Therefore, it is essential that the youth pastor have a long-term commitment to the church.

Because the model is a break from the average expectations of a youth group, it is necessary that the concept have the unqualified backing of the senior pastor and the church board.

URBAN MODEL

SCENARIO

When Tom first walked into the locker room at Roosevelt High School, the situation had seemed hopeless. Equipment was old and inadequate. Facilities were worn. There was not even a full-time football coach. "Bud" Johnson, the head coach, was really a math teacher who was paid a small stipend to head up the football program, but what could he do with so few resources? There was not even a weight room to use for developing the strength of the players.

During his first year as an unpaid assistant coach at the four thousand-student urban high school, Tom earned the right to be heard by the students both on and off the playing field. Relationships were built, even though he was candid about being the youth minister at the Jefferson Memorial Presbyterian Church. Yet few of his athlete friends ever showed up at church.

Then an idea occurred to the urban youth worker. The school had no weight room. Besides, even if it did, the school would be locked up as tight as a steel drum over the summer months, and that was the most important time for the football players to build up their strength. Why not buy a Nautilus machine, set it up at church, and sponsor a weight-training program for the athletes and their friends all summer long?

It took some convincing to get the church Session to go along with the idea and a lot of hard work to raise the money for the weight machine outside the church budget, but by July 1 the machine was in place and the athletes were streaming to the church.

Stipulations were made for people enlisting in the program, and soon Bible studies and discussion groups were filling the youth pastor's hours when the weight room was not open. Local Christian athletes were brought in at the end of the summer to address the program participants, and a number of students made personal commitments to Jesus Christ and began regular attendance at Jefferson Memorial Presbyterian Church.

That was four years ago. In the meantime, the weight machine concept has expanded to a year-round program that puts volunteer Christian youth workers in contact with urban teenagers and allows them to gain a hearing for the liberating news of the gospel.

PHILOSOPHY

Use the equipment and facilities of the church in conjunction with the presence of adults who have earned the right to be heard in the world of the urban high school student to reach high school students and build spiritually accountable relationships with them in the context of the local church.

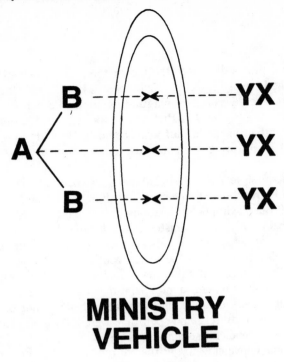

MINISTRY
VEHICLE

URBAN MODEL
Fig. 15.7

A=Youth pastor or senior pastor; B=Adult sponsor; X=Students (super-script indicates the ideal number of students); Y=Student leaders. Solid lines indicate accountable relationships; broken lines show advisory relationships.

BACKGROUND

Young Life Campaign and the Fellowship of Christian Athletes have employed the basic strategies of the urban model for years, so the strategies are not new.[15]

Ray Bakke attempted some of the same strategies when he formed the Innercity Athletic Mission to reach beyond the walls of a church on the North Side of Chicago in the late 1960s. More recently, Wayne Gordon at the Lawndale Community Church, on Chicago's southwest side, has blended the strate-

15. Bill Millikan, *Tough Love* (Old Tappan, N.J.: Revell, 1968).

gies of the parachurch agencies with the continuing presence of a local church and in the process has typified the urban model of youth ministry.[16]

MAJOR ACTIVITIES

Contact work on campus and on the streets by an adult youth worker builds a relationship between adult and student while earning the right to be heard.

Activities using a ministry vehicle, such as a recreation room, gymnasium, or weight machine, provide an opening to build relationships with students who may otherwise remain untouched by the church. The activities are not an end in themselves but are an opportunity to gain a hearing for the liberating power of the gospel.

Bible studies, which tend to be more like challenges from the Scripture by the adult leader, are tied closely to the activities using the ministry vehicle. Generally these must begin at a very basic level because of the absence of background in biblical teaching.

Camp, when possible, tends to be a vital catalyst in youth's breaking detrimental habits acquired in the streets of the city. The camp setting is conducive for experimenting with Christian principles for living.

LEADERSHIP ROLES

Pastor or *youth pastor* must be a person who gets out of the church building and meets students on their own "turf." He must be a risk taker, a visionary, and a person who is willing to do whatever is necessary to bring his dream to fulfillment.

Youth sponsors, frequently brought in from local colleges or from among young professional people, are an extension of the pastor's "presence" to more students. The activities are relational and discipleship oriented.

Student leaders perform a role within the peer groups with whom the pastor and sponsors are involved as they influence student opinions, bring their friends to meetings, and play an important part in maintaining discipline.

Parents for the most part have little active role in the urban model.

PREFERRED CONTEXT

Perhaps the best place for the urban model to function is in a new urban church or in a setting where the youth ministry to church families is nonexistent or at least limited to the Sunday school hour. Otherwise there will be

16. Cathleen Young, "Pastor, people send their hopes aloft." *Chicago Tribune,* 24 November 1983, Tempo section, pp. 1-2.

significant tension over with whom the pastor or youth pastor should be working.[17]

The Sunday school must not be a sacred cow in the urban model, or it is quite likely that it will not see significant growth. It simply does not seem compatible with the life-style of many of the urban youth reached through this model.

A supportive church board is essential in this model because usually the students brought into the church building through this kind of ministry do not have the same value system and respect for property that more established members of the church may have. Board members who see a hole in the wall of the gymnasium as a desecration of the church rather than an evidence of ministry may make the model difficult to employ.

YOUTH FELLOWSHIP MODEL

SCENARIO

It was Sunday afternoon at 3:30, and as usual, Bill and Sandy Wiggins's family room was buzzing with the sound of high school voices. Planning team number two was working on a program about witnessing that would be presented to the entire youth group the following Sunday at the Hi-Teens Youth Fellowship meeting just before the evening service.

Bill, an employee of the telephone company, and Sandy, mother of three and substitute school teacher, have been sponsors of the Hi-Teen group for the past six years. The Sunday afternoon planning meetings are a normal part of their weekly schedule. The procedure is simple. Each Sunday afternoon one of the four planning teams meet with the Wiggins to take the program materials provided by the church, adapt them to the specific needs of their group, and then assign team members to lead or participate in the various parts of the program for the following week. The preparation time is usually followed by a quick bite to eat before hurrying off to the weekly Hi-Teen meeting.

Because there are only about five or six people on a team, Bill and Sandy have a natural way to spend time with most of the students during the course of a month. Monthly socials and annual retreats are also part of the Hi-Teen schedule, but the heart of the youth program is the preparation and presentation cycle that starts in the Wiggins's family room.

PHILOSOPHY

Train students to serve the Lord through serving their youth group, specifically by means of the preparation and presentation of programs that relate to the Bible and its application to life.

17. See Glandion Carney, *Creative Urban Youth Ministry* (Elgin, Ill.: David C. Cook, 1984).

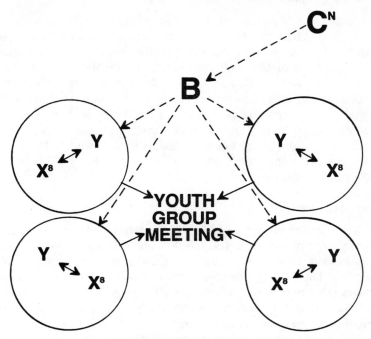

YOUTH FELLOWSHIP MODEL
Fig. 15.8

B=Adult sponsor; C=Parents; X=Students (superscript indicates the ideal number of students); Y=Student leaders. Solid lines indicate accountable relationships; broken lines show advisory relationships.

BACKGROUND

The youth fellowship model of youth ministry is the oldest of the approaches to youth work discussed in this chapter. Its roots date back to Francis Clark, pastor of the Williston Congregational Church, Portland, Maine, where in 1881 the Young People's Society of Christian Endeavor became a prototype of youth ministry for a variety of Protestant denominations.[18]

By the 1940s the Christian Endeavor style of ministry, with its multiplication of committees, commissions, and other institutional structures, had lost favor with young people and churchmen alike. A new emphasis called the

18. "Young People's Societies," in *The New Schaff-Herzog Encyclopedia of Religious Knowledge,* vol. 12, ed. Samuel Macauley Jackson (New York: Funk and Wagnalls, 1912), pp. 475-90.

youth fellowship had emerged. Oliver deWolf Cummings, its foremost advocate, explained that "Youth Fellowships have arisen out of a philosophy of Christian education which emphasizes: (1) the central place of the church as a true brotherhood of Christian community, and (2) the sacredness of human personality as over against an excessive stress upon organization."[19]

Designed to enable pastors and lay sponsors to assist adolescent youth in spiritual development, the model evolved into its present form as denominational publishing houses and later independent publishers began providing materials that could be used by lay sponsors in their work with church youth groups. It was the only significant model of youth ministry available during the middle years of the twentieth century.[20]

MAJOR ACTIVITIES

Youth group officers meet monthly at which time sponsors and elected officers choose program themes, schedule and plan social events, take care of the business matters of the youth group, and pray for the spiritual welfare of their peers. The meeting times are often used as a vehicle through which adult sponsors build nurturing relationships with emerging church leaders.

Small group preparation times allow adult sponsors to spend time with a different program team (usually there are four teams) each week in order to prepare a meeting on the theme assigned to them by the youth group officers. This tends to be key relational time for the students and sponsors.

Weekly meetings, usually an hour long, are most frequently held before or after the Sunday evening church service. At that time a planning team presents the topic it has worked on during the small group preparation time.

Social activities are wholesome events that allow students to develop social skills and enjoy structured time with church peer group members. Sometimes socials are used for evangelistic or community projects.

Retreats and camping activities are usually done in conjunction with other church groups and focus on evangelism and Christian living in a recreational context. Historically, many of the lifelong commitments to Christian service have been made in camping contexts.

LEADERSHIP ROLES

Adult sponsors serve as the coaches for the youth group. They facilitate, supervise, and support the activities in cooperation with the elected student leadership.

19. *The Youth Fellowship* (Chicago: Judson, 1956) p. 17.
20. See Gunnar Hoglund, *Better CYF Youth Groups* (Chicago: Harvest, 1960); Roy B. Zuck and Fern Robertson, *How to Be a Youth Sponsor* (Wheaton, Ill.: Scripture Press, 1960); Fern Robertson, "Sunday Evening Youth Programs," in *Youth and the Church,* ed. Roy G. Irving and Roy B. Zuck (Chicago: Moody, 1968), pp. 209-22.

Elected student leaders function as the captains of the youth fellowship. Their role is to provide planning and peer leadership for the activities of the group.

Planning teams are usually under the leadership of a team captain appointed by the elected student leaders. Though the primary function of a planning team is to prepare and present a program once a month, the sociological impact of the individual teams might be equally important, for the teams provide students a place to belong and a contribution to make to the group as a whole.

Parents play a supportive role in the youth fellowship model. Frequently they provide transportation and refreshments in exchange for the confidence that their teenaged children are benefiting by a wholesome youth group.

PREFERRED CONTEXT

The youth fellowship model tends to work best in churches where lay leaders are in charge of the church's youth ministry. These may vary in size from eight or ten to thirty students. Seldom does the group exceed thirty members or more than three or four adult sponsors.

Similarly, the model tends to work best where there is little competition from churches or parachurch ministries that have paid youth workers. Even national youth programs sponsored by the denomination with which the church is associated may lessen the effectiveness of the youth fellowship model unless those programs are philosophically compatible.

The model can be adapted for use with junior high school students through a careful selection of program material responsive to early adolescent needs and through close cooperation between adult leaders and junior high students. Adults, however, must remain sensitive to the insecurities of youth group members, especially when asked to speak in front of their peers.

CHOOSING A MODEL

The models presented in this chapter are not all appropriate for every situation. Some very sincere and enthusiastic youth workers could still fall flat on their faces in attempting to implement the model of their choice for one of three reasons:

1. The situation might not be appropriate.
2. The youth worker's abilities and gifts might not be suitable.
3. The Holy Spirit might be working to bring about something unforeseen by either the youth worker or the people in the church.

The first two reasons can be analyzed ahead of time. The final "obstacle" is the "checkmating" of the Holy Spirit and should be viewed as the starting point for a whole new set of lessons for both the youth worker and the church.

The following series of questions, when compared to the description of models presented in this chapter, should provide an adequate basis for selecting a model.

1. Does the church have a distinctive philosophy of ministry that must be reflected in the youth ministry? (Models 1, 3, 4, and 6 would be most likely to have such.)
2. Is the church willing to employ a youth pastor and provide an adequate budget to facilitate the model? (Models 1, 7, and 8 may not need these as much as the other models would.)
3. How well developed are the communication skills of the youth worker, especially in front of large groups? (Models 2, 3, 4, and 6 have greater need for this.)
4. How competent are the organizational skills of the youth worker? (Models 2, 3, 5, and 6 have strong needs in this area.)
5. How adept is the youth worker at meeting and gaining a hearing from non-Christian students? (Models 2 and 7 find this especially important.)
6. What kind of vision does the church have for ministering to the community immediately surrounding the church building? (Models 2, 4, and 7 would be most affected by this.)
7. How strong are the family ties within the church, especially as they relate to spiritual nurture? (Models 1, 3, 4, and 6 have strong needs for this.)
8. To what extent are mature and talented adults available to implement the model selected? (Models 2, 5, and 6 have special needs in this area.)
9. Are the students presently in the youth group sufficiently eager to make the changes necessary to implement a model that would have a significant spiritual impact on their lives? (This applies to all models.)
10. What kind of facilities does the church have that would enhance or weaken the model chosen? (Models 2, 5, and 7 might be most affected by this question.)

FOR FURTHER READING

Barker, Steve et al. *Good Things Come in Small Groups.* Downers Grove, Ill.: InterVarsity, 1985.

Carney, Glandion. *Creative Urban Youth Ministry.* Elgin, Ill.: David C. Cook, 1984.

Cousins, Don. "Son City: A Youth Program That Works." Robert M. Bland. "Involving Youth in Missions." In *Evangelizing Youth,* edited by Glenn C. Smith. Washington, D. C.: Paulist National Catholic Evangelistic Association; Wheaton, Ill.: Tyndale House, 1985.

Glovach, Vic, and Milford S. Sholund. "Parachurch Youth Movements and Organizations." In *Youth Education in the Church,* edited by Roy B. Zuck and Warren S. Benson. Chicago: Moody, 1978. `

Hestenes, Roberta. *Using the Bible in Groups.* Philadelphia: Westminster, 1983.

Peace, Richard. *Small Group Evangelism.* Downers Grove, Ill.: InterVarsity, 1985.

Stewart, Ed, and Neal McBride. *Bible Learning Activities: Youth.* Ventura, Calif.: Regal, 1978.

Yaconelli, Mike, and Jim Burns. *High School Ministry.* Grand Rapids: Zondervan, 1986.

Jim Burns

16

Starting a Youth Ministry from Scratch

Jerry and Debbie were bewildered. The previous week they had accepted the responsibility of starting a youth group from scratch at their new church. Now they were beginning to feel overwhelmed.

The two volunteers had never done anything like that before. In fact, only Debbie had been part of a high school youth group. Jerry had become a Christian during his college years. So the obvious place to start seemed to be by planning an activity that would allow them to get to know the students in the church.

Rapidly the plans took shape. An announcement about the Friday night party was made by the pastor. Debbie prepared the refreshments, and Jerry looked through party books at the library for games that would appeal to high school students.

Friday evening rolled around, but the students did not. Only one person showed up, a freshman whose mother dropped him off while she went shopping.

Jerry and Debbie's disappointment bordered on despair. "Why go to all the bother if the students aren't interested anyway?" they asked their pastor.

Wisely their pastor helped the couple draw up a list of questions that

Jɪᴍ Bᴜʀɴs, M.A., former minister to students, is president, Pacific Coast Study Center, Irvine, California.

needed to be answered before they ventured into their next attempt to start a youth group. Some of the questions included:

Which kids would be interested in a youth group?
Why would they be interested?
How much time will it take to be youth sponsors?
What should a youth group do?
What do we have to say to students?
How do we pay for all the refreshments that will be necessary? (The freshman had eaten all the food Debbie had prepared.)
Who could help work with the young people?
Are there any youth programming materials that make the sponsors' job easier?
Who wanted to start a youth group? Students? Parents? Pastor? Elders?

Before their next attempt to start a youth group from scratch, Jerry and Debbie had a lot of learning to do. Because initiating a youth program is much like planting a new church, the couple benefited by their pastor's experience. They began answering these questions by doing some basic research concerning the students of their community.

BACKGROUND INFORMATION

COMMUNITY

In gathering background information, be sure to look at the demographics of the community. Ask questions such as, What are the families like in our community and in our church? What activities are competing for students' time? What is the school system like?

SCHOOL

You can never underestimate the importance of the school environment. The average young person attends school more than 1,200 hours a year, or nearly forty hours a week. Compare that to the four hours a week in church for the active young person. It is not difficult to see that the impact a school campus has is often much greater than the church.

When starting a youth ministry, you should find out everything possible about the schools represented in your youth group. Learn about social cliques, "in" words, and the openness of the school administration to the spiritual environment. The better handle you have on the school environment, the better understanding you will have in meeting the needs of your group.

Simple suggestions would be to make an appointment with the school principal or vice-principal. Tell him or her that you are new to youth ministry and ask questions like, What are the biggest problems facing your students?

How can I be a positive factor in the lives of teenagers in the community? Treat the administration as the professionals; come to them as the learner and willing helper. My strong suggestion is not to compete with local school activities; rather, help to enhance those programs. The easiest way to keep informed is to subscribe to the school newspaper and get a district calendar of events. Be as visible as you can around the local school campuses.

STUDENTS

Ask questions. Almost all people like to talk about themselves. Ask questions about students' interests, school, family, and hobbies. Most young people have few significant adults interested in them as persons. At the beginning I would shy away from spiritual conversations and let them get to know me as a person, although you will be surprised at how many times they will bring up the spiritual dimension of life. Ask open-ended questions. Some good questions might include:

How are things going in school? Tell me about it.
Tell me about your family, how are things going at home?
What activities are you involved in outside school?
When I mention our church, what comes to your mind?
When did God become more than a word in your life?
What do you like to do for fun? With whom?

OTHER YOUTH WORKERS

To get better understanding of the environment and spiritual atmosphere, talk to other youth workers in the area. Far too often people start a youth ministry on the basis of their own past experiences, when, in fact, the need and challenges of a new youth work might be quite different. For example, a survey of youth pastors in a community in which I was seeking to begin a ministry revealed that their groups were filled with kids from single-parent families. Seeing this pressing need, the decision was made to emphasize dealing with the family.

DEVELOPING A PHILOSOPHY OF MINISTRY

Once a youth worker has a preliminary grasp of the context in which he or she is working, it is time to start developing a plan of attack. Much of this may have begun emerging through the conversations used to discover the background of the youth group. A philosophy is designed to answer the question, Why am I doing this? It controls the priorities of the youth worker, especially the volunteer who has only limited amounts of time to give to the ministry.

THINK RELATIONSHIPS

I recently asked 400 youth workers to list five sermons that had been extremely influential in their lives. Out of that large group there were only four people who could think of as many as five. The vast majority could think of only two. I then asked them to list five influential people in their lives. One minute later all 400 could produce a list of four or five influential people. The greatest impact you can make in the life of a student is in building a positive relationship with him or her.

Good youth ministries come in all shapes and sizes. Each program is different. Yet the one factor that remains true of every positive youth ministry in the world is that it is relational. Far too many youth ministries are centered on the program and not on relationships. As you start a youth ministry, think relationships. Spend less time worrying about program and numbers. It takes time to build relationships. Positive relationships will build a much healthier ministry than will a program focus.

As you begin a ministry, get to know the name of every person in your group or on your mailing list. Spend time with those students at ball games or drama events or whatever their interest might be. Let them know you are interested in them by visiting them on their territory with no strings attached. Jesus loves us not for what we do but for who we are. In building our foundation we need to make sure there is room for relationships with the unconditional love of Jesus as our example.

THINK ENCOURAGEMENT

It takes up to nine affirming comments to make up for one critical one. In our society many of our students receive very few encouraging words. Many parents have become too self-absorbed to affirm, and most teachers are over-whelmed or too busy with crowded classroom conditions to care. That places the ministry of affirmation with youth workers.

Young people today need youth workers who believe in them. One single-parent mother recently told me in my office, "I'm too tired to care." Most young people have an incredible amount of potential. They are waiting for someone to take the time to believe that they can become what they wish to be. Jesus believed Peter would become a leader of the Jerusalem church, and three years later, after many failures, the power of Jesus' belief paid off. Jesus made a habit of taking people like Zacchaeus, Matthew, and even Paul and looking beyond their bad points toward their potential. One of the cornerstones of building a youth ministry foundation is giving your students the gift of believing in themselves.

Young people also need youth workers who are liberal with praise. Mark Twain once said, "I can live two months on one good compliment." In the proper timing, we need to praise our students. When you see one of your students go out of his way to make the new person feel comfortable, go out of your way to praise him or her in return.

Finally, young people today need youth workers who are available. Reinforce the concept that you are available to listen or help when they are in need. Jesus allowed the little children to come even in His busy schedule. When your students know they mean so much that you will free up your busy schedule to be with them, you are giving them the gift of encouragement. Most often, when they have a need they will come.

However, even though we are to build availability into our youth ministry philosophy, we must also make sure we are taking enough time for ourselves, our families, and our relationship with God. What many kids call a crisis is simply a convenient time for them to talk. I would caution you to take care of your primary relationships in order to have a healthy, vital, available relationship with your youth group member who needs you.

THINK INVOLVEMENT

John and Donna are cousins. Their family backgrounds are very similar. Their church, school, social, and socioeconomic backgrounds are the same. Yet after high school John left the church, and Donna remained active. What made the difference? The answer comes in one word: involvement. John stayed on the fringe of the youth group, whereas Donna was an active participant, totally involved in the group. The important thing in youth ministry is not how many students are coming to your group, but rather, where your students will be five to ten years from now. Will they still be active in the Body of Christ? Involvement often makes the difference.

As we begin a youth ministry, we have to ask if we are creating mere spectators or if the kids are experiencing Christ firsthand. Many youth workers underestimate the contribution kids can make to their group. Many young people never get active in the youth group simply because they are never given responsibilities that really matter. Educators today remind us that people retain 5 to 10 percent of what they hear in a lecture and retain 80 percent of what they experience. Why has the Christian church most often chosen to continue to teach simply through the lecture method, creating a spectator mentality among the learners? Young people should learn through experience and involvement.

Youth workers are finally realizing that peer ministry is a very important foundational point to any philosophy of youth ministry. Increasingly we are finding that ministry to students can best be done by other students. True, we are taking a chance with theology and even methodology, but with correct supervision, that risk can be overcome, and there is no better influence than that of another peer.

A perfect illustration of this took place when our high school group invited a well-known evangelical leader to our winter camp. There are few more dynamic and powerful speakers in the evangelical world today. Yet on their evaluations at the end of the retreat, the majority of the young people said that the practical seminars given by fellow students were the most helpful part of the retreat. A typical response was "Lisa's talk on developing proper self-esteem was really helpful. She has just gone through what I am going through now." Students often prefer the less dynamic, if they can get input from fellow students. The credibility factor of students ministering to other students is perhaps the most powerful influence in your new youth group.

THINK SUPPORT TEAM

"For lack of guidance a nation falls, but many advisers make victory sure" (Prov. 11:14).

The Lone Ranger method of youth ministry is not a viable option. Even the Lone Ranger needed Tonto. Applying the preceding proverb to youth ministry means that students need adult role models and counselors. A youth group with good solid adult leadership is one with a very positive influence in the lives of the students it serves.

As you begin your ministry, look for a diversity of adult staff. A good staff will have a mixture of personalities and interests as well as job backgrounds and ages. These people will affect the kind of program that develops, and the wise youth worker will build around the strengths of volunteers. For a larger group you need a diversity of staff to meet the different needs of the group. Recruit a married couple, singles, college students, athletes, musicians, and in our mobile society even grandparents can be an excellent addition to the youth staff.

The athlete, of course, will tend to relate to the students more interested in athletics, whereas the musician will tend to influence the kids in the group with musical ability. With the breakdown of the nuclear family structure, it is important to have married couples as positive influences and role models in the area of Christian marriage.

One of the continuing challenges in starting youth ministry from scratch is the on-going exercise in faith for recruitment. Securing a good support team is one of the most important ingredients for a successful ministry. Recruitment never ends. You can never have too many positive adult role models for your students. If the adults are older than you, or approach life a little differently, you should not look at that as an obstacle. Instead, such diversity provides people who will be able to relate to some of the students you might find difficult to reach.

Here are two sure-fire recruiting ideas. First, use your elder board (deacons, session, church leadership) and senior pastor to make a list of potential support team personnel. Approach a person on that list and say, "Last week at our elders' meeting your name came up as a possible youth ministry support team volunteer. Would you ever be interested in joining our team? By using the authority of the church leadership or the senior pastor, you may relieve the person of any fears that he could not do youth ministry. After all, if the elders believe in him, he might as well try.

Second, ask your own youth group members to suggest who they would like as adult support team staff. After the kids have chosen several names, go with a few of the student leaders in your group and say, "Our youth group has unanimously voted to ask you to volunteer for the year with our high school youth ministry." That relieves the fear of not being accepted by the kids.

Once you have started to build a team, training is of major importance. I believe many good youth group volunteers leave the ministry quickly because they are not getting the training and support they need from the youth worker in charge of the ministry.

You can do much of the training yourself. Bring in other people for specialized areas. For example, if you want to give your volunteers basic counseling skills, ask a Christian psychologist in your area to instruct. Ask your pastor to teach Bible study techniques. The local parachurch leader can give evangelism training. Find out when one of the local or national youth ministry training events is scheduled in your area, and take your staff to an all-day training event. An important benefit will be that your people will stay as volunteers longer. They will sense your encouragement in their lay ministry.

THINK PROGRAM PLANNING

You have perhaps heard the saying that he or she who aims at nothing achieves it everytime. That certainly is true when it comes to developing a program in your youth ministry.

Initially, determine the needs of the group. Some programs that worked for you in the past may not be effective in your new ministry. Do not come with a preset program. Develop the program slowly, and build it around the specific relational and spiritual needs of your group. Spend the first few months asking questions about needs, wants, desires, the community, or anything else that might help you get started. As you begin to feel comfortable with the felt and real needs, plan the program to fit those specific areas.

Now it is time to think through a year's calendar. Far too many youth programs are not planned in advance. Spend at least one full evening with your adult volunteers and students brainstorming ideas for the year. Take each aspect of the ministry and write down ideas. Look individually at each area in the program: Sunday school, evening youth group meetings, retreats, special events, mission projects, and fund raisers. Then begin to schedule in your ideas tentatively on the calendar. Wait a week or so, then meet again to make final some of those dates.

When you have put a calendar together for a year, you can easily delegate responsibility to other members of the staff and youth group. Why should you plan the roller skating party for February when one of your students could easily organize the same event? Putting a program on the calendar will free you up for personal ministry, because you will not always be bogged down with administrative tasks.

One of the biggest complaints of veteran youth workers is that they are overwhelmed with program tasks and therefore are unable to spend time with the kids. The answer lies in cutting back on some program. No one ever said you had to have a social every two weeks. Over-programming can drown you. Delegating responsibility will also increase your effectiveness. As you start a youth ministry from scratch, such advice can save you from early burnout.

PRACTICAL QUESTIONS

Even with a solid philosophy worked out, many questions will remain. A few have been identified so that people like Jerry and Debbie will have some initial suggestions from which they can discover their own answers appropriate to their youth group as it develops.

Should I use my own material for Bible studies and programs or some other source?

Here is a great quote, "The essence of creativity is the ability to copy." One of the first agenda items of a new youth ministry is to get as many resources as possible. There are many curricula, workbooks, books, and other materials available. You can always adapt these resources to fit your own situation. In doing so you are saving yourself literally hours of preparation time and freeing up hours for ministry.

Where can I go for youth ministry ideas?

Besides the normal places—youth ministry books, conventions, and seminars—get acquainted with other youth ministers in your area. Exchange ideas, resources, programs, and anything else that might be beneficial. Look through experienced youth workers' libraries. Ask seminar speakers and professors what they are doing. Subscribe to youth ministry newsletters and magazines that will help you stay fresh.

I have a small group. Should we combine the junior high and senior high program?

Not if you can help it. Sometimes there are reasons that necessitate combining programs. If you must, then make the best of it. However, when you combine junior high and senior high you are doing a number of things wrong. First, you are stifling junior high leadership, because the high schoolers will tend to lead. Second, most high schoolers will not feel as comfortable bringing their high school friends to a group that includes junior highers. Third, you will have to "water down" your content for the younger person; and fourth, you will have to be much more careful with the guy/girl relationships. My suggestion is to split the groups as early as possible and do some of the events or experiences together.

What should I have accomplished in the first three months? The first year?

I believe most people have goals far too high for the first year and too low for the long term. The first year of ministry must be looked at as building a foundation. The way to build a firm foundation in youth ministry is to make sure you know the students in your group. When your students feel loved, affirmed, believed in, and personally cared for, then you have a foundation for bigger and better things. Relational ministry is a process; it takes time. Within the first year, if you have a core of adult volunteers and kids who are beginning to be excited about the youth group, then you have done a terrific job.

How can I get the students to feel ownership in the youth group?

The answer is involvement. Students who are involved in the group stay. Students who are merely spectators lose interest and leave. In order for your young people to feel ownership in the group they must have tasks that matter. There is no reason they cannot be a part of every aspect of the youth group. Artistic students could be doing the flyers and posters; others could be making phone calls. Everyone can help plan the retreats and have responsibilities for them. Even the spiritual discussions can at times be more effectively led by students because of the credibility factor. Ministry to students can best be done by other students because of the natural tendency to experience peer influence. A youth ministry should be done with positive adult direction and influence but with the students taking most of the responsibility.

How can I get the students to be serious about spiritual matters if all they want is fun and games?

I am not opposed to fun at all. However, I do know the reason I have stayed in youth ministry is because young people are at an age at which they are making spiritual decisions that will affect the rest of their lives. I believe students are really interested in spiritual matters but sometimes are not very vocal about it. There are a number of ways to get students more involved spiritually. One is to go on a mission trip. Give the students an opportunity to have their hearts break with what breaks the heart of God. Second, in a retreat atmosphere people are more open to spiritual things. Give your kids the opportunity to have a fun and exciting retreat, and do not apologize for the spiritual time. Third, make sure you are discussing topics that really are important to your students. If they show little interest, start with topics like sex and dating, getting along with parents, friendship, peer pressure, and then move toward deeper topics. Finally, do not expect too much too soon. Many students are not developing spiritually as quickly as others. One of the best suggestions would be to start with a small group Bible study. Let the students who are spiritually inclined begin to invite their friends as they get excited about learning more about the spiritual dimensions of life.

CONCLUSION

A year had passed since that first youth group "meeting" sponsored by Jerry and Debbie. For the past five weeks the attendance had been averaging a little over eighteen students, and there are now thirty-three names on the mailing list. That may not sound very impressive in an era when youth groups of two and three hundred are not uncommon, but none of them started off that large.

Most encouraging to Jerry and Debbie is that they have another couple working with them in the youth ministry, and a single young man will be joining the team in two weeks.

In addition, the original fears that the students would not accept them have proved unfounded. Many of them even bring their friends over to Jerry and Debbie's apartment for advice or just to talk.

"No program material is perfect," the pastor had told them, but just the same, the materials they had discovered through their Christian bookstore had made their year a lot easier.

One last note. That lone freshman who showed up at the first youth group "meeting" is still attending. He considers himself the "charter member" of the group.

FOR FURTHER READING

Barrs, Jerram. *Shepherds and Sheep: A Biblical View of Leading and Following.* Downers Grove, Ill.: InterVarsity, 1983.

Collins, Gary C. *How to Be A People Helper.* Santa Ana, Calif.: Vision House, 1976.

Corbett, Jan. *Creative Youth Leadership.* Valley Forge, Pa.: Judson, 1979.

Cosgrove, Francis M. *Essentials of Disipleship.* Colorado Springs, Colo.: NavPress, 1979.

Group. P.O. Box 481, Loveland, Colo. 80539.

Le Peau, Andrew T. *Paths of Leadership.* Downers Grove, Ill.: InterVarsity, 1983.

Little, Sara. *To Set One's Heart: Belief and Teaching in the Church.* Atlanta: John Knox, 1983.

Rerr, Ed, and Bobbie Reed. *Creative Bible Learning for Youth Grades 7-12.* Ventura, Calif.: Regal, 1979.

Son Power Idea Sheet. 1825 College Avenue, Wheaton, Ill. 60187.

Youthworker Journal. Youth Specialities, 1224 Greenfield Drive, El Cajon, Calif. 92021.

17

Scott W. Benson

The First Six Months
of a Youth Ministry

Welcome to real life. The following is not an excerpt from the best-selling, unabridged version of *The Life and Times of an Average American Youth Pastor.* Nor is it a hypothetical case study creatively designed to grab the reader's attention. No, it is reality. And the reality of this scenario is focused on the concept of transition. Transition involves change, and change is not easy. Yes, there is a sense of adventure and risk—the fresh realization of a new beginning. But change also means launching into an unknown future.

Like Abraham, who was called to leave behind all that was familiar and comfortable, God sometimes calls us to move on to newness and uncertainty. Imagine Abraham, seventy-five, his mid-life crisis behind him, reflecting on the good old days with his sweetheart Sarah, when all of a sudden he is told by God that he is to pack up and leave home. No maps from the auto club; no idea how long it would take to get there (wherever "there" was); just the assurance that God would be with him. What an intriguing character Abraham is. He encounters God's call and responds without hesitation in obedience and trust (Gen. 12:1-7; Heb. 11:8-10).

I, too, recently encountered God's call. My emotional response, however,

SCOTT W. BENSON, M. Div., is pastor of high school ministries, Lake Avenue Congregational Church, Pasadena, California.

was somewhat more hesitant than Abraham's. Verbally I was able to say, "Lord, I'll do it, if You want me to go," but on an emotional level there was a dramatic sense of loss.

To say good-bye to the high school students and families in whom I had invested my life over the past several years was traumatic. To realize that the dynamics of our interpersonal relationships would never again be the same was difficult to accept. And yet, there was the reality of God's call and the assurance that the same God who took care of Abraham would also be watching out for this young high school pastor as he moved through the dreaded process of transition.

So now the new adventure began. A brand *new* batch of students and parents with whom to interact and develop relationships, a *new* adult ministry team who joined me in dreaming how to become more effective in reaching out to high schoolers, a *new* pastoral staff from whom I could learn and be sharpened, and a *new* office in which to study, counsel, administrate, and laugh. So much newness; so much change. And although change still is not easy, I am confident in God's sovereign call.

But how do we launch into this new adventure? How do we begin to think through a strategy for the initial six months of a ministry to students? Coeditor Mark Senter helps us get a grip on a philosophy of ministry by suggesting a relationship-oriented approach to nurturing students toward spiritual maturity. In essence, he contends that as we spend time with individual students in order to understand what is going on in their personal lives (e.g., family and peer dynamics, contemporary trends in their youth culture, etc.), we will build relationships of trust. Such interpersonal contacts facilitate the process of drawing "students into a maturing relationship with God through Jesus Christ." (See also chap. 1.) The apostle Paul identifies the ultimate objective in discipleship as growing toward "unity in the faith and in the knowledge of the Son of God and [becoming] mature, attaining to the whole measure of the fulness of Christ" (Eph. 4:13).

If the ultimate goal in youth ministry is discipling students who live out the lordship of Christ, how do we begin to interact with them in the first six months? And beyond that, how do we lay down a solid foundation for long-term ministry? As a seasoned youth ministry veteran once said to me, "Nothing good happens fast." Productive ministry takes time to develop and, in reality, is constantly evolving. A long-range commitment and a marathon mentality are the essential nuts and bolts of youth ministry. But those first six months are significant as we begin to hammer out both ministry and personal life-style patterns.

Within the limited scope of this chapter we will look at several critical areas that will be helpful to consider in developing a wholistic strategy for the first six months.

UNDERSTANDING THE DYNAMICS OF TRANSITION

Transition and change are traumatic because they necessitate the "disruption of familiar communal patterns." Robert G. Kemper argues that physical place (where we are) and personal identity (who we are) are interrelated. He continues by noting that "we associate many events of personal significance with the particularities of place."[1] For instance, in my own experience Deerfield, Illinois, will forever be etched in my memory as the locale for my greatest struggles with the rigors of academia. Four years of my life were invested in seminary pursuits as Trinity Evangelical Divinity School became home. In moving to Southern California to begin an internship in high school ministry, I constantly noticed my tendency to refer to Deerfield as back home. Even though I wanted to live in the present tense, at least on a cognitive level, I had a difficult time convincing my emotions that Southern California was now home.

Kemper suggests a second dimension involved in the dynamics of transition is "the disruption of your network of interpersonal relationships." He states, "Moving makes you a dropout, a willing disassociate, maybe even a traitor to your former network of personal associates. By leaving one network for another, you betray the one you leave. That may make you feel guilty, and it may make the ones you leave feel resentful and angry."[2] The high school mentality of students struggles to understand, on an emotional level, why we would walk out of their lives. Even with a conceptual grasp of the intimate notion of God's call, they still feel abandoned. Initially, they want to deny the reality of the loss. They try to convince themselves that it is not really happening, that it is just an imaginative worst-case scenario.

But that sense of loss is not the exclusive experience of our students. We feel it deeply too. Or, at least we should, if we are honest with our emotions. We have invested long hours in the lives of our students. Much of our personal and professional identity is wrapped up in our involvement with them. For some of us "imbalanced, one-dimensional ministry machines," they have been our lives. Do not kid yourself, it hurts.

But the good news is that there is a healing process. We can express our pain and confront our loss. Robert Kemper insightfully comments that as we work through this healing process with our students, we are

> giving each other the recognition that (we) have loved and cared for each other. If (we) had not, then leaving would be painless and meaningless. (We) give each other tears to express the depth and power of the relationship (we) have had. (We) need to give verbal gifts by which to express (our) mutual appreciation for joys and

1. Robert G. Kemper, *Beginning a New Pastorate* (Nashville: Abingdon, 1978), p. 20.
2. Ibid., p. 21.

sorrows shared in intimate relationships. It is wrong to cut off the giving of those gifts to each other. It is good to be intentional about it.[3]

Let yourself be loved. Verbalize your hurt. It is all right to be human.

Some of you might be wondering, What does all this have to do with beginning a new ministry to students? Absolutely everything. If it is true that "we are what we have been becoming," then it is imperative that we examine the emotional baggage that we are bringing with us into the present tense.

Bruce Grubbs contends that "ministers underestimate the impact of termination from their previous pastorate on both themselves and their families." He suggests that we identify various aspects of our former ministry experience with a series of perceptive statements and questions:

1. These people will be missed from our former church.
2. These activities will be missed from our former community.
3. I liked the former house because . . .
4. We accomplished the following things in other places of ministry.
5. We had these problems in the former church.
6. I am grateful for these things out of our last experience.
7. What could cause our laughter or tears to flow easily?
8. What mistakes did we make that we want to avoid in our new church?[4]

By thinking through our responses to these statements and questions, we begin the process of becoming emotionally refocused so that we can move into the future.

Another dynamic involved in transition is the impact that change has on our families. Often there is an initial negative response to the prospect of disrupting family life-style patterns. Kemper, however, encourages us with the reality that through the adventure of moving, a family discovers that "they are more adaptable and flexible than they had thought. They do help one another; they do need one another. The big surprise is that family identity is portable. It is not dependent upon place; it is dependent upon sustained, nurturing, interdependent relationships."[5] Transition can be a significant bonding experience for our families if we take the time to explore and express our feelings about the implications of the move.

A final aspect of the transition process that is critical to understand is what Bruce Grubbs defines as the "three stages of ministry."

---

3. Ibid., pp. 84-85.
4. Bruce Grubbs, *The First Two Years: A Pastor's Guide to Getting Started in a Church* (Nashville: Convention Press, 1979), pp. 13-14.
5. Kemper, *Beginning,* p. 86.

1. Start-up stage: 12-24 months
2. Established ministry stage: indefinite period
3. Closure: days to months

He notes that "each stage influences each subsequent stage" in a "natural sequence."[6] Within the initial weeks (first four to twelve weeks) of the start-up stage, the proverbial honeymoon period sets in. As Grubbs describes with depth and insight, the honeymoon is a strategic time frame in which the youth pastor and the church will

> likely idealize each other. Human frailities may not be apparent. This time of idealizing lasts from two to four weeks. After that an awareness develops that neither party is really as perfect as first hoped. However, neither you nor the church is likely to admit this out loud. Because of an unwillingness to admit reality, an illusion is created based on denial. There is reluctance to give candid feedback to each other.
>
> The danger is not that feedback will occur but that, for fear of hurting each other's feelings, feedback is not given or received. It is easy to develop a false sense of security as a result of this. You may tend to operate with the assumption that people totally approve your actions. They may in fact be skeptical. You can easily mistake their silence for approval. . . . You may be afraid to see and hear the signals from people that say, "slow down," "not that way," "not at this time." The danger is that some mistakes of great substance may be made during this time. Wisdom says move slowly during these first few weeks and months.

Grubbs continues by observing that:

> The honeymoon period ends as you and the people begin to share your deeper feelings. Criticism may come. You may want to avoid hearing it, but it is best to hear and heed. Church members may lack the ability to share their feelings in a positive way. Both you and the church may be uncomfortable during this time. However, the end of the honeymoon marks the beginning of a potentially more mature relationship. . . . If you are aware of the need to listen and be open rather than to withdraw and be defensive, this period can be a time of growth. The more you resist the words and feelings of others, the more powerful and emotional this period will become. Seeking feedback says to people that you care about their thoughts and feelings. This open, approachable style is far better than one that is closed, inflexible and defensive.[7]

Simultaneous to the honeymoon experience is a process of testing. Students are traditionalists. They are not as adaptable and flexible as we often

6. Grubbs, *Guide*, p. 8.
7. Ibid., p. 16.

assume them to be. Before they will take the risk of owning us as their new pastor, they must examine our authenticity as a person and as a minister. Do we really know Jesus in a deeply personal relationship? Are we willing to be vulnerable about our own struggles and areas of weakness? Are we someone who will listen with compassion and understanding? Do we really care about who they are? Will we love and accept them unconditionally? Can we be trusted?

Change is not easy. The first six months can be terribly traumatic. But if we are committed to relaxing and even enjoying the dynamics of transition a day at a time, the process will become at least bearable, if not truly productive.

BUILDING RELATIONSHIPS WITH STUDENTS

If our ministry to students is to be based on a strategy of nurturing them toward spiritual maturity through interpersonal relationships, then how do we begin to interact with students in the first six months? Bill Muir clearly states, "Relationships can't grow unless people spend time with one another." He notes that "essential to 'redeeming' or building quality into time together" is our sensitivity to students. Referring to a research project designed to discover which interpersonal dynamics students look for in relating to significant adults, Muir suggests three crucial qualities: (1) the ability to listen and empathize with their feelings; (2) the ability to understand their concerns, values, interests, and desires; (3) the ability to communicate and interact with them as mature young adults.[8]

Muir develops a model for an incarnational style of youth ministry by looking at Jesus' approach to building relationships. (1) Jesus was a *lover.* To love means to give and to serve. In Mark 10:45 Jesus said that His purpose in relating to people was to serve and to give His life away. That is a radical step and involves a lot of risk, but it is what Christ calls us to do (John 13:12-17). (2) Jesus was the ultimate *example* of obedience to the Father. Students want to know how to live out the Christian life in contemporary twentieth century youth culture. They are not looking for models of perfection, but for people who are in process of becoming all that God intends them to be. As Muir asserts, "If our disciples are to grow we must 'flesh out' for them the life Christ demands that we live." (3) Jesus *accepted* people without any limiting conditions. There was no sense of "I'll accept you if." Muir reminds us that relating to students demands that "we dare not hold on to any preconceived mindsets that result in our discriminating against those who don't measure up in looks, performance, popularity and influence. We must accept students where they are in their own pilgrimage." In reaching out exclusively to the

8. Bill Muir, "The Youth Leader as a Model," in Gary Dausey, ed., *The Youth Leader's Source Book* (Grand Rapids: Zondervan, 1983), pp. 58-59.

"beautiful people," we are merely feeding our egos and engaging in a "subtle form of narcissism." (4) Jesus took the risk of getting *near* people in order to love them at close range. Jesus' style of relating with vulnerability enabled people to know Him as a real person.[9]

Bruce Grubbs picks up on this aspect of Jesus' transparency with people when he suggests,

> As you relate to persons, you can deepen your ministry relationship by letting them know that you too are human. You have doubts, frustrations, and struggles in your own life. You do not have all the answers. If you present yourself only at the points of strength and success, many will be frightened or intimidated and will avoid relating to you. It is important to realize that people generally relate to others most at the points of common limitations and weaknesses rather than at the points of mutual strengths.[10]

But I can hear someone asking, How do you get down to the business of actually building relationships with students? Spend time with them; meet them on their "turf"; tactfully move into their lives. Contact work, or going to where students hang out, can be intimidating. But it communicates "I really care about you."

Doug Stevens suggests a number of strategic locations for spending time with students:

on campus
parks
amusement centers
sporting events
theaters
recreational fitness clubs
extracurricular school activities
beaches
fast-food restaurants
parties
concerts[11]

Because students invest a lot of time at school, Stevens encourages us to check out the possibility of an on campus relational ministry. He states three helpful insights to consider before we investigate whether or not we can get access to the campus:

1. The youth leader must be committed to a consistent involvement that is frequent enough to ensure recognition and continuity. Showing up every other

9. Ibid, pp. 60-61.
10. Grubbs, *Guide*, p. 25.
11. Doug Stevens, *Called to Care* (Grand Rapids: Zondervan, 1985), pp. 119-20.

month qualifies us as strangers. Any cheating on the commitment will erode both our motivation and our accomplishments.

2. We must assume the burden of proving to the school authorities that we are an asset to them. They have an important responsibility to limit access to the property. Somehow, we have to convince the administration that we care about their school, that we are there to affirm and support the students we already know and to extend genuine friendship to their friends, and that we are not there to proselytize or hustle kids for our program. It is better to let kids invite other kids to our activities.

3. We need to sternly remind ourselves why we are there. We seek visibility without ostentation, proximity without intrusion and credibility without coercion. We are there to encourage the teenagers who are Christians. . . . We are also anxious to meet their friends and undermine any misconceptions about Christians and Christianity. . . . "Who are these guys, anyway?" they will ask. Their curiosity about us can work to our advantage.[12]

But what do you do when you are with students? How do you actually get to know who they are? How do you persuade them to open up and get beyond monosyllabic responses? The trust factor is critical. Students want to know if we are genuinely interested in them as individuals. Trust takes time to develop and mature. But slowly, students will detect your authenticity and will begin to take the risk of saying, "This is who I am."

With nonthreatening, open-ended questions, such as the following, we encourage them to share who they are: (1) How are things going in school? Tell me about it. (2) What school-related activities are you involved with? (3) What's going on at home? How do you relate to the members of your family? (4) How do you enjoy spending your free time? (5) What kind of music are you into? (6) Who are your closest friends? Do you feel you can be honest with one another?

As we build a sense of trust, students will begin to share more significant aspects of their lives (e.g., value systems that determine what is important to them and what motivates them; how they feel about their personal relationship with God; how secure they feel in peer relationships, etc.).

Developing relationships with other youth workers in the area (both local church and parachurch personnel) will provide further insight into the surrounding youth culture. Their experiences in interacting with students will give you a perspective on contemporary trends such as:

1. Does the school system demand high academic performance? How open is the school administration to our presence on campus?
2. Do students have heavy parental expectations to achieve scholastically?
3. What is the general socioeconomic background of the students?

12. Ibid., p. 121-22.

4. What kind of value systems do their life-styles reflect (e.g., materialistically oriented, etc.)?
5. What kinds of subcultural groups are represented (e.g., preppies, burnouts, jocks, etc.)?
6. How do students spend their free time (e.g., jobs, sports, clubs)?
7. What is the latest in hairstyle and clothes?
8. What fads are currently popular?
9. What are some of the slang words or phrases students currently use?
10. What kind of music are they into?
11. Where do students like to hang out (e.g., fast food places, beaches)?
12. Who are their heroes, role models, celebrities?
13. What about drugs and alcohol involvement?
14. Tell me about the party scene.
15. What are they watching on television and at the movies?
16. What about popular magazines and books?

By talking directly with key school administrators about current trends, subscribing to student school newspapers, obtaining school district calendars of the year's extracurricular activities, you will pick up a lot about the new student milieu. Other contacts in the community are also important. Police, social workers, and village managers can help the new kid on the block understand his new setting. All of this investigative background work will facilitate the relationships you build with students in those first six months.

GETTING IN TOUCH WITH THE CORPORATE CHURCH BODY

A ministry to students can not survive in a vacuum. It must be plugged into the corporate church family. The connectional aspect of the local church, in which a youth minister is integrally related to persons of various generations, should enable a youth pastor to feel a sense of support. And yet too often both students and youth pastor feel a lack of community with the larger church family. Students perceive themselves as unable to understand and/or relate to corporate church worship. That's for adults only, they assume. Students need to develop a separate group identity before they feel comfortable joining the larger congregation. However, without some integration into the corporate whole, their church involvement will likely end after high school or perhaps college.

As youth pastors, we often fail to invest the time to explain our strategy or philosophy of ministry, which initially might appear to be too radical or innovative. As a result, we feel lonely and alienated.

How then do you get in touch with the corporate church family? How do you begin that bonding process when you are the "new kid on the block"? Let us consider four initial areas.

INVESTIGATING THE PAST

Getting an historical perspective is helpful in understanding the present. Discovering how the church began, its initial goals and polity structure, growth patterns, significant points of crisis, transition shifts in theological outlook, and key leadership personnel changes will provide invaluable insight.

Researching the philosophy of ministry and program structure of the previous youth pastor is crucial. To spend time directly with your predecessor in talking through his or her ministry style and objectives is extremely helpful. Asking perceptive questions of the adult ministry team and the students will give you a further perspective of the former program.

It is crucial, however, that when you phrase your questions, you do not stimulate a lot of negative feedback. Your purpose is not to create a dramatic contrast between you as the new hero in town, complete with white hat and silver bullets, and that "other guy" who finally faded into the sunset. If possible, you want to affirm what has gone on in the past and express your desire to build on the foundation of the previous ministry.

TAKING THE PRESENT TEMPERATURE

What kind of contemporary scenario are you inheriting? Your analysis of the available resources (e.g., physical building space, audio-visual, curriculum and materials, financial budget) will give you an idea of the variables you can plug into your new ministry equation. An understanding of the church's power structure (e.g., how boards and committees interact, who has the authority to dictate policy) will enable you to know how to work within the system.

Bruce Grubbs argues that it is "important to develop a balanced perspective about (our) new ministry situation. We need to keep the beginning enthusiasm of seeing the church's qualities and opportunities." In order to "counteract disappointment and disillusionment," Grubbs suggests that we take "an assets and liabilities inventory."[13]

1. The following qualities of the church impress me:
   a. Positive factors about the church itself:
   b. Desirable qualities in individuals I have met:
   c. Things I like about the physical facilities:
   d. Impressions from staff/key leaders in the church lead me to feel that together we could have a good ministry here because:
   e. Terms of the call that I liked:
   f. Discoveries since I came that have excited or pleased me:
2. The following things do not please me about the church:
   a. Negative factors about the church:
   b. Undesirable qualities in persons I have met:
   c. Some disturbing feelings I have in talking with persons:

13. Grubbs, *Guide*, p. 21-22.

d. Some limitations I see about the physical facilities:
e. Impressions from staff/key leaders suggesting that we might have difficulties working together at these points:
f. Terms of the call that were less than desirable:
g. Surprises I have encountered that trouble me:

After we work through the inventory, Grubbs gives us some insightful comments to reflect on.

> How do you feel about these assets and liabilities? Your feelings are important. They need to be recognized and dealt with in prayer and conversation. If you ignore or stifle your feelings, they can become destructive. There is a need to keep in touch with the feelings you have about the church liabilities. They can become dissatisfiers if you dwell on them. The romance you have for your new church and its attractive points can turn to disappointment unless you respond to liabilities in a mature manner.

> The realities are not the cause of discouragement. Rather the feelings you have about them are. If you feel the liabilities were hidden from you, then you may feel betrayed. If you can see them only as problems, you may become critical. But if you see them as the realities of the situation, with counterparts in every church, then you can maintain a healthy attitude. Recognize that just as you have idealized the church, you have also been idealized. The fact is that the church is what it is and you are what you are. Efforts should be made to accept the congregation with both its strengths and weaknesses, its assets and liabilities.[14]

What is the heartbeat of the church? What dreams are the corporate body pursuing together? Why does the church even exist? A church's style of ministry will tell you a lot about its philosophy and direction. What do you feel when you come into the worship service? Is there a sense of warmth and acceptance? Is there an emphasis on a strict liturgical format or a more freely flowing approach? Does the senior pastor communicate with an expositional teaching style or is his preaching more relational? Does the church have a vision for covenant or support groups that focus on inductive Bible study and caring for one another?

Ask a lot of questions and be sensitive to what is going on around you. It might seem overwhelming at first. Everything is so new. But slowly you will begin to feel a sense of understanding and ownership of this new ministry environment.

BONDING WITH THE PASTORAL TEAM

A third dynamic in getting in touch with the church family is to begin the process of becoming integrated with the pastoral team. Whether you are

14. Ibid., p. 22.

joining a large team of diversified specialists or one other ministry partner, it is crucial that you invest time in building a sense of staff unity. The key individual on which to focus is the one who will be directly holding you accountable as your managerial supervisor. If you are involved in a larger multistaff ministry, more than likely that person will be the minister or director of Christian education. Begin by spending time together on a personal level. Hopefully you will be relating on both a friendship and a professional basis. Next, make sure you have hammered out the specifics of your written job description. It is imperative that both of you have the same understanding of your particular responsibilities.

Bruce Grubbs offers insightful comments on the notion of philosophical expectations. He says that too often both our expectations of what the church is and the church's perception of who we are are dangerously unrealistic. Because we bring a sense of newness and hope, we are easily perceived as the answer to questions and the solution to problems. He points out that when we readily take on a self-imposed messianic complex, we only create or encourage unrealistic expectations. He argues that "attempting to be a superhuman pastor can result in disappointment and disillusionment for yourself and others. Human inability to accomplish superhuman tasks can create an unnecessary sense of personal failure and guilt."[15]

Expectations cannot remain theoretical. They must be clearly defined statements that are both achievable and mutually accepted by you and your managerial supervisor. Try working through the following questions with the one who will be holding you accountable.

1. How do you perceive my role on staff?
2. How do you envision my ministry to students being integrated into the corporate educational program of the church?
3. How many hours do you imagine me investing each week in youth ministry?
4. What goals do you have for our youth ministry in these first six months?
5. How will I know whether or not I have accomplished these goals (criteria for measurement)?
6. What, if anything, would you like to see changed in these first six months?
7. How much authority do I have to change things? What kinds of issues do I need to talk through with you before I make any changes?
8. How do you see us working together to establish youth ministry goals and objectives for the future?
9. How often will we meet together on a regular basis? What will be the format of our meetings?

15. Ibid., pp. 4, 21.

10. What is your philosophy of youth ministry? Describe the basic components of a ministry to students.
11. What is your concept of discipleship? Describe a general profile of a discipled student.
12. How do you feel about cross-cultural student mission projects?
13. What kind of financial budget variables do I have to work with? What is the possibility of increasing the youth ministry budget?
14. What is the possibility of paid interns or staff assistants for our ministry?

Our intent is not to threaten with this formidable list of opening questions, but simply to initiate dialogue and facilitate understanding. Any hesitant feelings or a sense that something written between the lines has not been clarified must be confronted head-on. The establishment of a foundation of rapport and openness will be invaluable to a creative and productive relationship with the managerial supervisor.

Time should be spent with the other pastoral team members as well. You can begin to build relational bridges by asking them to share their own personal stories, how they came to be involved with the church staff, and what their dreams are for both their own area of specialized ministry and for the corporate church family.

Doug Stevens addresses the importance of developing an open and loyal relationship with the senior pastor. He cogently affirms:

> Without his full support, our objectives for youth ministry are in jeopardy. . . . Senior pastors don't like surprises. . . . It's our obligation to keep them informed and updated. To represent us intelligently, they must have sufficient information about our work. . . . Keep the information flow both consistent and manageable.
>
> Your senior pastor also needs to know the philosophy and objectives that guide our youth ministry. These should be outlined for him and periodically evaluated. When he responds to them, we need to listen intently to his affirmation, critique, and suggestions. Combined with other sources of evaluation, his suggestions should be carefully weighed.
>
> At the same time, the pastor wants a reasonable, honest and prompt response to his concerns for the youth ministry. Our consistent responsiveness is the most reassuring indication to him that our working relationship is on track.[16]

TEAMING-UP WITH THE HOME FRONT

A final aspect of identifying with the larger church community is to develop a sense of team ministry with parents. Parents are wondering, Who are

16. Doug Stevens, "Looking over Both Sides of the Fence," *Youthworker* 2, no. 3 (Fall 1985): 30-32.

you? and, What do you intend to do with our kids? We need to share our philosophy of ministry as well as the format of our program so that we can get their insightful feedback. Moms and dads need to know that they are not alone, but that we are partners together in ministry. And yet, as Paul Borthwick astutely notes, the biblical perspective is clear: parents hold the ultimate responsibility for raising their children (Deut. 6; Eph. 6). Therefore, Borthwick observes, youth pastors must perceive themselves "as assistants to the parents as they do their ministry."[17]

But how can we assist parents, especially in these first six months? Here are three ways to get the partnership rolling.

High School Parents, Inc. On a quarterly basis, call all shareholders (parents of students) to a meeting of this newly formed "corporation." By sending out formal invitations announcing the time you will convene in your very own executive boardroom, parents will be encouraged to come as you share with them your program agenda for the upcoming quarter. That is also a good opportunity to fill parents in on some of the latest trends in the contemporary youth culture. As Mike Yaconelli states, "Most . . . parents are not aware of the latest teenage cultural nuances. . . . Usually, youth culture is a real point of tension with parents (e.g., dress, hairstyles, music). We (youth workers) can diffuse that tension by being comfortable with the kids' culture and therefore be able to discern between harmless cultural fads and trends that really affect kids' spirituality."[18]

High school parents' prayer support group. Parents need a place where they can verbalize what is going on at home with their teenagers. Recently in our monthly support group, parents took the risk of sharing the struggles they were having in helping their teenagers work through the party issue. At first they were hesitant. But when they discovered that other parents were dealing with the same issues, they felt the freedom to open up and pray for one another. Yaconelli notes that

> most parents have no idea that the problems they face with their children are the same problems other parents face as well. Because we parents don't want to admit that we have problems with our children, we don't talk much about them with other parents. (But what we as parents need is to) realize that someone else has felt the same way we have, that we are not alone, and that maybe we are normal.[19]

High school steering committee. You, too, need to know that you are not alone in the ministry. You need a group of parents who will be committed to talking through the needs of your students and how your ministry strategy can

---

17. Paul Borthwick, "How I Cured My Parent-noia," *Youthworker* 2, no. 1 (Spring 1985): 17.
18. Mike Yaconelli, "Synchro-mesh Ministry: The Parent-Youth Worker Connection," *Youthworker* 2, no. 1 (Spring 1985): 22.
19. Ibid., p. 24.

most effectively be shaped to confront those needs. You need listeners, you need thinkers, and you need parents who are not afraid to give you honest feedback regarding whether or not your program is on the cutting edge. If you are on target in your ministry, these parents will be able to perceive it in the lives of their own students.

Also, you need their wisdom and prayerful counsel when making critical decisions. The unilateral approach is risky, especially when things do not go as planned. This group can also provide special support for you on a personal, as well as pastoral, level. Our monthly gatherings are always a breath of fresh air.

DEVELOPING A MINISTRY STRATEGY

The dynamics of transition and change are not easy to encounter. We struggle. Students struggle. As we proceed without pause into a new ministry context, we need to realize that these new lives with whom we are beginning to interact will be cautious and guarded. Some of them will still be working through the grieving process created with the loss of the previous youth pastor. They may feel betrayed. Their trust level may be at an all-time low. They are hurting. And the last thing they need is to be let down again by empty promises.

The issue at stake is integrity. Students want to know, When you express your intentions to stick around for the long haul, can we trust you? (Especially when the turnover rate for youth pastors is so high.) Can we really begin to take the risk and "own" you as "our" pastor? Will you really listen to our feelings about what is important to us? Do you want to hear our dreams about where we think the group should go?

There are two factors of which we need to be aware. The first deals with the threatening nature of change. I will never forget the negative impact of a youth pastor who barged into my junior high world with drastic and immediate change. "Who is this guy?" "What right does he have to change what is ours?" Suddenly it was us against him. It took a long and tenuous healing process to repair the relational damage.

A more recent incident comes to mind, much to my own embarrassment. A few months into my first high school pastorate, I presented to our student leadership team what I thought was a persuasive argument for changing the name of the youth group. From my perspective, the existing name seemed outdated and irrelevant to a 1980s high school student. What I failed to appreciate, being such a newcomer to the group, was the sense of identity and belonging the name provided. Even the kids' friends at school referred to the group by that name.

Especially when that "surge of energy comes with the stimulus" of a new challenge in ministry, Robert Kemper reminds us to slow down and take it easy. He wisely counsels us to "resist that urge to jump in. You do not know enough about the church; they do not know enough about you."[20] We need to be up front about our commitment to the status quo, at least for the first six months. What a great opportunity to pull together your adult ministry team, key student leaders, and interested parents to spend time dreaming, thinking, praying, and planning. Where are we now? Where does God want to take us? What will it take for us to get there? The operative phrase is *mutual ownership*. When you invest the time to do it together, no one feels the threat of imposed change.

A second factor in developing a strategy for ministry is to realize that an instant replay of the past will not work. Behold, you are in a new and different place. Do not forget that. People get tired of hearing about how it happened in your previous ministry. The issue comes down to identifying certain transferable principles that are foundational to your philosophy of ministry and then expressing them in new wineskins. Once again, those new methodologies, or wineskins, can be conceived together through brainstorming. Once again, the shared experience of innovating together takes away the threat of imposed change. And yet, at a philosophical level, you have remained true to your concept of biblical ministry to students.

DRAFTING YOUR ADULT MINISTRY TEAM

Doug Stevens has stated this truth:

> Youth ministry cannot be done long-distance. We must enter the world of the adolescent, just as Christ entered ours. We are sent into their turf. We must become accessible to them by intentionally placing ourselves in the midst of their subculture (I Cor. 5:9-12). In the same way that Jesus moved close enough to touch and be touched, so, too, we are called to minister to youth at close range.[21]

Students need to understand how Christianity as a theoretical belief system can be lived out in the here and now. They are asking this basic question: How does my relationship with Christ affect the everyday aspects of my life? That can happen most effectively when a student observes a significant adult who is modeling the real-life dimensions of what it means to be committed to the lordship of Christ. The need for a "life-on-life" discipling relationship is expressed by Larry Richards, who shares from the students' perspective when he states,

> For God's Word to catch at our hearts . . . we also need an intimate relationship with the teacher. We need to see ourselves (desire ourselves to be) like the teacher. We need to know the teacher well, to have access to his feelings and his values and

20. Kemper, *Beginning*, p. 96.
21. Stevens, *Called to Care*, p. 27.

his attitudes and his ways of responding in life. We need to be with the teacher outside the formal learning setting, in life. And the teacher needs to be a person who lives his faith, and who in his own personality reflects the meaning of truths Scripture communicates in words.[22]

As Richards has profoundly stated, "Truth flows through relationships."

If this up close and personal modeling style of ministry is to characterize our interaction with students, we must be convinced that we cannot do it alone. Jumping into a new ministry with a Lone Ranger mentality is not a viable option. Again, Stevens confronts us with the reality that "youth ministry is not a solo performance. . . . It is the team of leaders that carries out the ministry, not the omnigifted, edict-dispensing, quietly desperate, lonely figure of the youth minister. The one-man show is much less effective than the team."[23]

As we head into our first six months, we need to begin the process of building an adult ministry team. If our adult leaders are to model a growing, cutting-edge relationship with Christ, then a non-negotiable characteristic of each team member must be a love for God and a desire to know Him intimately. Other essential life-style qualities can be listed.

1. An unconditional love for students and a basic understanding of their youth culture
2. A teachable spirit that is open to new ideas and methods in ministry, especially in the areas of communication and relational skills
3. A willingness to be stretched, to take some risks in reaching out to students in the midst of situations that might be unfamiliar to the adult team member (e.g., loving a student through a difficult parental divorce when that has not been a part of your own experience)
4. An availability to spend time with students, because discipling relationships require time to develop
5. A faithfulness to the ministry for a minimum one-year commitment.

A balanced ministry team should be diverse in age and marital status. A team member should be at least two years out of high school (in working with high school students) in order to have developed a level of maturity that is necessary to relate to students as a role model. In interacting with students, there is a tension between relating to them as a friend and yet as a mature adult who is able to provide guidance and stability in their lives. Although single team members can often invest more time in the ministry, students need

22. Lawrence O. Richards, *A Theology of Christian Education* (Grand Rapids: Zondervan, 1975), p. 85.
23. Stevens, *Called to Care*, p. 151.

to be able to spend time with married couples who model a healthy family network.

After pulling your team together, what do you do? Working with students can be an intimidating proposition, especially if you have not had much experience on the front lines. The first thing we need to do in training the troops is to give them a clear understanding of their discipling responsibilities and the amount of time that will be involved. (It is hoped you will have filled them in on some of these details before they commit themselves.) Be sure to clarify any undefined expectations. Let them know that their primary focus will be to build relationships with students. (Having them distracted by programatic and administrative tasks that demand a lot of time should not be a part of the game plan.) Their objective is to get out there in the trenches with students.

The following ideas will sharpen their relational and ministry skills.

1. Share with them your philosophy of ministry so that they have a firm grasp of the direction in which you want to move.
2. Get them in touch with the contemporary youth culture so that they understand the students' world.
3. Bring in a Christian psychologist who can sharpen their active listening skills in initiating relationships.
4. Expose them to helpful ministry resource materials (e.g., books, films) that focus on the how tos of youth ministry. For example, if you are utilizing a small group approach, provide your adult leaders with resources that focus on how to ask inductive questions and how to facilitate conversational prayer.
5. Participate (as a team) in youth ministry seminars such as those sponsored by Youth Specialities.

Team members need to feel a sense of community and support from one another. Staff unity is developed through systematic time spent together in praying for personal concerns as well as encouraging one another in the ministry. A regular and consistent team meeting is absolutely imperative. But hanging out together as friends is important as well. Our students need to see a ministry team that enjoys being together and is committed to one another.

Do not try to do it by yourself. You need team workers. They are the arms and legs of your ministry. They will also give you invaluable feedback about the effectiveness of the ministry with the students. Team members need that sense of "ownership" in the ministry that comes when we really listen to their input.

Finally, remember that some of the adult leaders whom you inherit from the "last administration" might be somewhat hesitant to transfer their allegiance to you. Some of them will still be working through their own grieving process over the loss of the previous youth pastor. So give them time while they check you out. Do not feel threatened by a tenuous response to your leadership. Just like the students, it will take a while for them to adjust to your personality style and your philosophy of ministry.

A FEW CLOSING THOUGHTS FROM A SLIGHTLY SEASONED YOUTH PASTOR

Three final observations might stimulate your thinking as you get ready for those first six months.

First, one rather mundane but important aspect of getting started is that of organizing your office. You need to take the time to unpack, arrange, and decorate your office in the first week, or the process may drag on for months. Also, the filing system for the church's youth ministry must either be understood as is or revised to make it useful.

Second, establish a sense of open rapport with your secretary. Together you are a team. You need each other. But it will take time to understand the dynamics of your working relationship. Each of you has a particular style. Be up front about your expectations, but be willing to compromise during that initial period of adjustment to one another.

Remember, too, that there is a personal dimension to your relationship. Be sensitive to what is going on in your secretary's life. The office should have a professional feel, but as a pastor and as a friend, you need to express a genuine concern and interest.

Third, relax. It does not all have to happen in the first six months. Do not forget that nothing good happens fast. But there is always the temptation to rationalize yourself into a frenzy. Start-up always demands a big time commitment: "If I can just get this program off the ground with a little hard work, I'll be able to move into more of a maintenance mode." But do not kid yourself; there is no such thing as pure maintenance. (At least there should not be if you want to remain fresh and innovative.)

Sometimes we feel an unspoken expectation from members of the new church that we need to validate their confidence in us by investing long hours. We assume they want to know if they are getting their money's worth. Are we diligent? Are we tenacious? Well, let's go out there and show them. But that, too, is a trap.

The first six months is a new beginning. But we must realize there is no such thing as closure in ministry. There will always be more students to contact, more talks to prepare, and more parents to counsel. If our private lives are ever going to become ordered, *now* is the time to begin. As Gordon MacDonald so lucidly contends, we need to confront our drivenness and begin to build a sense of Sabbath rest into our cluttered lives. MacDonald defines this rest as

a time of looking backward, of loop-closing. We gaze upon our work and ask questions like: "What does it all mean?" "For whom did I do this work?" and

"What results did I expect, and what did I receive?" . . . True rest is happening when we pause regularly amidst daily routines to sort out the truths and commitment by which we are living.

We are daily the objects of a bombardment of messages competing for our loyalties and labors. We are pushed and pulled in a thousand different directions, to invest our resources and our time. By what standard of truth do we make these decisions? . . . Separating out the truths that are central to life is essential when one remembers that . . . we are vulnerable at all times to distortions of truth, to persuasions that the true is really false and the false really true. . . . Thus rest is not only a looking back at the meaning of my work and the path I have so recently walked in my life; but it is also a refreshing of my belief and commitment to Christ. It is a fine tuning of my inner navigational instruments so that I can make my way through the world for another week.[24]

The beginning is when we set life-style patterns. It is tough to shift gears in midstream. If we establish a precedent of investing an abnormal amount of hours in the first six months, it will be hard to back off. We need to get into the habit of perceiving our weekly ministry schedules with a sense of balance and rhythm. Earl Palmer advises us to consider "a representative week in our schedule and prioritize our time based on what is most important. Without this balance of priorities, our ministry can only last a few high-speed, non-stop years, after which we are exhausted and need to find an easier job."[25]

Palmer exhorts us to

take charge of our week, balancing times when we ease up with times when we work hard . . . so that during the intense and highly demanding days, we and our families can look forward to the ease-up days without intimidation by the pressures of the rest of the week.

Most people who burn out in ministry are nonrhythmic. Their souls go dry from imbalance, because they have little to look forward to beyond the sameness of fragmented, random days.[26]

We need to relax and remember that ministry does not happen all at once. Even if we feel totally overwhelmed with the reality of a new opportunity, we need to live one day at a time. Sit back and select one or two objectives that will determine how you invest your time. That means you will consciously ignore some seemingly pressing issues. But to institute a doctrine of benign neglect, as Palmer refers to it, will help us make wise choices and decisions in these first six months.

Finally, do not try to stand alone. As Bruce Grubbs observes, too often we fail to "recognize the importance of a personal support base during the transi-

24. Gordon MacDonald, *Ordering Your Private World* (Chicago: Moody, 1984), pp. 177, 179, 181.
25. Earl Palmer, "Strategy for Sanity," *Youthworker* 1, no. 2 (Summer 1984): 5.
26. Ibid., p. 6.

tion."[27] But that need goes far beyond those first transitional months. We cannot make it by ourselves, period. Doug Stevens reminds us that we need the support of our adult ministry team "who intercede for us and make us better than we could ever possibly be on our own. Both the support system that binds us to each other for ministry objectives and the private devotional pauses that root us in communion with God—both are necessary if we are to have the strength to press on and thrive."[28]

Every Tuesday afternoon for the past nine months, I have spent one-on-one time with another high school pastor in my area. Our vulnerability with each other and the hours we spent in prayer enabled me to realize that I was not alone in my struggles and concerns.

Every December, youth workers from the San Francisco Bay area gather at a Christian conference center to talk about ministries and personal lives. Once again, I realize I am not alone in ministry.

Investing time in establishing a support base is imperative. It is true, we cannot survive without it. But the primary foundation in that base of support must be the realization that it is God who has called us to that new place of ministry. And with that call is the assurance that through those first traumatic six months (and even after that), He will be there for us. "So we say with confidence, 'The Lord is my helper; I will not be afraid' " (Heb. 13:6).

FOR FURTHER READING

Blanchard, Kenneth, Patricia Zigarmi, and Drea Zigarmi. *Leadership and the One Minute Manager.* New York: William Morrow, 1985.

Greenleaf, Ralph K. *Servant Leadership.* Ramsey, N.J.: Paulist, 1977.

Grubbs, Bruce. *The First Two Years: A Pastor's Guide to Getting Started in a Church.* Nashville: Convention Press, 1979.

Kemper, Robert G. *Beginning a New Pastorate.* Nashville: Abingdon, 1978.

McCarty, Doran C. *Working with People.* Nashville: Broadman, 1986.

MacDonald, Gail, and Gordon MacDonald. *If Those Who Reach Could Touch.* Nashville: Oliver Nelson, 1984.

McDonough, Reginald. *Working with Volunteer Leaders in a Church.* Nashville: Broadman, 1976.

Palmer, Earl. "Strategy for Sanity." *Youthworker* 1, no. 2 (Summer 1984).

Stevens, Doug. *Called to Care.* Grand Rapids: Zondervan, 1985.

27. Grubbs, *Guide,* p. 36.
28. Stevens, *Called to Care,* p. 36.

18

William H. Stewart

Pulling Off the Long-Term Ministry with Youth

A while ago I interviewed a high school student whose church had recently lost its youth minister. She discussed with me her feelings about having four youth ministers in the church during her years in junior high and high school. The last one had stayed two years, which was a record for their group. Her comment was simply, "Just when we found out that he loved us, he left."

Some years ago a friend of mine went to a large church in Oklahoma. A high school student related to him how he, too, had seen three other youth ministry leaders come and go. The young man told my friend, "I am not going to commit myself to anything in this youth ministry until you have been here two years."

The underlying supposition for this chapter is that Jesus Christ does call men and women to spend their lives in youth ministry, especially in the local church. Without question, a person can make a career out of any one of a number of youth-related professions: public school teacher or administrator, probation officer, counselor, teacher in a Christian school, executive roles with the YMCA, YWCA, or Scouts, and the list could go on. The one, however, who would spend his or her life in youth ministry in the local church has been questioned again and again as to what he is going to do when he "grows up."

WILLIAM H. STEWART, M.Div., is associate minister, youth education, First Baptist Church, Modesto, California.

That question may have come from a well-meaning parishioner, another staff person, or a concerned mother-in-law.

Is it possible that the Lord Jesus Christ would call men and women to a life of youth ministry in the local church? It is apparently easier to believe that His call would come to someone in one of the parachurch organizations that work with youth. Perhaps the larger national influence of the parachurch organization seems to merit people who will give themselves to it for life. Again, men and women give their lives to teach in seminaries. That relatively small group of people is seldom queried about their spiritual, intellectual, or emotional maturity regarding their commitment to work with youth. However, the one who dedicates his life to working with students in a local church is questioned as to the wisdom of his decision and the permanency of such a position.

Youth ministry in the local church is really a question of faith. Jesus, in speaking to two blind men, told them, "According to your faith will it be done to you" (Matt. 9:29); so it has been in the local church. We have not believed that God could call men and women to youth ministry for life. Even though there are many models around us in our society, as mentioned above, *we have not believed and therefore we have not seen.*

Principles for a Long-Term Ministry

We need to establish the concept that God calls some to a local church ministry with youth *for life*. And what is required of such a person? Recently, I contacted at least six youth ministry people and asked the question, What has been required for your long-term commitment to working with students? None of those questioned had been in youth ministry less than twenty years. Two had been in their respective churches more than twenty years. Their responses are included in the following information.

The first principle for a long-term youth ministry is an all-consuming love for Jesus Christ. Anything short of a total and complete love for the Lord Jesus is a sure way out of the ministry to youth.

A second principle is a love for the Word of God. There is no other final source for our wisdom. There is no other book, be it on psychology, sociology, or history, to which we must totally commit ourselves. We have no other message to deliver. A properly studied, prepared, and presented message from the Word of God may well be used by the Holy Spirit to captivate young minds beyond anything they have known in the media.

Third, there must also be a love for the church of Christ. After years of involvement in a well-known parachurch ministry and, later, in my local church, I discovered that if I did not have a church in which to involve students who were reached, often no fruit remained (see John 15:16). The person who says that he will commit himself to the gospel of Jesus Christ and youth ministry but has no strong commitment to the local church is just kidding himself. Young people ultimately must be provided with a family and a life-support system.

Fourth, the individual who would work long-term with young people must love them. This may seem redundant. However, in my estimation, many have entered youth ministry for the wrong reasons. Some have wished to retain their own youth. Some have thought this would ensure their being in the middle of the action. Others have found ego fulfillment in working with youth. These motivations do not bring about long-term youth ministry. A person must love students whether the youth are in junior high school or high school. Tragic as it is, this love may be the only affection some youth ever receive.

Fifth, some love students, but demonstrate no love for parents. It has been my experience that some youth workers treat the parents of their young people as the adversary. At times it seems to become a tug-of-war between the parent and youth minister, with the young person in the middle. Love for young people must also include a love for their parents.

Finally, there must be love for the pastor. To work in the church without such love is to fall far short of that which our Lord intended. Genuine love for a pastor is developed in the same way that genuine love develops in a marriage. Many of us get married or go to church because of the benefits we see in it for ourselves. The test of either commitment comes when humanness is encountered. This is the real opportunity to make a conscious decision that *I will love*. If at this juncture I choose to live in anything less than love, whether it be out of self-pity or some other form of selfish concern, it is not what God intended (1 Cor. 5:14-15).

PRIORITIES IN YOUTH MINISTRY

We have discussed the youth minister's call and focus, or mind-set. Now we turn to his priorities. Speaking from the perspective of a parent of teenagers, and from many years spent in youth ministry, a system of priorities is absolutely essential to the one who would build a long-term work.

The first priority is Christ. There can be no rival; nothing can ever take the place of one's personal relationship with the Lord. That alone can sustain the youth minister over the long haul. It also makes all of the other priorites I will mention easier to maintain.

The second priority is the youth minister's family. Seldom does one meet an individual in youth ministry who has retained the Lord as first in importance that did not place the family second. If there is a fear youth ministers have, it is that their own children will not respond to the Lord and live lives that honor Him. It is important to note that perfection is not the main issue, but rather honesty. Will I admit my failures? Will I seek the forgiveness of my own children when I have wronged them? Will I model God-honoring confession before them when the Holy Spirit convicts me of sin?

Years ago, when our daughter was very young, I over-reacted and disciplined her too strongly for something she had done. I was wrong in the matter. I got down on my knees in front of her, looked her in the eyes, and asked her, "Cyndie, will you forgive your daddy and pray with your daddy that the Lord will forgive him?" My wife and I have consistently taken such an approach. As a result, we believe, our daughter has developed a tremendous sensitivity and willingness to forgive.

We must also find practical ways of showing that special love we have for our mates. One suggestion is to be a consistent source of encouragement. Because of the special pressures of the ministry and because we give much of ourselves to many people every day, it is a temptation to come home at night and vent our frustrations. There may be other things I feel like doing when I get home, but the first thing I must do is go to my wife and encourage her.

A third priority is income. A wife and family must be adequately supported and cared for in material ways. The apostle Paul indicated that a man who does not care for his family has denied the faith and is worse than an unbeliever (1 Tim. 5:8). There is no one I know who has become rich as a youth minister. However, God does expect His servant to meet the needs of his family. We shall speak of the church's responsibility in this regard later.

A fourth priority is education. One who neglects his education neglects his future and misses God's best. There has been a tendency on the part of some to rush off into youth ministry too soon. I became a youth pastor at eighteen. It is better to be closer to thirty. That gives a person more stability and maturity. It is significant that the apostle Paul, John the Baptist, and Jesus Himself all entered the ministry at about thirty years of age.

The fifth priority is youth ministry itself, working to see young people overcome the hassles of their adolescent years in order to stand on their own feet in spiritual maturity appropriate for their age. Youth ministry is enjoyable; it can even be fun. But the real joy of youth ministry comes not so much from fun-filled activities as from the satisfaction of seeing students grow into maturity in Christ. The apostle John wrote, "I have no greater joy than to hear that my children are walking in the truth" (3 John 4). The youth minister whose priorities are straight would agree.

CHALLENGES TO THE LONG-TERM MINISTRY

To pull off the long-term ministry with students demands much from the youth minister. But perhaps even more is required of the local church. In many churches the youth minister is not viewed as a professional but as a person who is in charge of activities. He is seen as one who must keep young people busy to keep them out of trouble. It is about a fourth or fifth step up from babysitting. He is given a few keys, a string around his neck with a whistle on it, and perhaps a bus driver's license. It is not surprising that youth ministers move in and out of the local church in a very short period of time.

Another view is that the youth pastor is an assistant to the pastor and parents. Of course, the youth minister is to a certain extent the pastor's associate or assistant, but he must also be seen as a minister in his own right. Again, the youth minister may well perceive himself as an assistant to the parents, but his role must be understood by the church as something reaching far beyond that also.

The youth worker's task is no less important than any other ministry. The people he works with are equally important. He certainly functions in a line of authority, but he has a distinct place on the church staff. He is recognized as a full-time minister.

Some churches place a denominational youth program or camp above the ministry to their own young people. I was once told I must sacrifice the local youth ministry in order to help a denominational program that needed the dollars our young people's participation would provide. The cause of Christ is not furthered in that way, nor is the local church enriched. We are responsible before the Lord for the youth in our churches and communities. If we do not provide an adequate program for reaching those young people with the gospel and bringing them to Christian maturity, we will be held accountable (cf. 2 Cor. 5:10).

In some churches, members place the educational needs of youth above the church's spiritual ministry. But a student who loses out spiritually also ultimately loses out in his educational enrichment. Even parochial Christian education is no substitute for the youth ministry of the local church.[1] It is designed for a different purpose. Public or parochial school programs and the church's youth ministry can complement each other. Parents and youth pastors must work together to attain the right balance.

On occasion other members of the church's staff express a low view of youth work. A statement like, "Oh well, that is just the youth department," may say a great deal more than appears on the surface. Respect and honor is vital in all directions. The pastor or staff person who does not speak well of another ministry in the church cuts the ground from beneath himself. His own ministry will probably suffer as a result.

The parent who disparages the youth ministry at home also does his or her young person a disservice. A better attitude is outlined in the following "Confession for Parents,"[2] written by my own senior pastor, William E. Yaeger:

1. See Paul Bubar, *The Jericho Wall* (Schroon Lake, N.Y.: Word of Life, 1982).
2. William E. Yeager, "A Confession for Parents" (First Baptist Church, Modesto, California, 1975).

1. My child was born with a sinful nature as I.
2. My child is influenced by others, but he has built-in problems of his own and is responsible for his own actions.
3. My child is a product of my home, and I must accept my responsibility for his conduct.
4. My commitment to Christ and His Word will enable the Holy Spirit to encourage my child to model himself after me.
5. My commitment will require me to serve in the ministry of my church and faithfully present myself for worship and the study of God's Word. My discipline will be reflected in my child's discipline.
6. My attitude toward the pastor and youth staff of my church will be reflected in my child's behavior.
7. The words of my mouth, spoken in the presence of my family, will be either blessings from God like raindrops from heaven or cursings from the Old Accuser, like the crustings of salt on the drought parched land.
8. May the words of my mouth and the meditation of my heart be acceptable in thy sight, O Lord, my rock and my redeemer.

THE LONG-TERM MINISTRY IN THE COMMUNITY

We come to the issue of the community in which the church exists. If the local church is greatly concerned about youth ministry, the youth minister must be concerned about some other issues outside the church.

The youth minister who is serious about a long-term investment of life must commit himself to ministry at the local Christian high school. He must make every effort to become well known to the administrators and teachers. The youth worker must overcome, at times, a feeling on the part of students in Christian schools that he is interested only in the public school students. He may find it more difficult to touch students in the Christian school for a number of reasons. Apathy may be a major problem. Then again, inaccessibility in reaching students may be a result of administrative policy. Opportunities such as speaking in chapel, counseling students, or being a guest classroom lecturer are possibilities.

The youth minister must not ignore the public school either. Inaccessibility is not an insurmountable barrier. I have lived in many areas of the country and have never found it impossible to gain access to the public schools. However, we must approach them in the right way. Too often we ask favors of the school and try to "dig everything and plant nothing."

There are many needs in every public school system. Committees cry for people to serve. The PTA and booster groups want help. Adults are required for chaperoning, assisting, and even campus supervision. Qualified individuals could look into substitute teaching. Sometimes the athletic teams lack adequate coaching personnel. If you have the background, why not help meet the need?

The youth minister who desires an extensive ministry must also acquaint himself with the law enforcement agencies in his community. That will assist you in getting a picture of the community seldom seen by others. You also will gain an appreciation of what is involved in that kind of work.

Most communities of any size have one or more parachurch organizations involved in touching the lives of students. We accomplish far more through cooperation than in competition. Work together with these organizations. Plan with them. But most of all, pray with them.

Do not neglect the political and social agencies serving in your area. There are opportunities in every community to the highest political level. Currently, there is a program in many congressional districts, called the Congressional Awards Program, that receives strong encouragement from the House of Representatives. It is designed for youth ages fourteen through twenty-three who are motivated by the challenge of voluntary public service and personal development activities. There are undoubtedly other awards programs, community agencies, service clubs, and opportunities that you will want to consider. These all provide good opportunities for youth and their witness for Jesus Christ.

Finally, meet regularly with other people in youth ministry in your area. Build a network. Encourage each other. Pray for each other. Lift up the hands of your brothers and sisters who serve.

At times youth ministers, like pastors, may get a little jealous of each other. Do not worry if someone from your ministry goes somewhere else because he has a friend in another church. Make it a point to be an open, loving, gracious minister of the gospel around whom young people can feel comfortable and know they are loved. Positive attitudes and ministries attract far more young people than they ever lose.

Strive to lend credibility and effectiveness to this special occupation to which God had called you. That starts by being worthy of your calling. Make sure your life and priorities are right before God. Be aware and prepared for the challenges that lie ahead. Learn to work within your community to bring young people into a saving relationship with Jesus Christ.

We need to establish roots within our churches and communities, and this can only be accomplished by a long-term ministry in one location. Experience the delight of seeing young people go through the junior high, high school, and college ministries, and then become strong adults serving Christ in His church.

The Body of Jesus Christ provides the only real home in our fragmented society. Knowing that makes the long-term ministry worth all it may cost.

FOR FURTHER READING

Benson, Dennis C., and Bill Wolfe. *The Basic Encyclopedia for Youth Ministry.* Loveland, Colo.: Group Books, 1981.

Campolo, Anthony, Jr. *The Success Fantasy.* Wheaton, Ill.: Victor, 1980.

Dobson, James. *Preparing for Adolescence.* Santa Ana, Calif.: Vision House, 1978.

Holderness, Ginny Ward. *Youth Ministry: The New Team Approach.* Atlanta: John Knox, 1981.

Hyde, Douglas. *Dedication and Leadership.* Notre Dame, Ind.: U. of Notre Dame, 1969.

Posterski, Donald C. *Friendship: A Window on Ministry to Youth.* Scaraborough, Ont.: Project Teen Canada, 1985.

Roadcup, David. *Ministering to Youth: A Strategy for the 80s.* Cincinnati: Standard, 1980.

Warren, Michael. *Youth and the Future of the Church.* New York: Seabury, 1982.

Part 4
Strategies for Church Youth Ministry

19

Rick Caldwell

Evangelism Through Youth Ministry

Perhaps nothing is talked about more, but actually done less, than evangelism. We plan elaborate, expensive choir tours for the purpose of evangelism. We conduct city-wide crusades featuring celebrities, sport personalities, and musical groups with the desire that evangelism will take place. We even hope it will be the end result of our church league softball, basketball, or bowling teams. But the truth is, not much evangelism is taking place in many youth groups.

For years I busied myself with the good things of youth ministry, ignoring the very best thing that Christ has called us to do: *evangelism*. It was after recognizing that I was working hard, yet failing to change the lives of youth for eternity, that I began to get serious about the role of evangelism in youth ministry. Since then I have sought to make evangelism my priority. Perhaps the best way to illustrate the change this has brought about is to recount the following experience.

Mike, a senior in high school, visited our Wednesday night youth celebration (called S.W.A.T., which stands for Spiritual Warfare and Training) over a year ago. He came at the invitation of Ricardo, a young man I was discipling and training for youth ministry. Three weeks after that first visit, Ricardo was

RICK CALDWELL, M.R.E., is minister of youth, Geyer Springs First Baptist Church, Little Rock, Arkansas.

able to lead Mike to Christ and into the church. Shortly thereafter Mike was giving his testimony publicly and reaching out to his friends with the gospel. He attended our basic discipleship seminar and learned to tell others of Christ. During the past year, an unbelievable chain reaction has taken place.

First, Mike's parents and older brother came to church. They were not attending church anywhere, nor were they professing Christians. Mike's new-found faith and radical change of life-style aroused their attention. Ultimately, the three of them received Christ and are now actively serving the Lord in our church. Mike's parents have just volunteered to become church youth sponsors, and his brother has become involved in a ministry group on his college campus.

This summer Mike reached out to a good friend named Greg. Greg has since come to receive Christ and has been instrumental in leading two of his friends, Kelly and Ken, to Christ. Greg, Kelly, and Ken have recently reached two other guys, forming a ministry team of five who come early each week and set up for S.W.A.T.

Just about a year ago this exciting process, which has resulted in seven conversions, was begun because Ricardo reached out to a friend for the purpose of introducing him to Christ. This incident is a classic example of several principles that will be discussed later in this chapter.

EXAMINING EVANGELISM

It is important here at the beginning to state my philosophy of evangelism. Simply put, evangelism does not happen mystically, apart from the actions of men. Three observations support that statement.

First, God is sovereign; He is able to bring His will to pass. But He has chosen to involve man on both sides of the process of proclaiming and receiving the gospel. So he has assigned us the awesome responsibility of sharing His redemptive message with the entire world. But it is extremely important that we give a clear and culturally relevant presentation, for those who receive it also will be held responsible for their response to that message.

Certainly the Holy Spirit must be at work through us if we are to evangelize youth in today's world, but it has been my observation that the Holy Spirit is more ready to do the task than we are. We must choose to make evangelism a priority in our ministries. I have discovered the hard way that evangelism does not happen automatically. That is the second observation.

Finally, Jesus began His ministry by saying, "Come, follow me . . . and I will make you fishers of men" (Matt. 4:19) and concluded His ministry with the words "But you will receive power when the Holy Spirit comes on you; and you will be my witnesses" (Acts 1:8). It is significant that the Lord emphasized our responsibility to evangelize at the beginning and end of His ministry.

In light of these observations, the following pages contain principles for

(1) establishing an evangelism awareness, (2) equipping people for evangelism, (3) planning event-oriented evangelism, (4) establishing relationships that result in evangelism, and (5) creating an environment for evangelism.

ESTABLISHING AN EVANGELISM AWARENESS

It is our responsibility to communicate to our youth that evangelism is something they can and should be doing. For months I bombarded our youth with films, speakers, and programs designed to help them see that evangelism was their job.

Here are some ideas that worked for us.

1. *Testimonies.* Almost weekly I had young people give testimonies of how they came to Christ and who was used by God to influence them in that decision.
2. *The tract.* I printed a personalized tract, using photographs of four group members accompanied by their testimonies and a gospel presentation. The tract cost less to print than the ones we bought from bookstores, and our students really began to spread them around.
3. *Ads in school newspapers.* We finally wised up and quit putting a picture of a staff member or the church building in our school advertisements. Instead we put pictures of young people and capsule versions of their testimony.
4. *Ten-most-wanted list.* Monthly we encouraged our youth to list ten of their friends that they wanted to see come to Christ or become involved in church. We focused on those kids through our outreach activities and visits.

EQUIP YOUTH AND WORKERS FOR EVANGELISM

After establishing an evangelism awareness, it became crucial that we train young people to do evangelism. This is where most of us fail. No amount of hype, guilt, or motivation will work if we fail to train thoroughly our people to speak of Christ with confidence. There are two methods that we have successfully employed.

THE SHORT TERM SEMINAR

This kind of weekend workshop is a great way to expose a lot of people to the basics in a short amount of time, but it should be followed up with a more lengthy program. Most short-term training programs focus on at least six basics of evangelism:[1]

1. The terms for witnessing
2. The techniques for witnessing
3. The testimony—having students learn to give their personal testimony

---

1. Rick Caldwell, "How to Bear Spiritual Fruit, Without Being a Spiritual Nut" (Prayer 'N Share Ministries, 5615 Geyer Springs Rd., Little Rock, AK 72209).

4. The tract—having them practice using a gospel tract
5. The transition—having them practice moving a conversation from a secular subject to a spiritual one without creating tension
6. The decision—actually leading the person in a prayer to receive Christ

In most cases, these brief seminars or workshops create an interest in learning more. In even the shortest seminar it is important to include time for actually going out to visit with someone who knows how to witness.

THE THIRTEEN-WEEK COURSE IN EVANGELISM

In my opinion this is the best method for evangelism training. This approach has been popularized by Evangelism Explosion, which was developed by D. James Kennedy. That particular program involves thirteen weeks of classroom time and actual weekly field experience under the supervision of a certified trainer.

Each participant must complete required homework as well as make assigned visits weekly. At the conclusion of the course, the participant is required to pass a certification test at which time he is qualified to train others, thus creating a multiplication effect. The advantages of this program are (1) its thoroughness, (2) its accountability, (3) its field training, (4) its emphasis on memorizing Scripture, and (5) its transferability.

Over the past two years we have seen more than 125 students and youth workers complete this kind of training. It has proved to be extremely effective in equipping our people for evangelism.

One exciting story that came out of this particular method of evangelism training involves Phil, a parent of two teenagers. He had been a deacon and Sunday school teacher for twenty years, but he had always lacked the confidence to witness boldly. Phil was anxious to overcome this weakness, so he signed up for our thirteen-week evangelism course. During his fifth week, while out on a routine Sunday afternoon call, he visited in the home of a sixteen-year-old runaway. She had returned home two days previously. She was strung out on drugs, malnourished, and pregnant. She had visited church that Sunday at the request of her family, who had become Christians while she was on the run. Much to Phil's surprise, Becky was eagerly open to his choppy gospel presentation. At the conclusion of what he calls a butchered version of the gospel, Becky gave her heart to Jesus.

Becky has been a Christian for just over a year now, but it has been quite a year. During that time Becky completely recovered from her drug habit. She also produced a healthy baby girl, which she chose to give up through a Christian adoption agency, re-enrolled in school, where she has become an honor student, led six classmates to Christ, and was elected president of her school's Christian Youth Council. Becky also completed the thirteen-week evangelism course and has served as a trainer for the past two thirteen-week sessions.

Whether you choose a short seminar approach to training, the thirteen-week seminar, or both, I cannot stress enough how important it is for you to begin immediately to train your people in evangelism.

EVENT-ORIENTED EVANGELISM

If evangelism is to be a priority within our ministry to youth, then it is time for us to wise up and begin planning our programs with a purpose. I used to spend much energy and time planning events and outings that I hoped would some day pay off in evangelism. Then I came to the realization that with just a little more effort, I could add an evangelistic edge to most of the programs. Since coming to that realization, more than 200 youth have received Christ through hayrides, concerts, cookouts, swimming parties, breakfast meetings, and even at all-night lock-ins.

To program for the purpose of evangelism requires several things. First, we must get unbelievers to the event. It is impossible to have an evangelistic thrust unless we can get non-Christians to attend. Here are several suggestions toward that end. Some may seem a bit sensational but can be handled in good taste.

Serve food at the event. Whether it is pizza, ice cream, hamburgers, or tacos, youth usually come in big numbers for free food.

Have your youth work hard to bring their nonchurch friends. One church I know charged the admission price of one nonchurch friend in order for its own kids to attend an activity.

Plan the event at a neutral site. Often a park or the backyard of a church member's home is a better location for attracting nonchurch youth.

Include youth in the program (especially new Christians). Non-Christians will come to see or hear their friends give a testimony or sing. At one burger bash, four new believers shared their testimonies. Each of them brought at least five friends who came out of curiosity.

Second, we must present the gospel at the event. For years I erroneously thought that the church was the place for spiritual things, and youth events away from the church were for social things. One day I recognized that more nonchurch youth attended the social outings than the spiritual meetings. Why not start presenting the gospel at events attended by youth who really need to hear it, instead of preaching it over and over at meetings attended by mostly Christian youth? Looking back now, I cannot believe how foolish my old approach was.

It is very important to present the gospel in a positive but non-pushy way, if you choose to program one of your social events for evangelism. You must clearly communicate the gospel to the students attending, but they should not be coerced into responding.

Youth listen to their peers better than they listen to the youth minister. This has caused me to begin to rely on young people to communicate the message of Christ at our evangelistic outings.

Recently we sponsored a late Saturday night outdoor concert on a mall parking lot, right in the middle of our community "cruising" zone. Even before the band began to play, a crowd of more than 100 young people gathered just because they saw sound equipment being unloaded.

As the band began to play, about 250 people crowded around. The vast majority of them were non-Christians, many were smoking, and some drinking. The band, which was composed of guys from our church, played very progressive, contemporary Christian music for twenty minutes, and then one of the band members told of his conversion and commitment to Christ. Many of the crowd knew him from his days as a leader while in high school and his involvement in a rock group. They listened intently to his powerful but non-preachy presentation. Then came the most important time of the evening. It was announced that the band would be back in fifteen minutes to play again, but during the break each person in the crowd would have a chance to talk with someone about their relationship with Christ.

As soon as the break began, almost one hundred students from our ministry began to witness to the people around them. By the end of the evening, nine people had prayed to receive Christ and were taken to a nearby truck where we registered their decision and gave them follow-up material.

The following factors helped make this event work.

1. The band was committed to making the event *evangelistic,* not just *entertainment.*
2. One hundred of our youth were willing to mix into the crowd, meet new people, and lovingly share Jesus with them by using a gospel tract.
3. Our young people had met earlier in the evening for prayer and a thorough explanation of what would happen at the event.
4. Proper security measures had been taken, and necessary legal arrangements were made with the city and the mall management.
5. The one-on-one witnessing was open and direct, but no one was pushed to make a decision or even to talk about Christ if the person chose not to.
6. Each person making a decision was visited and followed up by a team of workers from our ministry, which resulted in several of them getting involved in our church.

Another event that was programmed for evangelism was a backyard "burger bash." Students from several junior high campuses were given printed invitations at school. The invitations had the names and phone numbers of several people from various schools who were hosting the event. That made it more attractive to the non-Christian youth than if we had promoted it as a big church event.

As they began to arrive at the designated backyard, they were greeted by the smell of cooking burgers and the sound of contemporary Christian music. When the crowd of 150 was through eating, we had fifteen minutes of fun-oriented group singing led by a leader in our ministry. Then came the focus of the evening, a ten minute slide show highlighting our past summer events. The slides focused on youth well known to those in the crowd. At the close of the presentation four group members stood and told how they had met the Lord and how He had made a difference in their lives. Although I spoke at the conclusion, I am confident that it was the testimonies of the four students that God used to bring sixteen teenagers to Christ that evening.

Third, we must plan to draw the net at the event. Giving an invitation or extending an opportunity for students to receive the Lord is a very delicate area. We have used just about every method you can imagine. Some have proved effective; others have not. Two examples of our most effective ways of harvesting those who desire to make a commitment to Christ are the response card and the personal response.

The response card is a tool we use often in events such as the burger bash, lock-ins, or almost any activity. We call it an Evaluate the Event Card. On one side it allows the student to record his name, address, and phone number and make a comment on his opinion of the event. The other side of the card allows him to record what kind of decision, if any, he made that night.

Here is how we used it at the burger bash. After the four young people gave their testimonies, I spoke briefly asking each person to examine the tract and specifically notice the prayer of response printed toward the end. I prayed the printed prayer with the group, asking those who had never received the Lord to do so by praying silently. Following the prayer, the evening was concluded by instructing each student to fill out his Evaluate the Event Card. I especially encouraged them to share any decision they made or any need they had on the back of the card. This card has provided a simple but valuable means for recording decisions, and it gives the information necessary for follow-up.

The personal response is another method we often use. This simply is extending an opportunity for the youth to receive Christ and then indicate it by raising their hands while heads are bowed in prayer. Following the prayer, I encourage those who made decisions to obtain a follow-up booklet from one of our youth staff. We mention a designated place where we will be standing and always go directly to that place. I never go into the crowd to button-hole a person who lifted his hand. If he is sincere, he will come to me. When we give him the follow-up booklet, we record his name and address and attempt to schedule a time when we can come by and visit him.

The public invitation is an approach used only occasionally.[2] It is most appropriate for youth crusades and concerts.[3]

Programming with a purpose is the key to event-oriented evangelism. We must pray through and plan out the occasion, all the while thinking about what we can do to give it an evangelistic edge.

ESTABLISHING RELATIONSHIPS THAT RESULT IN EVANGELISM

We are being a bit idealistic when we expect large numbers of nonchurch-oriented youths to flock to our weekly worship services, drop their emotional defenses, and embrace our messages with repentant hearts. Most unchurched high schoolers feel like fish out of water when they attend the average evangelical worship service. In most cases, they even feel uncomfortable at our high-energy youth meetings.

A nonchurch-oriented youth is like a newly captured animal in a cage. He is tense, on the defensive, and frightened. His new environment threatens him and prevents him from being open or at ease. The one element that can make a radical difference in his anxiety level is the security of a familiar face, especially if it belongs to a person that has cared enough to initiate and develop a personal relationship with him. So if we are to breach the emotional walls surrounding their hearts, our ammunition must be relationships rather than religious rhetoric. That may be more threatening to us, but it is the most effective way. The process of building relationships with kids outside our youth group and church comfort zone may seem frightening to many youth ministers and volunteer workers, but it is a hurdle that must be overcome if we are to establish a vital ministry of evangelism to the nonchurch-oriented youth.

Barry St. Clair developed the Reach-out Strategy several years ago while serving as youth consultant to the evangelism department of the Southern Baptist Home Mission Board. Barry's strategy included an element called the touch ministry, which he describes as "a visitation program of the adult leaders on the high school campus. The purpose of the Touch Ministry is outreach—to put youth leaders in touch with high school young people. In order to do that, youth leaders must go consistently where high school kids are! Since kids spend the majority of their time at the high school, that is where youth leaders are committed to be."[4]

This idea of penetrating the youth culture simply means taking the gospel to the world instead of expecting the world to come to the gospel. That is not to suggest that we march into the youth culture armed with tracts and trumpets, but, instead, that we lovingly reach in to establish a relationship that will result in evangelism.

2. John R. Bisagno, *The Power of Positive Evangelism* (Nashville: Broadman, 1968).
3. Roy D. Fish, *Giving a Good Invitation* (Nashville: Broadman, 1975).
4. Barry St. Clair, "The Youth Leader's Strategy to an Effective Ministry" (Reach Out Ministries, 3117 Majestic Circle, Avondale Estates, GA), p 14.

Belinda was a senior at a high school near our church. She had never visited our church nor was she actively attending any church. I visited her school campus weekly to eat lunch and meet students. I spoke to her, learned her name, and after a period of weeks I would have a brief conversation with her each time I visited. I made it a point to remember her name and always recalled bits of information from previous conversations we had together. Although I never talked to her about spiritual things on campus or even invited her to church, she knew I was somehow related to the church. She was totally overwhelmed when she arrived at our large Wednesday night youth meeting and found out I was speaking. She had previously told her friends that she could never feel comfortable at such a big church.

Although Belinda was completely out of her normal environment at our Wednesday night meeting, I somehow sensed she was comfortable. Later she came bouncing up to me and told me how surprised she was to see me speaking to three hundred youth. She said "I knew you worked here, but I didn't know you were a real preacher."

Within a matter of weeks Belinda discovered she could be comfortable in such a big church and has become a very supportive part of our youth group. I am convinced that the key to reaching Belinda was that a friendship was established before religion was ever discussed.

The high school lunch room is an excellent place to establish relationships, but several guidelines must be followed.

1. Always meet the principal of the school you wish to visit and gain permission to visit the campus. Make sure he knows you will not be passing out literature or recruiting kids for your church program. Make sure he knows that your purpose simply is to build relationships with students.

2. Talk to the students about their favorite subject—themselves. Kids will flock to an adult whom they sense is really interested in them, but they will run from one who is out recruiting for his program.

3. Learn names. There is nothing more important than remembering names. It lets people know you consider them important.

4. Boldly stretch out beyond your comfort zone. It is easy to visit with kids who attend your activities every week and never reach out beyond that group. Make a point to meet a set number of new kids every time you visit a campus.

In some cases, you may find that a school's cafeteria is not open to you. That does not mean that the campus is closed; it just means that you must be more creative. For example, pep assemblies, athletic events, concerts, and plays are almost always open to the public. Wherever students go is where we must go to establish relationships that result in evangelism.

In many schools I have found that coaches can be very receptive to allowing a youth minister to serve as chaplain to one of his teams. This usually consists of visiting the locker room before the game to have prayer with the team, but it can include quite a bit more responsibility. I know of one youth minister who visited the afternoon practices of a particular team almost daily until he became known as the team's most loyal fan. Finally the coach asked him if he would like to become the official chaplain. He took the responsibility seriously, even to the point of traveling with the team to away football games. His availability and genuine devotion to the guys soon earned the team's respect and trust, which later resulted in several athletes coming to Christ.

In another case I know of, a church made its facilities and vehicles available to a school for use by any of its clubs. The church had a large Greyhound-style bus that was used for long trips. They offered that vehicle and its youth minister to drive the school's athletes to a Fellowship of Christian Athletes conference and also transported its journalism students to a national journalism convention. Although this cannot be done in many cases, it does illustrate how we can build relationships with students and school officials even if we do not have an open door to visit the school campus weekly.

While serving a church near Birmingham, I had a problem securing access to a school campus. I was told that my presence on campus during lunch might set a precedent that could open the door for radical religious groups and even cults. After a time of prayer and creative brainstorming, my wife and I thought of a solution. She applied as a substitute teacher. Almost daily she was called on to teach, which afforded me access to the campus as the husband of a teacher. I would come to the campus to have lunch with my wife and visit with several students in the process. This was in no way a deceptive ploy. The principal knew of my purpose and supported me. By having my wife serve as a substitute, it enabled him to have just cause for allowing me access to the campus.

Even today I still have to work hard to push myself to leave the security of my office and plunge into the high school campuses. It is easy to become too busy to spend two or three hours a week on a school campus, especially during lunch, but I know how valuable it is, and I must do it. Students know we really care when we take time to come to them and develop personal relationships.

It is important to remember that establishing relationships with youth is only the beginning. Much care must be given to make the most of that relationship and to follow through with a gospel presentation at the right time. We must always remember that we cannot ease students into the kingdom of God by merely getting involved in their lives. There must be a communication of the gospel to them and an opportunity given for them to respond.

ESTABLISHING AN ENVIRONMENT FOR EVANGELISM

We have all heard people say that when they walked into a meeting they could sense something special. Regardless of the terminology used, what we are talking about is a sense of spiritual warmth that can be a very important factor in evangelism. I have talked at length with youth who said they felt such a warmth when they visited our youth meetings. Summarized here are some of their statements.

> I sensed love in the atmosphere. People came up to me that I didn't know and began to talk to me. I even saw a girl that I used to do drugs with. She came over and hugged me. She seemed really different. (A seventeen-year-old runaway who visited our services)

> I felt good at first, kind of at ease by the welcome I received and the fun music. But then things began to get serious, and I felt funny. It was heavy, like God was speaking to me inside. (A fifteen-year-old boy who had never been to an evangelistic worship service)

> I feel loved here, accepted, safe. Things are pretty bad around my house. (A senior in high school who was abused by a parent)

The temple of God is not a building but the people who dwell in that building. One of the keys to successful youth evangelism lies in creating a genuine sense of Christian love and warmth in meetings and at activities. When lost or nonchurch-oriented kids visit church events, they need to sense the acceptance and genuine love of the group. Too often visitors come and go without ever experiencing a personal encounter from someone who bothers to communicate with them.

An environment of warmth can grow out of several important elements.

1. A group of trained youth workers that has strong personal relationships with the regular church youth thus allows members to recognize a visitor when he arrives.
2. Develop a mature nucleus of students on whom you can count to be on the lookout for visiting high schoolers. I ask these leaders to identify visitors each week and introduce them to several of their friends.
3. Plan your youth meetings to include interaction. Crowdbreakers, skits, mixers, and participation songs relax the atmosphere and can make an outsider feel more comfortable.
4. The most important element is prayer. I have groups of youth and leaders assigned to pray prior to our youth meetings. We pray that God's Spirit will be sensed by all who are present.

I have seen the Holy Spirit work in some very unusual circumstances and some far from perfect environments, yet creating a proper spiritual climate is very important in evangelizing youth. I have attended many youth meetings in elaborate facilities that were sorely lacking in spiritual warmth. We need to evaluate our group's temperature and begin working to attain a warm atmosphere that will be conducive to evangelism.

One of the best illustrations of this and other principles mentioned occurred recently. A girl named Wendy had been visiting our youth events for about three weeks. She professed to be a Christian, and we had no reason to doubt her. However, late one Wednesday I received a phone call. Wendy was calling from a pay phone at a miniature golf course where she had gone with some friends following S.W.A.T.

Our youth service that night had consisted of music and testimonies. There had been no evangelistic message or invitation, yet Wendy had come under the conviction of the Holy Spirit. She wanted me to pray with her to receive Christ, so I talked to her for some time and then led her in prayer. The following day we met to discuss what had happened. Her exact words were, "Right in the middle of the service, I began to realize I didn't have Christ in my heart. I've been counting on my church membership to get me to heaven, but the more I was around the kids in the youth group, I began to notice something missing in my life."

Wendy's conversion was the result of three very important principles. First, she noticed a difference between her life and the lives of the other kids in the youth group. Nothing is more important in youth evangelism than the lifestyle witness of your church's youth group. Second, the service she was in, although not evangelistic in nature, had the spiritual warmth necessary for her to come to grips with her condition. And then, finally, she felt secure enough to call. Although we had talked only briefly on three occasions at the most, we had established a relationship that enabled her to call late at night for help.

Evangelism is not a distant spiritual goal to be dreamed about by our youth ministries. It is well within our reach. In fact, it is what we have been commissioned to do. It certainly cannot be all that we do, but it must be high on our list of priorities.

FOR FURTHER READING

Aldrich, Joe. *Lifestyle Evangelism.* Portland, Ore.: Multnomah, 1981.

Barber, Cyril J., and Gary H. Strauss. *Leadership: The Dynamics of Success.* Greenwood, S.C.: Attic Press, 1982.

Eims, Leroy. *The Lost Art of Disciple Making.* Colorado Springs, Colo.: NavPress, 1978.

Engel, James, and Wilbert Norton. *What's Gone Wrong with the Harvest?* Grand Rapids: Zondervan, 1975.

Hendricks, Howard G. *Taking a Stand: What God Can Do Through Ordinary You.* Portland, Ore.: Multnomah, 1983.

Kuhne, Gary. *The Dynamics of Personal Follow-Up.* Grand Rapids: Zondervan, 1976.

Ortiz, Juan Carlos. *Call to Discipleship.* Plainfield, N.J.: Logos International, 1975.

Stearns, Bill. *How to Build a Youth Outreach Ministry.* Wheaton, Ill.: Victor, 1984.

20

Dan Webster and Jana Sundene

Speaking to High School Students

Step with me into the First Church of the Sanctimonious, room 27B, where Youth Pastor Poindexter is speaking to his group of twenty-five high school students. He is saying, "We may note in this passage that what is incidental to the primary intent of the narrative may indeed reflect an inspired author's understanding, but its didactic value . . . "

Wait a minute. How do you respond to this deeply insightful communication? How do you think the students are responding? Pastor Poindexter may have some rich content in his message, but the students do not seem to be appreciating it. In fact, many of them are nodding off.

Now come with me to another church, the Happy Day Everything's Great Total Joy Community Church. I have heard there is a more lively group there. As we walk into the fairly-full auditorium, we observe Youth Pastor Joe Bob relating a humorous story about high school life. He really seems to understand students, because he has them doubled over with laughter. For a half an hour straight he has us entertained—kids are pleading for mercy because their sides are aching so badly. Even though Joe Bob understands how to get the attention of high school students, as we talk with him afterward, we discover

DAN WEBSTER, B.A., is director of Son City Ministries, Willow Creek Community Church, South Barrington, Illinois.

JANA SUNDENE, M.A., is associate director of girls' ministries, Son City Ministries, Willow Creek Community Church, South Barrington, Illinois.

that he is concerned because too few of his students seem serious about putting energy into really living out the Christian faith.

At the Church of the Common Way, our last stop, Youth Pastor Ron Of-the-Mill is speaking to his students on Defensive Thinking in a Manipulative World. Sounds gréat. Despite Pastor Ron's ability to connect important biblical truths to relevant issues for students, however, we are disappointed to find that he lacks the skill to communicate his ideas. His message is dry, formal, and delivered in a monotone voice. The students are getting restless.

Do any of these scenarios sound familiar? Have you noticed similar responses from students and wondered what was wrong? Each scenario illustrates some characteristic of effective speaking. Youth Pastor Poindexter knows the importance of drawing his content from the Word of God; Youth Pastor Joe Bob has the speaking skills necessary to capture the audience; and Youth Pastor Ron Of-the-Mill understands students well enough to relate God's truth to them. The problem is that each of the strengths of those speakers needs to work *in conjunction with one another* in order to create effective communication. To be an effective communicator one should seek to *understand his target audience* (the students), know how to *apply biblical truths to a student's life,* and *develop practical communication skills.* However, even these three characteristics will not be effective unless they are connected with an ongoing, personal knowledge of the power of God's Spirit working in and through you.

YOUTH MINISTER AS COMMUNICATOR

Before examining each of the characteristics of effective communication, consider the responsibility of the youth minister as a communicator. Is it necessary for a youth pastor to have certain spiritual gifts (such as teacher, prophet, or knowledge) in order to be an effective teacher? Certain spiritual gifts may definitely enhance your ability to teach effectively, but we have a responsibility that goes beyond our natural abilities and gifts. Consider the following passages from Scripture:

> And the Lord's servant must not quarrel; instead, he must be kind to everyone, *able to teach,* not resentful. Those who oppose him he must gently instruct. (2 Tim. 2:24-25*a*, italics added)

> Therefore go and make disciples of all nations, baptizing them in the name of the Father and of the Son and of the Holy Spirit, and *teaching* them to observe everything I have commanded you. (Matt. 28:18-19*a*, italics added)

Youth workers of today must rise to the high calling involved in shaping the church of tomorrow by becoming responsible teachers. No matter what spiritual gifts we possess, we have the responsibility to develop our abilities as communicators. The goal of this chapter is to aid the development of those abilities.

The four characteristics of effective speaking can be visualized as four overlapping circles.

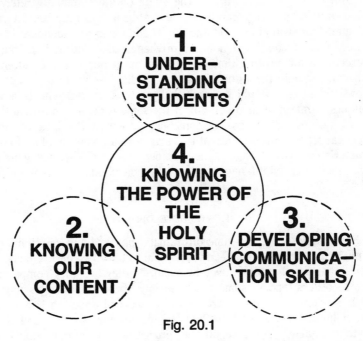

Fig. 20.1

Each of the circles represents an equally important idea, but each idea is ultimately dependent on its interaction with the middle circle. We must personally know the reality of God's power in each area to be effective. Each of the circles will be examined separately. See chapters 2 and 3 for additional materials on understanding students (circle one).

THE TARGET AUDIENCE

The first circle represents a need to understand *who* we are communicating with. Matthew 16:1-3 records Jesus' rebuke to the Pharisees and Sadducees because they did not know how to interpret the signs of the times. How desperately we need to be aware of the signs of our own times in order to understand our students. Jesus knew what was in man (John 2:25), and no one needed to testify to Him concerning man because He was sensitive to all that humankind was experiencing. It is only as we develop our sensitivity to the inner and outer world of today's students that we can begin to communicate effectively to them. Specifically, we need to understand (1) the characteristics of their stage of development, (2) the influencing forces of today's society, and (3) the distinguishing characteristics of the group of students we are addressing.

High school students are in the stage of life commonly referred to as *adolescence*. Adolescence can be thought of as a culturally based term denoting the age between childhood and adulthood when an individual has neither the freedoms of childhood nor the privileges of adulthood. In our society, adolescence is a confusing time because we are ushering our children into the adult world rapidly through fashion and media. We are also giving them the responsibilities that would normally belong to a parent (who is now absent through separation or divorce), but at the same time denying them the status that goes along with those responsibilities.[1] Often the lack of status and respect causes teenagers to resent this stage of life. As we explore four general characteristics of this stage of development for students, ask yourself what impact each area might have on the way you choose to communicate with students.

FOUR GENERAL CHARACTERISTICS OF DEVELOPMENT

First, adolescence is a time of dramatic physical and emotional changes. The physical changes of the teen years seem to have two basic effects. Kids are either embarrassed and confused by them, or they are busy comparing themselves to others (and in some cases terribly afraid the changes might never occur). Students are very aware of and concerned about their bodies at this stage of life. As voices change, bodies become more shapely, and acne medicines take on new importance, another process is also set in motion: the formation of sexual drives and desires.

Irene and Merton Strommen state from their studies of 8,156 church young adolescents:

> The increased sex drive that accompanies onset of puberty is shown in the rising percentage of young adolescents who are interested in the opposite sex. . . . The percentage who think "often" or "very often" about sex increases each year, from 24 percent for fifth-grade boys to 50 percent of ninth-grade boys. Though two years behind girls in their physical development, boys do not lag in the number who think often about sex. They respond more readily to sexual stimuli when alone, in contrast to girls, who respond more readily to affectional stimuli.

> With thoughts of sex come an increased percentage who frequently talk about it. The number who talk "often" or "very much" with their friends about sex steadily increases from 26 percent (fifth grade) to 48 percent (ninth grade). It is a topic

1. See David Elkind, *All Grown Up and No Place to Go: Teenagers in Crisis* (Reading, Mass.: Addison Wesley, 1984).

that new drives and emotions make exciting and daring. For many, talk about sex becomes a way of coming to understand and accept this new phenomenon in their lives.[2]

It is not hard to discern the greatest preoccupation of high school students. If you listen to their conversations, you will hear one very dominant subject of discussion: for guys, it is girls, girls, girls; for girls, it is boys, boys, boys. Students are beginning to test their standing with the opposite sex, which often results in subtle power games between them.

Men, do you remember the tremendous fear you experienced when you asked a girl out for the first time? You told yourself that she could not possibly resist you, but you felt differently inside. So, you played it really cool when you asked her—making sure you did not display too much interest. That way you could still feel as though you had the upper hand if she rejected you. Hopefully, the cracking in your voice would not give you away. If she said yes, you would be elated. If she said no, you would feel like you were going to die. That is characteristic of the drastic emotional fluctuations that accompany this period of hormonal development. One moment students act like mini-adults, and the next moment they respond to one another with childish emotional outbursts. The average high school girl can have her whole day made *or* ruined by just one casual comment from that special guy at school. Knowing that students are preoccupied with the opposite sex and that they are undergoing many changes, how will you help them understand God's perspectives on relationships and find peace in their development?

Partly because teenagers' bodies as well as personalities are undergoing these changes, students will usually experience a self-worth crisis. That is a second characteristic of this age. They begin asking themselves, Who am I? Often they receive inadequate answers from parents or peers or the media. How can we help our students in the midst of their struggle to find their value as people? What kind of topics will aid them in forming a balanced understanding of themselves? Which passages of Scripture will clarify God's view? It is important to be aware of the feelings of inferiority and insecurity that accompany adolescence.

If you have ever spent any amount of time in a foreign culture where you did not know the language or the customs, then you will understand a third characteristic of adolescence—the high school student's desire to fit in. In a foreign country, even the most basic activities are uncomfortable and sometimes impossible for an outsider who does not have a knowledge of the rules of that culture. Most students are taking great pains to avoid the discomfort of being an outsider by speaking the language of their peers. Ridicule and rejection, many feel, can be avoided only by going along with the prevailing opin-

2. Merton P. Strommen and A. Irene Strommen, *Five Cries of Parents* (San Francisco: Harper & Row, 1985), pp. 55-56.

ions of the crowd. To defy the will of the crowd on trivial matters (such as clothing fads) represents a risk for many students. A study by Ruth Beranda found that 75 percent of the students tested conformed to the judgment of the majority of other students even when the judgment was *obviously wrong.*[3] Do our messages help students learn to make godly choices instead of conforming to those arbitrarily endorsed by the crowd?

Adolescence is also a time of mental confusion. Perhaps one of the reasons students struggle with the pressure to conform has to do with confusion about how to make their own decisions and value judgments. They are begining to contrast "what I've been told" with "what I believe." Because many students are not properly equipped to make those decisions with any degree of confidence, they adopt the values of the crowd. It is difficult for them to realize that they are only replacing "what I've *been* told" (by adults) with "what I am *being* told" (by peers). Beyond conforming to a different set of values, many students are genuinely examining accepted concepts and ideas and are trying to determine whether they should reject them or accept them. Two common questions during this stage of development are, Why should I do it your way? and, Why are you always right? Perhaps we should examine the messages we are giving them to determine whether we are helping students form new conclusions or just telling them what they should believe.

Experiencing physical and emotional changes, struggling with self-worth, and tending toward conformity and mental confusion are some of the common ailments of adolescents, but the students of today also face circumstances unique to their generation. Whereas the common offenses in public schools used to be talking, making noise, and running in the halls, public school offenses for 1982 were listed as rape, robbery, assault, burglary, arson, murder, and suicide.[4] We will examine four of the major forces that shape the enviroment of today's students.

FOUR MAJOR INFLUENCING FORCES

First of all, students face *fragmentation.* As society becomes fragmented through divorce (the divorce rate has risen 700 percent in this century) and the breakdown of community, students become fragmented.[5] They are broken apart inside and disjointed. That is evident in the *tripling* of the suicide rate for fifteen to twenty-four-year-olds in the last thirty years.[6] The students of today are more depressed and exhibit deeper psychological problems than in previous

3. Ruth W. Berenda, *The Influence of the Group on the Judgment of Children* (New York: King's Crown, 1950).
4. "Offenses in Public Schools," *Indianapolis Tech Challenge Newsletter* (January 1983).
5. *The World Almanac and Book of Facts 1986* (New York: Newspaper Enterprise Assoc., 1986), p. 779.
6. John Janeway Conger and Anne C. Petersen, *Adolescence and Youth* (New York: Harper & Row, 1984), p. 655.

years. That is not hard to believe when you realize that literally millions of kids are victims of violence in the home, whereas others face emotional abuse or alcoholic parents. The frequency of sexual abuse in the home is just now coming to the surface. The Bureau of the Census "projects that 48% of all children born in 1980 will live 'a considerable time' with only one parent before they reach the age of 18."[7] Our hearts go out to the single mothers or fathers who have no other option but to work and therefore can devote less and less time and energy to their children. Unfortunately, it is destroying the emotional stability of our young. Kids desperately need to know about a stable, consistent God who loves them. They also need to be introduced to an environment that reflects that kind of God. We should not be asking our students to change (clean up their language, stop listening to certain kinds of music, etc.) before we accept them. Recall Jesus' example in Matthew 9:36 where He felt *compassion* for the multitude because they were "harassed and helpless, like sheep without a shepherd."

Second, students are surrounded by a *me-istic* culture. A *me-ist* is one whose world revolves around his own personal needs, wants, and desires. Second Timothy 3:2 warns us that in the last days people will be lovers of themselves. A me-istic culture encourages people to turn away from social issues and world problems and toward personal comfort and affluence. In an article about rearing families, a university professor claims that our culture has produced parents who "are excessively concerned with self-fulfillment to the detriment of family life."[8] Me-istic parents are self-oriented and not willing to sacrifice for their children.

Christopher Lasch, in his book *The Culture of Narcissism*, defines meism as a form of self-love that results when people are afraid to love other people and hence turn all their affections in upon themselves.[9] From these sources we can point to two possible contributors to a meistic culture: (1) self-oriented parents who lead kids to the conclusion that everyone must learn to care for his own needs first and (2) fragmented and destructive home environments that cause children to turn inward instead of outward because of an abnormal fear of possible rejection when loving other people. A meist lives without concern for the future, lacks self-control, refuses personal responsibility, and is sexually self-centered. No wonder we see kids spending forty dollars on concert tickets, fifteen dollars on beer or wine, and another fifteen dollars in gas in one evening but looking at you as if you are crazy if you ask them to contribute a mere one dollar to the poor. What a contrast this attitude is to Christian

---

7. B. F. Brown, "A Study of the School Needs of Children from One-Parent Families," *Phi Delta Kappan* 61 (April 1980): 537.
8. Edward Wynne, "The U.S.: It's No Place to Raise a Family," *The Wall Street Journal*, 23 August 1982, p. 14.
9. See Christopher Lasch, *The Culture of Narcissism: American Life in an Age of Diminishing Expectations* (New York: Norton, 1978).

values: "Greater love has no one than this, that he lay down his life for his friends" (John 15:13).

Students also live in a *relativistic* society. This mindset encourages people to make decisions without regard for absolute truths but only on the basis of comparison. One time I was talking to a student in my office, and in the midst of a frustrating counseling session I asked her if she thought there was anything that was wrong for everyone. Without hesitation she replied no. Then she added that maybe murder was wrong.

Kids do not have the same conception of absolutes as their elders and therefore conclude that no one way is more right than another. This is frustrating because students do not buy it when I appeal to absolute truths. Students are more apt to understand a matter according to its practicality. They do not ask if it is true; they ask if it works. But relativism does not work. I am reminded of the ethics professor who taught relativism but screamed foul when a kid in his class got his fifteen-year-old daughter pregnant.

On a flight to the East Coast for a speaking engagement, I asked a Harvard professor sitting next to me what he thought were the most important absolutes. He told me it was absurd to believe in absolutes and stated that there were none. I paused for a moment, then turned to him and said, "Excuse me, sir, but that sounded like a very absolute statement you just made." He did not have much to say to me after that. Our messages to our students must be based on the absolute truths of God, and yet we must be aware that we are addressing a generation of students that has been educated on relativistic thinking.

A final aspect of this society is its gravitation toward *escapism*. Our culture abounds in providing ways for people to avoid reality. So, instead of focusing on their hurts or responsibilities, more and more students are turning to drinking and partying (the number of problem drinkers in high school is increasing),[10] or to their TV sets or video games (the average student spends more time in front of the TV than in front of his or her teachers). Rock music can also be an escape from thinking about reality. Most of this music only reinforces the hedonistic mentality of meism and encourages participation in sexual activity, drugs, violence, and satanic worship.

Finally, you must be aware of the specific social/economic background, emotional and intellectual maturity level, and median age of the particular group you will be speaking to. We have discussed the big picture, but you will want to ascertain the small picture as well. It is obvious that Satan is battling for the hearts and minds of today's students, but our awareness of what is

10. A self-report of a cross-section of U.S. high school students was conducted yearly using approximately 16,000 students. Daily use of alcohol was reported by 5.7 percent of the students in 1975 and 6.9 percent in 1979. The percentage of students who reported heavy drinking on a weekly basis in 1983 was 46.7. See *Drugs and American High School Students 1975-1983* (U.S. Department of Health and Human Services, 1984), pp. 311-13.

going on is the first step in understanding how to reach students in a life-changing way.

THE CONTENT

The second circle of effective speaking is the content of our message. That content needs to be based on the Word of God. We will use 2 Timothy 4:1-5 to glean some more specific advice.

> In the presence of God and of Jesus Christ, who will judge the living and the dead, and in view of his appearing and his kingdom, I give you this charge: Preach the Word; be prepared in season and out of season; correct, rebuke and encourage— with great patience and careful instruction. For the time will come when men will not put up with sound doctrine. Instead, to suit their own desires, they will gather around them a great number of teachers to say what their itching ears want to hear. They will turn their ears away from the truth and turn aside to myths. But you, keep your head in all situations, endure hardship, do the work of an evangelist, discharge all the duties of your ministry.

The content of our message expresses not man's opinion but God's truth. Realizing that roots of each message should be grounded in biblical truths, what are some specific truths that need to be addressed when speaking with high school students? As we have implied earlier, that is dependent on your audience. What kind of students are you talking to? It is important to discern what the needs of your particular group of students are and to discover how the Bible approaches those needs.

Over the years we have found that students we have spoken to know little of (or have a distorted view of) the identity of God and the nature of man. Yet they have intense relational and social needs at their stage of development. For that reason, we often present biblical perspectives on such topics as getting along with parents, dealing with friendships, love, sex and dating, loneliness, self-esteem, standing up for what you believe, and making right decisions. The topics *you* pick and your treatment of them should take into account not only the needs of the group, but their level of spiritual and emotional maturity. If you have a mature group, you will want to tackle more difficult issues of faith and doctrine than you would with a less mature group.

Another important consideration in deciding what your content will be is to understand your own level of skill in communicating. If you decide to speak on doctrine, do you have the skill and creativity to make that doctrine understandable for the average student? If you are speaking on the Old Testament, can you make the content relevant to the lives of your students? Appropriate content is rooted in the Word, depends on the needs as well as the emotional and spiritual maturity of your audience, and takes into account the communication skills of the speaker.

Verse two of our passage says that the work of preaching is to reprove, to rebuke, and to exhort. Reproof implies that one is to show God's standards next to the standards of the world. The result of reproof is that the hearer will have an understanding of what constitutes incorrect living. He will therefore be able to point out areas of sin in his or her own life. The speaker may bring his audience to a point of conviction.

Rebuking resembles a sincere, loving scolding. This scolding should be from an accurate authority (i.e., the Bible) along with the sense that the speaker can have a certain level of identification with his hearers. The goal is to give members of the audience an understanding of where they need to be as well as how to get there. Any speaker who is in touch with the values of today's society will not find it hard to put these first two areas into practice. Biblical values stand in stark contrast to life in modern society. We must help our students recognize the differences.

The third area is exhortation. Exhortation implies an urging or pleading. All three of these areas need to be blended for effective messages. We need to balance the severity with gentleness and encouragement.

Paul adds two more important ingredients to the work of preaching: patience and instruction. Anyone who has had any experience in youth ministry will know how necessary patience is. In this instance, patience seems to indicate the ability to endure under pressure. We must learn to have patience in our preaching and with our hearers. Finally, we are to instruct. What good would it do for us to point out sin or urge our young people toward right living if they do not know how to apply what they hear?

DEVELOPING COMMUNICATION SKILLS

Once we are aware of some of the considerations necessary in content development, what are some of the skills we need to develop in order to present that content in an effective way? Unfortunately, there is no formula available to guarantee that students will listen to the messages given to them. In fact, one of the most effective ways to get students to listen is often to develop relational integrity with the leaders of your group. If they listen, then their friends usually listen also. In general though, if we, as speakers, can learn to say things that make sense, are interesting, and apply to the lives of our students, then we will have a good chance of having them listen. Develop a good track record with your students: live what you teach, develop integrity, speak the truth, share illustrations that identify you with them, be transparent and honest with your own life. We have taught our group of Christian students how to have an authentic walk with God. As a part of that, we taught about spending time with Him daily. One of us shared some of the entries from our spiritual journal with the students. They then had an idea that we were really trying to live the things we were teaching them, as well as what kind of things we bring before God (including some personal confessions and areas of needed growth). Another suggestion is to break up your serious content with humor. If you are losing the kids' attention, humor can bring them back into the message, and then you can lead them into the more serious aspects of your talk.

Some of the skills involved in putting together an effective message can be broken down into three areas: (1) topic selection, (2) message preparation, and (3) message presentation.

TOPIC SELECTION

There are two progressions you may go through to develop a topic: (1) identify one of the needs of the group, discover a passage in Scripture that speaks to that need, then form your message, or (2) study Scripture and let the Holy Spirit identify one of the group's needs, and then shape your talk. In the first progression, one of the needs of your group may be revealed in a counseling session with one of your students, in corporate discussion with your students or your leaders, or as you consider some of the universal needs of high school students.

We once conducted a survey of our core group of Christian students to help identify some of their needs. We asked questions regarding their thought life, their devotional and relational life, as well as what kinds of pressures hinder them in their walk with God. We were amazed to discover that one of the constantly recurring needs was a topic on which nothing had been taught. Many of our students were discouraged about the apathy they faced from other students in school. They did not know how to respond to it. God used this survey as a means of opening our eyes to a need and giving us a topic for a series of messages.

Under the second progression, the Holy Spirit may reveal a need or topic for your message through personal devotions (prayer or study), through your own experience living the Christian faith (sometimes God may bring things into our lives so that we can share what we learn from them with our students or so that we can transmit a God-given burden to them), or through some other reading in which you may be involved.

As speakers with various tendencies, temperaments, and gifts, we should be careful to implement what can be referred to as the "rotation principle." That will prevent us from getting locked into preparing messages that reflect only our predisposition. For instance, we may gravitate towards giving challenging messages that motivate but neglect giving comforting messages that point out the benefits of being a Christian, or evangelistic messages that present the gospel, or instructive messages that encourage growth in specific areas. Identify your own tendencies so that you can rotate to other kinds of messages. One of the most important principles to remember in topic selection is that our messages should be born out of the needs of the group and the Word of God, not simply out of topics with which we feel comfortable.

MESSAGE PREPARATION

Once we have discovered a need and corresponding passage of Scripture, we are ready to begin message preparation. As you dig into the passage, do not hesitate to use tools such as commentaries, concordances, Greek word studies, dictionaries, and the like. Discover the context of the passage, and ask yourself other relevant questions about its content or implications. Writing down important thoughts that pertain to the topic will give you a large pool of ideas to use in forming the outline of your message. Identify a key idea, or thesis statement, and decide what other information or ideas will help to drive it home. That should give you a rough outline and enable you to ask three important questions of your material.

1. What does the key idea mean? Spend some time *explaining* your idea.
2. Is it true? How is this key idea evidenced in history and science? Explore the *validity* of your idea. Can you reason from logic or experience to make your point believable? Remember that students are at a skeptical age.
3. Who will care? What difference will this make? The ability to *apply* your idea is important.

Rethinking your purpose will give direction to your message. Remember that a message should seek to change a life in some specific way, so it is important to ask yourself what you are hoping will happen in the lives of your students. Do you want to see a change in knowledge level, attitudes, or behavior? Be specific about what you want to accomplish. For example, 1 Peter 5:8 has a key idea (Satan desires to destroy God's work), out of which you can identify a purpose for your message (to increase the students' awareness of Satan's work) and then form a specific goal (to help students identify and learn how to resist the attacks of the enemy).

Larry Richards uses the word *hook* to describe the introduction, which conjures up the image of taking fish from the water into the boat.[11] That is an important function of an introduction; it should draw your students into your topic by arousing their interest, stimulating their curiosity, or commanding their attention. As speakers, we come prayed up and excited about the truth that we will be addressing, but our students are not usually in the same frame of mind. A fight with Mom, the frustration of a math exam, or the lingering memory of a conversation with that special person is still holding their attention. It is important to find a way to usher them into your topic.

Some examples of hooks include: setting up a situation to be solved,

11. Larry Richards, *Creative Bible Studies* (Grand Rapids: Zondervan, 1979), p. 108.

telling a real life story, using a news quote, having the students think of the last time they encountered a specific situation, using an intriguing or enlightening definition of your subject, expressing your concern over the topic, or asking questions that require some kind of audience participation. Your introduction should also lead naturally into the body of the message. It is not only an attention getter, but also a *lead-in* to your subject.

In the body of the message, it is good to phrase major points in such a way that they reinforce the key idea. Careful phrasing will enhance the overall effect as well as enable your students to recall information later. After you note a main point, additional information can be used to *restate* (in different words, for emphasis or clarification), *prove* (with facts, observations, examples, statistics, or quotes), *explain* (with illustrations, definitions, or visual demonstrations), or *apply* (through explanation, illustration, or question asking). Everything in the body of the message should direct the listener back to the key idea. A message can be illustrated as follows:

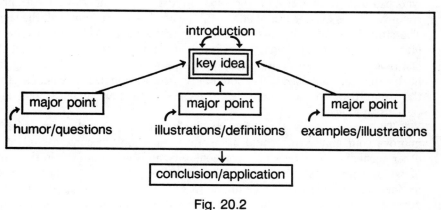

Fig. 20.2

Illustrations and humor are two essential ingredients in speaking to high school students. An illustration should throw light on a subject by proceeding from the factual to the visual, the conceptual to the practical, or the abstract to the concrete. Illustrations can be used to restate, validate, explain, or apply a truth. In the Bible, Jesus spoke with parables and also provided word pictures for His listeners ("It is easier for a camel to go through the eye of a needle," Matt. 19:24). In 2 Timothy 2, Paul uses the images of the soldier, the athlete, and the farmer to illustrate his point. Both drew their illustrations from everyday life.

Illustrations have tremendous potential for validating truths psychologically. That is especially true in a media-oriented society. Our students have been brought up with a medium (TV) that communicates graphically, not conceptually. The use of illustrations allows you to restate and clarify your concepts without wearying your students with abstractions. (That is not to say your message should lack logic or factual material.)

Where can you find illustrations for your message? The best way is to learn to keep your eyes and ears open. Read books, observe life as it unfolds around you, listen to the way people talk to one another, keep up with the news (in all forms), and finally, be in touch with your own life experiences. (When one of us talks about love, sex, and dating, we always include a few personal illustrations.) Be sure you keep up on the news that your students would be aware of, too. The lives of rock stars, as well as lyrics from various songs to which they are listening, can provide effective illustrations.

Good illustrations display truth in action. They should be developed so that they hold the attention and stir the emotions of your audience. However, the most important aspect of your illustration should be its ability to be applied to an idea. For instance, we sometimes share a story about a Canadian trapper who has a dog for a close companion. At the end of the story, the trapper shoots and kills his dog out of anger. But he acts before he knows all the facts. The story is emotionally involving, but its real strength is its application to Matthew 7 (about not judging). I will ask students in the group to recall the last time they were a victim of judging, then stress the point that judging can be destructive. So illustrations should be shared, then applied. Remember that the strength of an illustration lies in its ability to drive home a point in a responsive moment.

There is no doubt that effective illustrating takes practice. In order to improve your ability to recount a narrative you should become a student of other speakers. When you hear someone give an illustration, get in the habit of asking yourself why it worked. What did the speaker say or do that made me feel and respond to what he or she was saying? What aspects of the story penetrated, and why did they? Look for pacing, phrasing, humor, and the elements of surprise or suspense.

The second essential ingredient, humor, can break tension and lower the defenses of your audience. Humor is great, but it should be used purposefully. It should either direct attention to an idea in your message or be used to build a bridge between you and your listeners. Also, be careful with the use of humor. You do not want to be written off as a comedian; you want to be known as a speaker of truth. Make sure your humor is not destructive or degrading and that you do not sacrifice your integrity just to get a few laughs. Use humor that is suitable for you and most comfortable for your personality type.

Skills at developing relevant material for the body of your message will be enhanced as you learn to be a student of good speakers and of those things to which high school kids are currently responsive. As you listen to various speakers who are effective with students, discern what need of the audience they are meeting. Why do kids grow from listening to one speaker, or feel loved by another? This will help you get a feel for the dynamics of effective speaking.

Become a student of the things today's students respond to in popular culture (entertainment, fads). If kids are spending hours and hours hanging around in shopping malls, determine what it is that keeps them interested. Is it meeting a social need, or does it meet a need for status or accomplishment they are not getting anywhere else? If a movie has a huge teenage following, become familiar with the movie and ask yourself what there is about it that attracts teenagers. Find out why kids like certain comedians or rock stars. Studying those things will help you identify various needs and allow you to apply truth to the trends of today's youth. It is also a good way to discover relevant illustrations to support your points.

The conclusion of the message should be a means of tying everything together, not just as a stopping point. Because your end goal is obedience to God, the conclusion should do more than summarize, however. Like a lawyer, ask for some kind of verdict or personal application. This is the time in your message when you will let the students know what to do with what you have just said.

It is helpful to realize the progression that people go through in response to new information. First a person will change his mind, then he will change his attitude. Only after those two changes have occurred is a person ready to change his behavior. If we make a call for action without giving the audience the opportunity to make changes internally, that is manipulation.

If we deliver a message about bad habits or self-esteem in which the particular content does not specifically lead up to salvation, we may make a challenge regarding the topic. Or we may simply state that the truth we have covered is the truth of Jesus Christ and challenge our listeners to investigate Christianity. In messages for nonchurched students, we have a progression in which we do a series of messages that lead up to a call to salvation. That allows the students to make internal changes before they are challenged to act. So the conclusion of each message should be based on its content. You also should keep in mind where your listeners are in determining what kind of application you ask them to make.

MESSAGE PRESENTATION

The last communication skill is message presentation. Adopt a style of presentation that is consistent with your personality. Be willing to be authentic and human with your students. You do not need to degrade yourself in order to be vulnerable with them. Just be real—students hunger for that. It is helpful to avoid the word *you*, if it is being used in a condescending way. That will alienate students. Finally, be confident enough in your content and the work of the Holy Spirit to be able to speak in a positive manner.

UNDERSTANDING THE POWER OF GOD

We will now consider the importance of the last circle of effective speaking: a personal knowledge of God's power. Recall that each of the other circles is completely dependent on its interaction with this fourth circle. First Corinthians 4:20 reminds us, "The kingdom of God is not a matter of talk but of power." An effective communicator understands that his or her words are nothing if the power of God is not in them. As speakers, our greatest challenge is to be the kind of people through whom God's power can flow. We must not waste the opportunities God has given us by neglecting to prepare our hearts.

How can we meet the challenge to become those who speak with the impact of the Holy Spirit? First, by affirming our call to youth ministry. Why is it that so many regard youth ministry as a stepping-stone to big-time ministry (adult ministry)? Is it that God cares more about the spiritual development of adults than He does for youth? We know that is not true. Have you ever heard it said, "The youth of today are the church of tomorrow"? Youth ministers are an important part of God's plan in reaching the world and in the growth of the church. Reaffirming your call to ministry to students will increase your passion for God and for the students' spiritual welfare. You are called to a holy calling (2 Tim. 1:9) and should live with that awareness.

Second, we should strive to live up to our calling by living a life that is pleasing to God. Does this sound basic? It is, but unfortunately many of us do not seek to "find out what pleases the Lord" (Eph. 5:10) as diligently as we seek to learn what will make us a successful leader in the eyes of the church or our youth. It is possible to have a successful youth ministry and a reputation among other youth workers by learning how to be popular with kids. But that does not always equal a life that is pleasing to God. Who are you serving in your ministry? Serve the Lord, and He will teach you how to serve others in a much more profound way than you can imagine.

This leads to the third aspect of becoming one who speaks with the impact of the Holy Spirit. We must learn to wait on the Lord in prayer. It is in prayer that we can begin to gain the heart of God. It is in prayer that we can be filled with the power to speak His truth. And it is in prayer that the Lord can speak to us concerning what and how we should speak to others.

Finally, we must become humble servants of our Lord. No matter how gifted we may be, or how many skills we may develop as communicators, it is only through God's power that we will have any effect at all for the kingdom of Christ. In our own strength we may be able to have some kind of temporal impact on those around us, but only God is able to help us make any eternal impact on others. Paul says in 1 Corinthians 2:4-5, "My message and my preaching were not with wise and persuasive words, but with a demonstration of the Spirit's power, so that your faith might not rest on men's wisdom, but on God's power."

Perhaps it would be wise to step into one more youth group meeting before we end. The youth pastor seems to be normal enough, and the students do not look much different from others we have seen. But we are amazed at the understanding this speaker seems to have of his students. He is saying things that really matter, yet sprinkling his truths with illustrations that are able to reach the students. He has well-developed communication skills and knows how to keep the attention of his audience. Most important, we sense that the Holy Spirit is working in the life of the youth pastor as well as in the hearts and minds of all those present. This scenario does not have to be the exception. In fact, if you have been putting some of these principles to work, it is possible that we just observed *your* youth group!

FOR FURTHER READING

Baumann, Dan. "Speaking to High School Students." In *The Youth Leader's Source Book,* edited by Gary Dausey. Grand Rapids: Zondervan, 1983.

Brilhart, John K. *Effective Group Discussion.* 4th ed. Dubuque, Ia.: Wm. C. Brown, 1982.

Conger, John Janeway, and Anne C. Peterson. *Adolescence and Youth.* New York: Harper & Row, 1984.

Hurley, Pat. *The Great Teen Robbery.* Wheaton, Ill.: Victor, 1987.

Lasch, Christopher. *The Culture of Narcissism.* New York: W. W. Norton, 1978.

LeFever, Marlene. *Creative Teaching Methods.* Elgin, Ill.: David C. Cook, 1985.

Le Francois, Guy R. *Psychology for Teaching.* 4th ed. Belmont, Calif.: Wadsworth Publishing, 1982.

Richards, Larry. *Creative Bible Studies.* Grand Rapids: Zondervan, 1979.

———. *69 Ways to Start a Study Group and Keep it Growing.* Grand Rapids: Zondervan, 1973.

Strommen, Merton P. *Five Cries of Youth.* New York: Harper & Row, 1974.

21

Charles O. Bradshaw

Working with Parents of Youth

"Our youth program is not as good as the one at the church down the street." "The youth seldom leave or return from an activity on time." "Our youth pastor is never serious." "The youth pastor has no control over the kids." "He really needs some mature adults to help him." "You would not believe how noisy it gets at the youth meetings." "The youth don't have enough Bible study." "Our youth director relates only to the popular kids in the youth group." "He never spends time with my son." "You have no business correcting my child at the youth meetings." These are just a few of the comments I have heard from parents of teenagers in youth groups.

Youth pastors dread it when the senior pastor calls them into his office and says, "I've been getting some complaints about your handling of a situation in the youth group. The parents have asked me to talk with you and get the problem solved." This situation is repeated over and over again in churches across America. Unhappy complaints from parents about the youth pastor are commonplace. For many youth leaders, the idea of working with parents is frightening and at best discouraging.

At times, parents can be your greatest support; at other times, they can be your worst enemy. There is the joy of victory when you hear parents relate how

CHARLES O. BRADSHAW, Ph. D., is a Christian education consultant living in Rowland Heights, California.

344 The Complete Book of Youth Ministry

helpful the group is to their teenagers. There is the agony of defeat when parents complain when a trip, study, or project does not go as expected. The youth leader has, on one hand, the demanding parents who expect him to mend the rifts between them and their teenagers and, on the other hand, the grateful parent who states, "I'm so glad you are here; I am sure you can help my daughter," which reflects his or her desire for you to be a miracle worker. Excessive demands, unrealistic expectations, and unjustified criticisms all keep one from wanting to work with parents.

PARENTS AS FRIENDS, NOT FOES

For good or for bad, a youth worker must learn to work with parents. You will need to win their friendship rather than alienate them. People who have worked with youth pastors for years have observed over and over again that a critical test of a youth ministry's long-term effectiveness is the ability of the youth worker to work effectively with parents. Because it is *their* values, attitudes, and relationships that will have the greatest long-term effects on youth, to build a youth ministry without concern for the parents is to neglect the most influential people in the lives of the youth.

The competent youth worker recognizes that working with youth also means working with adults. He must decide to structure his ministry to reflect the strong influence that parents are exerting on their children. Though peer pressure is significant, children are still largely the product of their homes. Friends gain influence with age, but the most recent study done by the Search Institute of Minneapolis shows that students look principally to parents for guidance during the early teen years.[1] Psychologist John Conger has concluded: "An impressive body of research and clinical investigation makes it clear that the single most important influence in helping or hindering the average adolescent to cope with the developmental demands of adolescence in today's world is his or her parents."[2] In order to be most effective with youth, the role of the youth worker should be that of a caring friend, an adult peer, an interpreter of youth to parents and of parents to youth. Youth are not always aware of just how important parents are, and parents often feel as though they have no real influence on their teenager. However, parents are primary influencers of the teenagers, both now and in later years when the youth worker has faded out of the picture.

It is also necessary to work with parents because youth ministry has an unavoidable limitation. Youth workers need to be aware they have only a limited exposure to the young person. Young people are like icebergs. A youth

---

1. Merton P. Strommen and A. Irene Strommen, *Five Cries of Parents* (San Francisco: Harper & Row, 1985), p. 76.
2. John Conger, *Adolescence: Generation Under Pressure* (New York: Harper & Row, 1979), p. 47.

worker sees only the tip and perhaps only one side of it. Parents, however, see many facets. "Who would have more to share with the youth leader than the parents of the kids?" a parent asked when being interviewed by Marlene LeFever. "Yet never once in three years has our youth worker sought us out to talk about our daughter or the program."[3] Parents are involved with their teens in the problems of education and of social adjustments in and out of the home. They see the moods, strengths, and weaknesses of their adolescents. Because of normal family intimacies, a parent sees far more deeply into the young person than often is realized. The youth worker who knows his own limitation, and sees how parents can help him in understanding young people, will be far more effective.

For a youth worker it is vital to make parents his friends, not his foes. A first big step is to understand them. Youth workers take courses, read books, and attend seminars on how to understand adolescents, but one should also learn about the parents of teenagers. The youth pastor needs to understand what developmental issues and what fears parents are dealing with at this time in their own lives.

UNDERSTANDING PARENTS

For those without teenage children, it is difficult to imagine the pressures and fears parents experience as their children grow up. Parents' critical words or high expectations of the youth pastor often are caused by those pressures and fears. The youth leader who aspires to win the support of parents must be willing to be a sounding board, a counselor, or a support to parents, who are often in great pain.

DEVELOPMENTAL ISSUES FOR PARENTS

Both parent and adolescent are simultaneously in unique cycles of growth and change. Children are in adolescence, and the parents are in what some psychologists call middlescence, the years between thirty-five and fifty. Gail Sheehy writes that wives past the age of thirty-five often experience a movement toward more independence.[4] During these same years, according to Eda LaShan, the husband may become more aware of unfulfilled aspirations, mistaken decisions and choices, things left undone. He may realize that there will be no "big time" in his career. Hence, this period of married life is ripe for anxiety, impatience, and misunderstanding."

> I feel like a drowning man with all these people clinging to my neck. My father died of cancer last year, and my mother has been helpless ever since. Then

---

3. Marlene LeFever, "Parents Rate Their Youth Workers," *Youthworker* (Spring 1985), p. 26.
4. Gail Sheehy, "The Crisis Couples Face at 40," *McCall's Magazine* 103 (May 1976): 107.

my wife decided to return to the university to complete her degree, which means me picking up many of the household responsibilities. At this same time my older daughter starts her college career that demands large sums of money for tuition. Everyone tells me now is the critical time for professional advancement. Help!! It feels like I'm going down for the last time.[5]

This man's complaint is not a cry of self-pity but an accurate reflection of reality for the father of many of the teenagers in your youth group. For most men and women, the responsibilities that come with being in the prime of life are truly staggering. We are aware of the conflict with the younger generation, but there is another generation that puts the squeeze on the mid-life parent. This is actually the time when husband and wife must parent two generations, the young and old. Their children are becoming adults, and their parents are approaching death. The mothers and fathers of teenagers are often being squeezed in a viselike grip by two generations, while other demands are also multiplying. Suddenly they have to take care of everyone, but nobody is there to care for them.

The teen years often collide with parents' mid-life reassessment, that critical time of life when marriages, careers, life pursuits, values, and priorities are questioned, turned around, and often drastically altered. Dreams are re-examined. This is a period of identity development for both the parent and the adolescent child. Adolescents must establish themselves in the larger social context, whereas the family must regroup into a smaller context to face the eventual loss of these teens. Middle-aged homemakers face the prospect of the empty nest just as they sense a not-so-subtle cultural message that they may have wasted their lives and have been cheated out of a career. Most people realize that teenagers are going through the turmoil of forming an adult identity; few realize that middle adults have identity problems, too. In mid-life, parents must learn how to avoid stagnation and rigidity and to value wisdom more than physical power, among other things. Parents of teenagers must decide who they are and who they will be for the remaining years of their lives.

Teenagers in the family are discovering sex in technicolor, just at the time their parents are feeling a little gray. Adolescents, just discovering their sexuality, may be envied subtly by their parents, who may be experiencing menopause and periods of psychological impotence.

The same adolescent is faced with an overwhelming number of career choices at the same time his or her parents are beginning to face vocational stagnation, change, or possibly retirement. The middle-aged parent may be haunted by career goals unachieved, unfulfilled dreams, mistaken decisions, and things left undone. The child moving into adolescence becomes a reminder to the parent that he or she is moving into old age. The parents are at a point

5. Eda LeShan, *The Wonderful Crisis of Middle Age* (New York: McKay, 1973), p. 83.

where they may be feeling more aches and pains and are witnessing the illnesses and deaths of parents or even contemporaries. This may cause them to realize they may be the next to die.

FEARS OF PARENTS

Merton and Irene Strommen in their book *Five Cries of Parents* present and interpret the findings of current research on the parenting of adolescents. Their book focuses on the massive study called the Adolescent-Parent Study done by Peter L. Benson and the research team of Search Institute in 1983. This study involved 8,165 young adolescents and their 10,467 parents. Parents of adolescents, they found, often have searching and sometimes urgent questions. These searching questions were called cries because they represent the strong desires of parents.

Initially, the Strommens considered making fear one of the five cries of parents. On closer examination, however, they came to see that fear is not a separate cry, but rather a quality that gives urgency to the others. Parents have many fears because they know how susceptible children and young adolescents are to the social infections of our culture. This fear has been intensified by the many tragic accounts reported daily in the news media. It is important to realize this feeling of fear in parents. The fear alone can explain a lot of parental behavior and emotions. In the Adolescent-Parent Study, four out of ten parents admit they worry "very much" about the child's future, and an additional three in ten worry "quite a bit."[6]

A parent's need for answers during this period is perhaps more urgent than at any other stage in the family life cycle. It is important, then, for a person working with youth and their parents to be aware of what the Strommens call the five cries of parents. These five cries will be examined with the emphasis on what we can do to help as youth workers.

"Cry for understanding your adolescent." Parents need at least two things to help them know and understand their teenager. First, they need a simple conceptual framework to help them understand the changes typical of this stage of growth, and, second, they need listening skills to help them tune in and discover where their adolescent is in the maturing process. The importance of good parent-youth communication was evident in the Adolescent-Parent Study. More than 2,000 youth filled in answers saying, "I wish I could talk to my folks about some of my problems." The frequent response of 2,000 parents to the same item was, "I wish I could talk with my teenager about the things troubling him."[7] Those responses point up the impasse in communication that both parents and adolescents wish could be broken.

6. Strommen and Strommen, p. 4.
7. Ibid., pp. 72-73.

The youth minister can do much to help in communication. In an interview done by Marlene LeFever, one parent said, "A youth leader could help educate parents. Ours did have a parent night, and he preached a sermon on his philosophy of youth ministry. But there was no room for dialogue, and I've got a lot I need to get off my chest."[8]

The youth worker has a responsibility to those parents who cannot understand their developing son or daughter. Most parents feel some sort of responsibility for their teenagers, but many find that their attempts to show love are short-circuited. They cannot link their parental feelings with the adult-teen relationship. The youth pastor has the opportunity to provide a support system and information to assist the parents in communicating with their teenager. Many churches have developed programs for training adults to communicate and to gain listening skills. Training sessions usually include opportunities for adults and teens to work in separate groups. Then participants have a gathered time when each group shares what it has learned about the other group. At the same time, listening skills can be practiced.

"Cry for close family." This is something we all would like. Those who work with troubled youth report that "quality of human relationships is the most powerful determinant of successful programs in the education and treatment of troubled children."[9] The principle applies to all kinds of adolescents. Nothing is as powerful as the love of parents. Youth workers need to keep the perspective that parents are more important than the youth worker. One mother interviewed said, "I'd like the leader to structure some participatory programs between kids and parents. A lot more could be done to strengthen the parent/child relationship."[10]

A youth minister needs to do everything possible to build and strengthen family relationships. He can do this by watching his scheduling of activities, making positive comments about parents, and supporting the parents as much as possible. Sensitivity to parents' needs may also mean being cautious with our youth activity schedule. Parents are appreciative when we do not over-schedule and take the youth away from home too often. Also, it is good when starting or ending times are set that reflect a thoughtfulness for family meals. Activities should be scheduled well in advance, especially in the summer, so that family vacations can be planned. The youth leader who always sides with the youth against the parents will fail. Promoting an "us versus them" mentality is destructive.

"Cry for understanding yourself as a parent." We have already seen that parents are going through their own developmental issues. They need to be in touch with their own feelings, drives, and motivations. Many years ago Carl Jung noted that we have schools and colleges to help people prepare for young

8. LeFever, p. 28.
9. Larry Brendto and Arlin Ness, *Reeducating Troubled Youth* (New York: Aldine, 1983), p. 63.
10. LeFever, p. 28.

adulthood, but there are no colleges for forty-year-old parents who need to be educated into the complexities of living as an older adult. The church, or ideally the youth pastor, can help parents in this area. When serious storms are approaching, there is less damage and loss of life if the weather bureau issues a warning in time for residents to get ready and take cover. It can also be helpful if people in their mid-thirties are warned that the mid-life transition is coming. Such warning need not be frightening. Mid-life is a time of problems, especially during the early forties, but mid-life is also a period filled with rewards and challenges. There is a sense of being settled, of having found one's place in life, and of being freed from the demands and responsibilities of raising small children. When compared with younger adults, mid-life people often have more financial security, positions of prestige, more opportunity to travel, and increased wisdom. Parents can be helped to anticipate both the negative and positive aspects of this period in life that usually includes teenagers in the family.

"Cry of moral behavior." One of the issues here is helping parents decide what is moral. What is right and wrong for their teenager? Parents desire support and help in limit-setting. Bruce Narramore, in *Adolescence Is Not an Illness,* suggests that parents should "compare their standards to those of a variety of other parents." He says this can help avoid narrow decisions.[11] It can also help a parent see what limits to set that other parents have not. One parent interviewed commented, "I need to feel the security of knowing the youth leader is treating the parent/child relationship with dignity and respect. He or she needs to reinforce my values with my children. He or she doesn't always have to agree with me, but he or she does need to reinforce what is good and right in my relationship with my child."[12] Another parent said, "I would like to meet with people who have kids the same age as mine. We could share problems; it's nice to know I'm not the only parent going through something."[13] Parents need a place where they can compare notes. The youth pastor can establish the forum for that to happen.

"Cry for a shared faith." Parents and adolescents in the Search Institute study expressed similar convictions as to the importance of religion. One might assume, then, that people are discussing their faith at home. The enigma, however, is that though religion is identified as important by both parents and adolescents, it is almost a taboo subject in the home. When asked, How often does your family sit down together and talk about God, the Bible . . . or other religious things? 42 percent of the young adolescents said this never happens; 32 percent said this topic is discussed once or twice a month; 13 percent said it is discussed once a week. And this, it must be noted, is the finding from a survey of largely church-connected families, of whom 97 percent are members

11. Bruce Narramore, *Adolescence Is Not an Illness* (Old Tappan, N.J.: Revell, 1980), p. 68.
12. LeFever, p. 28.
13. Ibid.

of a church. Though religious discussions are rare, most parents of the 10,467 wished it were different.[14] The youth pastor who helps in this area will be called blessed.

"Cry for outside help." Parents cannot do it alone, and they know it. That is one reason they hired a youth minister in the first place. Thus he must be available to both teenagers and parents. A seminar on how to control your teenager is not the only thing a parent wants or needs to know about. Marriage seminars and couple retreats that help to revitalize, stabilize, and readjust marriages would be worthwhile. Support groups for parents could also be established. For example, a social support group could serve as a buffer during times of stress brought on by problems within the family. At the same time, it could provide healing and strength. Parents should realize that the youth worker is not, and will not be, a substitute parent. Instead, he is a significant adult whose function supports the parent as well as the youth. When this dual relationship becomes apparent, parents will appreciate more than ever the crucial ministry that has been undertaken.

LISTENING TO PARENTS

Being aware of the developmental issues of parents and their fears will greatly assist the youth pastor in building solid relationships with parents. Something that will help the youth worker understand the parents of his kids, and also reduce conflicts between parents and himself, is active listening. Youth leaders need to spend more time enabling the parents to talk, rather than monopolizing every encounter. When parents know their youth minister cares about their feelings, it will be easier to get their cooperation and support. To make parents friends, a youth worker should listen to them.

One parent responding to the question, What would you include in a youth leader's job description? said, "I would require good listening skills."[15] The youth worker needs to communicate to parents that he is willing to listen to them; ignoring their wisdom and experiences will cause one to sacrifice a great deal of insight into working with youth. If he gets defensive, failing to listen genuinely to parents with concerns and problems, he is putting up a major roadblock to long-range effectiveness in working with the teenagers. Therefore, a desirable quality in an adult leader is the ability simply to listen.

ACTIVE LISTENING

Listening for feelings comes under several labels, depending on the psychologist or counseling method you follow. Thomas Gordon, founder of Parent Effectiveness Training (P.E.T.) and author of a book by the same name, calls it

14. Strommen and Strommen, pp. 133-34.
15. LeFever, p. 27.

active listening.[16] Being an active listener is an extremely important factor in having good relationships with parents. Norman Wakefield talks about the values of being an active listener. (1) It helps others express their feelings. (2) Active listening helps others talk out ideas, problems, and decisions that need resolving. (3) It is one of the best means of expressing unselfish love. (4) Active listening provides the foundation for wise counsel. (5) It is one of the most basic ways to convey a sense of respect, to treat another with dignity.[17] Active listening says, I want to understand you; I want to know you; you are important.

The main idea in being an active listener is to listen for feelings and then send back a message of empathic understanding. Empathy is putting yourself in the other person's shoes. You don't evaluate, offer advice, or try to problem-solve. You try to feed back a comment that lets parents know you are trying to understand what they mean and how they feel. Most people need to listen more and talk less. By being an active listener, the youth worker can help parents understand themselves and their teenagers better because active listening helps those listened to to get in touch with their own feelings. It also helps the talker ventilate emotions that are causing problems.

To be a good listener one must first act like a good listener. To act like a good listener one should (1) maintain good eye contact; (2) sit attentively, even lean forward at times; (3) look as if he is enjoying listening; (4) ask questions; (5) appear alert, but not tense; and (6) react. People like recognition. You can give it to the one talking by verbal comments such as "I see," "That's interesting," "I never knew that." However, it is not enough that you simply *act* like a good listener. You must *be* a good listener. Most people listen, but few hear. A good listener listens to understand. A good listener hears. Most people do not listen; they just take turns talking. A person may act like a listener but be thinking only of what he is going to say when it is his turn to talk.

To be an active listener who listens for understanding, one must ask probing questions, get more information, and give feedback. Ask only questions that seek to clarify, not intimidate. The youth worker should talk only 20 to 30 percent of the time and allow the parent to verbalize his or her feelings, attitudes, and impressions. In so doing, one will be able to understand objectively the dynamics of the situation.

When working with parents, one should not give advice until he has earned the right to be heard. Earn that right by listening, asking questions, and restating their thoughts until you know what they feel and they know that you know. When you are able to restate the other person's feelings, you have reached what Wakefield calls a shared meaning.[18] The Bible expresses these

16. Thomas Gordon, *Parent Effectiveness Training (P.E.T.)* (New York: Peter H. Widen, 1970).
17. Norman Wakefield, *Listening—A Christian's Guide to Loving Relationships* (Waco, Tex.: Word, 1981), pp. 18-19.
18. Ibid., p.62.

thoughts about shared meaning: "He who answers before listening—that is his folly and his shame" (Prov. 18:13).

MANAGING CONFLICTS

Youth workers will cut their problems in half and worries in thirds if they become active listeners. But what happens when you run into a real conflict or problem with a parent? In spite of your best efforts at prevention, conflicts do arise. A parent comes to you with a complaint. A conflict is on the horizon. What should be done? First, continue listening and communicating empathy, understanding, worth, and concern. Second, accept the resentment without making a defense of any kind. That does not mean you agree with them, but that they have a right to their feelings. Do not get defensive. Third, share concern by finding points you and they can authentically agree on. Find the common ground. Fourth, reflect their emotions by putting those into your own words to demonstrate your understanding. Again, continue to ask questions and restate their thoughts until you can clearly reflect their feelings. When you have reached a shared meaning, you have earned the right to speak. At that point you can advocate additional information in order to give parents a reason to end the conflict. Also, you should be willing to accept responsibility for any mistakes you may have made. All sides bear some responsibility for most conflicts. Face your weaknesses honestly and openly. Parents will develop deep respect for you when you admit your own vulnerability. Finally, you should conclude by asking for a verbal agreement to confirm their willingness to end the conflict. You might also want to close the time with prayer.

In working with parents of your youth, remember to pay attention when they express their needs, concerns, and fears. Encourage them to express their feelings. Do not condemn or discount their feelings. Do not refer them to someone else; take them seriously. When rumors of conflict reach you, listen closely, and then go directly to the source. Do not get defensive. Be an active listener. It is important to realize that people will be heard. If you do not listen to parents, they will find someone else who will, and it will probably be the wrong person. If you are an active listener who tries to reach the point of shared meaning, parents will come to you with their feelings, concerns, and suggestions. They will come to you with their cry for outside help. You will be their friend and, in turn, an effective youth worker.

CONCLUSION

Ministry to the parents of the youth with whom you work is extremely crucial. Obviously it cannot take a dominant section of your time. Nevertheless, you have a responsibility to be aware of their developmental needs and pressures. They are torn with the demands placed on them. Some are not able to communicate with their children, and their frustration is at a high level. As a result, on occasion you may become the person on whom they unleash their feelings. Being cognizant of their problems and tensions may assist you in ministering to them as well as their youth.

For Further Reading

Brownstone, Jane E., and Carol J. Dye. *Communication Workshop for Parents of Adolescents.* Champaign, Ill.: Research Press, 1973.

Campbell, Ross. *How To Really Love Your Teenager.* Wheaton, Ill.: Victor, 1981.

Gordon, Thomas. *Parent Effectiveness Training.* New York: Peter H. Wyden, 1970.

Hart, Thomas N. *The Art of Christian Listening.* New York: Paulist, 1980.

LeFever, Marlene. "Parents Rate Their Young Workers." *Youthworker* (Spring 1985).

Narramore, Bruce. *Adolescence Is Not an Illness.* Old Tappan, N.J.: Revell, 1980.

Oraker, James, with Char Meredith. *Almost Grown: A Christian Guide for Parents of Teenagers.* San Francisco: Harper & Row, 1982.

Sell, Charles M. *Family Ministry.* Grand Rapids: Zondervan, 1983.

Strommen, Merton P., and A. Irene Strommen. *Five Cries of Parents.* San Francisco: Harper & Row, 1985.

White, John. *Parents in Pain.* Downers Grove, Ill.: InterVarsity, 1979.

22

Jayne Price and Richard C. Price

Effective Youth Retreats

Not all successful retreats are effective, and an effective retreat does not always look successful. What is the difference, and how can we ensure that all our retreats are effective in the areas that count?

We all have a picture of the successful retreat: well planned, smoothly run, all elements of the retreat going on schedule, dynamic speaking, many decisions made for Christ for new life and renewed commitment, kids singing songs of praise on the way home, parents excitedly waiting in the church parking lot to greet exuberant students. Successful.

Another picture comes to mind: the retreat disaster. Things did not go as planned: bad weather, transportation breakdowns, confused reservations, sick students, a no-show speaker. Unsuccessful? Maybe, but also potentially effective. It depends on your definition of an effective retreat.

Retreats are most effective when we see them as being used by God to provide teachable moments. Our goal for retreats need not be smoothness or success but opportunities for growth. In that goal we can expect failures, interruptions, and inconveniences that will facilitate teachable moments.

STRATEGIZING: CAPTURING THE VISION

Whether you are planning for an overnight campout or an extended time away with students, there are some simple steps to ensure that at the very least you know why you are out there.

JAYNE PRICE, M.A., and RICHARD C. PRICE, M. Div. Richard is youth pastor, University Baptist Church, Santa Cruz, California.

SPIRITUAL PREPARATION: PRE-PLANNING DIRECTION

In order to do God's work we must have God's mind. However, in the rush of ideas and excitement of planning a retreat, we often forget to seek it. Beginning the process of planning with prayer, both personally and as a team, is a direct means of inviting God to be an active participant in the retreat process. In team ministry this is an essential opportunity to build faith in the volunteer leaders who will see God work not only at the retreat, but through the planning stage as well. With all the detail work that needs to be done before any sort of trip, it is actually easy to leave for the retreat already burned out. We need to maintain the spiritual disciplines in order to go through the retreat with maximum spiritual power and energy.

PHYSICAL PREPARATION: DEVELOPING A FOCUS

Discovering the basic needs of the group. The most elaborate or intricately programmed retreat cannot be effective if it does not meet the needs of the students. Determining those needs will set not only the specific retreat goals but also give direction to the overall youth program. Ask anyone in the group what that person perceives the group needs to be and you can end up with as many needs as you have students.

One method of finding group needs quickly is to use the process of group brainstorming. We have had our students and volunteer leaders, either separately or together, write down on three-by-five cards as many needs as they can think of, one idea per card, as fast as they come to mind. No discussion, no comments. After five minutes, two people tally the ideas, one reading each idea aloud, another recording. Any need that repeats is marked as such. This process is quick and generates the most ideas in the least amount of time. It moves the discussion of ideas to the next phase, which is that of setting priorities.

The brainstorming process should reveal both real and felt needs of the group. A real need is something of a subjective nature, or inside oneself, such as a person's need to know Christ. A felt need is more objective, or outside oneself, such as "our group needs to draw closer together."

Setting priorities. Once you have a list of needs you can begin to put them into priority on a scale from one to ten, with ten being the highest priority. It may be difficult to come up with one need. You may have to take a vote to determine it. The discussion that comes as a result of the priority setting will help to clarify the needs. This process should also help to eliminate the time generally spent on discussing low-priority needs.

Focusing in on what you want to accomplish. Any needs-assessment, regardless of the process used, will reveal more needs than you could possibly hope to meet on a retreat. Selecting the top one or two will set the focus for the retreat. If you have used the process to set the tone for the entire year's youth program and the top needs are being met within that program, you might single out another need that cannot be met within that program and focus your retreat there.

Developing creative ways of meeting needs. Once you have the retreat focus in mind, you can begin the process of answering the question, What kind of retreat would best meet these needs? The process of brainstorming can be used in this stage as well, getting the most ideas out in the shortest amount of time. If your team is short on ideas, look for helpful resources.[1]

It is easy to become excited by a great retreat idea even when a more simple one might be more effective in meeting the specific group needs. Evaluating each idea by the criterion of how it will best meet the retreat focus will help keep the planning team on track.

PLANNING: FITTING THE FOCUS

Committing the leadership team to designing the retreat around the one or two group needs you have decided on may be the most difficult part of the planning process. Because we tend to view retreats as great opportunities for seeing God work, we generally structure the schedule so tightly that we give the students too much program. Keeping the retreat focus in the forefront at all times will help avoid that problem.

DETERMINING WHO PLANS THE RETREAT: GIVING OWNERSHIP

There is nothing more discouraging to a youth leader than to have a well-planned program criticized. When we have put so much time, energy, and creativity into a retreat it is hard to hear comments from students like, "This weekend is boring," "Last year's trip was better," or worse yet, "We had more fun with our last youth pastor." For the sake of the youth director's morale, and even survival, it is essential that volunteer leaders and students have ownership in the retreat planning process. It also ensures cooperation and supportive attitudes from all the participants.

During an overnight retreat we had, a junior high girl took on the responsibility of dividing up the groups for a scavenger hunt. Her own personal needs overcame the group's best interest, and, of course, all the "best" kids were in her group. The whole evening preceding the event she was inundated by requests from students who wanted to be in a different group. They came to us hoping we would interfere. We felt it was important to resist, knowing that the learning process for the young lady and our group as a whole was more important than a smoothly run and fair scavenger hunt.

It is at these critical times that we need to evaluate the teachable mo-

---

1. Creative ideas for retreats may be found in Anthony Campolo, *Ideas for Social Action* (El Cajon, Calif.: Youth Specialties, 1983), and Arlo Reichter, et al., *The Group Retreat Book* (Loveland, Colo.: Group Books, 1983).

ment. Our goal is to provide opportunities for students to learn biblical truths in everyday situations. But we must be sensitive enough to know when a lesson has been learned and be careful not to have an ownership situation become so disheartening for a student or leader that it discourages them from future participation.

SELECTING THE SITE: TAHOE TO TIMBUKTU

Site selection is always difficult, yet it is crucial to the success of the retreat. Lay leaders and students can be helpful in this process as the group begins to decide what aspects of a site are important.

Our annual ski retreat has been a problem since the group outgrew a family cabin we had always used. We struggled to find a facility that was not too far from the church, not too far from site to ski area, reasonably priced for the group, and available on a three-day weekend.

Questions to ask when selecting a site might include:

What is the maximum distance we should expect the group to travel?
Do the camp fees fit into our budget for the retreat?
Is it available on the dates we need it?
Is it important to do our own cooking or to have meals prepared for the group?
What are the sleeping arrangements? Will they enhance or detract from relationships between students and leaders, and students and students during the cabin times?
Is the site itself a distraction? Too close to other groups or people? Cluttered facilities that may result in destruction of property?
What are the attitudes of the caretakers of the facility? Will they enhance and enable you to minister, or will their demands and restrictions be a distraction?

An evaluation sheet may help remind the leaders of the kinds of questions to ask. One is provided at the end of the chapter.

It is not always possible, but a preinspection tour of the facility is extremely important before committing the group to a weekend. Such an inspection takes time, but taking a student or fellow leader with you allows you to use that time wisely and gives others the chance to participate in the input and ownership of the program.[2]

Our problem of a ski camp was solved when one of us took a senior high guy along to the site to check out the facilities. We not only had ten hours of travel time to build a friendship, but the student's enthusiasm and confirmation of the facility was brought back to the rest of the group. We have been able to use the facility for the past three years because it continues to meet the criteria

2. *Journal of Christian Camping: Official Guide to Christian Camps and Conference Centers.* P.O. Box 646: Wheaton Ill. 60189; (312) 462-0300.

we originally established. Taking the time and effort to find the right facility has its own rewards, for we are then able to focus the program more on the needs of the students rather than the physical plant. Students feel secure when a pleasant tradition has been established; they know where they are going and what to expect because of the previous years' positive experiences.

As the group's needs change, a new facility may need to be chosen. But change just for the sake of variety is rarely helpful. Remember, students and lay leaders can and should be involved in the decision-making process if a site change is needed. You will need their support because, for most people, change is a difficult process.

PLANNING THE PROGRAM: NO EASY WAY

Developing a plan for spiritual input. Strategic planning is hard work. It takes discipline, time, energy, and lots of prayer. Deciding on the structured spiritual input for the weekend is a tough assignment and can be done best when the planning team knows the needs of the young people attending the retreat.

A youth group of church kids might want to emphasize spiritual renewal or capturing a fresh vision of the character of God, whereas a group of predominantly non-Christian students may respond better to an evangelistic approach. But the essential thing is to know your young people and their needs.

There are many options available for spiritual input that fit the retreat setting. An outside speaker, when informed of the group profile and needs, can bring a fresh approach that differs from your weekly program. On our summer houseboat trip we have a tradition of reading books geared to the teen audience, such as Anthony Campolo's *You Can Make a Difference*[3] or Fred Hartley's *Growing Pains*.[4] We were able to reinforce the concepts in *You Can Make a Difference* by reading the book on the houseboat trip and then showing the film series "You Can Make a Difference" on our winter ski trip.

We have used a variety of mini-seminars for the shorter attention span of junior highers. The activity-centered Bible learning provided in David C. Cook's *Young Teen Action* series has been helpful.[5] Our girls' and guys' support groups usually deal with topical issues or inductive Bible studies on their retreats. Another group does short weekends that are centered on service projects.

Choosing leadership. No matter how well planned the formal spiritual input is, the informal input from the modeled life-style of your retreat leaders is

3. Anthony Campolo, *You Can Make a Difference* (Waco, Tex.: Word, 1984).
4. Fred Hartley, *Growing Pains* (Old Tappan, N.J.: Revell, 1981).
5. *Young Teen Action* (Elgin, Ill.: David C. Cook).

essential. One of us encountered much confusion during our own adolescent years when, after a biblical talk given to the group on a retreat, the counselor invited our cabin out to the parking lot. The ice chest in the trunk of his car was packed with malt liquor.

Ministry will be taking place in the lives of the adult leaders as well as in the lives of the teens. The adult leadership should not be seen as people to be used, abused, and manipulated. Help them catch a vision of how their own lives can be enriched by being on the retreat team.

Spiritual maturity should be a primary characteristic of the leader. We all have the ideal spiritual leader in mind, and each adult will be at a different point in his relationship to Christ. But remember, it takes a spiritually mature person to withstand the trials, temptations, and disappointments that can come when working with teenagers away from home.

Retreats are also a great time to try out or develop an interest among potential leaders for your year-round volunteer staff team. Without committing yourself to long-term involvement, the youth pastor can see firsthand how a potential leader responds to teens, and how they relate to him or her. It also gives a first-time adult leader the chance to see for himself how he fits into youth ministry. The potential leader will find it easier to build quick initial friendships on a retreat than in one or two Sunday school classes or a mid-week program. Upon returning from the retreat the youth director has the freedom to approach the interested adult, affirm him for his performance, and encourage him to continue on the team for the year.

The need for variety. In solidifying the retreat plan, variety needs to be considered as a key element. Again, this is where an adult leadership team and/or a student core group can help in the process.

Variety and healthy change tends to motivate, whereas sameness and repetition produce apathy and boredom, especially among adolescents. Strive to leave most of the weekly program at home. Try to inject newness and freshness into the weekend getaway. The change in environment will be a major factor in this variety, but seek to use different speakers, vary the meeting format, teach some new songs, and experiment with a new worship format.

THE SCHEDULE: PLAN TO BE TENTATIVE AND FLEXIBLE

Tentative and *flexible* are the watchwords when implementing the program of a retreat with teens. But a schedule is essential and helps to put the focus of the retreat into time slots. Those programs and activities that are the highest priority should be put in first and so forth down the list. The schedule needs to be seen as a servant to the adult leadership and students, not the other way around. The schedule should not be set in concrete and should be tentative and flexible enough to change with the needs of the weekend.

More times than not, retreats are so overprogrammed that a lot of the energy and enthusiasm they generate are dissipated. The retreat should not reflect the chaotic busyness of our culture. Give the young people a break.

When developing a schedule, take several aspects into consideration.

The role of free time. Unstructured discretionary time fulfills two main roles. First, it allows teens to build friendships with one another. Peer relationships are paramount to adolescents and take place best in natural, unstructured settings. If developing new and better friends is a focus of your retreat, then unstructured chunks of time are essential. Second, it allows your leadership team time to seek opportunities to be with the students. If the adult volunteers are expected to care for and build friendships with kids, they need uncluttered natural blocks of time in which to minister.

Free time can be a scary element of the retreat. It may mean that for a period of time the adults will not have control over what goes on among the young people. But it is invaluable for building significant friendships.

The need for rest. We live in a culture that in many ways uses busyness as a measure of success. We forget that the word *retreat* implies a coming away for rest (Mark 6:31). Sending students and leaders home from a retreat without providing time for rest is contradictory to the whole retreat philosophy.

Building into your program an end-of-evening "wind down," and perhaps even a cabin group sharing, will help facilitate getting the students in bed at a reasonable hour. We have found that by the final morning of a weekend retreat everyone is tired. By arranging for an 11:00 A.M. brunch instead of an 8:00 A.M. breakfast, we can give everyone an extra hour of sleep and start the program at 9:00 A.M.

MAKING THE LOOSE ENDS FIT: SURVIVING THE HASSLES OF RETREATS

Transportation. Getting there can be half the fun. It can also be disastrous. Panic set in as the lights suddenly went out on one of the vans in our caravan. It was late. We were on our way to Lake Tahoe for a ski retreat. Fortunately there was an off ramp with a truck-stop nearby. For the youth director or trip leader this can be the first indication of a possible weekend disaster. Yet, God is still in control.

We were surprised at how the hour-and-a-half delay facilitated group cohesiveness and modeled servant leadership by the driver-mechanic in our group. Modeling good driving habits and attitudes is also essential as the next generation of drivers looks on. A retreat is like the Christian life. It is not how quickly we get there, but how well we do in the process.

Food. Food and adolescents seem to be inseparable, and the food on a retreat plays a crucial role. Can the preparation of the food meet any of your retreat goals? With students coming from nine high schools in our youth group we continually have the need to provide opportunities for students to get to know one another and develop a sense of working together. Using small cooking units of leaders and students has provided an excellent vehicle for small group interaction. At times the groups have been responsible for the entire process of menu planning, shopping, preparation, and clean-up, or just for clean-up duty. When the program has centered on meeting other group needs we have sought a facility that provides food service as part of the package. Cooking for large groups is not difficult, but it does take a great deal of planning. Dividing up the work among leaders and students or taking a crew along will ease the load. The *Church Kitchen Handbook*[6] is a helpful guide.

Regardless of the direction you decide to go with the food preparation, the menu should reflect adolescent preferences. This is another time when student involvement in the planning process is essential.

A potpourri of concerns. Much of the effectiveness of retreats comes from our response to the unexpected. However, there is only so much of the unexpected that we care to deal with on any given trip. In preparation, think through what could go wrong. This enables one to eliminate some of the potential surprises. Taking extra tire chains on ski trips, bulbs for the projector, and even renting a spare projector when it is key to the program helps you to feel free from some of the anxiety that can limit your energy for ministry.

CONCLUSION

It is entirely possible to do a retreat without going through a detailed planning process. But it is the process that becomes a valuable teaching and modeling tool for our lay leaders and students. It is not worth the shortcut to pass up philosophy of ministry discussions. Instead, give others opportunities to contribute and experiment with their gifts in a variety of roles. Most of all, it is great to see God work in an orderly, unifying way among a group of focused believers.

IMPLEMENTATION: MOVING FORWARD

The temptation is always there to see the retreat as an end in itself instead of being the means of providing teachable moments. This is particularly the case when we have spent hours strategizing, planning, and focusing the retreat to meet specific needs. It is at this point that something unanticipated can strike, and we can think all is lost.

Our attitude in dealing with the unexpected, whether it be in student behavior or the unforeseen disaster, can provide the greatest growing experi-

6. Marilee Mullin-Marshall and Virginia Meers, *Church Kitchen Handbook* (St. Louis: Concordia, 1985).

ence for both students and leaders, if we see the unexpected as an opportunity and not a distraction.

PICKING YOUR BATTLES: TO WIN THE WAR

Each of us has only so much energy and time to deal with all the problems and hassles that come up on a retreat. Some problems may even have to be ignored. Know yourself and your strengths and weaknesses. Let your focus of the retreat set your priorities in the battles you fight. If you are dealing primarily with nonchurched kids on an evangelistic retreat, you may need to back off on the bathing suit issue. If your goal is building group closeness and cohesiveness, hit the cutting remarks and put-downs hard.

Discipline should be viewed as an opportunity for ministry rather than an inconvenience. Proper discipline and problem solving takes time. If a problem arises that needs to be dealt with, it should not wait, and the other leaders should realize that it will take a large chunk of time to work through the problem and consequences.

Misbehavior and discipline problems are times to teach teens that there are consequences for their actions, that their behavior does not take place in a vacuum, and that what they do affects the feelings and relationships of others. Most deviant behavior is only a surface indication of a deeper struggle. It takes patience, time, and good listening and problem-solving skills to get to the deeper issues.

An experience with Phil was a classic example. He had been in camp for the three summers we were working as counselors, and had been in Richard's cabin one year. His last summer at camp Phil became a behavior problem. It was nothing serious, just several outbursts of anger and rebelliousness. After one particular incident, Richard called him in to try to sort out the problem. Not long into their discussion it came out that the week before Phil arrived at camp his mother had walked out on the family. He did not know where she had gone or if she was physically OK. His outbursts had been a direct result of the anxiety about his home situation. Richard listened to him for a long time until he was able to come up with a solution that would help ease Phil's anxiety. The outbursts ceased. He still needed to accept the consequences of his earlier misbehavior, but the relationship between Phil and Richard had grown stronger through the situation.

The paramount idea to keep in mind is that no matter what happens, it is important that the relationship between student and leader be maintained. That means the leader needs to be vulnerable about his love and concern for the student. We must avoid power struggles and take initiative in seeking forgiveness and reconciliation when the student has been hurt or ill-treated by a leader. It takes a discerning heart to know when a quick warning or reprimand is in order over against a lengthy problem-solving session. Keep praying.

DEALING WITH THE UNEXPECTED: THE SUBTLE KEY

Murphy's law states: "If anything can go wrong, it probably will." Retreats are a prime example. Fear of failure breeds a need to be in control. The more we fear God and not failure, the more we can give the control over to the Lord. The students are watching us, and they are learning how to react in tense, tough situations by our example.

Releasing control may be the first hurdle to overcome in developing a creative retreat. When he begins to think about the possibility of potential problems, the youth leader may become debilitated with fear. He or she will not be able to be the driver of all the vans, be the counselor in each cabin, cook all the food, solve all the problems, keep track of all the finances, and drive all the ski boats. Therefore, the thought of not being in control may dissuade the youth leader from even attempting a retreat.

From beginning to end the retreat process is a series of situations in which one must allow God to have control. Our initial reaction or response in a situation can often set us up to effectively or ineffectively deal with a problem or a need. When we *react,* the situation is controlling us. When we *respond,* God is in control through us. A response is characterized by honesty and vulnerability. A reaction produces confusion and defensiveness.

THE ROLE OF THE LAY LEADER: WHAT WOULD WE DO WITHOUT THEM?

God never intended one youth pastor to possess all the gifts necessary to operate an effective youth ministry. We need to surround ourselves with adults who have a variety of gifts to do a variety of tasks. Our main goal as equippers of lay leaders is to ensure that they are successful in their ministry experience.

We must make every effort not to set up a volunteer leader for failure. Because we were pressed to fill a teaching spot, we prematurely moved a leader into a teaching role before he had the skills or the relationships with the students. The experience wiped him out, and we had to spend a lot of time backtracking and explaining to students what was going on. The leader soon became overwhelmingly discouraged and left the team.

Each person has strengths and weaknesses. We want to put people in roles that will maximize their strengths and minimize their weaknesses. The retreat is an ideal place both to abuse and accomplish that objective.

It is important that those who do better with student relationships than administrative details be put in a pastoral role. Some do both well, but we should not sacrifice the leader and his enthusiasm in order to take care of an annoying detail. The youth leader's role as enabler should free the members of the adult lay leadership to do what they enjoy and do best.

Along with the speaker, cook, and music leader, there can be another person who is invaluable to the youth leader and the team. That is a person who has the organizational skills to pull details together before, during, and after the retreat. This may or may not be a person who is a great youth worker, but he must be a person who can free others to be with kids on the retreat. Gilbert has been that kind of gifted person for our youth group. He arranges for the transportation, sees that there are enough drivers, organizes the chain crew when required on ski retreats, secures the rental trailer for the gear, arranges for ski boats in the summer, and takes care of all the little details regarding the rented equipment.

Gil also has a love for teenagers and lately is doing more as a youth leader and small group facilitator. Now it is time to find someone else to take on those administrative tasks. But that is youth ministry—always changing, fluctuating, and moving. As leaders, we must also have that same attitude.

WRAP-UP AND EVALUATION: KEEPING THE MOMENTUM GOING

We have all experienced those feelings that "the party's almost over, it's been great fun, oh, the cleanup, and we're so tired—was it worth it?" We need to realize that the conclusion of our retreat and the move down from the mountain is the enemy's last stand. He still has an opportunity to frustrate what God has done and will attack at the time when both leaders and students are most vulnerable. Being aware of this possibility is half the battle. Preparing our students can help them be victorious.

END OF TRIP DANGERS: THE ENEMY'S BATTLEGROUND

Being aware of what's happening. Our first defense against attack is in being aware of the danger. Be honest with yourself about your energy limits and that the end of the retreat is a vulnerable time. The spiritual disciplines become of the utmost importance. We must allow God to have total control of the situation both emotionally and physically, or we could blow it.

We find the hardest time is when the group needs to be getting on the road and kids are tired. They do not want to pack, load up, or clean up, and they are involved in having that last little bit of fun before going back to the real world. This is when impatience, anger, and frustration start coming to the surface, and we know we are in danger of reacting in a way that may hurt what we have been working so hard to build during the retreat.

We find it worthwhile to go off and take a five to ten minute break. A brief time out is refreshing. We want to become centered on God again to gain perspective and to draw on those last energy reserves before the push home. The key to surviving last-minute battles is to know yourself. Where are your pressure points? What pushes certain emotional buttons? How do you deal with it in the midst of the battle?

Exposing the enemy. One way to deal with Satan's attacks and strategy is to expose openly what is happening. Most teens do not understand spiritual warfare and need to be reminded that there are times when we are particularly vulnerable. Share Satan's strategy with the group, expose his methods, and pray together that what has been accomplished on the retreat will be preserved and protected by God during the vulnerable time.

MAKING THE RETREAT LAST: FOR A WEEK OR A LIFETIME

Most often students get as much joy from talking about an activity after it is over as they do from the experience itself. Reliving the retreat experience with students not only reinforces the spiritual input but builds excitement and enthusiasm for the youth program as a whole.

There are a number of ways to extend the retreat time into your yearly program. Covering the walls of the youth room with picture boards, having slide shows after the retreat and again prior to another trip, and presenting memory albums to graduating seniors are all ways to relive the retreat experience. Reliving recalls God's work and gives vision for new students coming up through the youth program. It also provides a sense of history, tradition, and security in the youth group.

THE ROLE OF AFFIRMATION IN THE EVALUATION PROCESS: SOMETHING GOOD MUST HAVE HAPPENED

Evaluation is important, but because it has to be last it is usually forgotten as other programs come up and the tyranny of the urgent surpasses the need to bring closure on the past. The evaluation is a time to ask What was helpful, positive, and good? What changes need to be made next time?

There should be a time for individuals to be affirmed, gifts recognized, the body encouraged and built up. Each of us has a need to be stroked and affirmed. Do not pass up this unique opportunity to give to your leadership team that which only the Body of Christ can genuinely give.

POST-PROGRAM DEPRESSION: THE ENEMY'S LAST STAND

In youth ministry we are always asking ourselves if it was worth it, because working with teens is hard work with many disappointments and few signs of fruit or success. Youth ministry is a seed-planting work, and fruit does not appear in some cases for many years. It may be different for others, but the times we start thinking about another line of work is usually right after a big program push or a retreat. Yet we must not become discouraged. This is God's work, and God is faithful.

CONCLUSION

The elements of strategizing, planning, implementation, wrap-up, and evaluation can all work together to ensure an effective retreat. The power to make the total experience of a retreat an effective ministry tool lies in God's faithfulness to work in us and through us as we live out our lives in front of our students.

Fig. 22.1 Choosing a Retreat Site

Comparison worksheet for leaders:
Helping you to make the best choice for your retreats.

	Camp:	Camp:	Camp:
Availability: *Fall weekends *Winter weekends *Christmas break *Spring weekends			
Facilities & Site: *Will take groups of what size: *Large meeting rooms *Smaller meeting rooms *Bathrooms *Dining room size *Sports field/volleyball court *Lighted broomball rink *Snack & ice cream shop *T-shirt shop *Kitchen & food service area *Snow cover (winter retreats) *Heated ski house *Sleeping accommodations *Tennis court(s) *Gymnasium (heated) *Obstacle course *Surroundings			
Equipment: *Sound system *Movie projector *Slide projector *VCR player *Television *Push ball *Screen *Overhead projector *Other: *Other: *Other:			

	Camp: _____	Camp: _____	Camp: _____
Winter activities: *Sleigh ride *Horseback rides *Cross-country skiing *Ice skating *Innertube run(s) *Downhill skiing *Snowmobiles *Rental ski equipment *Ping Pong			
Fall or spring activities: *Hayride *Horseback rides *Canoeing *Sports field/Volleyball court *Ping Pong *Archery			
Programming & staff: *Years of experience *Song leaders *Activity coordinators *Cooks & kitchen people *Saturday eve activities *Cross-country ski instructors *Sleigh/hayride drivers *Experienced trail guides *Available speaker(s)			
Additional helps: *Helps in producing a handout *Promotional videotape *Phone consultation/planning *Rental coach buses available			
Price breaks & discounts: *Leader (& family) *Discount for fall/spring *Charge for any speaker(s) *Other discounts offered *Discounted coach bus rates			

	Camp:	Camp:	Camp:

Prices:
*Winter—2 nights, 5 meals &
  many of the activities
*Spring/fall—2 nights, 5 meals
  & many of the activities
*Leader and group discounts			

Camp phone:			
Camp address:			
Booking person: Program person:			

Adapted from advertising piece for Fort Wilderness.
By Mark H. Senter III, February 1986.

FOR FURTHER READING

Clapp, Steve. *Retreat Guide.* Sidell, Ill. 61876. 1981.

Conner, Ray. *A Guide to Church Recreation.* Nashville: Convention Press, 1977.

Graendorf, Werner G., and Lloyd Mattson, eds. *An Introduction to Christian Camping.* Chicago: Moody, 1979.

Kamstra, Doug. *The Get-Away Book.* Grand Rapids: Baker, 1983.

MacKay, Joy. *Creative Camping.* Wheaton, Ill.: Victor, 1984.

Nelson, Virgil, and Lynn Nelson. *Retreat Handbook: A Way to Meaning.* Valley Forge, Pa.: Judson, 1976.

Reichter, Arlo. *The Group Retreat Book.* Loveland, Colo.: Group Books, 1983.

Troup, Richard. *Mini Camps.* San Diego: Success with Youth, 1974.

23

Michael J. Risley

Strategies for Summer Camp as Part of the Church Ministry

Ken was higher than a kite as he bounced enthusiastically into my office and started chattering. "Mike, the most awesome, incredible experience is happening right before your eyes! Remember what we learned at summer camp about 'Thank Therapy'? How we should look for twenty things to be thankful for each day?" I nodded. "Well, I've been practicing it, and it works. I can't remember when I have had more joy from the Lord!"

Something Ken had learned from a camp experience was obviously changing his life. Camp does that. It takes us out of our life's ruts, provides us the time to reevaluate ourselves, and gives the Lord a foothold to change us. But let us back up a little and ask an important question. What was Ken's life like before his great summer-camp learning experience? Or, in other words, How did this summer camp fit in with the total year-round youth ministry in Ken's church?

MICHAEL J. RISLEY, M. Div., is pastor of college ministries, Lake Avenue Congregational Church, Pasadena, California.

A PHILOSOPHY OF YOUTH MINISTRY:
HOW SUMMER CAMPING FITS INTO THE TOTAL YOUTH PROGRAM

The essence of youth ministry is discipleship (Matt. 28:19-20)—discipling students to become Christlike in character (Eph. 4:13; Rom. 8:29) and disciplers of others who will in turn disciple other people (2 Tim. 2:1-2; Mark 1:17). We might say that our ultimate purpose in discipling students is that they become "Christlike multiplying disciplers."

The essence of discipleship is a modeling relationship. As we examine how Jesus, Paul, Silas, Timothy, and others in Scripture approached ministry, we see they discipled others by modeling, or demonstrating, in their life-styles the principles of God's Word and by building intimate, loving, and thus significant relationships with their disciples (Mark 3:13-14; 1 Thess. 1-3).

These two key concepts of the discipleship process bear a closer examination.

MODELING

Scripture teaches over and over again that modeling the truth is critical in the process of teaching. The apostle Paul teaches, "Follow my example, as I follow the example of Christ" (1 Cor. 11:1) and, "Whatever you have learned or received or heard from me, or seen in me—put it into practice. And the God of peace will be with you" (Phil. 4:9). The writer of Hebrews exhorts, "Remember your leaders who spoke the word of God to you. Consider the outcome of their way of life and imitate their faith" (Heb. 13:7) Jesus said, "A student is not above his teacher, but everyone who is fully trained will be like his teacher" (Luke 6:40). Therefore, anyone discipling students must be living what he or she wants the students to become. That is, they must be mature believers, or Christlike multiplying disciplers.

Who are these models of maturity in a youth ministry? Basically, they are the students' parents (Deut. 6:4-7; Eph. 6:4) and the youth ministry staff (Eph. 4:11-13). Thus a great deal of the church's emphasis in youth ministry needs to be on helping those adults be strong in their faith and, therefore, good models of the Christian life.

RELATIONSHIPS

We must have enough mature believers to make the leader-to-student ratio small and therefore conducive to intimate and loving relationships. It is through these kinds of relationships that the truth flows. Think back on how your own life has grown in Christ. Probably your most significant growth happened through spending time with and getting close to a more mature Christian than you. You found yourself starting to emulate his or her love and devotion for prayer, the study of God's Word, witnessing, listening to others, and so on. Truly, Christianity is more caught than it is taught.

Jesus, of course, is our ultimate example of a relational, intimate ministry style. According to Mark 3:14, Jesus "appointed twelve . . . that they might be with Him." That is, Jesus had a one-to-twelve ratio with His disciples. In light of this, Walter Henrichsen writes:

> While on earth, our Lord Jesus Christ was God in the form of man. He was endowed with every spiritual gift, He did not have any of our weaknesses or failings, nor did He have the heavy responsibilities of being married or running a business; His time was devoted completely to the ministry. And yet, with all of these advantages, He felt that He could effectively train only twelve; and even out of those twelve, to really major in three.[1]

When the leader-to-student ratio is small, strong relationships are built, and thus the modeling-teaching process will be most effective. For example, having one leader discipling every seven students would be outstanding. Pray for the quality and quantity of youth workers that will help you disciple students biblically and effectively (Matt. 9:36-38).

With an understanding of this philosophy of youth ministry, let us answer our question, How did this summer camp fit in with the total, year-round youth ministry in Ken's church? And how should discipling be implemented within the context of camp?

During the entire year, Ken belongs to a support group of seven guys who meet weekly to study God's Word, pray, and encourage one another. This group is led by Joel, a twenty-five-year-old graduate student who has been a Christian for eight years and seeks consistently to trust and obey Christ. Joel loves the guys in his group and desires for them to become Christlike multiplying disciplers as he models the Christian life and spends time with them in studying and applying God's Word, praying, helping them evangelize and disciple their friends, playing racquetball and basketball, eating, and camping.

Summer camp turns Joel's and Ken's support group into a cabin group. Camp gives the group members an extended time together to do many of the things they do during the year, but also to hike in the wilderness, listen to a challenging speaker (besides Joel), have pillow fights, and reach out to potential new guys to love and disciple. This extended time together and the additional experiences and input truly enhance Joel's ongoing discipleship ministry with the group.

Of course, when the support group gets larger as others are added, the staff-to-student ratio grows. That is when a new staff member needs to be added to the group, and eventually the one support group becomes two, thereby keeping the staff-to-student ratio small so there is an intimate and loving relationship to each student.

1. Walter Henrichsen, *Disciples Are Made—Not Born* (Wheaton, Ill.: Scripture Press, Victor, 1974), p. 145.

THE PURPOSES OF SUMMER CAMPING

The foundation for summer camping is its purpose. Purpose determines if a camp will be geared for recreational fun, educational achievement, or strictly spiritual growth. Purpose determines the camp's direction in regards to personnel, programming, and facilities.

As we observed in Ken's life, the purpose of summer camping should be seen as an integral part of the total year-round youth ministry. Werner Graendorf explains, "Understood as Christian education, camping becomes a key part of a total ministry whose results are planned for, anticipated, and are part of an ongoing effort. Here Sunday school and camp point toward common goals. Each part of the church's program strengthens the other parts."[2] Lloyd Mattson writes, "The goals of Christian camping and the church are identical. Only the locale and methodology differ."[3]

In light of the youth ministry philosophy already stated, a good summer camping purpose would be "to use as fully as possible the camp experience as an opportunity for discipling individuals toward maturity in Christ."[4] As a part of this concept of maturity in Christ, students need to catch a vision and be trained to disciple others. Training students to be disciplers might not happen at every camp during the summer, but it certainly needs to be at the forefront of our thinking in youth ministry.

Some other purposes of summer camping that are part of the overall purpose include:

1. To grow in the faith through Bible study, prayer, challenging and inspiring talks, and discussion. Camping takes students into an atmosphere that is free from distractions (TV, homework, telephone, etc.) and allows them to examine their own lives and to focus on their relationships with God and others.
2. To build stronger relationships between the youth sponsors and the students through the extensive time together and the variety of activities. Here the important role-modeling of Christian values and behavior by the youth ministry staff is critical.
3. To build love and unity in the youth group. As people sing, recreate, study God's Word, pray, eat, and brush their teeth together, God draws them closer as a family.
4. To evangelize. As friends of the students come to a camp, they hear the gospel, experience the love and unity of the youth group, and often become Christians. John 13:34-35 and 17:21 teach us that love and unity are

---

2. Werner Graendorf and Lloyd Mattson, *An Introduction to Christian Camping* (Chicago: Moody, 1979), p. 21.
3. Lloyd Mattson, *Build Your Church Through Camping* (Duluth, Minn.: Camping Guideposts, 1984), pp. 39-40.
4. Graendorf and Mattson, p. 25.

strong arguments for the Christian faith.
5. To have fun. An invigorating change of pace with friends, including recreational activities and the great out-of-doors, gives laughter to lives.
6. To learn new skills. How to disciple others, how to backpack, how to rock climb, how to play volleyball—these are some of a variety of skills that can be taught when camping.

RUNNING YOUR OWN CAMP VERSUS PARTICIPATING IN THE CAMPING PROGRAM OF A DENOMINATION OR AFFILIATED CAMP

As a youth program grows, there comes a time when the leaders will begin feeling camp "growing pains." Perhaps there will be so many students from a church that other campers feel intimidated by the camaraderie (sometimes viewed as cliquishness) of one group, and unnecessary tension will result.

In another situation, a youth group may have matured spiritually and socially to such an advanced level that a camp program targeted at the average high school student will even retard the group's development. Or, a youth minister may want to use his own volunteer leaders as camp counselors so that relationships can be built for the coming year of ministry.

How can the decision on best camp program be made in order to assist the progress of the youth ministry? The following questions might be used to stimulate your thinking and bring about a wise decision.

1. Which camp would have the best staff expertise? Do you have the personnel to run an excellent camp, or does the denomination or affiliated camp have better "know how" in its staff?
2. Which campgrounds would have the facilities best suited to the purposes of your camping experience?
3. What is the proximity of the campgrounds? How much time and money do you want to spend in getting to camp?
4. Does the philosophy of the denomination or affiliated camp correspond with your church's youth philosophy? Can you gear the camp to meet your students' needs?
5. Do the denomination or affiliated camp dates fit well with your church and youth ministry schedule?
6. Do your students need time to be by themselves or with other Christians outside of your group? For instance, sometimes you need time by yourselves to develop group unity and identity. Sometimes you need to be with other youth groups to be encouraged and sharpened by them (Prov. 27:17).
7. Will you be using your own counselors, or will the camp supply them? How many of your adult leaders will be able to take time off from work or school to serve as counselors? Obviously, if you want to enhance the modeling relationship of your youth ministry staff, you will want to use your own counselors.
8. What kind of a ministry could you have with other youth groups if you participated with them in a denomination or affiliated camp?

9. Would it be a better use of your youth group's leadership time to go to a denomination or affiliated camp where much of the work is done for you and you can concentrate on other things (encouraging students to go to camp, building relationships, and counseling students at camp, etc.)?

10. At which camp could you develop your student and staff leadership best? When you run your own camp, you can give your students and your youth ministry staff more of an opportunity to lead in activities like Bible studies, recreation, multimedias, announcements, and singing.

11. How would a move to establish a camp program exclusively for your youth group be perceived by the leadership of your church? More important, would it produce more problems than it solves in terms of the students' total development?

It is not always an easy decision whether to run your own camp or to participate in the camping program of a denomination or affiliated camp. If you can, you might want to have both kinds of camps. For instance, at our church we have our winter camp with other church youth groups at a nearby Christian conference center. The conference center runs the program, and our youth ministry staff and student leaders concentrate their time and energy on getting as many students to camp as possible, especially non-Christians. But in the summertime, our big resident summer camp is at a different location and is run entirely by us. Doing it both ways gives us the best of both worlds and a nice balance.

DIFFERENT KINDS OF SUMMER CAMPING

When thinking about different kinds of summer camping, let your mind run with creativity, for the opportunities are almost limitless.

Resident camping has a permanent campsite, and the campers spend the majority of their time there. This is the more traditional summer camp approach and is excellent for bringing your whole group together. Most students thoroughly enjoy this kind of camping.

Travel camping is a motorized, mobile camp that includes campers traveling by car, bus, motorhome, train, motorcycle, or motorboat. The youth group members visit sites of special interest to help fulfill their goals.

Trip camping is a nonmotorized, mobile camp that includes campers traveling by bicycle, hiking, horseback, skateboard, canoe, or boat.

An aspect of trip camping would be wilderness trail camping. The goal of this kind of camping is to keep warm, dry, and well fed regardless of weather or trail difficulties. Confronting the wilderness with your food and shelter in your pack is a special challenge.

Wilderness stress camping is like a wilderness trail camp in that the camper learns to live comfortably with minimal gear, but it adds the extra dimension of physical and mental stress. The camper grows as he is tested beyond his normal endurance in activities like whitewater rafting and canoeing, rock climbing, rappelling, long hikes, and extended periods of isolation (usually called a solo).

Family camping is a great way for your students to build a stronger relationship with their parents and sisters and brothers. Here, the family gets away from TV and other distractions to recreate and learn together.

PLANNING FOR CAMP

The key to a great camp experience is great planning. The planning process needs to start six to twelve months before the camp date, depending on the length, size, and purpose of the camp. In planning your camp, you will want to ask several questions.

WHY?

Why have a camp? You need to answer this question by determining the needs of your group and setting goals to meet those needs. One way to evaluate the needs is to think about your students in light of three basic aspects of life.

1. *Their commitment to God.* How are the students growing in their relationship to God? What aspects of Scripture should we emphasize?
2. *Their commitment to the Body of Christ.* Would outsiders know that we are disciples of Christ by our love for one another (John 13:34-35)? How can we help the youth group grow closer and more caring for one another?
3. *Their commitment to service.* How can we prevent "me-ism" and "ingrown eyes" and stimulate students to reach out in evangelism and service?

Another way to help evaluate your students would be to examine their needs spiritually, mentally, physically, and socially.

Once you have determined the needs, then you want to set goals that will meet those needs. Goals should be *specific* (they should not ramble on and on, but be right to the point), *achievable* (they must be realistic for the resources you have), and *measurable* (you need some criteria to know when you have accomplished the goal).

The following is a sample format to help set good goals.

A YOUTH MINISTRY GOAL[5]

NEED   For this reason: *The high schoolers are very self-centered and complacent and have the need of reaching out beyond themselves in serving others.*

---

5. Adapted from Ted W. Engstrom and Edward R. Dayton, "Operational Goals Form," "Managing Your Time" seminar, Monrovia, Calif.: World Vision International.

GOAL   We plan to accomplish this: *Have a five-day camp to paint the homes of the missionaries in Tecate, Mexico.*

By this date: *August 5, 1987*

We will know it has happened because: *All the missionary homes in Tecate will have a fresh coat of paint on them!*

STEPS We plan to take these steps:

1. *Find out how many missionary homes are in Tecate and whether or not we can paint them.*
2. *Determine dates, transportation, costs, housing.*
3. *Get adult leadership.*
4. *Publicize camp with high schoolers and parents.*
5. *Have registration.*

PEOPLE These people are responsible: *Jason Michael and Joanie Risley*

COST   It will cost this amount: *$1,500*

WHEN?

When is the best timing for summer camping? It is good to have a number of camps throughout the summer because the students are available, the weather is great, and "a camp setting is the greatest environment for learning today."[6] At our church we run a number of special interest camps that involve missions, wilderness and travel camping, and service projects. Each of these is usually for a smaller group of students and is done throughout the summer. But we also have our big resident summer camp. This is the camp that we diligently strive to have all of our students and their friends attend to build group unity and identity. Timing for this camp is critical. Two American institutions that we try to avoid are summer school and the annual family vacation. Summer school dates are not negotiable, but if we publicize our camp date early enough, that is, starting in the fall, and educate parents on how important this big camp is to their teens, then the family vacation can be planned at a time that does not conflict with it.

We like to do more expensive mission-camps at the beginning of the summer, have moderately-priced wilderness and travel camps in the middle of the summer, and conclude the summer with our big summer camp. This timing means our big camp avoids summer school, and we can use the building summer momentum from our smaller camps and other activities to get many of our church's students and their friends to the big camp. This timing also gives our small group discipleship ministry, which is emphasized at the big camp, a real boost when we start the school year.

6. Ted Ward, in Graendorf and Mattson, p. 7.

Whatever the timing of your camps, be sure to think it through carefully in regard to summer school, family vacations, costs, building momentum, and your philosophy of ministry.

WHERE?

Where you go for your summer camping is obviously important. Find out the alternatives by checking with other youth leaders, city and state departments of parks and recreation, YMCAs, Boy Scouts, Girl Scouts, Camp Fire Girls, college campuses, and Christian Camping International. Also be on the lookout for good motels in locations you would like to go to or for someone's cabin or cottage.

Once you have some potential camping sites, investigate them. In resident camps, notice how long it takes to get to the camp, the size of large rooms, the number of small rooms, sleeping capacity, recreation facilities, and the quality of the food. Find out what the temperature is like in the summer and what the camp's executive director expects of you.

An important factor to consider in selecting your campsite is how you are going to get there. This can be an attractive aspect of any camp. Will you go by car, van, bus, bicycle, foot, boat, train, or plane? Our youth group has used all of these modes of transportation. For instance, we have taken a plane on a mission trip to Mexico City, a train to the beach in San Clemente, and a boat to camp on Catalina Island.

WHAT?

What will the summer camp program look like? Notice the needs of your youth group and the goals that you have established to meet those needs. Take your major goal or a number of related goals and develop a theme. For instance, if your major goal relates to having a deeper understanding and experience of God's power in the life of your youth group, your theme might be The Holy Spirit. This theme would be the unifying thread that ties every aspect of the program together: the speaker's topic, the devotionals, songs, and maybe even recreational activities (though you may choose to have a separate recreation theme). Of course, it is best to think of a catchy title for your theme so it helps in the promotion of the camp.

Schedule. Now with your goals and theme in hand, think through how and when to implement them in the camp schedule. The schedule is your agenda. It describes the what, where, and when of each camp event. The following are some suggestions for planning a schedule.

1. Plan very carefully, but be sure to be flexible and adaptable. Often your well-laid plans will not happen, and you will need to adapt. Be sensitive to the needs of the campers and to the leading of the Holy Spirit.

2. Have balance. Think carefully about how much structured time versus free time, meeting time versus recreational time, small group discussions versus large group celebrations, and so on.
3. Be sure to allow adequate time for getting to camp, reaching your goals, and developing your theme, meals, sleep, recreation, and free or unstructured time.

Rules. Rules help the students stay involved in what the camp is seeking to accomplish. State the camp rules (we usually call them traditions) at the beginning of camp. Keep the rules simple and clear—for instance, The Three Ps: *privacy* (no guys in the girls' cabins and vice versa); *property* (take care of it; if you break it, you buy it!); and *program* (all meals, meetings, and activities are mandatory). Remember, if breaking the rules does not have any consequences, then you might as well not have rules. Enforce the rules and discipline with love those who break them.

Budget. Whatever your plans may be, they will definitely cost money. The following are some items to consider when you are seeking to keep a balanced budget:

INCOME	*Projected*	*Actual*
Campers' fees		
Budget from church		
Scholarship gifts		
Fund raiser		
EXPENSES		
Campground fee		
Transportation		
Recreation supplies		
Honoraria		
Food (if not included in campground fee)		
Insurance		
Publicity		

WHO?

The who involves the camp participants: the students, the youth ministry staff, and the program staff.

The students. The kind of students you seek to attract to a camp will depend on your camp goals. Some camps are for evangelism, and you will want to bring as many of your students and their non-Christian friends as possible.

Other camps might involve missions work, leadership training, welcoming a new ninth-grade class, service projects, surfing, skiing, and other interests that dictate whom you bring. Just be careful not to be too exclusive.

The youth ministry staff. The counselors or cabin leaders should be those people that disciple the students year-round so there is continuity in the important staff-student discipling relationship. Camp is also a good time to get new staff involved because relationships with the students can be built quickly.

Qualities. The kind of youth ministry staff you want will: (1) have a time-tested dynamic relationship with Jesus Christ. Therefore, he or she models what you want the student to become; (2) have a love for students and enjoy being with them. This involves being a good listener and having a sense of humor to help in building significant relationships.

Many other qualities are useful in working with students, but most of them can be taught. A love for God and for students are the two critical qualities that must be present from the start.

Recruitment. There are basically two approaches to recruiting youth ministry staff: the open approach and the selective approach.

The open approach involves making a church-wide announcement that you need staff and those interested should contact the youth pastor or come to an information-training meeting. This approach might get a lot of people, but it also gets a lot of people who lack the qualities you seek. This approach necessitates weeding through and even disappointing many people.

The selective approach involves going to the church leaders and asking them who they would suggest to disciple the students. Then you need to pursue these suggested people, being prepared to explain just what you expect if they were to join the youth ministry. You should also interview them to see if they really are qualified to work with youth. Remember, whichever approach you use, saturate the process in prayer.

Job description. The youth ministry staff, which will also be the camp counselor staff, needs to know clearly what is expected of it. At our church, we recruit our staff for a one-year period, which is renewable. During the year there are three ministry semesters, and at the beginning of each semester we review our goals, or ministry expectations, which we call a job description. When our staff prepares to go to our big resident summer camp, we also review a job description that would typically have some of the following goals:

1. In seeking to allow Christ to be Lord, and to model Christlikeness, I will start each day before breakfast by confessing any known sin and yielding my life to God's control (1 John 1:9; Eph. 5:18).
2. I will invest myself in my cabin group by:
   a. Being involved with them in the daily activities that they enjoy.
   b. Endeavoring to have a personal one-on-one encounter with each of them during camp to discuss his life and his relationship to Christ.

3. I will support and implement the camp goals, theme, and schedule by:
   a. Conducting a "quiet time" each morning with my cabin.
   b. Leading devotions each evening.
   c. Sitting with my students during chapel services.
   d. Correcting and disciplining any student violating camp rules and/or letting the camp dean know of problems.

Other training and input that the staff needs to discuss and review before summer camp includes camp goals and theme, schedule, quiet times and devotionals, camp rules, how to counsel, and how to lead someone to Christ.

The program staff. The program leaders include the camp dean, the recreation director, the speaker, and the music leader.

The *camp dean* is the main coordinator of the camp. It is his job to make sure that the students, youth staff, speaker, recreation, music, facilities, and transportation all work together to carry out the theme and reach the goals of the camp.

The *recreation director* coordinates all recreation including games, skits, talent night, and skill workshops. Since fun is the chief reason students come to camp, his job is crucial.

The *speaker* teaches the Word of God in a large group setting. It is important that you pursue the best youth speaker available for your summer camp because the speaker has the important responsibility of teaching and challenging all of the students—which is no easy task. Sometimes you, as youth pastor, might want to do the speaking. But usually it is good to allow the students to hear someone else teach, as they have the opportunity to hear you throughout the year.

Music is such an important part of our lives, and this is especially true for our students. Whether you use a contemporary Christian band or someone leading with a guitar or piano, make sure the *music leaders* are youth-culture relevant and they exalt Jesus Christ.

PROMOTION

You can have the best camp location, the most gifted youth ministry staff, an incredible speaker, and a program that would make Disneyland look dull, but if the promotion is poor, so will be the attendance. It is really worth the time, energy, and money to be excellent in your promotion because good promotion motivates.

Here are some promotion ideas and a possible schedule.

1. Camp date sent in parent letter (five to eleven months prior to registration deadline)
2. Initial announcements, posters up in your youth room, and camp brochures (include who, what, where, when, and how much) sent to every student two

to three months prior to the registration deadline

3. Announcements, church bulletin notices, and funny skits about camp every week for the four to five weeks prior to the registration deadline
4. Multimedia or videos on previous camps—two weeks prior to the registration deadline
5. Phone calls—continually the last two weeks prior to the registration deadline
6. Key student leaders telling the youth group what they enjoy about camp (one week prior to the registration deadline)
7. Adult leaders urging the students with whom they work to attend

ASSORTED INSIGHTS

- Eat good food. It really helps a camp to have food that is nutritionally balanced and enjoyable to eat. Even if you have to spend extra money, it is worth it.
- Do some recreation that students would not normally do when they are at home. Be creative and make camp a special time.
- Give the students something to wear that they can use when camp is over. Hats, T-shirts, and sweatbands with a special logo on them are a few articles that students enjoy and help build youth group unity and identity.
- At the end of camp, warn students that they might be physically and emotionally low or depressed for a time after camp. Remind them that camp has been action packed and emotionally high and now their bodies require time to rest.

WHILE AT CAMP

BUILDING A COMMITMENT TO GOD

Helping the students grow in their relationship to God should be your highest priority. You can do this by practicing some of the following suggestions.

1. Be devoted in prayer for the camp (Col. 4:2). Have your church leadership, parents, youth ministry staff, and students pray diligently that God will change lives for His glory.
2. Meet daily with your youth ministry staff. Focus on what God is doing, even the little breakthroughs into lives. Discuss the daily schedule and any logistical or camper problems, but do not let the discussing of problems control and put a damper on the meetings. Encourage the staff; be enthusiastic; pray together.
3. Have your camp speaker constantly have the students look to God's Word. This will teach them to have a dependence on the Scripture rather than on

the speaker. Remember, the Scripture and its application give your students substance for their lives.

4. Have your cabin groups meet for Bible study, prayer, and discussion. Also, it gives effective continuity if the cabin study is on the same theme as the camp speaker's topic.

5. Use the discipline of silence. Give students time during camp when they can be alone and silent for thirty to sixty minutes to pray, think, and/or read their Bibles. This might be in the morning or evening, especially after a meeting where they have been presented with a lot of content.

6. Keep sports and fun times in perspective. Do not allow competition or games to dominate the camp, but use this time to build Christlike character. This is a critical time in which your staff and student leaders should be especially alert to model love and graciousness.

7. Prepare your students to continue their spiritual growing when they leave camp. Discuss the potential struggles they will face and the spiritual helps they must use, such as:

   a. Their cabin group will continue to meet as a support group.

   b. They need at least one or two close friends who are growing Christians.

   c. It is important to be actively involved in church and the youth group.

   d. They must seek regular communication with God involving Bible study and prayer.

BUILDING A COMMITMENT TO ONE ANOTHER

Next to growing in their relationship with God, helping the students grow in their relationship with one another is your top priority. Here are some suggestions to help make this happen.

1. Have fun together. Recreation, singing, eating, and laughing draw people together.

2. Work together. When you are working together, whether painting a missionary's house in Mexico, trying to climb a mountain in Colorado, or putting together a skit, you will grow close.

3. Pray together. It is hard to be distant with someone with whom you are praying. Pray in large groups and definitely in the intimacy of small groups.

4. Touch each other. I know this sounds strange, but in our culture we do not touch each other enough, and it is a need we all have. Therefore, one of the best ways we can have our students express love, caring, and warmth to one another is to be sensitive. Know when it is appropriate to have the students join hands, link arms, give a hug, or in some way nonverbally express love for one another.

5. Express love and affirmation verbally to one another. Whether in a big meeting or a small cabin group, give students an opportunity to express love to those they are growing close to at camp. One effective way that we

have done this at our church is through a candle ceremony. The last night of our big summer camp, we have residents of each cabin sit in a circle. Then we give each group a lit candle. One by one each person in the cabin group holds the candle, and the other students express what they appreciate about them. What a time of love!

6. Seek forgiveness from one another. It is impossible to worship God sincerely when you know there is something wrong between you and your friend (Matt. 5:23-24). Give the students an opportunity to become reconciled with those with whom they are at odds. Confession and forgiveness bring people together.

Shared experiences and loving communication will draw your campers together, and they will experience what the Body of Christ is all about.

SUMMARY

Summer camping certainly provides the church with one of the best educational tools available. Because students have more time in the summer, a variety of camping experiences can have a dynamic impact on winning students to Christ, building them up in their faith, and teaching them to have an impact on others. But remember, camping needs to fit in with the total year-round youth ministry strategy. I am sure you recall higher-than-a-kite Ken, who was so enthusiastic about what he learned at camp and was applying to his life. Well, to make sure that his growth in the Lord continues, Ken, Joel, and the other guys from his cabin continue to meet as a support group for Bible study, prayer, and encouragement. Yes, camp is over, but because it was so interrelated with the total youth ministry, the relationships and biblical concepts Ken experienced at camp will not fade, but will be built upon.

FOR FURTHER READING

Kamstra, Doug. *The Get-Away Book.* Grand Rapids: Baker, 1983.

Mackay, Joy. *Creative Camping.* Wheaton, Ill.: Victor, 1984.

Madsen, Erik. *Youth Ministry and Wilderness Camping.* Valley Forge, Pa.: Judson, 1982.

Mattson, Lloyd. *The Camp Counselor.* Duluth, Minn.: Camping Guideposts, 1981.

Pearson, John. *Recruit, Train and Love Those Volunteers.* Christian Camping International, Box 646, Wheaton, Ill. 60187. Reprints available.

Reichter, Arlo. *The Group Retreat Book.* Loveland, Colo.: Group Books, 1983.

Smith, Frank Hart. *Reaching People Through Recreation.* Nashville: Convention Press, 1973.

Willey, Ray, ed. *Working with Youth.* Wheaton, Ill.: Victor, 1982.

Wright, Norman. *Help . . . I'm A Camp Counselor.* Ventura, Calif.: Regal, 1968.

Sonny Salsbury

24

Music in the Young Church

"Why should the devil have all the good music?" is a question asked in an old Larry Norman song. It is a question, however, that is extremely relevant today for anyone who is interested in effective youth ministry. For in the minds of many, there is a vast gulf between the bulk of today's music and the appropriate position of the church. My answer to Larry's question is, "If the devil *has* any good music, he borrowed it." Satan does not create anything. He can, however, engineer anything's misuse. It is Jesus Christ who has created all things, including music. He has given people the ability to devise melodies, create poetry, and He has put it into the hearts of people, at one time or another, for one reason or another, to *sing*.

Music, in one sense, is like sex. Both are beautiful creations of God. Jesus thought them up, entirely. But they can be used properly, or they can be misused. Even when they are misused, they are still ultimately God's creation. And just as there are instructions in God's Word for the experiencing of our human sexuality, there are also guidelines for the uses of God's wonderful gift of music to us.

MUSIC FOR TEACHING

As a youth minister in my thirty-first year of working with kids, I see music, first of all, as a powerful teaching tool. In Colossians 3:16, we are

SONNY SALSBURY, B.A., minister of music and junior high pastor, Community Fellowship Church, Santa Clarita Valley, California.

instructed to teach each other by the singing of songs. This command is filled with obvious wisdom. Almost everyone can remember the lyrics of a song much longer than a mere verbal statement of fact. Songs very often stay with us for a lifetime. Hence it is common practice to set Scripture to melodies to aid us in recalling it.

Our hymnals and chorus books are filled with other great "teaching songs," whereby we remind each other of the great truths of our faith. (There are also some, both ancient and contemporary, that should be discarded.)

I want to propose another wonderful use of music in this regard. I suggest using music of the youth culture as effective discussion material, and including some well-known and beloved "evergreens" in our singalong repertoire. Remember that this music is the creation of God. What a joyous victory if we can reclaim it for a righteous purpose. In any event, there is no sacred/secular distinction in the life and teachings of Jesus Christ. He is lord of everything. Truth is truth, wherever you find it. So is falsehood. If the group "Duran Duran" makes a true statement in one of its songs, it is true. Period. If the holiest of gospel ministers makes a false statement, nothing can make it true.

Conversely, there is great benefit in examining and discussing the false values put forth in many current hits. To work with young people today is to be aware of rock 'n' roll, with all its trendy categories. We can have several responses toward this music.

To discount its importance or influence. "I don't listen to the words, anyway" say some kids. But the message is far more than the lyrics alone. It is the very life-style of the rock stars. Tony Campolo labels this life-style the most dangerous negative influence among young people today, which is also the unanimous conviction of the entire sociological community, both inside and outside the church.

To crusade against it. This stand is characterized by the casting of album collections into bonfires or attempting to insulate young people from secular music and expose them to Christian music only, whether rock and roll or other forms. This brings us to the question of which is evil—just the lyrics and the musicians, or is it the music itself—the melody, the beat, and the instrumentation? I see music as a language. For ten years, my brother, Ron Salsbury, headed a Christian rock and roll band called "The J.C. Power Outlet." They were pioneers in the field of Christian rock, and they took a lot of flak. But it was their conviction that the good news needed to be expressed in this emerging "language." One might ask: Why not use another language if the existing one is truly distasteful to the communicator?

Let's say someone goes to Brazil as a missionary. Upon arrival, he discovers that the Portugese language is very unpleasant to his ears. It is really distasteful, so he determines to avoid its use in communicating the gospel. Ridiculous, of course, and yet I believe it is a fair analogy to what happens when one crusades against certain music. Our young people are going to hear today's music, whether they want to or not, and most of them want to. I believe the best alternative is the next approach.

To train students to be discerning and discriminating. We ought to teach them to choose wisely and boldly when they *can* choose what to listen to; to listen for and evaluate the messages, both verbal and nonverbal. I have found many valuable lessons in the Top 40 to share with high school and junior high kids.

A frequent approach is to build a lesson around such a title as "JESUS CHRIST and MADONNA." Phrases from lyrics of several of the star's songs are put on the board, alongside quotes from the sayings of Jesus. I believe it is good to find at least one example of a lyric that is stating a truth, even something right and good, and to demonstrate that you affirm, even applaud, the truth. This disarms the idea that you might just be out to demean the artist. It also makes any of that artist's fans who may be in your group feel more at ease.

You will, however, find other statements that are obviously opposed to the position of Jesus, and discussing them can be a very relevant and effective learning time. This may seem radical to some. But did Jesus not do something very similar? He talked to fishermen about catching fish and to farmers about sowing seeds. He used subject matter with which His listeners were familiar to communicate a deeper spiritual truth. I see using music of the youth culture in this way as doing the very same thing.

At this point I like to turn the radio off and erase the chalkboard. I believe our verse in Colossians says that we are to teach *each other* by singing. Yet this is an age when music in the young church is all too often characterized by a "musician" performing while everyone else listens. Group singing has suffered a great deal as a result of this. I have visited youth groups in the last few years that have abandoned completely the practice of singing together. The reason is usually that there is no one to lead, or that the kids just do not want to participate.

I recently spoke for a week of chapel services at a large Christian junior high school. I prepared songsheets (copyright permission included) and started each day's service with some group singing. They started slow, but by the end of the week were really singing great. It was then that the faculty informed me that they had done no singing in chapel for two years, but our week together had convinced them that they should start again.

If they are successful, indeed if any of us is having positive group singing experiences, it will most likely be because the following ingredients are present.

1. *The song leader is familiar with the songs* and is obviously enthusiastic about every chance to sing together. If it's really fun for the leader, it will tend to be contagious.

2. *The words will be available for everyone.* Too many groups sing from memory all those songs they learned at camp last summer. The trouble is, the new kids may never have heard them before. What a way to build a wall! Everyone knows that we learn more quickly when we see *and* hear, as opposed to just hearing. Whether it is songbooks, song sheets, slides, or overheads, we should have the lyrics there.

3. *Provide lyrics only.* Some thought should be given to the need for musical notes in your group. More than 75 percent of today's young people have no use for them because they cannot read music. Worse than being of no use, research has shown that the notes are actually a hindrance to some kids. They say, "This is music, this is technical. I'm no musician. I'll just listen." Providing the lyrics *only* is much better for the majority of our young people.

4. *Be prepared.* Have more songs ready than you will need for the time allowed. Then you can be flexible. If someone requests a song you do not feel comfortable leading but you think it is a good suggestion, promise to have it ready in a few weeks. And never ask for favorites unless you have a song on the tip of your tongue. If no one responds right away say, "Well, I've got one, and here it is." Wasted time can really injure your group singing.

5. *Go for variety.* Fast-slow: Sometimes fresh meaning can be given to an old favorite by changing the tempo. Old songs-new songs: Welcome suggestions of new songs, but request that they be given to you on the side. When you have a new song to teach, consider these suggestions. Teach it to a small group that can then demonstrate for everyone. If the song is recorded, create a video-like introduction—play it along with a little slide show you put together to interpret the lyrics visually. When teaching a new song from scratch, always have the words available and go with portions they can handle. I've heard leaders sing an entire song and then say, "Now, let's try it together."

    Sacred-secular (there's no distinction, remember). I've no room here for a list, but here are a few suggestions: "Cat's in the Cradle" (giving time to people who need it), "You've Got a Friend" (Jesus is the only one who can fulfill the promise of this song), and "Raindrops Keep Fallin' on My Head" (victory through adversity). No recent hits these, but evergreens that have a lot to say—spiritually.

6. *Go for quality.* Consider all the suggestions from your kids, but use only the good ones. Explain thoughtfully if you cannot use one. And do not misuse songs. I have been with groups whose members would never think of singing anything but "sacred" songs, but they add variety by hamming up Christian songs. I do not encourage using songs that way.

7. *Be committed.* A committed core of your group, and absolutely all of your leaders, will need to acknowledge the importance of group singing and

enthusiastically follow the leader. Kids on the fringe will notice this and be more quickly involved. Singing out thus becomes a valuable ministry.

MUSIC FOR EVANGELISM

Many a gospel performer has taken Psalm 40:3 as his theme: "He put a new song in my mouth . . . many will see and fear and put their trust in the Lord." I believe there is a place for telling the gospel in a song. I just do not think the place is as large as we have made it. Jesus said the gospel would be communicated by how we live. In his classic song "Pass It On," Kurt Kaiser wrote a beautiful invitation to the Christian life ("I wish for you, my friend, this happiness that I've found"). But the *power* of the invitation is the life in Christ that Kurt and his family have been living out in Waco, Texas. Sometimes, unfortunately, the song gets sung without the life being lived.

I am not downplaying music for evangelism. Far from it. Just as Paul became "all things to all men so that by all possible means I might save some" (1 Cor. 9:22), I believe we have opportunities to use music to establish common ground with other people, toward the goal of winning them. Various kinds of music, therefore, become legitimate evangelistic tools. I am talking about singing "Five Foot Two" and "Daisy, Daisy" in a convalescent home. Sure, those old folks will enjoy your kids singing *anything*, but if your songs of faith are mixed in with some familiar oldies, I believe the elderly will recognize that you are really caring and reaching out to them.

I am talking about including a few Top 40 songs in your concert ministries with young people. When I took my first youth choir on tour in 1964, our concerts were for vacationing high schoolers across southern California. Our program included several Beach Boy tunes. *What?* "Surf City, U.S.A."? We were building rapport—coming alongside those kids in a fun way that was opening doors for the gospel to be presented. I am also talking about any opportunity to serve the community with music, for example, Christmas carolling in malls and hospitals and anywhere else. Programs for service clubs and high school assemblies have provided us many opportunities to advance the cause of Christ, even though they consisted largely of "secular" music.

MUSIC FOR PRAISE

In the church today, "praise" music has become a distinct category in itself—usually consisting of simple, repetitive choruses. We can and should praise God by the singing of such songs, but we should also praise Him by *every* song we sing. Colossians 3:17 and many other Scriptures command us to do *everything* to God's glory. We should help young people realize they are doing something valuable and significant when they sing. I love what Eric Liddell's father said in the film *Chariots of Fire:* "You can praise God by peeling a spud if you peel it to perfection!"

A YOUTH CHOIR—THE ULTIMATE YOUTH MINISTRY CLASSROOM

I have just come from a great high school football game. I came home thinking about discipline, for there were evidences of it all around me. The teams on the field, the cheerleaders, and the marching bands all demonstrated the commitment they had given to their endeavors. High school kids are no strangers to discipline. When they are motivated by a goal, they can experience and achieve an incredible amount of discipline. If we can motivate young people to achieve this discipline in a spiritual context, as they so often do in athletics, academics, music, and student leadership, we will see the results in strong discipleship.

I see the youth choir as my best chance for helping young people achieve discipline. I also see a first-class "on-the-road experience" at the end of the school year as a goal that will motivate kids to spiritual discipline through the coming school year. I used to call them choir tours, but in recent years I have chosen the broader term "travel camp." Then again, our tours used to be an endless cycle of bus ride, performance; bus ride, performance. Now my goal is to offer an adventure that will have tremendous appeal (even to nonmusicians), and will involve kids in the full spectrum of the Christian life.

Luke 2:52 has been an important guideline for me since my early days in Youth For Christ. "Jesus grew in wisdom and stature, and in favor with God and men." This verse, describing Jesus as a teenager, outlines the four basic areas of our lives: mental, physical, spiritual, and social. A truly valid travel camp will involve all four areas with equal emphasis. Rather than theorize at this point, I will describe a sample itinerary.

Day One. We left San Diego at noon after a morning of careful loading and checking. All thirty-seven kids had a specific assignment for departures, and each one would keep those assignments for the entire trip. (Those kids not singing in the choir had supportive responsibilities for the nights—ten out of twenty-one—we gave concerts. Support duties include such things as lighting, sound, passing out programs.) We arrived at Calvary Community Church in Thousand Oaks, California, in time to set up for our first concert. At dinner, we introduced the Travel Camp Library: a trunk full of about one hundred great Christian books. I had assigned one of these books to every individual, depending on his age and spiritual maturity. Each person was required to read this book plus one other of his own choosing (from the library) during the first sixteen days of the trip. At day sixteen, a great reward awaited the disciplined.

Our housing that night was in homes. On a few occasions I let kids choose their roommates, but most of the time I ask our hosts to choose random pairs or groups from our roster ahead of time. This really aids the building of community in the entire group. We pray about this housing, knowing that some homes will be Christian, others not. We will have chances to minister and be ministered to. *In every home we will have more of a chance to witness authentically than we ever will on stage in a concert.* Thoughtfulness and courtesy were stressed. (Make those beds! Leave those thank-you notes!)

Day Two. The day started with group Bible study, led by the youth director at Calvary Community Church. We had arranged ahead of time to spend an hour or so with great teachers and youth leaders all along our route. Such wonderful communicators as Earl Palmer, Bruce Larson, John Fischer, Ken Medema, and dozens of others have been happy to talk with us. We could never bring them all to our youth group, so we just go to them. That afternoon we arrived at Bass Lake in the mountains of California. After water-skiing for a while, we set up for our concert in the outdoor amphitheater of the public campground. We donned Western costumes for the musical we were to present that night and strolled through the campsites, attracting a great deal of attention and inviting everyone we met to the concert that evening.

Day Three. As we climbed aboard the vans for the next leg of our journey, everyone was instructed to sit by someone with whom they were least acquainted. The next thirty minutes were spent in an exercise we call "The Two of Us." Actually, this exercise was repeated every morning, always with a different partner. Sometimes it was done en route, and other times in a church pew or under a tree. The idea is simply to get better acquainted with this one other person. To take turns asking and answering questions—about anything and everything—family, goals, pastimes, likes, dislikes, faith. The time is concluded by each one's praying aloud for the other. This experience not only builds community, it sharpens communication skills in a practical, non-threatening setting. No single exercise has drawn as much praise from my high school groups across the years as "The Two of Us."

Following our concert at First Presbyterian Church, Berkeley, California, that night, we bedded down on the floor of the church's high school department. I have known youth choir leaders who never house their kids anywhere but in homes. They want them to get their best rest so they can be at their peak for the concerts. I believe balance is a better learning experience—a balance between comfort and the lack of it, a balance between the importance of the "performance" and every other aspect of the trip.

Days Four and Five. We left the hustle of the San Francisco Bay Area and traveled to the little logging town of Happy Camp, California, where we were the guests of the Happy Camp Assembly of God Church. This time the girls slept in homes and the boys on the church floor. But we all spent the next day taking kayak lessons and cruising down the beautiful Klamath River. Recreational activities are a valuable part of a tour. Naturally, they will be the major attraction for some kids. But it is important for them to see this, too, as part of the well-balanced Christian life. Check the areas you will be traveling in for the chance at some recreation that will be really new and out of the ordinary for your kids.

Well, what an opportunity to share the gospel that night! A little town of 2,000 people, without even a movie theater, and we were big news. More than half the town came to our concert on the elementary school field, and a number became Christians. I thought of all the times I had presented "evangelistic" programs for audiences that were almost entirely Christian. This was far more fruitful—and so much fun.

Days Six, Seven, and Eight. Leaving that picturesque hamlet on the California-Oregon border, we traveled north to another one—Woodland, Washington. And leaving the purely recreational, physical activity, we made our way to physical activity of another kind—from play to work. For the next three days we were painting buildings, cutting firewood, and clearing pastures. We were serving a small Christian camp with our gift of manual labor. This strenuous work was mingled, of course, with Bible study, "The Two of Us," and quiet time to read assigned books and work on personal journals. A week prior to the start of the trip, each student was given an empty clothbound book. In it students were instructed to keep a diary of the trip, their thoughts, feelings, and responses. They were to take notes of all the Bible studies in their journals. They were encouraged to let their creativity run wild. They could paste in post cards, photos, concert programs, as well as draw pictures, cartoons, and the like. We provided a journal workbox with plenty of scissors, glue sticks, and such. These one-of-a-kind journals have become prized possessions for most of the kids, and valuable reminders, for years to come, of the lessons they learned on travel camp. On our final night in Woodland we presented a concert in the public high school auditorium. (A much better location than a church building, for our purpose.)

Day Nine. The ninth day found us driving slowly through the breathtaking Columbia River Gorge. I always want to give kids a chance to see the sights, and I encourage them to *see.* We stopped at Multnomah Falls and had a fantastic picnic lunch. We planned for more food than we needed and had the freedom of inviting other sightseers to join in our informal meal. We took group pictures, swam, laughed, and sang. On the spur of the moment we stopped at a you-pick berry farm and picked five quarts of blackberries. The sundaes that night were "awesome," and we had them with our hosts at Nellie Campbell Farm in Wapato, Washington.

Days Ten and Eleven. Nellie who? Well, Nellie Campbell Farm is owned by the Presbyterian church and is a self-supporting work-study center. For city kids who had scarcely ever seen a farm, it was a unique and challenging experience to live and work on one for two days. Up at 4:00 A.M., they put in three hours of feeding pigs and hoeing cornfields before breakfast. They sat under the teaching of Craig and Barb Gilbert, the innovative young ministers who are leading this pioneer project. They rode horses bareback, had "The Two of Us" on hay stacks, drove tractors, performed in a large high school auditorium and worshiped in a little country church. Physical. Social. Mental. Spiritual. The well-balanced life.

Days Twelve, Thirteen, and Fourteen. We left civilization behind and stepped into a three-day backpacking trip in Olympic National Park. We chose the wilderness beach area of the park and hiked along miles of beautiful coastline with no sign of any other human beings. Every now and then the trail would take us up into the rain forest to bypass a headland, and we marveled at the number of streams and the huge ferns. At night we sat around a driftwood campfire, singing only for God and each other, and then we went to sleep on the sand. It added a wonderful new dimension to our entire trip.

Day Fifteen. Seattle, Washington, is a fascinating city. It's the kind of place where high school kids would love to have a free afternoon. And so they did, following our participation in the worship service at University Presbyterian Church. They were instructed to go nowhere in groups of less than three and to be back at precisely 6:00 P.M. (Wherever a strict return time was necessary, a dollar-per-minute late fine was employed, with great success.) That night we went to St. Mark's Episcopal Cathedral for the Compline service. It was just Scripture reading and singing in Latin by a men's choir, but it was at the top of the list of spiritual highlights for most of the kids. I believe in intentionally exposing young people to as many denominations and church families in the course of a tour as possible—to experience different styles of worship and expressions of faith.

Day Sixteen. Remember the reading assignments? By this morning, students were to have finished their two books and handed reading reports to me. If they did, they were treated to a once-in-a-lifetime breakfast at Snoqualmie Falls Lodge (three-month reservations and sixteen dollars per person). The two who did not make it, despite frequent encouragement, waited outside and watched the waterfall. The meal was a genuine feast. We also fasted a meal during the trip and discussed the significance of feasting, fasting, and moderation. Regarding food, we also emphasized the importance of truly giving thanks for everything, whether we cooked it ourselves over an open fire, or whether it was served to us at a church potluck supper.

Our final week on the road continued to present a flavorful mixture of all the aforementioned kinds of experiences. I have found that this kind of tour creates great enthusiasm for more of the same. And when we have this kind of motivation, we can experience much greater success throughout the school year. Just as a good football coach expects a lot from his players, we can expect and require certain disciplines of our choir members. Here are some I have found beneficial.

1. A personal interview with each prospective choir member. There is no audition. Vocal talent is not a prerequisite. But this interview gives me a good start at getting personally acquainted with each one of the prospective

members. I learn something of their families and their interests and get a sense of where they are spiritually. They do not have to be a Christian at this point. I believe more kids have become Christians as members of my youth choir than by any other means. If they join before they are Christians, however, they must accept the choir's code of conduct and disciplines, and understand that we are going to be praying for them.

2. We require 75 percent attendance at all choir rehearsals and performances, worship services, and youth activities.
3. A monthly reading assignment is required of all members, October through May. Everyone reads the same book in this assignment.
4. We start every rehearsal with a session of "The Two of Us."
5. We undertake monthly service projects. I feel one of the best is to involve my kids in the life of a local retirement home. We make regular visits to sing for and with the residents, and then we sit and visit with them. I encourage kids to "adopt a grandparent" on an individual basis and pay them visits on their own. We do special things like taking a bunch of ice cream makers to the home, making ice cream on the lawn while all the residents watch, and then serving everybody, staff included. What a great way to love people.

There is one problem inherent in a strong youth choir program. Those kids who do not choose to sing in it will nevertheless feel left out. The best we can do is to make sure there is plenty going on aside from the choir and to foster a spirit of community that eliminates any walls between choir members and non-choir members.

Whether choir members or not, our young people have so much to gain by singing, and so much to give, too. A great musician lay on his deathbed. Surrounded by loyal friends and family, he uttered these despairing words, "The song I came to sing has gone unsung. I have spent my life tuning and retuning my instruments." How terribly sad. But it need not be true of us or of the young people we are charged with leading. We all have a song to sing—in our words, our actions, and our daily lives. While I am speaking figuratively, I am convinced that the most effective sharing of this "song" with a world that is dying to hear it will be accompanied by joyful music throughout the young church. Let's be making that music.

FOR FURTHER READING

Anderson, Yohann. *Group Singing Dynamics.* San Anselmo, Calif.: Songs and Creations.

25 *Ridge Burns*

How to Plan and Lead
a Student Mission Trip

Some people find it hard to believe that 2,500 high school students from the United States would give up their Easter vacations to serve God. More incredibly, these students endure extreme temperatures, high winds, sleeping in tents, no running water, and traveling in church buses and vans in order to bring their faith in Jesus Christ in a practical way to the people of the Mexicali Valley, just south of the United States border.

As I have worked alongside students at Mexicali and other mission sites, I have discovered feelings of intentionality, mission, and purpose that cannot be generated at any summer camp or retreat. Short-term missions projects like Mexicali and many others around the country have become the very essence of ministry to many youth groups. Short-term missions projects in this chapter are defined as *cross-cultural mission trips* (either at domestic or foreign sites) *that take place during school vacations, lasting one to eight weeks in duration.*

RIDGE BURNS, M.R.E., is pastor to youth, Ocean Hills Community Church, San Juan Capistrano, California.

THE IMPACT OF SHORT-TERM MISSIONS

Short-term missionary projects have been viewed as an educational process to allow a student to evaluate his values and life's direction. It is particularly important to provide these opportunities at the high school level because high school students are very pliable and just beginning to reevaluate and formulate lifelong values.

There are three reasons a church should become involved in short-term mission projects. The first is *education*. I do not expect students to become missionaries as a result of these trips. Rather, I want them to acquaint themselves with the mission process. As they are educated, they may become career missionary candidates. Churches must realize that these trips do not become an end in themselves; they merely feed the spiritual appetite of the students so that some can begin to make plans to become career missionaries. I try to plan mission trips at the high school level so that students will be able more appropriately to select colleges and curricula to fulfill their mission goals.

The second reason churches should become involved in short-term missions is the benefit of *entry-level missions experiences for students*. Short-term projects that are appropriately designed can be the first real outreach experiences for young people. The days of the student's completing his college education entirely within one country, then getting on an airplane or boat and committing himself to four years of ministry in a foreign country, have gone the way of the trolley car—still possible but rarely experienced. Today's approach is to give students exposure to other cultures and get them thinking about outreach ministry.

Churches should also be involved in short-term missions because they give students an *opportunity to express their faith*. Too many times our programs are designed to teach students *about* their faith instead of providing opportunities for them to *express* their faith. The genius of these projects is that students are forced to articulate their faith and express their life-styles in the context of another culture. To do this, a student must reevaluate his own culture and life-style to see if any inconsistencies exist.

PLANNING A MISSION TRIP

One way to schedule a trip is through a missions agency that specializes in taking groups of high school students. Some agencies are listed at the end of this chapter. They are specialists in preparing and sending students for short-term ministries all over the world. It does not matter whether the youth group has only one person or a number who wish to go, the organization will put together well-supervised ministry teams and send them out.

A problem may arise from this approach, however. Remember, students need to be sociologically comfortable (see Axiom 7, chap. 13). Some students who go by themselves on short-term mission trips may have a hard time fitting back into the youth program when they return because they have had experiences that are not common to the rest of the group. My suggestion is, even if your group is small, run the project yourself. Following are some steps to help you plan a short-term mission trip.

STEP 1: SHARE YOUR VISION WITH THE CHURCH AND STUDENT LEADERSHIP

Before sharing your vision with your pastor, mission board, or Christian education committee, develop a short mission statement to use as a basis for your discussion. Our mission outreach is called Project Serve. Prior to the trip, we developed the following mission statement: "Project Serve is a mission project for high school students of the Wheaton Bible Church. It provides students with an opportunity to experience cross-cultural missions, which will in turn allow them to grow, build, and strengthen their relationships with God, each other, and the world."

Get complete approval for the concept from your pastor, Christian education committee, and/or missions board before proceeding. If the committees of the church can sense the philosophy behind your actions, they will be much more open to the specifics of your program later on.

Some missions committees may be slow to see the value of such trips. They may view the investment in "immature high schoolers" as a waste of the already limited missionary budget. Fortunately, their hearts are in the right place. Unfortunately, their perspectives on discipleship are limited. Be patient with them, but do not let them kill the idea. If the pastor and board are behind the idea, find another way to accomplish it.

It is equally important to share your vision with key student leaders. Get full conceptual approval from your youth group cabinet or student leadership team before proceeding. Short-term mission projects require a high degree of student ownership. Failure to bring students into the planning process will cause problems for you later.

All my trips are student-led. In other words, students administer, direct, and are accountable for the entire project. I am a firm believer that the success of a mission trip is directly proportionate to the amount of student ownership and leadership. Each year, a Project Serve student director is appointed by the unanimous vote of the student leaders from the previous year. This appointment is made by students who understand and have experienced the process. In my situation, I have two student directors and seven site leaders. I meet with that group of nine students every week throughout the year to talk over the mission trip and disciple them. I become their role model, and they become very serious about their responsibilities as I delegate them.

STEP 2: SELECT A MISSION SITE

Your mission site is determined by the structure of your project. I divide our projects up into thirds. One-third of the time is spent in a physical project—structures that allow the local ministry to continue after our students leave. Another third is invested in person-to-person ministry. Even in situations where students do not know the language and have to work through interpreters, vacation Bible schools and backyard Bible clubs provide them with effective ways to articulate their faith on a one-to-one level. The last third is invested in group-building, making students feel like a team.

To select a site, communicate with your church-supported missionaries. Often they know of projects in their city or country with which you can help. International Teams, in Prospect Heights, Illinois, is a great resource for contacts on mission sites. Once the initial contact is made, establish who the site manager will be and stay in touch with that person on a regular basis.

You can never prepare too much for your on-site activities. Without adequate preparation it is quite likely that the planned work project, vacation Bible school location, or proper supplies will not materialize. After initial plans have been made, periodic phone calls to the host missionary will help minimize breakdowns. If possible, you should visit the site several months prior to your trip to make sure the site can actually accommodate your group.

STEP 3: SECURE ADULT SPONSORS

Try to recruit adult sponsors at least four months before your trip. This helps the sponsors arrange their vacation schedules and also provides time for training.

I call my adult sponsors "coaches" because I feel that name describes their role. A coach does not play in the game; he merely makes sure that the game is played appropriately. Here is a sample job description for an adult coach/sponsor.

ADULT COACH/SPONSOR

I. The purpose of an adult coach is to participate in a project the same way a coach would participate with his team. That is, he trains, facilitates, encourages, shepherds, and pastors students to enable them to accomplish their work.
II. We are looking for Christians who have flexible, open life-styles; will encourage others; have a servant's heart; are optimistic; like high school students (and have proved themselves in working with high school youth).
III. The tasks include such things as serving as a guide for all matters on your site. You will also be involved in such tasks as renting vehicles, food services, medical emergencies, safety assessment, relationships with the local people (including border crossings, visas, etc.). You will be the final authority in discipline in agreement with the Pastor of High School students. You will facilitate appropriate site manager/student leader communication. As an adult coach you will be responsible to: (a) attend all training sessions; (b) make your commitment by the deadline date; (c) commit a specified amount of time to the youth group; (d) attend the monthly meeting of the project staff; (e) attend a high school winter retreat (highly recommended, as it provides great student contact).

STEP 4: DEVELOP A BUDGET

The greatest source of controversy for a short-term mission project is the cost. Ask the treasurer of your church to set up a budget and an accounting procedure for your particular trip. Last year we spent $47,000 on Project Serve. Most of it was spent in foreign currency, making it difficult to have an accurate accounting procedure. But because we worked as a team, we were able to come up with an adequate system that provided the necessary information for businessmen at our church to appreciate the stewardship that took place on Project Serve. A sample budget is provided in figure 25.1.

Fig. 25.1 PROJECT SERVE BUDGET

Transportation

Air fare	$18,700.00		
Van	650.00		
Cars in Mexico:			
$450.00 per car, 7 cars	3,150.00		
Gas	750.00		
Mexican auto insurance (10 vehicles):			
$5.50 per day, 13 days	715.00		
		Subtotal	$23,965.00

Food

Breakfast	$ 1,360.00		
Lunch	2,040.00		
Dinner	2,720.00		
		Subtotal	$ 6,120.00

Miscellaneous

Camp rental	$ 1,000.00
Publicity	550.00
Training:	
Tom Spears	350.00
Food	100.00
Obstacle course	375.00
Leadership expense	450.00
Administration:	
Pre-trips	700.00
Car rental	500.00
Office supplies	364.50
Lodging	441.00
Phone expense	500.00
Azusa	600.00
Winnebago expense	1,176.32

Stove rental		180.00		
Shirts				
11.25×85		956.25		
			Subtotal	$ 8,243.07

Ministry expense

	VBS Expense	Construction Expense		
Door of Faith	75.00	200.00		
Ranch delos ninos	100.00	300.00		
Orfanatorio 29	75.00	300.00		
Ramon	75.00	200.00		
Dump	200.00	150.00		
Miracle Ranch	100.00	200.00		
Site No. 7 Church	100.00	200.00		
			Subtotal	$ 2,275.00
			Contingency	500.00
			Grand total	$41,103.07

Income

45 percent Church budget	$18,496.38
10 percent Fund raisers	4,110.31
45 percent Student fees	18,496.38
Total Income	$41,103.07

My church pays 45 percent of the entire cost of our mission projects. We also ask the students to pay 45 percent of the cost, and we raise 10 percent as a group. Our fund-raising procedures have included a refugee camp, a bicycle motorcross, a concert series, and servant days, as well as selling items to produce a profit.

Money is not your greatest obstacle—motivation is. If students are properly motivated, they will raise money for any project. If you need some good ideas on how to raise money, ask students who have raised funds for their band uniforms, cheerleading camp, or other school activities. They are the "experts."

STEP 5: ENCOURAGE TOTAL CHURCH INVOLVEMENT

The goal of a summer mission trip is to make it a total church experience. Though it seems easiest to leave on a Friday evening after adult sponsors get off work, try to schedule your departure after the Sunday morning worship service. At my church, the students and sponsors are commissioned in front of the whole church, and, on several occasions, we have had buses and vans waiting outside to take us to the airport. There is a unique sense of excitement as the church sees the chancel full of high school students committed to serving God.

Print prayer cards for each student so each can give those to his friends and enlist prayer support. Set up a prayer partners' program in which church families can pray each day for a specific student while he is on the trip. Have your students write to those prayer partners during the project to give the partners a first-hand report.

STEP 6: PROVIDE ADEQUATE TRAINING

The most common complaint from missionaries about short-term mission projects is that we send ill-prepared, ill-trained students who are more of a hindrance than a help for them. The missionaries have a good point. Unless we are willing to put time and effort into training students, we have no business sending them into cross-cultural situations.

Begin your training with a very thorough application and interview process. Our Project Serve application is twelve pages long, and it takes an average of two hours to fill out. We require an essay from each student on the culture of his site and 100 percent attendance at all training sessions.

Orientation should include a cross-cultural experience like visiting an inner-city church if your group is from a suburban church or vice-versa. We include such things as an obstacle course, Bible verse memorization, evangelism training, cultural orientation, and construction work training to prepare students spiritually, physically, and socially. Mission organizations such as The Evangelical Alliance Mission, Greater Europe Mission, and International Teams can provide you with training materials.

STEP 7: FOLLOW UP THE TRIP TO SOLIDIFY THE IMPACT

After planning several mission trips, I have discovered that as students' appetites are whetted for missionary service, I need to provide year-round opportunities to satisfy that hunger. At Wheaton Bible Church, that opportunity came in the form of our Sidewalk Sunday School—a daily outreach to latchkey children, funded and directed by high school students. Be sure not to compartmentalize missions into a two- or three-week summer approach. Provide your students with integrated activities to solidify the impact of their short-term trip.

Overcoming Problems

The most common problem for students on mission trips is homesickness. For some, the short-term mission project may be their first trip out of the country. They feel trapped, far away from home. There is also a sense of inadequacy. If students are in a foreign culture, they may not speak the language, and difficulty in communication coupled with homesickness reflects the importance of close interpersonal relationships. That is why we spend one-third of our time building team wellness. We want to make sure that the team members feel good about each other and that interpersonal conflicts are resolved.

Other problems are usually related to the missionaries' expectations of high school students. The students who come may not be as mature as the missionary expected. Sometimes missionaries forget that students want to buy T-shirts that are not appropriate and wear them home. At the same time, students have difficulty understanding the reasons for restricted dress or behavior when they are in a cross-cultural situation.

Another problem is that of time. Occasionally, missionaries are not aware of the time involved in managing a group of students at a site. Try to help your missionary/site manager be aware of the time commitment needed for your project. Explain that they are participating in the educational process of the church that supports them.

Short-Term Dreams

Taking students on mission trips is a dream. Some people may not understand that dream. We need to educate people to understand. Expect criticism as part of the educational process. Help your students work through criticism and accomplish the dream. The three most common dream-killer statements are:

1. "There are needy people right here in our city. Why don't you do a project here? Why go so far away and spend money on people we don't even know?" There is an element of truth to this statement. Do not start a missions program by sending students overseas; start in your own city or high school. Build a sensitivity toward outreach in all areas of life. If you begin with the dramatic programs, students respond to just the travel and excitement of the different cultures and not to the dream of expressing their Christian faith.
2. "It costs so much. Couldn't we just send them the money and let the missionaries we support use that money to accomplish the same things?" The people who give this kind of criticism do not understand that this is a missions *education* project. We are not pretending that we are involved in total missions, but we are trying to invest some money in students while they are pliable so that they retain a concern for missions six or seven years down the road.
3. "My aunt is a missionary and she had some high school students come over for the summer and she said it was more bother than it was worth." Students who are inadequately trained can create problems and more work

for the missionaries. Not all missionaries can handle short-term missionaries. You have to be sure that the environment in which you are placing your students is the kind of environment that can handle the high-energy activity that high school students produce.

The most important thing to remember about short-term mission work is that it begins with a heart broken for the hurts of the world. You cannot take students further than you have been yourself. The trips I have taken with students have not only affected the students, but in a much deeper way, they have affected me.

SOURCES OF MISSIONS CONTACTS

International Teams
P.O. Box 203
Prospect Heights, IL 60070

The Evangelical Alliance Mission (TEAM)
P.O. Box 969
Wheaton, IL 60187

World Team
P.O. Box 343038
Coral Gables, FL 33134

Greater Europe Mission
P.O. Box 668
Wheaton, IL 60187

Compassion International
P.O. Box 7000
Colorado Springs, CO 80933

Mountain Top
P.O. Box 128
Altamont, TN 37301

Institute of Outreach
    Ministries (Mexicali)
Azusa Pacific University
Azusa, CA 91702

Tom Spears
403 Fourth Avenue
Haddon Hgts., NJ 08035

Ridge Burns
Ocean Hills Community Church
San Juan Capistrano, CA 92675

Paul Borthwick
Grace Chapel
Worthen Road
Lexington, MA 02173

FOR FURTHER READING

Borthwick, Paul. *How to Plan, Develop, and Lead a Youth Mission Team.* Lexington, Mass.: Grace Chapel, 1980.

Keyes, Ralph. *Is There Life After High School?* Boston: Little, Brown, 1976.

Klein, Chuck. *So You Want to Lead Students.* Wheaton, Ill.: Tyndale House, 1982.

Larkin, Ralph W. *Suburban Youth in Cultural Crisis.* New York: Oxford U., 1979.

Little, Paul. *How to Give Away Your Faith.* Downers Grove, Ill.: InterVarsity, 1970.

Zehring, John William. *Preparing for WORK.* Wheaton: Victor, 1981.

26

David E. Carlson

Principles of Student Counseling

You are a youth worker because you are convinced you have answers that teenagers need to hear. You have found these answers in God's Word. You have learned them from your own experiences. As you teach Scripture, relate your own spiritual journey, and illustrate from the lives of others, you hope it makes a difference in teens' lives. You are thankful when it does. Yet there are times when giving the answer does not result in a solution. What do you do then?

In youth work, we use two primary styles of ministry in helping people change—selling and telling. The ability to persuade (selling) is a powerful gift for ministry. To move teenagers to belief in Christ, or to change their behavior or actions through gentle coercion, is a desirable skill.

Many effective youth workers have charismatic personalities that make "selling" a possibility. Other successful youth workers are better at teaching (telling). They have the ability to make clear the truths of Scripture. Relating biblical and theological perspectives to teen life is their talent.

Yet there are times when selling and telling are limited or ineffective. The teen is not sold or taught. He is, however, willing to talk over the questions, issues, problems, or needs. This is where counseling, a third ministry style, is useful.

DAVID E. CARLSON, B.D, M.A., M.S.W., has a private practice and is visiting professor of counseling and psychology, Trinity Evangelical Divinity School, Deerfield, Illinois.

Whether you are a good teacher, preacher, or salesman, you can add the counseling (priestly) approach for effective ministry. Remember, I am not asking you to give up what you are doing, only to add another approach to your repertoire. The goal of this chapter is to teach you the "what" and "how" of counseling.

The prophetic and priestly models are summarized below.[1]

Prophetic

		Priestly
Telling	Preaching	Facilitating
Teaching	Exhorting	Counseling
Explaining	Inspiring	Empathizing
Instructing		Imagining
Confronting		Comforting
Proclaiming		Processing
Emphasizing rules		Emphasizing relationships
Law giving		Love giving
Selling		Listening

Undoubtedly, one of these approaches predominates your ministry. That is understandable, since ministry style is the result of personality, training, and spiritual gifts. The challenge facing youth ministers is this: to match your style of ministry to the teenagers' needs.

A priestly response takes effort. It takes time and patience to discern what the teen needs, to assess his readiness to listen to what you have to say, to identify his resources to implement your suggested plan of action. Your natural style of ministry may get in the way of responding to your students' needs. Unless God specifically instructs you to approach someone in a certain way, *begin where the teen is.* This means that you will need to be flexible in your approach. Take a moment to reflect on how Jesus approached the blind man on the road to Jericho (Matt. 20:29-34), the woman at the well (John 4:5-29), or how Paul approached the men of Athens (Acts 17:22-23).

Sometimes you will be prophet, and other times you will be priest. If your spiritual gifts and personality do not match the needs of the teen, you should ask another person to counsel him or her. But it is possible to develop attitudes and skills beyond your spiritual gifts and natural style. Encouragement to be a flexible minister is found in Jesus' training of His disciples. The apostle Paul eloquently argues for matching the method to the person's needs when he writes, "To the Jews I became like a Jew . . . to the weak I became weak . . . I

---

1. David E. Carlson, "Jesus' Style of Relating: The Search for a Biblical View of Counseling," *Journal of Psychology and Theology* 4(1976): 181-92. Reprinted in J. Roland Fleck and John D. Carter, *Psychology and Christianity: Integrative Readings* (Nashville: Abingdon, 1981), pp. 231-46.

have become all things to all men, so that by all possible means I might save some" (1 Cor. 9:19-23).

To have choices in ministry, then, we must be willing to try something different when what we usually do is not working. Unfortunately, most humans solve problems by *trying harder* rather than *trying differently*. That is, they repeat what they have been doing even when it is ineffective. Counseling is helping people learn to think, feel, and behave differently. It is assisting teens to talk to themselves differently, to look at themselves and their world differently, to experience and express their feelings differently, and to act differently.

STAGES IN THE COUNSELING PROCESS

The counseling process is used when a teen is not able to translate the answer into action. This process has at least six stages.

ENGAGING

A rule of thumb: Before you explore or question, you need to initiate with the teen an understanding, empathic, nonjudgmental relationship. I assume you have read about this first step in ministry and are practicing and developing your skills in this area. If not, what you are about to read will be of little use until you are willing to become a warm, kind, respectful, genuine, trustworthy person who can feed back accurately what you hear and feel. These characteristics are needed to establish and maintain a relationship. Without rapport, counseling is seldom effective. Ask yourself:

> How well do I fulfill the characteristics of the "Lord's bond servant"? (See Luke 6:42; Col. 3:12-17; 1 Thess. 2:7; 1 Tim. 3:2-13; 2 Tim. 2:24-26.)
>
> How warm and kind am I?
>
> How respectful can I be to those who act and think in ways that are illegal, immoral, unspiritual?
>
> How genuine am I? Do I feel free to be myself? How much do I hide who I am?
>
> .How trustworthy am I? Do I keep confidences, not sharing my counseling sessions in social situations?
>
> How well do I listen? Does the other person feel listened to and understood? Can I express for him what he has a hard time putting into words?

After answering each question, ask yourself, *How do I know?* In addition to self-observation, ask a close friend, spouse, youth sponsor, or pastor to help you monitor the accuracy of your perception of yourself.

EMPATHIZING

I consider empathy the primary skill in counseling. Without empathy, counseling and ministering are performances more than relationships.

Preachers and teachers characteristically have an easier time talking than listening. You may need some training in the skills of listening and relating. *Empathy* is the capacity to imagine the teen's experiences (what he is saying, seeing, feeling, doing) as well as to express those experiences to show understanding. Empathy is not feeling sorry for another person. It goes beyond sympathy in the sense that the counselor maintains objectivity—he does not get caught up in the emotions of the teens.

I have found that most people can figure out another person's thinking easier than they do his feelings. To help you identify and express feelings, I suggest the following list: scared, angry, sad, happy, excited, tender. The acronym SASHET may help you remember these six feelings (see fig. 26.1).[2] Of course, there are more "feeling words," but these encompass the range of emotions. Pay attention to the many synonyms teenagers use for these feelings.

Consider the messages your students have given you this week. Could you identify both their thoughts and their feelings? Give yourself permission to guess what a teen is feeling. Your attempts will be rewarded with establishing rapport, even if you guess wrong. You will convey that you are trying to understand, and that is a gift for which the teen is looking. Ask teens if what you heard is what they meant. Called a *perception check*, this is an excellent and necessary tool in good communication.

Many counselors find that their ability to identify others' feelings is directly related to their capacity to identify their own. To aid you in this discovery, keep a feeling journal this week. Select a time each day when you will write what you feel. You will find the following chart helpful.

EXPLORING

After you have begun to understand the teens' needs, feelings, problems, and concerns, the next step is to begin working on these by developing understanding for both you and the individual teen. This process is called *exploring* or *purposeful questioning*. Five questions will assist you in this process.

1. *Determining the goal: What do you want?* Much counseling ends in frustration and failure for two reasons—one, because the problem has been discussed to the exclusion of the desired outcome, or two, because the goal/outcome has not been specifically established. We need to keep in mind what is

---

2. Frank Morris and Dixie Morris, *The Recognition and Expression of Feelings* (South Bend, Ind.: TMAC, 1985).

Fig. 26.1 *Feeling Recognition Exercise*[3]

What am I feeling?	How did I recognize this feeling?	When/where did I have this feeling?	What did I do with the feeling? express/implode/explode	Whom does the feeling involve, if anyone?

Scared
Panic-stricken
Terrified
Frightened
Anxious
Startled
Afraid
Stress-filled
Nervous
Jittery
Tense

Tight down the
back of the neck
and in shoulders,
tight across
chest, constricted
breathing

Angry
Violent
Rage-filled
Irate
Furious
Inflamed
Mad
Resentful
Upset
Disgusted
Frustrated
Irritated
Depressed

Tight jaw,
clenched fists,
arms want to hit

Sad
Grieved
Mournful
Melancholy
Heartbroken
Dejected
Distressed
Mopey
Blue
Down
Funky

Tightness in throat,
behind the eyes,
and down the center
of the chest

3. Adapted from Morris and Morris and from Sherod Miller, Elam Nunnally, and Daniel B. Wackman, *Alive and Aware* (Minneapolis: Interpersonal Communication Programs, 1975).

Fig. 26.1   *Feeling Recognition Exercise*[3]

What am I feeling?	How did I recognize this feeling?	When/where did I have this feeling?	What did I do with the feeling? express/implode/explode	Whom does the feeling involve, if anyone?
Happy				
Joyous	Relaxed			
Complete	muscles			
Fulfilled				
Optimistic				
Satisfied				
Content				
Relaxed				
Pleased				
Peaceful				
Glad				
Excited				
Ecstatic	Jumpy and			
Energetic	shivery all			
Aroused	over, fast			
Effusive	pulse			
Bouncy				
Perky				
Sparkly				
Antsy				
Nervous				
Jittery				
Tender				
Intimate	Soft tears			
Loving	around eyes,			
Warm-hearted	"full" sensation			
Gentle	around heart, arms want			
Soft	to hug			
"With you"				
Touched				
Kind				
Empathic				
Sympathetic				

motivating this teen to talk to us. What is he hoping to get out of this conversation? The goal can be determined by asking such questions as, "What do you want? Need? Hope for? What brings you here today? If you could change anything in yourself or your life, what would it be?" For biblical examples, see Jesus' conversation with the blind man on the road to Jericho: "What do you want me to do for you?" (Mark 10:51). And with the paralyzed man at the pool of Bethesda: "Do you want to get well?" (John 5:6). Expect the answer to be a broad generalization, maybe fuzzy, usually negative, at times unrealistic. Frequently teenagers want someone else to change. Your next step in counseling will be to help the teen develop a specific, positive, achievable, self-initiated goal.

Ted comes to you after the party and says, "I need to talk to you. My parents are really bugging me. They fight all the time. What can I do to stop them from fighting?" Here is a real problem for Ted. But you know nothing about how it is a problem for him. He is requesting help, which you desire to give; yet the problem seems bigger than you and Ted may be able to deal with immediately.

So where do you start? Begin by clarifying what Ted really wants. Notice the generalizations in Ted's statements, "My parents are really bugging me. They fight all the time." Determining the goal in this situation is to specify his generalizations. "Ted, you said that your parents are bugging you. Can you tell me how they are doing this?" Or, "I know you are really concerned for your parents and want to help them. What would your life be like if they stopped fighting?"

Another rule of thumb: When your counseling seems to be going nowhere, chances are that both of you have lost sight of the desired outcome, or you have not established one. Ask yourself, "What is the desired goal here?" Or ask, "Have I helped this person establish a specific goal, or is it still a broad generalization?"

The next step in determining the desired goal is to make sure you have stated it in positive language. It is easier to achieve the positive than to stop the negative. For example, think about a habit or behavior you would like to quit. Now remember the struggles you went through attempting to stop. How successful were you? Probably not too successful. Now think about what you would like to do in place of that habit. Reflect on how much easier it seems to be to do the positive than to refrain from the negative. Ted wants his parents "to stop fighting." This is a negative statement. To get at the positive side of what he wants, ask, "What would you rather have your parents doing?"

The third important consideration in developing the positive goal is to determine if the desired outcome is *achievable* by the person seeking help. In Ted's case we need to ask, "Can you realistically stop your parents from fighting?" Probably not. So what can Ted do? He can consider how he might be a catalyst for them to get some help. Does he have the relationship and communication skills to talk with them about his concerns for them? Or can he tell them what he wishes for them? Or can he tell them what he is experiencing when they fight; in other words, the feelings, fears, and anxieties that get stirred up in him?

None of these approaches may be effective even if Ted has the skills to engage his parents in a positive conversation. So what can Ted do if he cannot influence his parents? He can begin to deal with his own feelings—tenderness, fear, sadness, anger, hopelessness. He may need to consider calling the police when his parents fight. Some domestic disputes can only be stopped by external authority. Trying to stop one's parents from fighting can be dangerous and should only be attempted when a person has assurance that his intervention will be responded to positively. If not, then some authority needs to be called in. This may be the only direction possible for you and Ted to pursue.

Many counseling sessions end in frustration because the counselor has not recognized that the goal is not achievable—in other words, self-initiated. A self-initiated and self-maintained goal is one that the person can achieve through his own efforts. Ted wants to help his parents stop fighting. He may not be able to do that. But he can do something for himself: for example, learn how to feel safe when his parents are fighting. We cannot change anyone except ourselves. This is a significant lesson for youth ministers to accept and learn. It will save much frustration.

A well-determined goal, then, is a desired outcome that is specific rather than a broad generalization, positive rather than negative, and self-initiated and self-maintained rather than initiated by others.

Before moving on to the next exploratory question, practice determining the positive goal. Think about a conversation with a teen, and write the goal as you hear it. Ask how specific, positive, and self-initiated it is. Use the following outline as a guide for this empathy exercise:

- Generalized form of goal
- Specific form of goal
- Positive form of goal
- Self-initiated form of goal

2. *Documenting the evidence: How will you know when you reach your goal?* A frequent problem in counseling arises when people say they want something but have no basis for knowing when they will have achieved the goal. A teen may say, "I want to be happy." When you ask him how he will know when he is happy, he may not be able to tell you. If this is this case, then your next step in counseling is to consider with him what happiness is. To do this you may ask, "Have you ever been happy?" or, "Tell me what you thought and felt when you were happy." Occasionally, a person may not be able to describe this kind of evidence; so you will need to ask him to "imagine what happiness is like" or "describe someone you know who is happy."

In our example, Ted wanted to know how to stop his parents from fighting. We asked him what he would have if his parents stopped fighting. We did this as a way of establishing a specific, self-initiated goal. He might have told us, "I wouldn't be bugged so much." This is a negative result that needs to be translated into a positive goal so it is clearer and more achievable. His positive goal would be a statement about himself: "I would feel more secure. I wouldn't be so embarrassed by the neighbors' hearing their fighting. I'd feel like I could share my problems with them." These responses begin to tell you how he will know when he reaches his desired outcome.

As a youth minister, you will also want to develop the skill of documenting evidence for your ministry. Earlier in this chapter, I asked you to gather evidence regarding your personal characteristics and skills in counseling. How well did you do? To answer this question, you will need some way of measuring your capacities and skills. This is the same process you will be asking teens to go through with you. In the empathy exercise outlined above, I asked you to write the messages you thought you heard teens send you. I also asked you to check the accuracy of your listening. Now, using those same messages, consider what evidence the teen gave you for knowing when he would reach his desired goal.

3. *Discovering the ecology: How will your life be different when you reach your goal?* Remember we asked Ted, "How will your life be different when your parents stop fighting?" This question was used to develop a more specific and positive goal to work on in counseling. This third positive outcome exploration is a way to discover the desired emotional, social, physical, or spiritual atmosphere. It is a way of uncovering the hoped-for quality of life. And it will frequently enable the teen to tell you more specifically his desired goal in sensory-grounded terms what he wishes he could say, see, feel, do.

Consider how Ted's life would be different if his parents stopped fighting. Differences for him might include security, safety, respect, pride, accessibility, and availability. Again, determining the ecology gives you, as a helper, direction for the counseling session. You will have a map that tells you what directions to take with the teen. Utilizing this question of ecology will save you from attempting to help someone with a problem that cannot be solved and, therefore, will reduce frustration for both of you.

Let us go back to our example of someone who says, "I just want to be happy." You could ask either, "How will you know when you are happy?" (evidence) or, "How will your life be different when you are happy?" (ecology). Notice that these questions do not need to be asked in any special order. The importance of the question you ask is this: will it give me what I need to know to help this person achieve a desired goal? But for the sake of illustration, we will ask the ecology question, "How will your life be different when you are happy?" We can anticipate these kinds of responses: "Oh, I'll never be sad again; nothing will ever get to me; I won't be hurt when I am put down." Are these achievable goals? No. So how do you develop achievable goals? You could ask, "Do you really think you'll be able to avoid ever being sad again?" or, "Do you really believe you can never, ever let someone get to you?" Or you can translate the goals for the teen. "I can't help you never be sad again, but I can help you learn how to deal with your sadness." Or you might say, "Making sure nothing will ever get to you is not something I can help you acquire. Would you like to learn how to cope when things do get to you?" Another possibility is, "I can help you learn how to deal with put-downs, but I don't know anyone who can help you avoid hurt."

Teens who come to you for help want their lives to be different in some way. It is our job as youth ministers to help them determine realistic ways their lives can be changed. Hope for the better life is rooted in reality. The desired goal a teen brings to you may be unrealistic and unachievable. What do you do then? Look for and develop specific, positive, achievable (realistic and self-initiated) goals.

4. *Detecting the context: When, where, and with whom do you want to accomplish your goal?* The context is the life situation in which the teen wants the goal to be experienced—family, friends, church, youth group, school.

Ted, for example, wanted his parents to stop fighting so he could feel secure and so he could talk to them about his problems. Although this goal is specific and positive, it may not be self-initiated or self-maintained. Therefore, counseling will be directed toward helping him recognize and accept his parents' limitations if he is to be free to ask others to help him meet his needs. That is, Ted's family may not now, or ever, be what he would like it to be. He may not be able to bring about the desired changes in his family. But that does not leave him in a hopeless situation. He will need to find another context, in this case "family," who will listen.

Betty came to me and said, "My father will not let me explain my side of the story. No matter what happens, it is my fault and his view is always right. I am so angry that I am about to explode. I can't tell Dad what I'm feeling without getting put down or punished." The way Betty represents her problem may be accurate. It may be true that Dad will never be able to listen to her side of the story. Therefore, a different context will need to be chosen.

Before jumping to the conclusion that Betty's dad will never be able to listen to her, however, it would be appropriate to find out how Betty talks to *him*—her tone of voice, facial expression, body posture. It may be that the problem is more the way Betty is attempting to talk to her father than what she is saying. So the context question can open the door to other counseling interventions that will make the achievement of the desired goal possible.

5. *Discovering the resources/blockages: What do you need to reach your goal? What stops you from reaching your goal?* Notice the two directions the counselor can take. One pursues what the person needs in order to meet his goal; another pursues the hindrances that prevent him from meeting

his goal. You will need to be flexible to determine which question will give you the information necessary to be helpful.

What did Ted need to stop his parents' fighting? Maybe the police or some other powerful authority, such as the pastor of Ted's church if the parents respect him. Ted could learn how to talk to them in ways that would have a positive impact on them. And yet, there is the possibility that he could do very little. That is for the counselor and Ted to explore together.

Resources can be internal or external. That is, they can be qualities, characteristics, perspectives, or skills that come from either within a person or outside the person (e.g., people, money, contacts, skills). It is the counselor's job to help determine what resources are needed to reach the desired goal. Much counseling ends in frustration and failure because the needed resources were not identified or developed. Also, counseling will end in frustration if the hurdles and blockages to the desired outcome are not observed and eliminated.

Consider the teen's *faith* as an important resource in counseling. Has this person made a commitment to Christ? What is the maturity of that relationship with Christ? Does he read Scripture regularly? How much of God's Word is hidden in his heart? What capacity does the teen have for implementing the teachings of the Bible in daily life? Can the teen pray humbly, with a forgiving spirit, considering his part in the problem? Is he willing to be accountable to others in a spiritual walk?

Betty may have needed to develop her ability to talk in a way that did not sound or look as though she were "talking back." A youth minister could help her learn how to do that through role playing. He could also help her talk differently by assisting her to deal with her frustration and rage. This could be done by her talking to the youth minister or praying her frustrations and rage out to God as the psalmist prayed. The youth worker could also help Betty develop realistic expectations of her father. He could be an external resource for her. The father's response to her would also help the youth minister assess the potential for the father to respond positively to Betty. As a bridge between Betty and her father, the youth minister could meet with them and facilitate the conversation by playing coach, referee, supporter, and external resource for both Betty and her dad.

EXPERIMENTING

Throughout this chapter I have encouraged you to experiment with what you are learning because little learning takes place without practicing. This is as true for you as it is for the teens you minister to. Do not ask teens to do something outside the counseling conversation without first having them practice it with you. To send a person out to do what he has not practiced is like sending a person out to fly a plane with only ground instructions.

Experimenting is part of the counseling process that enables teens to deal with their fears and resistances to change—to listen, talk, look, see, feel, and act in ways that help them reach desired goals. Experimenting is an extension of exploring. Through experimenting, the teen will clarify his positive goal or develop new goals. His situation will be explored in more detail as new feelings, perspectives, and understandings come to light. A greater appreciation for the meaning of the problem and the wish for change will often develop. As counselor, you will find it easier in the experimenting phase to explore in greater detail the parts missing from the desired outcome. It is often true that threats and anxieties become clearer during this phase. And creative alternatives are frequently uncovered.

You will spend time role playing with the teen to develop his or her confidence and skill. Consider your counseling contacts. How much experimenting do you encourage and participate in? Take time now to reflect on and plan experimenting that should be done in your counseling contacts this week. Experimenting leads to and involves the next stage in counseling, which is evaluating.

EVALUATING

Evaluating is another form of exploration. It is a part of the process of gathering evidence to determine where you and the teen are in the journey to reach his desired destination. Evaluating is a review of what the teen came to you for in the first place, how far you and he are in achieving that goal, and what is left to be expressed, perceived, and done.

As counselor, you are not only reviewing the student's progress toward a desired outcome, you are monitoring your own participation in the process. You are asking yourself questions like, "How am I facilitating this person's quest for a solution? What else do I need to ask, say, look for, conceptualize, confront, support, that will assist this teen to reach his goal?"

You are also asking the teen to review his progress. It may be an exploration as you start a follow-up session, such as, "What do you need or want to accomplish today?" Or at the end of a session, "Let's review where we have gone today." Incidentally, summarizing the session is an excellent communication tool that serves as a perception check for both of you.

The responsibility for the summarizing can be shared. For example, you can suggest, "I want to pause for a moment and make sure that I have heard you correctly. This is what I understand we have talked about today. . . . How close am I to what you have experienced?" Or you can ask the teen, "As we end our time together, I wonder if you can tell me what you have gotten out of our conversation?" Or during the counseling session, you can pause and say, "Before we move on would you please tell me what you have heard me say to you so far?"

Choose a recent counseling session and review it. Write out your progress, using the outline that follows.

Engaging. What level of rapport is between this teen and me? How much does he trust me? How well have I shown him respect and confidence? Have I demonstrated a loving, nonjudgmental attitude? Is he willing to talk to me again? How would he describe our relationship?

Empathizing. What do I understand about this teen's feelings, perspectives, and behaviors? How does his response to me demonstrate that I have communicated my understanding? What feedback does he give me that suggests he feels understood?

Exploration. What do I think is this teen's desired goal? Have I checked it out with him and received confirmation? What other goals does he have that I need to explore with him? Have I established a positive, specific, self-initiated goal? What evidence confirms that I know when he will have reached his outcome? Does he have a clear picture of the evidence?

How will this teen's life be different as a result of our interactions? If he achieves his goal, what will be the positive result(s)?

Have we established when, where, and with whom the teen wants this goal?

How well have we established the resources he needs to reach his desired goal? What hindrances have we dealt with? Are there any remaining obstacles?

Experimenting. What have we practiced? How proficient has the teen become in his trial runs? What else should be explored, experienced, or practiced before we terminate these regularly planned conversations?

Answers to these questions will tell you when exiting, the last stage of counseling, can be initiated.

EXITING

Someone said, "All good things must come to an end." This is also true of counseling. Counseling is a special, time-limited relationship that considers how to meet the needs, feelings, and desires of a person more effectively. In youth ministry, a relationship with a teen usually is ongoing even when the counseling terminates. This is a unique aspect of ministry that professional counselors do not have.

Therefore, setting parameters on the counseling relationship is crucial from the beginning contact. This might be done by agreeing to meet with the person for a set number of sessions—three or four contacts is reasonable for most youth workers. It is also important to establish referral sources. What professional counselors in your community appreciate and respect a person's faith? Will they work cooperatively with you? Will they provide consultation and supervision when you need it?

A word of caution: *Be careful to what you commit yourself.* Is it feasible for you to meet as often and long as the teen is requesting and needing? Given the demands of your position, how many students can you see in an ongoing relationship? Can anyone else in the church—youth sponsors, other adults or teens—be helpful to you and the student you are counseling? Also, be aware of the possibility that the person might feel rejected or abandoned as you set limits on the relationship. Some students will cling to a relationship with you. It is important to assess what is involved for you and the teens. Take their feelings and needs seriously, but be realistic about what you can offer. You cannot be the perfect parent or friend that they are longing for. But you can help them learn how to ask for what they need and how to receive what they get in ways that are satisfying to themselves and to the giver.

Remember you are a shepherd, not the Savior. You cannot meet all of a student's needs even if both of you share the fantasy. So giving up the special relationship a teen has with you may be difficult. Take time to process this experience as you are terminating counseling. It is possible that letting the young person go may be difficult for you. When this happens, explore what meaning this relationship has for you. Seek the services of a professional counselor or colleague to help you deal with your grief or unmet needs.

A second word of caution: Make sure that your own needs are met before you minister. *Do not use these young people to meet those needs.* It is absolutely crucial that you sort out your motives for being in ministry. You will be useless and terribly hurtful to teens if you are not dealing with your own unmet needs outside of the ministry context. Friends, family, and fellow ministers are resources to meet your needs—the students are not. In addition, make sure that you are dealing with your temptations, depravity, and sinfulness. As a minister you have a grave responsibility to be a model of Christian character and living. Watch your tendency to rationalize your corrupt side. By all means, *get out of a helping relationship when you are tempted to use it merely for your own satisfaction.*

PUTTING IT ALL TOGETHER

By the time you read this paragraph, it is very possible you feel overwhelmed. You are probably asking yourself, "How in the world am I going to digest all of this?" You can do it, slowly, one step at a time. Learning to counsel is a *process* that is not learned immediately. You will need to practice, make mistakes, ask for help, experiment some more, read, and consult with a competent counselor before you master these strategies. If you are a teller or seller, you will find it easier to continue using the style that is comfortable to you. But I hope you have been teased into thinking that your ministry could be enhanced by adding counseling skills.

If you have practiced the exercises as you read this chapter, you have begun learning counseling methods. You have discovered that counseling is not giving advice, but listening, understanding, reflecting, exploring, experimenting, and evaluating with the teen. Counseling is not something you do to the young person. It is thinking, feeling, and behaving *with* him. Counseling is a partnership in which you and the teenager learn how to live a more fulfilling life, to solve his problems in different and more effective ways, and to achieve his desired goals.

To give advice, suggestions, or answers may be helpful toward the end of the counseling process when you have a grasp of the teen's needs, feelings, values, and resources. A frequent mistake tellers and sellers make is to advise before they understand what the goal is; how the person will reach the goal; in what way the teen's life will be different; when, where, and with whom the person wants the goal; and what resources the teen has or needs to develop in order to reach his desired goal.

It is difficult to engage, empathize, explore, and evaluate patiently when you know what the answer is. But remember that your answer to the teen's problem is only *your* answer to his problem until he can make it *his* answer to his problem. To accomplish this, a *process* of learning and experimenting is often necessary. Teens who are puzzled, confused, overwhelmed, unable to take what you say and live it out—those are the ones who will ask you for help. To teach and preach again to those teens will result only in frustration for both of you. For those teens, *giving the answers is not the solution; processing is the solution.*

FOR FURTHER READING

Bandler, Richard, et al. *Changing With Families.* Palo Alto, Calif.: Science and Behavior Books, 1976.

Carlson, David. "Relationship Counseling." In *Helping People Grow,* edited by Gary Collins. Santa Ana, Calif.: Vision House, 1980.

———. "Principles of Informal Counseling." In *The Youth Leader's Source Book,* edited by Gary Dausey. Grand Rapids: Zondervan, 1983.

Collins, Gary. *How to Be a People Helper.* Santa Ana, Calif.: Vision House, 1976.

———. "Counseling Adolescents." In *Youth Education in the Church,* edited by Roy B. Zuck and Warren S. Benson. Chicago: Moody, 1978.

Egan, Gerald. *The Skilled Helper.* Monterey, Calif.: Brooks/Cole, 1982.

———. *Exercises in the Skilled Helper.* Monterey, Calif.: Brooks/Cole, 1982.

Welter, Paul. *How to Help a Friend.* Wheaton, Ill.: Tyndale House, 1983.

Wright, Norman. *Training Christians to Counsel.* Denver: Christian Marriage Enrichment, 1977.

27

Jon Byron

Youth in Personal Bible Study

I stood before a small group of students and adults who were endeavoring to get a better grasp on what it means to be involved in youth ministry. The format of the session had not given much opportunity to answer questions from the floor. Yet one older woman caught my attention as she waved her hand and called my name. Her question was something like this: "How do you help your children (in this case a high school son) live according to the right set of values?"

As her words rang out, nods of agreement spread across the room, and I knew that the question of not just the hour, but possibly a lifetime, had been asked. She had touched upon what I believe is the nerve center of our culture, the determining and living out of values. My answer was slow in coming, but I finally replied, "I believe we need to motivate and challenge them to live their lives in obedience to the Scriptures and the Lord they reveal to us."

The culture today is not just immoral; it is amoral, or valueless. There is no prevailing standard by which actions or attitudes are judged, good or bad. From one moment to the next, according to cultural whim, that which has been basic to life's foundations may change. It is within this context of shifting and unstable values that the minister is led to ask the question, How do I help the person of this valueless age emulate and hold to Christian values?

JON BYRON, M. Div., former minister to high school students, is currently a youth speaker and musician in Anaheim, California.

The only logical answer must involve the Book of the Christian—the Bible. It is in the Scriptures that we are introduced to the mind of Christ and His purpose and plan for our lives. It is in the Scriptures that we find the only authoritative rule for faith and practice. Therefore, it is to the Scriptures we must go if we are to express the values associated with Christ and His kingdom. John Calvin put it this way: "Faith ought to be upheld with such firmness as to stand unconquered and unwavering against Satan and all the devices of hell, and the whole world. We shall find this firmness solely in God's Word."[1]

PERSONAL STUDY IS NOT OPTIONAL

Although the clarification of values is a major reason to be involved in the study of Scripture, an even more basic reason is that we are commanded to do so by God Himself. In chapter 6 of Deuteronomy, Moses says, "Hear, O Israel: The Lord our God, the Lord is one. Love the Lord your God with all your heart and with all your soul and with all your strength. These commandments that I give you today are to be upon your hearts. Impress them on your children. Talk about them when you sit at home and when you walk along the road, when you lie down and when you get up. Tie them as symbols on your hands and bind them on your foreheads. Write them on the doorframes of your houses and on your gates" (Deut. 6:4-9).

In this passage one is confronted with God's sole right as sovereign Lord of all creation. This affirmation is followed by a command that defines how Israel is to respond to God's sovereignty—with a love that encompasses her whole existence. This is, to most of us, fairly familiar ground, and yet there is also given a strong command to interact with Scripture in an intimate fashion.

The people of Israel were first instructed to have Moses' words, spoken on behalf of God, "on their hearts." This in itself was a radical shift from words written on tablets of stone. They were to be *involved* with God's words in such a way that His spoken impressions influenced their thoughts, intentions, and emotions. Only as one is a student of the Word of God can this kind of heart-moving change be manifested to its fullest extent.

Israel is then commanded to teach the Word of God diligently to her children. The word *diligently* in the Hebrew language comes from a verb that means "to sharpen," and in this instance carries with it the idea of penetrating deeply. The Scriptures were not to be taken lightly but instead were to penetrate and influence all areas of the people's lives. In this family approach of passing on the faith, the study of God's Word became a multigenerational and intergenerational discipline. It was more than an archaic tradition of early Israel.

The people of Israel were called to bind God's Word to their hands,

---

1. John Calvin, *Institutes of the Christian Religion*, 2 vols. (Philadelphia: Westminster, 1960), 1:1158.

foreheads, and doorposts. Through a figurative expression God was identifying the sphere of influence His Word was to have. To bind God's Word to one's hands and forehead was to submit the mind, will, and actions to the authority of Scripture. In fact, in ancient Near East societies a very common way to identify one's slave was by marking him on the hand and on the forehead. God was calling the Israelites to be slaves to His lordship and the authority of His Word. This could only be realized as their thoughts and actions were saturated with the Scriptures. That intensity of saturation demanded personal time studying the Word of God.

We are those to whom this biblical tradition has been passed, and as such we have the same call to study God's Word that it might influence our hearts, penetrate our lives, and be the authority over our thoughts and actions. We are called to be and to produce students of the Bible, not for a grade but for the transformation of our very lives. And yet, the dilemma is often not a lack of motivation but rather a lack of understanding regarding the skill of Bible study.

Often we, as ministers, are the very ones at fault because we challenge our congregations and small groups to study the Bible, yet leave them cripples without the skills to do so. Therefore, not only should we motivate God's people to study His Word but also give them an understanding of how to do so.

Study for Change

The primary goal in teaching the skill of personal Bible study to Christians should not be restricted to the gaining of information but rather to bring life change for the glory of God. Our call is to search the Scriptures that we might come face to face with the one of whom they bear witness, Jesus Christ (John 5:39).

Personal Preparation

Since personal Bible study is ultimately a spiritual experience, it is logical and important first to take time to prepare oneself spiritually. Praise and petition will assist us in this process.

Praise is the vehicle by which we remove the focus from ourselves and place it on God. We recognize our finitude in the presence of an infinite God. It is in the prayer of praise that one begins to experience the holiness of God that demands holiness of all His creation, and the power of God that can bring one's life into conformity with His righteousness.

I have found that in caring for the lives of students, praise is the tool that frees them to believe that God, through His Word, can make a difference in their lives. Encourage students to list different attributes or characteristics of God by using the alphabet as a catalyst to their thinking, that is, list one characteristic of God for each of the first five letters of the alphabet. Or have them identify some of the more obvious attributes of God, such as love, kindness, and care. Then help them see some of His less obvious characteristics, for example, holiness and omnipresence. With a list of God's attributes in hand, it is easier for the student to focus his/her worship.

The second integral part of this spiritual preparation process is the prayer of petition. Prayer is the means by which the Holy Spirit is called upon to guide us as we confront the revelation of the plan of God in the Scriptures.

There are four reasons the student of Scripture should petition God before beginning to study.

First, we should confess our sins and ask God's forgiveness for them (1 John 1:9). Without the cleansing of God we remain incapable of receiving the illuminating work of the Holy Spirit due to the impediment of sin. This is often forgotten when we open up the Scriptures.

Second, pray for clarity of thought and the illumination of the Holy Spirit. This implies both a freedom from distraction and an ability to concentrate on the task at hand. Spiritual insight is needed. The Holy Spirit will provide it (1 Cor. 2:9-16).

Third, pray that the experience of personal Bible study is an enjoyable one. There is so much about the word *study* that seems to alienate people from the idea of enjoying God's Word. My father brought this point home to me through the following vivid illustration from his years as a physician living in San Francisco.

> Some years ago I was riding a street car in San Francisco, seated in the central section facing the passengers on the other side. My casual glance became riveted on a teenage girl who was reading her Bible with great enthusiasm. It was soon apparent what she was doing; she would read a verse and then look up all the cross references. I thought, "That's great!" Suddenly she came to the end of the chapter, slammed the Bible shut, gave a big sigh, and mumbled, "That's done! Now I don't have to do it again until tomorrow!"

The reading of God's Word should not become a distasteful discipline. Rather, it should be viewed as an opportunity to gain an inside look at God's unfolding plan.

Fourth, pray for a receptive and obedient heart. Often our enjoyment of God's Word is diminished not by lack of clarity or understanding but by our failure to be obedient to the truth revealed.

Assuming that the leader has nurtured this attitude of prayer in a student's life, there are specific skills that can be passed on to enhance the study of the text itself. A key method of study is known as inductive Bible study. It is the process whereby the text is allowed to speak with a minimum of predetermined biases. It differs from deductive Bible study at this very point. One who is involved in deductive Bible study generally comes to the text with a particular framework or theology that structures the way Scripture is approached. Inductive Bible study is the orderly method of investigation in which correct theology, or principles of life, come as the result and not the presupposition of one's study.[2]

BASIC STEPS FOR INDUCTIVE BIBLE STUDY

The following steps are presented to provide structure to develop one's personal search of Scripture.[3]

STEP 1: SELECT AN APPROPRIATE UNIT FOR STUDY

How does one initiate an inductive study of the text of Scripture? This can be done by taking the whole Bible, a book of the Bible, a chapter, or even a verse as a unit of study. All of these will have merit under a variety of circumstances, but it is most important to choose an amount that is manageable, such as a chapter or a paragraph of the text.

We also need to encourage students to read large portions of Scripture to get the flow of biblical events and the breadth of God's activity over time. We will focus on the shorter portions of a chapter or a paragraph for our inductive model.

STEP 2: READ WITH UNDERSTANDING

After choosing the portion of Scripture to be studied, read that section several times. The more times it is read, the better the comprehension. This process is known by different terms, such as skimming, rapid reading, or previewing of the passage, yet the intention is the same in that one is trying to get a very basic grasp of what is going on in the passage.[4] This process should enable us to determine the main theme or intention of the author. It is not the time to try to understand *all* the relationships, concerns, and ideas put forth in the passage.

Two brief questions are helpful in the process of previewing. The first is purely observational: What words or concepts seem to recur? The second question builds on the first and is more interactional: Is there a particular theme that might be suggested by these recurring words or concepts?

· Remember that the preview is not supposed to answer all of our questions, but should illuminate the basic direction of the passage. This should enable us to do a more analytical reading of the text.

2. James F. Nyquist, *Leading Bible Discussions* (Downers Grove, Ill.: InterVarsity, 1967), p. 7.
3. Adapted from David H. Roper, "Youth in Personal Bible Study" in *Youth Education in the Church*, ed. Roy B. Zuck and Warren S. Benson (Chicago: Moody, 1978), pp. 237-45.
4. Mortimer J. Adler and Charles Van Doren, *How to Read a Book* (New York: Simon & Schuster, 1972), p. 43.

Having previewed the passage, we are ready to engage in the more analytical side of inductive Bible study. As a good detective desires to let no clue go unnoticed, so the Bible student seeks to uncover as many clues as he can to shed light on the meaning of the passage.

Basic to effective reading of the Bible is the ability to observe the details of the text. The following excerpt is a good example of the process of careful observation, illustrated by Alexander Agassiz, a great naturalist and teacher.

It was more than fifteen years ago that I entered the laboratory of Professor Agassiz, and told him I had enrolled my name in the scientific school as a student of natural history. He asked me a few questions about my object in coming, my antecedents generally, the mode in which I afterwards proposed to use the knowledge I might acquire, and finally, whether I wished to study any special branch. To the latter I replied that while I wished to be grounded in all departments of zoology, I purposed to devote myself especially to insects.

"When do you wish to begin?" he asked.

"Now," I replied.

This seemed to please him, and with an energetic "Very well," he reached from a shelf a huge jar of specimens in yellow alcohol.

"Take this fish" said he, "and look at it; we call it a Haemulon; by and by I will ask you what you have seen."

With that he left me, but in a moment returned with explicit instructions as to the care of the object entrusted to me.

"No man is fit to be a naturalist," said he, "who does not know how to take care of specimens."

I was to keep the fish before me in a tin tray, and occasionally moisten the surface with alcohol from the jar, always taking care to replace the stopper tightly. Those were not the days of ground glass stoppers, and elegantly shaped exhibition jars; all the old students will recall the huge, neckless glass bottles with their leaky, wax besmeared corks, half-eaten by insects and begrimed with cellar dust. Entomology was a cleaner science than ichthyology, but the example of the professor who had unhesitatingly plunged to the bottom of the jar to produce the fish was infectious and though this alcohol had a very ancient and fish-like smell I treated the alcohol as though it were pure water. Still I was conscious of a feeling of disappointment, for gazing at a fish did not commend itself to an ardent entomologist. My friends at home, too, were annoyed, when they discovered that no amount of eau-de-cologne would drown the perfume which haunted me like a shadow.

In ten minutes I had seen all that could be seen in that fish, and started in search of the professor, who had, however, left the museum; and when I returned, after lingering over some of the odd animals stored in the upper apartment, my specimen was dry all over. I dashed the fluid over the fish as if to resuscitate it from a fainting fit, and looked with anxiety for a return of a normal, sloppy appearance. This little excitement over, nothing was to be done but return to a steadfast gaze at my mute companion. Half an hour passed, an hour, another hour; the fish began to look loathsome. I turned it over and around; looked it in the face—ghastly; from behind, beneath, above, sideways, at a threequarters view—just as ghastly. I was in despair; at an early hour I concluded that lunch was necessary; so with infinite relief, the fish was carefully replaced in the jar, and for an hour or so I was free.

On my return, I learned that Professor Agassiz had been at the museum, but had gone and would not return for several hours. My fellow students were too busy to be disturbed by continued conversation. Slowly, I drew forth that hideous fish, and with a feeling of desperation again looked at it. I might not use a magnifying glass; instruments of all kinds were interdicted. My two hands; my two eyes and the fish; it seemed a most limited field. I pushed my fingers down its throat to see how sharp its teeth were. I began to count the scales in the different rows until I was convinced that that was nonsense. At last a happy thought struck me—I would draw the fish; and now with surprise I began to discover new features in the creature. Just then the professor returned.

"That is right," said he; "a pencil is one of the best eyes. I am glad to notice, too, that you keep your specimen wet and your bottle corked."

With these encouraging words he added,

"Well, what is it like?"

He listened attentively to my brief rehearsal of the structure of parts whose names were still unknown to me; the fringed gill-arches and moveable operaculum; the pores of the head, fleshy lips, the lidless eyes; the lateral line, the spinuous fin, and forked tail; the compressed and arched body. When I had finished he waited as if expecting more, and then, with an air of disappointment:

"You have not looked very carefully. Why," he continued more earnestly, "you haven't seen one of the most conspicuous features of the animal, which is as plainly before your eyes as the flesh itself. Look again, look again!" And he left me to my misery.

I was piqued; I was mortified. Still more of that wretched fish. But now I set myself to the task with a will and discovered one new thing after another, until I saw how just the professor's criticism had been. The afternoon passed quickly, and when towards its close, the professor inquired:

"Do you see it yet?"

"No," I replied. "I am certain I do not, but I see how little I saw before."

"That is next best," said he earnestly, "but I won't hear you now; put away your fish and go home; perhaps you will be ready with a better answer in the morning. I will examine you before you look at the fish."

This was disconcerting; not only must I think of my fish all night, studying, without the object before me, what this unknown but most visible feature might be, but also, without reviewing my new discoveries, I must give an exact account of them the next day. I had a bad memory, so I walked home by Charles River in a distracted state, with my two perplexities.

The cordial greeting from the professor the next morning was reassuring; here was a man who seemed to be quite as anxious as I that I should see for myself what he saw.

"Do you perhaps mean," I asked, "that the fish has symmetrical sides with paired organs?"

His thoroughly pleased, "Of course, of course!" repaid the wakeful hours of the previous night. After he had discoursed most happily and enthusiastically—as he always did upon the importance of this point, I ventured to ask what I should do next.

"Oh, look at your fish!" he said, and left me again to my own devices. In a little more than an hour he returned and heard my new catalogue.

"That is good, that is good," he repeated, "but that is not all; go on." And so for three long days he placed that fish before my eyes, forbidding me to look at anything else, or to use any artificial aid. "Look, look, look," was his repeated injunction.

This was the best entomological lesson I ever had—a lesson whose influence has extended to the details of every subsequent study; a legacy the professor had left to me, as he left it to many others, of inestimable value which we could not buy, with which we cannot part.[5]

Suppose someone revealed the location of a fabulous treasure chest, out-fitted ten young people with shovels, and sent them out to dig. However, he failed to tell them the depth at which the chest would be found. Those who located it would not do so because they had a special shovel, but because they persisted. In a similar manner, effective Bible study requires observation and persistence. It is an arduous and time-consuming process, but the results are certain for those who persist. Encourage teens to read and reread a Bible passage until they see "wonderful things from [the] law" (Psalm 119:18, NASB). Encourage them to have paper and pen handy to jot down their observations or note their observations in their Bibles as they read.[6]

STEP 3: BE AWARE OF THE STRUCTURE OF LANGUAGE

Several aspects of grammar and syntax need to be considered for a clearer understanding of the words of Scripture and their relationships to one another. Words that are unclear should be defined. Although a dictionary is of value, one should remember that English was not the original language of the Bible. Some of the meanings of words may have changed over time, so a method of determining the original, intended meaning of words is needed. A helpful tool at this point is a Bible or expository dictionary that gives the biblical defini-tions of key terms and concepts.

Also note the context of the sentence or paragraph in which the word is used. This will probably shed a great deal of light upon the author's intended meaning. Another helpful tool in this respect is a Bible concordance that lists the different biblical references in which a word is used. This can be helpful in comparing an author's usage of a particular word in different situations.

The part of speech that any given word holds within a sentence must be

5. Appendix, *American Poems* (Houghton Odgood, 1880).
6. Roper, p. 240.

determined when studying the grammar and syntax of the text. This means that one must be able to identify whether a particular word is a noun or a verb, a direct or indirect object, the subject of the sentence or a modifier of some other word or phrase. To do this one may need to remember the following simple definitions.[7]

A *noun* denotes a person, place, or thing and can be singular or plural, masculine, feminine, or neuter. A *verb* tells or asserts something about a person, place, or thing and can indicate past, present, or future time of action, as well as the attitude of the one performing the action (described as the *mood* of the verb) such as questioning, commanding, doubting. *Pronouns* substitute for nouns to avoid repetition within the sentence. They follow the same patterns of gender (masculine, feminine, and neuter) and number (singular and plural) as the nouns they replace.

Adjectives modify nouns as *adverbs* modify verbs, adjectives, or other adverbs. *Prepositions* are placed before nouns or pronouns to relate them to other words. They are represented by words such as *in, by, through, with,* or *on. Conjunctions* join together words, phrases, or clauses for the purpose of expressing or explaining thoughts within a sentence. They are represented by words such as *because, and, for,* and *therefore.*

Although these definitions do not give all the variations of the parts of speech and their usage, they do provide a framework that can be helpful to the study of Scripture.

The student of Scripture will need to be aware that each Bible author had his own style of writing. Some, like the apostle Paul, were very complex in their formulation of sentence structure. Others, like John, wrote with less of the complexities, choosing instead a more readable style. However, both were unique instruments of the Spirit of God. In dealing with each author's stylistic differences one very helpful way to grasp the relationships within the structure of a sentence is to make an outline of the paragraph. To do this, differentiate between the main point of the paragraph and the various supporting points. Remember, words like *because* and *for* will usually indicate reasons for a statement made and thus probably will not introduce the main point. Conjunctions such as *and* or *also* will often indicate a phrase that is of equal importance and thus might highlight the presence of *several* main thoughts or supporting thoughts of equal value.

STEP 4: EXAMINE THE IMMEDIATE CONTEXT

The next major step is to see the passage in its proper context. In order to do this, have the teens read the paragraphs immediately before and after the unit. Then enlarge the setting by reading the chapters that precede and follow

7. Ibid., pp. 242-43.

the unit. In some cases it may be necessary to read the entire book. And ultimately, of course, the entire Bible forms the setting for any unit of study. However, for practical reasons it is usually sufficient to read the immediate context (paragraph or chapter surrounding the section being investigated). It is helpful to note particularly any conjunctions or connective devices that introduce the unit. For example, 2 Timothy 2:1 (NASB) opens with the statement, "You therefore . . . be strong in the grace that is in Christ Jesus." The chapter division would suggest a new subject. However the presence of the conjunction "therefore" would indicate that the new material in this chapter is a conclusion based on certain facts given in chapter 1. Thus, in order to interpret chapter 2 correctly, the student would need to know the facts given in chapter 1. Context is very important because much of Scripture is a reasoned argument rather than a homily of isolated facts. Understanding the context of any passage will help young people grasp the flow of the passage.[8]

STEP 5: BE AWARE OF THE HISTORICAL/CULTURAL SETTING

Up to this point we have dealt with only one side of the grammatical-historical method. We have considered the selection of the passage to study and the importance of reading the text with the precision and scrutiny of a scientist. Then we examined the language structure and the immediate context of the passage. Now we turn to the aspect of the historical setting that surrounds the particular author and his writing.

The Bible was written over a period of fifteen hundred years with a variety of authors. Each wrote out of his unique historical context. For instance, when Jesus used the metaphor of the good shepherd in John 10, His audience was a society and culture in which sheep herding was a common occupation. Everyone could easily follow His metaphor. Today, the number of people involved in the business of caring for sheep is far less. So to better understand the words of Jesus in John 10, it might be helpful to learn more about first-century sheep herding.

The student should ask: Who is the author of this book? When was it written? Who was the intended audience? What were the historical or cultural trends? Most of these questions can be answered by careful observation of the text itself. A good example of this is found in the epistles of Paul. In most of his introductions he identifies himself as the author and also specifies the audience for whom the letter is intended. In the book of Philippians, Paul states that he is writing from prison (Phil. 1:7, 13).

STEP 6: INTERPRET BY USING SOUND HERMENEUTICAL PRINCIPLES

Historically there have been two fundamental principles utilized in the process of analytical observation and interpretation of the Scriptures. All

8. Ibid., pp. 243-44.

correct biblical interpretation in some way incorporates these two basic guidelines. The first is called the analogy of faith, which means that Scripture is to interpret Scripture. The principle assumes the fundamental unity of the Word of God and implies that no interpretation of a passage will conflict with what is clearly taught elsewhere in Scripture. Scripture agrees with itself.

The second principle is, we should assume the normal, socially accepted meaning of words. After all, Scripture is literature. We should not interpret poetry as though it were historical narrative, wisdom literature, or legal documents. Although each type or style of writing will demand different methods of interpretation, it does not mean that a verb is any less a verb or a noun any less a noun. The style may vary, but rules of grammar will remain constant.

Interpreting the Bible as literature does not impugn the fact that Scripture was inspired by God. Rather, it affirms that the agency through which God chose to communicate was human language with all of its grammar and literary styles.

Outside resources that assist in Bible study are of great value. These include a Bible or expository dictionary, a commentary, a concordance, and a Bible atlas. Many of the study Bibles printed today include both maps and historical introductions to each book of the Bible. It is important to remember that all these tools are not to replace the text of Scripture, but only to enhance our understanding and application.

STEP 7: APPLYING THE TRUTH

Bible study is never complete until we personally apply the Word of God. It is the most important part of the whole process. We are not only to *comprehend* the truth but also to *obey* it. Christ summarized this in John 14:15: "If you love me, you will obey what I command."

If application is so crucial, the how-to of it becomes paramount. David H. Roper has suggested seven applicational questions to use in Bible study:

Is there some command here which I must obey?
Is there some promise which I may claim?
Is there some sin I must avoid?
Is there some danger to which I must be alert?
Is there some fact to share with a friend?
Is there some truth which I should ponder?
Is there some encouragement for the days ahead?[9]

A key to application is to pray for God's power to carry it out. It is the Holy Spirit who sets the Christian in motion as an instrument of the living God. Thus reliance on God's power and His Spirit within our lives is central to the life of obedience (Eph. 1:15-18*a*).

9. Ibid., p. 245.

John Welsey was committed to be "a man of one book," and that was the key to his success in life and ministry. As shepherds and teachers we should instill in the lives of students a love for God's Word. By our own words and walk we model the truth and challenge them to respond in obedience to Scripture.

For Further Reading

Adler, Mortimer J., and Charles Van Doren. *How to Read a Book.* New York: Simon & Schuster, 1972.

Ezell, Mancil. *Youth in Bible Study/New Dynamics.* Nashville: Convention Press, 1970.

Gower, Ralph. *The New Manners and Customs of Bible Times.* Chicago: Moody, 1987.

Nyquist, James F. *Leading Bible Discussions.* Downers Grove, Ill.: InterVarsity, 1967.

Richards, Lawrence O. *Expository Dictionary of Bible Words.* Grand Rapids: Zondervan, 1985.

Roper, David H. "Youth Personal Bible Study." In *Youth Education in the Church,* edited by Roy B. Zuck and Warren S. Benson. Chicago: Moody, 1978.

Sproul, R. C. *Knowing Scripture.* Downers Grove, Ill.: InterVarsity, 1977.

Wald, Oletta. *The Joy of Discovery in Bible Study.* Rev. ed. Minneapolis: Augsburg, 1976.

Emory Gadd

28

Youth and the Sunday School

The speaker at a seminar for youth ministers began his presentation by listing the elements of a "successful youth ministry" in the local church. Among those listed was "exciting Bible study."

For months I had been frustrated trying to evaluate our Sunday school program. Serious complaints of boredom and dislike came from our young people, and I had become sensitive to the frustration of our lay people as they worked in Sunday school. These were good people, both youth and adults, honestly sharing their concerns with me. I could no longer rationalize away their comments, nor could I ignore their observation of the ineffectiveness of what we called "Sunday school." That is why the phrase "exciting Bible study" caught my attention.

I raised my hand and asked the speaker, "Are you talking about Sunday school, on Sunday morning?" He explained that he was referring to a Bible study at another time of the week. My hand went up again. "It seems to me that one of the main purposes in Sunday school is to teach the Word of God, and that what we should do is turn Sunday morning around instead of going to another night of the week." The speaker responded, "If you can do it—good luck!"

At that moment I began to be challenged to do just that—turn Sunday morning around. I wanted Sunday school to be worth attending—a place to hear something worth writing down; a place where the Word of God becomes

EMORY GADD, B.A., is director of Youth Ministry Imperative, Houston, Texas.

applicable. I wanted our Sunday school to be somewhere young people not only were taught the Word with authority and enthusiasm, but also somewhere they wanted to be and wanted to bring their friends—a place to be with adults who were willing to love and minister to them.

MAINTAIN THE BASIC PURPOSES OF SUNDAY SCHOOL

The ultimate purpose of Sunday school is to relate biblical truth to life needs. Even if large numbers of young people attend a program early in the year, they will not continue to come unless their needs are being met. Unless Bible study results in changed lives, Sunday school is not achieving its ultimate purpose (2 Tim. 3:16).

The five specific purposes of any biblically-based Sunday school are relatively easy to state.

TEACHING BIBLICAL REVELATION

The Sunday school is the Bible-teaching arm of the church. Its purpose is to teach the Word of God and what it says about salvation and the Christian life. Teenagers are becoming more and more biblically illiterate. We need to teach the Bible with authority, credibility, and enthusiasm. It is a sin to bore students with the Scriptures.

INTERACTION FOR APPLICATION

Not only must we teach the Word of God, but we must also apply it to the lives of our students. What good does it do to teach James 1:2-3 (or any other passage) if we cannot apply it to our students' lives? There must be a time and an atmosphere that is conducive to discussion of the application of God's Word.

RELATIONSHIP BUILDING

Sunday school is an organization that takes the entire group of students and in some manner divides them into small groups. Each class is headed by an adult whose basic responsibility is to care for the students assigned to that group. The name *Sunday school* carries with it a Sunday morning connotation, but if we really want to minister to our students it will take more than just Sunday morning. The leader must be knowledgeable about their lives and responsive to their needs.

CREATING AN ENVIRONMENT

Students learn best in a loving environment in which relationships are built with fellow students as well as adults. They are not simply heads for storing biblical information, or "worker bees" who want to rush right out and put into practice what they have learned. We must develop a sense of expectation and confidence in the leaders, in friends, and in what will happen during their time in a Sunday school class.

OUTREACH TO NON-CHRISTIANS

Our Sunday schools can and should be evangelistic. When the Bible is taught with clarity and authority, when application of the Bible is made to the students' lives, and when students are being ministered to and loved, the Holy Spirit has the opportunity to do His convicting job regarding sin, righteousness, and judgment (John 16:8) in an atmosphere conducive to trusting Jesus Christ as one's Lord and Savior.

REASONS FOR ATTENDANCE

There are many reasons teenagers come to Sunday school, but to keep things simple, let me note three basic reasons they attend.

PARENTAL PRESSURE

Some young people will be at your church on Sunday morning because they were forced to come. Some of them just lost World War III, and somebody said, "You're GOING!" This group may have a bad attitude, but I would rather have them there with that attitude than for them not to be in Sunday school at all. When a parent leaves the decision of whether or not to attend up to the student, he may have eliminated one of the few spiritual influences on that child. But be aware that this group can affect the atmosphere of your whole group. Recognize that many in this category have never come into a right relationship with God through faith in Christ. That is why it is imperative that Sunday morning be quality time.

PEER PRESSURE

There are two sub-groups under this reason for attendance. One is the group that is present because they were *invited to attend* by friends. That is positive peer pressure, which is good. The number of visitors in Sunday school is largely dependent on the confidence students have in the quality of this ministry. They are reluctant to invite friends if the adult leaders are boring or if the other students in their group cannot be trusted with their responses. Bringing a friend can be a risky situation.

The second group is there because *it's the thing to do*. I do not mean that it is a fad or the "in" thing, but that it is just something we do. That is called nominalism, religiosity, or going through the motions. Many young people are straddling the fence, and they see church and Sunday school attendance as just something one always does on Sunday morning. These young people usually have a pretty good attitude. Some of them are Christians. They usually do not give you any trouble but are generally nominal in their response.

PERSONAL CHOICE

There are young people who attend Sunday school because they have had an encounter with Jesus Christ: He has changed their lives, and they want to study God's Word and be with God's people. They want to be there. The group whose parents make them attend and even some in the peer pressure group do not understand this third group. The first two groups think anyone who really wants to come is "weird." Yet this third group consists of those who are present at every youth activity or event. They are the core of your youth group.

There is a fourth group we must mention; however, they cannot be listed in the reasons young people come to Sunday school. These are the students whose names are on the roll, but who never come.

Your youth group resembles the amoeba—some students are inside the circle called the nucleus; others are just "around"; some are on the periphery and are as far away from the action as they can get; and some are outside the group. The wall of the amoeba has no definite form—it flows in and out. That is the same way with your youth group. We need to reach these four groups with the gospel of Jesus Christ.

EVALUATION

There must come a time in any program or structure that involves evaluation and adjustment. Honest evaluation can be not only revealing but also painful, especially if change is demanded. In many churches it is difficult to advocate or promote change. Any changes made should relate to the five purposes of Sunday school. Be flexible and open to possible changes that allow you to accomplish these purposes with less frustration and greater effectiveness. Enlist key students and adult lay people to assist you in evaluating your existing Sunday school program. Following are some basic areas that should be evaluated.

WHOM YOU ARE FEEDING—YOUR YOUTH GROUP

What are the group's strengths and weaknesses? What are the members' dominant attitudes? What are their needs?

WHO IS FEEDING THEM—YOUR ADULT LAY LEADERS

Do the adult leaders see their positions as jobs or as ministries? Why did they choose to work with students? Do your adult lay leaders really know one another? What is their attitude?

HOW YOU ARE FEEDING THEM—YOUR METHODOLOGY

Is your methodology accomplishing the five purposes? Is it exciting? What changes could be made to make it more effective? Be sure to listen to opinions of students and leaders.

WHAT YOU ARE FEEDING THEM—YOUR CURRICULUM

What should students know about the Bible by the time they graduate from high school? What should students be doing that reflects Christian attitudes?

LEADERSHIP

The quality of the Sunday school's ministry depends, to a great degree, on the selection of individual teachers. The church that takes seriously the obligation to provide the best possible leadership for its youth Sunday school is already on the road to effectiveness. Some churches select their leadership in an insensitive and inadequate manner. Others have selection committees that do the choosing. Still other churches believe that as long as they are fully staffed, everything else will take care of itself. Whatever system is used should result in a group of adult lay workers who have sensed a call to work with students:

- They understand youth and their culture.
- They desire to minister to students and their needs.
- They have hearts for God.
- They have teachable spirits.
- They function well on a team.

Before a person takes on leadership responsibility, he should weigh the matter carefully. "Not many of you should presume to be teachers, my brothers, because you know that we who teach will be judged more strictly" (James 3:1). That one thought should constantly be placed before adult leaders.

In looking for leaders for youth Sunday school, keep in mind these following three qualities.

GOAL ORIENTED

Do you want to follow someone who is going nowhere? Young people do not. They can spot, a mile away, someone who has direction, vision, goals, and purpose, and they are willing to follow such a leader. Goal-oriented youth workers:

- Know where they are going in their own lives and with the young people God has given them to lead.

- Are keenly motivated by an idea or cause, especially that of winning and discipling young people for Christ. They tend to have adventuresome spirits.
- Have dreams—instead of having nightmares about ministering to students. They look forward to being with students, and they communicate it.
- Hang in there when the going gets tough. One of the saddest facts about youth ministry is that so few workers stick it out.

PEOPLE ORIENTED

Would you want to be placed into the care of someone who really does not like people? Young people can sense whether or not youth workers really care about them and their personal lives. People-oriented youth workers:

- Genuinely care about young people (Phil. 2:20). Such youth workers are willing to find out what is happening in the student's world—by listening.
- Are sensitive to the needs of young people. Like Jesus, they hurt for people who are hurting (Matt. 9:36; 1 Thess. 2:8). They do not have to be told that a student is hurting.
- Spend time developing relationships with young people. These workers spend time beyond Sunday morning.
- Go where students are (school events, practice, concerts, games, etc.). Students are pleased that an adult leader is interested enough to act.
- Know where their young people are—spiritually, physically, mentally, and socially. They know their students' world and are responsive to it.

CHRIST ORIENTED

These workers are dedicated Christians, not just church attenders. They are people who can say with the psalmist: "My heart is steadfast, O God" (Psalm 108:1). They are people of commitment:

- to their own personal study of God's Word. They can say with Jeremiah, "When your words came, I ate them; they were my joy and my heart's delight" (Jer. 15:16).
- to a consistent, personal devotional life. Things happen when you pray, and often they happen within you.
- to keep a clear conscience (1 Tim. 1:5; Heb. 13:18).
- to their own families (Eph. 5:22-25). Young people are looking for a model of a Christ-centered home.
- to other youth workers.

Young people do not remember much of what we say, but they do remember *us*. They are crying out for examples who have their act together. The effective Sunday school depends on adult lay people, called of God to minister to students. Be selective; be sensitive. Be sure of those you ask to take on the ministry to students.'

SUNDAY SCHOOL STRUCTURES

I believe the following structure is the most effective for accomplishing the five basic purposes of Sunday school. Each department is set up in this pattern:

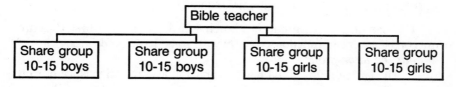

Fig. 28.1

The following is an outline of the time frame we use: 25 minutes—Bible teacher instructs in biblical truth; 5 minutes—transition; dismiss to share groups; 30 minutes—share group leader guides discussion and helps students apply material to their lives. Of course, this is a suggestion. You can adapt the times to meet your situation.

STAFF ROLES

Bible teacher. This person does not have a name list or group on which to follow up. His main responsibility is to be prepared on Sunday morning to make the Word of God come alive—to communicate the truths of Scripture with enthusiasm, clarity, and authority. The Bible teacher must have charisma, an infectious personality that inspires others. He must be a student of the Word and excited about communicating the assigned Scripture for each Sunday, using all the resources available to him to prepare and teach.

Share group leader. The share group leader has two basic responsibilities—to lead discussion and minister to the group apart from Sunday morning.

After the Bible teacher has presented the assigned Scripture, the large group is dismissed into share groups. Here the teaching technique changes from lecture to application of the Scripture to life situations. The purpose of this small group time is to encourage each student to participate. This is the opportunity to clarify any misunderstanding, reinforce any truths, and apply the principles. The adult leader becomes the facilitator, directing but not dominating the discussion.

The share group leader must spend time with his students apart from Sunday morning if they are to open up and share with the group. The teacher must know the students' world—what they do and what their interests are. The more an adult leader develops relationships with his students, the more likely they are to participate in the share group. The share group leader must be willing to minister to students and respond to them, regardless of their attendance patterns.

SETTING UP THE LARGE GROUP AND SMALL GROUPS

The size of a youth group or church will determine the best structure. Any combination can function properly with some basic guidelines.

For the large group.

1. The large group should have a minimum average attendance of thirty or more. This allows for an atmosphere of excitement and intensity. But good things can happen with a smaller number.

2. The group may be co-ed. The teaching of God's Word in this situation is universal.

3. Announcements can be made at this time, if needed. Announcement sheets concerning youth activities work well.

4. The Bible teacher *must not* exceed the allotted teaching time. He should get to the point and give the share groups something to discuss. When Bible teachers go overtime, the share group leaders lose important discussion time with their groups. It also can make the leaders expect to have less time and therefore become lackadaisical in their preparation.

For the share group.

1. Each share group should have no more than fifteen students on its roll. An adult may be able to teach more than fifteen students, but he will not be able to minister adequately to more than fifteen.

2. It is usually more effective to have separate male and female groups. If planned, there is nothing wrong with occasional co-ed share groups on Sunday mornings. But when a male leader is responsible for ministering to an all-boys group, or a woman to an all-girls group, there is more freedom to form close group relationships through activities (e.g., campouts, sleep-overs, special trips).

3. Share group leaders must know their students. A card filled out by each student, similar to figure 28.2, gives the leader ministry information. The important thing is what gets done with the information on the card. The share group leader must be wise and responsive. Students want to have their presence and accomplishments acknowledged.

4. Make the love of God central.

5. Make the application of Scripture primary, but do not do all the work for the students. Allow them to make specific applications.

6. Learn small-group dynamics by reading, for example, Navpress's *How to Lead Small Group Bible Studies*.[1]

7. Find the young people in your group with potential leadership ability. Spend time explaining what you are trying to do in the share group on Sunday and also during the week. Communicate your vision to them. Show them ways they can help you during discussion time and during the week. Key young people need to know their role and also their value in making the Sunday school ministry work.

8. Get to know the parents of your students as quickly as possible. Visit or call them when the young person is not there. Give them the opportunity to meet you and hear your intentions. Develop lines of communication with parents.

9. When talking or visiting with your students in the share group, do not refer to their attendance patterns. Plug into their lives. Be responsive to their world. Show them you care. Remember, the Holy Spirit brings conviction better than you do.

Fig. 28.2

NEW MEMBER INFORMATION CARD

The Sagemont Baptist Youth Ministry Is Glad You're Here!

Date: _____   School grade: _____   *You're*

Name: _____ Phone: _____ Birthday: _____   *important*
                                       Day/Month/Year   *to God*

Address: _____ City: _____ Zip _____   *and to me.*

School: _____ Parent or guardian: _____

Is parent a church member? _____ Where? _____

Are you a church member? _____ Where? _____

Brothers/Sisters? _____ Grade: _____

_____ Grade: _____   _____ Grade: _____

_____ Grade: _____   _____ Grade: _____

Do you work? _____ Where? _____

Clubs, hobbies, interests, etc.: _____

Are you a Christian?   Yes: _____   No: _____   Not sure: _____

Department: _____ Share Group Leader: _____

---

1. Navigators, *How to Lead Small Group Bible Studies* (Colorado Springs: Navpress, 1983).

CURRICULUM

EMPHASES

The Sunday school curriculum begins and ends with God's revelation to humanity as found in the Bible. This is a natural as well as a supernatural book, so both must be considered in teaching (1 Cor. 2:9–3:9). Humans wrote the Bible using the language of their day. Therefore, human teachers must communicate the Bible in the context of our time (Matt. 28:16-20; 2 Tim. 2:2). The Holy Spirit is active in the teaching process (John 14:26). Our part of the teaching-learning process can be enhanced by making the following emphases.

Christ centered. The basic curriculum of the early church was Christ. He is still the core of Christianity. Sunday school must present the historical truth of Jesus Christ—His life, ministry, miracles, death, resurrection, and ascension into heaven. But students must also be brought into personal experience with Christ; He must live in their lives by faith (Eph. 3:17).

Bible grounded. If you teach Christ apart from the authority of the Bible, you will probably drift into heresy or emotionalism. The objective basis of our faith is grounded in the Word of God. A Christian cannot grow in Christ without knowing the Bible; therefore, our Sunday school curriculum must include Bible facts and content.

Pupil related. The ministry of Christ was centered on individuals. He continually related to the needs of those around Him. The Bible lesson must begin with the needs of students and end meeting those needs. The Great Commission commands, "Teaching them to observe"—the student must practice the Bible.

CRITERIA FOR SELECTING CURRICULA

A great deal of informative study, prayerful consideration, and honest evaluation must go into the choosing of a Sunday school curriculum. The evaluation should include several sets of curricular materials within the church's theological emphases. Some denominations have their own publishing houses, but evaluate literature from an interdenominational or independent publisher for a complete understanding of what is available.

There must be criteria for deciding which materials should be used. Some materials may be theologically sound, yet not meet the personal needs of students. Another set may be geared for a specific denomination. Any literature worth using should be able to stand the test of careful scrutiny. Some guidelines for making the crucial decision are as follows.[2]

---

2. Elmer Towns, *How to Grow an Effective Sunday School* (Denver: Accent Books, 1979), p. 107-8.

Theological content. The evaluator is responsible to test the curriculum's doctrinal agreement with the church's doctrinal statement.

Lesson content.

- Do the lessons challenge dedication of life on the student's part?
- Is the content relevant?
- Does each lesson build upon previous lessons?
- Is each lesson biblically based?
- Does the content cause students to want to use their Bibles?
- Do the lessons include character building as well as Bible facts?

Appearance.

- Are materials attractive?
- Does the format appeal to students?
- Are pictures contemporary and colorful?
- Are materials durable?

Teacher helps.

- Does material give leaders tools for application?
- Does it give suggestions for the use and most effective variety of approaches for both large group and small group sessions?

Evangelistic.

- Will the planned lessons lead to decisions for Christ, spiritual growth, and Christian action?

Student helps.

- Is there provided adequate learning material such as student books, activity sheets, and take-home papers?
- Does the written work encourage active Bible study?
- Does the material encourage and stimulate discussion?
- Are illustrations authentic and pertinent?
- Are student materials readable and interesting?
- Are student materials worth keeping after the study is over?

Evaluations of Sunday school curricula may reveal that no one curriculum provides all the desirable features. Try to choose one that gives the best balance of Bible content, learning activities, and application of truths to life. Do not be willing to accept a substandard curriculum for your students.

YOUTH LEADERSHIP FAMILY

The effectiveness of your youth Sunday school in its attempt to accomplish the five basic purposes will be greatly dependent on the team of lay workers. For this team to function properly, there must be a regular, consistent time and place in which these leaders come together.

Youth Leadership Family is a good name for this group of lay workers because it *is* the "youth leadership," and you want them to become like a family. Your leaders need to come together for planning, evaluating, sharing, learning, and equipping.

The time, place, and day of the week are not as important as *agreeing* on them. Many churches find different workable combinations, realizing that it is not important *when* you meet, only *that* you meet. Your leaders must not see this as just another meeting; they must see it as imperative for the team to function properly. Here are some guidelines for an effective and worthwhile youth leadership family.

One hundred percent attendance. The lay leaders must be committed to being at meetings. When they are absent, they have let the other youth workers down. That is why it is important to choose a time, place, and day that does not have built-in obstacles. Let the group members decide when and where to meet. When it is their decision (in unity), the chances of having 100 percent attendance increase.

Announcements. This is a good time to make any important announcements to your leaders concerning items of interest. Keep your leaders informed. Give them an opportunity to ask questions. This will keep the machinery oiled.

Honest evaluation. We must be willing to evaluate our effectiveness. This is a good opportunity to review the preceding Sunday with one another. Bible teachers need to hear comments from share group leaders regarding the teaching time. Share group leaders need to express frustration or success with the discussion time. We need to hear from one another in order to provide mutual encouragement and accountability.

Planning. After evaluating the previous week, look ahead to next Sunday. The Bible teacher can announce the emphasis or direction he will take with the assigned Scripture. Share group leaders can contribute ideas and techniques they are going to use. Many heads are better than one.

Ministry report. Each group leader needs time to report any pertinent student information to the other leaders. All adults in a department need to be informed of events and situations involving their students. This is also a good time to mention names of new students. The other adults may have some insight or knowledge of that individual or family that would enable the share group leader to make a positive follow-up visit.

Share time. This is a special time in which the youth leadership family begins to bear one another's burdens. Relationships are built and strengthened when people become transparent and caring. "All men will know that you are my disciples if you love one another" (John 13:35). If a leader cannot confide in fellow leaders, he will probably not be able to facilitate sharing on Sunday morning.

Prayer. This is not just a "word" of closing prayer to end your meeting but an opportunity to pray specifically concerning all that has been discussed: evaluations, plans, students, prospects, workers, and so forth. "Do not be anxious about anything, but in everything, by prayer and petition, with thanksgiving, present your requests to God" (Phil. 4:6). "The prayer of a righteous man is powerful and effective" (James 5:16).

Nothing can be accomplished apart from prayer. You can change your concept, literature, and workers, but without prayer it is the work of man (flesh). Why do we do the most important things the least often?

Youth Leadership Family is the oil that keeps the machinery running. It is imperative that all the adults that staff your youth Sunday school be a part of the leadership family. A Sunday school program without the consistent coming together of its staff is fragmented, disjointed, and ineffective.

CONCLUSION

Remember the five purposes of the Sunday school:

- Teaching biblical revelation
- Interaction for application
- Relationship building
- Creating an environment
- Outreach to non-Christians

God has promised to bless His Word. Sunday school, therefore, has a bright future when its programs and methods are based on Scripture. But when innovative ideas are not biblical, or old ideas are not relevant to the times, Sunday schools have declined in attendance.

We can turn Sunday morning around. If a church wants its Sunday school to be worth attending, it must teach the Scriptures and apply them to life situations. Take an honest look at the existing program, and change, if necessary. No program in the church is set up to teach the Bible, minister to people, and reach students for Christ as is the Sunday school. Do not shortchange its potential. Breathe fresh life into it. Make Sunday school exciting!

For Further Reading

Beechick, Ruth. *A Biblical Psychology of Learning.* Denver: Accent Books, 1982.

Coleman, Jr., Lucien E. *How to Teach the Bible.* Nashville: Broadman, 1979.

———. *Why the Church Must Teach.* Nashville: Broadman, 1984.

Delnay, Robert G. *Teach as He Taught.* Chicago: Moody, 1987.

Ford, LeRoy. *A Sourcebook of Learning Activities.* Nashville: Broadman, 1984.

Grassi, Joseph A. *Jesus as Teacher.* Winona, Minn.: St. Mary's College Press, 1978.

Highet, Gilbert. *The Immortal Profession: The Joys of Teaching and Learning.* New York: Weybright and Talley, 1976.

Johnson, Kent L. *Paul the Teacher.* Minneapolis: Augsburg, 1986.

Reed, Ed, and Bobbie Reed. *Creative Bible Learning for Youth Grades 7-12.* Ventura, Calif.: Regal, 1977.

Shafer, Carl. *Excellence in Teaching with the Seven Laws.* Grand Rapids: Baker, 1985.

Westing, Harold J. *Evaluate and Grow.* Rev. ed. Wheaton, Ill.: Victor, 1984.

Willis, Wesley R. *Make Your Teaching Count.* Wheaton, Ill.: Victor, 1985.

29

Denny Rydberg

Dynamics of Small Group Bible Studies

Terry Winters is a youth worker—a rookie worker. This is his first church as a paid staff member. He did graduate from a Christian college where in his senior year he served as a volunteer intern with the youth director at a local church. And one year he served as a camp counselor. And in high school he attended Young Life some. But that was different. Now he's responsible.

Now he's on his own at Westfield Community Church—a growing church in a suburban area. Three high schools nearby. Five junior highs. Terry is *the* youth director. He's in charge.

And he's a bit nervous, somewhat anxious. He's not immobilized, just concerned. He wants to do a good job. He feels responsible for the kids in the church and the surrounding area. He knows that the ministry belongs to the Lord, but he also knows he's paid by the church to be a good shepherd, and he wants to do what's right. He wants to disciple young people and help equip them for the long road ahead.

Members of the youth committee at Westfield Community Church are supportive. They want to do all in their power to make Terry's first year a success. But the committee members are not very experienced in youth work either. That is why they hired a full-time youth director.

DENNY RYDBERG, B.A., is director of university ministries, University Presbyterian Church, Seattle, Washington.

The senior pastor, Ralph Tomasin, is supportive, and he has had experience in youth work. But his role as a youth worker ended fifteen years before, and he feels a bit out of touch with recent trends in youth ministry and in his understanding of the youth culture today. And besides, Pastor Tomasin is extremely busy. That is one of the reasons he was so excited when Terry was hired. He wants someone to share the load, not add to it.

Terry would like to begin small group Bible studies in the junior high and senior high groups at Westfield. He was in a small Bible study group in college that encouraged him a great deal. He got to know four other guys very well and enjoyed studying Scripture with them and praying with them. But that was college. And they were all upperclassmen—fairly responsible, mature people.

Terry is leery about starting small group studies with high school and junior high kids. He knows how beneficial small groups have been for him, but he does not understand their dynamics and, consequently, does not know whether they will be effective in his new situation. He has no idea what to use for content. Terry believes he is a good small group leader, but he does not know how well the groups would do in which he was not directly involved. He knows he could lecture adequately to the entire youth group, but he doubts the effectiveness of that teaching/learning style over the long run.

These concerns are not minor to Terry because he wants to minister creatively and effectively. Small groups seem like a gamble that could self-destruct. Deep in his heart, Terry would like someone to guarantee that they would "win." And he does not need answers to his questions just for himself. He also needs them to reassure Pastor Tomasin, the youth committee, and the parents of the youth. None of them has ever done small groups with youth either.

CAN SMALL-GROUP BIBLE STUDIES WORK WITH JUNIOR AND SENIOR HIGH STUDENTS?

The answer is an enthusiastic yes. Parachurch groups and church groups representing a wide variety of denominations from many different geographic areas have used small groups with success. Urban and suburban, homogeneous and heterogeneous youth groups have gathered together and been helped by interacting with the Word in small groups. Almost every major publishing house involved with youth materials has incorporated small group strategies into its curricula, and one publisher, Serendipity House, has devoted its well-received Serendipity Youth Series entirely to small-group Bible study and discussion groups. Young Life has for years used small groups (called Campaigners) in its discipleship, and other church and parachurch organizations have done the same. Small groups are not new to junior and senior high ministry. They can work.

What Can I Tell My Youth Committee Will Happen in Small Groups?

The answer, of course, is that anything can happen in small groups. Students can become distracted and talk about the current issues of school and forget the Bible altogether. Or they can interact with the Word and really get something out of it. They can emerge from a small group more committed to one another, more in prayer for one another, more in love with the Lord and His Book. In other words, small groups can be a winner or a loser depending on the structure and direction. But there is a more significant question than, What works?

Are Small Groups Essential?

Small groups are very necessary. They are beneficial in growing disciples—young people who are committed to Jesus Christ and are willing to be identified with Him, young people who are maturing in their faith and serving Christ faithfully.

The groups are beneficial in many ways. First, the size of the group provides the opportunity for a student to be known and loved. In a small group, a person can no longer hide. In a *good* small group, that student will be accepted. In that group, members will be able to communicate honestly enough with each other that they will be able to fulfill the New Testament command to "bear one another's burdens and so fulfill the law of Christ." In a small group, members will begin to pray for one another specifically because they know one another well. They will begin to recognize and call forth one another's gifts. In a small group, members will be able to ask "dumb" questions without having to feel foolish in front of the larger group. *Small groups are not only workable; they are essential.*

What Could Go Wrong with Small Groups?

Almost everything *could* go wrong in small groups. Just because they can work does not mean they always will. For instance, small groups can become cliques if left alone for too long. If the group is immature and the leadership is weak, small groups can be a waste of time. If the small-group leader is insensitive, sensitive kids can be hurt. If the youth director is not well grounded in doctrine, once in a while even a heresy can develop. But the good generally outweighs the bad.

What Kind of Leadership Do I Need for the Groups to Be Effective?

We need trained leadership in order to have effective small groups. Tim Dearborn, a former associate of mine, describes the perfect missionary to Haiti as a person who loves Christ and loves Haitians. This definition can be adapted to describe the perfect small-group leader as one who loves Christ and loves kids and knows a little bit about small-group dynamics.

The age of such leaders depends on the maturity level of the group and how open they are to peer leadership. It also depends on how much time the youth leader is going to spend with the small-group leaders.

What Leadership Style Should I Use?

There are basically three leadership styles with small groups. The first is the *mentor approach*. Here, an older, wiser leader facilitates the group. The second model is the *facilitator.* This is a leader who really does not control the group at all. Instead, he or she guides the group and facilitates interaction. The third model is called *rotation leadership.* Here the leadership is passed around each week. Usually rotation does not work very well with younger groups. Not everyone is skilled or confident enough to do that. But the facilitator role can work where, for instance, a more mature high school senior can lead a high school small Bible study group or a junior high one.

So, Terry Winters needs to decide on the leadership style he wants. His decision might be based on availability. A new youth director often does not know what people resources he or she has available. Until Terry knows, he may have to use small groups sparingly or draw upon his older students for leadership.

How Do I Train Small Group Leaders?

In training small group leaders, the trainer probably should begin by reviewing some of the points in this chapter. Then he or she needs to meet with the leaders regularly. A good time is just before the general meeting where small groups will take place. For example, if the small groups meet on Wednesday night at 7:30, it might be good for the leaders to bring a sack dinner and come at 6:00 or 6:30. At this regular meeting, leaders would discuss the study content for the groups, talk about what is happening within the groups, what needs the leaders themselves have, and so forth. Leaders can pool their ideas and experiences and help one another. They can also pray for each other and the members of the individual small groups.

The leaders also need to be reminded of four important principles in small group Bible study leadership. *First, the leader must be a listener.* An intent listener. The leader must give the person speaking his or her undivided attention, "warmest eyes," and most open ears. The leader also must be a loving and accepting listener. Every person has worth, and every idea from that person has worth. Every idea might not be right, but it carries weight and deserves to be heard.

Second, the leader leads through openness. Whenever a leader has a personal question he or she wants to ask of the group, the leader should proceed with that question. Going first does two things. It demonstrates leadership openness and sets the stage for how open group members will be. It also allows members of the group to think about an answer before feeling compelled to speak.

Third, a leader is prepared. If the group leader wants the group to study Philippians 1, he or she must study it in advance.

Finally, the leader must be committed to the members of his or her group and also to the whole youth group leadership team, including, of course, a loyalty (in this example) to Terry Winters as the youth director. John Mott, a former missionary statesman, said he valued the characteristic of loyalty most on a ministry team. Mott's perspective should be valued by every small-group leadership team as well.

WHAT IS THE PURPOSE FOR THIS SMALL-GROUP BIBLE STUDY PROGRAM?

Does the small group exist to help members get better acquainted with the Word and to check in briefly with one another? Or is Terry trying to put together more intensive discipleship groups that will develop a high commitment mentality—a high commitment to group members, a high commitment to the Word, a high commitment to ministry, and so forth? That purpose should be clearly in Terry's mind because it will determine the make-up of the individual groups, the commitment required of them, and even the length of time each group will be together.

For instance, if Terry is looking for an all-out discipleship group where members create a covenant of accountability, Terry's small-group program would not involve many people, because not a large number of students at Westfield would probably be ready for that kind of commitment. If he did go with that kind of group, it would probably meet weekly for several hours, maybe monthly for a mission project, and would be involved together for the whole year.

On the other hand, Terry's purpose might be to give the kids in his church an experience in which they could ask questions about the Word without being intimidated by the larger group, in which they could begin to know five or six other people better, and maybe sometime in the course of the group's experience they would even begin to pray for one another. If those were the objectives, the commitment and time levels would not be so high. Terry might have groups together for eight weeks dealing with a smaller book or a topic or a character from Scripture. So purpose is important, and Terry needs to define what that is.

After working through the purpose question, Terry is ready to move back to the nuts and bolts of small-group dynamics.

WHAT IS THE OPTIMUM SIZE FOR SMALL GROUPS?

There are minimum sizes as well as maximum sizes for small groups. There is a certain "critical mass" for a small group to be effective. That minimum size is four. When a group has fewer than four people, discomfort can set in. Shy people feel more forced to speak than normal. The pressure is on. The maximum size is eight. Above eight the group begins to have a "too large" feel. So, with the four to eight configuration, what specifically must be done when it comes to setting up a small group? The best answer is: "Think in terms of eight-person groups plus a leader." On any given day, one member of the small Bible study group will be gone. If more are absent, you will not move below your critical mass number. If everyone shows up, you are very close to eight. In setting up a small group, the leader should think not only of committed, core kids who always come, but also of those who "float" in and out.

WHAT IS THE OPTIMUM MIX FOR A SMALL GROUP?

We are prompted to ask the following kinds of questions when considering a group's proper mix. Do you mix girls with guys? Upper classmen with underclassmen? How about junior high students with senior high ones? And, if you do a guy-girl mix, what about couples who are dating? Should they be in the same small group? The answers to these questions are "it varies, sometimes, sometimes, seldom, sometimes." To elaborate: the optimum mix depends on what the purpose is for the small group. And it also depends on the length of time the leader wants the groups together. Obviously, the dynamics of a small group Bible study change somewhat when the mix moves from a same-sex grouping to a co-ed one. Most youth workers would like girls and guys to be able to profit together from being in the same group—to enjoy the friendship and camaraderie of a co-ed group, to hear the different perspectives of men and women. But there are drawbacks to co-ed groups. One is that shy males and shy females have a more difficult time expressing their thoughts in a co-ed group. Underclassmen have even more of a difficult time doing so when there is an upperclassman of the opposite sex in the group. Those difficulties exist until the barriers are broken down, with some difficulty.

So what is the answer to Terry's multiple question about the optimum mix? *The general principle is that variety is good for a youth group.* Small Bible study groups should change throughout the year to allow students to interact with more students than they would meet in one small group. An eight-to-ten week period seems to be a long enough time to accomplish this in a group before changing the mix. (Unless, of course, the goal is an intensive discipleship group with high demands. Then the group would probably exist together for the whole year. See discussion above.) During the year, the leader should strive for variety. During some ten-week periods, the grouping would be same-sex. In other periods, co-ed groups could be the norm. However, with sensitive topics and with junior high students in particular, the more sensitive the topic, the more a same-sex grouping the youth director should have.

When students are dating each other, another dynamic exists. If a student is fairly mature, being in a small group with the person he or she is dating does not detract from the group. But if difficulties arise in the relationship that the couple are afraid to address, tension arises, and the small group suffers. If the couple dating is immature and in the "only us" stage of a relationship and constantly clinging to one another, they will not be very effective as small-group members. The best way to control these dynamics is to establish the above-mentioned eight-to-ten week pattern and rotate people in the groups, including those who are dating. Sometimes couples would be together. Sometimes they would not.

WHAT SHOULD BE THE GROUP GUIDELINES?

As mentioned before, the level of commitment relates to the purpose of the group. In the beginning, the rules should be simple and probably not even written for the average high school or junior high small group. The leader can state them before the groups begin meeting and then occasionally mention them in the weeks that follow. For instance, the leader might say, "We've got a few guidelines we want to follow in our small groups. Only one person speaks at a time. Everyone gives the person speaking his undivided attention. This means looking at the person speaking as well as listening to that person. All comments are given equal worth, including those of the leader. We are all co-learners. We are all in this together. Those are the guidelines. Now let's have a great time in small-group Bible study together."

Later, some of those rules might be written down and even signed by the students. Again, the commitment level is less for a group that meets eight weeks and then disperses than it is for the more intense discipleship Bible study group. For the eight-week group, the covenant will probably cover the following points: (1) to attend the small-group meeting except in unusual cases; (2) to listen intently to the person speaking; (3) to respect everyone's comment (no put-downs, ridicule, etc.). If people are going to check in weekly and share some of their life, a fourth commitment would be included: (4) to keep whatever's been said in confidence—no repeating outside the group what has been said.

With a more committed group, rules would include: (1) to attend every group function except in extreme cases and, if such a case should arise, to call another member and explain (this commitment underlines the importance of each member to the group); (2) to prepare in advance for the study; (3) to listen intently to each person speaking and to respect everyone's comment; (4) to pray daily for each member of the group; (5) to maintain confidentiality; (6) to encourage each person weekly in some way as he or she seeks to know the Lord better and seeks to obey and serve Him. Other covenants could be established depending on what a leader wanted to accomplish with his or her group.

WHEN SHOULD A SMALL GROUP MEET?
HOW DOES IT FIT INTO THE TOTAL YOUTH PROGRAM?

There are several models of how you can fit small groups into your total program. My favorite one is the "midweek expanded model," which I believe is close to the optimum. The entire youth group gathers on a midweek night and begins the meeting with dinner. Dinner can be prepared by a parent or a young person, and all attending can pay a couple of dollars to help defray expenses. When dinner is over, the total group enjoys some crowd-breakers, singing, and the like. Then the large group breaks into individual small groups for interaction and Bible study. After about thirty to forty-five minutes of checking in with one another and studying the Word, the small groups return to one large group for prayer, a couple of praise songs, and a quick wrap-up.

In this model, the small group Bible study would begin with a quick time of commenting by group members on how their week had gone. For example, When did you feel the most lonely this week? The most joyful? The most misunderstood? What was the high point of your week? Why? What was the kindest act anyone did for you this week? Why did it make you feel good?

The point of these kinds of questions is to help group members learn a little bit about each person's life away from the group—so that members can more intelligently and energetically pray for one another. These questions break the ice without intimidating the members.

Another model, which is less effective than the midweek expanded model, is the "Sunday morning church school model." It obviously involves less time. The group meets as a whole for a few announcements and/or worship. The leader can set up the study with a few words, and then the total group breaks up into small groups for forty-five minutes of study.

Another effective model is one in which small groups meet on their own at homes or near their campuses before or after school. Let's call this the "home group model." In an area similar to Terry Winters's where students from several high schools are involved, the home group model has good possibilities. Each of Terry's three high school campuses could have groups meeting nearby. Terry could lead some of these, or other volunteer leaders could. In home groups, it is advisable to have an adult meeting with the groups rather than having strictly peer leadership.

HOW SHOULD THE BIBLE CONTENT BE STRUCTURED?
WHAT SUBJECTS ARE MOST CONDUCIVE FOR SMALL GROUPS?

Probably the most helpful kinds of Bible studies for youth are Bible stories. People learn from stories—stories about each other, stories from the Word. That category would include stories of Jesus and the disciples from the gospels, parables, stories from Acts, and many of the stories from the Old

Testament. Even though young people have heard some of these stories before, they have probably never really dissected and discussed them as they will in their small groups. Topical studies are also helpful, such as temptation, friendship, leadership, love, forgiveness, and the like.

If the content involves stories or specific passages, the leadership team selects which story or passage the small groups study. Study questions would be written to help facilitate group discussion. With topical studies, the leadership team (or the youth director himself) would have to develop both the questions and the combination of passages to study on that topic. In selecting scriptural references, stories about that theme and characters who faced that topic should be included. For example, on the topic of forgiveness, the group should probably look at David's experience with forgiveness after the Bathsheba incident; Peter's experience of forgiveness after the denial; and Paul's experience after persecuting so many believers.

How Do You Write Questions That Cover the Material and Still Interest Youth?

The key for writing good questions is to think in terms of "flow questions," ones that naturally develop. Think of questions at three levels. The first level is composed of nonthreatening, easy-to-answer questions that bridge the gap between the text and the lives of the group members. These are the "open questions." The next level of questions is used to discover what the text has to say and to help us think more deeply about those answers. This level could be called "dig questions." The deepest level is level three, where questions are designed to help students reflect on what they have learned and apply it to their lives. "Reflect questions" are at this level. For example, if Terry's group was studying the familiar passage of Scripture, Acts 9:1-19, in which Saul is confronted by the Lord on the Damascus road, Terry might write some questions like the following examples.

Open: If you knew you were losing your sight tomorrow, what would you want to see today? What does this tell you about yourself? Everyone can take a stab at that question. It opens up the group, breaks the ice. You do not have to be a Bible scholar to answer it.

Dig: In verses 1-2, do you think Saul is sincere in his beliefs? What do you think motivates him? How deep would you say is his love for God? Why do you think God would want to reach a man like Saul? To use a man like Saul? How might his past be helpful in God's plans to spread the gospel? Why do you think God used such dramatic means to get Saul's attention? What is significant about the three days of blindness for Saul? How hard would it have been for Ananias here?

Reflect: Where has been the Damascus road in your life—the place where God first got your attention? How does Jesus usually get your attention now?

Where is your Straight Street—the place where it's tough to obey the Lord? What makes this place so difficult? Who has been an Ananias in your life? What did that person do for you? To whom have you been an Ananias? How? What are you motivated to do because of what you've read in this passage?

If Terry did not want to write his own flow questions, he could add to his resource library the *Serendipity Bible Study Book* published by Zondervan and Serendipity House. The book contains the New Testament text in the NIV edition as well as introductions to every New Testament book and flow questions for every section of the New Testament. The point is that with the resources available and with personal creativity, content will not be a problem.

IN CONCLUSION

Terry Winters has some of his answers now. He is still a bit apprehensive, but he has confidence—confidence in his Lord and confidence that small Bible study groups are essential and can work. He is ready to recruit some leaders, train them, and help the youth in their discipleship process through the use of small Bible study groups.

FOR FURTHER READING

Barker, Steve et al. *Good Things Come in Small Groups.* Downers Grove, Ill.: InterVarsity, 1985.

Brilhart, John K. *Effective Group Discussion.* 4th ed. Dubuque, Ia.: Wm. C. Brown, 1982.

Duck, Lloyd. *Teaching with Charisma.* Boston: Allyn and Bacon, 1981.

Griffin, Em. *Getting Together: A Guide for Good Groups.* Downers Grove, Ill.: InterVarsity, 1982.

Hesteves, Roberta. *Using the Bible in Groups.* Philadelphia: Westminster, 1983.

Hyman, Ronald T. *Ways of Teaching.* 2d ed. Philadelphia: J. B. Lippincott, 1974.

Navigators. *How to Lead Small Group Bible Studies.* Colorado Springs, Colo.: NavPress, 1982.

Peace, Richard. *Small Group Evangelism.* Downers Grove, Ill.: InterVarsity, 1985.

Stewart, Ed, and Nina Fishwick, *GroupTalk!* Ventura, Calif.: Regal, 1986.

Zuck, Roy B. *The Holy Spirit in Your Teaching.* Rev. ed. Wheaton, Ill.: Victor, 1984.

30

David Busby

New Christians—
Delight or Dilemma?

In the past fifteen years of ministry with junior high, high school, and college students, I have been increasingly aware of a serious problem concerning working with new Christians. It is a problem that has taken a number of years to admit and has become a very embarrassing question, especially to those who gauge the success of their ministry on baptisms. "Where are those young men and women who were baptized six months ago?" is a very significant question for the youth worker whose focus is to see kids' lives changed into the image of Jesus Christ.

It is not only our goal to introduce students to faith in Jesus Christ, but also to help them grow to be stable, mature, reproducing Christians. We must face the problem of attrition among new babes in Christ. Where are they six months after they have made their profession of faith? Is our focus really to see that a student prays a prayer, or is it to see his life change into the image of Jesus Christ? A man once said that a problem well-defined is a problem half solved, and I agree. What is at the root of the problem? Why are so many new Christians not pressing on to maturity?

David Busby, M. Div., is minister to youth, Grace Church, Edina, Minnesota.

FALSE ASSUMPTIONS

Part of the difficulty is that we youth workers may have made some wrong assumptions. One is that *follow-up is primarily informational.* For some reason we believe that if we present the right content the student will be able to make the transition from a secular to a spiritual mind-set. In recent years I have discovered that this is the wrong approach; the follow-up of a new babe in Christ is not primarily informational but *relational.* The first 168 hours of that new Christian's life are critical.

It seems as if from the second of new birth we race against the clock to see how much information we can pour into new baby "Joe." "Have you read the gospel of John yet?" "How about prayer?" "Have you established a quiet time yet?" "Who were the twelve disciples?" Just as a new infant must have pats, hugs, and soothing words, the new Christian must be encouraged relationally. Coming from darkness into light can be staggering and overwhelming initially. It is at this time that Satan and the powers of darkness would most enjoy erecting barriers to prevent the new Christian's stability and maturity in Christ. So wrong assumption number one is that follow-up is mainly informational rather than relational.

The second wrong assumption is that *follow-up is real-need centered, not felt-need centered.* So many times our first conversation with a new Christian goes something like this. "Joe, if you want to make it as a new Christian it's critical that you memorize Scripture, have a regular quiet time, witness to your friends, and hang around with other Christians who have the same values as you do. Remember now, Joe, if you don't do that, you won't make it in your Christian life."

I am not saying that those disciplines and basics are not essential for someone who wants to mature in his walk with Jesus Christ. They are, and they must be applied if that babe is to be well-grounded in his faith. But many times the real-need issues can only be addressed and dealt with in the new Christian's life as we are willing to address the pressing felt-needs in his life. I will explain further the importance of meeting felt-needs versus real-needs later in this chapter.

The third wrong assumption is that *spiritual failure is the new Christian's fault.* Apparently, his decision was insincere, or he just was not willing to pay the price of following Jesus Christ. I have found that the attrition rate within the new Christian community is not always the fault of the new Christian, but rather it is often the fault of the youth worker who is not prayerfully equipped to help this babe grow into maturity. Of course, the responsibility is shared between the new Christian and the follow-up leader. Even the best-equipped worker cannot penetrate a heart set against growth. Even so, it is a two-way responsibility, and therein lies the necessity of finding God's solution to this whole problem.

Toward a Solution

THE LORDSHIP OF CHRIST

I have found four basic solutions to help with the problem of dropouts among new believers. Solution number one in creating a growth environment is to make *sure* that the babe in Christ has understood and personally appropriated the biblical gospel. Many people who profess to be new believers in Christ are not believers at all. So the very first step in this transition process is to explain salvation clearly, making sure that the person has an understanding of what it means to be committed to the Lord Jesus Christ. The basic error of the "easy believism" gospel that flourishes in the student community today is a gross misconception of what it means to repent. Repentance was one of the first topics that Jesus, John the Baptist, and Peter presented in their ministries. Jesus stated it this way, "Repent or perish." John the Baptist said, "Repent, for the kingdom of God is at hand." Peter proclaimed, "Repent and be baptized." We must not leave repentance out of the gospel, or we have no gospel at all. It is imperative in the presentation of salvation to a potential believer that we explain what repentance means—to change one's mind about who will be the lord of his life. An exchange of gods is critical for that new relationship in Jesus Christ. Without lordship there is no relationship.

The rich young ruler account (Mark 10:17-31) is a critical theological discussion in terms of youth ministry. Youth workers need to understand it clearly. As I have reviewed that passage, I believe that the rich young ruler could be president of most of our youth ministries. He had always honored his mom and dad, the Scripture says. Yet Jesus let him walk away because he was not willing to exchange the god of his life (riches) for the God of the universe (Jesus Christ). So the first solution in helping new Christians grow is to take the time to make sure they have a clear, biblical understanding of repentance and the lordship of Jesus Christ.

EXISTENTIAL NEEDS

The second solution in reducing the attrition rate for new babes is to meet the new Christian right where he is. Many times a new Christian cannot move into a position to grow because of the immediate barrier he faces (for example, his present peer group or non-Christian parents who forbid him to come to church). If the felt-needs are not initially addressed and resolved, his future growth is hindered.

To amplify further—it is vital for a new Christian to develop a quality quiet time in order to grow in Christ, his new-found friend, confidant, and Lord. Let's say his parents are in the midst of a bitter divorce, however. His home atmosphere is shredded and unstable. His felt-need is to find a workable answer for how to live in the home and survive without himself becoming a victim of bitterness, anger, and hate—*now.* Yes, the real need of developing a quiet time along with a thousand other content-needs is there. But do not lose the felt-need; address it, calm the storm, quiet the fears, before attempting giant strides in the real-need area.

I surveyed our "spiritual nursery" to find out what felt-needs existed and compared them to our follow-up format. The lists were very different. The new Christians had a list of felt-needs. We had a list of real-needs. I was so preoccupied with the real-needs that the felt-needs caused the young Christians to become disheartened. They were not interested in seeing the real-needs met until their felt-needs were satisfied.

In order to identify and harness those felt-needs, take a transitional survey of your new Christians (those who have come to Christ in the last six months), and ask them four or five questions that will help to surface the *first* felt-needs they encounter. A survey could be composed of these five questions:

1. How long have you been a Christian?
2. What problems or areas of discomfort have you had?
3. Which people were the most difficult to tell of your decision?
4. What areas of the Christian life seem to be the most confusing to you as a new Christian?
5. What things or people help you to resolve some of these difficulties?

After you survey your new Christian group, design material that will focus on some of the tough issues new Christians face during their transition into their new faith and the church. It is imperative to get answers to those first, almost frightening, questions to help settle their minds about Christianity—What have I done, anyway? Will I lose my friends? Later, after their fears are calmed, come questions about prayer, quiet time, doctrine, Bible study, and discipleship. But if we do not meet those pressing felt-needs, the new Christians will not wait around until week number seventeen of our follow-up program when we finally begin to deal with issues such as, "How do I respond when my friends react negatively to my new faith in Christ?" It is critical that we first meet that young Christian where he is and then help him move to where he needs to be.

RELATIONSHIPS

Solution number three concerning the new-Christian dilemma is that we *must* focus on relationships. Initially we must view the new Christian's primary need more from a social rather than a spiritual transition. Keep in mind his dilemma is that he is coming into a group of people with a Christian mind-set who have totally different values and perspectives. He is also leaving a peer group—intimate relationships that reflect the secular world view. For all practical purposes he is a man without a country. If we do not address his pressing social needs immediately, we will not have to concern ourselves with addressing the informational needs. He will not stay around long enough for that.

Because the relational need is primary, the follow-up worker needs to include the new Christian in as much of his life as possible for those first weeks. Regular contact via phone, asking the young Christian to sit with him at church, contacts after school (and the list goes on) are absolutely critical.

FORMULATING THEIR OWN SOLUTIONS

The fourth solution is to understand how to challenge the new Christian to solve felt-needs. Many times we attempt to challenge people by offering a drink of water when they are not thirsty. We present solutions to people without needs. We try to hold them accountable for things to which they have not committed their inner hearts. Instead, we need to be a partner with the Holy Spirit in creating a thirst within that new Christian to see felt-needs met.

One of the ways to do that is to make a list of several of the most common felt-need issues the typical Christian faces. Ask the new Christian to identify his most pressing need. Next, say something like, "John, would you be interested in meeting together to talk about this particular need you feel so strongly in your life right now?" If he says, "Yes, I would be interested in having you help me meet this need," then we have a commitment. This is the point where I have penetrated his willingness so that I can hold him accountable to meet with me. When he feels ownership, his motivation level has increased.

SUMMARY

We have discussed the attrition problem, talked about the dilemma facing new Christians, and tried to face the embarrassing question, "Where are they?" Be sure to present a clear, biblical gospel. Meet the felt-needs that deter growth for new believers. Focus on their relational needs during those critical early days of the journey with Jesus. Know how to challenge the new Christian to see those needs met. Then following up new Christians can be a delight as we observe them pressing on to maturity (Phil. 3:13-14).

SECOND-GENERATION CHRISTIANS—HOT-HEARTED OR HEADACHES?

The other category of people on which this chapter focuses is the second-generation Christian. I am defining this person as one who has grown up in a Christian home, sometimes has gone to a Christian school, and has lived in a Christian atmosphere. As I speak in Christian schools and look at kids in our own youth group, I become very troubled as I view the "typical" church kid. Here is what I generally observe: (1) no passion and warmth for God; (2) the "right" vocabulary and many Christian clichés, but little reality; (3) an incredible knowledge level but a very low application level; (4) and a boring, apathetic perspective of the Christian experience with few real convictions. These are just a few descriptive adjectives of the typical church kid. The more I see the kind of student that our youth groups are developing, the more I fear that we are truly missing the whole point of youth ministry.

How do we actually know if a student ministry is successful? One of the criteria of a quality ministry is the *kind* of student that ministry produces. Of course, students make their own choices. At best, all we can do is create an environment for life change. At the same time, however, I am deeply troubled at what many student ministries are producing as an end result. What is one of the key reasons second-generation Christians are so bored and apathetic? Why do their convictions change with the weather?

INCREASE IN KNOWLEDGE, DECREASE IN OBEDIENCE

I have spent many hours thinking and praying through the second-generation issue and have found that hard-heartedness exists because there is often an increase in knowledge but a decrease in obedience. These young men and women have heard the Spirit's call for obedience through the Scriptures, Bible classes, retreats, and camps, yet they have resisted it. Hebrews 4:7*b* says this, "Today, if you hear His voice, do not harden your hearts." When we hear the voice of the Spirit through the Scripture, through spiritual leaders, through other Christians, through the events and circumstances of our lives, and we do not obey His voice, our heart cools a few degrees and becomes insensitive. The deceptive thing about the second-generation Christian is that he does not *immediately* sense this hardening effect taking place. But after numerous decisions have been made to disobey, a callousness forms in the mind, will, and heart. It becomes very difficult for that young person to hear the voice of God, much less obey it. In many Christian circles our knowledge level is at its peak, resulting in pride and "puffed-upness"—but the application level is at its all-time low.

A nonpersonalized and theoretical faith is another reason for spiritual callousness. It is Mom's faith, it is the youth worker's faith, it is their Christian peers' faith, but it is really not their own. Two particular passages of Scripture illustrate this point. One is in Hebrews 11:23: "By faith Moses' parents hid him for three months after he was born, because they saw he was no ordinary child, and they were not afraid of the king's edict." The faith that is targeted here obviously was not Moses' faith as a child, but his parents' faith. But notice the transition in verse 24. "By faith Moses, when he had grown up, refused to be known as the son of Pharaoh's daughter. He chose to be mistreated along with the people of God rather than to enjoy the pleasures of sin for a short time." The passage goes on describing specific choices *he* made, based upon his *personalized* faith. Students often try to live on Mom's or Dad's faith without making it their own.

Another passage is Acts 19:13. Some of the Jewish exorcists were trying to cast out evil spirits in the name of the Lord Jesus, saying, "In the name of Jesus, whom Paul preaches, I command you to come out." In verse 15 the evil spirit answers those men and says to them, "Jesus I know and Paul I know about, but who are you?" These men tried to use someone else's faith. Faith is not transferable; it is personal. So many times kids do not have a faith of their own. It is a knowing *about* but not a knowing *personally*. Consequently, we should help the second-generation Christians to personalize their faith.

MORE APPLICATION THAN CONTENT

We need to focus on solutions in helping those students from Christian homes take positive steps in living a vibrant day-by-day walk with Jesus Christ. First of all, we must direct our teaching and ministry toward application rather than mere content. For some reason we think that if we can just teach the content we will see lives change. Psychologist Lawrence Crabb has discovered that life change occurs most effectively in the context of a relationship. We need to get the second-generation person into a relationship with a hot-hearted Christian who will focus on applying the truth.

THE SALT PRINCIPLE

Another principle in helping these second generation students make a transition is learning how to challenge them to grow spiritually. Not enough time is spent "salting" students to enable them to develop a thirst for what they will receive. We move too quickly and too directly to the information. Then we try to hold the students accountable for the content when they have not volitionally and emotionally agreed to be held accountable. In giving a proper challenge we should include these four basic elements: (1) "salting," (2) presenting the information, (3) penetrating their wills, and (4) holding them accountable to their commitment. We must be aware, however, that only the Holy Spirit can accomplish the changing of their wills. Intercessory prayer is therefore of tremendous consequence.

A friend of mine, working with a number of second-generation Christians in Phoenix, was frustrated that his students did not have a tenderness and an openness to hear God. He was struggling to help them see their spiritual condition. Even though he had taught many Bible studies on the subject, they still did not see their need. He decided to be a partner with the Spirit in salting them and in creating a thirst. He invited them to take some severely mentally disabled children to a rodeo. They cared for those children all day long in the heat of the Phoenix sun. They met the children's needs in spite of much inconvenience.

At the end of the day on the bus ride home, after they had delivered the children back to their residence, the students discussed how they felt about the day. Several expressed anger and frustration in feeling that all of their work and service had been in vain. The youth pastor questioned them and said, "Why do you feel that way?" They vehemently retorted that disabled children did not even know they were being loved and cared for. They were not aware they were at a rodeo. They neither appreciated the ability of the performers nor the sacrifice of the students.

At that point the youth pastor took the moment to create a thirst (salt) in the hearts of those young people. He asked, "Has it ever occurred to you that sometimes God feels the same way about you? He reaches out for you, He loves you, He cares for you, He provides for you, and yet you are not even aware of His presence. You are not aware of His voice; you are not aware of His love. Could it be that you have seen a parallel of where you are in a spiritual relationship with Jesus?"

That is an example of salting. The youth pastor then provided the opportunity for the students to get into a Bible study (information) and experience the presence of God. About sixty students responded. Because of their willingness, he held them accountable and saw life changes. The Spirit had moved their wills. The youth pastor had established the environment.

CHRISTLIKE PEER MODELS

A third area in seeing second-generation Christians respond is having godly peers, who are modeling a sincere walk with Christ. Students can dismiss Bible studies, they can dismiss prayer times, they can dismiss mission trips, but they have a very difficult time dismissing a peer (an equal) who is demonstrating the Christian life in power. Consequently, the development of a godly core group of students is a nonnegotiable item for your program.

THE INDISPENSABLE SOLUTION

A fourth solution to this second-generation problem is one to which we often give assent but practice little. It is prayer. Someone has stated that intercession is love on its knees. That is true. It is critical that we as youth workers present our students name by name and day by day to Christ. We must fight against apathy and employ our spiritual weapons (2 Cor. 10) against the strongholds of the enemy.

LOVING CONFRONTATION

The principle of loving confrontation is another essential for the second-generation Christian. Lives are often changed through challenge. We may be confronted with the Scriptures, the Holy Spirit, a godly person, or a message. It is not an encounter in anger or frustration by the youth worker, but by a loving approach of asking penetrating questions rather than making accusations. That young person can then see his own heart and spiritual condition without feeling threatened. Jesus asked twice as many questions as He gave answers. We should follow that pattern as well.

Another tendency of the second-generation Christian is to focus on the outward rather than the inward. Recently I have been challenged with the Bible's focus on the inward man. God does not look at outward appearances as man does, but rather on the heart (1 Sam. 16:7). It is crucial that we youth workers get excited about the right things—about character changes in the inward person. As we work with kids who have grown up in a Christian environment, we sometimes find there is a high degree of overprotectionism from the parents, the Christian school, or even the youth worker. We deeply desire to prevent failure of any kind. I am not saying that we should encourage them to fail. But failure is not always a negative in the spiritual journey. Failure may well be a motivational force toward growth for the student, *especially* a second-generation Christian. Kids who fail are kids who are more teachable.

TEACHABLE MOMENTS

Teachable moments do not always come when we expect them. The perfect opportunity to seize the vulnerable, instructable moment with youth and communicate the reality of truth may occur when they fail. Numbers of second-generation kids with whom I have had conversations feel almost disappointed that they have not been able to experience the dramatic "life of sin." As Psalm 37 states, they are "envious of the wicked" and believe they have not been able to enjoy the pleasures of sin even briefly. We must continually point these students to where Psalm 37 concludes its treatise, "Don't be envious of the wicked," but consider their end.

Can we not stress sin's consequences without being overprotective of our kids? We need to teach them to think, because so many contemporary youth do not take the time to think. There is a mental dullness that has been developed through the media—a spectator mentality.

Another way to minister effectively to second-generation students is to prod them to get outside their "comfort zones." Students who live in a Christian environment have an untested belief system and consequently tend to become weak and anemic. Dare kids who live within the secure Christian community to step out and into an arena where God's strength is required. In every statement of the Great Commission God's unique presence is promised. Christ pushed His followers beyond their "comfort zones." God delights to see us come to the end of ourselves, because it is there that we will find Him and learn to depend on Him.

Finally, teaching students to recognize, remember, and record God's activity in their lives is imperative. Forgetting the mighty acts of God has been characteristic of His people throughout the ages. Deuteronomy 11:2-3 states it this way: "Remember today that your children were not the ones who saw and experienced the discipline of the Lord your God: his majesty, his mighty hand, his outstretched arm; the signs he performed and the things he did in the heart of Egypt, both to Pharaoh King of Egypt and to his whole country."

God is addressing the parents who *had* seen the deliverance of the Lord. The children had *not* seen God at work. The parents were responsible for rehearsing God's activities to their children so that later on their children would recognize and know Jehovah for themselves. Consequently in verses 18-21 of the same chapter the Scripture says:

> Fix these words of mine in your hearts and minds; tie them as symbols on your hands and bind them on your foreheads. Teach them to your children, talking about them when you sit at home and when you walk along the road, when you lie down and when you get up. Write them on the doorframes of your houses and on your gates, so that your days and the days of your children may be many in the land that the Lord swore to give your forefathers, as many as the days that the heavens are above the earth.

It is critical to help students from this environment recognize and begin to thirst after God and practice His presence.

Motivating second-generation Christians should be a top priority for youth workers. Their apathy and boredom can either frustrate us or motivate us to be partners with the Spirit for life change.

FOR FURTHER READING

Arn, Win, and Charles Arn. *The Master's Plan for Making Disciples.* Pasadena, Calif.: Church Growth Press, 1982.

Bruce, A. B. *The Training of the Twelve.* 1898. Reprint. Grand Rapids: Kregel, 1978.

Bruce, F. F. *The Pauline Circle.* Grand Rapids: Eerdmans, 1985.

Coleman, Robert E. *The Master Plan of Evangelism.* Old Tappan, N.J.: Revell, 1980.

Fleischman, Paul., ed. *Discipling the Young Person.* San Bernardino, Calif.: Here's Life, 1985.

Hadidian, Allen. *Discipleship.* Chicago: Moody, 1979, 1987.

Hull, Bill. *Jesus Christ Disciplemaker.* Colorado Springs, Colo.: NavPress, 1984.

Kuhne, Gary. *The Dynamics of Personal Follow-up.* Grand Rapids: Zondervan, 1976.

Mayhall, Jack. *Discipleship: The Price and the Prize.* Wheaton, Ill.: Victor, 1984.

McAllister, Dawson, and John Miller. *Discussion Manual for Student Discipleship.* Chicago: Moody, 1980.

Petersen, William J. *The Discipling of Timothy.* Wheaton, Ill.: Victor, 1980.

31

Richard Ross

Denominational and Interchurch Activities

Buses, vans, and cars from twenty-three states cooled their engines in the parking lots of the University of Wisconsin at Whitewater. Twenty-four hundred people representing 160 churches had gathered for the week-long Evangelical Free Church Youth Fellowship annual conference. Music, drama, Bible quizzing, workshops, and messages by nationally-known youth speakers were the features that attracted so many students and their sponsors to this small town.

In another town, the front page of the local newspaper featured a picture and article about a youth worker and several high school students celebrating 7-Eleven Appreciation Day. The occasion? The store had agreed to stop selling certain pornographic magazines. For months the Suburban Youth Ministers' Association had led a boycott of the store that included picketing actions and press conferences on the issue. Their efforts had resulted in an 18 percent reduction in sales.

As the sun quietly slipped above the rugged mountains, the occupants of nearly a thousand tents and campers began to move about in preparation for a warm spring day. But this was not a scenic national park in Wyoming. It was Ejido Cuernavaca, twenty miles below Mexicali (a border town in Mexico just

RICHARD ROSS, Ed.D., is youth ministry consultant, Sunday School Board, Southern Baptist Convention, Nashville, Tennessee, and part-time youth pastor, Tulip Grove Baptist Church, Hermitage, Tennessee.

below Calexico, California). Instead of fishing poles, tourist brochures, and maps of hiking trails, the inhabitants were decked out with paint brushes, ladders, and carpentry tools. This was "Mexicali Outreach," a project that annually attracts nearly fifteen hundred students from all over the western United States to invest their spring vacations in serving orphanages, churches, and a variety of other ministry opportunities south of the California border.

What makes these situations special is not their size of impact alone. They are important because young people and their leaders from many churches cooperated to achieve carefully defined goals for the glory of Jesus Christ. A personalized contrast might help to put the examples into biblical perspective.

Even though Mark is fifteen years younger than I, he is one of my best friends. Mark is a believer with a sharp sense of humor and a winsome smile. He also has cerebral palsy. His mind is clear. His brain sends signals that could result in a long-distance run or a rippling backstroke. However, Mark's handicap makes it impossible for all the parts of his body to work together. His limbs move without purpose, and his speech is barely understandable. When Mark arrives in his wheelchair, children stare and adults look the other way.

Jesus is the head of His Body, the church. His leadership is clear. The parts of His Body can respond with coordinated action or with a flailing of limbs that frightens and turns off the world. The youth ministry of a local church needs to sense being part of the broader Body. Coordination is more likely when the big picture is clearly in focus.

There are a number of advantages in doing youth ministry in concert with other churches and denominational groups—advantages to the youth, the volunteer youth workers, and the youth minister or youth pastor—each of which deserves consideration.

Advantages to Youth

GROUP SUPPORT

Doing joint programming with other churches in the immediate area has great potential for good. Youth are encouraged by discovering other students from their world who share their faith and life-style.

Teenagers are at a point developmentally where it is difficult to stand alone. Even though courage to be true to one's own convictions is a valid goal of youth ministry, adults must realize that this represents a significant struggle for most teenagers. On the average, ego strength is lower during the teenage years than during any other period of life. Ego strength is closely related to the ability to take an unpopular stand. Even conscientious Christian youth face a significant challenge.

A rally or retreat that brings together Christian youth from the same schools or community can strengthen individual teenagers. Youth may be amazed at how many other young believers there are in their world. Those teenagers may return to their schools willing to support one another and to effect change. Such mutual support may give them courage to begin a morning prayer group or to vote down a keg party for their school club.

STRENGTHEN SELF-CONCEPT

Sharing life with believers from other denominations and churches can strengthen the self-concepts of teenagers. Teenage self-concepts are seldom formed in a vacuum. The peer group is most important in shaping how a teenager will view himself. Youth often find a sense of self through identifying with the values of those around them.

A teenager in a coliseum full of Christian teenagers can reasonably conclude, "I'm not the nerd after all. A lot of people believe as I do." A teenager who develops more positive feelings about his beliefs and values will likely develop more positive feelings about himself.

APOLOGETIC VALUE

Participating with large groups of believers has apologetic value for teenagers. It is normal for Christian teenagers sometimes to wonder, "Have I placed my faith in something that is real? What if this Christianity thing is all made-up?" Having fellowship with believing youth from many other churches and denominations can help a doubting teenager conclude, "All these people have put their trust in the same thing I have. It must be true."

Youth who wonder if they believe only because of the family they were reared in will be impressed with testimonies of youth from terrible home conditions. Youth who wonder if they are Christians only because they were reared in a "Christian" nation will be impressed with testimonies from youth who chose the Christian faith in another setting.

A SENSE OF COMMUNITY

Teenagers have a need to experience an almost overwhelming sense of community from time to time. Some forces in society have learned to manipulate this need for selfish ends.

For example, rock concerts artificially produce a strong sense of "weness" among those who attend. Cult leaders use group hypnotic techniques to cause the individual to feel one with the group.

The Body of Christ produces the only genuine sense of community. Youth singing, praying, and sharing together in large gatherings that cross geographical and denominational lines can experience priceless moments of true oneness. In those moments, the words "One in the Spirit" move from cliché to reality. And unlike a rock concert, the spell is not broken when the house lights come on.

DENOMINATIONAL IDENTITY

Participating in events beyond the local church can help young people understand the denomination of which they are a part. The concept of a denomination is difficult for many youth to grasp. The terms *Southern Baptist* or *United Methodist* have hazy meanings to youth who have grown up in the church and no meaning to new believers with no church background.

Participating in denominational youth events can help build identity. Assemblies of God is theoretical. Assemblies of God summer youth camp is concrete. Presbyterian is theoretical. Presbyterian hunger relief project is concrete. Shared events help teenagers grasp the family of which they are a part.

Youth who feel positive about denominational events may develop a sense of loyalty that will last a lifetime. Feeling positive about denominational membership can complement a sense of community with all believers.

Carrying some sense of loyalty to denominational programming into adulthood can have value. When young adults outgrow the youth ministries of their churches, or when they move to new communities, they need to feel a loyalty to an adult community of believers for spiritual growth. Otherwise, spiritual orphans will result. Building lifetime churchmanship is part of the youth discipleship process.

BROADER PROGRAM

Participating in denominational and interdenominational youth events can involve teenagers in programming that would be impossible on the local church level. This is not to say that bigger is always better. Nor is it to say that more money always leads to bigger blessings. The consistent ministry of the local church is the source of most genuine spiritual growth among teenagers.

Even so, there is value in bringing youth under the ministry of leaders with special gifts in unique settings. By combining their resources, churches can provide opportunities that none could provide alone.

WIDER MINISTRY POSSIBILITIES

Denominational and interchurch events can make a dramatic impact on young people. The reverse is also true. Young people can have a dramatic impact on their world through cooperation among churches.

For example, youth in a Southern Baptist camping experience in the summer of 1985 donated $85,000 toward world hunger. A gift of that size can make a difference. Similarly, the aforementioned Mexicali project, sponsored by the Institute for Outreach Ministries, annually draws hundreds of students from otherwise unrelated churches. The impact on both students and nationals is dramatic.

Denominations have supported youth as they have built basic housing in the Appalachians or refurbished mission centers in the inner city. The needs of the world require the combined resources of churches and denominations.

ADVANTAGES TO VOLUNTEER LEADERS

NEW VISION

Cooperative programming with other churches can be a genuine source of inspiration for volunteer leaders. It can give them a new vision of the ministry of which they are a part.

Some leaders serve in churches where the response of the youth is disappointing. Adults put in long hours but see few teenagers respond. A teacher who usually meets with two or three needs to see a group of two or three hundred from time to time.

Events that bring together the youth of many congregations remind workers that the Christian church is making an impact on teenage society. The progress of the church can be uplifting even when the response in a particular congregation is disappointing.

CONTINUING INSPIRATION

Fellowship among leaders of many congregations can be a continuing source of inspiration. If looking across a sea of teenage faces can be inspiring, then seeing those youth accompanied by a small army of committed leaders can be doubly inspiring.

Many congregations struggle with a significant shortage of dedicated youth leaders. It is a fact that most adults would prefer not to be with teenagers, even at church. With some adults, their personalities make it difficult for them to give youth the unconditional love, affirmation, and acceptance that is needed. Still other adults have found a comfortable life-style that cannot be disturbed with the time commitment that young people require.

No one feels the shortage of youth workers more keenly than the few adults who are serving. They become discouraged both because of the extra time pressures placed on them and because they realize many youth needs are going unmet. Temporary or permanent burnout of committed leaders is often the result.

Fellowship among leaders from many churches is one answer to this troubling situation. In such settings leaders can find new inspiration for service in their own congregations.

Joint events can foster an esprit de corps among workers. It can remind leaders they are part of a significant group of adults who are making a difference in the world. It can remind leaders that others are also making personal sacrifices in order to minister in Christ's name.

REDUCED COMPETITION

Participating in denominational or interchurch events can also reduce the sense of competition among church youth leaders in an area. Building close relationships among youth and adults from churches in the community makes it harder to feel it is "us against them."

Participating in events together reduces the desire to "out-program" the other churches in order to reach youth. And it certainly takes away the desire to lure active youth from other believing congregations.

Distrust and prejudice are usually based on ignorance and misunderstanding. Bringing youth and adults together reduces ignorance and increases understanding.

The church is certainly in competition. It is in competition with the world. Competition within the church is similar to the handicapped person who hits himself uncontrollably. Personal relationships and shared experiences are the best solution to struggle within the Body.

SHARPENING SKILLS

Events provided by denominations or interchurch groups are ideal for training volunteer leaders. Working with youth is a calling, but it is also a constellation of skills that need continual sharpening.

Volunteer leaders are more likely to find their work satisfying when they feel competent in what they are doing. They are more likely to become discouraged and resign when they feel poorly prepared for their responsibilities.

Certainly, the local church needs ongoing training for volunteer leaders. Every church needs to provide experience to equip the saints further for the work of the ministry. Training provided by the denomination or other groups should complement and strengthen what is already being done.

In churches with a very small group of youth leaders, it may be difficult to generate enthusiasm and excitement in training sessions. This component can be added through large training experiences that bring together the leaders of many congregations.

In churches with small training budgets, it may be difficult to use top quality media or other learning aids. Joint events can provide access to resources that will make the training session a quality experience.

In churches without a professional staff, it may be difficult to find leadership for training events. Experiences provided by the denomination or interchurch group often feature leading authorities in specific areas of youth ministry. Local church workers are able to have contact with leaders with special gifts and insights through whom God can speak in significant ways.

Gifted leaders can give new insights to youth workers, but so can fellow sponsors. There is value in workers in various churches sharing insights with one another. And those who are "in the trenches" sometimes understand more about their work than outside observers.

Workers come to training times with questions like: How do we motivate youth to participate in our activities? How do we communicate our objectives to parents? What teaching methods actually lead to learning? How do we create a sense of unity in our diverse group? How should discipline problems best be handled? Youth workers in scattered churches may feel alone as they struggle with questions such as these. Most will profit from lively sharing times with other workers from a variety of backgrounds and churches.

CURRICULUM TRAINING

Denominational training experiences can be especially helpful in denominations that produce youth curriculum pieces. A teacher who is handed material without instruction is no better off than a soldier with a gun he cannot fire.

Even teachers with a well-written curriculum need to know: What are the developmental characteristics of teenagers this material is based on? How are issues selected for study? What approach is taken to Scripture? What learning experiences are designed to motivate youth to become mentally involved in this study? Which will help youth struggle with issues or the meaning of Scripture passages? Which will help youth make practical applications to their daily lives? What preparation will make a quality learning experience more likely?

Training designed specifically for a particular curriculum can answer such questions directly. Such events can even model the effective use of that curriculum in a realistic setting. If denominational training events are available, they can make a measurable difference in the effectiveness of youth learning experiences.

ADVANTAGES TO THE YOUTH MINISTER OR YOUTH PASTOR

OUTSIDE SUPPORT

All church staff members need personal support groups outside their congregations. Staff members who relate to youth have a special need for such a group.

Ministering to and with young people is emotionally taxing. The effective minister to youth cannot be a detached administrator. He or she must be personally involved in the endless variety of complex issues facing society's in-between ones. Teenagers do not always choose to get into trouble during convenient hours. And church events that will appeal to them can seldom be planned during business hours.

The complexity of teenage home situations is also emotionally and physically draining. Frightened and frustrated parents seldom react to leaders in a calm and logical fashion. Parents who have made their children the center of their lives can place unrealistic expectations on youth ministers.

Leading a core of volunteer youth workers can be draining as well. Each worker represents a complex assortment of gifts, fears, hopes, frustrations, joys, and sorrows. Ministering to the needs in each leader's life is rewarding, essential, but tiring.

Relating to the church family as a whole calls on inner reserves of strength. Because the local church is made up of humans, it is less than perfect. The sanctification of Christians is still a process.

Life experiences have caused some church members to be bitter about life. They sometimes express that bitterness by lashing out at staff members in inappropriate ways.

Other members have carried severe self-image problems from adolescence into adulthood. Some may depend on a church-elected position to prop up a sense of personal significance. Because of all the emotional complexities involved, a staff member may eventually do something that threatens the arrangement and will pay a price for doing so.

Many pastors are mentally healthy individuals. Some are not. Some are insecure in their leadership roles. Others must depend on their central position to meet many ego needs. Personality weaknesses in a pastor almost always create added tension for the minister to youth.

Relating to youth, parents, workers, church members, and fellow staff members can be spiritually and emotionally draining. Talking with others during times of struggle is essential to emotional and spiritual health.

Often it is inappropriate to make known relationship problems to fellow church members. Most church problems are compounded as word begins to spread. Staff members who relay confidential information can find the door closed to further ministry.

The solution to easing all the aforementioned tensions is to find a support group outside the church. Fellow youth leaders in other churches can become that group, and a denominational or interchurch fellowship of youth ministers can provide emotional support and a listening ear. They can also provide an objective viewpoint during emotionally troubled times. They can share insights from their own days of struggle, and they can help develop a redemptive action plan.

CONTINUING EDUCATION

Professional-level training provided by the denomination or interchurch groups can provide continuing education for the minister to youth or youth pastor.

Decades ago it may have been sufficient to know a few guitar chords and a couple of punch recipes. Today, however, youth ministry is tremendously complex and requires a variety of high-level skills. Coasting on a college or seminary degree is not adequate.

Here are a few of the skills that need continual sharpening:

- Ability to keep four or five youth program organizations functioning effectively
- Ability to understand and minister to the complex problems facing parents of youth
- Ability to handle hundreds or thousands of dollars of budget funds responsibly
- Ability to counsel youth in a variety of complex problem areas
- Ability to handle the Scriptures without violating principles of biblical interpretation
- Ability to communicate effectively with a variety of audiences both verbally and through the printed page
- Ability to do long- and short-range planning, and the ability to implement those plans
- Ability to use sports and recreation as components in a balanced program of ministry
- Ability to function well with a multiple staff, complex office operations, and numerous committee relationships
- Ability to train and inspire adults to perform a ministry to youth through their elected positions[1]

Joint training experiences are essential if effective ministry is to be done.

Denominational training events have several advantages. First, the model of youth ministry presented at a denominational training session is already consistent with the theology and traditions of those attending. The youth minister does not have to "cut and paste" concepts to make them fit his or her situation.

Second, discussion can be very specific concerning church youth organizations, programs, and curriculum. All who attend will be speaking the same youth ministry vocabulary.

Third, denominational training events can lead to joint programming involving numerous churches. A structure for cooperation and coordination is already present.

Even though continuing education provided within the denomination is central, there is also value in participating in interdenominational training. Hearing concepts of ministry from leaders from diverse backgrounds can be a mentally invigorating experience. Such events can also build friendships that may open the door to joint programming for youth.

1. Richard Ross, "The Minister of Youth: Calling, Qualifications, and Preparation," in *The Work of the Minister to Youth*, comp. Bob R. Taylor (Nashville: Convention, 1982), pp. 28-29.

ACTION PLAN

Here are several steps to help the youth worker experience the advantages of denominational and interchurch activities.

First, build personal friendships with denominational staff who provide support services for youth ministry. Denominational staff members on the local, state, and national levels will do a better job of supporting a church's youth ministry if they know the youth workers personally. This also makes it easier to learn more about how to take advantage of their resources as friendships are built.

Most denominational leaders are eager to know on a personal level those whom they serve. Aloofness is uncommon. Formality is uncommon. For example, more than 1,300 of us serve at the Southern Baptist Sunday School Board. Each of us answers his own phone. Even though I relate to nearly 8,000 youth ministers, I am happy I receive calls from several of them every day.

Second, get on every appropriate mailing list. Participating in denominational and interchurch activities is impossible if you do not receive notice of those events. Most organizations are eager to have you on their list. All you have to do is ask.

Third, be willing to invest time putting together denominational and interchurch activities. If it is true that shared projects have value for youth, youth workers, youth ministers, and churches, then it is worth the investment of time. Events that may bless the lives of hundreds will never happen if every youth minister is "too busy at my church" to be involved.

Fourth, try to have an impact on denominational programming related to youth ministry. Some youth ministers boycott weak denominational events without seeking to upgrade what is being offered.

Most denominational leaders work with committees of staff members from local churches. Making oneself available to serve on such a committee can give a youth minister direct input into the quality of denominational youth events.

Even if a youth worker does not serve on a planning committee or board, honest evaluations of denominational programming can carry weight. Even in an organization as large as the Sunday School Board, every letter of evaluation is circulated and receives careful attention.

Of course, an evaluation will carry even more weight if the evaluator actively supports the events he is seeking to improve. A planning committee will be more impressed with comments concerning summer camp if the critic brings a group to camp every summer.

Fifth, work to encourage your denomination to increase budget and staff support for youth ministry. Many denominations are experiencing a decline in youth enrollment. A denomination can respond in one of two ways: "Because we have fewer youth, we can cut back on our support of youth ministry," or,

"Because youth enrollment is down, we need to strengthen our support for those who work with youth." Input from concerned youth workers can make a difference.

Finally, take the initiative in forming a support group among youth ministers in the local area. As noted earlier, this group can meet significant personal needs experienced by those committed to teenagers. Also, this group can become the force behind a series of interchurch events planned for youth, youth parents, and youth workers. It is worth your effort.

Introducing teenagers to Jesus Christ and growing them up in His image requires all the resources of the church. Cooperation and coordination within and across denominations is essential if the Body of Christ is to work without handicap.

FOR FURTHER READING

Ross, Richard. *31 Truths to Shape Your Youth Ministry.* Nashville: Convention Press, 1984.

———. *Youth Ministry Planbook 3.* Nashville: Convention Press, 1985.

Stone, J. David, ed. *The Complete Youth Ministries Handbook.* Vols. 1 and 2. Nashville: Abingdon, 1980, 1981. Vol. 2 is entitled *Catching the Rainbow: A Total Concept of Youth Ministry.*

Stone, J. David. *Spiritual Growth in Youth Ministry.* Loveland, Colo.: Group Books, 1983.

Taylor, Bob. *The Work of the Minister to Youth.* Nashville: Convention Press, 1982.

32

Wayne Rice

Junior High Ministries

Everybody is afraid of something. Some people are afraid of high places; others are afraid of the dark. *Ochlophobiacs* are afraid of crowds. *Kakorrhaphiophobiacs* are afraid of failure. *Thanataphobiacs* are afraid of death.

There are many people, youth workers included, who are afraid of junior highers. I call them "eardolescaphobiacs." They can handle youngsters under ten, or high school and college students, but they fear, and therefore avoid, human beings who are between the ages of eleven and fourteen—early adolescents. As a result, perhaps the most underserved group in the church (or in society, for that matter) are junior highers,[1]

But we in the church cannot afford to neglect junior highers. These young people are at a very critical turning point in their lives when they need more, not less, of our time and attention. Urie Bronfenbrenner of Cornell University, a well-known expert in the field of human development, has stated that no other time of life is more important in terms of human development than early adolescence—the junior high years.[2]

Most people fear and therefore avoid things they do not understand. I am convinced that "eardolescaphobiacs" fear junior highers because they do not

---

1. Joan Lipsitz, *Growing Up Forgotten* (Lexington, Mass.: Lexington Books, 1977), p. xv.
2. From an interview conducted by National Public Radio entitled "Options in Education: A Portrait of American Adolescence." Transcripts are available by writing to National Public Radio, Washington, D.C. 20036, and requesting programs 92-96.

WAYNE RICE, B.S., is president of Youth Specialities, El Cajon, California.

understand them very well at all. In this chapter we will take a closer look at this age group so that we might become more effective with, and less afraid of, junior highers.

WHY JUNIOR HIGH MINISTRY IS SO IMPORTANT

There is no question that every phase of life carries with it an importance of its own, but there are several realities that make early adolescence especially significant.

EARLY ADOLESCENCE IS A TIME OF TRANSITION

It is during this time of a person's life that he or she literally changes from a child into an adult. It only happens to a person once, and for most people, it happens during the junior high years. Like the caterpillar, people change into something they were not before: an adult human being. Before, they were children; after, they are capable of having children. And the difference is much more than merely physiological. As the apostle Paul put it in 1 Corinthians 13:11, "When I was a child, I talked like a child, I thought like a child, I reasoned like a child. When I became a man, I put childish ways behind me." The change is sometimes startling in its totality.

But it is ironic that this reality (transition) is also a primary reason junior highers are neglected. There are many people who are quick to point out that because junior highers are in transition—neither one thing nor the other— then it would behoove us simply to wait for them to "grow out of it." Why try to hit a moving target? Instead, wait for them to settle down into something we are more familiar with and better equipped to handle.

The problem with that line of reasoning, of course, is that they do not grow out of it. Junior highers are not merely passing through a stage of life that is neutral. It is during these few years that lives are shaped, values are chosen, and important decisions are made. What happens to young people during early adolescence significantly affects the rest of their lives.

The reality of transition during early adolescence offers us a unique opportunity to make a difference in a young person's life at a very important crossroads.

EARLY ADOLESCENCE IS A TIME OF OPENNESS AND VULNERABILITY

Because junior highers are leaving their childhood behind them and are looking forward to adulthood, an entire new world is opening up before them. With wide eyes and unbounded enthusiasm, they want to try out all the new options and possibilities they see. That is why junior highers are viewed as a primary "target group" by advertisers and marketing people. They know this age group is willing to try almost anything once, just to find out what it is like. Junior highers show little restraint or good judgment. Whether it is the latest fad or the philosophy and life-style of a new rock idol, junior highers will usually be first in line.

On the negative side, that means junior highers are extremely vulnerable. They can be hurt. But on the positive side, it means they are very open and can be influenced in positive ways. They have not yet set themselves in concrete. They are willing to change, to experiment, and to discover all God has in store for them. They are quite flexible, giving junior high workers a unique opportunity to play an important role in the shaping of someone else's life.

As a junior high worker, I have always felt especially privileged to be in the position to make an impact on almost every major decision the young people in my care will ever make. The same is not true for those who work with older youth and with adults. By the time a person reaches his or her senior year in high school, most important life-style, personality, and value choices have been made already. Not so with junior highers. All of these choices still lie ahead of them. They are open, flexible, and ready to find out how Christ can make a positive difference in their lives.

EARLY ADOLESCENCE IS A TIME FOR DECISION-MAKING

Most people look back on their early adolescent years as the time when they made a number of important decisions that changed their lives. As junior highers approach adulthood, they are eager to exercise the one adult privilege and right that up to this time has been withheld from them: the ability to make their own decisions. As children, all their decisions were made for them. Now, as they see themselves no longer children, they want to be able to choose for themselves and to make their own decisions.[3]

This, of course, frightens many parents. Parents are not used to getting so much resistance from a child when they make decisions for him or her. They fear that their child is becoming rebellious and unmanageable. But in actuality their child is simply growing up. He or she desires autonomy. They are not rebelling in most cases, nor are they seeking absolute independence. All they want is the opportunity to make a few important decisions for themselves. That is both healthy and normal. As careful studies have shown, though young adolescents do turn to their peers for companionship, they continue throughout their adolescent years to turn to their parents for models and advice.[4]

Erik Erikson, the renowned adolescent psychologist, has said that junior

3. That was the finding of a survey of more than 8,000 young people between the ages of eleven and fourteen conducted by Search Institute in 1984. Young people were asked to rank a list of twenty-four "values" according to importance. The value that showed the greatest change (increase) between the fifth and ninth grade was the value "to make my own decisions." From the Project Report "Young Adolescents and Their Parents" (Search Institute, 122 West Franklin Ave., Minneapolis, Minn. 55404), p. 133.
4. Charles E. Bowerman and John W. Kinch, "Changes in Family and Peer Orientation of Children Between the Fourth and Tenth Grades," in *Adolescent Development*, ed. Martin Gold and Elizabeth Douvan (Boston: Allyn and Bacon, 1969), pp. 137-41.

highers are not yet ready to make any kind of permanent or life-long commitment to anything.[5] In his view, all decisions made during early adolescence are of the trial and error variety—temporary at best. And in many respects, he is correct. In their zeal to make decisions, junior highers make many they are simply not ready to make. They do not, however, hold themselves to their own decisions, and neither should we. Still, we should never underestimate the long-range impact of decisions made during the junior high years. Their cumulative effect is significant indeed. Because junior highers possess few decision-making skills, we need to help them learn how to make the right kinds of decisions.

EARLY ADOLESCENCE IS A TIME OF PREMATURE ADULTHOOD

Thirty years ago, junior high school students were still considered to be children. But times have changed dramatically. According to Bronfenbrenner,

> the adolescents today are the 12 year olds and the 11 year olds and the 10 year olds. That is, they are having the experiences that five years earlier, adolescents didn't have until they were 13, 14, and 15. And they, in turn, are having the experiences that adolescents used to have when they were 16, 17, and 18.[6]

In other words, kids are getting older at a much younger age.

David Elkind, in his book *All Grown Up and No Place to Go,* puts it this way:

> They have had a premature adulthood thrust upon them. Teenagers now are expected to confront life and its challenges with the maturity once expected only of the middle-aged, without any time for preparation. . . . The special stage belonging to teenagers (that they once had) has been excised from the life cycle, and teenagers have been given a pro forma adulthood, an adulthood with all of the responsibilities but few of the prerogatives. Young people today are quite literally all grown up with no place to go.[7]

Marie Winn, in her book *Children Without Childhood,* agrees. She says:

> Something has happened to the limits of childhood. An advertisement for a new line of books called "Young Adult Books" defines a young adult as "a person facing the problems of adulthood." The books, however, which deal with subjects such as prostitution, divorce, and rape, are aimed at readers between the ages of ten and thirteen, persons who were formerly known as children.[8]

5. Erik Erikson, *Identity, Youth and Crisis* (New York: W. W. Norton, 1968), p. 91.
6. National Public Radio, "Options in Education."
7. David Elkind, *All Grown Up and No Place to Go* (Reading, Mass.: Addison-Wesley, 1984), p. 5.
8. Marie Winn, *Children Without Childhood* (New York: Pantheon, 1984), p. 4.

Because early adolescent growth has accelerated so much in recent years, we as youth workers must respond in a decisive manner. We need to begin to give junior high ministry a much greater priority than we have in the past. We can no longer afford to put these young people on hold or to "warehouse" them until they become more predictable and manageable. If we do not minister to them now, we will lose them. They will not wait around for us to decide they are worthy of our time and efforts. Twenty years ago, youth ministry was aimed primarily at the high school or the college campus. But today, if we are serious about youth ministry, then we must take junior high ministry seriously and give it our highest priority.

KEY DEVELOPMENTAL CHARACTERISTICS OF EARLY ADOLESCENTS

There are certain characteristics that make junior highers different from other people. It is important that youth workers understand what they are and how they affect junior high ministry. Though we will not deal with all of them, we will highlight a few key developmental characteristics and draw some implications for ministry from them. Keep in mind that these are all sweeping generalizations about an age group that defies being categorized. It has been said about junior highers that "the abnormal *is* the normal," which is probably as accurate a generalization as one can make about this age group. There will be lots of exceptions—kids who are way ahead, way behind, or completely off the map. That is normal.

PHYSIOLOGICAL DEVELOPMENT

The most obvious thing you can say about physiological development in early adolescents is that their bodies are changing dramatically. That is because of the onset of puberty, the adolescent growth spurt, which is second only to infancy in velocity of growth.[9] Before puberty, one has the body of a child; after puberty, one has the body of an adult. The onset of puberty for girls occurs, on the average, at 9.6 years of age. The adolescent growth spurt peaks for girls at about 11.8 years. The average age for menarche, when a girl has her first period, is 12.9 years. Comparable milestones for boys occur almost two years later.[10]

During this time, many dramatic changes take place in a young person's body. These changes can be a source of considerable anxiety for many junior highers. They are, in their own secret fears, growing too rapidly, too slowly, too unevenly, too tall, or developing too much in the wrong places. And for many, their fears are justified. Physical growth can be very uneven and unpredictable during early adolescence.

9. Gilman D. Grave, *The Control of the Onset of Puberty* (New York: John Wiley & Sons, 1974), p. xxiii.
10. Ibid., p. 409.

During the early adolescent years, girls begin to take on the appearance of women. The hips widen, the waist narrows, and breasts begin to develop. Boys also grow and change very rapidly. Some will grow as much as six inches in a single year. Their voice changes, their muscular development changes, and pubic and facial hair begins to appear.

Keep in mind that the range of "normal" is very wide when it comes to physiological development (as well as development in other areas). It is not unusual to have two junior highers who are exactly the same age, yet as much as six years apart in terms of physical development.[11] For example, one might be a very slow developing boy (who will eventually catch up), and the other might be a fast developing girl (who will slow down). In reality, the best word one can use to describe this age group is *variability*. About the only thing predictable about one's age during early adolescence is grade placement in school. Everything else is up for grabs. That is one good reason we may need to find better ways to group junior highers than by chronological age. Age is hardly ever an accurate indicator of need or interest level during the early adolescent years.

With the onset of puberty comes a new awareness of the body. Junior highers typically will spend hours in front of the mirror, constantly comparing themselves to others. They want to be as "average" as they possibly can, not too tall or too short, too fat or too skinny. But of course, they cannot all be average, and the reality of this can be a source of real frustration for many kids.

The reason junior highers are so concerned with their bodies and their appearance is that they are concerned with being accepted by others. Junior high schools are notorious for their rigid caste systems. There are "popular" kids and there are "unpopular" kids. What usually separates the popular from the unpopular are obvious physical differences. Good-looking, attractive girls are naturally more likely to be popular. Handsome, fast-developing boys are also more likely to be popular. No one wants to be in the unpopular or "out" group.

Some junior highers who are slow developers, or who have low self-images, will try to compensate for their lack of physical prowess in other ways. Some will try to "prove their manhood" (or "womanhood") by smoking, drinking, drugs, sex, rowdy behavior, foul language, fighting, joining gangs, running away from home, or breaking the law. This is not uncommon. But others will find the same sense of fulfillment in more positive forms of behavior if they are given the opportunity. Art, music, writing, program planning, teaching, sports, youth activities, and serving others are just a few ways junior highers can build their sense of self-esteem and have positive feelings.

---

11. Joan Lipsitz, *Successful Schools for Young Adolescents* (New Brunswick, N.J.: Transaction Books, 1984), p. 6.

SEXUAL DEVELOPMENT

With the onset of puberty comes the advent of adultlike sexual activity: attraction to the opposite sex, touching, hand holding, experimentation, everything up to and including sexual intercourse. Recent surveys of early adolescents who regularly attend church youth groups have revealed that 20 percent of all ninth graders already have engaged in sexual intercourse.[12] Other studies have shown that the only age group experiencing a rise in the birthrate is the eleven to fourteen group.[13] A significant percentage of the abortions performed in this country are performed on girls under the age of fifteen.

Despite the increase in sexual activity among early adolescents, young people are still as ignorant and confused about the subject as they ever were. Junior highers desperately want to know the "straight scoop" about sexuality, yet they rarely get it. Parents still find it difficult to talk to their children about sex. Public schools deal with the mechanics of sex but cautiously avoid discussions of sexual morality and values. And the church has not been very helpful either to parents or to young people in the area of sexuality, even though sex is rightly recognized as a gift from God. It is no wonder that many young people are given the impression that sex is "filthy, dirty, and nasty—save it for the one you are going to marry."

Most of the information that junior highers pick up about sex is gleaned from the media, their peers, and the rock music culture.[14] Rarely does any of it reflect Christian values. Author and sex educator Eric Johnson, of Philadelphia's Germantown Friends School, has said that sex education for this age group must begin by helping young people to *unlearn* all the myths and half-truths they have come to believe over the years.[15]

However we approach the subject, youth workers need to realize that we cannot remain silent. We need to be a resource to our junior highers and their parents. We need to be open, honest, realistic, and biblical about sex. We cannot let the world do our sex education for us.

It is during early adolescence that young people also begin to establish a sexual, or gender, identity.[16] They begin to come to grips with what it means to be a man or a woman. For this reason, it is important that we provide for our young people positive male and female adult role models whom they can emulate and admire. Without them, junior highers naturally have no choice

---

12. Search Institute, "Young Adolescents and Their Parents."
13. Joan Lipsitz, "The Age Group," in *Toward Adolescence: The Middle School Years,* ed. Maurice Johnson (Chicago: U. of Chicago, 1980), p. 8.
14. From a survey I conducted with junior high school students in 1977. See Wayne Rice, *Junior High Ministry* (Grand Rapids: Zondervan, 1978), p. 55.
15. Johnson elaborated on this in a seminar he conducted at the Search Institute "L.E.A.P." (Learning from Early Adolescents and Their Parents) Conference held in Nashville, Tennessee, in February 1984.
16. Winn, *Children Without Childhood,* p. 155.

but to turn to celebrity role models, such as television personalities or rock musicians. It remains to be seen what the long-range impact of today's androgynous rock heroes will have on the lives of our young people.

SOCIAL DEVELOPMENT

With early adolescence comes a marked increase in social awareness and social maturity that parallels the many physical changes taking place. Peer relationships become very important to junior highers. Prior to this age, they only needed playmates, but now they need friends. Having friends is the very lifeblood of adolescence.[17]

As junior highers move from childhood into adulthood, they seek out others besides their parents who will help them to make this transition. In many ancient cultures it was the adult community in the village or the tribe who would take these young people under their wings and welcome them into their world. But in modern society there are few adults who are willing to be a friend to someone else's adolescent child. David Elkind writes:

> The children who were rushed through childhood are now abandoned as teens. Parents, schools, the media, and society as a whole seem unable to accept the fact of adolescence, that there are young people in transition from childhood to adulthood who need adult guidance and direction.[18]

This accounts for the rise of the peer group as the single most powerful influence on young people outside the home. Kids today have no one else to turn to. The peer group has always been important to young people, but in today's fast-paced society, the peer group has become a substitute for a community of adults who cares enough about the members of the next generation to get involved in their lives.

The peer group as an important bridge from childhood into adulthood is a true axiom of adolescent development.[19] It cannot be denied, nor can it be reversed as a modern social phenomenon. In many ways, it serves a very important function. As mentioned earlier, kids need to have friends whom they can trust, who will listen to them, and who will take them seriously. They need a safe environment outside the home where they will be accepted and where they can try out all their newly developed values and beliefs.

But junior highers also need and want to have adult friends. Youth workers in the church play an important role in this regard. We must take the time to enter into personal relationships with our junior highers and not simply be adult babysitters who put on programs, entertain them, and keep them in line.

17. Lipsitz, *Growing Up Forgotten*, p. 75.
18. Elkind, *All Grown Up and No Place to Go*, p. 4.
19. Alvin W. Howard and George C. Stoumbis, *The Junior High and Middle School: Issues and Practices* (Scranton, Pa.: Intext Educational Publishers, 1970), p. 34.

INTELLECTUAL DEVELOPMENT

There are very basic structural differences between the way a child thinks and the way an adult thinks, and once again, we find that it is during the junior high years when most young people begin to develop adult minds. The brain shifts gears, so to speak, and a whole new way of thinking begins, much more complicated than before, yet wonderfully exciting.

Much of the research in the field of cognitive development (how the mind develops) has been done by the late Swiss genetic epistemologist, Jean Piaget. Following years of study and research he came to the conclusion that one's intelligence during life does not increase at a steady rate, but rather in spurts. On a graph this increase would look like a staircase rather than a gently sloping hill. What is especially significant for the junior high worker is that Piaget found that whereas the child reasons on the basis of objects (a stage he calls "concrete operations"), at some point during early adolescence the young person begins to reason on the basis of abstract symbols and principles ("formal operations"). That stage of reasoning is the final, adult stage of intellectual development that will be with young people for the rest of their lives. They enter this stage during the junior high years.[20]

This of course has a profound impact on how junior highers understand themselves, the world, and their faith. Before, they thought as a child, but now they think as an adult. They begin to give some kind of order and meaning to all the childlike thinking and learning they have done previously. They begin to reason about the future (an abstract concept), to formulate philosophies, to struggle with contradictions, to think about thought. They begin to doubt and to question much of what they have been taught. All of this is a normal part of growing up.

What this means for youth workers is that we must no longer treat junior highers like little children. Many junior highers are capable of thinking and reasoning on an adult level. They may at times revert to an immature level of thinking, but that is to be expected. We need to stimulate their thinking, to push them a little bit intellectually, and help them as they begin to think for themselves. They may not understand or "get it" every time, but there is no place to go but up.

PSYCHO-EMOTIONAL DEVELOPMENT

It is important to know, despite rumors to the contrary, that junior highers are no crazier than anybody else. If we perceive them as being "crazy," it is only because we do not understand them, or more accurately, we do not remember what it was like to be a junior higher.

Most adolescent psychologists agree that the primary psychological task

20. Bärbel Inhelder and Jean Piaget, *The Early Growth of Logic in the Child* (New York: Harper & Row, 1964).

of early adolescence is building self-esteem. Junior highers want to feel good about themselves in relationship to others. "Am I OK?" is without doubt the most important question on their minds.[21]

According to psychologist Bill Wennerholm (a former junior high pastor), the process of building self-esteem includes the following steps.

1. The achievement of emotional and psychological independence from parents
2. The achievement of a separate personal identity
3. The development of personal values and beliefs
4. The ability to motivate oneself and to set one's own goals and direction
5. The ability to participate in intimate reciprocal relationships
6. The establishment of an appropriate sexual identity
7. The ability to function in a work capacity (competence)[22]

Youth workers can be very instrumental in helping junior highers to develop healthy and positive self-images. We need to build up and encourage them whenever we can. We need to give them responsibility and opportunities for success. We should praise them whenever they are doing well, and avoid putting them down for their mistakes and failures. They need to know that we hold them in high esteem and that they are indeed "OK."

David Elkind has described another unique psychological characteristic of this age group. It is an egocentrism that is characterized by two mental constructions: *the imaginary audience* and *the personal fable*.

The imaginary audience is the perception that "everyone is watching me." Junior highers typically feel they are on stage and that everything they do is being observed and judged by everyone else. That is why they will try on fifteen different outfits in the morning before school or spend hours combing their hair. They are positive that *everyone* will notice what they are wearing.

The personal fable is the belief that "I am unlike anyone else," or, "I am immune to the kinds of things that happen to others." This is why kids will often say, "You don't understand me." It is because they believe they are so unlike others that it would be impossible for you to understand them as you understand others. This is also the reason that appeals to this age group based on the concept "it *can* happen to you" are not very effective. Junior highers also often think of themselves as immortal: "I cannot die. Other people may get cancer or die in auto accidents, but that will never happen to me."[23]

A final characteristic of the psycho-emotional development of junior highers

---

21. In a survey of more than seven hundred junior high school students I asked, "If you could ask any question and get a straight answer, what would it be?" The most common responses were, "Do you like me?" and, "Am I OK?" See Wayne Rice, *Junior High Ministry*, p. 31. This finding was also confirmed in the Search Institute study "Young Adolescents and Their Parents."
22. Bill Wennerholm, "Adolescence: The Bridge from Self-Esteem to Self-Esteem," in *Changes*, ed. David Pollock (Atlanta: Vision Media, 1982), 1:2-3.
23. Elkind, *All Grown Up and No Place to Go*, pp. 33-37.

is their propensity to "try on" many different personalities to see which one fits them best. They are in a process of trial and error personality development, which accounts for their moodiness, their abrupt changes in behavior patterns, their unpredictability. A junior higher might be very cooperative and well behaved one day and unexplainably belligerent and disruptive the day after. That is normal. It is not until later, often much later, that young people settle into more predictable patterns of behavior.

These strange shifts in behavior are not limited to individuals, they are found in groups also. It is not uncommon for the dynamics in a group of junior highers to change dramatically from one week to the next. This, of course, requires the ability to shift gears on a moment's notice.

SPIRITUAL DEVELOPMENT

Junior high young people are making a spiritual transition that parallels the many changes taking place in other areas of life. When they were children, they had a faith that was simple, almost mythical, one that provided clear-cut answers to life's most difficult questions. It provided them with invincible heroes of the faith to admire and to emulate. They believed simply because their parents and their teachers believed. But now, with the advent of adulthood, they realize that the faith of their childhood will no longer do. They must develop a faith that is personal and that makes the transition from childhood to adulthood along with them. Unless the church is willing to help junior highers make this transition, it is in danger of losing them. Many young people reject their faith and leave the church during their junior high years because they are still being asked to believe in a God they literally have outgrown. It is important to help junior highers to see God in completely new ways and to see how their faith in Christ relates to the world that is opening up before them.

Not all junior highers reject their faith or the church, but almost all of them begin to have serious doubts and questions that need attention. Early adolescents generally lack the confidence actually to express those feelings, and so they tend to keep them locked up inside. They need to know that their doubts and questions are permitted, that they are normal and God approves of them. They need to know that though they may doubt God, God never doubts them. Wise youth workers will try to provide an environment of safety where junior highers have the freedom to open up, to ask questions, and to mine their faith for answers that make sense to them.

That is one of the reasons relationships are so important in junior high ministry. Junior highers need a person, not a program, someone they can talk to about the questions and problems they are dealing with in their lives. They need someone in whom they can confide, an adult friend who cares enough about them to listen. In many cases, parents are unable to fill this role completely. An adult other than their parents is needed, one who will take them seriously and allow them to express their feelings and ideas without criticism.

I have found that the best opportunities for ministry with junior highers are not meetings and Sunday school classes. These formal meeting times merely provide the possibility of informal contact with students. The best opportunities are when you are with a junior higher at home, in the car, on a hike, or at a ballgame. It is at times like those that a junior higher will be ready to learn and to ask questions. Recently I was helping a junior high boy with his math homework, when out of the blue he asked me a very serious question about the nature of God. It was a question that had been on his mind for a long time, but he chose that particular time to unload it. It gave me a great opportunity to discuss some important issues of the faith with him.

In classroom situations we need to learn how to conduct good discussions rather than "quizzes." In a discussion, young people can begin to express their opinions and feelings, explore the bigger issues of life, and learn how their faith relates to those issues. Good curriculum needs to allow for that kind of learning and discovery.

Effective Christian education for junior highers must also have a strong experiential component. As junior highers move into adulthood, they no longer want to accept everything at face value; instead, they want to try everything out for themselves. They want to be "movers and shakers." They would rather be doers than hearers, which, of course, is very close to the heart of Christ. Junior highers will be much better off *doing* Christian education than hearing it. Field trips, service projects, role playing, simulation games, and other learning activities have a far greater impact on junior highers than sitting in a classroom hearing a teacher talk or simply filling in the blanks in a workbook.

David Elkind, collecting the ideas of Jean Piaget, has said that junior highers might be better off not attending school at all, but instead being allowed to go build a boat, put on a play, work in a hospital, or teach. My thirteen-year-old son does not attend a junior high Sunday school class at our church. Instead, he helps teach the primary class. He is probably learning a good deal more than his students, and of course, how this affects his self-esteem cannot be matched in any junior high curriculum I have ever seen.

Curriculum also must relate to the world the junior higher is living in. It must be relevant. Many junior highers have a difficult time making the connection between their faith and the real world. That is why so many junior highers in the church will, in effect, lead two different lives: the one that comes to church and acts like a Christian and the one that goes to school and acts like all his or her friends.

Here we can see the importance of ministering the whole gospel to the whole person. Junior highers should not be taught that religious experience and religious truth are set apart from everyday experience and everyday truth.

Programming and curriculum for junior highers should always have some practical applications and should relate to the present as much as possible. Early adolescents are not going to be very interested in church history, eschatology, or theological issues. But they will be interested in understanding how to make friends, how to get along with their parents, how to handle peer pressure, how to listen to rock and roll music, or how to watch television. These are all important issues for junior highers, and they need to know how their faith makes a difference in all those areas.

Junior highers are also dyed-in-the-wool hero worshipers. They are easily led (or misled) by those who are able to capture their attention, admiration, and allegiance. Usually they are rock singers, film and television stars, or sports heroes. Young adolescents need someone to look up to and to pattern themselves after. For that reason, we need to transfer some of that hero worship to the Person of Christ. One of the best subjects for junior highers is a study of the life of Christ, allowing kids to see Christ from a new perspective. A study of other "Superheroes of the Faith" would also be appropriate. Junior highers need people with whom they can identify, models they can admire and emulate. We should give them some good ones.

Spiritually, junior highers are exploring their faith. They are open and responsive to the good news of the gospel, but in most cases, they are not ready to make final decisions about it. As was pointed out earlier in this chapter, most of the decisions made by this age group are of the trial and error variety. Very few of their decisions last very long. But still, they are learning how to make decisions about themselves and about their faith, both good ones and bad ones, and the cumulative effect of those decisions makes an enormous impact on their lives. We cannot and should not force junior highers into making decisions about their faith prematurely. But we should teach them how to make good decisions and give them every opportunity to make the kind of choices that ultimately will change their lives.

CHARACTERISTICS OF AN EFFECTIVE YOUTH PROGRAM

An effective program for junior highers will take the needs and characteristics of early adolescents seriously. What we know about junior highers should make a positive difference in how we design programs and how we go about implementing them. The following characteristics of an effective junior high program are based on current adolescent research and good common-sense knowledge of eleven- to fourteen-year-olds.

PROVIDE VARIETY AND DIVERSITY

Because junior highers are growing and changing very rapidly, and at a variety of rates, an appropriate activity for one young person might be completely inappropriate for another. Therefore, when programming for groups of junior highers, it is best to provide a wide variety of experiences and activities.

PROVIDE INVOLVEMENT AND PARTICIPATION

As junior highers develop more mature social, physical, and intellectual skills, they need opportunities to use them. Involve kids in the planning of programs, in the leadership of them, in discussion, in creating things, working on things, playing, and interacting. Do not allow junior highers to come and be mere spectators. This, by the way, is the best way to eliminate or to prevent the so-called discipline problem with junior highers. Get them involved, and there will be much less time or need for them to create problems.

PROVIDE MEANINGFUL RESPONSIBILITY

Junior highers need opportunities for success and competence. It has been said that this age group is omnipotent in imagination but impotent in action. Unfortunately, we give them few chances to express their inherent idealism and desire to do something meaningful with their lives.

PROVIDE POSITIVE INTERACTION WITH PEERS AND ADULTS

Junior highers are very relational human beings, and we need to give them a place where they can develop many friendships, both with adults and with peers.

PROVIDE OPPORTUNITIES FOR PLAY AND PHYSICAL ACTIVITY

Junior highers need to wiggle, stretch, and exercise their rapidly growing bodies. They need and desire times when they can go full blast and have fun. Play a lot of games and keep them moving. Do not force them to sit in one place for more than about fifteen minutes at a stretch.

PROVIDE STRUCTURE AND CLEAR LIMITS

Young adolescents are aware that they live in a society governed by rules, and they want to understand their limits within that system. They want freedom, but they also want to know the limits of that freedom. They need to be given well-defined rules and limits; but unlike younger children, they are capable of helping to formulate them, and they require that they be fair and equitable.

PROVIDE ADULT ROLE MODELS

The key to the success of any junior high program is the quality of adults who are working with them. We need to surround our junior highers with capable people who understand them, care about them, and enjoy being with them. We need to involve as many adults as possible as sponsors and counselors, as helpers or chaperones. We can invite adults to participate in panel discussions or to share their talents and skills with the group. We need to expose our junior highers to as many Christian adults as we can in a positive and genuine way.

PROVIDE HELP FOR PARENTS

Many parents begin to panic as soon as their children reach early adolescence. Youth workers can be a tremendous resource to them. We need to acquaint ourselves with the families of our junior highers and establish a relationship of trust and friendship with them.

Every junior high program will include a variety of meetings, activities, big groups, little groups, fun times, serious times, noisy times, quiet times, and much more. Almost anything will work with junior highers so long as it takes them and their needs seriously. Most important, anything will work so long as they have youth workers who understand them and are willing to be good listeners and good friends.

FOR FURTHER READING

Elkind, David. *Children and Adolescents*. 3d ed. New York: Oxford, 1981.

Farel, Anita. *Adolescence and Religion: A Status Study*. Carrboro, N.C.: Center for Early Adolescence, 1982.

Frans, Mike. *Are Junior Highs Missing Persons from Your Youth Ministry?* Wheaton, Ill.: Victor, 1980.

Holderness, Ginny Ward. *The Exuberant Years: A Guide for Junior High Leaders*. Atlanta: John Knox, 1976.

———. *The Junior Hi's: A Manual for Youth Ministers*. Winona, Minn.: St. Mary's College Press, 1978.

Johnson, Lin. *Teaching Junior Highers*. Denver: Accent Books, 1986.

Jones, Stephen D. *Faith Shaping: Nurturing the Faith Journey of Youth*. Valley Forge, Pa.: Judson, 1980.

Kesler, Jay, with Tim Stafford. *Breakthrough: Questions Youth Ask About God*. Grand Rapids: Zondervan, 1981.

Rice, Wayne. *Junior High Ministry*. Grand Rapids: Zondervan, 1978.

Spotts, Dwight, and David Veerman. *Reaching Out to Troubled Youth*. Wheaton, Ill.: Victor, 1987.

33

Jim Adkins, with Mitchell Smith

The Use of Video in Youth Ministry

The room is humming with low, excited voices. About twenty to twenty-five high school youths are sitting around on bean bag chairs and carpeted steps. Despite the lounge chairs, everyone is leaning forward in anticipation.

In front of the room sits a television set, the screen clouded with snow. When the lights go down, the room fills with a shushing sound as if a hundred snakes had just slithered in. Then, all is silent as the youths wait for an image to appear on the screen. Suddenly, there it is. The picture of a bedroom appears, looking as if a whirlwind had just gone through it, and the camera slowly pans 360 degrees.

"Oh, no! It's my room!" cries a single, pained voice in the darkness of the lounge.

The camera locks in on the group's youth minister, who is holding a microphone and giving the camera a wry grin. "That's right, Mike" he says, having anticipated this reaction several days before. "It's your room, so welcome to "The Bedroom of the Week," and boy have we caught a live one this time!" The group is broken up with laughter again and again for the next twenty minutes as the youth minister and Mike's mother examine the various facets of Mike's room.

JIM ADKINS, M.A., is junior high youth pastor, Emmanuel Faith Community Church, Escondido, California.

"The Bedroom of the Week" has become a regular feature of the youth group's weekly meetings. Sometime during each week, their minister meets with conspiring parents to do a short video tour of the selected group member's room and house. Then, at the regular meetings, the group sits in anticipation, each student wondering if this night is his room's turn to be on the show. Every week the response is the same—sighs of relief or groans of agony. Either way, the kids love it.

This is just one example of how video can become an exciting and successful tool in youth ministry. In this chapter we will explore other examples that further illustrate how video can be successfully employed in teaching Christian values and building community relationships. In addition, an overview of various areas of use will suggest reasons churches should take advantage of this new methodology. Finally, some practical information on tools and techniques will be given to help a church start teaching through video. But first, a word about the philosophy of incorporating video into the teaching ministry of the church.

THE POWER OF VIDEO IN TEACHING

In itself video is just another method of teaching students and guiding them to find truths for themselves. Its value is that it can teach through involvement. Instead of just handing out information, video allows students to be part of the teaching process. They can work behind or in front of the camera, or they can take advantage of an opportunity to view the teaching. A student learns a limited amount from hearing. He retains more if he sees as well as hears. But learning is maximized by seeing, hearing, and actually being involved in the way that video permits.

Also, as Lyle Schaller, author of *Understanding Tomorrow* and a foremost leader in church growth and management has indicated, members of today's younger generation are particularly attuned to visual learning. They have grown up watching television, and much of their informal instruction has been acquired through that medium. The information the church wishes to convey is God's Word and the values resulting from a Christian world view. But these values often can be taught better if the church stays current with the methodologies of processing information. It is prudent for the church to convey its message through the most modern and readily acceptable means. In the words of Kenneth Gangel, we must either visualize or fossilize.

Note too that advances in technology have made video so much cheaper and easier to operate that for the first time church leaders have ready access to its use. Ministers can employ the very means of communication young people today find most appealing and understandable. The opportunity to utilize video has never been greater.

Finally, there is the challenge of understanding and dealing with the way video is shaping the consciousness of young people. Children and youth are watching rock videos and movies that are becoming increasingly spectacular in their use of special effects. Many new messages and values are being spread to young people through these means. The church can be aware of these changes and respond to them by learning about video. Then the teaching of the church will remain current and effective.

SOME EXAMPLES OF SUCCESSFUL TEACHING WITH VIDEO

One church, through a seminar, dealt with one of the new concerns created by video and, at the same time, took advantage of the new technology to catch the attention of the young people. The youth minister combined tapes of rock music videos (video cassettes with the top ten current videos can be purchased at various record and tape stores) with those of his own making, which introduced material, highlighted issues, and pointed out certain aspects of the videos. The final product was a program composed of current, popular material that could be used to teach students how to analyze values. The introductions and discussions were fast-paced, full of pertinent statistics and thought-provoking questions. During the presentation, there were three pre-programmed stops that gave the youths a chance to discuss what they were seeing with their group leaders. This was a crucial step, eliminating the possibility that the session would become merely educational entertainment.

In the first segment, the youths, who were arranged into groups with a leader in each to help them through the discussion, analyzed the technique and special effects used in the videos. Then, after seeing how complex the commercial videos were, each group was asked to discuss the kind of messages the videos were trying to communicate through the use of those techniques. Finally, the leaders worked hard to help the groups identify what kind of values the videos were espousing and whether those values coincided with a Christian world view. Great care was taken to let the young people think for themselves. The point was to make them understand that they should be aware of the content of what they watch and try to analyze its message. Sometimes church leaders make the mistake of ripping into videos because of the obvious immorality that is in them. But it is important to remember that these videos represent to young people their generation's form of artistic expression.

The seminar was well received by the students, who became fascinated with analyzing the rock videos. Having the actual videos was an invaluable asset. They could be replayed as often as necessary so there could be no question as to what they contained. In addition, the program was simply fun to watch. The youths were excited by the music and the images, and sometimes they laughed when they saw through the intent of certain videos. The success of such a program opens up other possibilities. Advertisements, movies, and television programs all could be analyzed similarly, with young people learning and enjoying it.

(It is important to remember when doing any sort of video analysis that proper permission must be obtained to use commercial videotapes. See the section of this chapter concerning copyright law.)

A second example of the high impact video can have in creating involvement is found in an educational program on suicide for a church youth group. The church that made this program is located in Southern California, but its youth minister went on a two-day trip to San Francisco. He decided to take his video equipment with him to tape the introductions he was going to make for the various speakers who were to appear in the video program. Using the Golden Gate Bridge as a background, the minister recorded himself introducing the program and announcing each speaker. In the final version of the tape, the program switched locations repeatedly from the church leaders speaking in Southern California to the youth minister introducing them in San Francisco.

When the program was aired, the youth group was delighted and impressed. The impact of having the Golden Gate Bridge in the background was increased when in his introduction of the show, the youth minister told how many people committed suicide each year by jumping off that bridge. Then, after each church leader spoke about some aspect of suicide, the scene switched back to the youth minister at the bridge, providing visual reinforcement of what was being said. In addition, the youth minister was back in town when the video aired, which somewhat mystified the group. How could he have been introducing the speakers from San Francisco when it had been only a week since they had seen him last? Of course, it was the capabilities of video that had allowed him to work quickly and efficiently enough to take advantage of the short time available. The result was a colorful, involving show that took full advantage of changing scenes to make the lesson effective.

Videos also can be a good tool for establishing personal relationsips. At least that was the experience of one youth minister at a track meet. This minister had learned that it was advantageous to have video taping equipment with him whenever he went to any special event. One never knows when something noteworthy might occur. In this case, he used the equipment to record a high jumper, Dennis Lewis, a Long Beach City College student. After each jump, Lewis would come over to examine his form played back on the video monitor. Noticing that he had a couple of inches to spare each time he cleared the bar, Lewis started raising the bar more than he might have otherwise. He ended up jumping 7 feet 7¼ inches, breaking Dwight Stone's American record. Without the on-the-spot capability of video, Lewis might not have realized his full abilities. This incident became a springboard for the minister to build relationships with students.

Finally, churches have been successful in building community relationships through the use of video. One California church has done this by volunteering to record local high school football games. The youth ministers first discussed the program with local high school coaches. They told the coaches they wanted to play a part in enhancing the performance of the football teams. Using several cameras and monitors provided by the church, high school students were able to capture the games from several angles. The finished tapes were both professionally done and useful for the teams, which in the past had been filming their games with a single hand-held camera that provided black and white film without sound. Team members had been uninterested in reviewing their performances in those films, and indeed, because they record only one angle, the films were of limited value. But the players liked the videos so much they began making copies of the team tapes, which have sound and graphics like actual television replays, may be played in slow motion, and provide the valuable added angles.

The result for the church was a closer relationship with the coaches and the players. Many boys who did not know much about the church were exposed to it in a positive way. A number have become interested in getting more involved. Coaches as well have had a favorable response. Some who did not attend church in the past have begun coming to services at the church. One coach and his wife decided to seek counseling after meeting one of the ministers through the program. Now talk is starting of the church's providing chapel for interested players before each game. Overall, the program has shown another way that the church can get into the community and get involved.

SOME AREAS OF USE FOR VIDEO

For churches interested in incorporating video into their programs, there are many possibilities. One of the simplest and most obvious uses is the documentation of special events. High school students can be trained to film regular events at the church, such as weddings and baptisms, either for the church or as a keepsake for the families. Special musical or dramatic productions put on by the church could be recorded for those unable to attend. All that is really necessary for this kind of taping is a camera, a microphone, and a recorder. The tapes themselves might be kept in a church video library for congregation members to check out at their convenience.

A more elaborate use of documentation could involve editing taped events. An example of this can be found in one church that records special sermons and then edits in sections to give the tape another dimension beyond the sermon itself. In one instance, a panel discussion was added after the sermon. The panel, made up of church leaders, discussed the points of the sermon in a conversational way, adding personal views and conflicting opinions. In another instance, the sermon was intercut with various role playing episodes. Members of the congregation acted out skits to highlight certain points of the sermon. That made the sermon more memorable, especially for the younger members of the congregation, by visually reinforcing the message.

In another area, sports celebrities can have a great effect on youth when they describe their own faith. One youth minister discovered this after attending a conference for evangelism in Dallas, Texas, where Tom Landry, head coach of the Dallas Cowboys, was a member of the panel of speakers. Afterwards, Landry was available for questions. The youth minister asked him if he would be willing to give a testimony of his faith on videotape, and Landry agreed. Using a video camera and a mobile recorder, the minister made the tape on the spot. Since then the minister has shown that tape to his youth groups and interested members of the congregation. Their first reaction is wonderment at how he got an interview with Tom Landry. But the youth also show a deep respect for Landry's testimony. They are accustomed to seeing the Dallas coach on television, so in their minds he is a familiar authority. That gives his testimony an added validity.

Video can also be used to promote the church and its activities for the congregation and the community at large. These promotions can be in the form of video packages showing highlights from previous special events. For example, many churches take part in supporting summer youth camps. Because these camps provide Christian teaching in the context of summer fun, some churches have put together video promotions for them.

Another video promotion done by one church concerns its Mexico outreach program. This program involves training young people in evangelism, then sending them into Mexico to put the training to use. The church tapes the young people during training, then interviews each of them right after they return, while the experience is still fresh. Each person gives one short, key observation. The completed report is presented in the church's sanctuary using a large-screen video projector. Viewers get a condensed and powerful impression of the program.

Video can provide the flip side of promotion, feedback, as well. One church has managed this by doing video interviews of random members of the congregation. The interviewers ask them their reactions and feelings about sermons, musical features, and other church activities. Then the church leaders watch these tapes to gauge the effectiveness of their work, and also to look for suggestions for changes. The interviews bring out a candor that might not be found in a formal, written survey. It also brings out the views of people who have not been involved in other church functions that might give them more voice.

Counseling is another area in which video may be used. One minister tapes all his counseling sessions. When talking to a husband and wife, the wife might tell her husband that he is reacting with too much anger. The husband might deny this. The minister is then able to rewind the tape to review it so the couple could see and hear the husband's reaction. In another instance of counseling, one church recorded a discussion between a pastor and his wife as they recounted before the congregation their various struggles and changes through thirty years of marriage. The resulting tape was made available through the church library. It became quite popular because it showed two respected church leaders offering insights from their own experience, which the viewers could apply to their own lives.

One area of use that cannot be overlooked for youth groups is enjoyment. Most video programs include that as an element in maintaining interest, but some programs can be made for pure fun. "The Bedroom of the Week" program described earlier is an example. Another church conducts a game show in which the young people are recorded as they play. The winners get prizes, but everyone enjoys seeing himself on the video screen. Promo tapes for summer camp are included in the program, offering the youths another chance to view themselves in amusing situations.

A major use for video in church programs is education. This can take the form of educational programs. Many subjects appropriate to teens could be discussed in video format, for example, emotional changes or teenagers and alcohol. Video can provide more color and different scenes to keep interest high. It also can utilize creative teaching methods such as role playing to emphasize a point more effectively. With graphics, a program can provide clear statistics and figures. Speakers normally inaccessible, like Tom Landry, can be made available to the group. And their performance can be improved, for mistakes and pauses can be deleted.

One church produced a program about Halloween that incorporated the elements of good video use. The program opens with shots of vivid Halloween paintings taken from the windows of local businesses. Eerie music begins to play. The youth minister, standing in front of the windows, introduces various speakers, who are interviewed in other locations. The speakers point out that though Halloween ghouls and demons are presented in fun, they do have a realistic and serious side. When the program was aired, the interest generated by the format increased the young peoples' attention to the message. In fact, they paid more attention to one speaker on screen than when he came in and spoke in person.

Education with video can be an interactive process as well. Youth groups can make their own videos, writing, acting, taping, and editing. From this process they learn skills relating to the equipment, but they also get a deeper understanding of whatever educational material they are dealing with. Instead of passively taking in the information, they work with it and try to present it successfully. Video can show them things about themselves they might not always see. One youth minister took his group to a military cemetery on Veterans' Day. Afterwards, he asked some members how they felt about seeing so many graves of men and women who had died while serving their country.

Many of the youths described how thankful they were for what these men and women had done. The tape was edited and included in a Thanksgiving program. Often young people say they do not know what they should be thankful for on Thanksgiving. But this youth group watched members describing something they were thankful for.

Tools and Techniques for Church Video Programs

A church can begin working in video with very basic equipment. With just two components, a video cassette recorder (VCR) and a television set, a church can rent movies to show or borrow programs other churches have made. By adding a camera and a microphone, a church can start working more creatively. A second VCR opens up editing possibilities.

A decision that must be made early concerns which video format to choose, VHS (Video Home System) or Beta. Beta has a higher quality, less grainy picture. But VHS is by far the more common choice, and VHS cameras have more features, such as graphics. The availability of each in a particular area might determine this choice. Many people have equipment of their own, so a church might begin its program based on what members of the congregation are willing to lend.

The limits on what can be done with video depend more on the imagination of those involved than on the equipment. A church need not be concerned whether its productions are professional looking or not. Most churches have found their youth groups and congregations were satisfied by home movie quality. The real thrill of video comes in seeing oneself on screen. An added pleasure is that one can see himself quickly. There is no need to wait for anything like film development.

Of course, video can be misused. If it is used too much, the excitement is diminished. It also is possible to tape the wrong kind of events, in which few people are interested. Again, the quality may be poor. This is not necessarily due to the lack of equipment. One can get by, for example, without editing equipment by "shooting in the can," that is, by setting up everything to be taped ahead of time and getting it all in one take. Another possibility is to edit by simply recording over things.

As skills increase, churches might want to expand their equipment. A video screen is better than a television for showing programs to large groups. Additional recorders and an enhancer would give even greater editing capabilities. A church could add more cameras or perhaps buy higher priced and better quality equipment. Each small step opens up new possibilities. By incorporating a computer cataloguing system one could keep up with who and what is on each cassette. That way, if someone was to be the recipient of a special honor, a tape might be made featuring him in some way. The same principle could be applied in locating tape sequences for a memorial tape.

The key to video is involvement. Individuals who have their own video equipment might get involved in church programs by lending their equipment. A church might also build involvement by starting a video library. The congregation would not only take part in offering the service, it could also see many dimensions of the church through its educational or promotional programs. Finally, there is the involvement in the actual making of the videos, script writing, acting, camera work, editing, and the like. People can offer their time and skills and have fun doing it. Most of all, this methodology can make the teaching of God's values more effective.

COPYRIGHT CONSIDERATIONS*

Before a youth worker begins using commercial video tapes and video tapes made from television broadcasts, there are certain guidelines of which he should be aware. The purpose of these standards is not to frustrate the work of the Lord but to protect the copyright owner and allow him to gain a fair return from his creative effort, at the same time permitting the educator (or in this case, youth minister) fair uses of educationally significant materials.

On January 1, 1978, a new federal copyright law became effective, after the old one had stood for seventy years. The Xerox copier had either made many parts of the older law obsolete or had made a majority of people in the nation petty criminals through their use of copying machines. But even as the law was being written, videotape recorders (VCRs) were making parts of the law obsolete. They were doing for television what the Xerox machine had done for books and articles.

Rather than rewrite the new law, Congressman Robert W. Kastenmeier, chairman of a House Judiciary Committee sub-committee, in 1981 brought together representatives from education and the media to hammer out guidelines that would interpret the law and provide a balance between the money-making rights of the owners and the instructional rights of educators.[1]

The rights of owners affirmed the 1978 copyright law. Owners were protected by being given sole authority over duplication rights. That means they have the exclusive right to grant permission for a program or film to be copied. It should be noted, however, that the Supreme Court (*Sony* vs. *Universal Studios, Walt Disney Productions*) has ruled that private citizens may tape programs from television for their own private use.[2]

Similarly, owners have transmission rights and thus can control the use of

---

*This section was written by Mark H. Senter III.
1. U.S. Congress, House, *Congressional Record* (14 October 1981) 127, no. 145E4750-4752).
2. F. William Troost, "When to Say No to Off-Air Videotaping," *Instructional Innovator*, January 1985, p. 26.

copyrighted material by commercial and public television, cable television firms, hotel and apartment cable systems, as well as educational transmissions within and between instructional agencies.

Derivative works may provide the youth minister some headaches, for these, too, are the exclusive right of the owner. This implies that materials from a television show may not be used in another form, such as using puppets in the place of real people, without receiving the owners' permission.

Performance rights (both for profit and for nonprofit purposes) as well as distribution rights are also controlled by the owner. With the prices of video projectors falling, there may be a temptation to use segments of television programs in church socials or on retreats as a cheap substitute for rented films or videotapes. Yet this, too, is stealing from the owner income that is rightfully his.

Even the use of videotapes rented from the local video store violate performance rights, for such rentals are intended for home use, not institutional use. The same videotapes may be rented for use at a church youth group social, but they must be rented from an agency that is licensed for such purposes. Most state universities have film and video rental libraries for this specific purpose, and the process remains very reasonable.

Yet the creative use of videotape is still a live option. Christian educators have the right to copy and use public domain programs, that is, programs whose copyrights have expired as well as works of the federal government, such as addresses by elected officials, congressional hearings, or informational programs produced by governmental agencies. But this will not exactly provide hours of dynamic youth ministry instructional aids for most youth groups.

In addition, educators were able to gain concessions from the media representatives. Nine guidelines provide the youth worker with standards to direct his use of materials videotaped from television. These are described as "fair use" guidelines.

The first is not a problem for most church youth ministries, for it states that these rules apply only to nonprofit educational institutions. Most churches and parachurch youth ministry agencies fit the nonprofit criterion through state charters, whereas the discipleship and moral development activities of the program would fit the educational part of the definition.

The second guideline limits the amount of time that a tape made from television can be saved. It states that copies can be retained for no longer than forty-five days for the purpose of evaluation. The intent of this guideline is to give the educator enough time to determine whether he would like to have the educational institution purchase the tape or if he would like to rent it in the future.[3]

---

3. Rentals and purchasing information can be obtained from The Television Licensing Center, 1144 Wilmette Avenue, Wilmette, Illinois 60091.

Guideline three further restricts the use of the tape made for or by the youth worker to the first ten "instructional days" after the program is aired. For churches, the arguments can be made that only Sunday is an "instructional day." However, the forty-five-day limit that the tape can be kept adequately restricts the youth worker even under such an interpretation. The spirit of this guideline is to limit the direct educational or ministry use of the tape to two weeks.

Furthermore, says guideline three, the off-air recording may be used only once, with the possibility of once for review purposes, and it must be in an instructional setting such as the church or church school. This apparently eliminates the use of tapes made by or for the youth pastor at youth group functions in private homes unless those homes are the normal meeting places for religious instruction.

The fourth guideline may stimulate more planning on the part of the youth worker. It states that all copies of television material must be made *at the request* of the teacher who wishes to use the materials. Random taping and recording of large amounts of televised materials in hopes of finding usable material is forbidden. Intentionality is the key. Apparently even time shifting (recording something now so that I can view it when I get home after club) is not an adequate basis for using materials in the educational program unless the original intent was to record it for use at church.

Furthermore, say the fair use guidelines, a youth worker may not have a program copied more than one time. If a segment of a televised program was used as the starting point for a discussion on family relationships with junior high students and the youth worker wants to use it during the summer with students' parents at a family camp, he cannot just tape the same segment of the program from the summer rerun. He must rent it as he would any other film.

Only in churches where curriculum for youth ministry requires multiple classrooms or the entire educational program is coordinated would the fifth guideline apply. It allows copies of the original off-air tape to be made for several teachers as long as the other criteria are maintained. An example of how this might be valid is when the youth minister tells his teaching staff about an upcoming special on drugs to be aired on television. Several of them in turn request that a copy of the program be made available to them so they can use it in their Sunday school classes. A tape is made and then duplicated for each teacher who requested it in advance of the time the program was aired on television.

At the end of the forty-five day period that the youth minister is permitted to keep the copied program, the tape must be erased according to guideline six. A fine line exists between the youth pastor as a private citizen (in which case he can keep the tape indefinitely) and the youth pastor as an educator. Remembering the other guidelines, the youth worker after the forty-five day limit should erase a tape made off television if the tape has been used in a youth group educational function or if the original intent of the tape was for educational purposes.

In addition, the tape may not be given to students for their use or for any other nonevaluation purposes without the express permission of the copyright owner. Using such tapes for mere entertainment purposes, especially when it involves youth group members, similarly violates the guidelines.

The seventh guideline permits the youth worker to use only a portion of a program but restricts him from electronically editing or altering its content without the permission of the copyright owner. This means that a series of illustrations from copyrighted material cannot be strung together electronically. The youth worker can, however, remove one tape from the VCR, insert another tape, and repeat this process as often as he wishes in order to provide a series of visual illustrations. That would not violate the copyright.

The eighth guideline simply states that all tapes made from television must contain the copyright notice. The reason for this would appear to be proper credit and remuneration for professional work should the youth minister decide to purchase or rent the tape and make it part of the church's youth ministry curriculum.

The final guideline puts the church on notice that it is vulnerable to legal procedure if it does not provide appropriate control procedures for maintaining the integrity of these guidelines. Because youth pastors are the agents acting in behalf of the church in the ministry to students, legally they are viewed as carrying out the policies of the church. Violations on a youth pastor's part constitute violations on the church's part. Thus the church could be sued for the actions of a careless or unethical youth worker.

FOR FURTHER READING

Kemp, Jerrold E. *Planning & Producing Audiovisual Materials.* 5th ed. New York: Harper & Row, 1985.

Troost, William F. "When to Say No to Off-Air Videotaping." *Instructional Innovator* (January 1985).

Index of Subjects

Index of Persons

Moody Press, a ministry of the Moody Bible Institute, is designed for education, evangelization, and edification. If we may assist you in knowing more about Christ and the Christian life, please write us without obligation: Moody Press, c/o MLM, Chicago, Illinois 60610.